CHAPTER 217

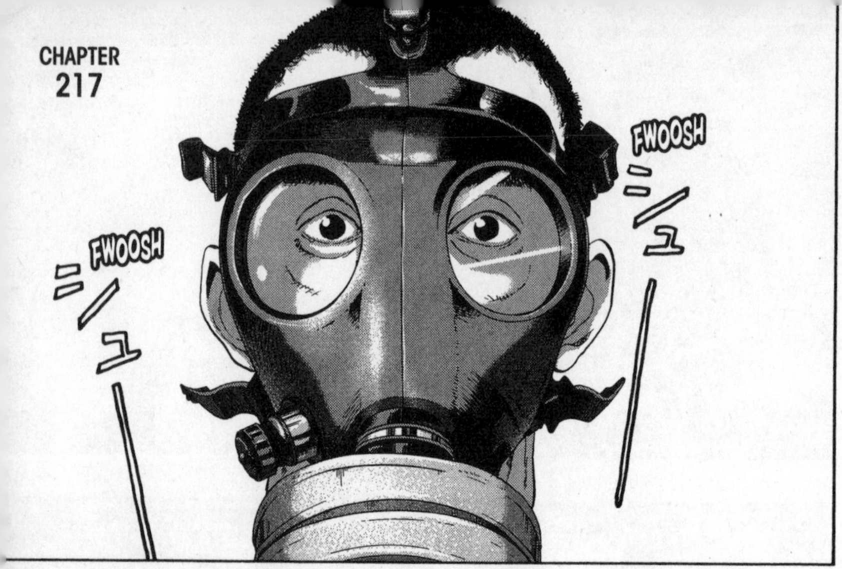
FWOOSH
FWOOSH

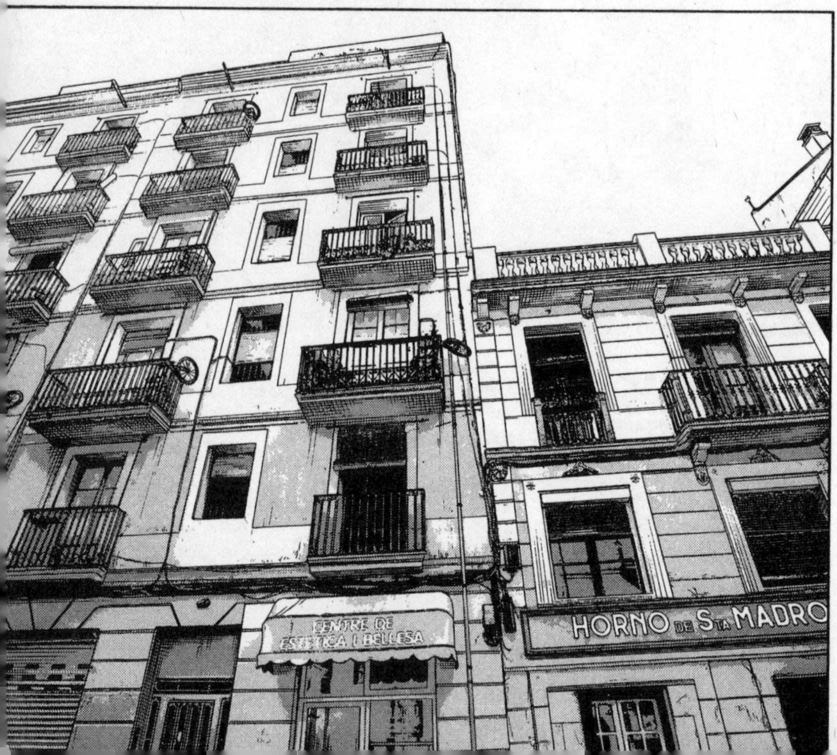
HORNO DE Sta MADRO
CENTRE DE ESTETICA I BELLESA

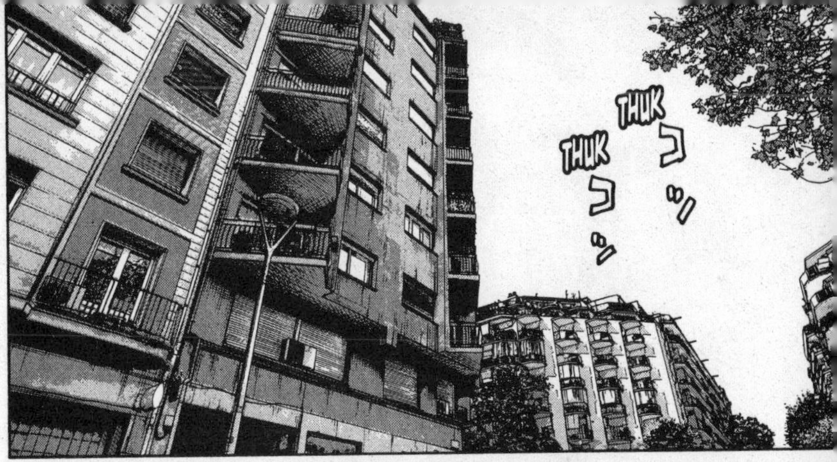
THUK
コッ
THUK
コッ
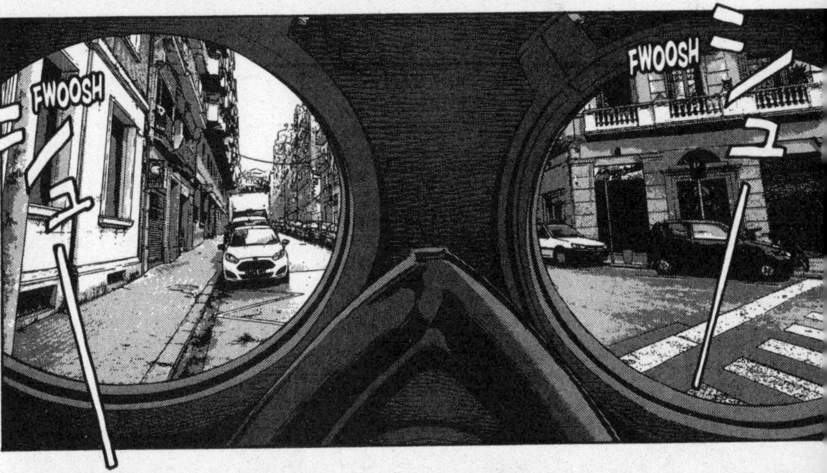
FWOOSH
FWOOSH
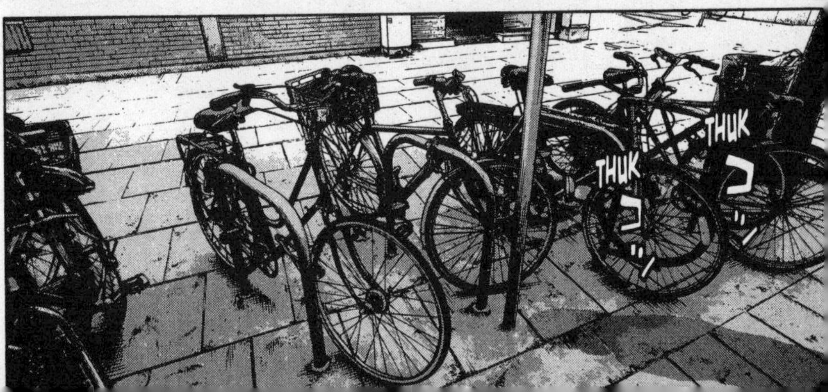
THUK
コッ
THUK
コッ

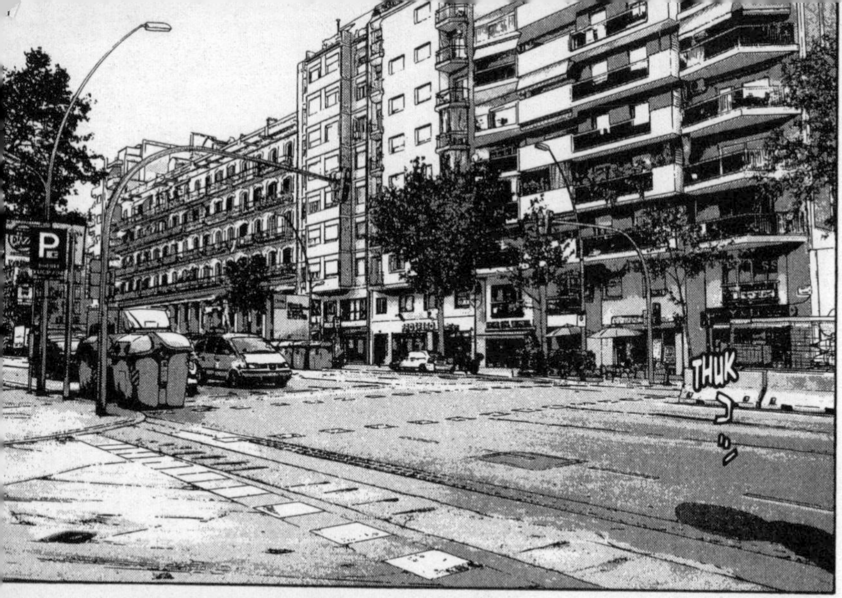
THUK

NOTE: SPOKEN SPANISH WILL FALL WITHIN POINTED BRACKETS, <LIKE THIS>.

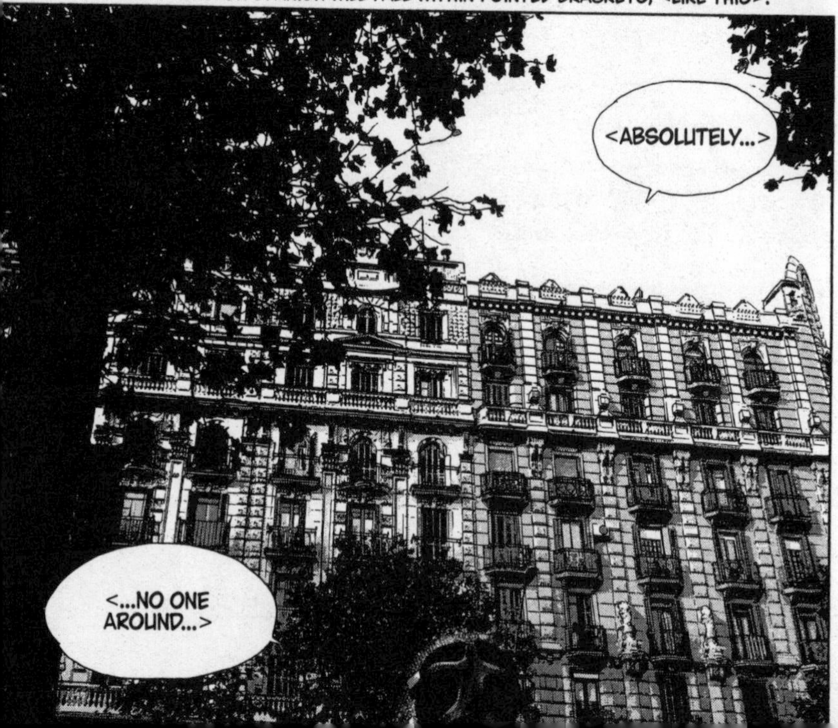
<ABSOLUTELY...>
<...NO ONE AROUND...>

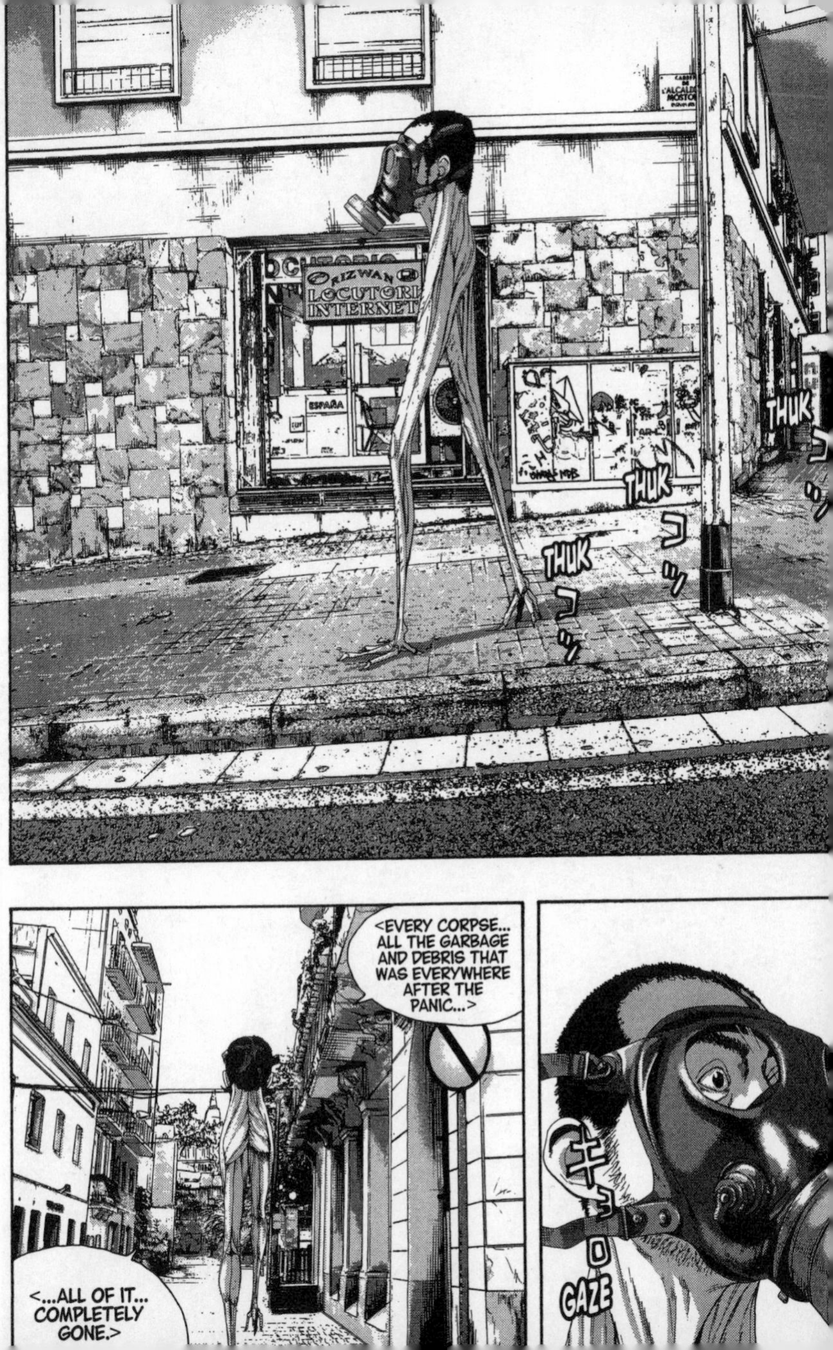

RIZWAN
ESPAÑA
THUK
THUK
THUK
GAZE
<EVERY CORPSE... ALL THE GARBAGE AND DEBRIS THAT WAS EVERYWHERE AFTER THE PANIC...>
<...ALL OF IT... COMPLETELY GONE.>

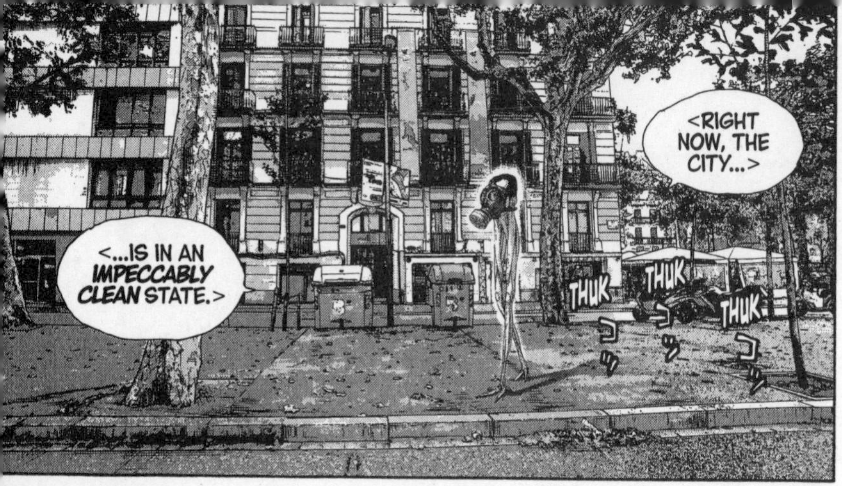
<RIGHT NOW, THE CITY...>
<...IS IN AN IMPECCABLY CLEAN STATE.>
THUK
THUK
THUK

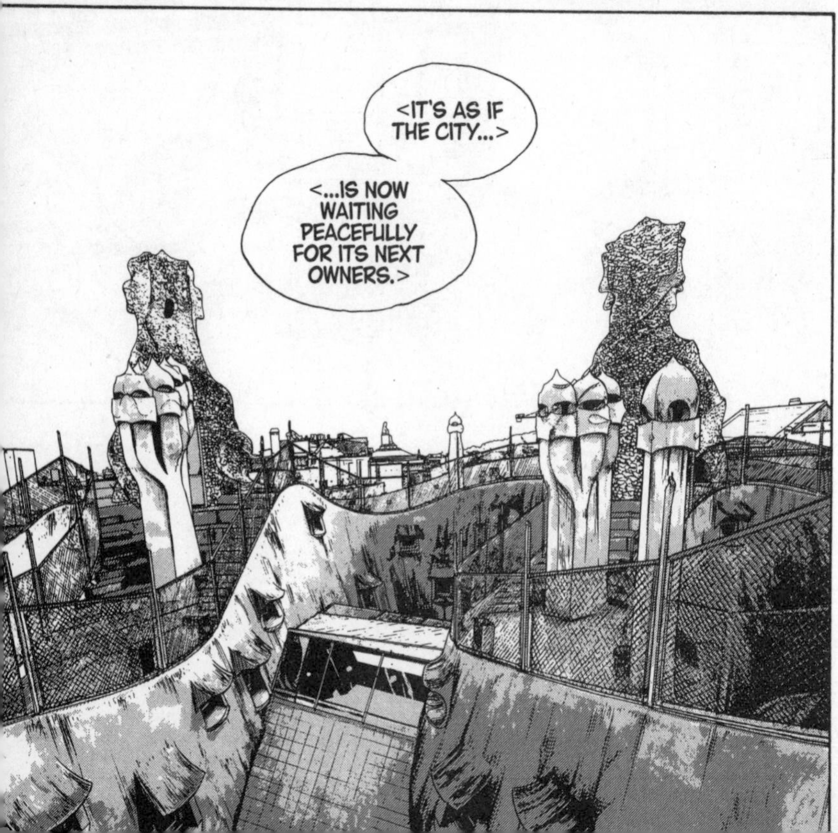
<IT'S AS IF THE CITY...>
<...IS NOW WAITING PEACEFULLY FOR ITS NEXT OWNERS.>

ADRONA
SOL
SHRFF
SHRFF
SHRFF
SHRFF
SHRFF
THUK
THUK
THUK

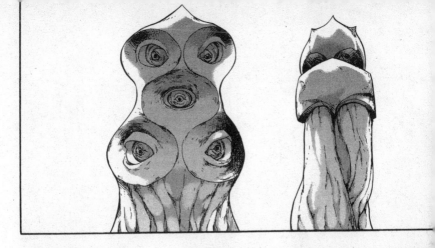

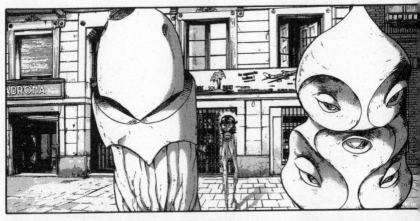

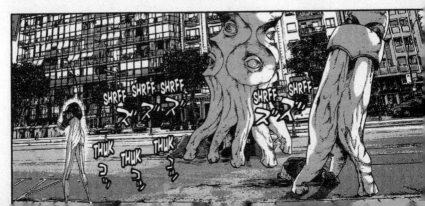

<SO THERE ARE BASICALLY *THREE* TYPES OF ZQNS.>

<THE NUMBER OF THOSE SO-CALLED *HUMANOID ZQNS* HAS DRASTICALLY DECREASED...>

<...AND ZQNS RESEMBLING TYPES OF BARCELONA'S ARCHITECTURE ARE CLEANING UP THE CITY.>

<FIRST, THE HUMANOID ZQNS WHICH SPREAD THE INFECTION.>

<I DON'T SEE THEM AROUND. PERHAPS THEIR TASK IS COMPLETE.>

<AND SECOND-- THE ZQNS OF THE TYPE I CAME ACROSS JUST NOW. THEY ARE IN CHARGE OF CLEANING UP THE CITY, AND THEY PATROL TO MAINTAIN ORDER.>

<ACTING METHODICALLY AND MECHANICALLY, ONE COULD CALL THEM *CONSTRUCTIVE-TYPE ZQNS.*>

THUK

THUK

THUK

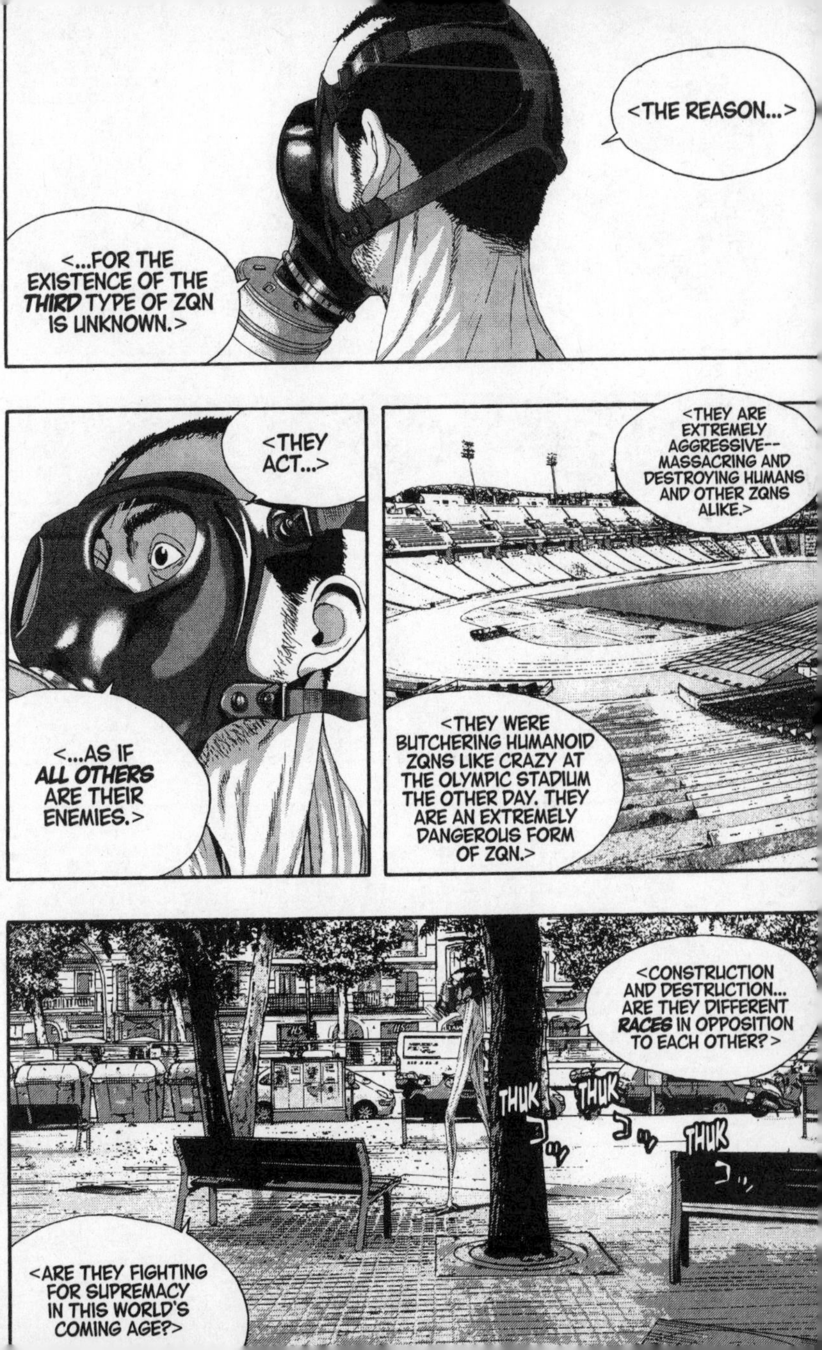
<THE REASON...>
<...FOR THE EXISTENCE OF THE *THIRD* TYPE OF ZQN IS UNKNOWN.>
<THEY ARE EXTREMELY AGGRESSIVE-- MASSACRING AND DESTROYING HUMANS AND OTHER ZQNS ALIKE.>
<THEY WERE BUTCHERING HUMANOID ZQNS LIKE CRAZY AT THE OLYMPIC STADIUM THE OTHER DAY. THEY ARE AN EXTREMELY DANGEROUS FORM OF ZQN.>
<THEY ACT...>
<...AS IF *ALL OTHERS* ARE THEIR ENEMIES.>
<CONSTRUCTION AND DESTRUCTION... ARE THEY DIFFERENT *RACES* IN OPPOSITION TO EACH OTHER?>
THUK
THUK
THUK
<ARE THEY FIGHTING FOR SUPREMACY IN THIS WORLD'S COMING AGE?>

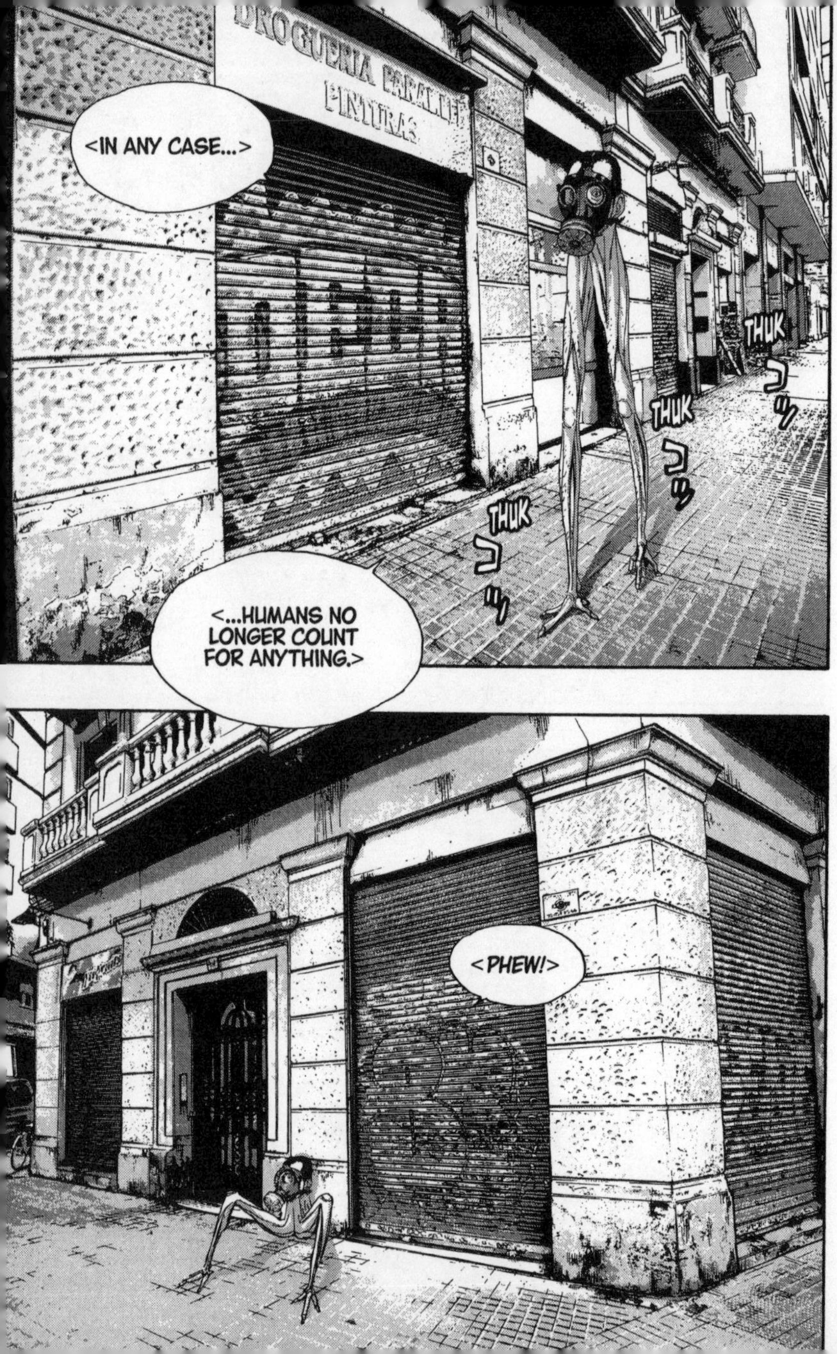
<IN ANY CASE...>
THUK
THUK
THUK
<...HUMANS NO LONGER COUNT FOR ANYTHING.>
<PHEW!>

<BUT I HAVE NO HANDS, SO I CAN'T SCRATCH IT.>

<DOES THAT MEAN I NO LONGER HAVE ANY NEED TO SCRATCH MY HEAD?>

<THE TOP OF MY HEAD.>

<SEEMS LIKE IT'S ITCHY.>

<BUT SPEAKING OF REASONS FOR ONE'S EXISTENCE BEING UNKNOWN...>

<...I'M IN THAT CATEGORY TOO.>

<I AM A HEAD WITH LEGS.>

<I SEEM TO BE SPECIALIZED SOLELY FOR THINKING AND WALKING.>

<...BUT MY CAPACITY TO THINK IS CLEAR. I DO NOT FEEL THAT I'M BEING LIMITED BY ANYONE. ALTHOUGH...I HAVE NOTHING TO COMPARE THIS WITH...>

<I HAVE LOST ALL MEMORIES OF MY PAST...>

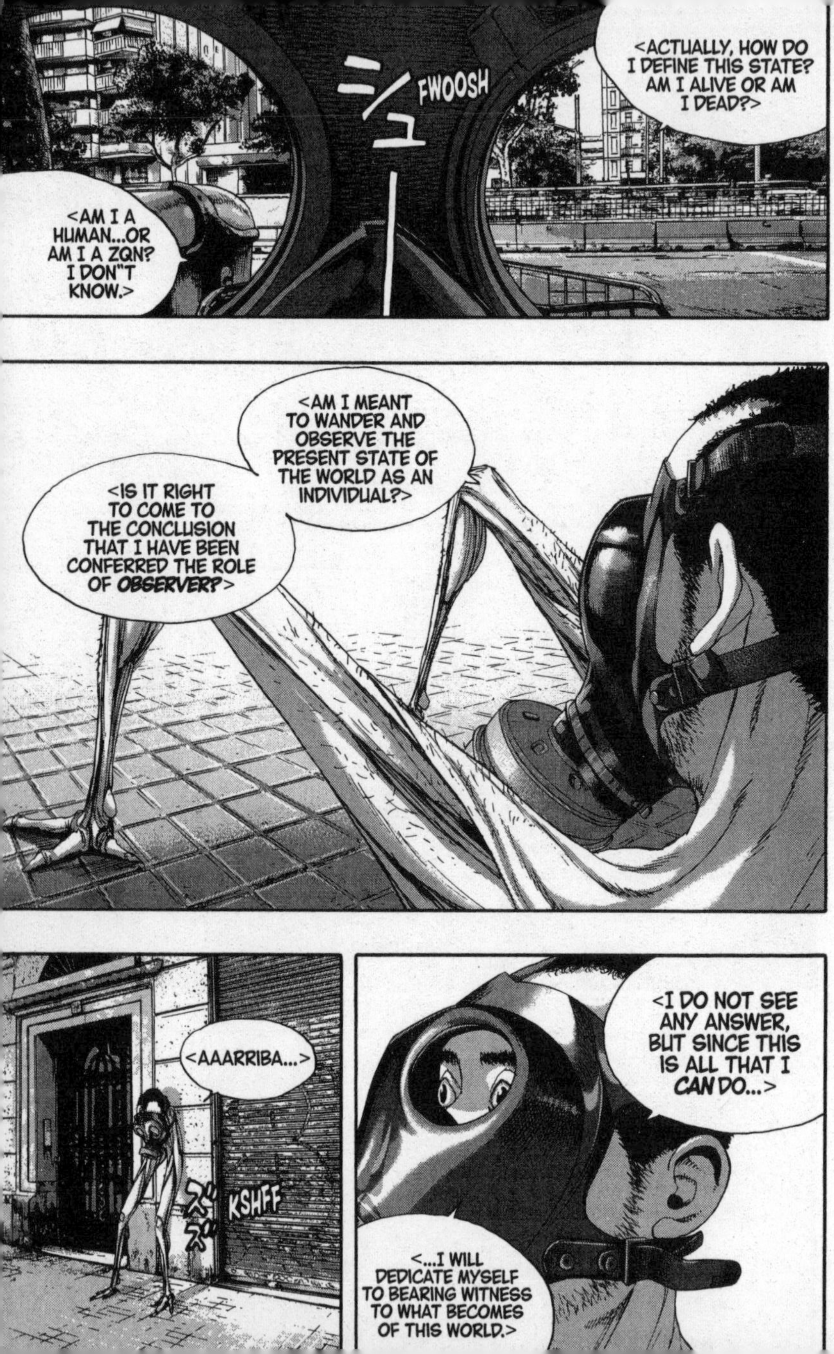
<ACTUALLY, HOW DO I DEFINE THIS STATE? AM I ALIVE OR AM I DEAD?>
シュ
FWOOSH
<AM I A HUMAN...OR AM I A ZQN? I DON"T KNOW.>
<AM I MEANT TO WANDER AND OBSERVE THE PRESENT STATE OF THE WORLD AS AN INDIVIDUAL?>
<IS IT RIGHT TO COME TO THE CONCLUSION THAT I HAVE BEEN CONFERRED THE ROLE OF OBSERVER?>
<I DO NOT SEE ANY ANSWER, BUT SINCE THIS IS ALL THAT I CAN DO...>
<...I WILL DEDICATE MYSELF TO BEARING WITNESS TO WHAT BECOMES OF THIS WORLD.>
<AAARRIBA...>
ズズ
KSHFF

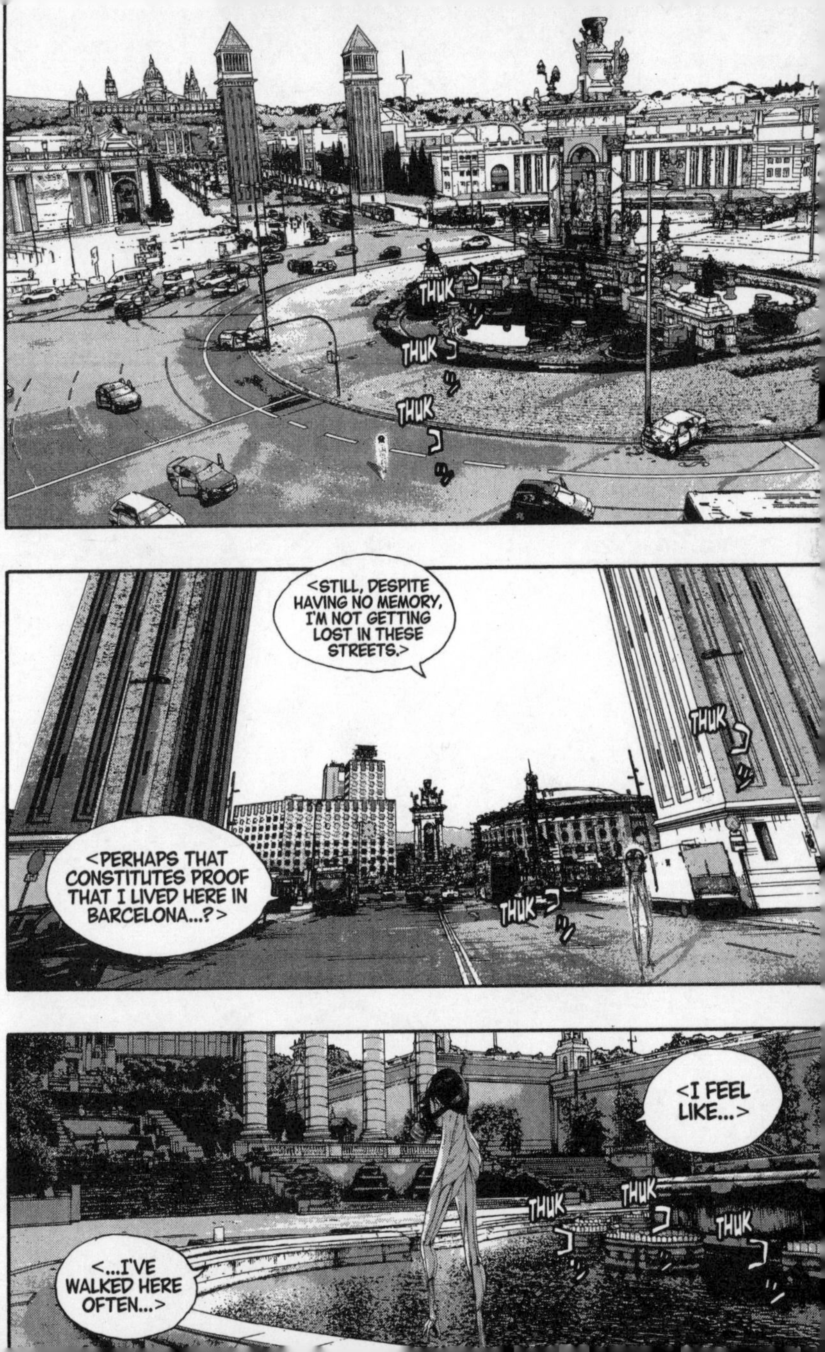
THUK
THUK
THUK
<STILL, DESPITE HAVING NO MEMORY, I'M NOT GETTING LOST IN THESE STREETS.>
THUK
<PERHAPS THAT CONSTITUTES PROOF THAT I LIVED HERE IN BARCELONA...?>
THUK
<I FEEL LIKE...>
THUK
THUK
THUK
<...I'VE WALKED HERE OFTEN...>

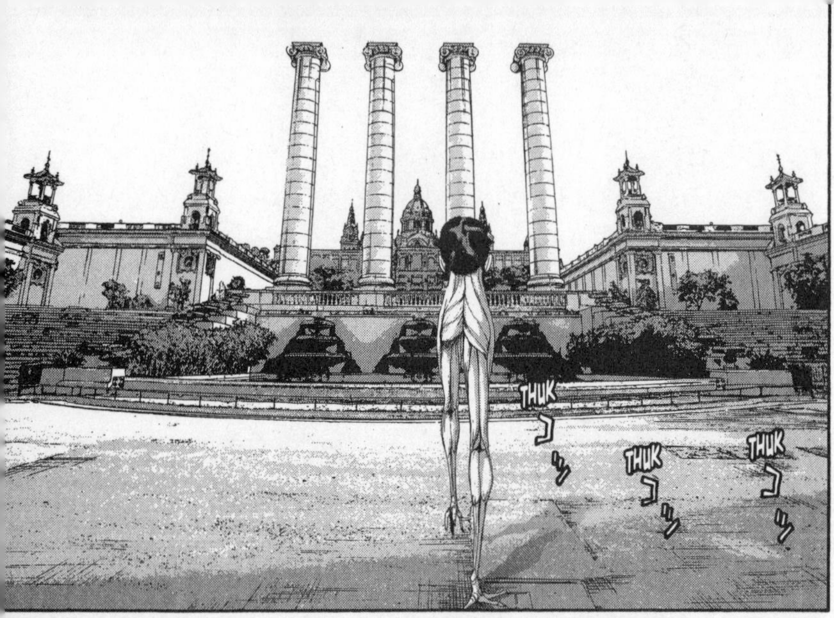
THUK
ゴッ
THUK
ゴッ
THUK
ゴッ

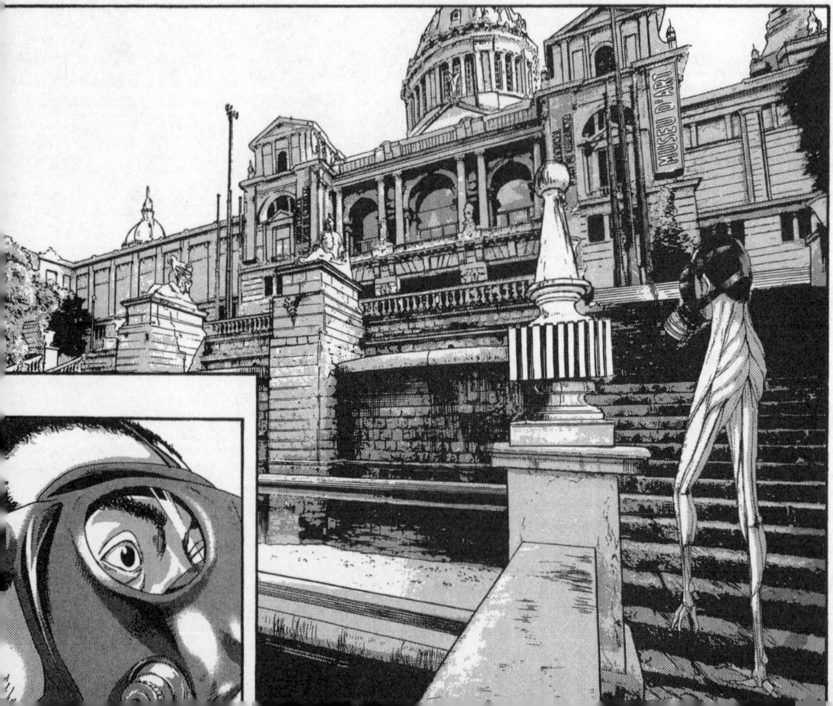
MUSEU D'ART

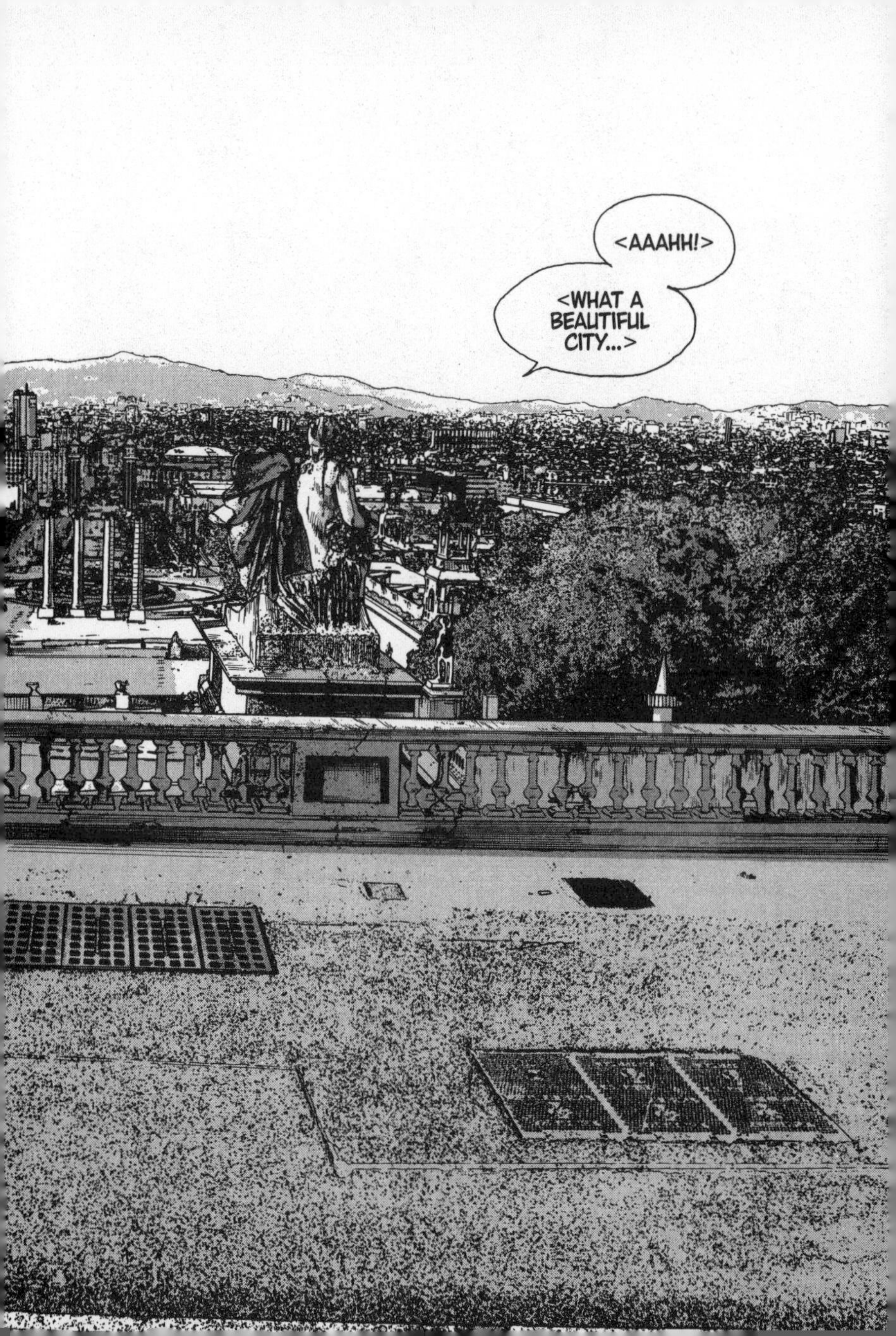
<AAAHH!>
<WHAT A BEAUTIFUL CITY...>

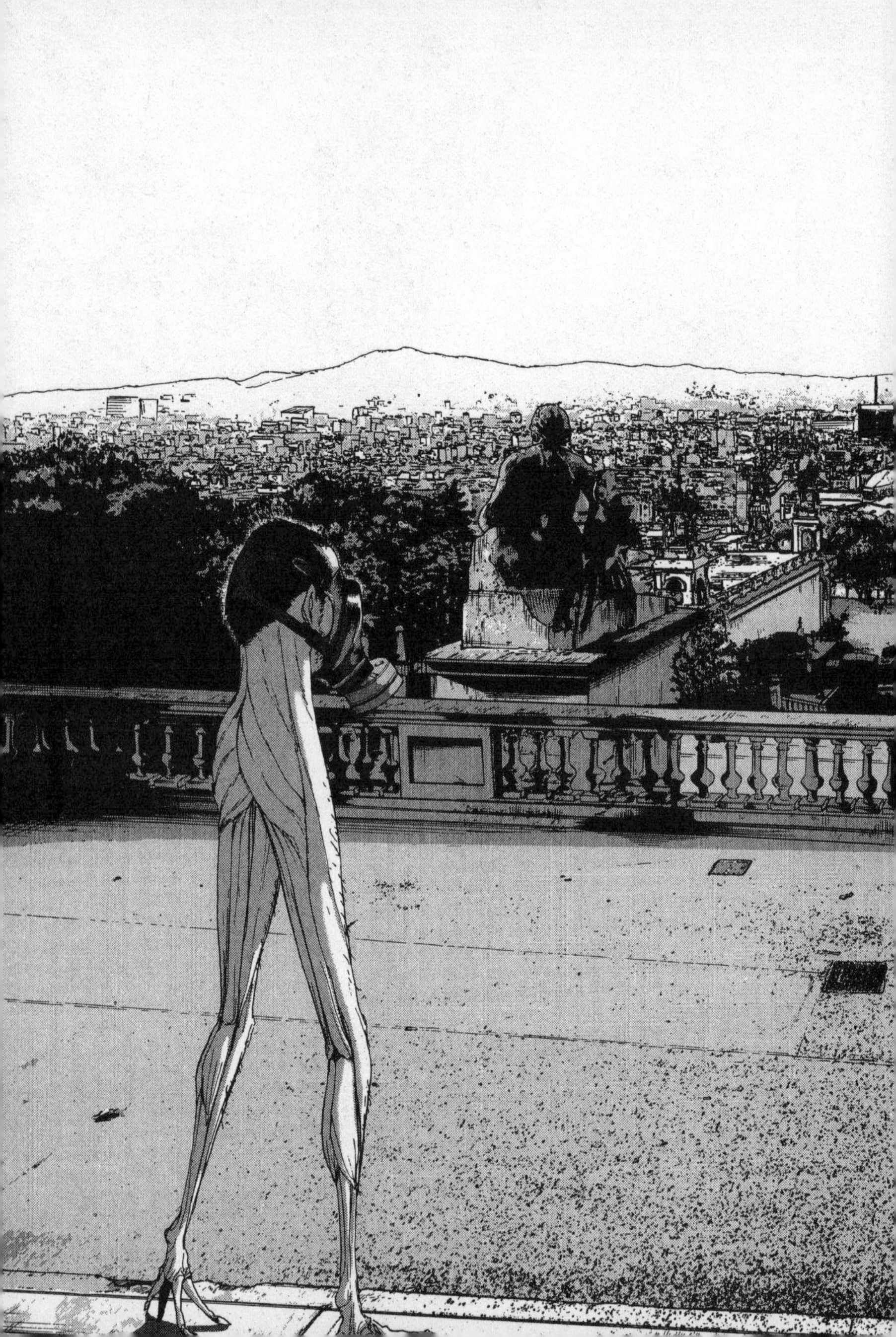

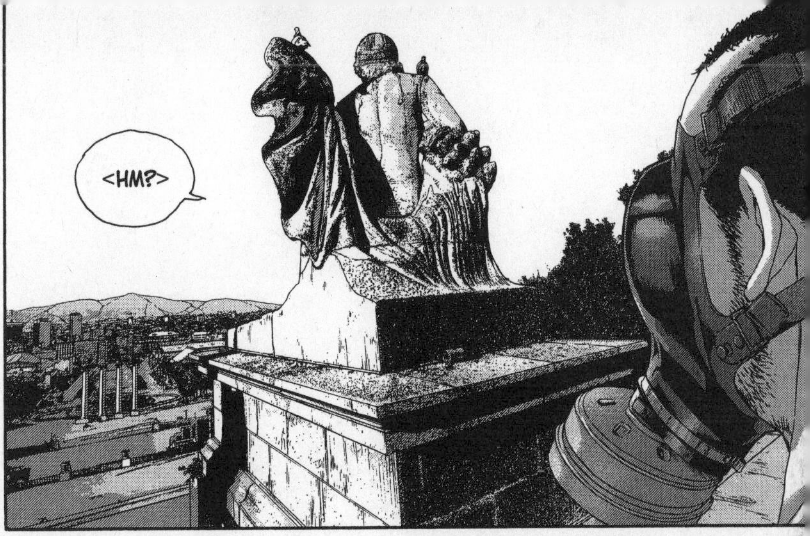
<HM?>

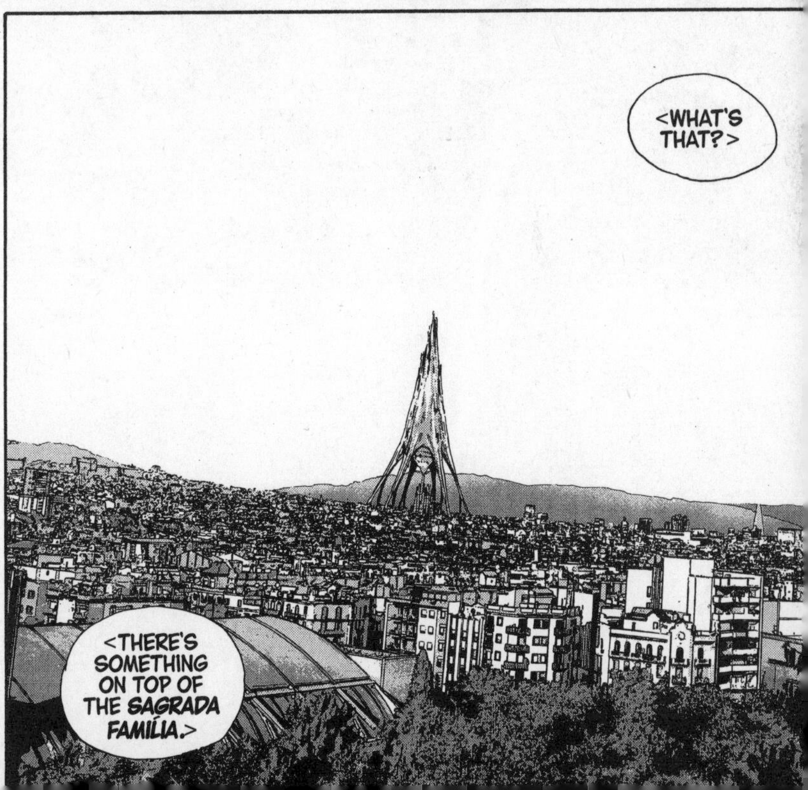
<WHAT'S THAT?>
<THERE'S SOMETHING ON TOP OF THE SAGRADA FAMÍLIA.>

CHAPTER 218

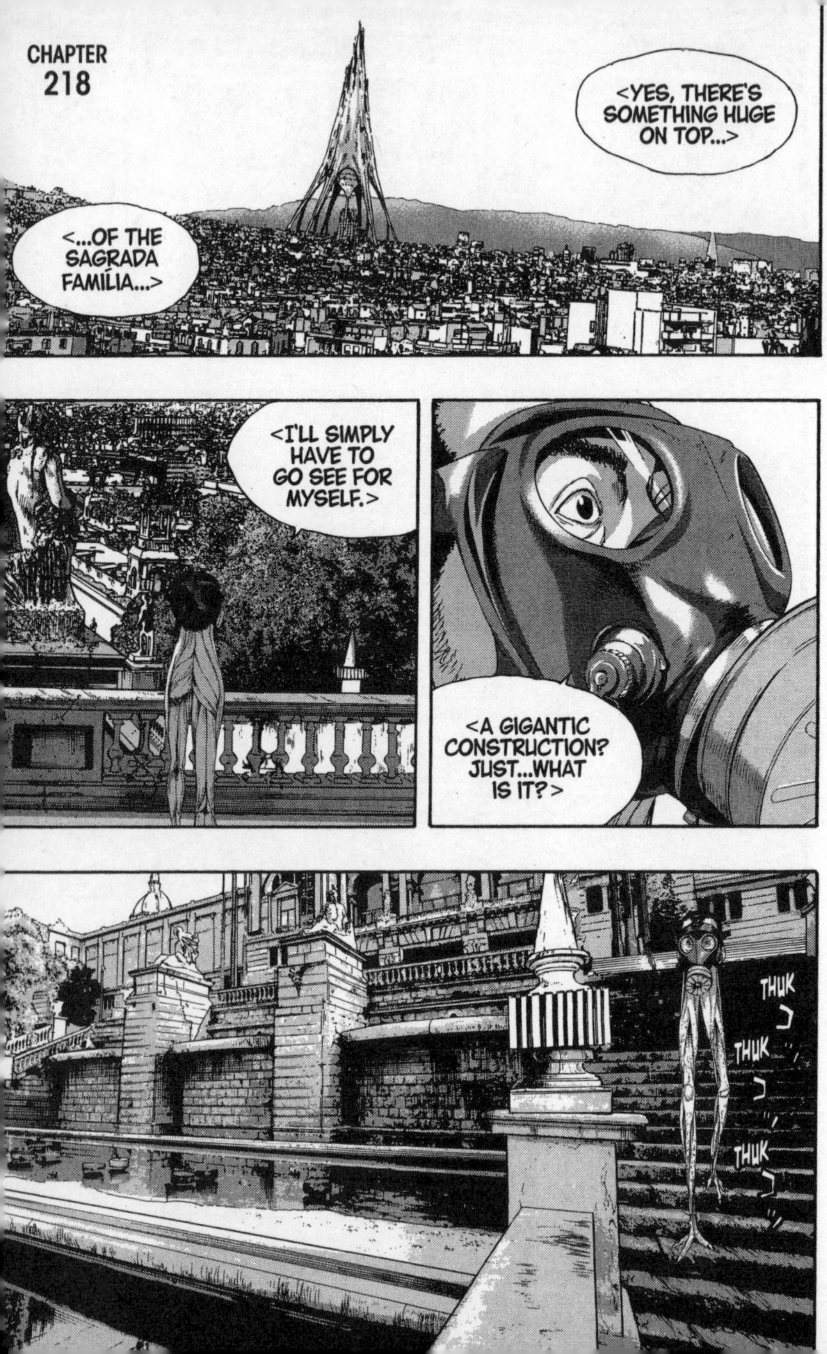
<YES, THERE'S SOMETHING HUGE ON TOP...>
<...OF THE SAGRADA FAMÍLIA...>
<A GIGANTIC CONSTRUCTION? JUST...WHAT IS IT?>
<I'LL SIMPLY HAVE TO GO SEE FOR MYSELF.>
THUK
THUK
THUK

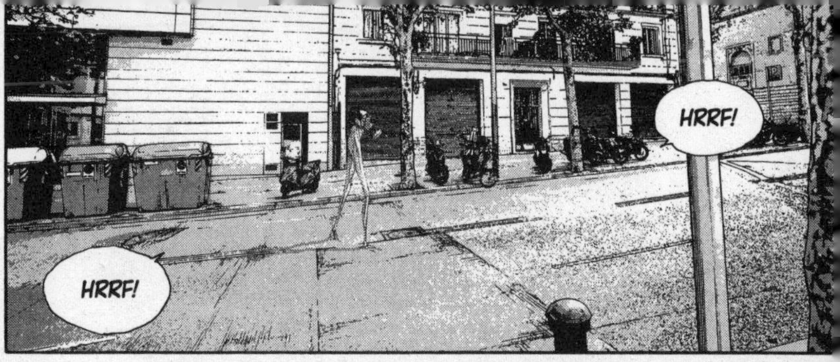
HRRF!
HRRF!

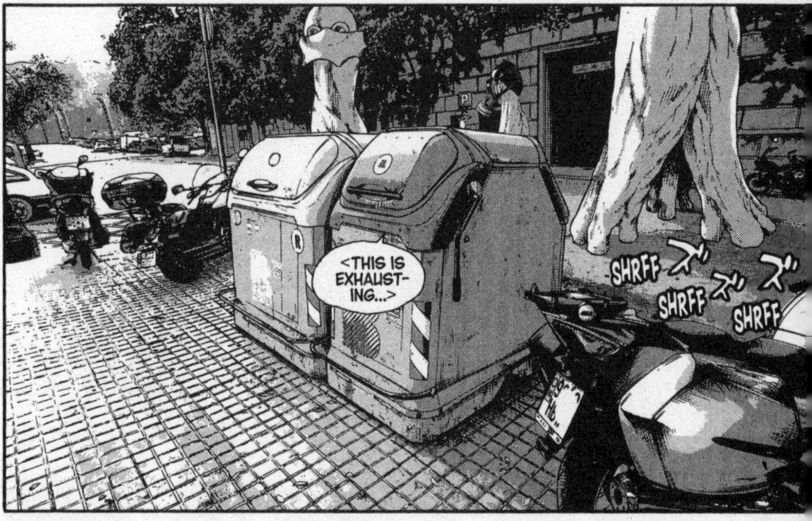
SHRFF ズ
SHRFF ズ
SHRFF ズ
<THIS IS EXHAUST-ING...>

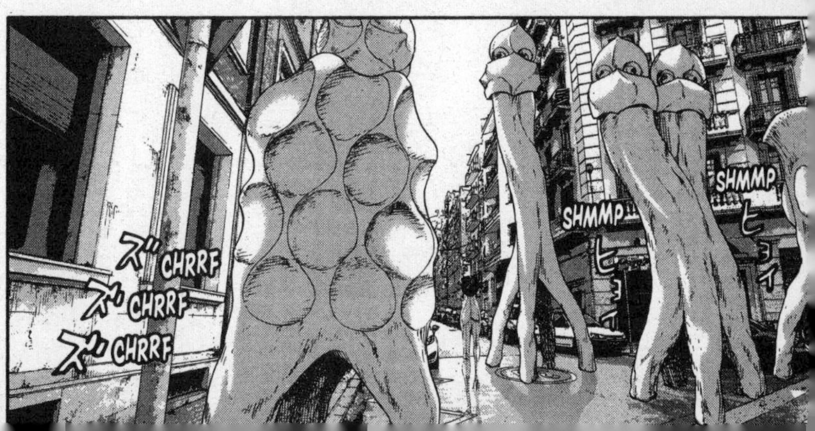
SHMMP ヒョイ
SHMMP ヒョイ
ズ CHRRF
ズ CHRRF
ズ CHRRF

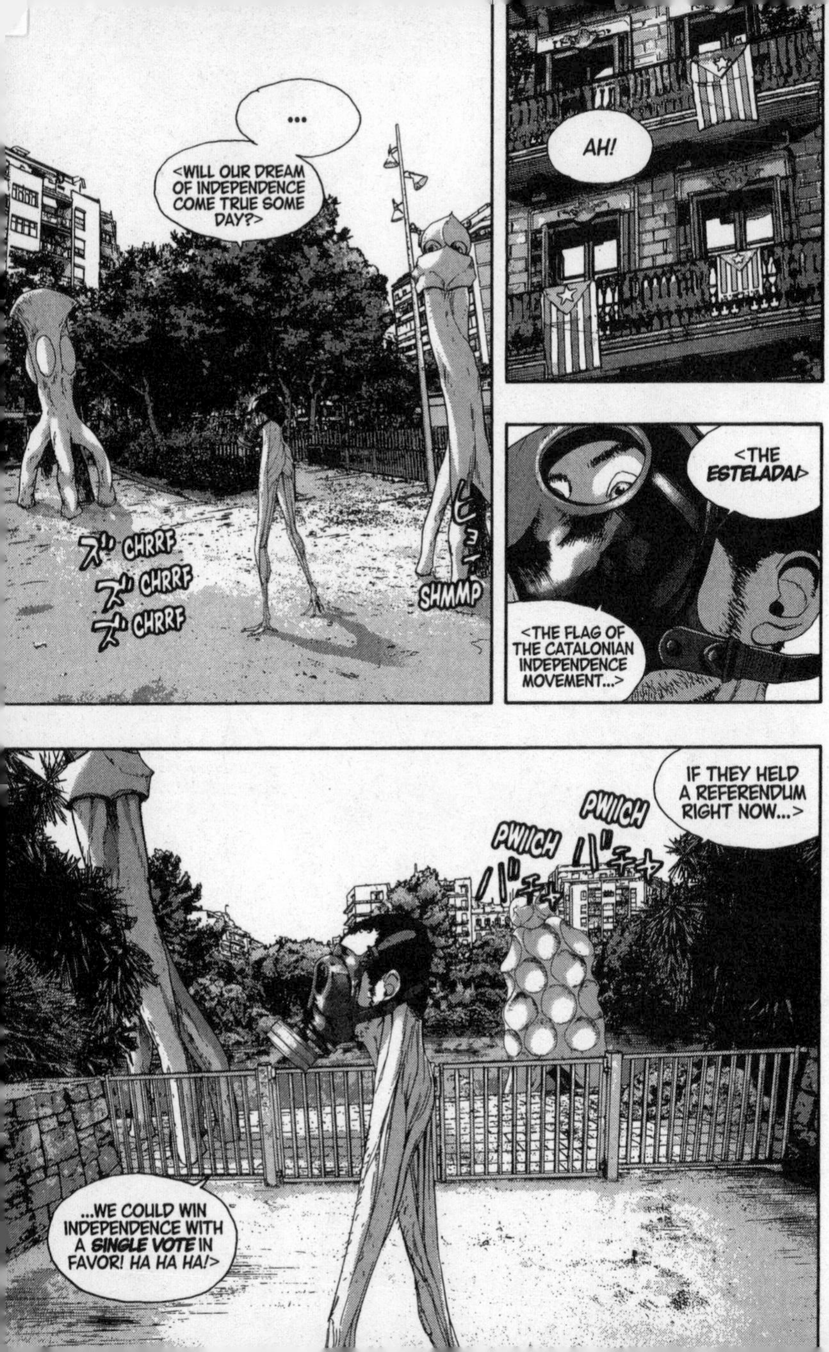
AH!
<THE ESTELADA!>
<THE FLAG OF THE CATALONIAN INDEPENDENCE MOVEMENT...>
...
<WILL OUR DREAM OF INDEPENDENCE COME TRUE SOME DAY?>
SHMMP
CHRRF
CHRRF
CHRRF
IF THEY HELD A REFERENDUM RIGHT NOW...>
PWIICH
PWIICH
...WE COULD WIN INDEPENDENCE WITH A SINGLE VOTE IN FAVOR! HA HA HA!>

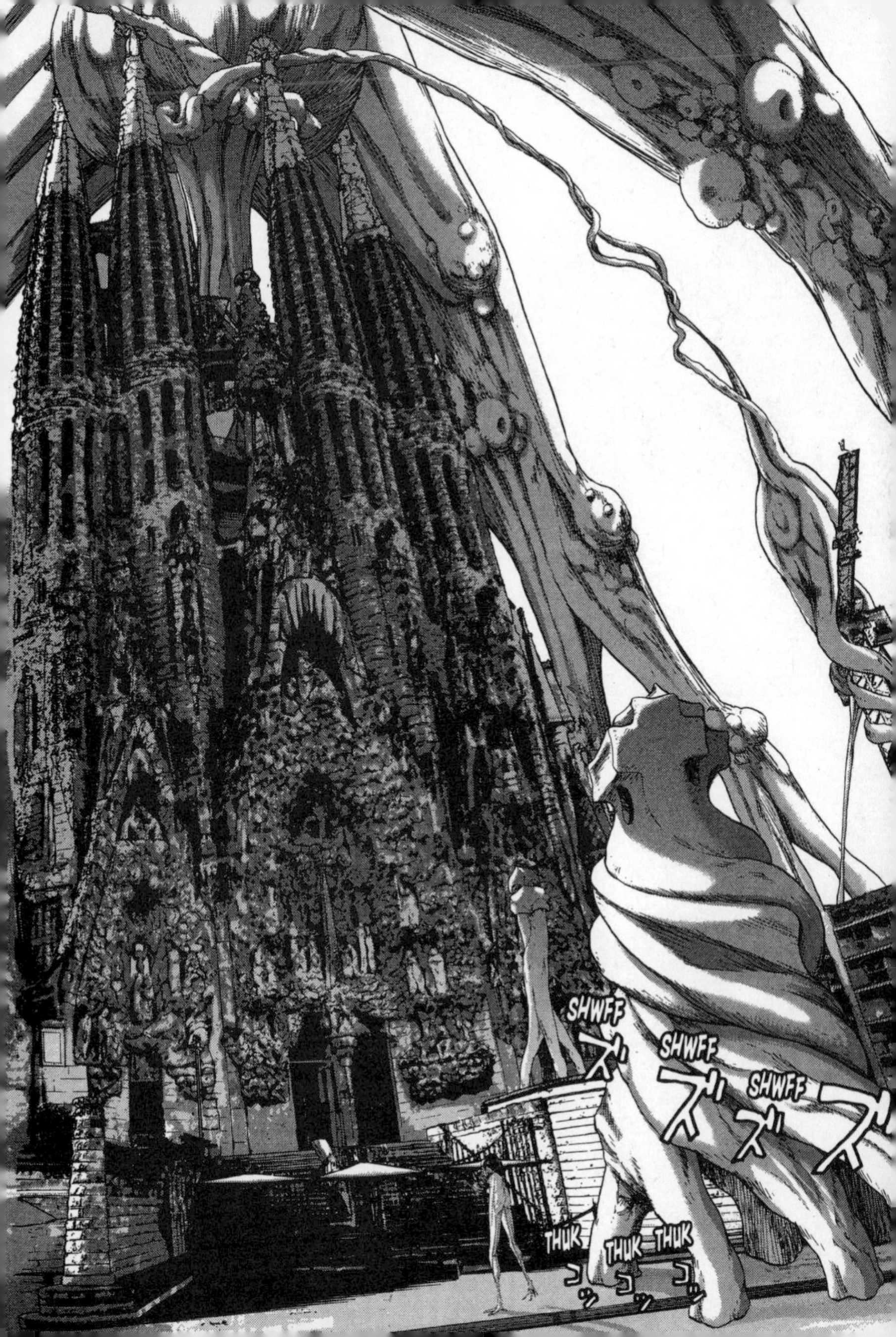
SHWFF
ズ
SHWFF
ズ
SHWFF
ズ
THUK
ゴッ
THUK
ゴッ
THUK
ゴッ

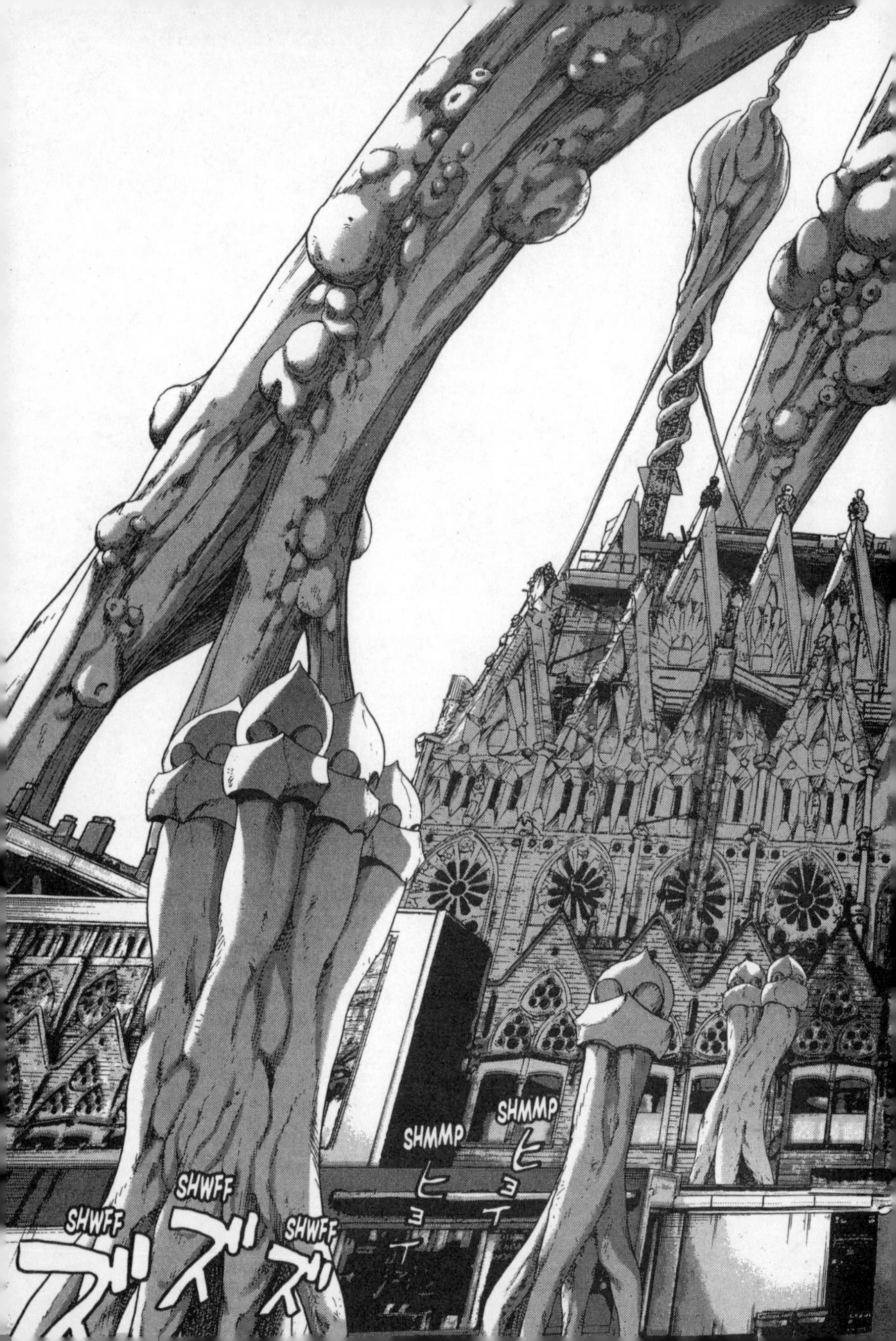
SHMMP
ヒョイ
SHMMP
ヒョイ
SHWFF
ズ
SHWFF
ズ
SHWFF
ズ

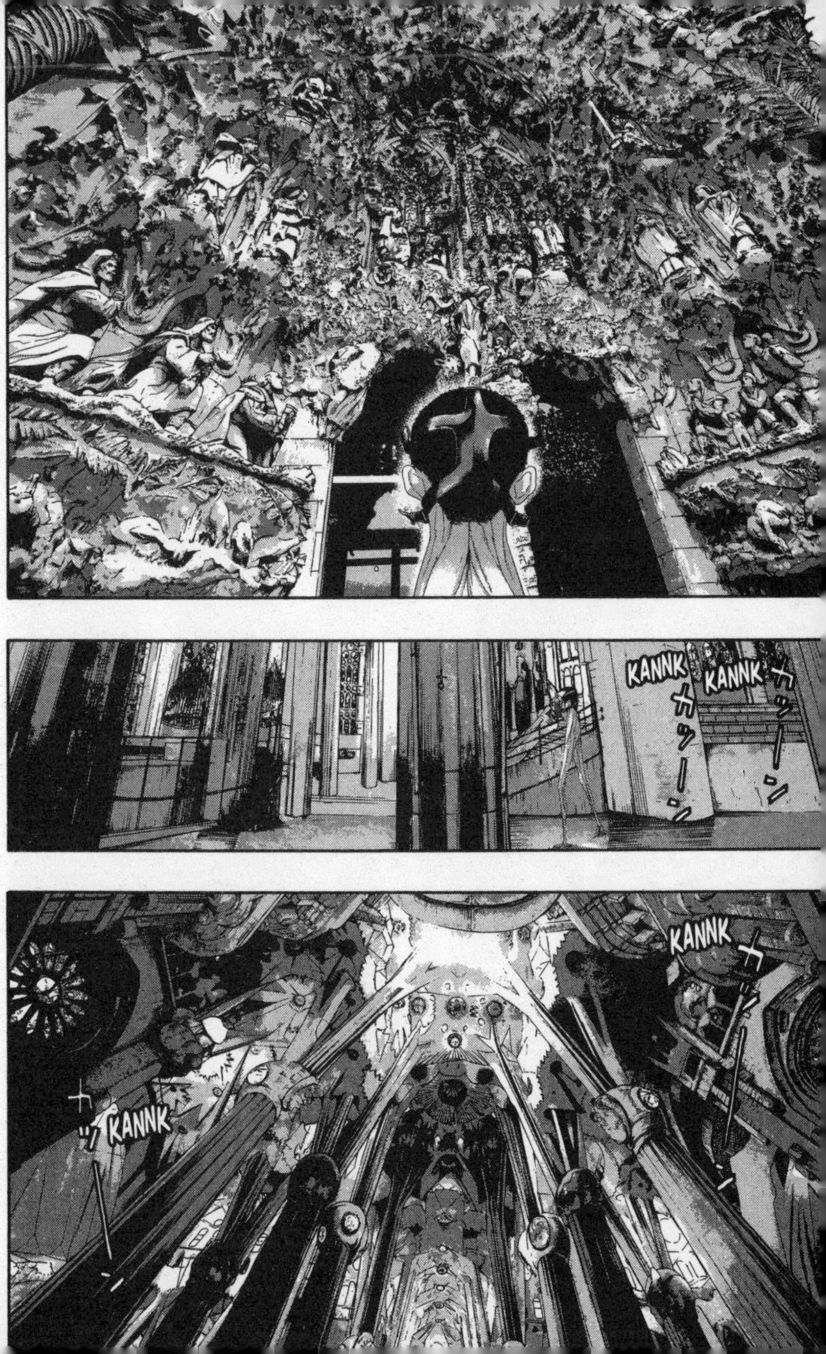
KANNK
KANNK
KANNK
KANNK

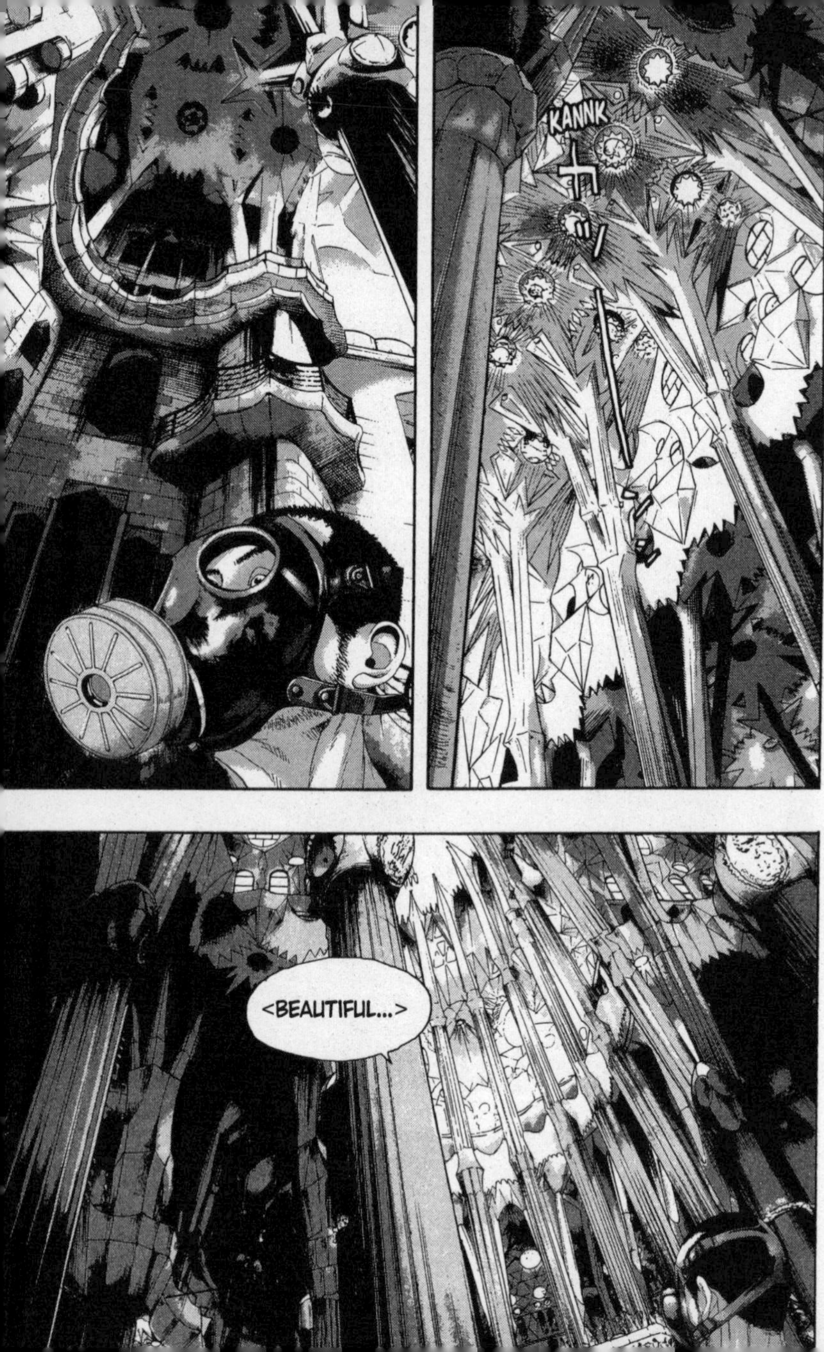
KANNK
<BEAUTIFUL...>

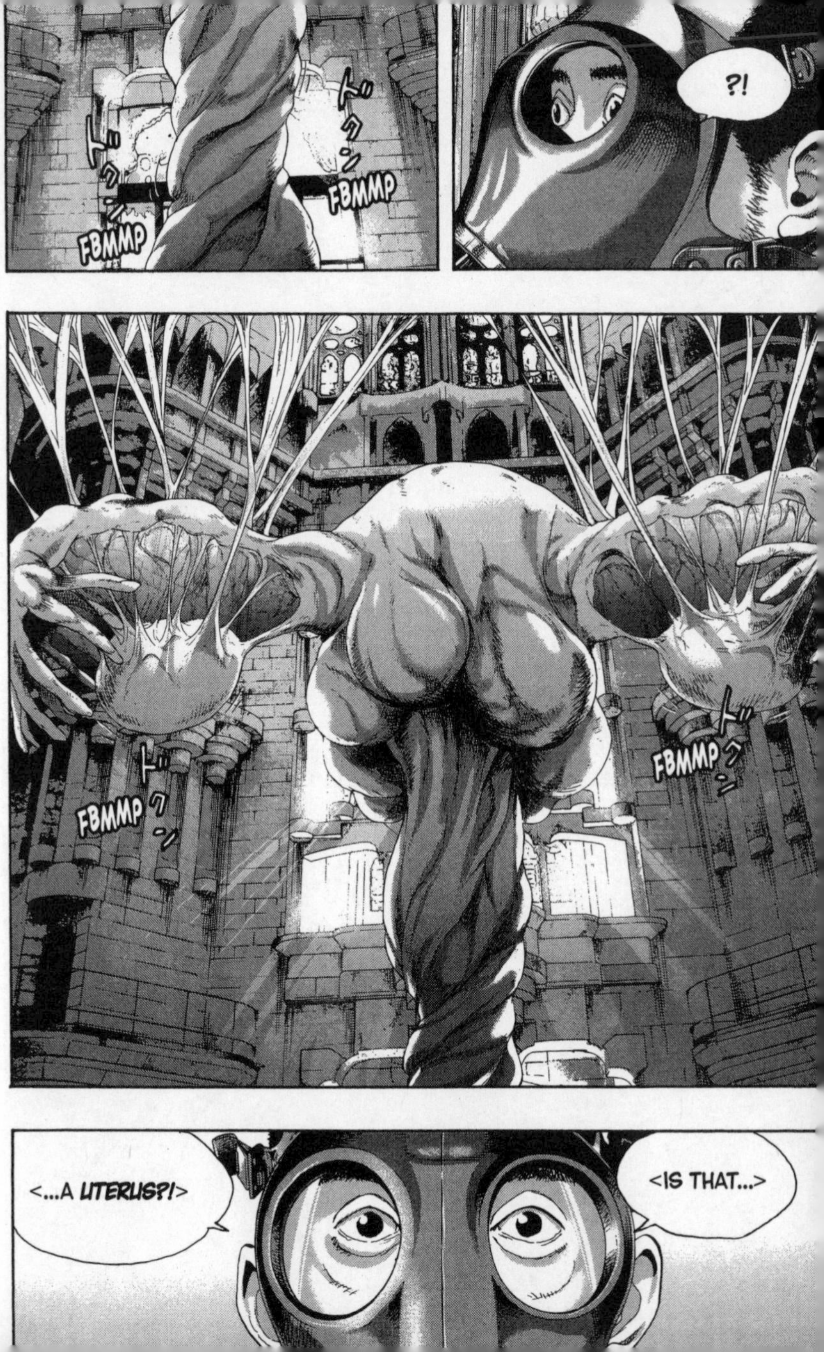
?!
FBMMP
FBMMP
FBMMP
FBMMP
<IS THAT...>
<...A *UTERUS*?!>

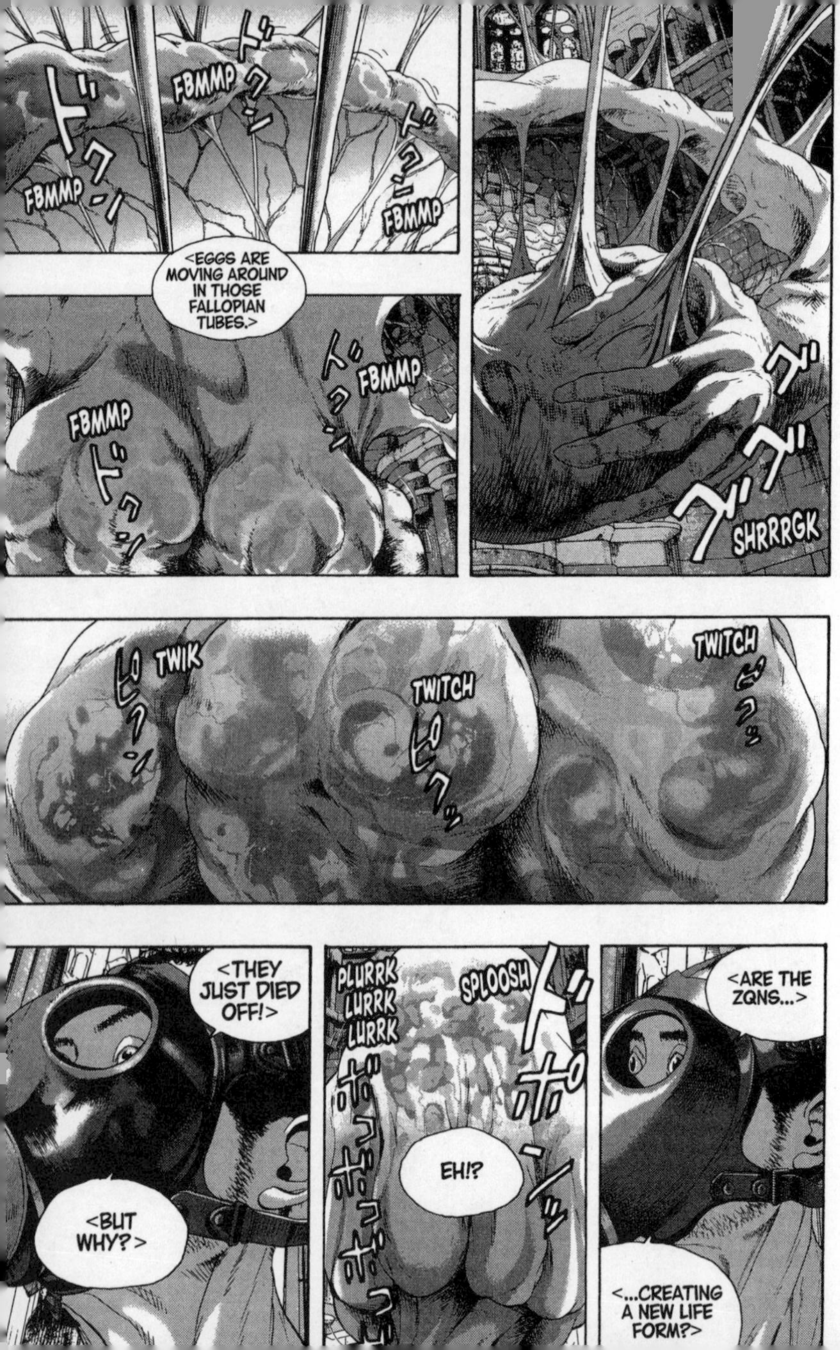
SHRRRGK
FBMMP
FBMMP
FBMMP
FBMMP
<EGGS ARE MOVING AROUND IN THOSE FALLOPIAN TUBES.>
FBMMP
FBMMP
TWITCH
TWITCH
TWIK
<ARE THE ZQNS...>
<...CREATING A NEW LIFE FORM?>
SPLOOSH
PLURRK LURRK LURRK
EH!?
<THEY JUST DIED OFF!>
<BUT WHY?>

<IS IT ALTERNATING BETWEEN LIFE AND DEATH?>

生和死没有 Ni la vida ni n sentit
Leben 和死没有 과 죽음이
ohne LIFE AND 는 없다
DEATH HAVE
NO MEANING. nificato.
non hanno significato.
tienen sentido.

<ARE YOU...>

<...A HUMAN BEING?>

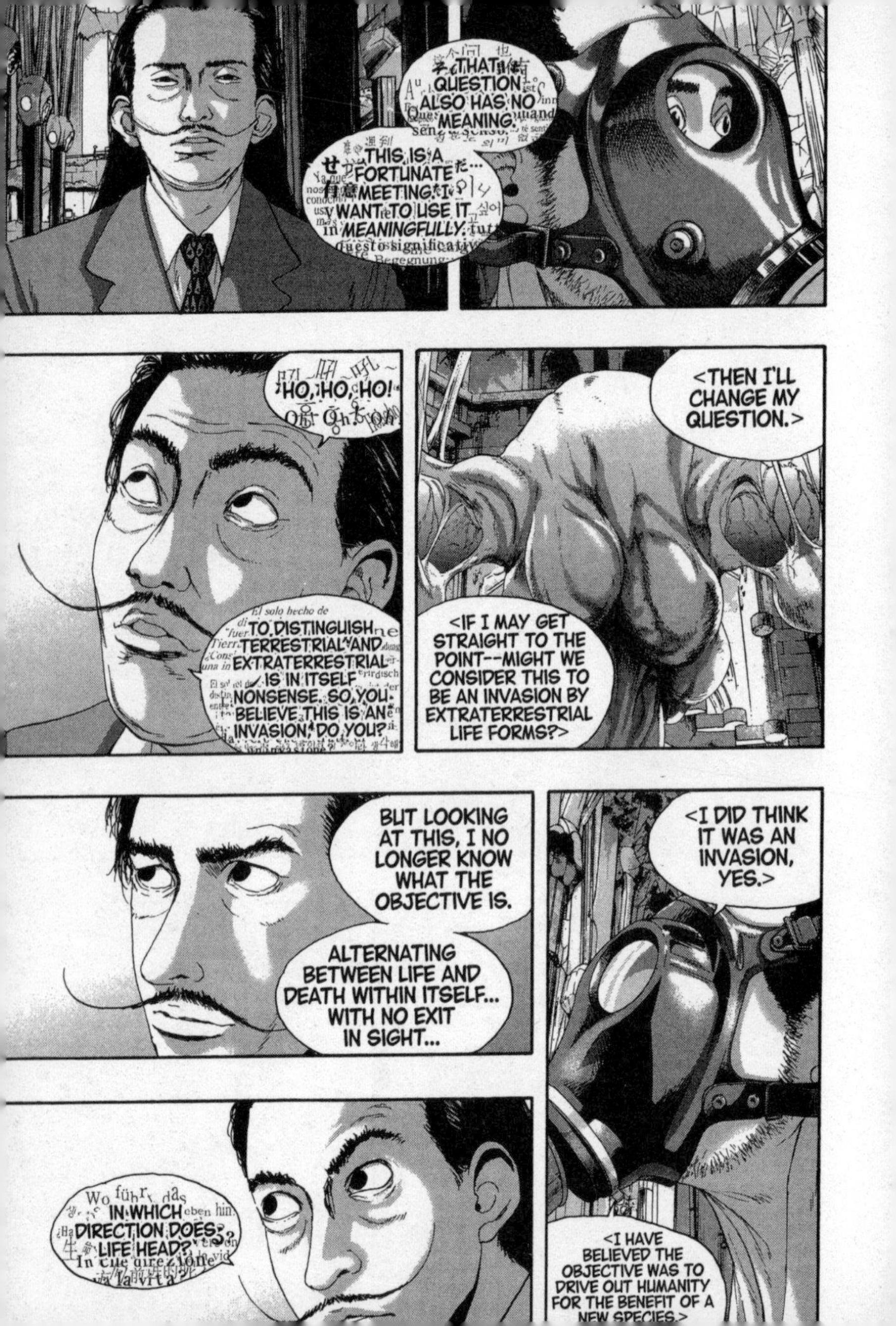
THAT QUESTION ALSO HAS NO MEANING.
THIS IS A FORTUNATE MEETING. I WANT TO USE IT MEANINGFULLY.
<THEN I'LL CHANGE MY QUESTION.>
<IF I MAY GET STRAIGHT TO THE POINT--MIGHT WE CONSIDER THIS TO BE AN INVASION BY EXTRATERRESTRIAL LIFE FORMS?>
HO, HO, HO!
TO DISTINGUISH TERRESTRIAL AND EXTRATERRESTRIAL IS IN ITSELF NONSENSE. SO YOU BELIEVE THIS IS AN INVASION, DO YOU?
<I DID THINK IT WAS AN INVASION, YES.>
<I HAVE BELIEVED THE OBJECTIVE WAS TO DRIVE OUT HUMANITY FOR THE BENEFIT OF A NEW SPECIES.>
BUT LOOKING AT THIS, I NO LONGER KNOW WHAT THE OBJECTIVE IS.
ALTERNATING BETWEEN LIFE AND DEATH WITHIN ITSELF... WITH NO EXIT IN SIGHT...
IN WHICH DIRECTION DOES LIFE HEAD?

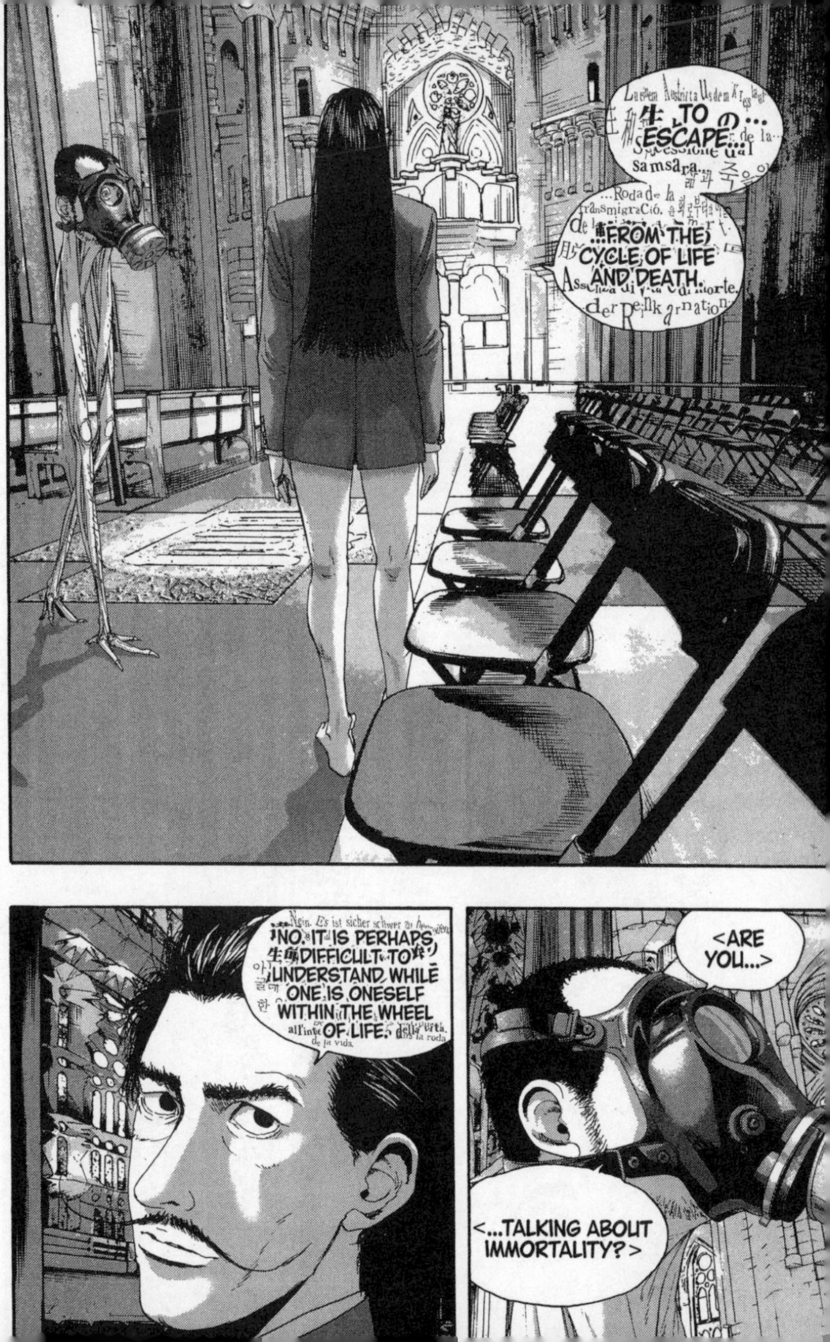
TO ESCAPE...
...FROM THE CYCLE OF LIFE AND DEATH.
<ARE YOU...>
<...TALKING ABOUT IMMORTALITY?>
NO. IT IS PERHAPS DIFFICULT TO UNDERSTAND WHILE ONE IS ONESELF WITHIN THE WHEEL OF LIFE.

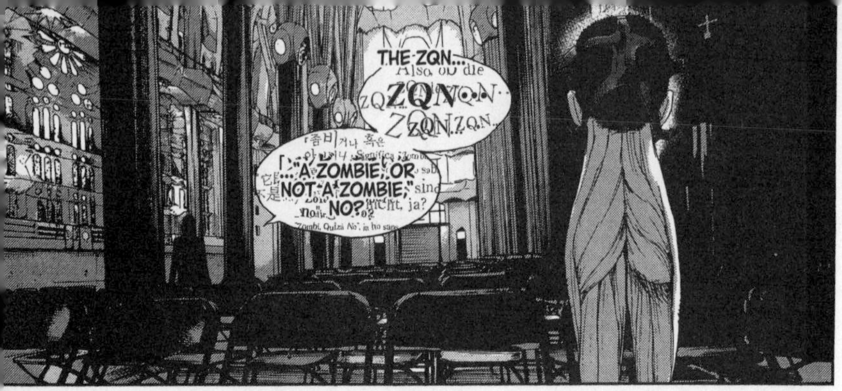
THE ZQN... ZQN
...A ZOMBIE, OR NOT A ZOMBIE," NO?
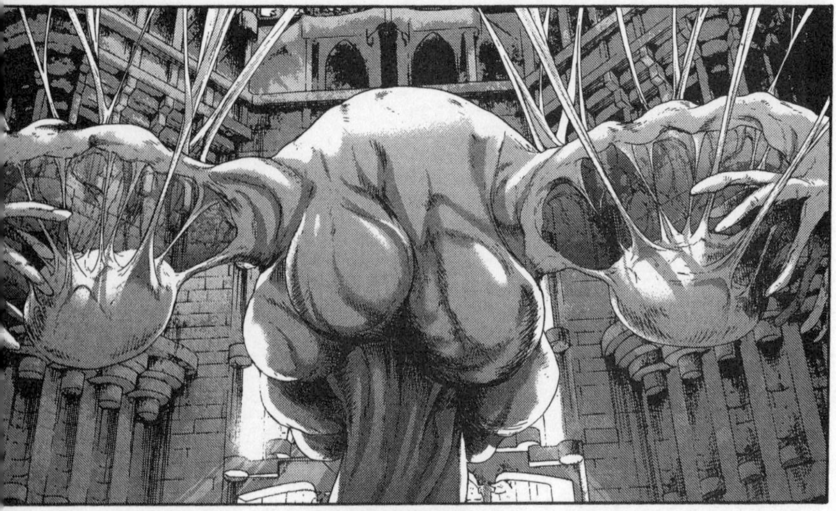
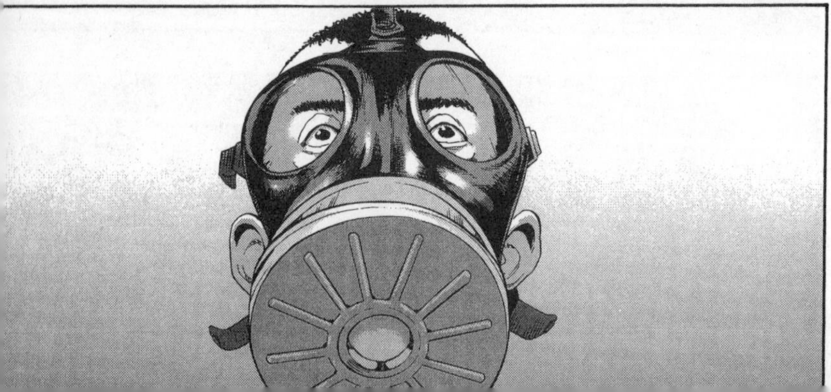

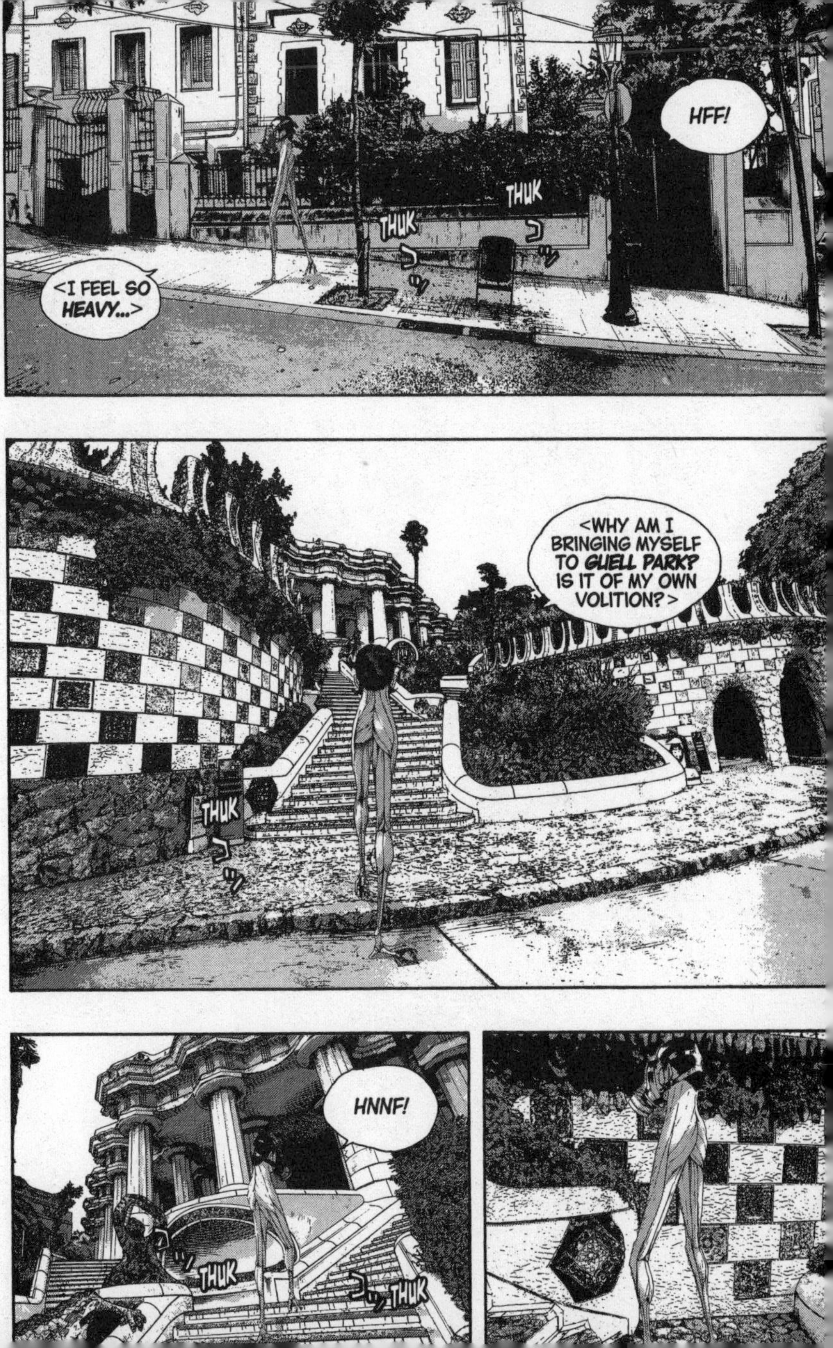
HFF!
THUK
THUK
<I FEEL SO HEAVY...>
<WHY AM I BRINGING MYSELF TO GUELL PARK? IS IT OF MY OWN VOLITION?>
THUK
HNNF!
THUK
THUK

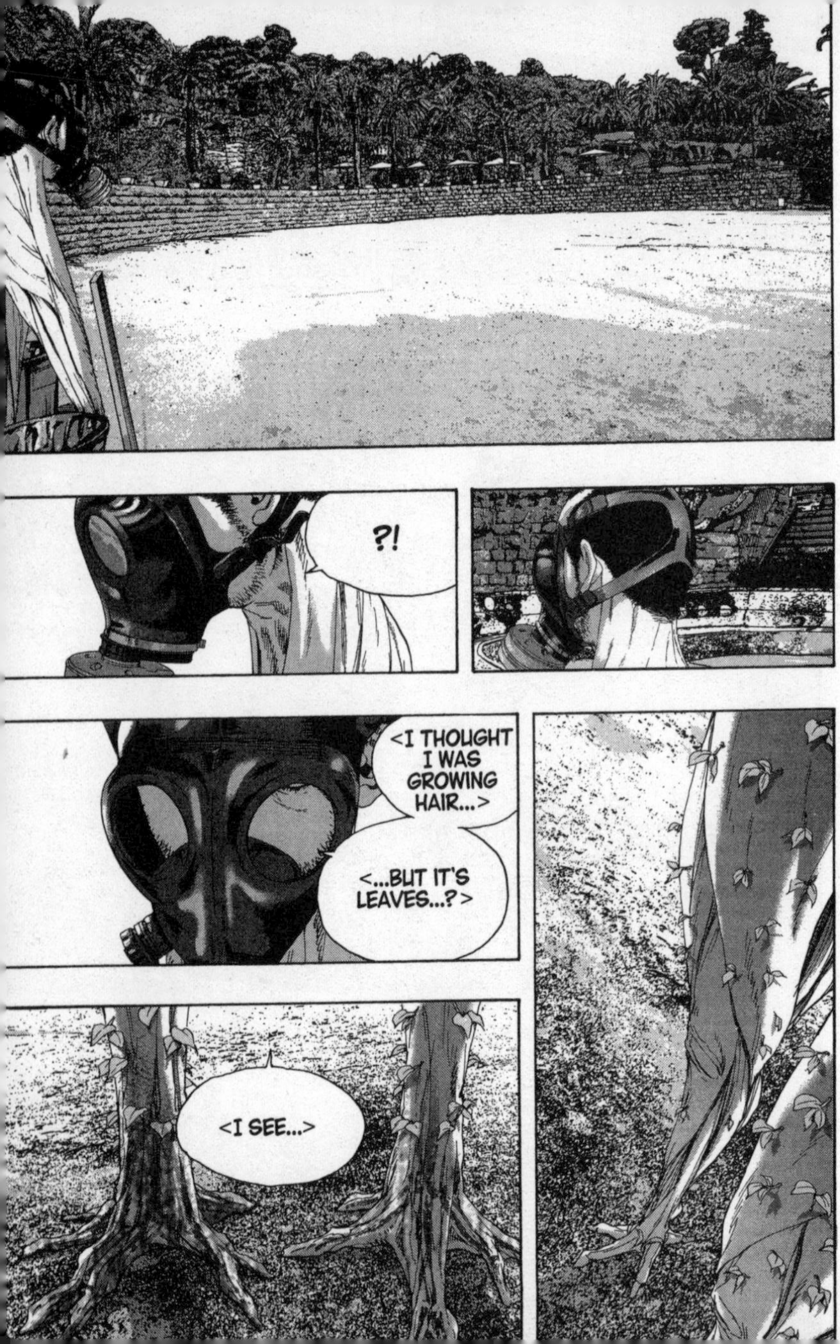
?!
<I THOUGHT I WAS GROWING HAIR...>
<...BUT IT'S LEAVES...?>
<I SEE...>

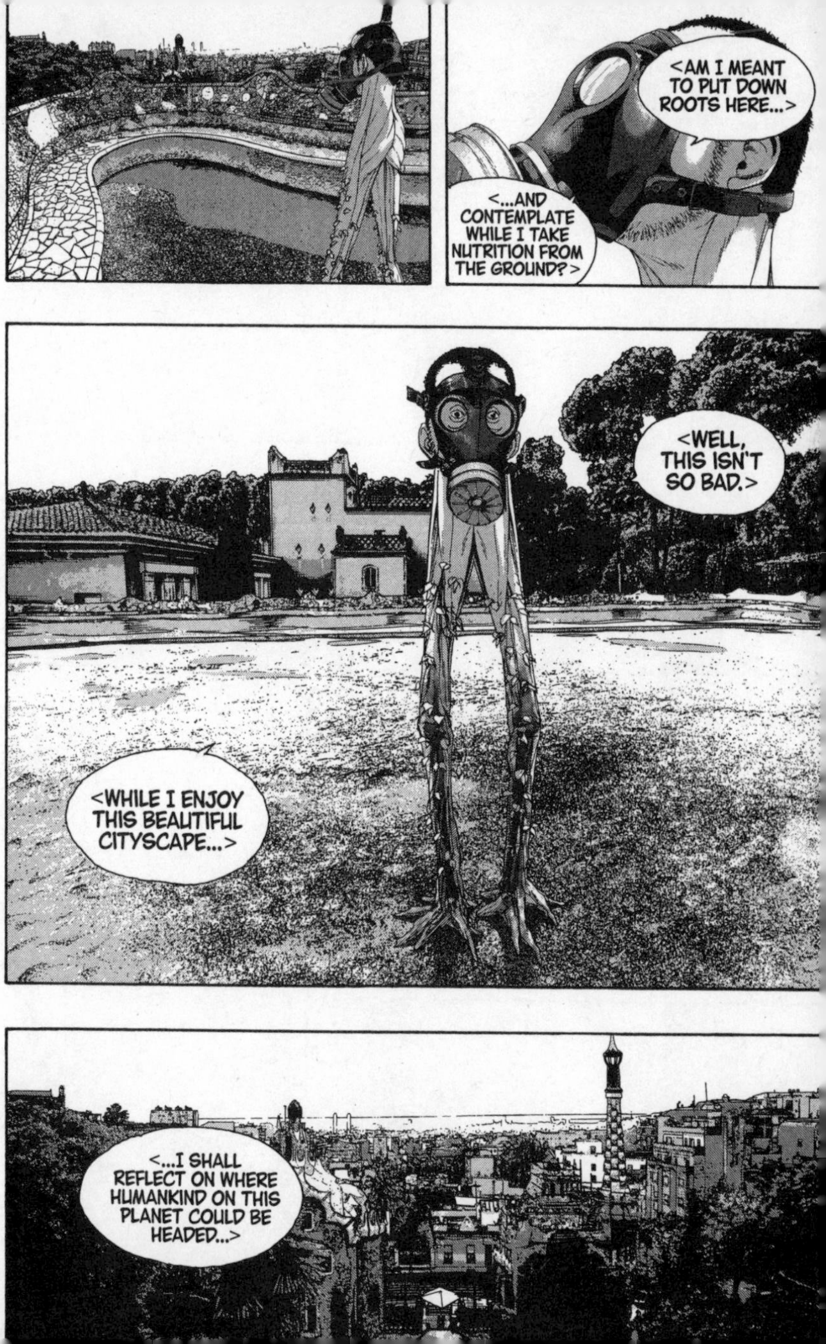
<AM I MEANT TO PUT DOWN ROOTS HERE...>
<...AND CONTEMPLATE WHILE I TAKE NUTRITION FROM THE GROUND?>
<WELL, THIS ISN'T SO BAD.>
<WHILE I ENJOY THIS BEAUTIFUL CITYSCAPE...>
<...I SHALL REFLECT ON WHERE HUMANKIND ON THIS PLANET COULD BE HEADED...>

CHAPTER 219

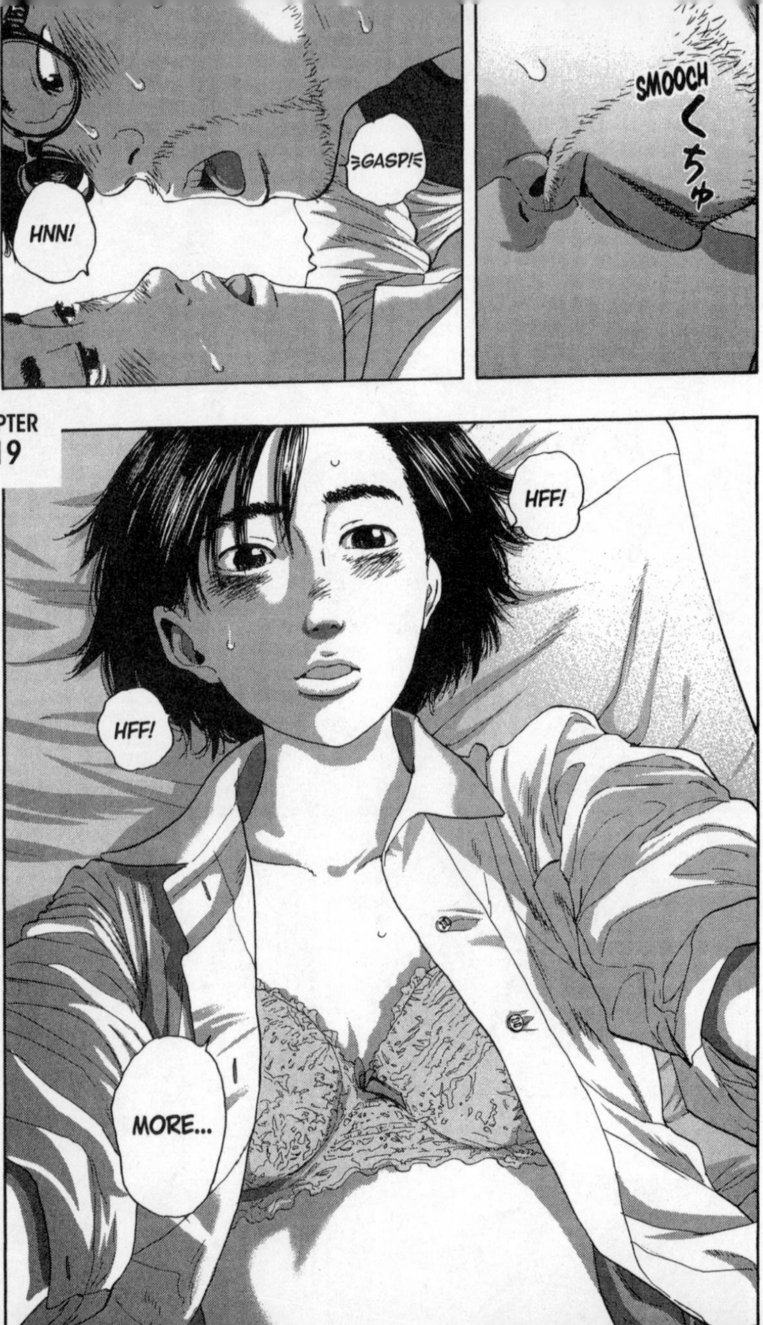
SMOOCH
くちゅ
GASP!
HNN!
HFF!
HFF!
MORE...

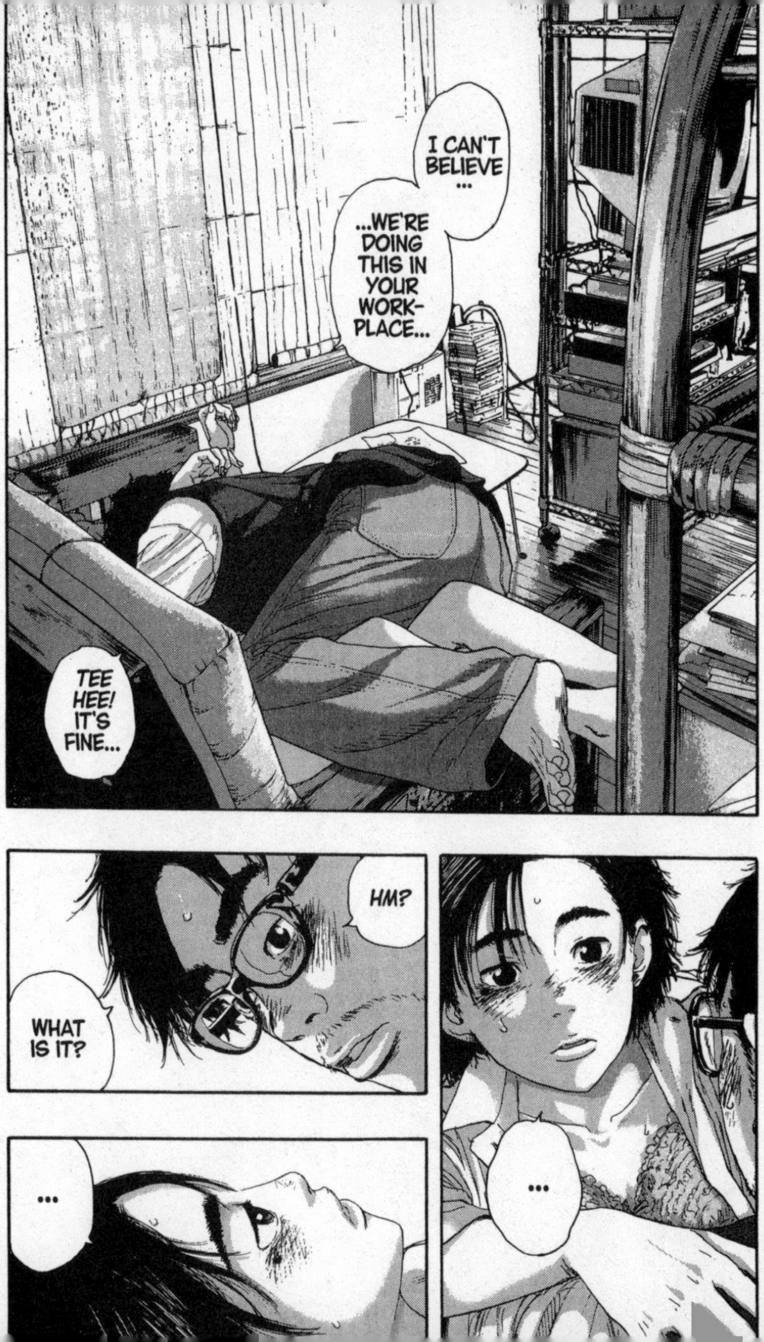
I CAN'T BELIEVE ...
...WE'RE DOING THIS IN YOUR WORK-PLACE...
TEE HEE! IT'S FINE...
...
HM?
WHAT IS IT?
...

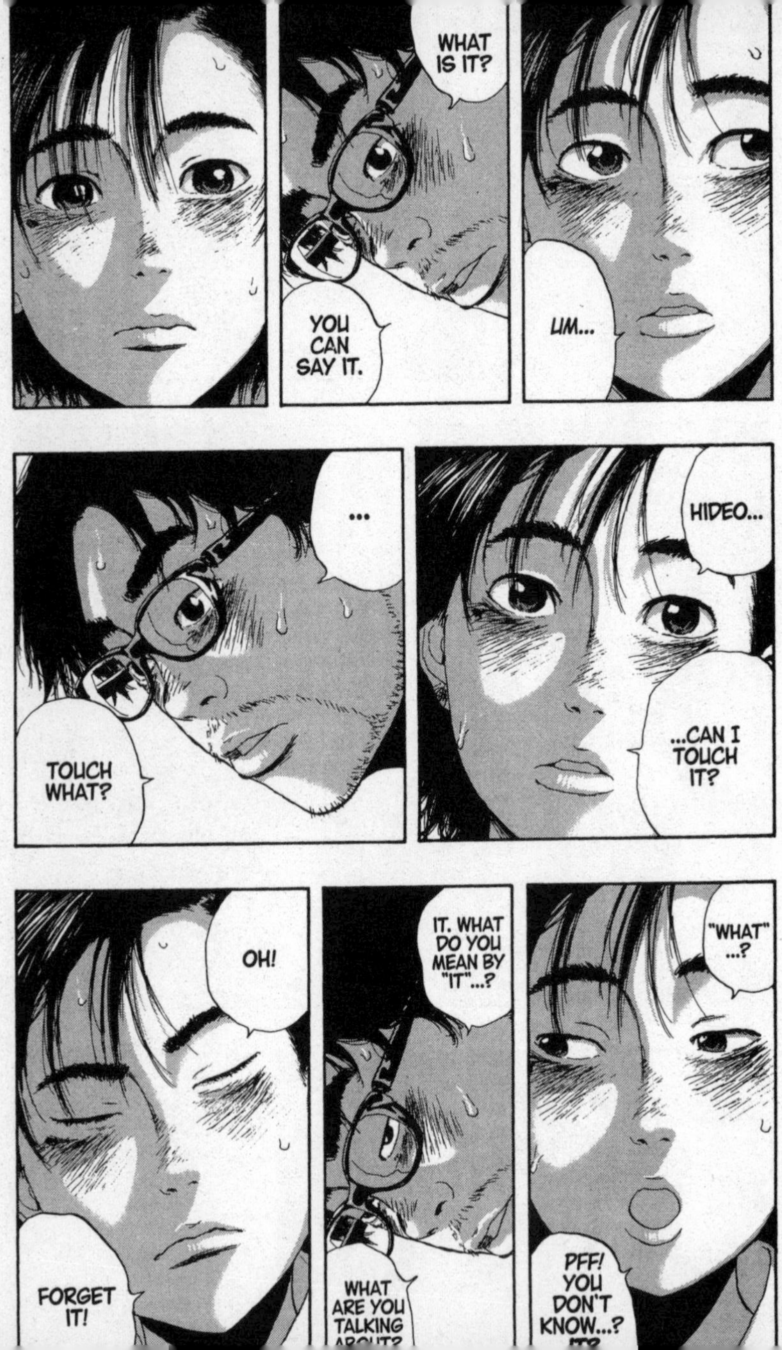
UM...
WHAT IS IT?
YOU CAN SAY IT.
HIDEO...
...CAN I TOUCH IT?
...
TOUCH WHAT?
"WHAT" ...?
PFF! YOU DON'T KNOW...?
IT. WHAT DO YOU MEAN BY "IT"...?
WHAT ARE YOU TALKING
OH!
FORGET IT!

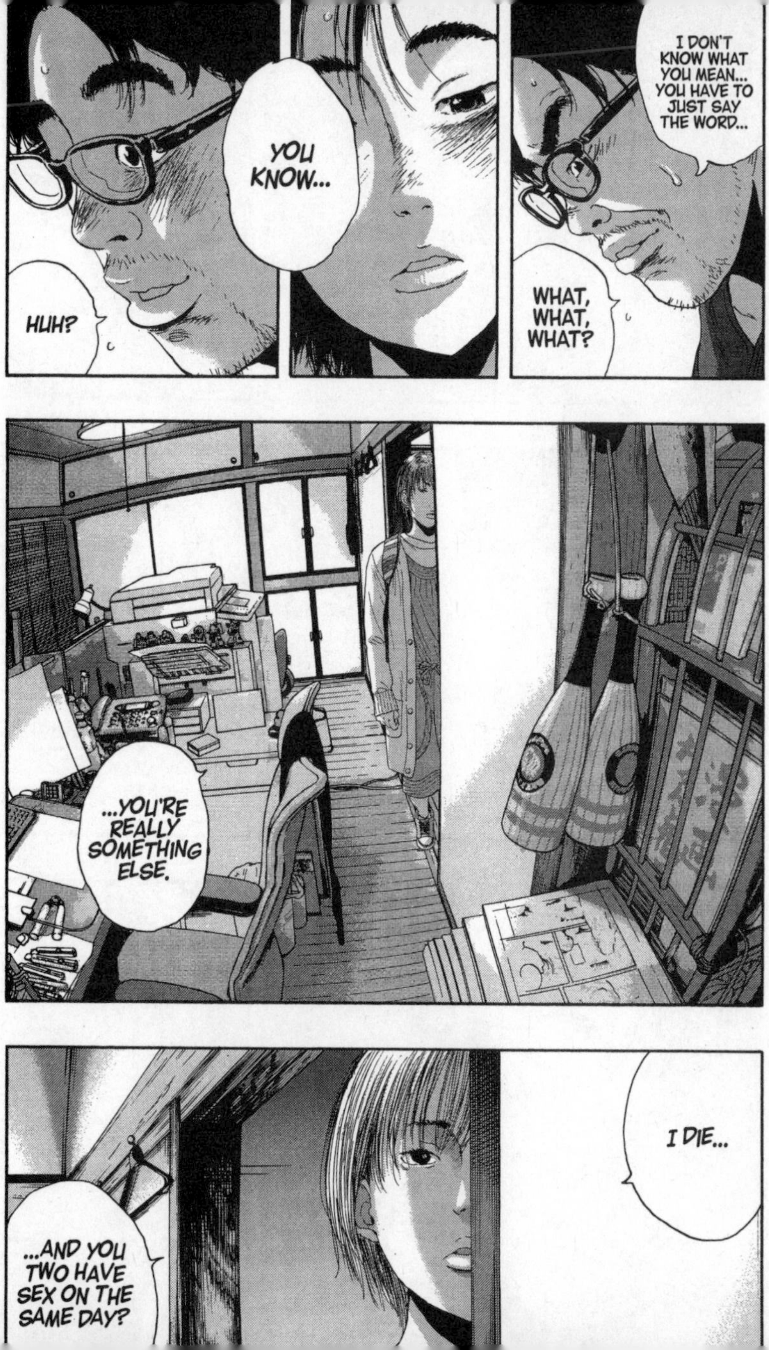
I DON'T KNOW WHAT YOU MEAN... YOU HAVE TO JUST SAY THE WORD...
WHAT, WHAT, WHAT?
YOU KNOW...
HUH?
...YOU'RE REALLY SOMETHING ELSE.
I DIE...
...AND YOU TWO HAVE SEX ON THE SAME DAY?

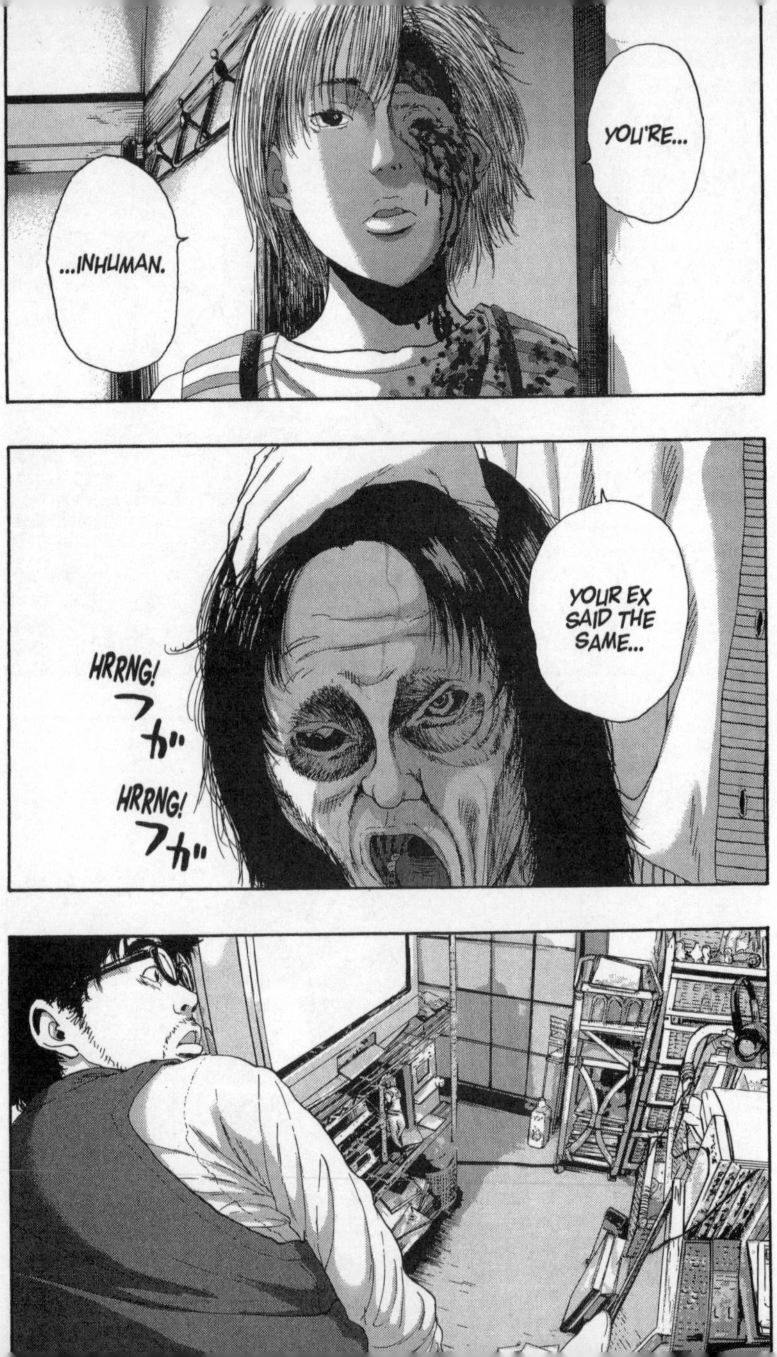
YOU'RE...
...INHUMAN.
YOUR EX SAID THE SAME...
HRRNG!
フガ
HRRNG!
フガ

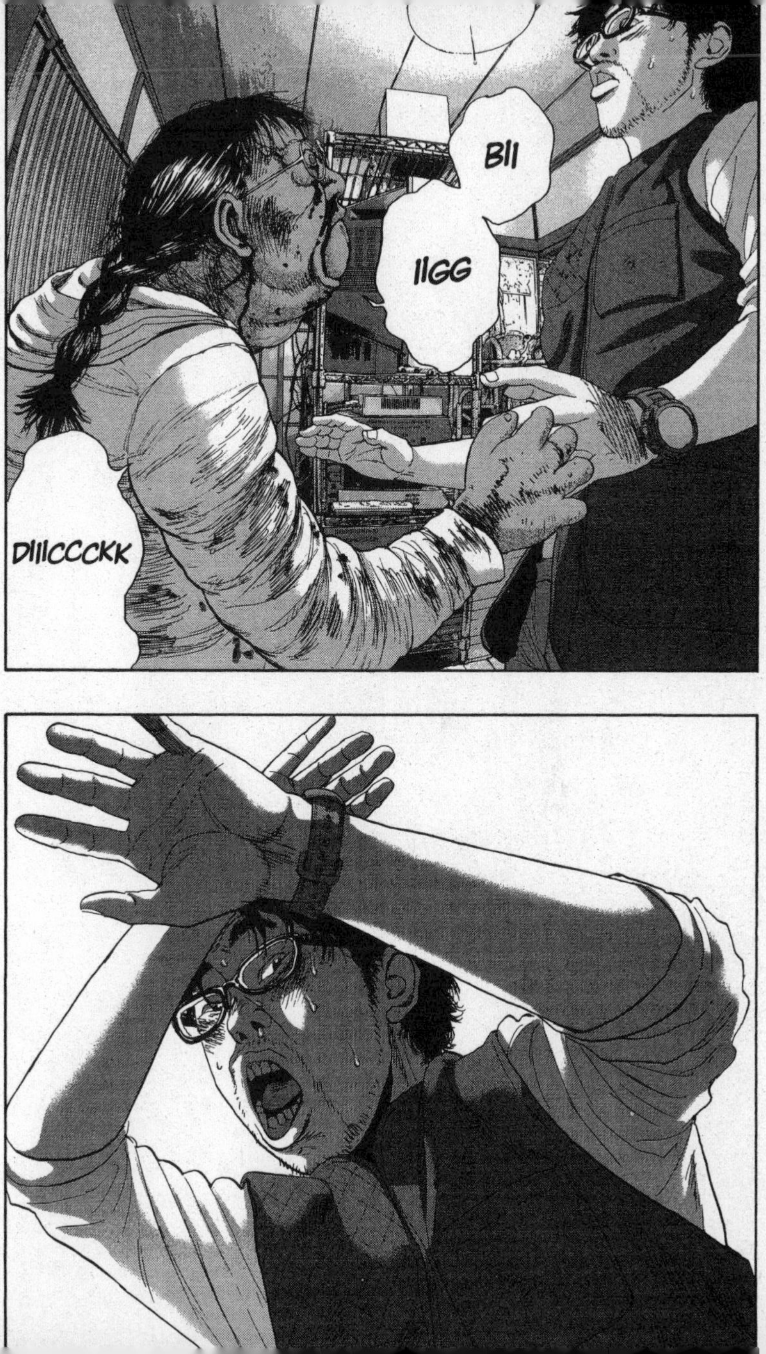
BII
IIGG
DIIICCCKK

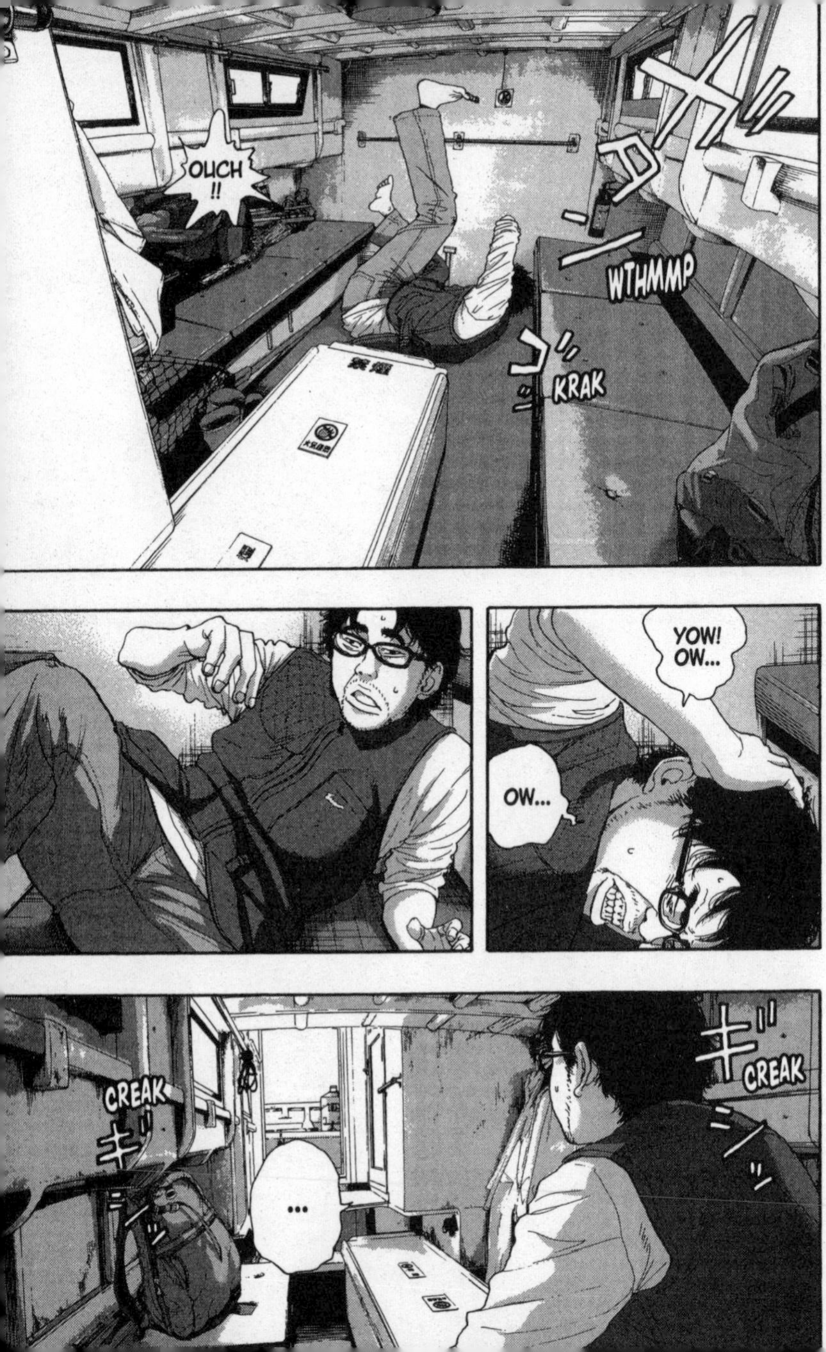
WTHMMP
KRAK
OUCH !!
YOW! OW...
OW...
CREAK
...
CREAK

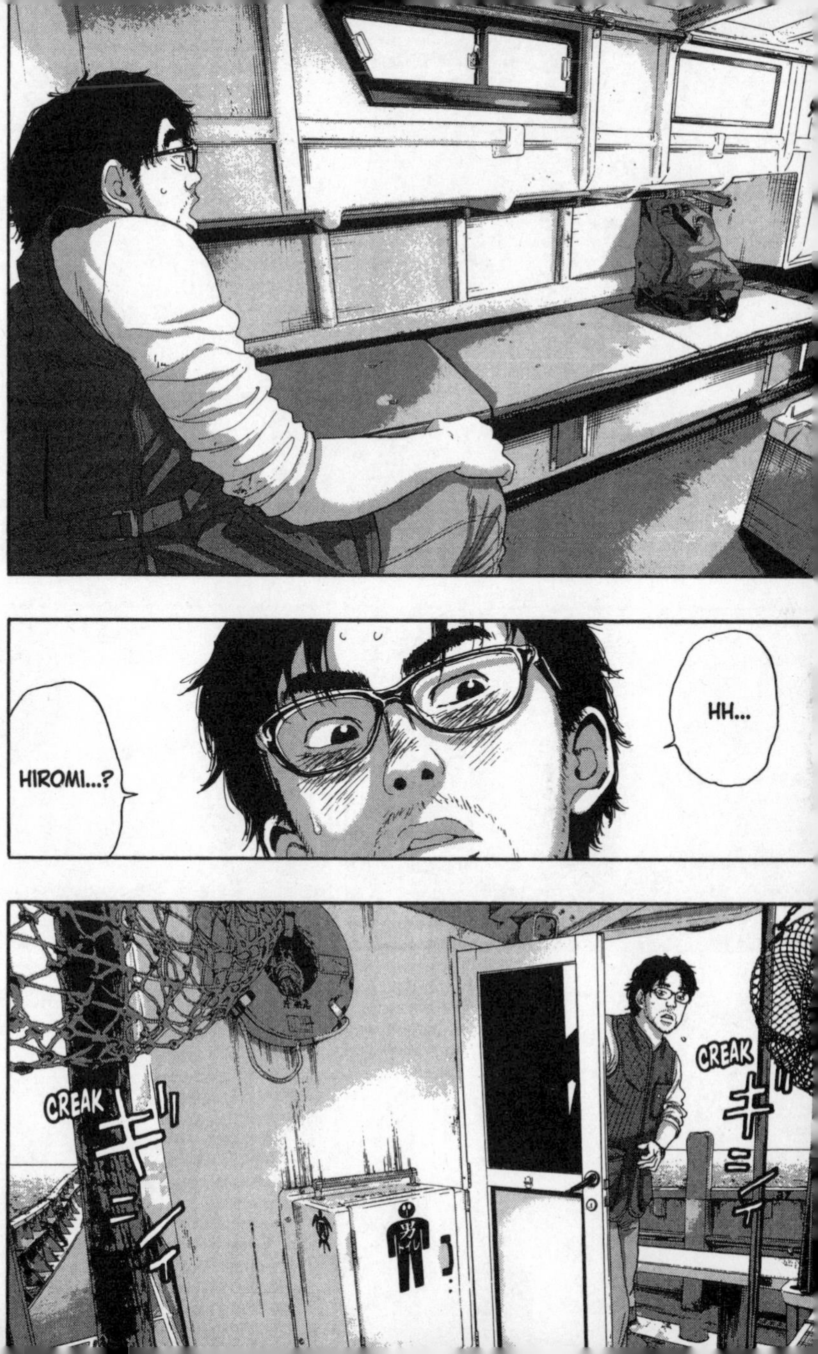
HH...
HIROMI...?
CREAK
CREAK

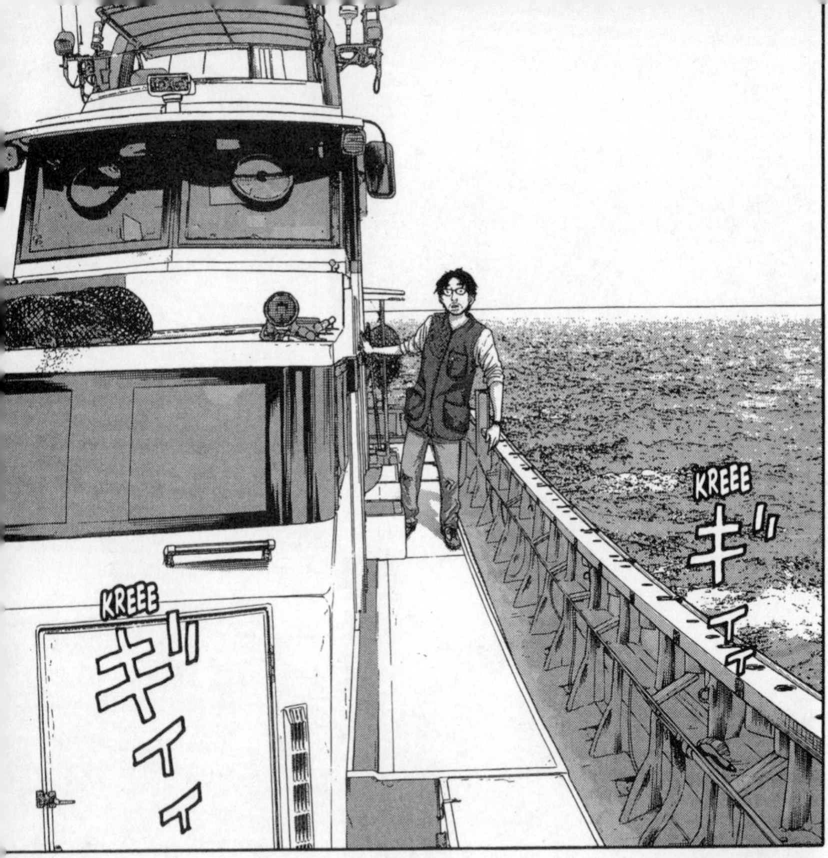
KREEE
ギィィ
KREEE
ギィィ
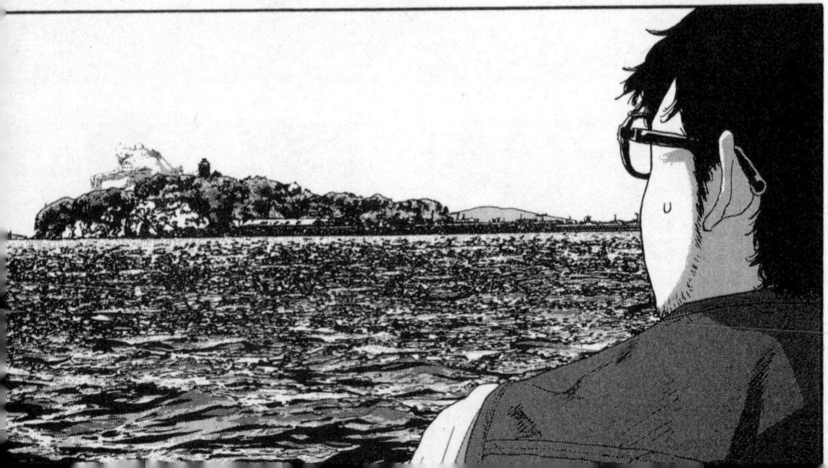

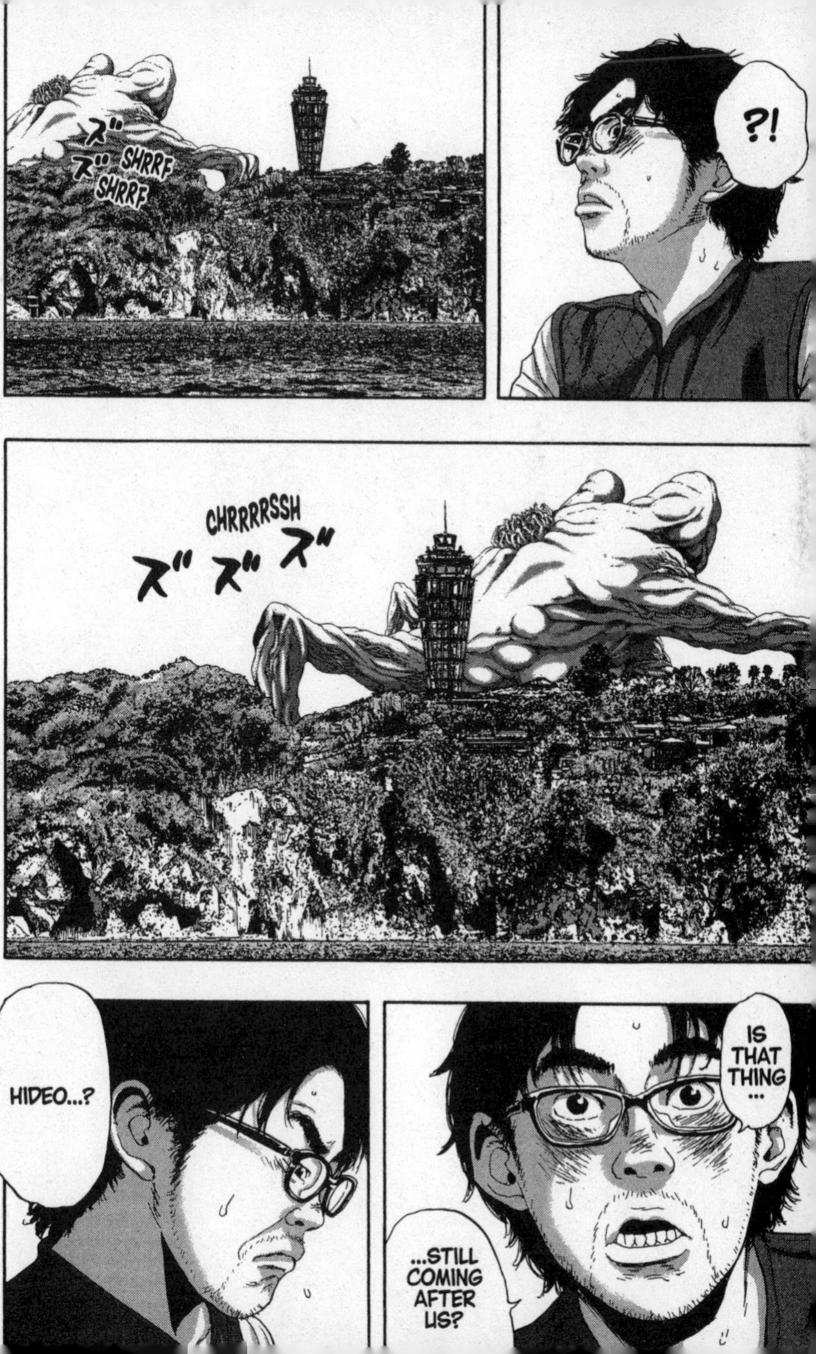
?!
ズズ
SHRRF SHRRF
CHRRRRSSH
ズズズ
IS THAT THING...
...STILL COMING AFTER US?
HIDEO...?

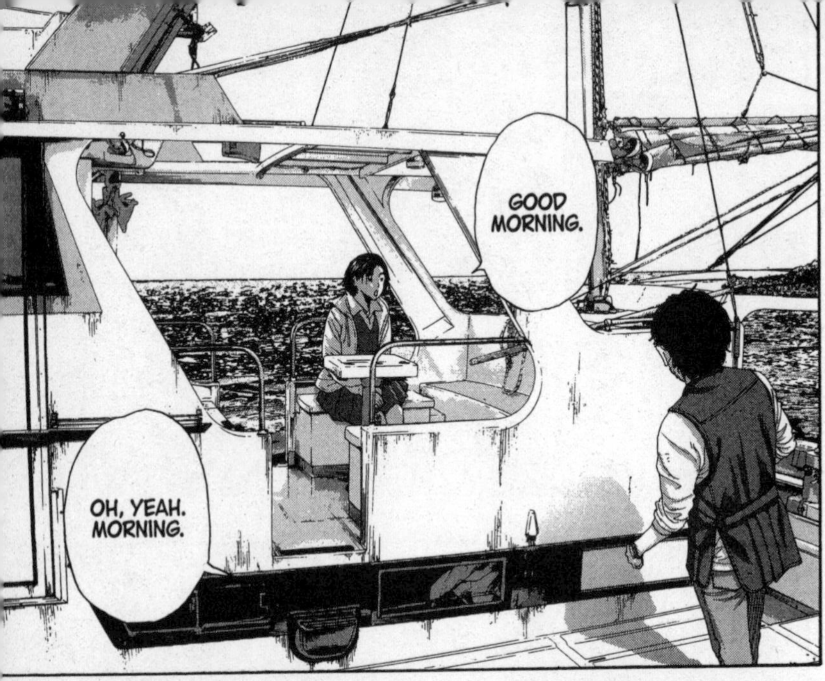
GOOD MORNING.
OH, YEAH. MORNING.
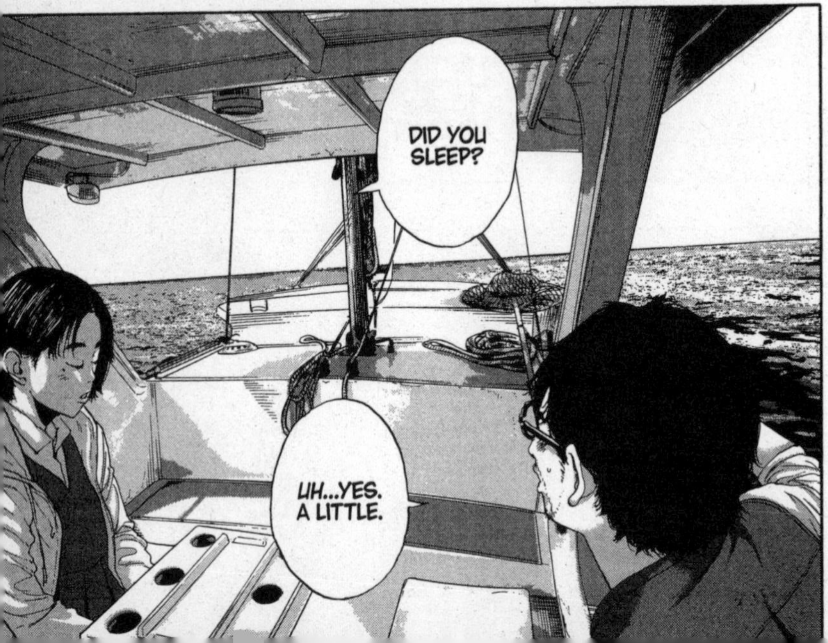
DID YOU SLEEP?
UH...YES. A LITTLE.

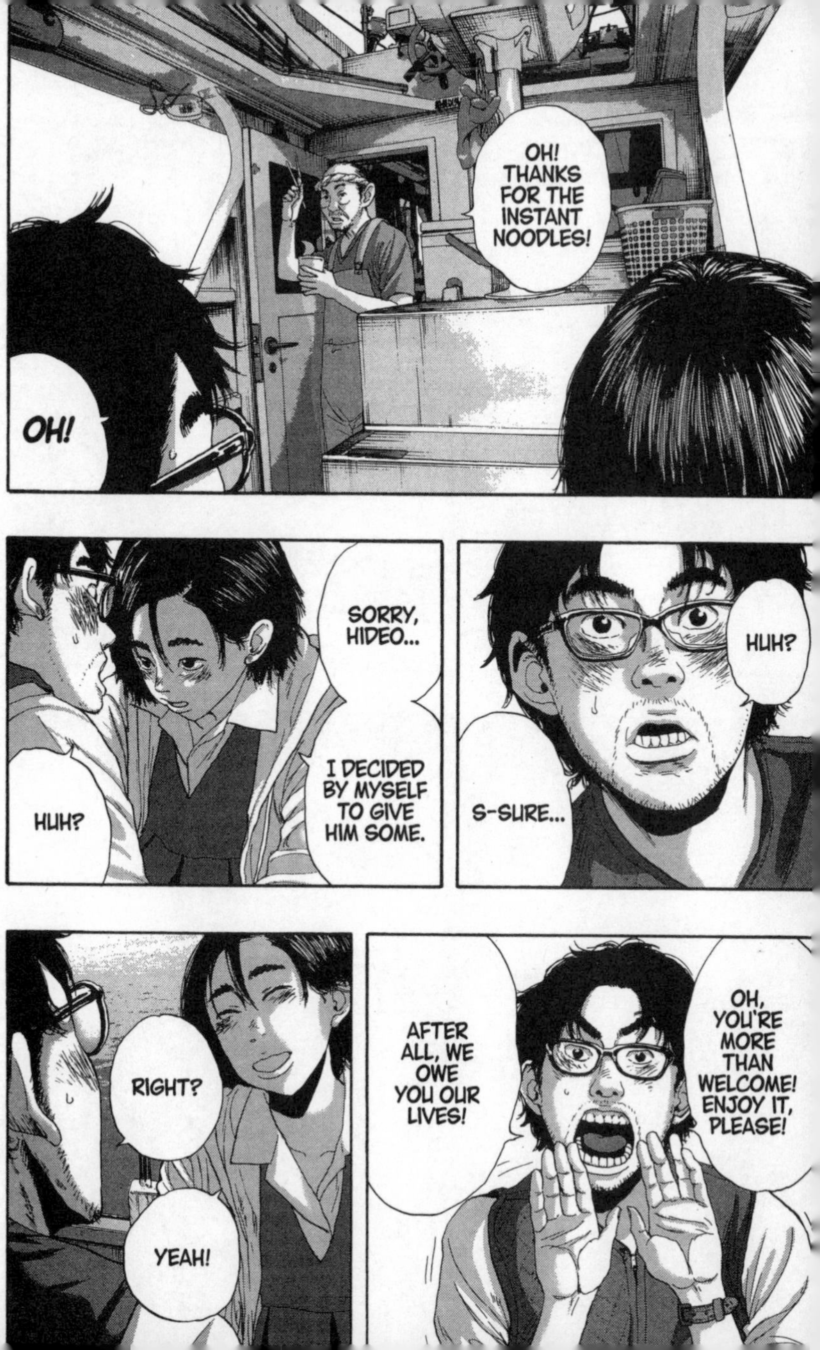
OH!
OH! THANKS FOR THE INSTANT NOODLES!
SORRY, HIDEO...
I DECIDED BY MYSELF TO GIVE HIM SOME.
HUH?
HUH?
S-SURE...
RIGHT?
YEAH!
AFTER ALL, WE OWE YOU OUR LIVES!
OH, YOU'RE MORE THAN WELCOME! ENJOY IT, PLEASE!

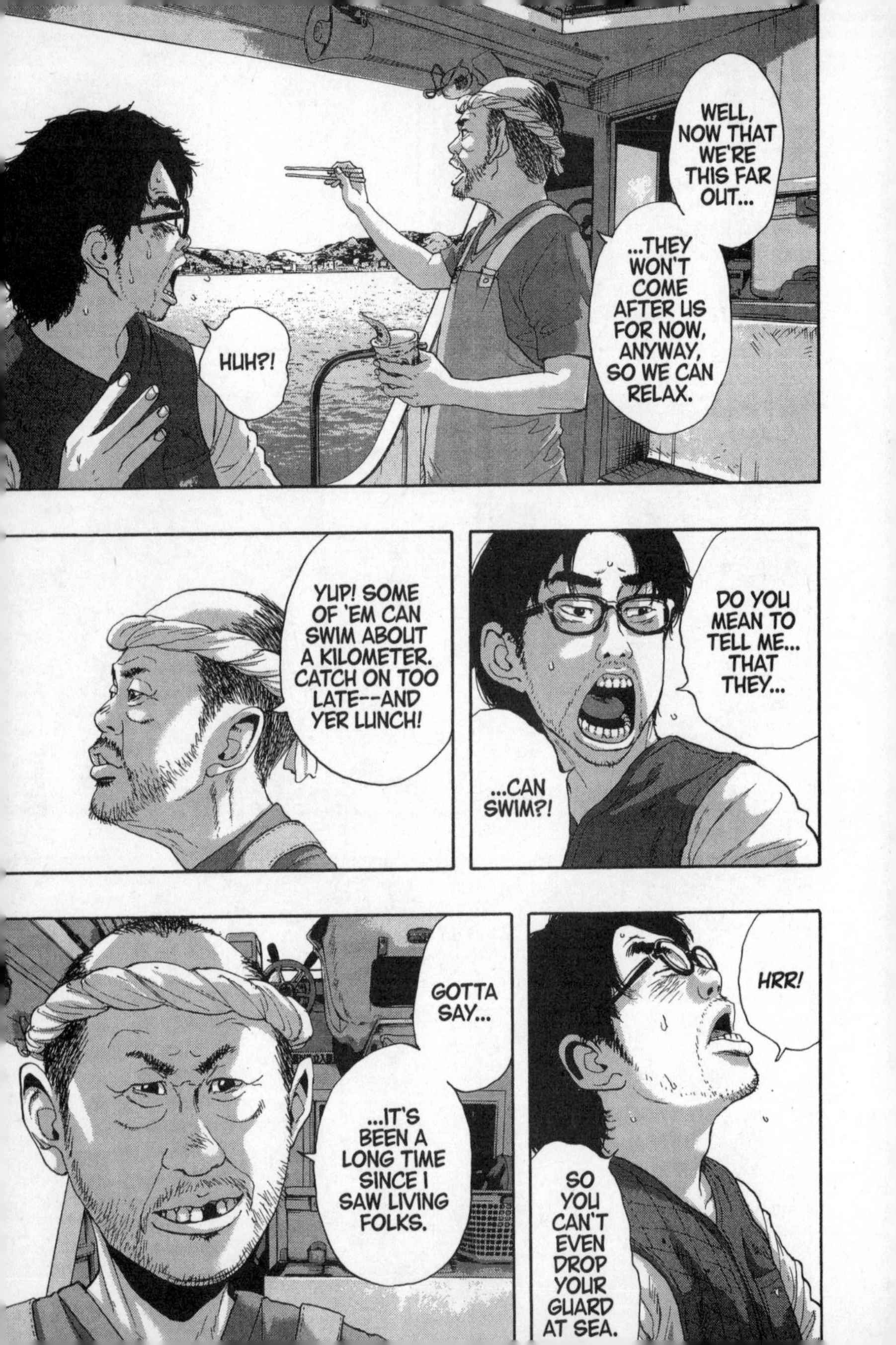
WELL, NOW THAT WE'RE THIS FAR OUT...
...THEY WON'T COME AFTER US FOR NOW, ANYWAY, SO WE CAN RELAX.
HUH?!
DO YOU MEAN TO TELL ME... THAT THEY...
...CAN SWIM?!
YUP! SOME OF 'EM CAN SWIM ABOUT A KILOMETER. CATCH ON TOO LATE--AND YER LUNCH!
HRR!
SO YOU CAN'T EVEN DROP YOUR GUARD AT SEA.
GOTTA SAY...
...IT'S BEEN A LONG TIME SINCE I SAW LIVING FOLKS.

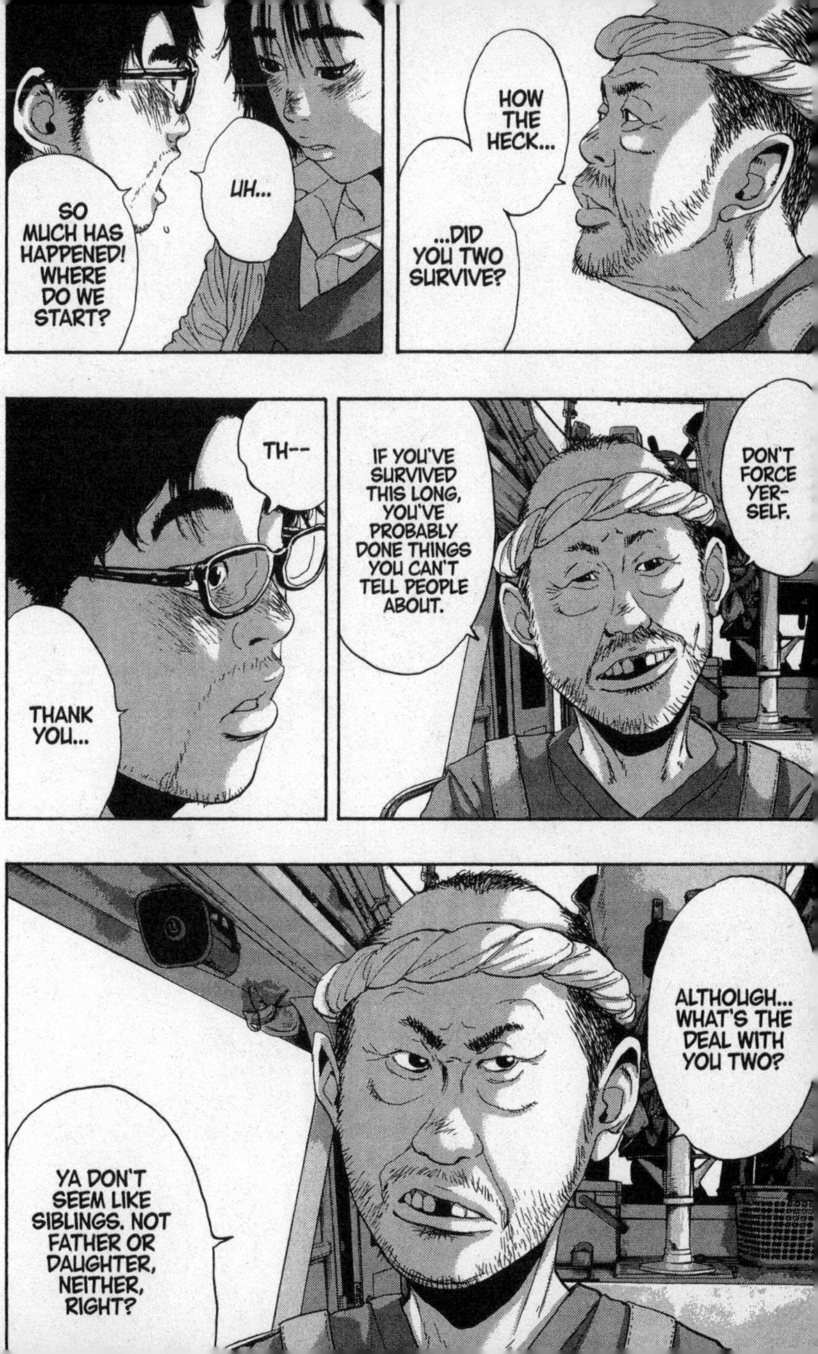
HOW THE HECK...
...DID YOU TWO SURVIVE?
UH...
SO MUCH HAS HAPPENED! WHERE DO WE START?
DON'T FORCE YER-SELF.
IF YOU'VE SURVIVED THIS LONG, YOU'VE PROBABLY DONE THINGS YOU CAN'T TELL PEOPLE ABOUT.
TH--
THANK YOU...
ALTHOUGH... WHAT'S THE DEAL WITH YOU TWO?
YA DON'T SEEM LIKE SIBLINGS. NOT FATHER OR DAUGHTER, NEITHER, RIGHT?

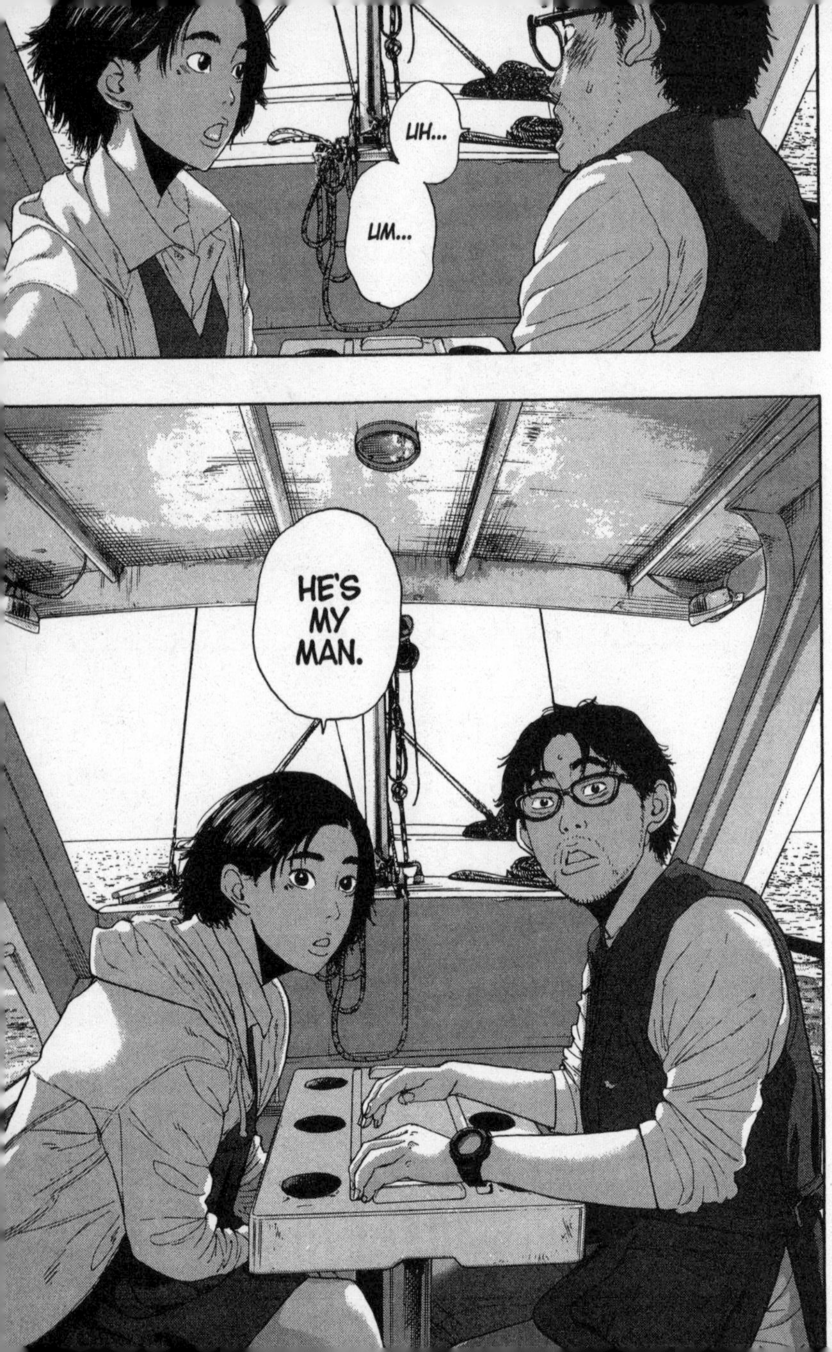
UH...
UM...
HE'S MY MAN.

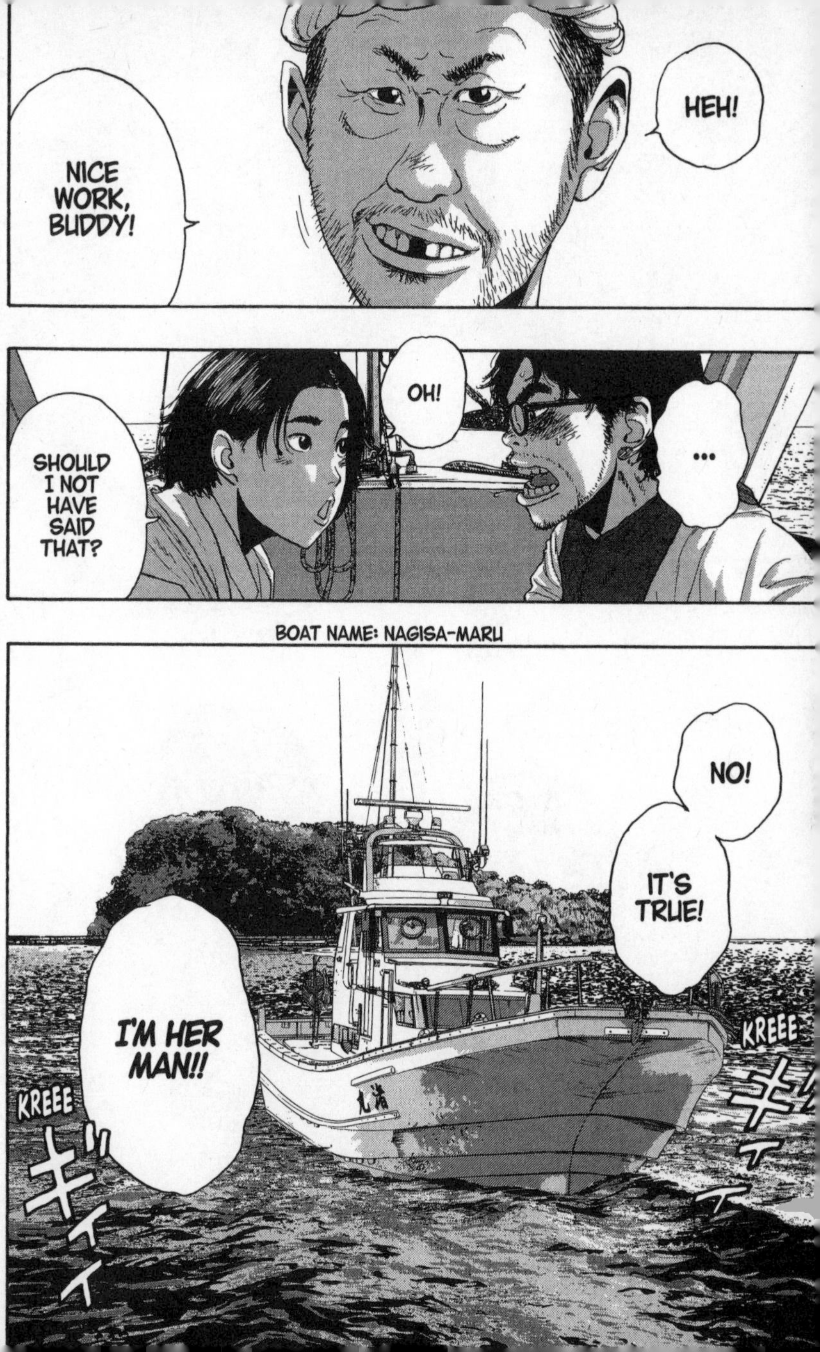
HEH!
NICE WORK, BUDDY!
...
OH!
SHOULD I NOT HAVE SAID THAT?
BOAT NAME: NAGISA-MARU
NO!
IT'S TRUE!
KREEE
I'M HER MAN!!
KREEE

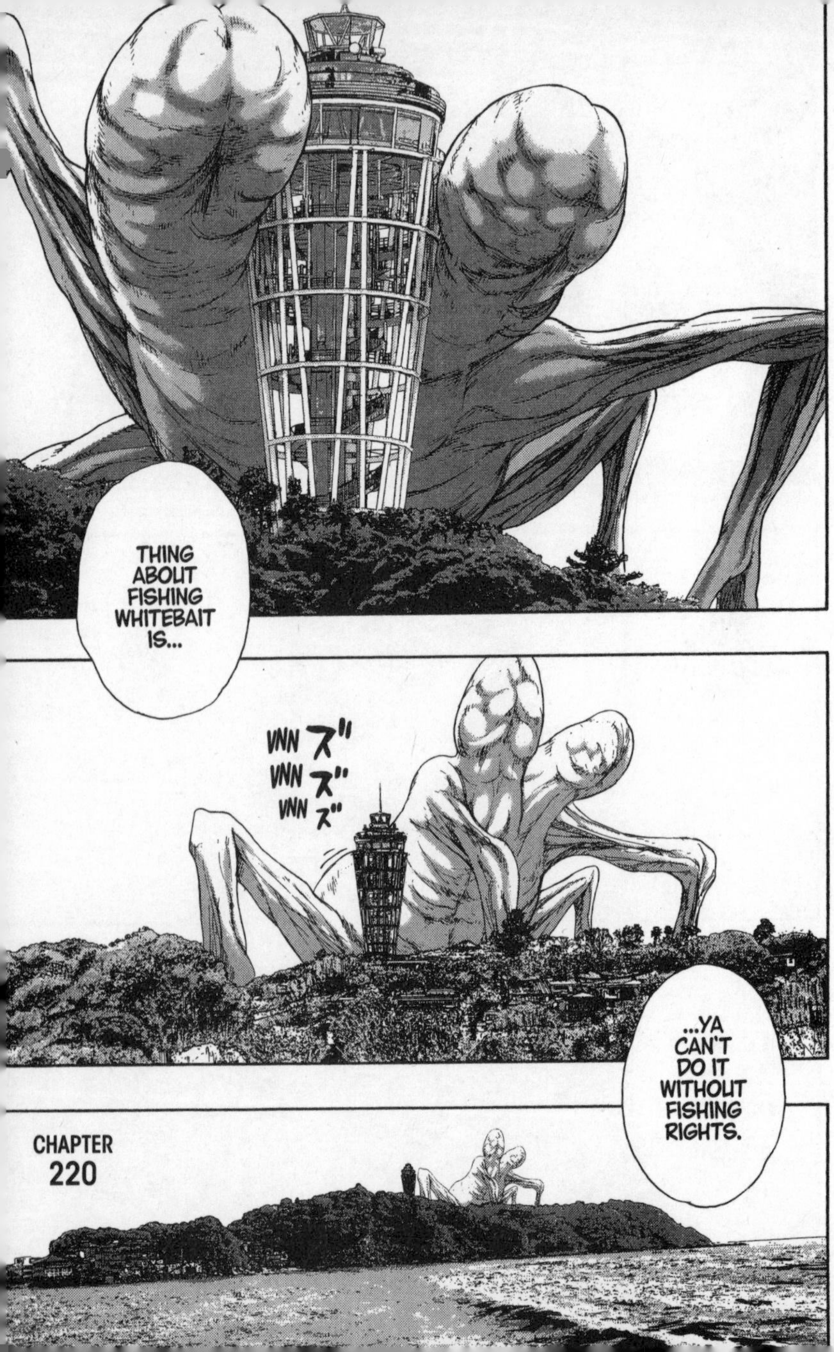
THING ABOUT FISHING WHITEBAIT IS...
VNN ズ
VNN ズ
VNN ズ
...YA CAN'T DO IT WITHOUT FISHING RIGHTS.
CHAPTER 220

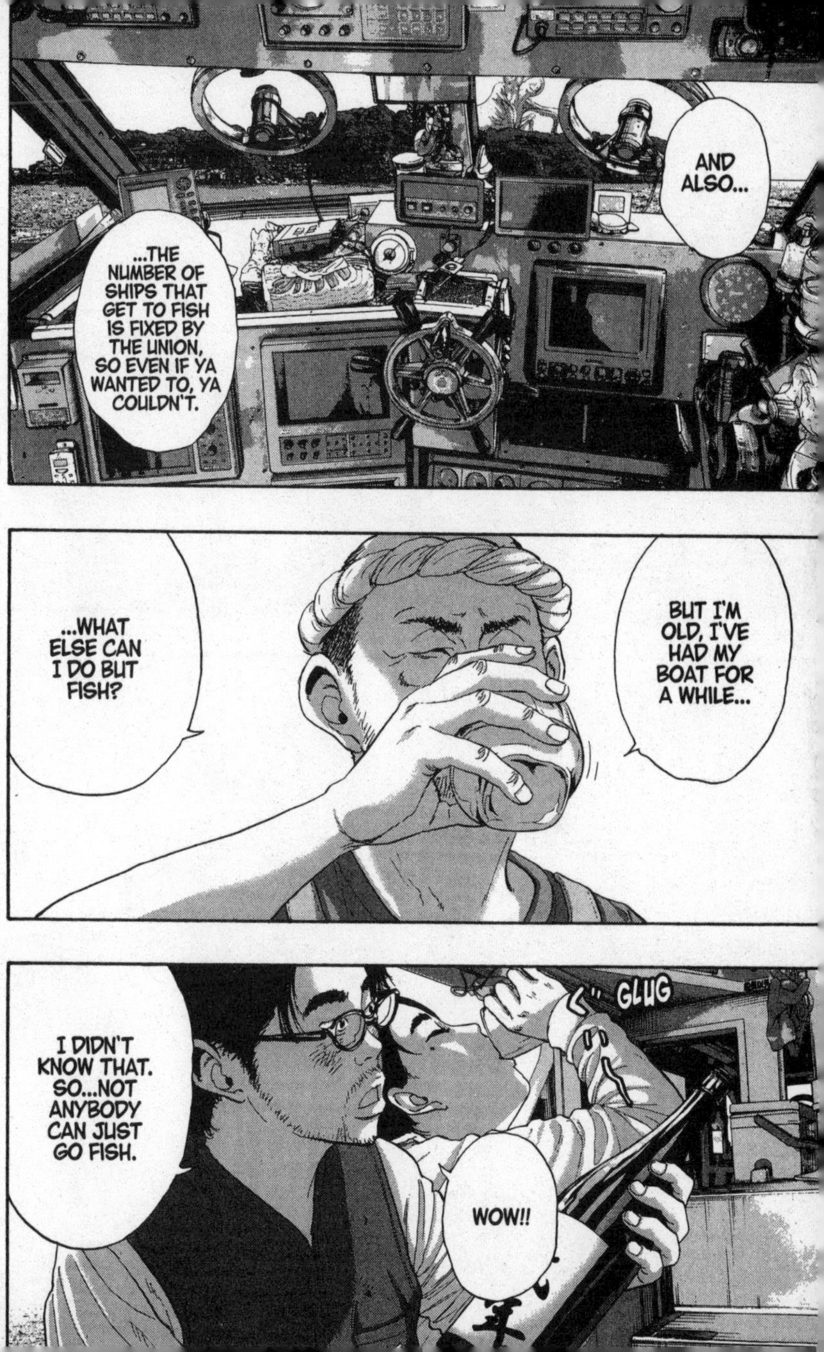
AND ALSO...
...THE NUMBER OF SHIPS THAT GET TO FISH IS FIXED BY THE UNION, SO EVEN IF YA WANTED TO, YA COULDN'T.
BUT I'M OLD, I'VE HAD MY BOAT FOR A WHILE...
...WHAT ELSE CAN I DO BUT FISH?
GLUG
I DIDN'T KNOW THAT. SO...NOT ANYBODY CAN JUST GO FISH.
WOW!!

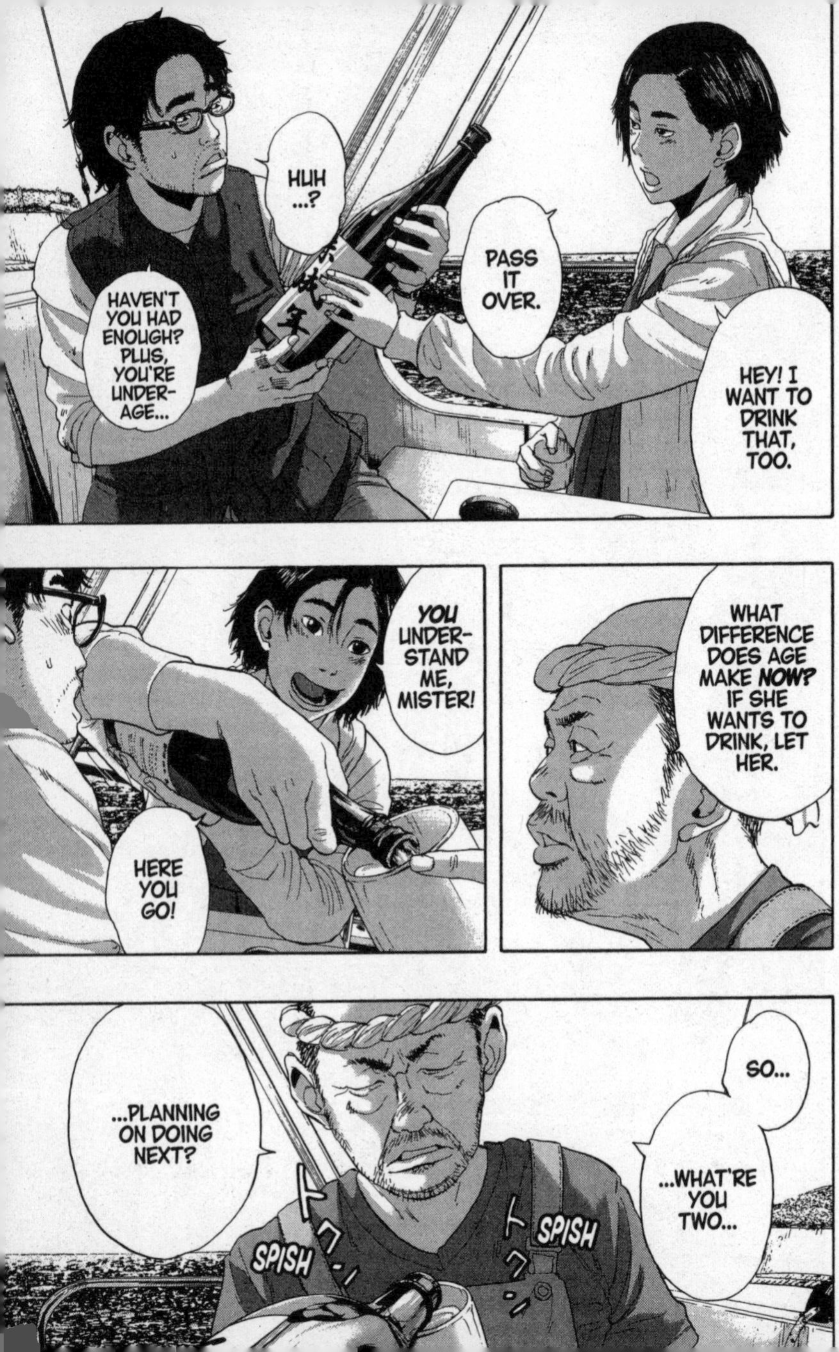

HEY! I WANT TO DRINK THAT, TOO.
PASS IT OVER.
HUH ...?
HAVEN'T YOU HAD ENOUGH? PLUS, YOU'RE UNDER-AGE...
WHAT DIFFERENCE DOES AGE MAKE *NOW?* IF SHE WANTS TO DRINK, LET HER.
YOU UNDER-STAND ME, MISTER!
HERE YOU GO!
SO...
...WHAT'RE YOU TWO...
...PLANNING ON DOING NEXT?
SPISH
SPISH

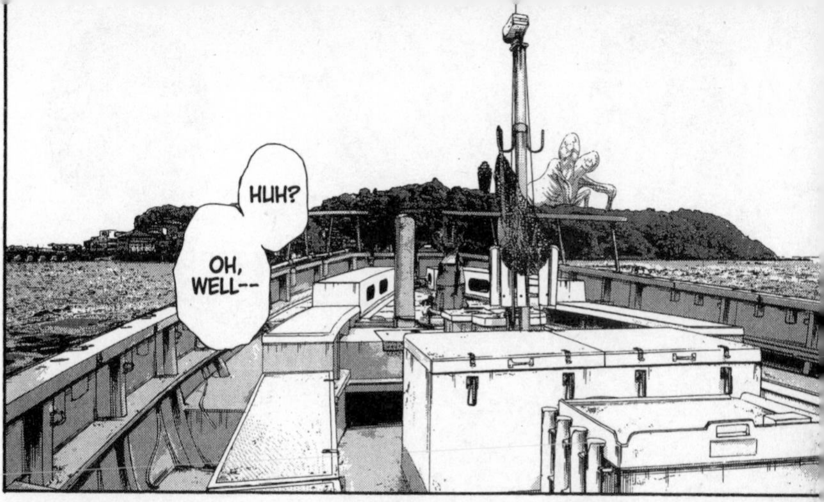
HUH?
OH, WELL--

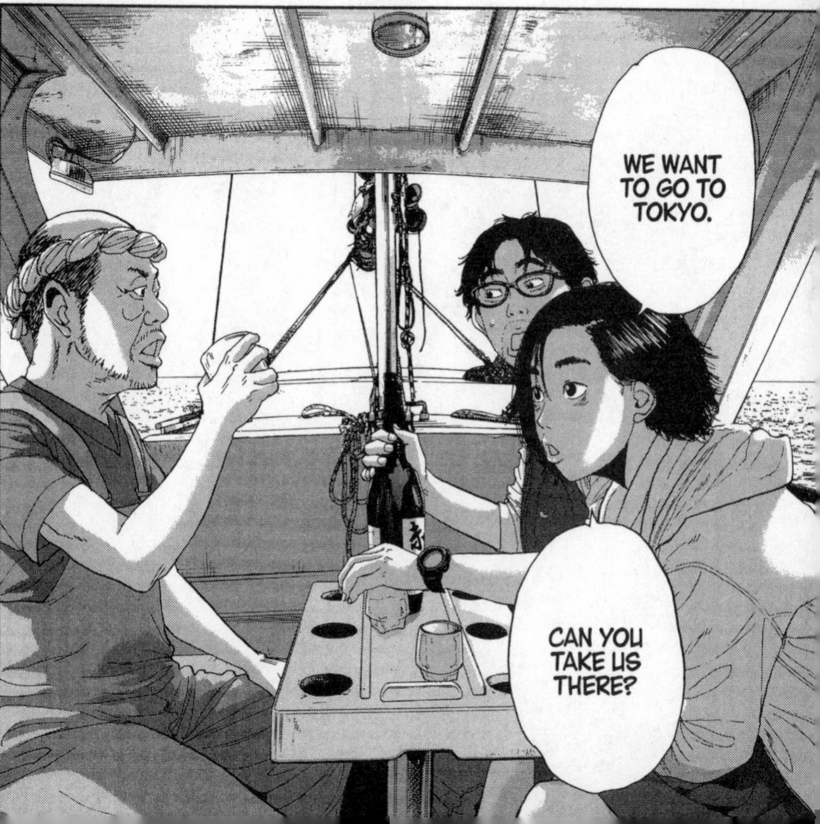
WE WANT TO GO TO TOKYO.
CAN YOU TAKE US THERE?

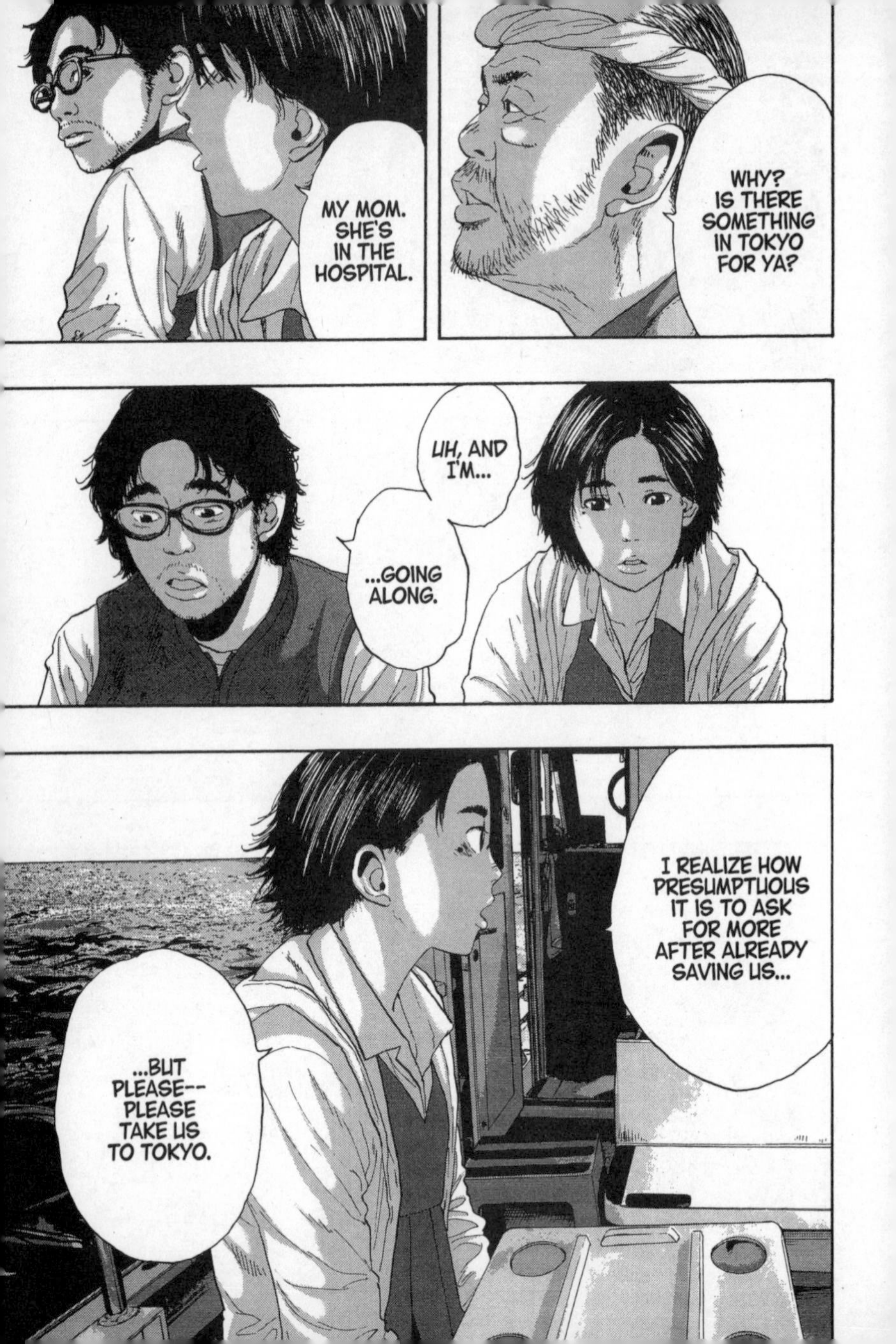
WHY? IS THERE SOMETHING IN TOKYO FOR YA?
MY MOM. SHE'S IN THE HOSPITAL.
UH, AND I'M...
...GOING ALONG.
I REALIZE HOW PRESUMPTUOUS IT IS TO ASK FOR MORE AFTER ALREADY SAVING US...
...BUT PLEASE-- PLEASE TAKE US TO TOKYO.

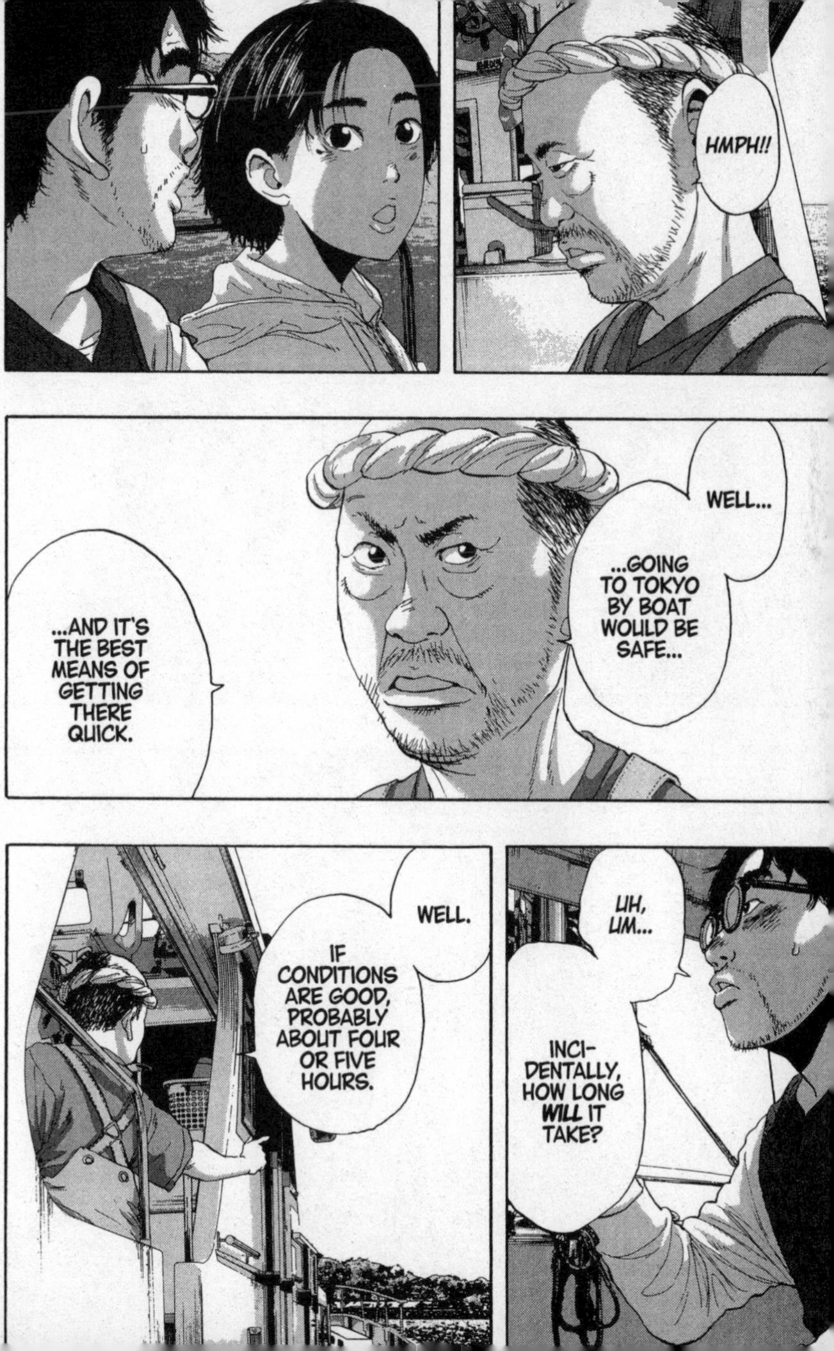
HMPH!!
WELL...
...GOING TO TOKYO BY BOAT WOULD BE SAFE...
...AND IT'S THE BEST MEANS OF GETTING THERE QUICK.
UH, UM...
INCI-DENTALLY, HOW LONG *WILL* IT TAKE?
WELL.
IF CONDITIONS ARE GOOD, PROBABLY ABOUT FOUR OR FIVE HOURS.

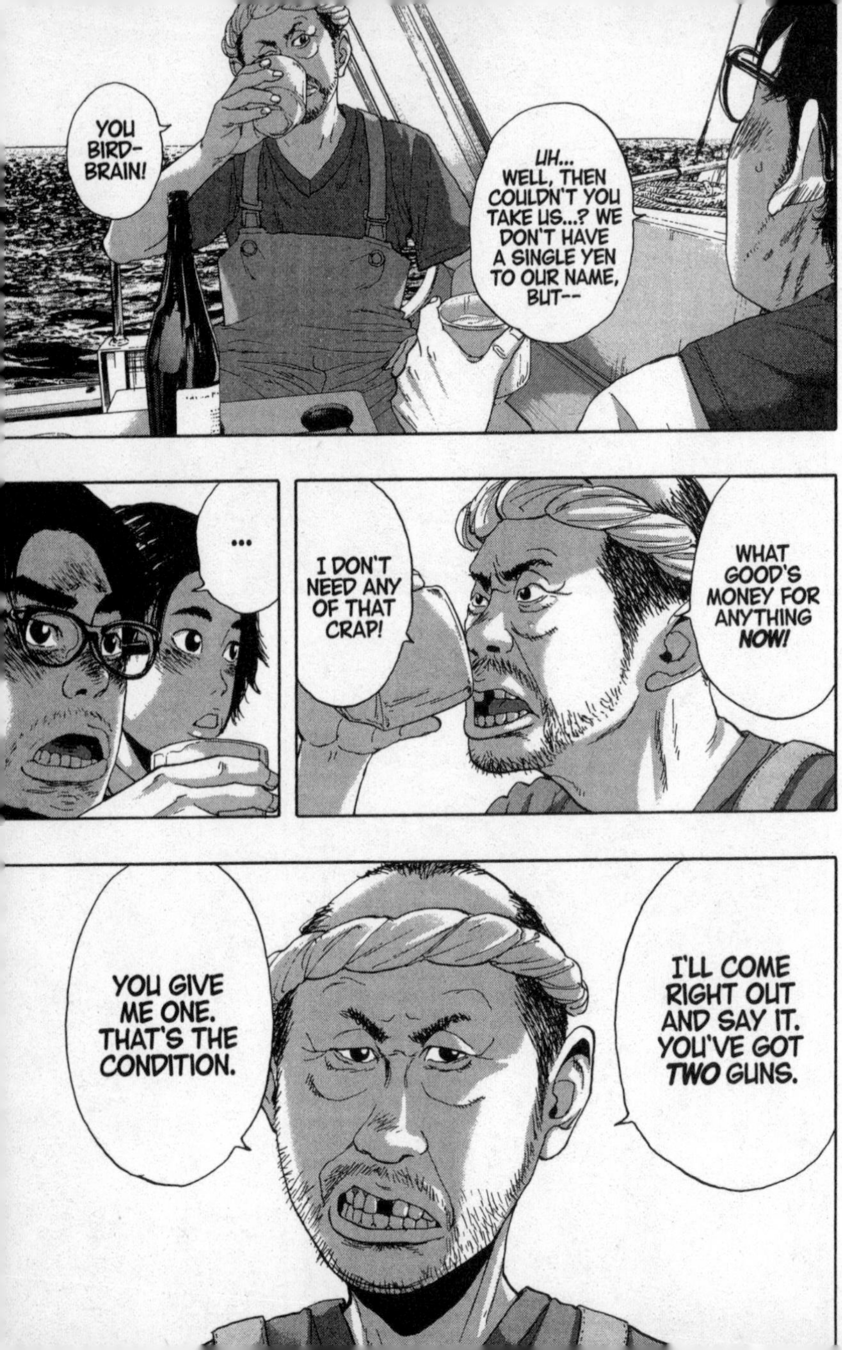
UH... WELL, THEN COULDN'T YOU TAKE US...? WE DON'T HAVE A SINGLE YEN TO OUR NAME, BUT--
YOU BIRD-BRAIN!
WHAT GOOD'S MONEY FOR ANYTHING *NOW!*
I DON'T NEED ANY OF THAT CRAP!
...
I'LL COME RIGHT OUT AND SAY IT. YOU'VE GOT *TWO* GUNS.
YOU GIVE ME ONE. THAT'S THE CONDITION.

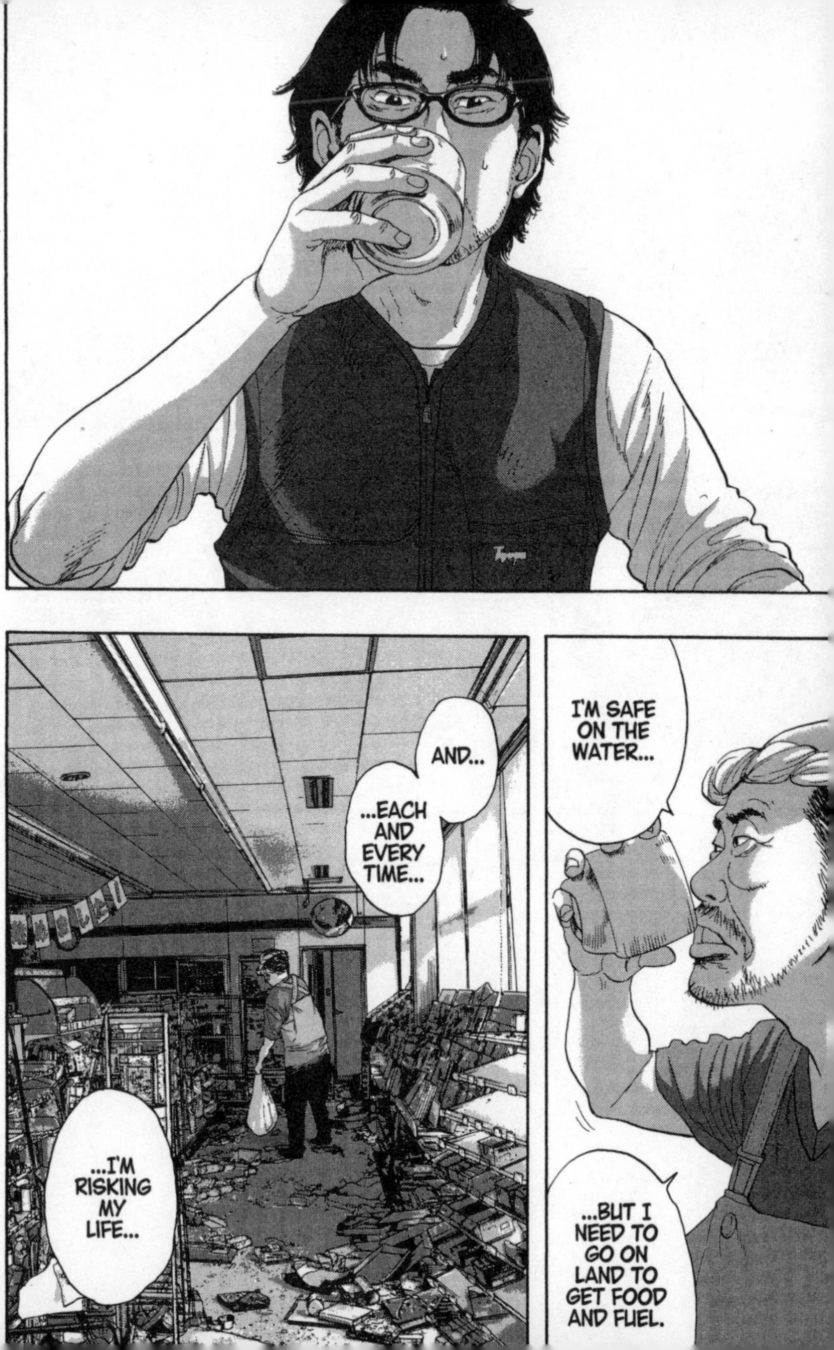
I'M SAFE ON THE WATER...
...BUT I NEED TO GO ON LAND TO GET FOOD AND FUEL.
AND...
...EACH AND EVERY TIME...
...I'M RISKING MY LIFE...

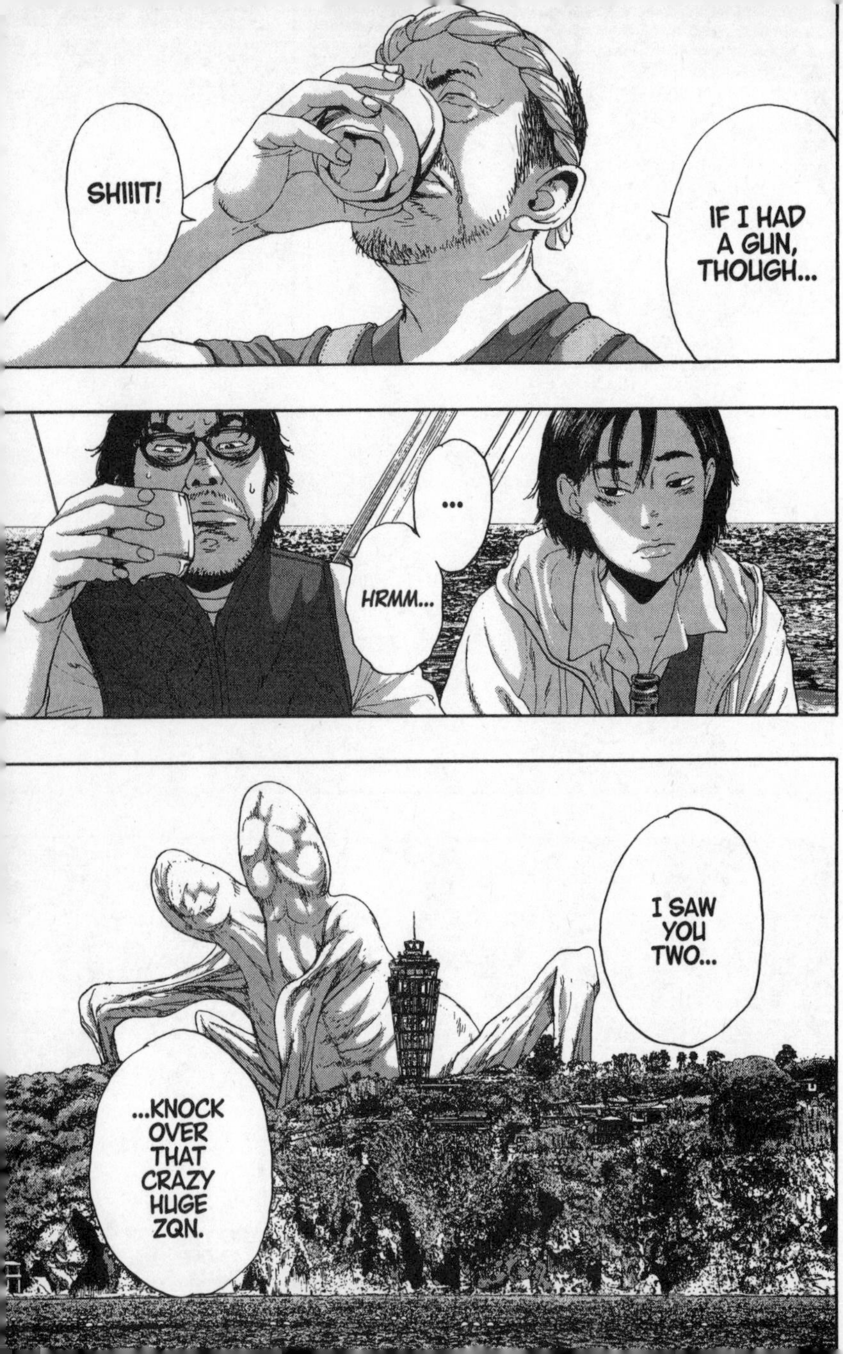
IF I HAD A GUN, THOUGH...
SHIIIT!
...
HRMM...
I SAW YOU TWO...
...KNOCK OVER THAT CRAZY HUGE ZQN.

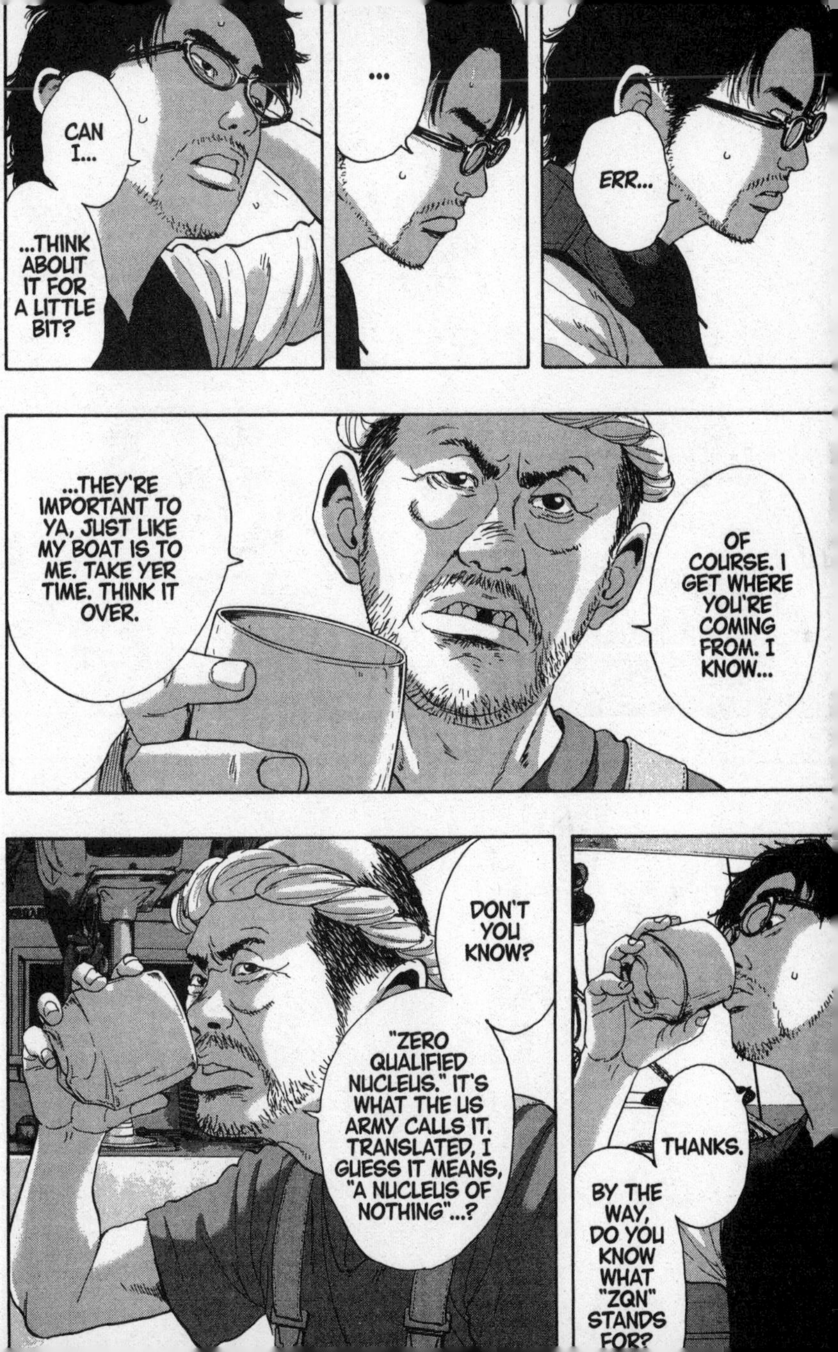
ERR...
...
CAN I...
...THINK ABOUT IT FOR A LITTLE BIT?
OF COURSE. I GET WHERE YOU'RE COMING FROM. I KNOW...
...THEY'RE IMPORTANT TO YA, JUST LIKE MY BOAT IS TO ME. TAKE YER TIME. THINK IT OVER.
THANKS.
BY THE WAY, DO YOU KNOW WHAT "ZQN" STANDS FOR?
DON'T YOU KNOW?
"ZERO QUALIFIED NUCLEUS." IT'S WHAT THE US ARMY CALLS IT. TRANSLATED, I GUESS IT MEANS, "A NUCLEUS OF NOTHING"...?

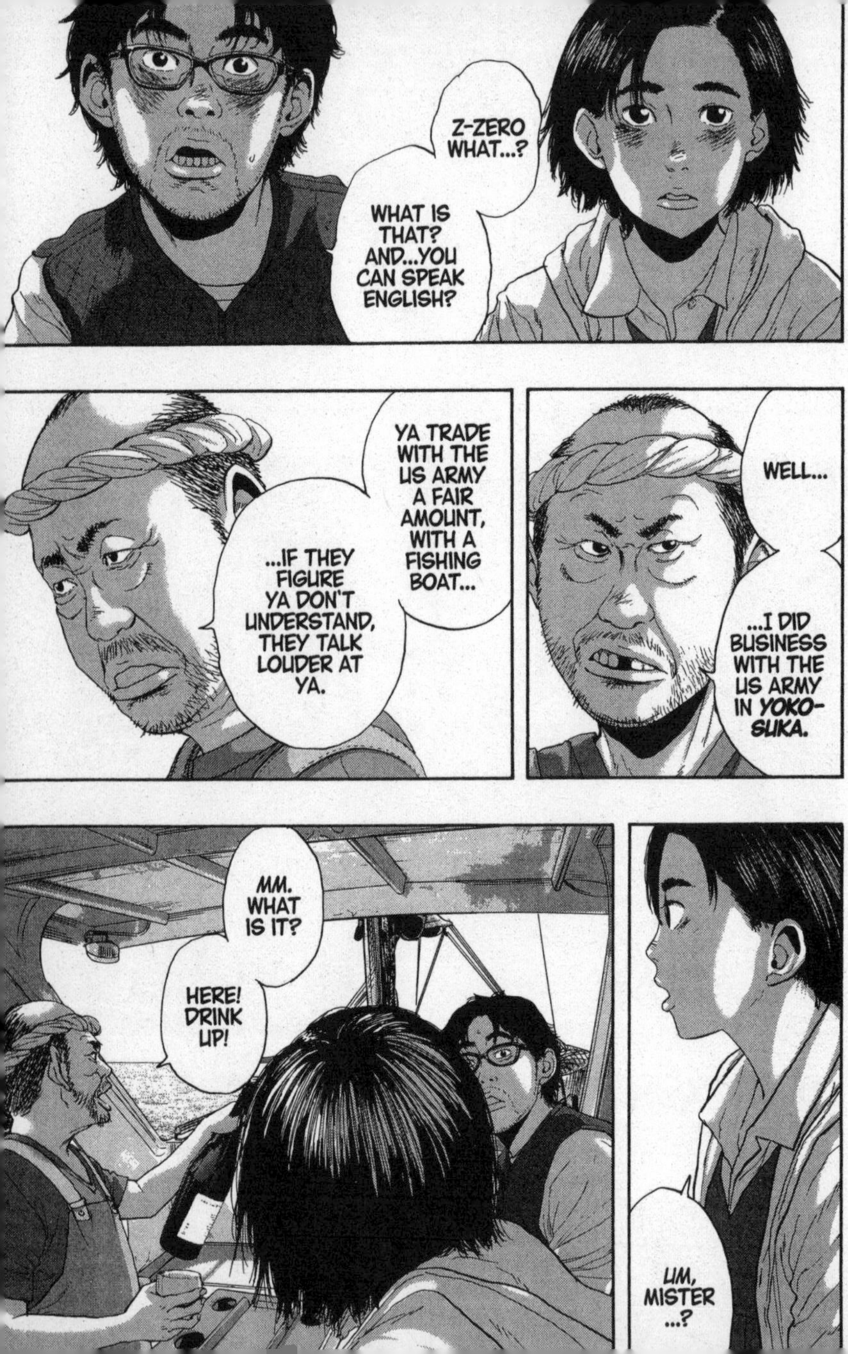
Z-ZERO WHAT...?
WHAT IS THAT? AND...YOU CAN SPEAK ENGLISH?
WELL...
...I DID BUSINESS WITH THE US ARMY IN *YOKOSUKA.*
YA TRADE WITH THE US ARMY A FAIR AMOUNT, WITH A FISHING BOAT...
...IF THEY FIGURE YA DON'T UNDERSTAND, THEY TALK LOUDER AT YA.
UM, MISTER ...?
MM. WHAT IS IT?
HERE! DRINK UP!

THERE'S...

...ANOTHER PERSON ON THIS BOAT, ISN'T THERE?

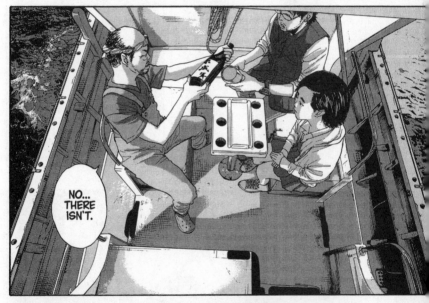

NO... THERE ISN'T.

OVER THERE... DOWN BELOW...?

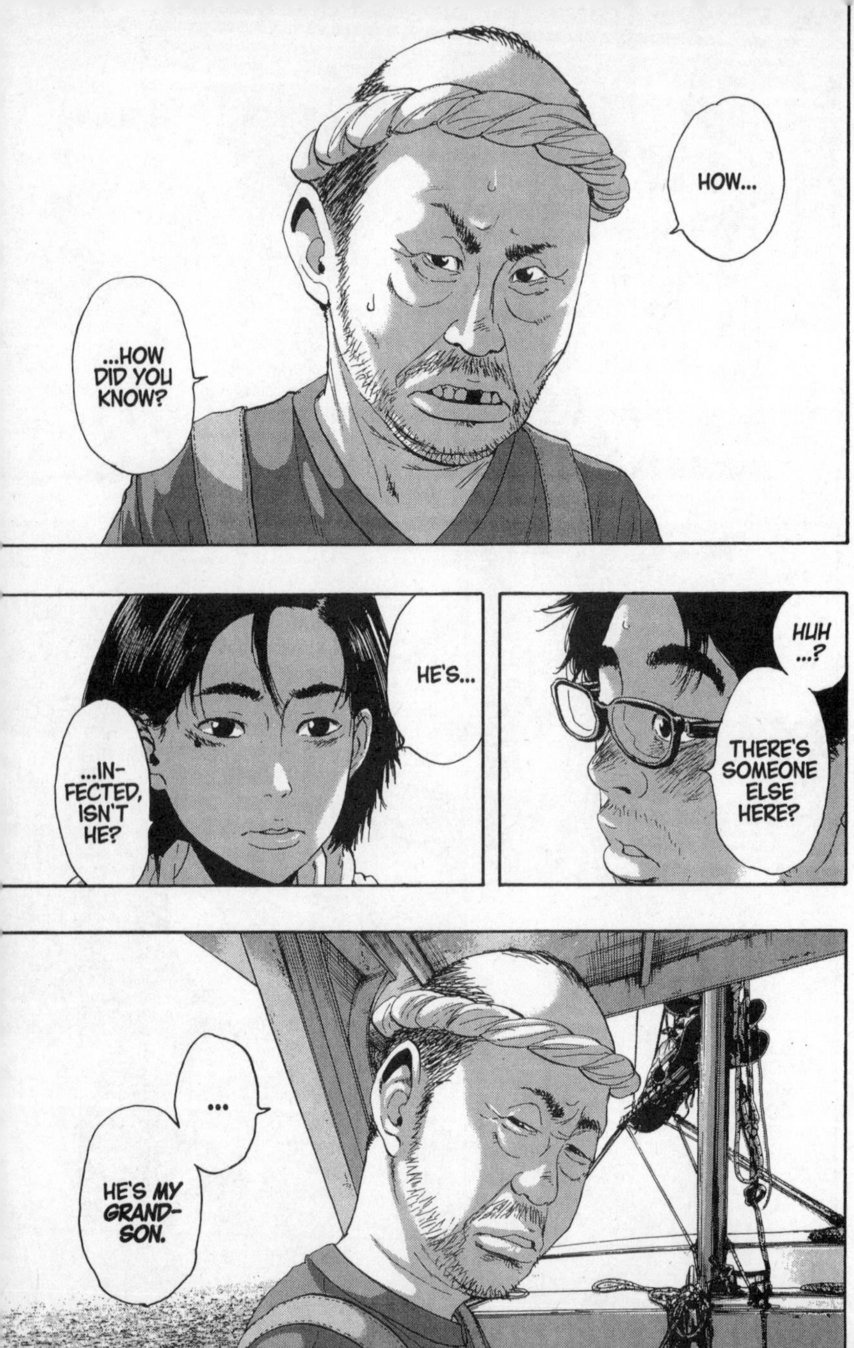
HOW...
...HOW DID YOU KNOW?
HUH...?
THERE'S SOMEONE ELSE HERE?
HE'S...
...INFECTED, ISN'T HE?
...
HE'S MY GRANDSON.

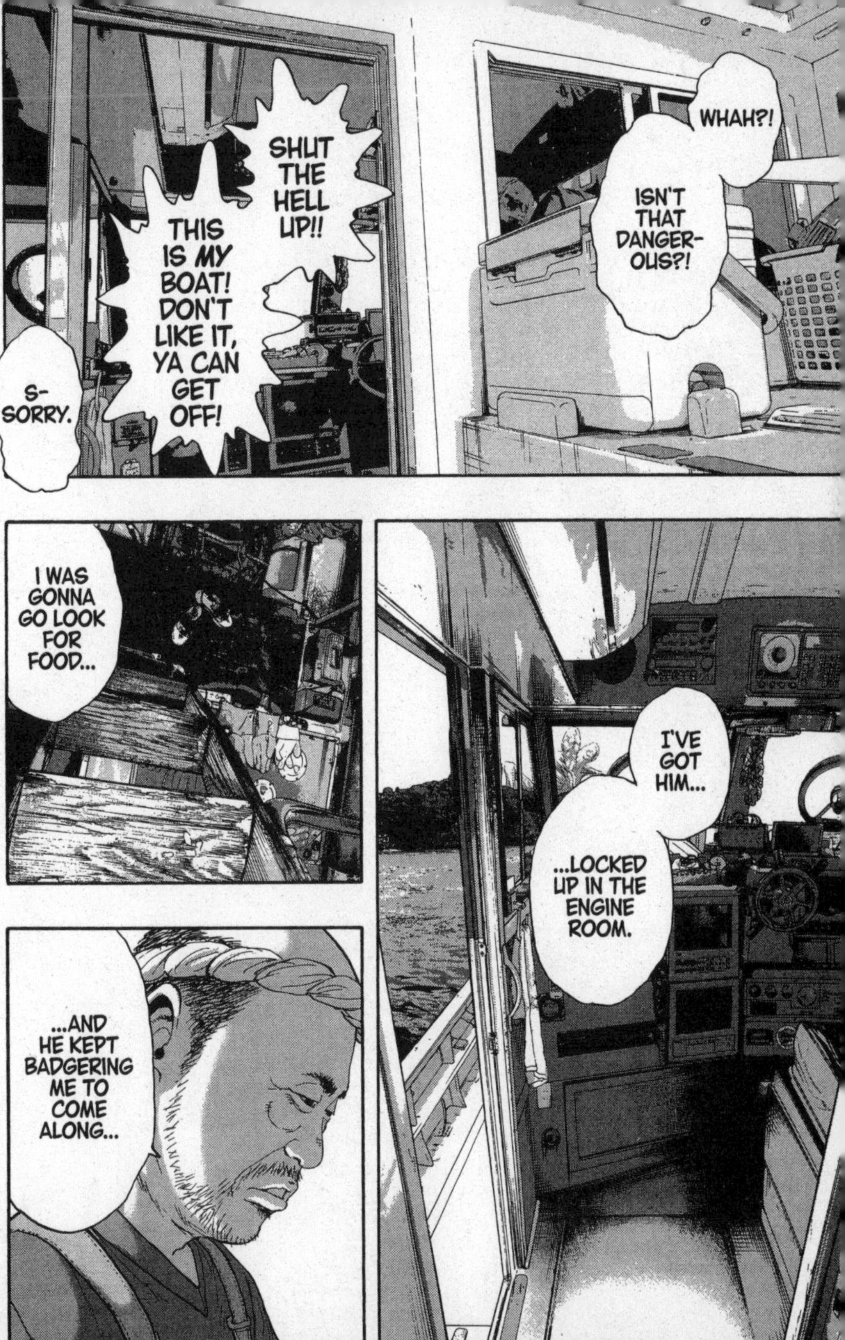
WHAH?!
ISN'T THAT DANGER-OUS?!
SHUT THE HELL UP!!
THIS IS MY BOAT! DON'T LIKE IT, YA CAN GET OFF!
S-SORRY.
I'VE GOT HIM...
...LOCKED UP IN THE ENGINE ROOM.
I WAS GONNA GO LOOK FOR FOOD...
...AND HE KEPT BADGERING ME TO COME ALONG...

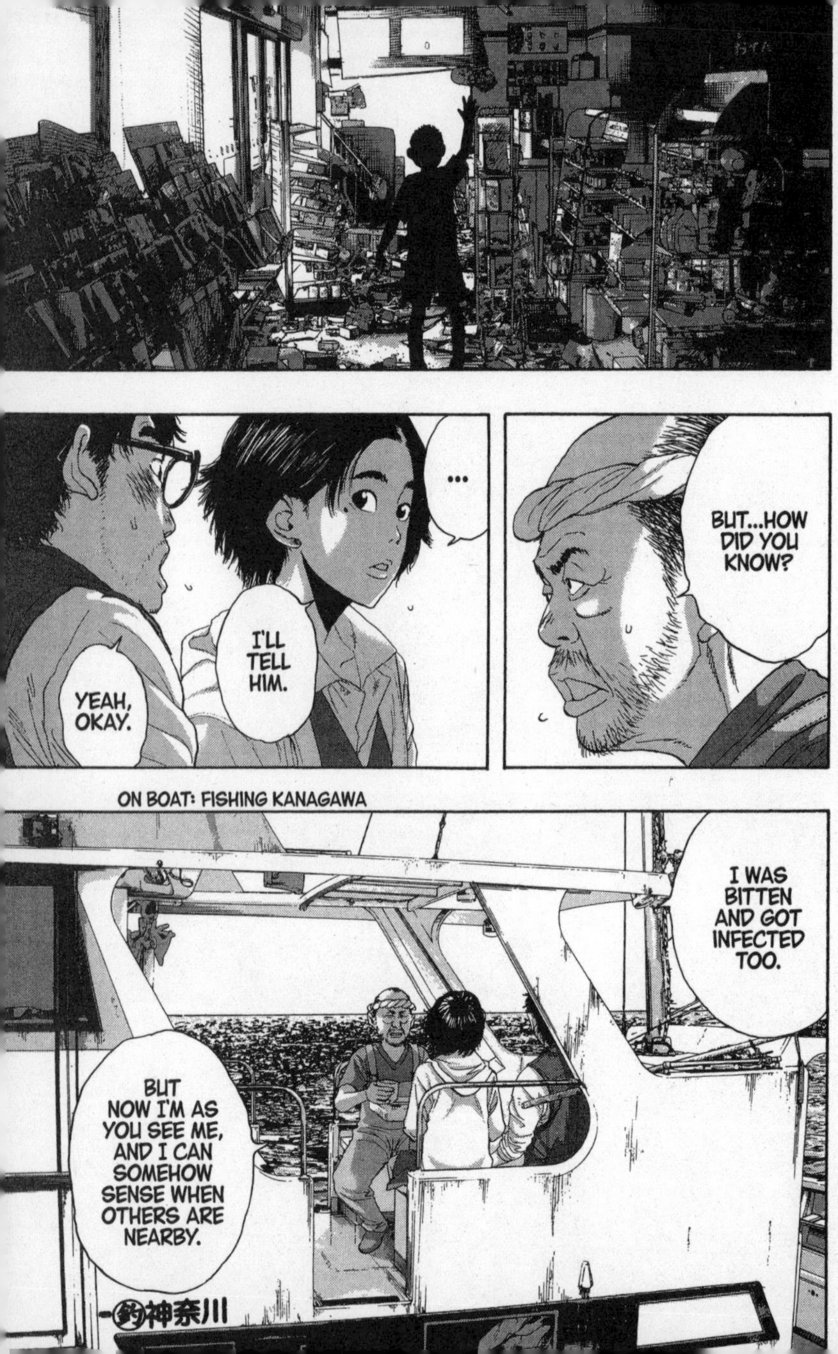
BUT...HOW DID YOU KNOW?
...
I'LL TELL HIM.
YEAH, OKAY.
ON BOAT: FISHING KANAGAWA
I WAS BITTEN AND GOT INFECTED TOO.
BUT NOW I'M AS YOU SEE ME, AND I CAN SOMEHOW SENSE WHEN OTHERS ARE NEARBY.
釣神奈川

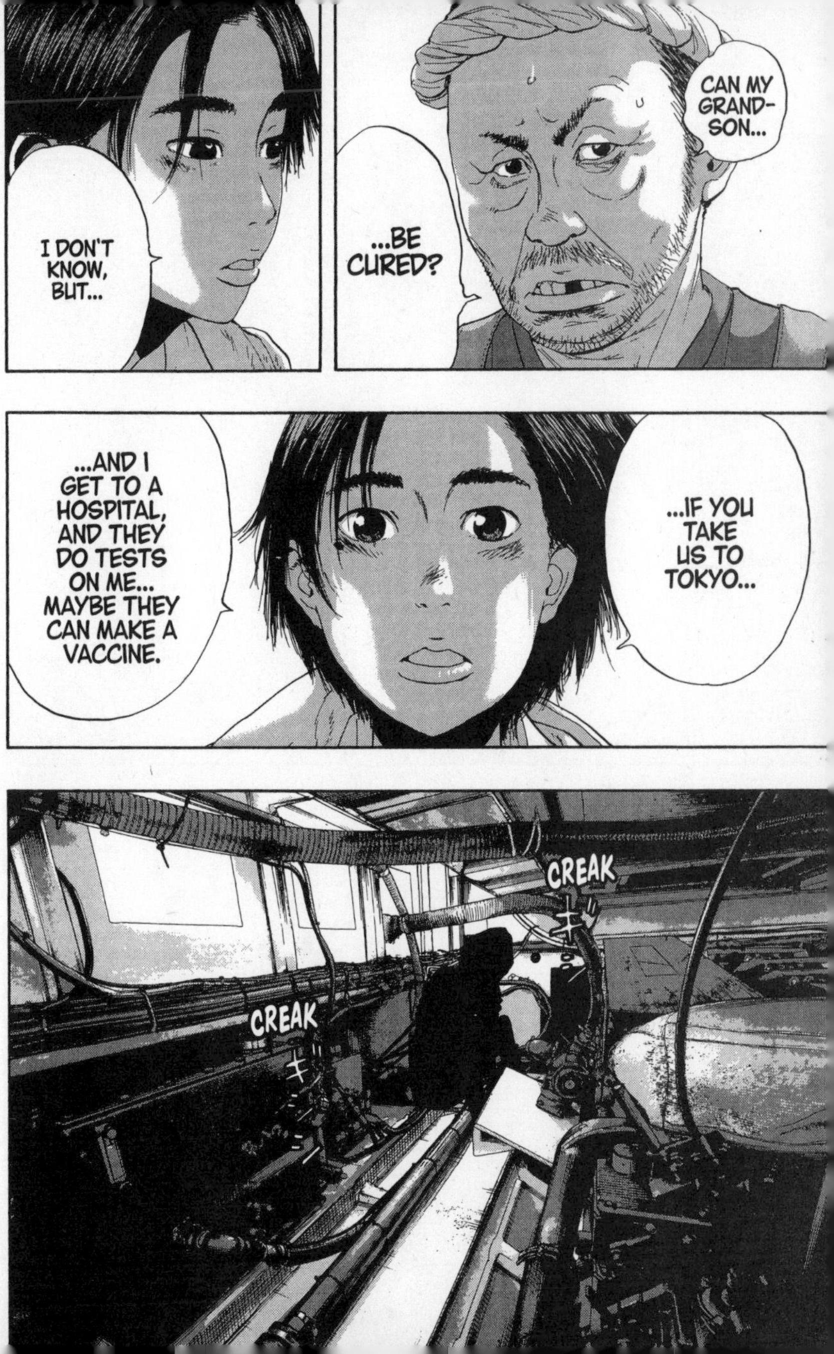
CAN MY GRAND-SON...
...BE CURED?
I DON'T KNOW, BUT...
...IF YOU TAKE US TO TOKYO...
...AND I GET TO A HOSPITAL, AND THEY DO TESTS ON ME... MAYBE THEY CAN MAKE A VACCINE.
CREAK
CREAK

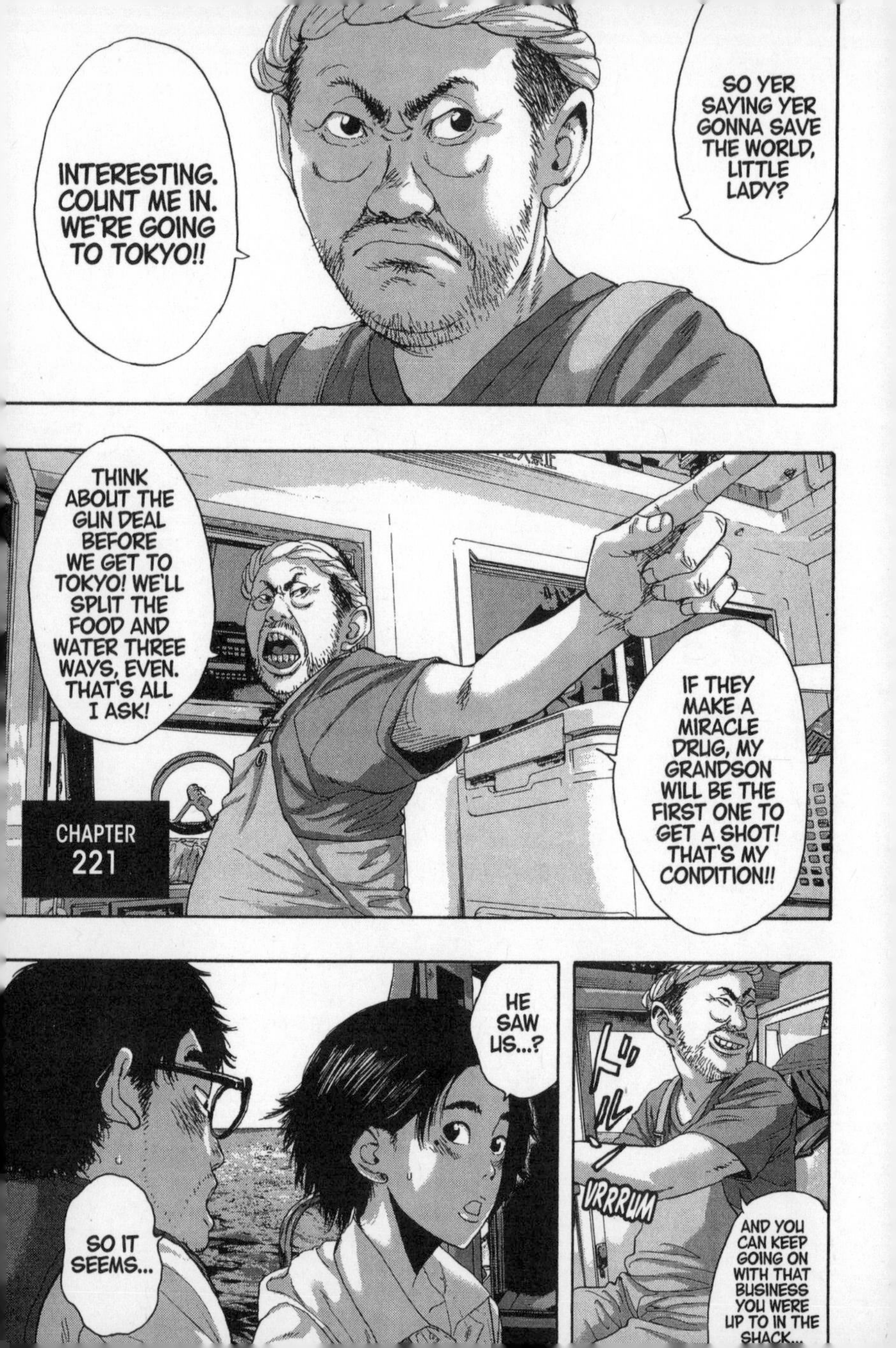
SO YER SAYING YER GONNA SAVE THE WORLD, LITTLE LADY?
INTERESTING. COUNT ME IN. WE'RE GOING TO TOKYO!!
THINK ABOUT THE GUN DEAL BEFORE WE GET TO TOKYO! WE'LL SPLIT THE FOOD AND WATER THREE WAYS, EVEN. THAT'S ALL I ASK!
IF THEY MAKE A MIRACLE DRUG, MY GRANDSON WILL BE THE FIRST ONE TO GET A SHOT! THAT'S MY CONDITION!!
CHAPTER 221
VRRRUM
AND YOU CAN KEEP GOING ON WITH THAT BUSINESS YOU WERE UP TO IN THE SHACK...
HE SAW US...?
SO IT SEEMS...

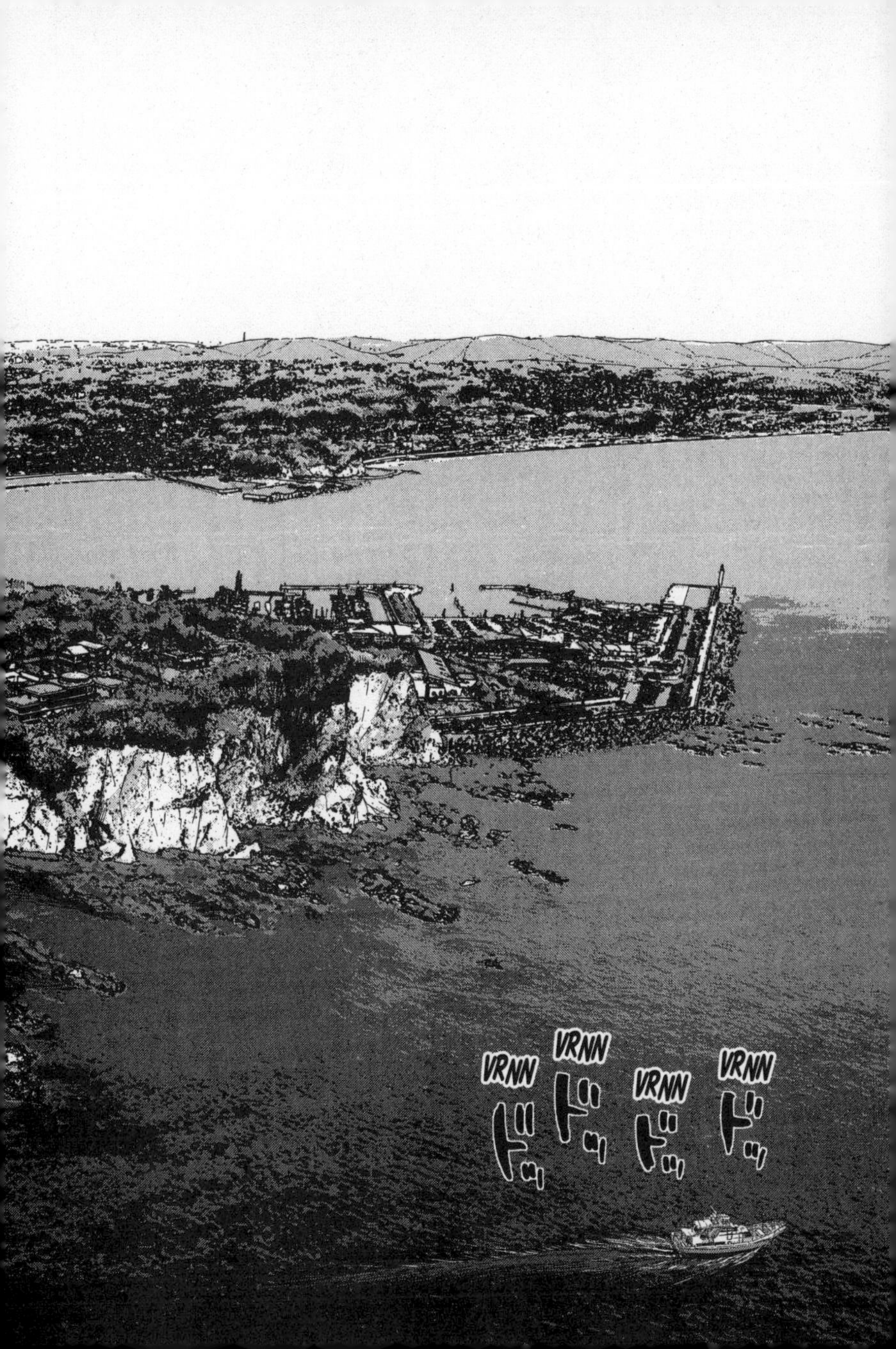
VRNN
ドッ
VRNN
ドッ
VRNN
ドッ
VRNN
ドッ

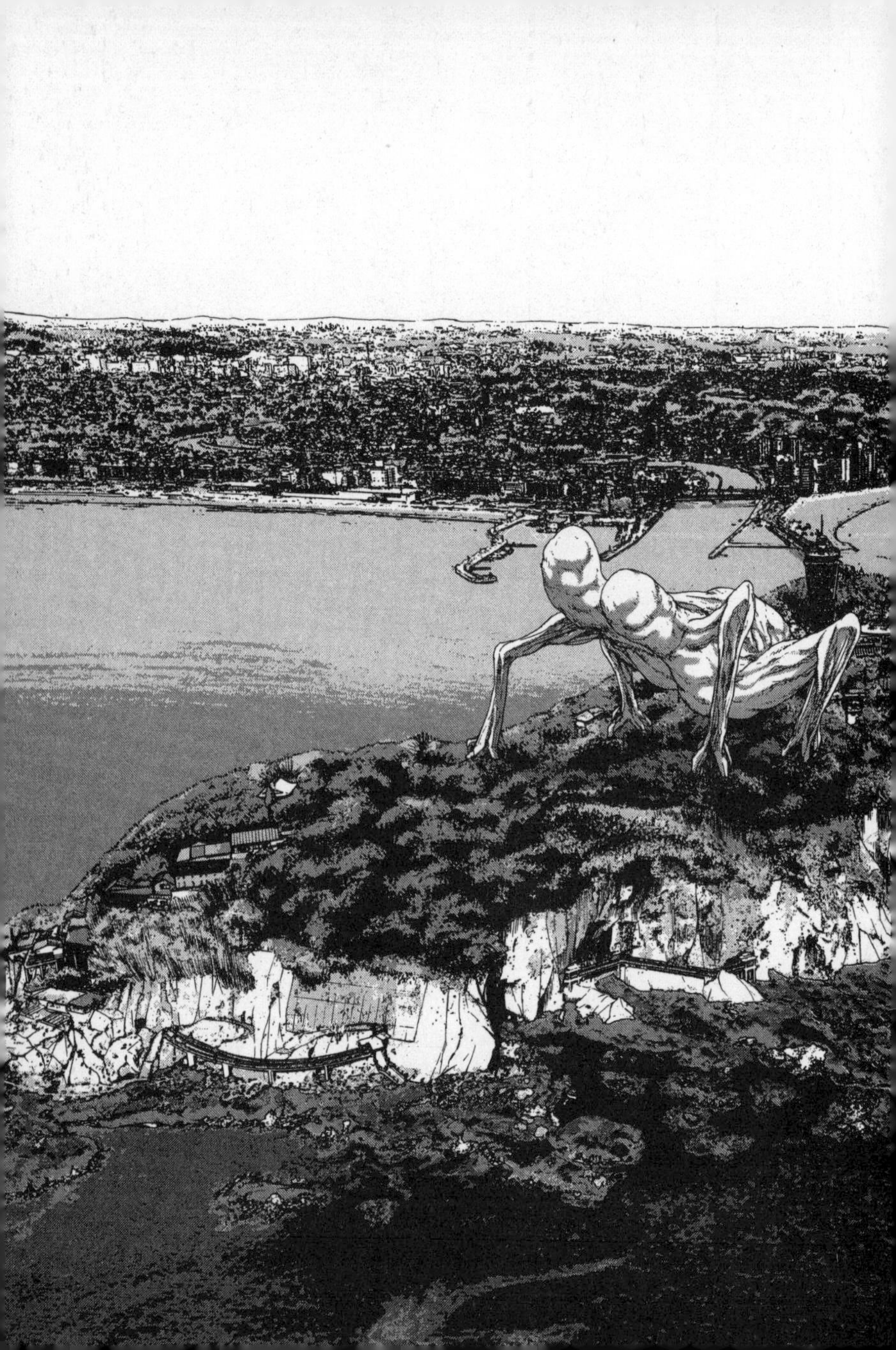

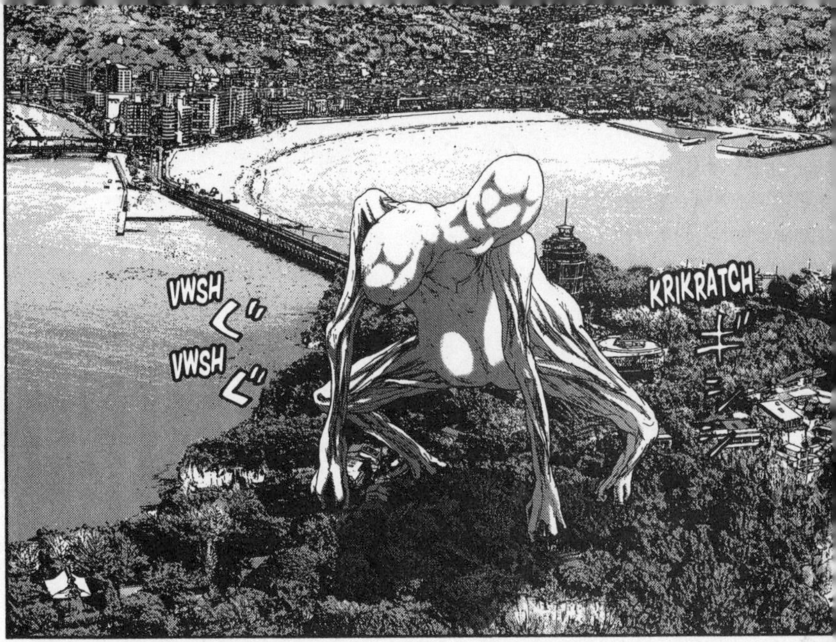
KRIKRATCH
ギ
VWSH
ぐ
VWSH
ぐ
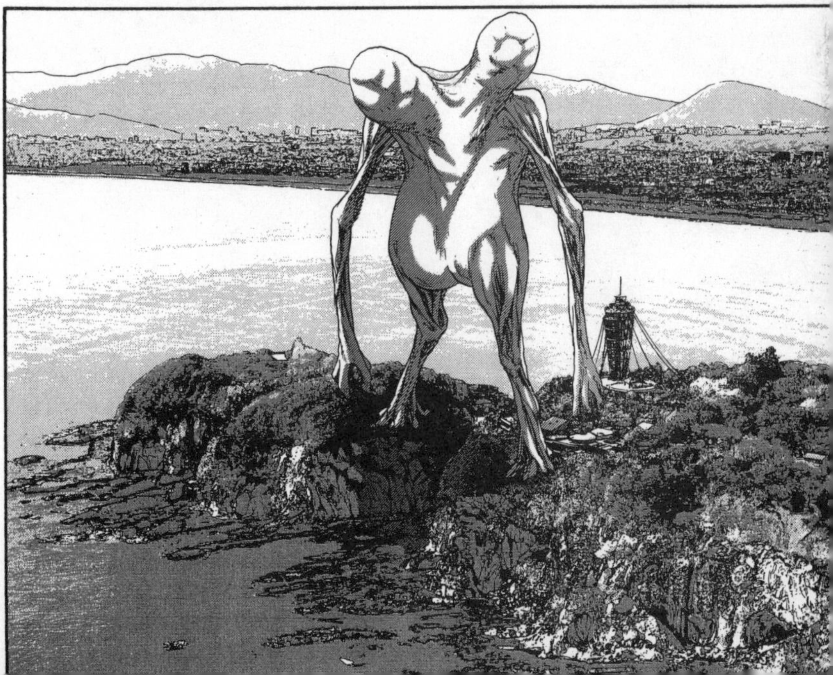

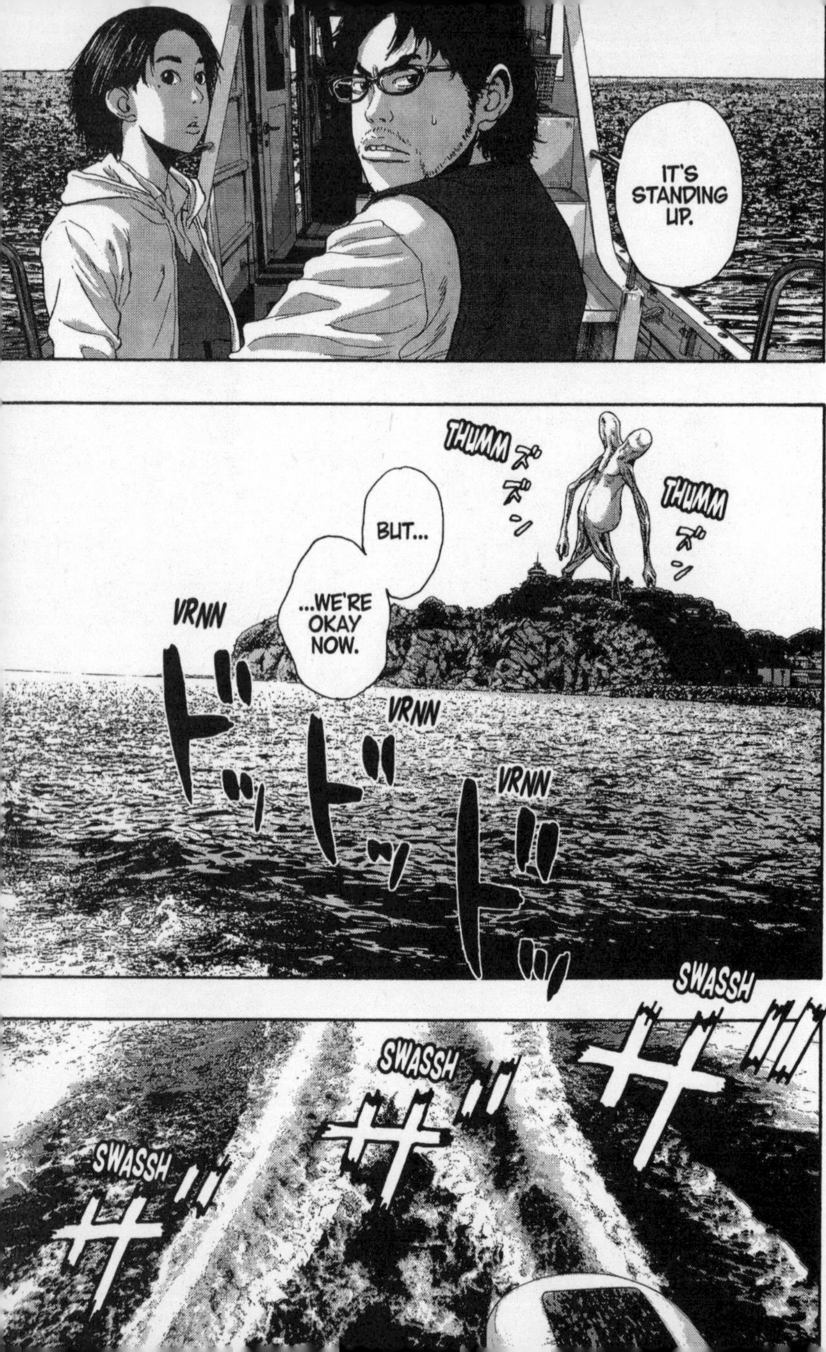
IT'S STANDING UP.
THUMM
ズン
THUMM
ズズン
BUT...
...WE'RE OKAY NOW.
VRNN
VRNN
VRNN
ドッドッドッ
SWASSH
SWASSH
SWASSH
ザザッ

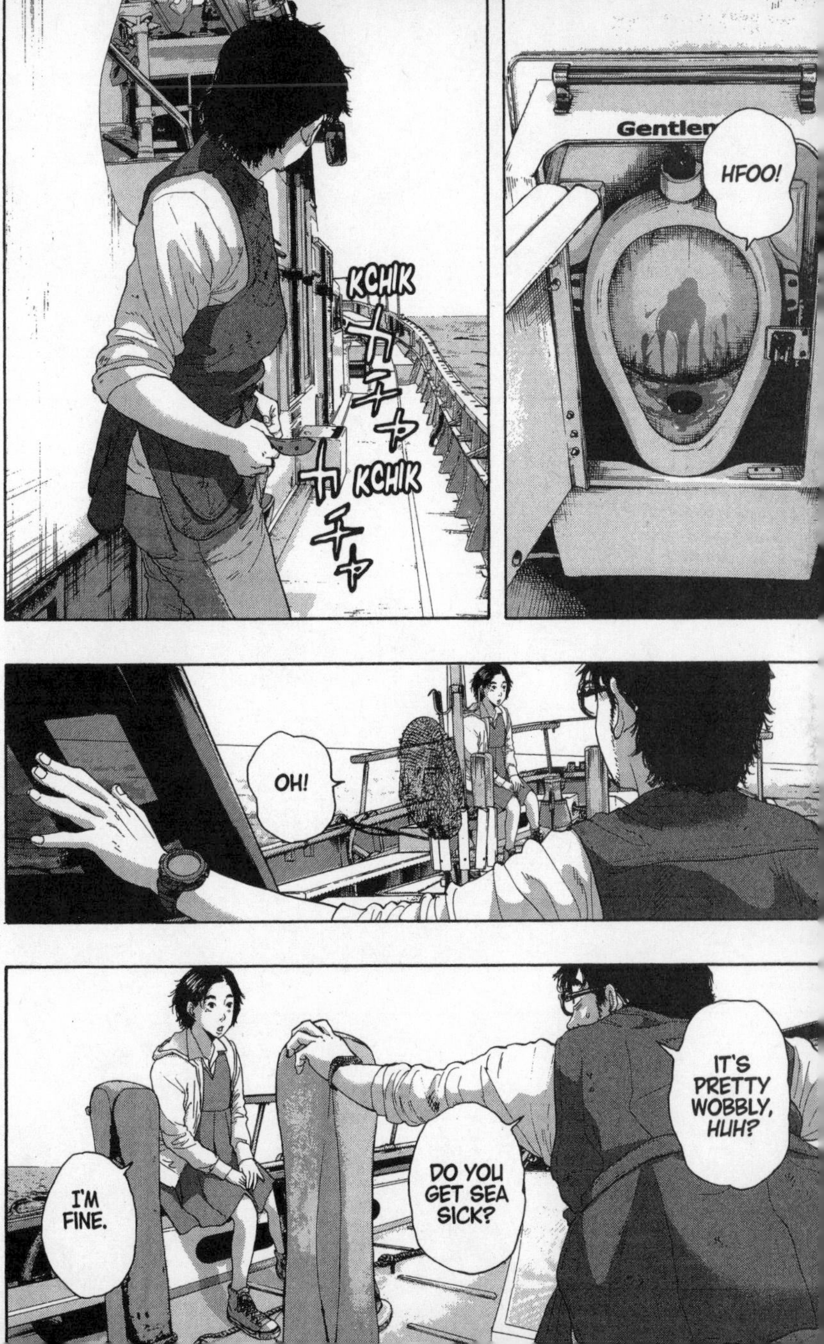
Gentlem
HFOO!
KCHIK
カチャ
KCHIK
カチャ
OH!
IT'S PRETTY WOBBLY, HUH?
DO YOU GET SEA SICK?
I'M FINE.

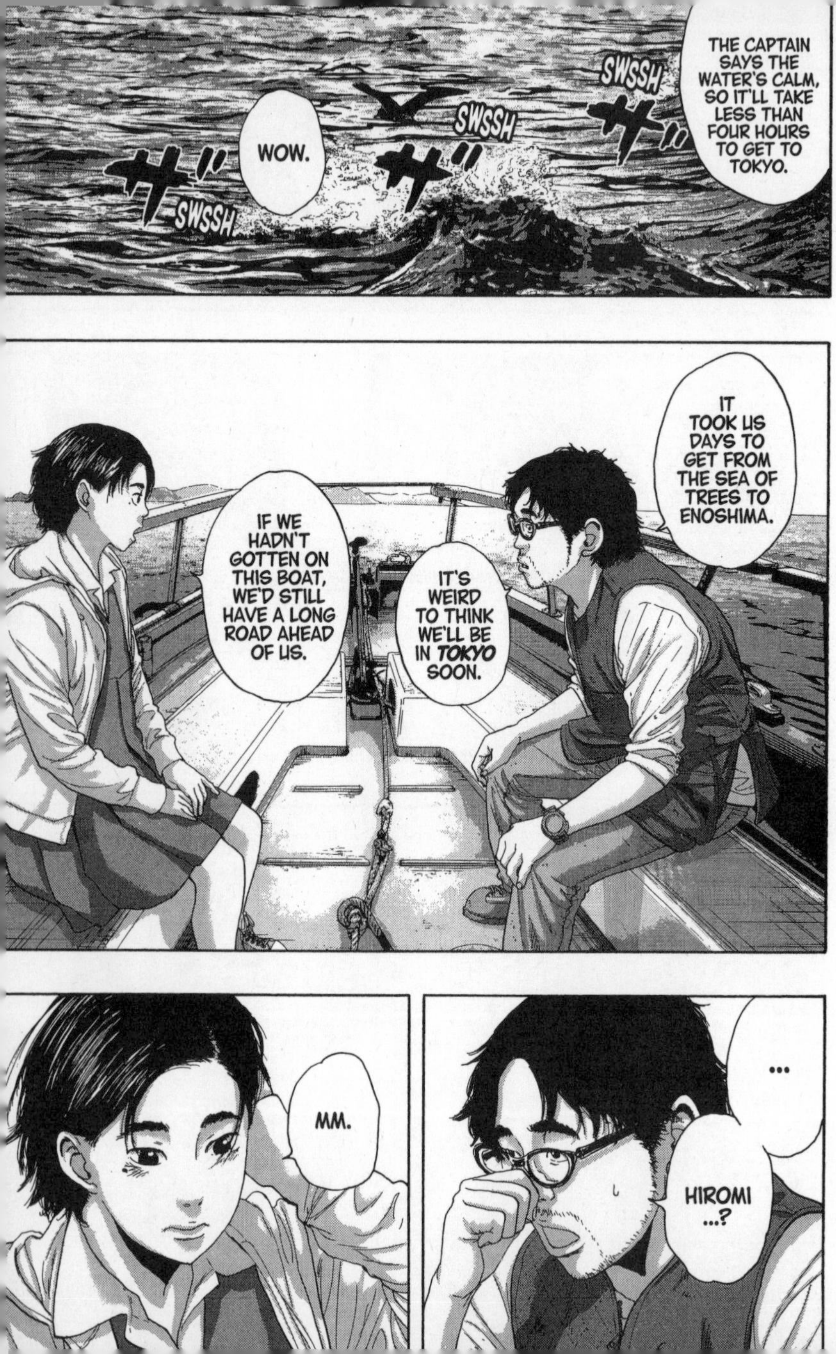
THE CAPTAIN SAYS THE WATER'S CALM, SO IT'LL TAKE LESS THAN FOUR HOURS TO GET TO TOKYO.
SWSSH
SWSSH
WOW.
SWSSH
IT TOOK US DAYS TO GET FROM THE SEA OF TREES TO ENOSHIMA.
IT'S WEIRD TO THINK WE'LL BE IN *TOKYO* SOON.
IF WE HADN'T GOTTEN ON THIS BOAT, WE'D STILL HAVE A LONG ROAD AHEAD OF US.
...
HIROMI ...?
MM.

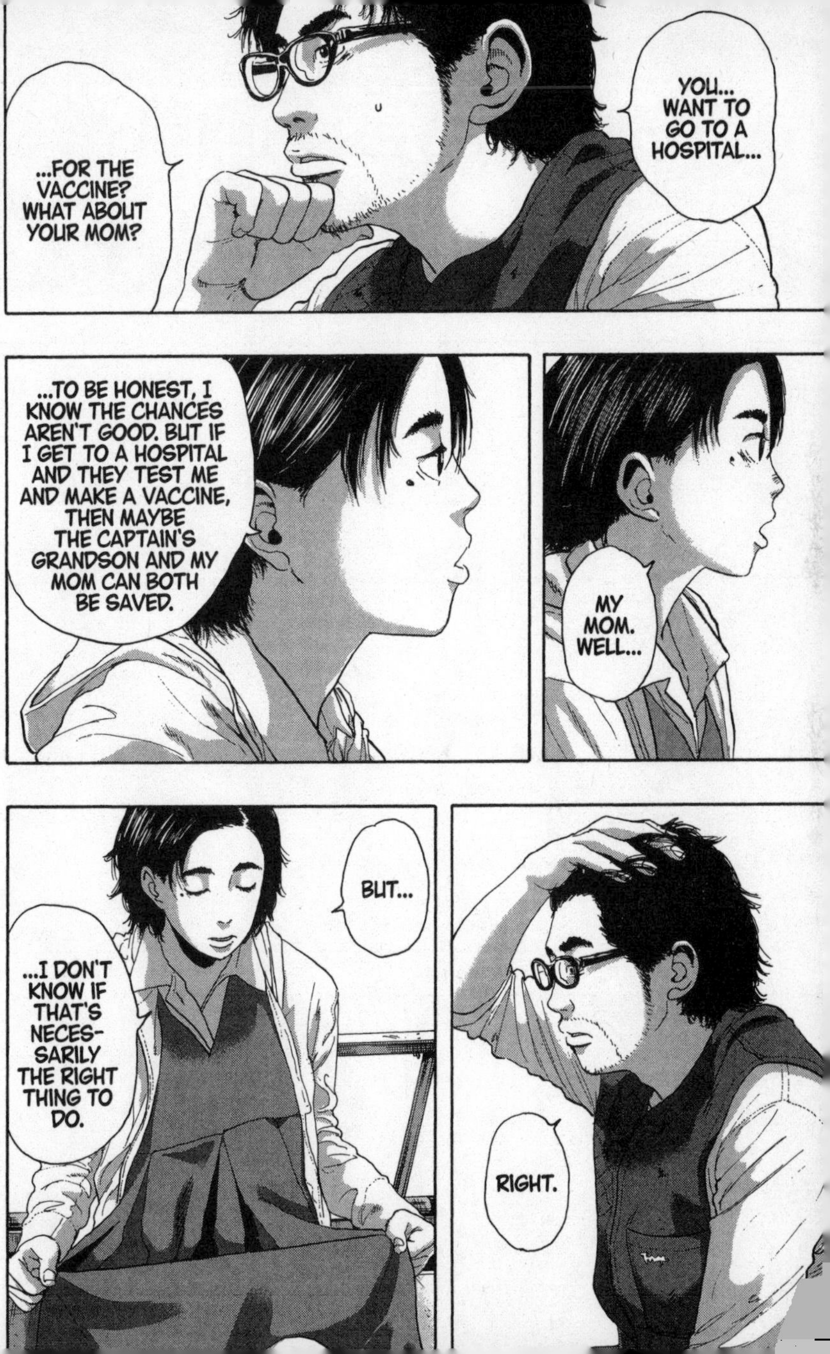
YOU... WANT TO GO TO A HOSPITAL...
...FOR THE VACCINE? WHAT ABOUT YOUR MOM?
MY MOM. WELL...
...TO BE HONEST, I KNOW THE CHANCES AREN'T GOOD. BUT IF I GET TO A HOSPITAL AND THEY TEST ME AND MAKE A VACCINE, THEN MAYBE THE CAPTAIN'S GRANDSON AND MY MOM CAN BOTH BE SAVED.
RIGHT.
BUT...
...I DON'T KNOW IF THAT'S NECES-SARILY THE RIGHT THING TO DO.

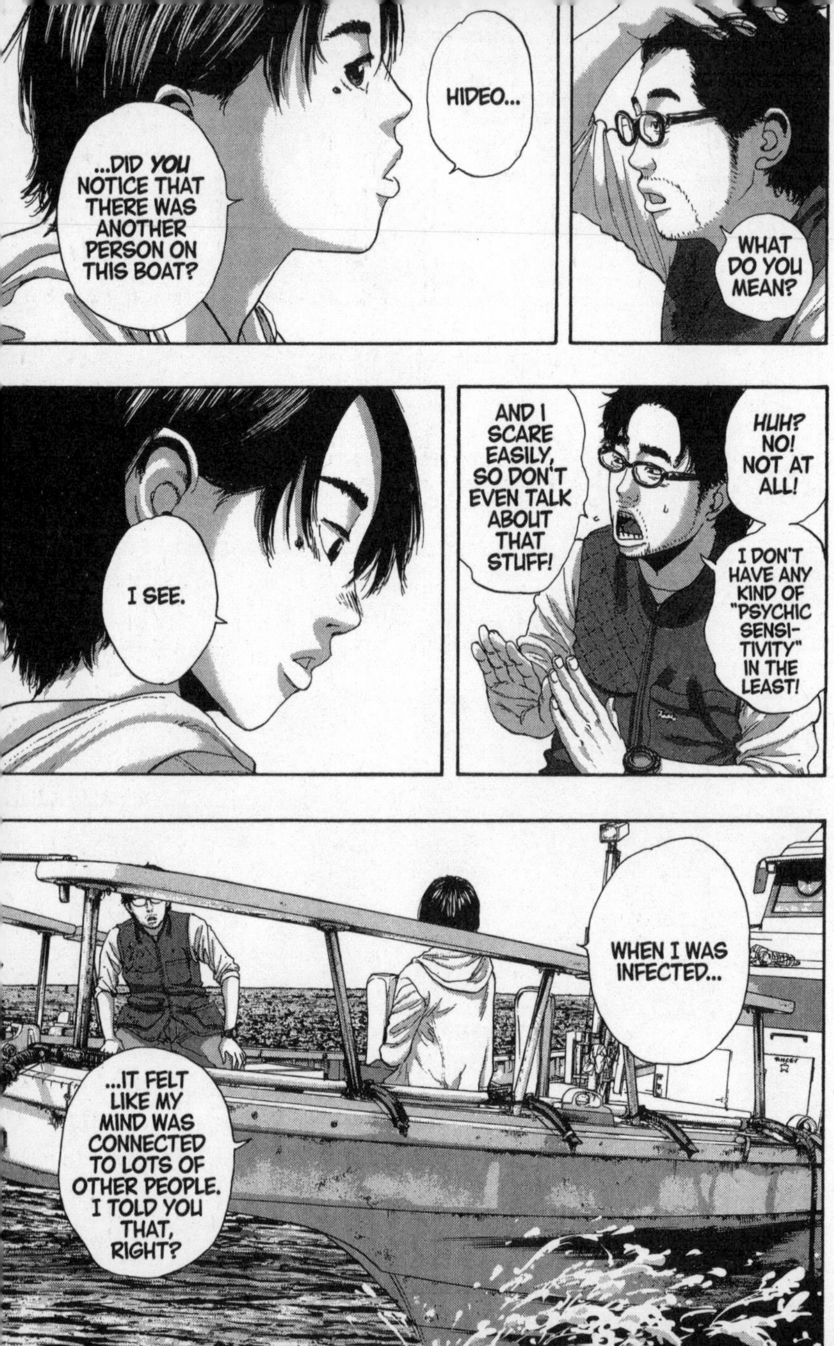
WHAT DO YOU MEAN?
HIDEO...
...DID YOU NOTICE THAT THERE WAS ANOTHER PERSON ON THIS BOAT?
HUH? NO! NOT AT ALL!
I DON'T HAVE ANY KIND OF "PSYCHIC SENSI-TIVITY" IN THE LEAST!
AND I SCARE EASILY, SO DON'T EVEN TALK ABOUT THAT STUFF!
I SEE.
WHEN I WAS INFECTED...
...IT FELT LIKE MY MIND WAS CONNECTED TO LOTS OF OTHER PEOPLE. I TOLD YOU THAT, RIGHT?

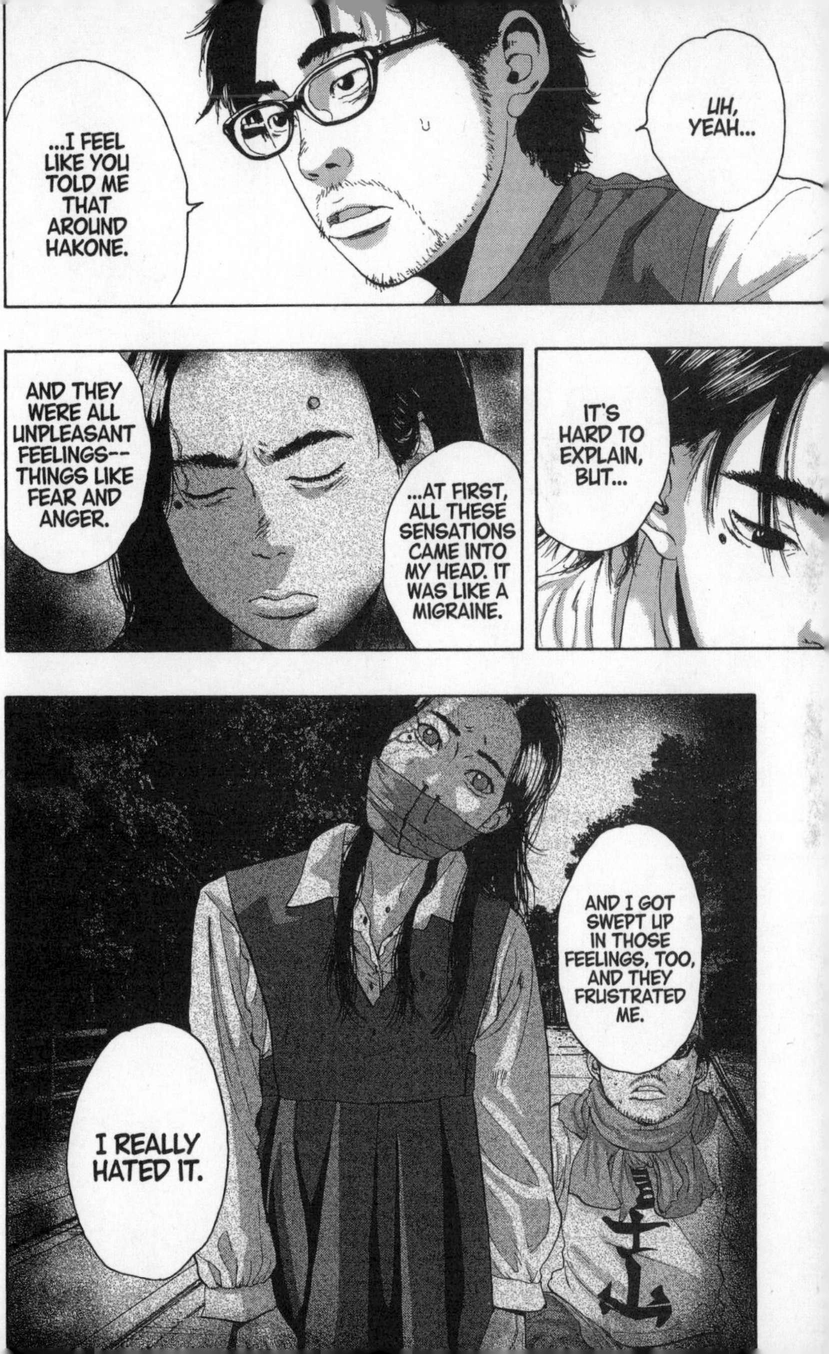
UH, YEAH...
...I FEEL LIKE YOU TOLD ME THAT AROUND HAKONE.
IT'S HARD TO EXPLAIN, BUT...
...AT FIRST, ALL THESE SENSATIONS CAME INTO MY HEAD. IT WAS LIKE A MIGRAINE.
AND THEY WERE ALL UNPLEASANT FEELINGS-- THINGS LIKE FEAR AND ANGER.
AND I GOT SWEPT UP IN THOSE FEELINGS, TOO, AND THEY FRUSTRATED ME.
I REALLY HATED IT.

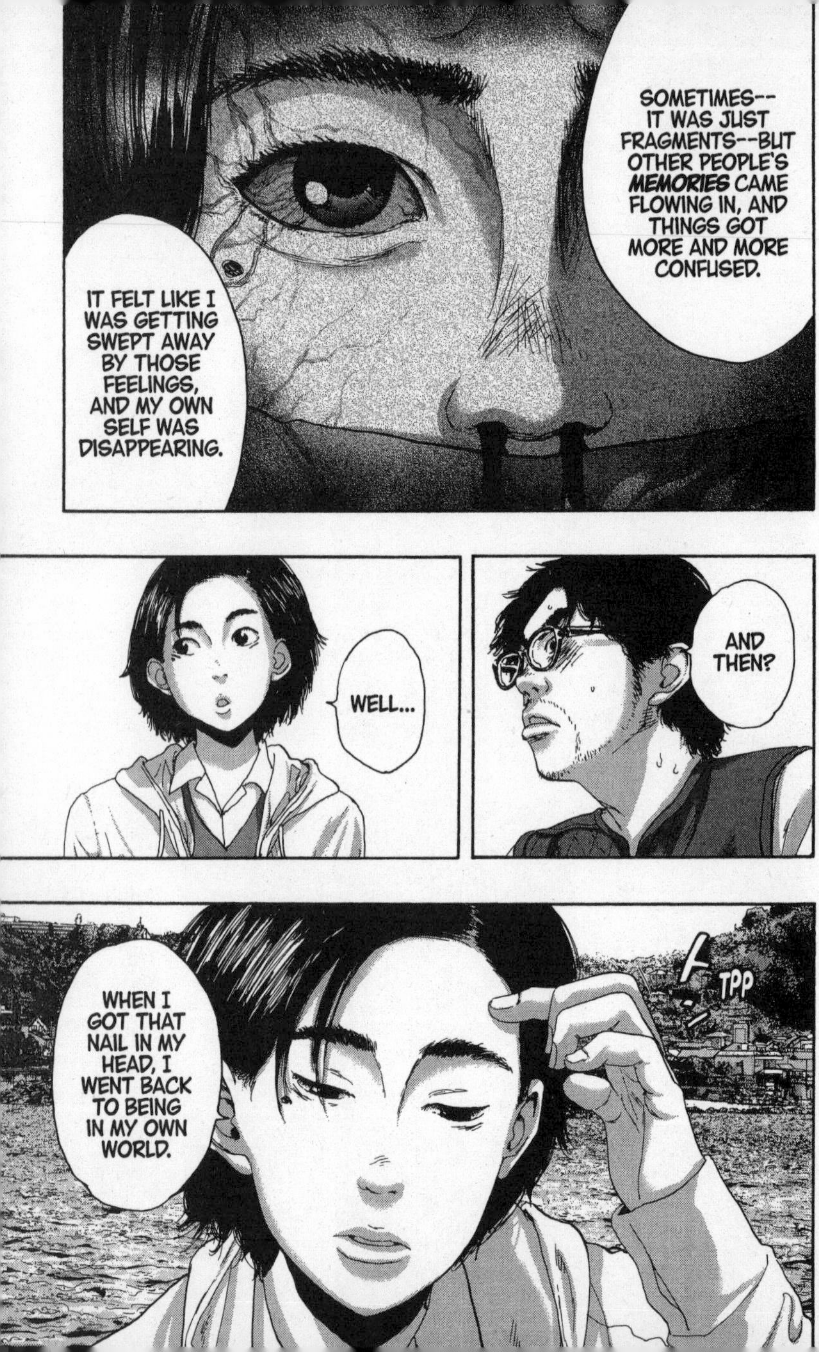
SOMETIMES-- IT WAS JUST FRAGMENTS--BUT OTHER PEOPLE'S **MEMORIES** CAME FLOWING IN, AND THINGS GOT MORE AND MORE CONFUSED.
IT FELT LIKE I WAS GETTING SWEPT AWAY BY THOSE FEELINGS, AND MY OWN SELF WAS DISAPPEARING.
AND THEN?
WELL...
TPP
WHEN I GOT THAT NAIL IN MY HEAD, I WENT BACK TO BEING IN MY OWN WORLD.

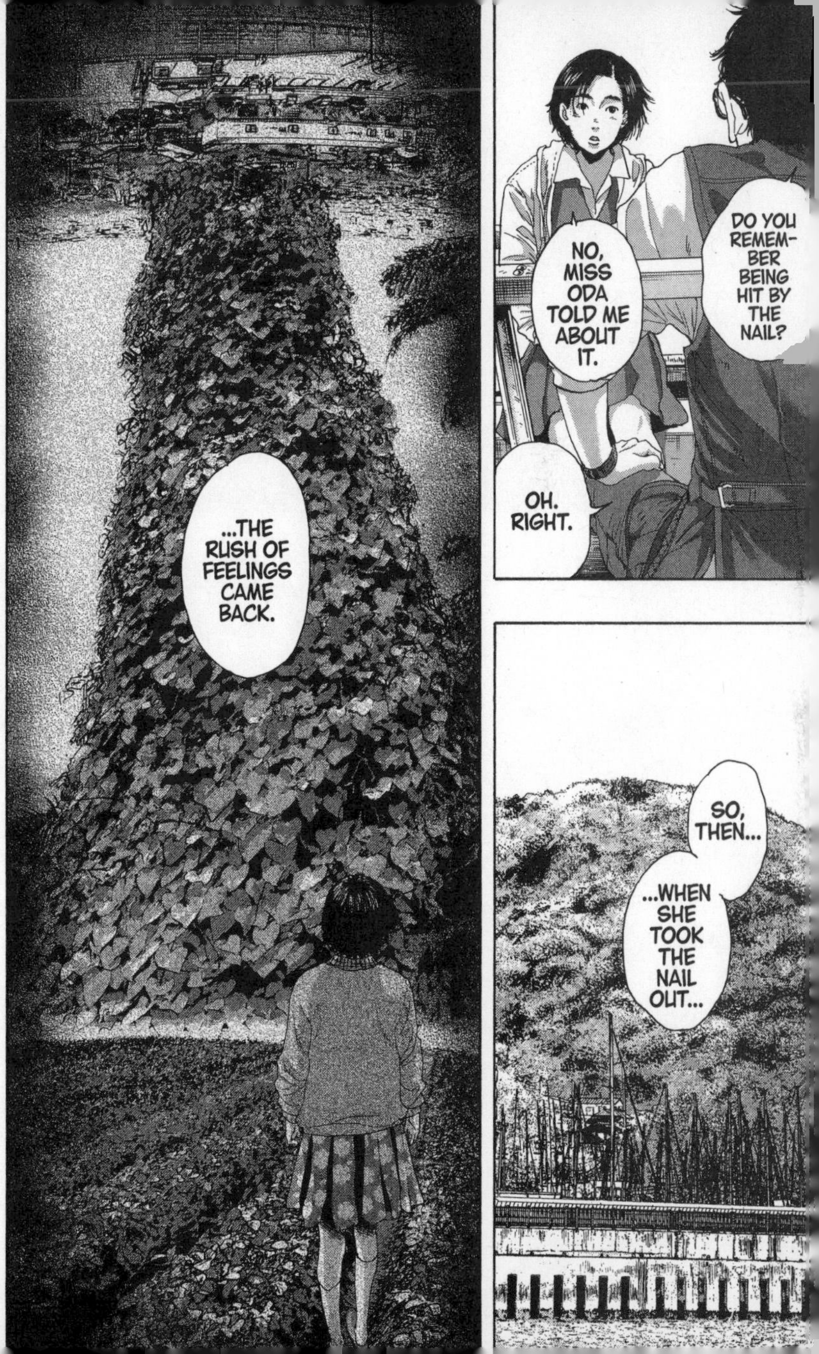
DO YOU REMEMBER BEING HIT BY THE NAIL?
NO, MISS ODA TOLD ME ABOUT IT.
OH. RIGHT.
SO, THEN...
...WHEN SHE TOOK THE NAIL OUT...
...THE RUSH OF FEELINGS CAME BACK.

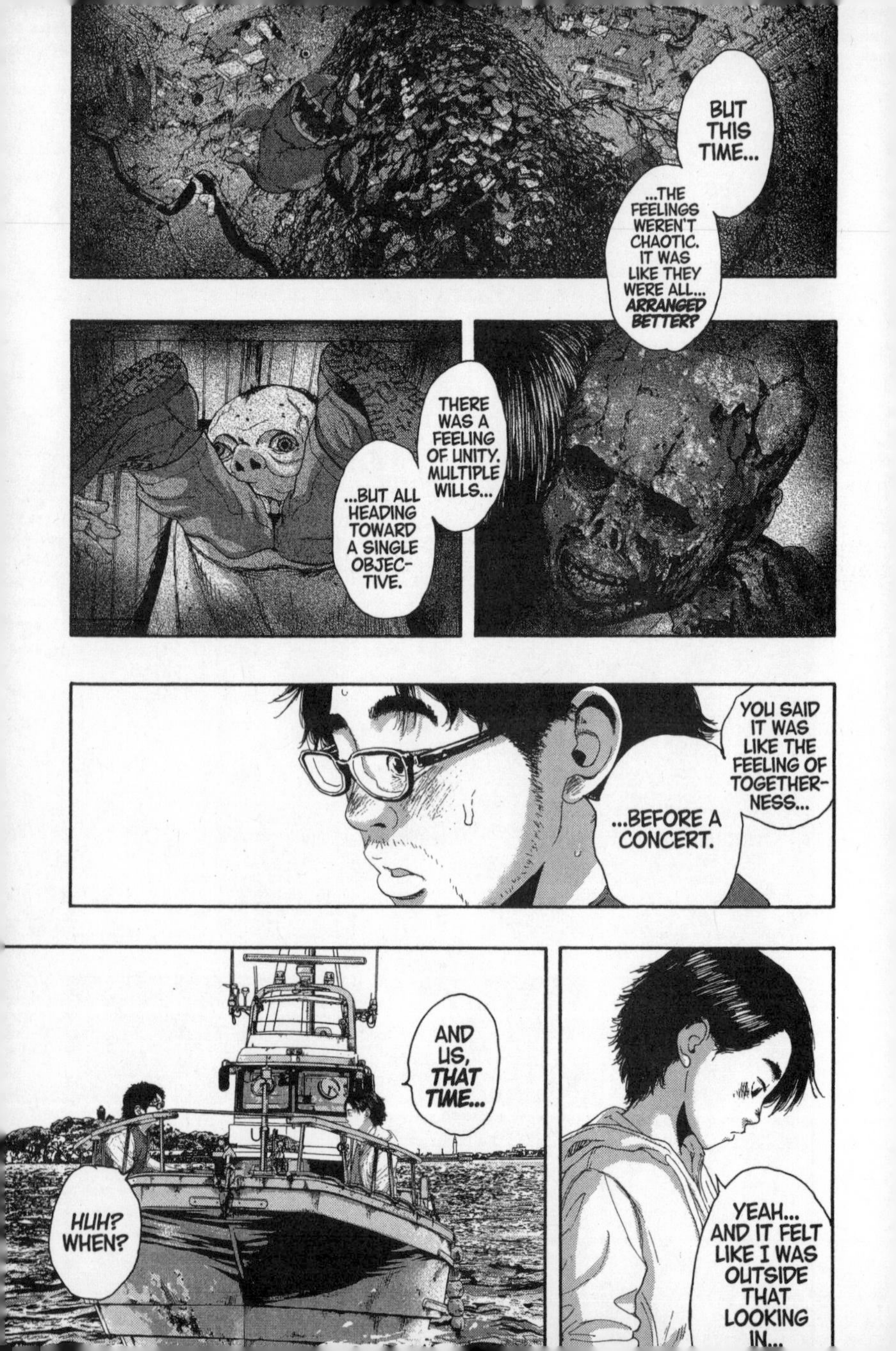
BUT THIS TIME...
...THE FEELINGS WEREN'T CHAOTIC. IT WAS LIKE THEY WERE ALL... *ARRANGED BETTER?*
THERE WAS A FEELING OF UNITY. MULTIPLE WILLS...
...BUT ALL HEADING TOWARD A SINGLE OBJECTIVE.
YOU SAID IT WAS LIKE THE FEELING OF TOGETHERNESS...
...BEFORE A CONCERT.
YEAH... AND IT FELT LIKE I WAS OUTSIDE THAT LOOKING IN...
AND US, *THAT TIME*...
HUH? WHEN?

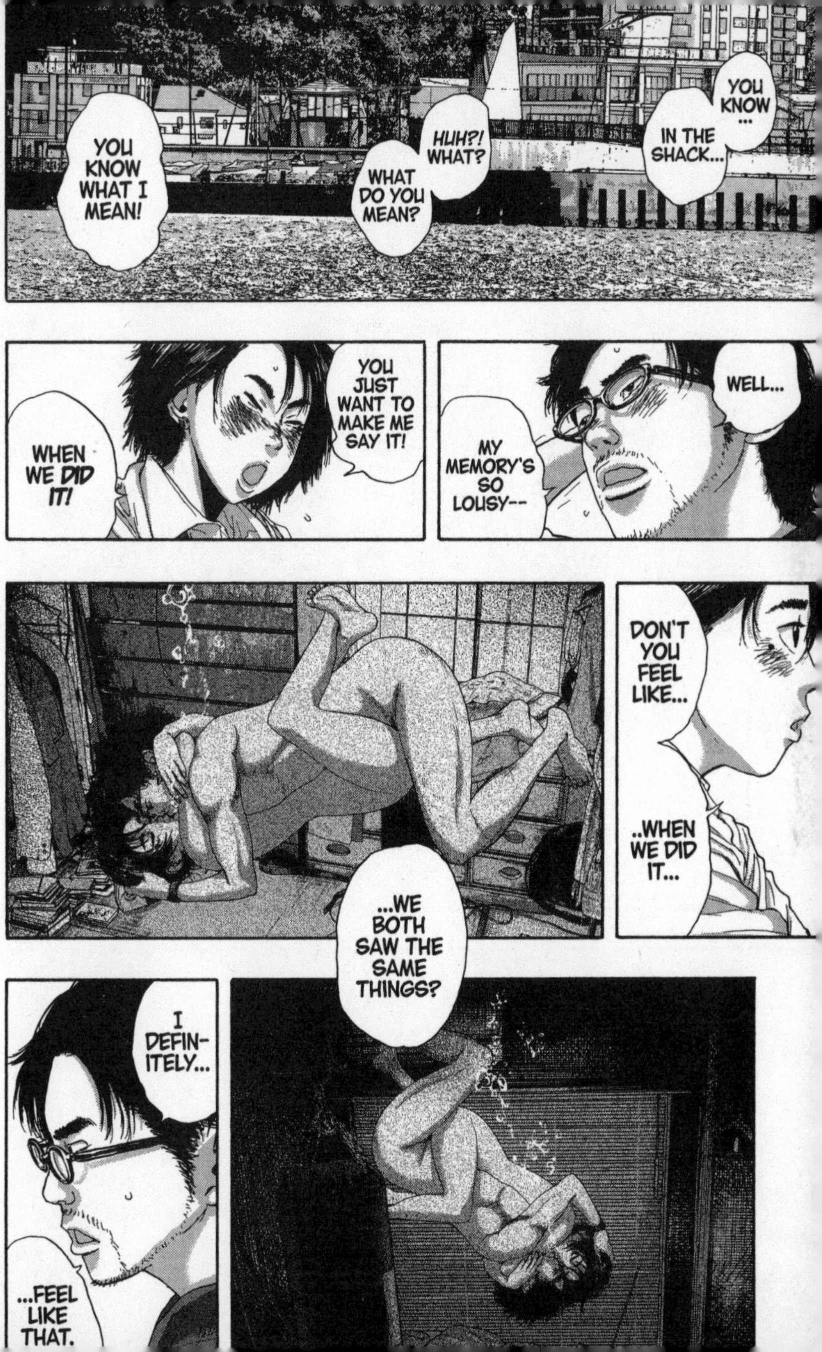
YOU KNOW ...
IN THE SHACK...
HUH?! WHAT?
WHAT DO YOU MEAN?
YOU KNOW WHAT I MEAN!
WELL...
MY MEMORY'S SO LOUSY--
YOU JUST WANT TO MAKE ME SAY IT!
WHEN WE *DID* IT!
DON'T YOU FEEL LIKE...
..WHEN WE DID IT...
...WE BOTH SAW THE SAME THINGS?
I DEFIN-ITELY...
...FEEL LIKE THAT.

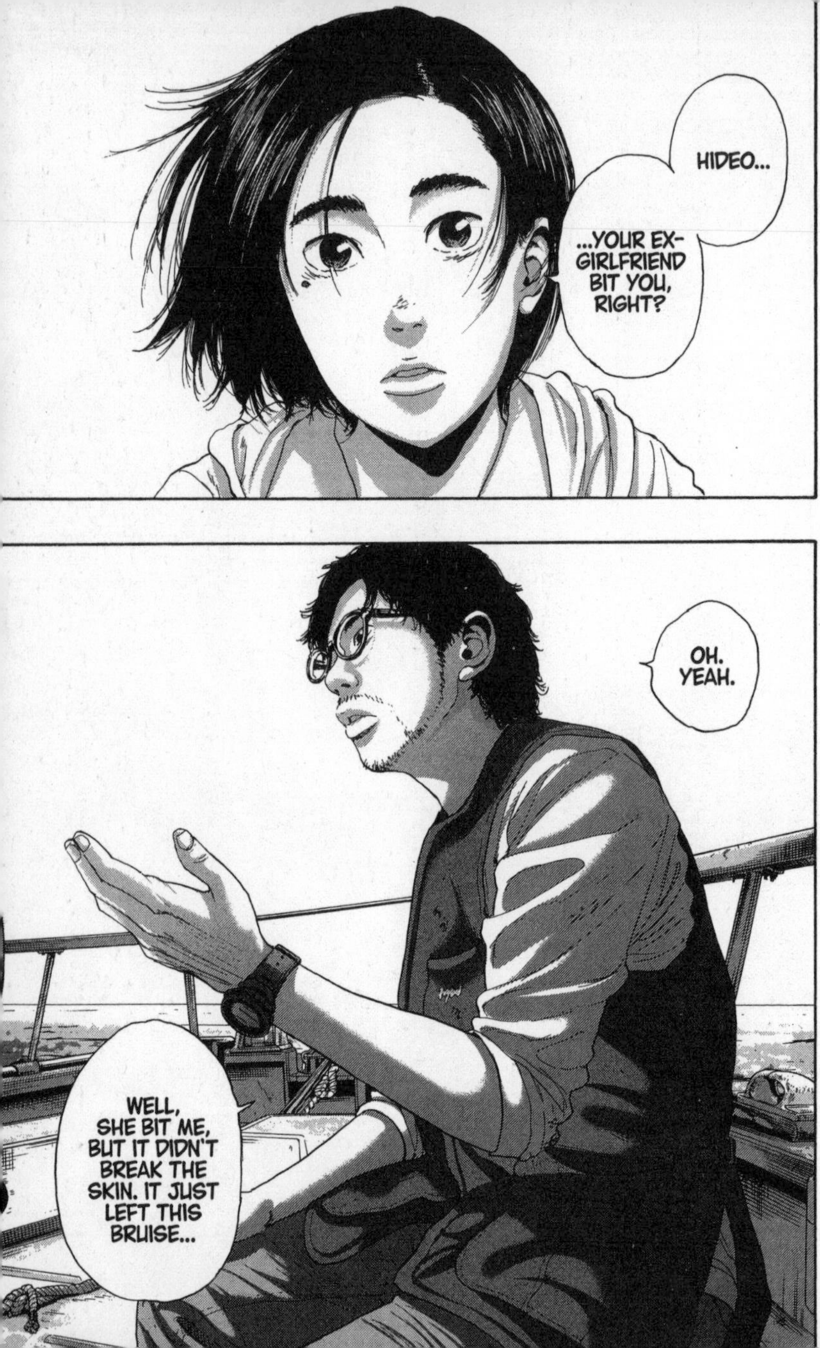
HIDEO...
...YOUR EX-GIRLFRIEND BIT YOU, RIGHT?
OH. YEAH.
WELL, SHE BIT ME, BUT IT DIDN'T BREAK THE SKIN. IT JUST LEFT THIS BRUISE...

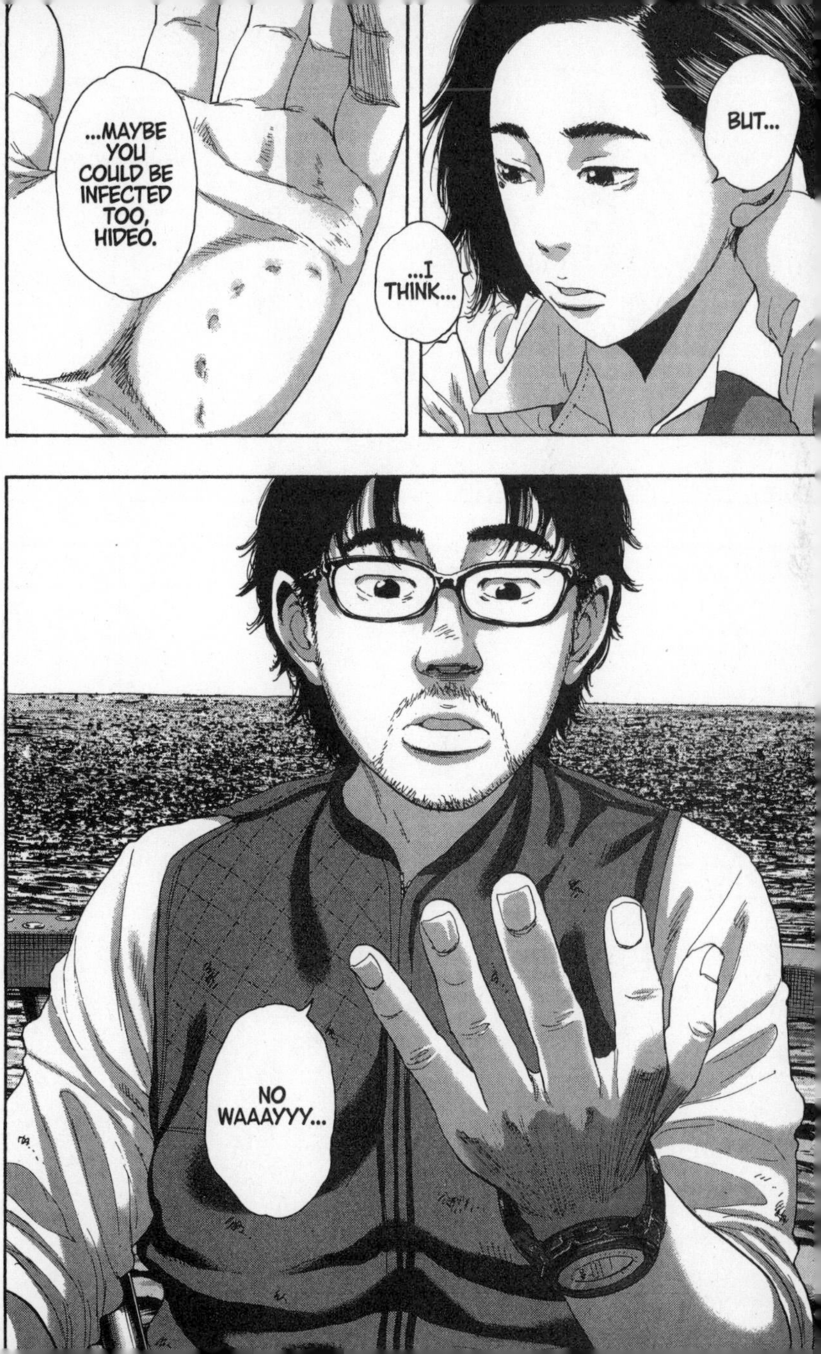
BUT...
...I THINK...
...MAYBE YOU COULD BE INFECTED TOO, HIDEO.
NO WAAAYYY...

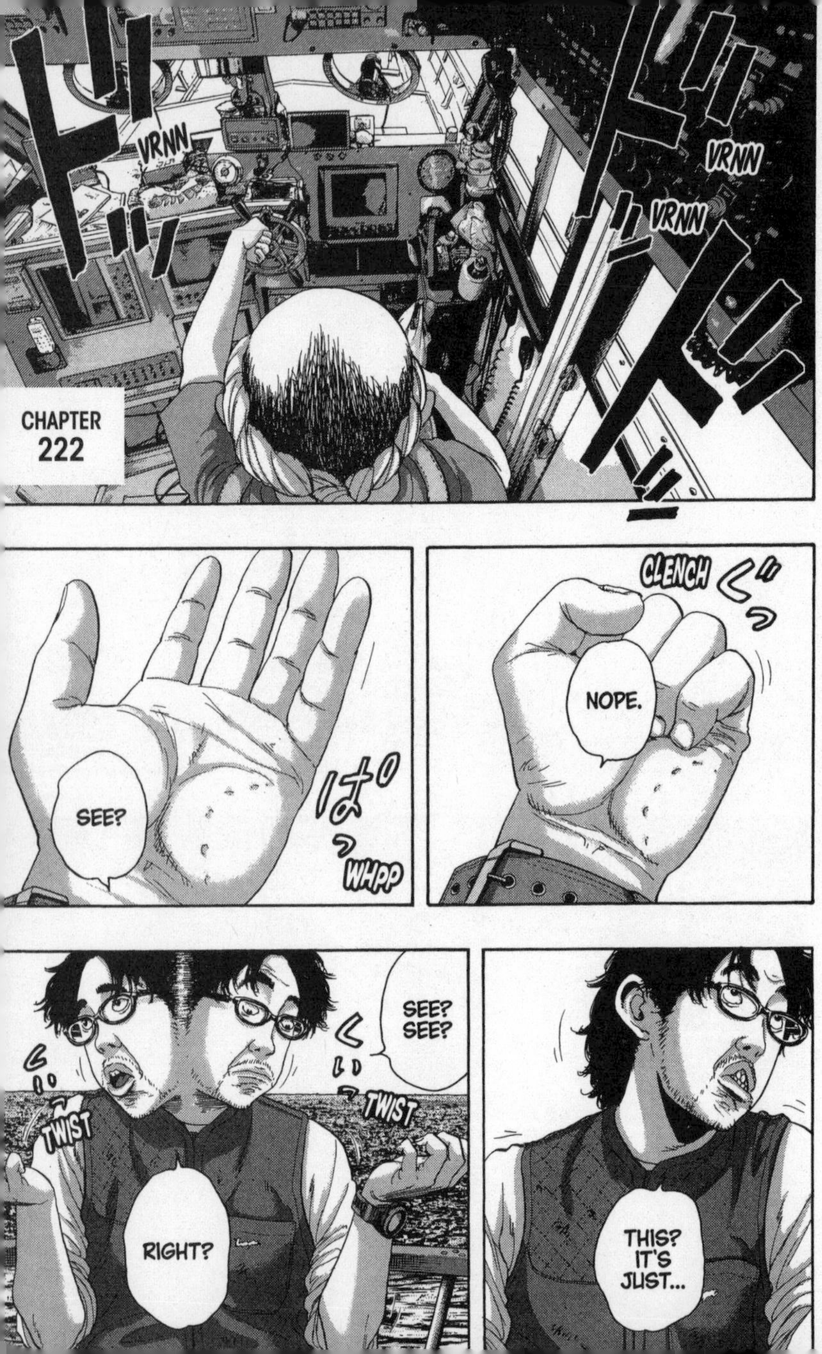
VRNN
VRNN
VRNN
CHAPTER 222
CLENCH
ぐっ
NOPE.
はっ
WHPP
SEE?
THIS? IT'S JUST...
SEE? SEE?
くいっ
TWIST
くいっ
TWIST
RIGHT?

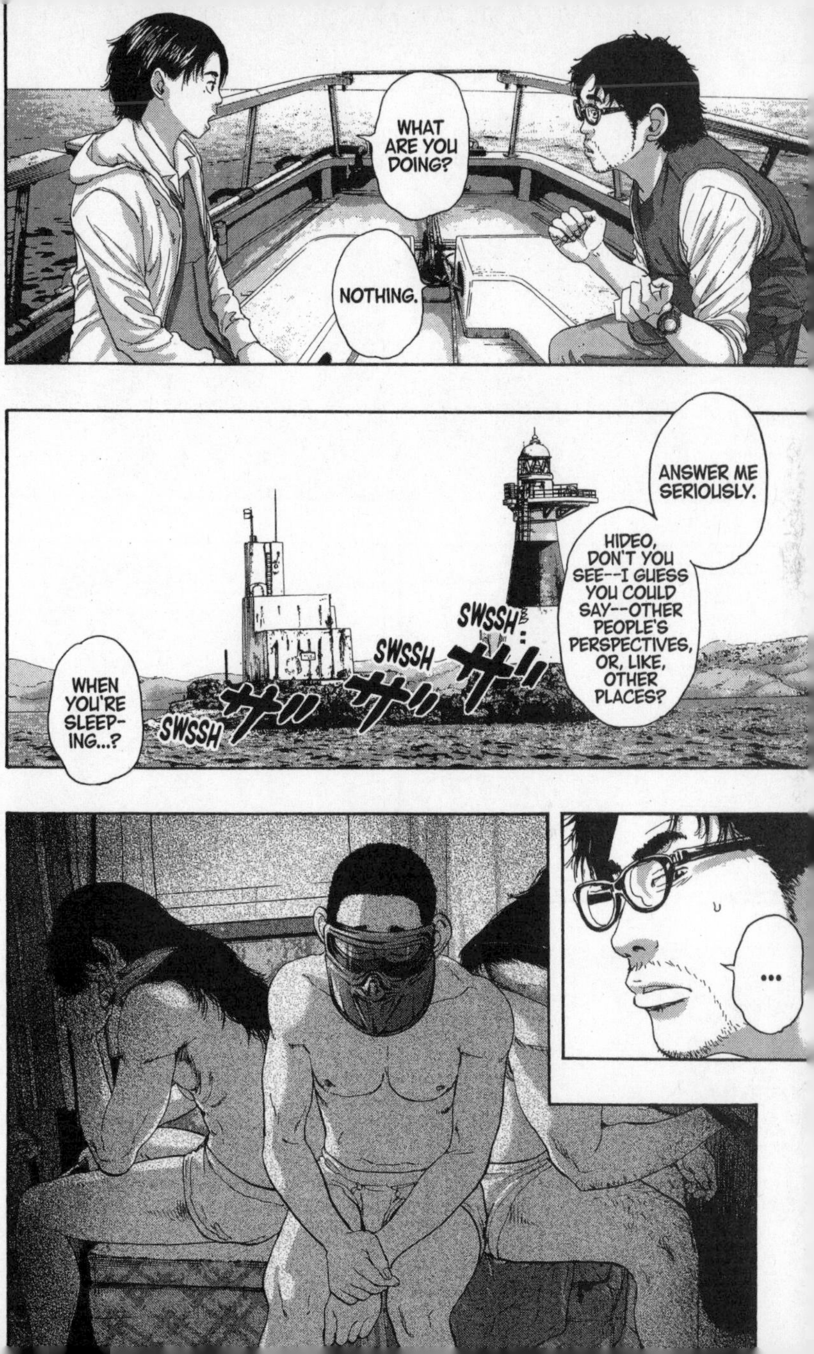
WHAT ARE YOU DOING?
NOTHING.
ANSWER ME SERIOUSLY.
HIDEO, DON'T YOU SEE--I GUESS YOU COULD SAY--OTHER PEOPLE'S PERSPECTIVES, OR, LIKE, OTHER PLACES?
SWSSH
SWSSH
SWSSH
WHEN YOU'RE SLEEP-ING...?
...

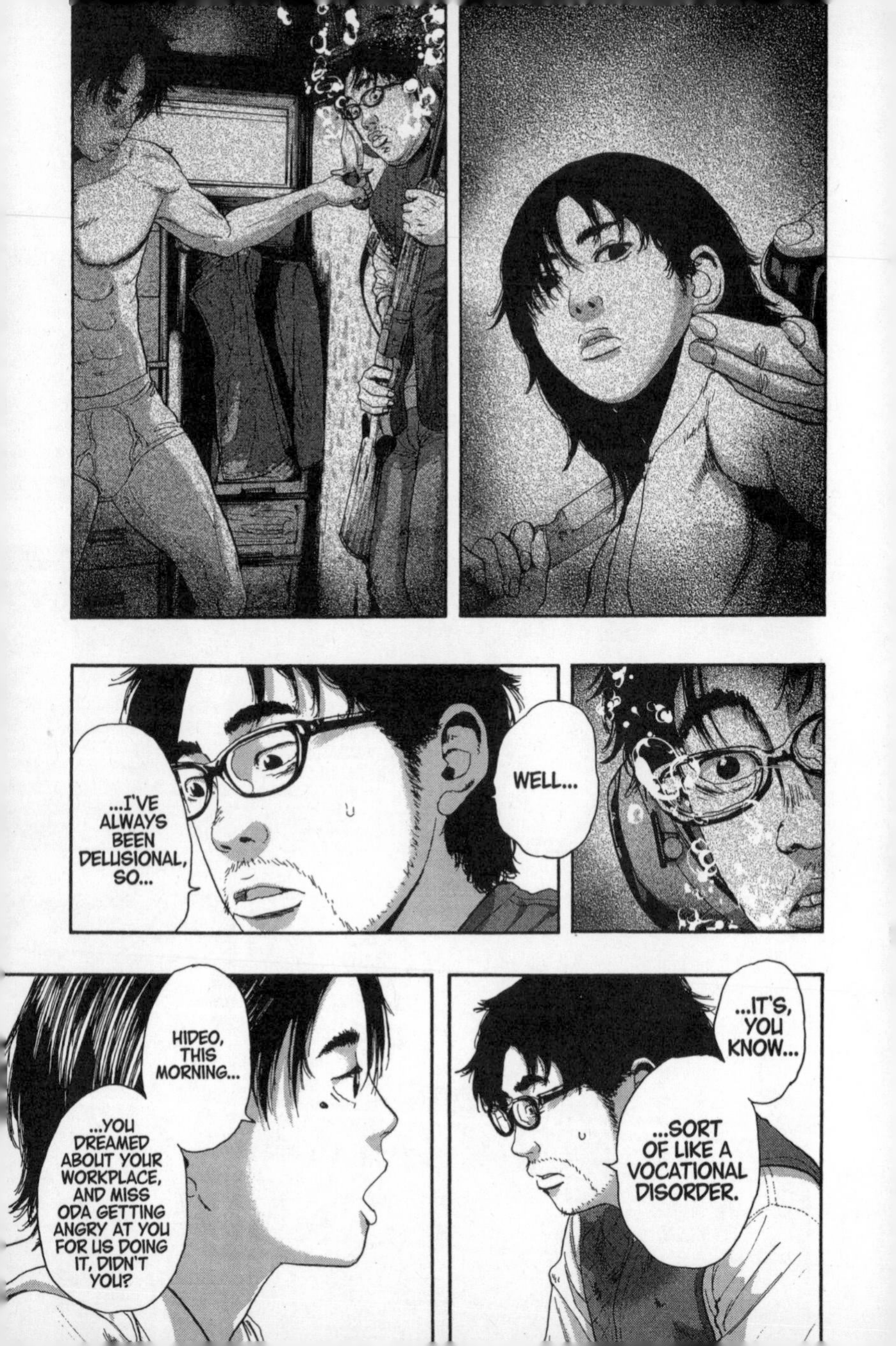
WELL...
...I'VE ALWAYS BEEN DELUSIONAL, SO...
...IT'S, YOU KNOW...
...SORT OF LIKE A VOCATIONAL DISORDER.
HIDEO, THIS MORNING...
...YOU DREAMED ABOUT YOUR WORKPLACE, AND MISS ODA GETTING ANGRY AT YOU FOR US DOING IT, DIDN'T YOU?

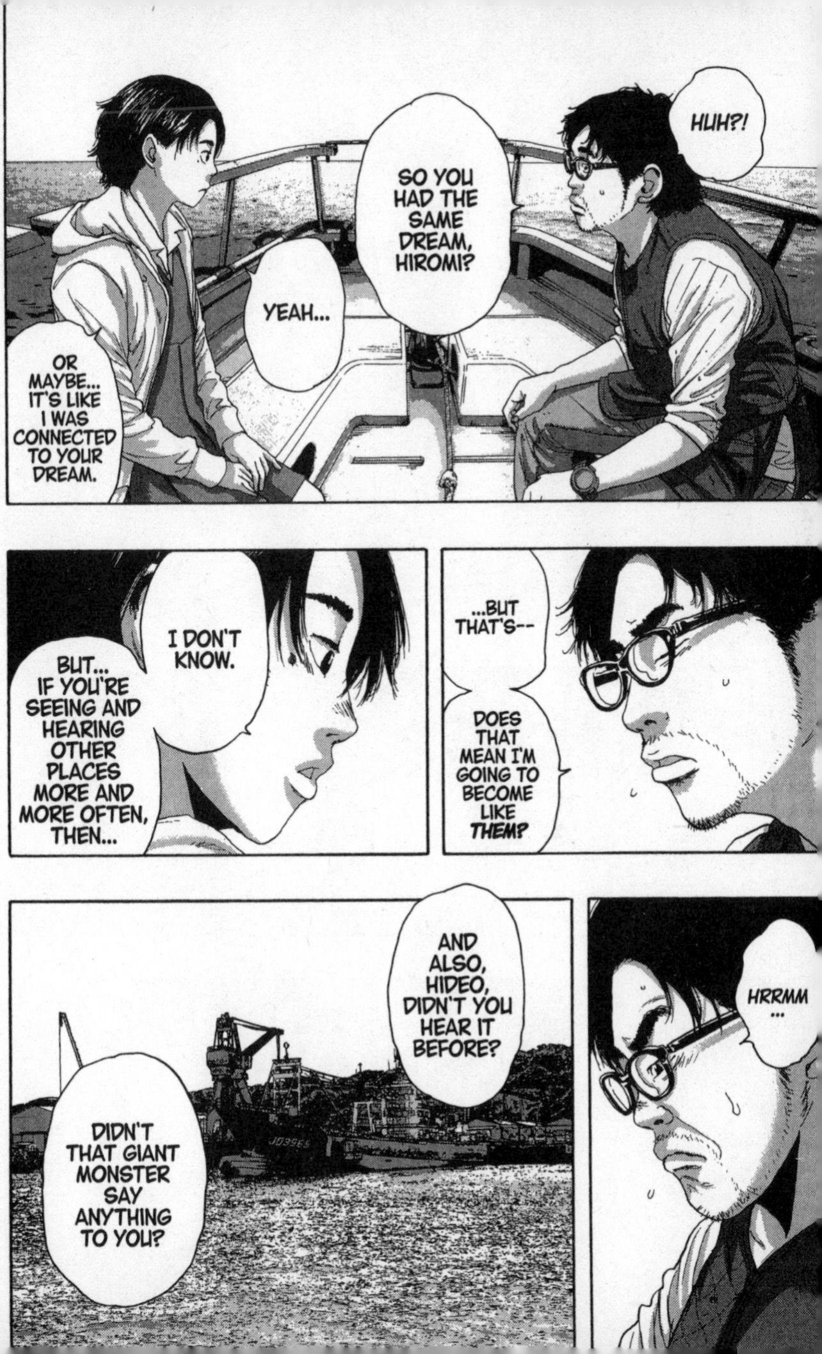
HUH?!
SO YOU HAD THE SAME DREAM, HIROMI?
YEAH...
OR MAYBE... IT'S LIKE I WAS CONNECTED TO YOUR DREAM.
...BUT THAT'S--
DOES THAT MEAN I'M GOING TO BECOME LIKE *THEM?*
I DON'T KNOW.
BUT... IF YOU'RE SEEING AND HEARING OTHER PLACES MORE AND MORE OFTEN, THEN...
HRRMM ...
AND ALSO, HIDEO, DIDN'T YOU HEAR IT BEFORE?
DIDN'T THAT GIANT MONSTER SAY ANYTHING TO YOU?

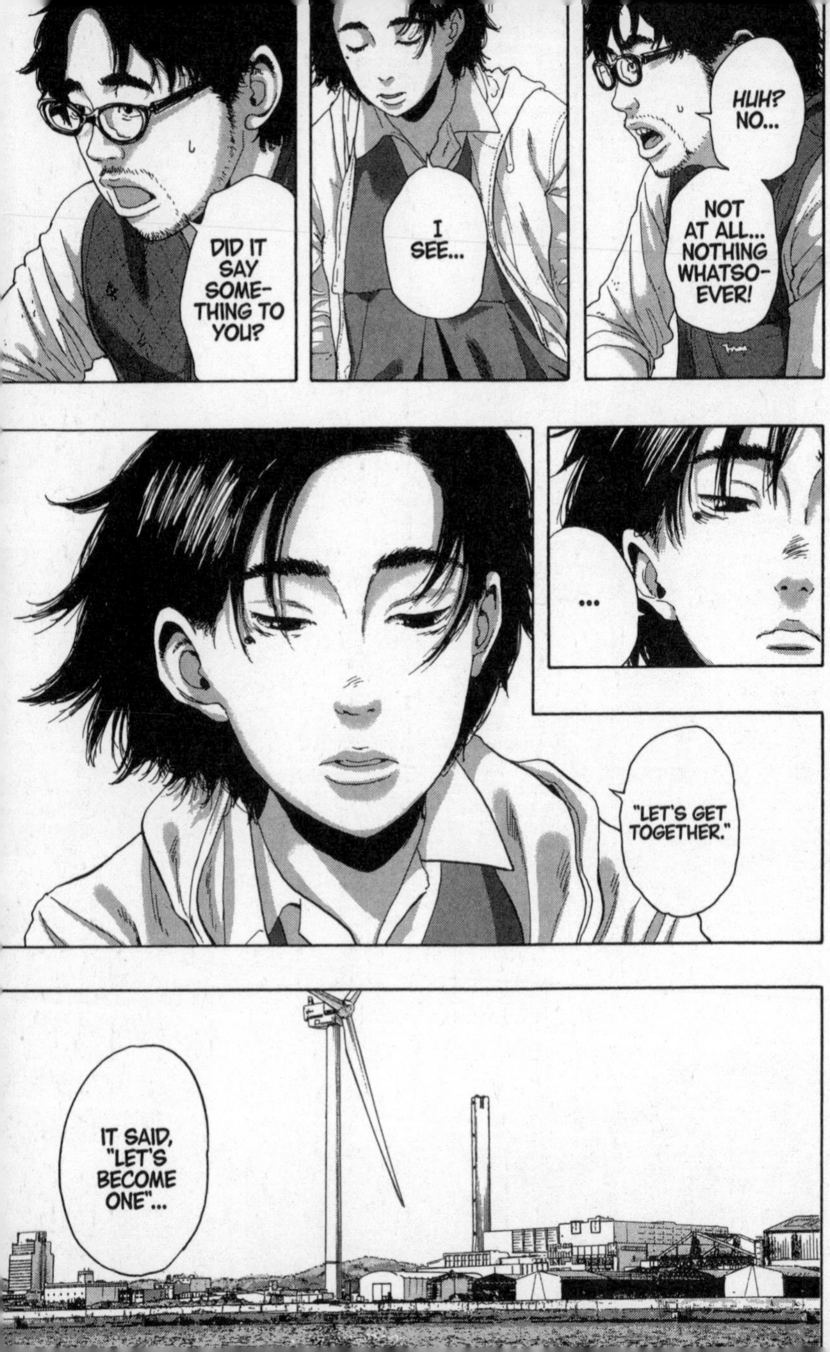
DID IT SAY SOME-THING TO YOU?
I SEE...
HUH? NO...
NOT AT ALL... NOTHING WHATSO-EVER!
"LET'S GET TOGETHER."
...
IT SAID, "LET'S BECOME ONE"...

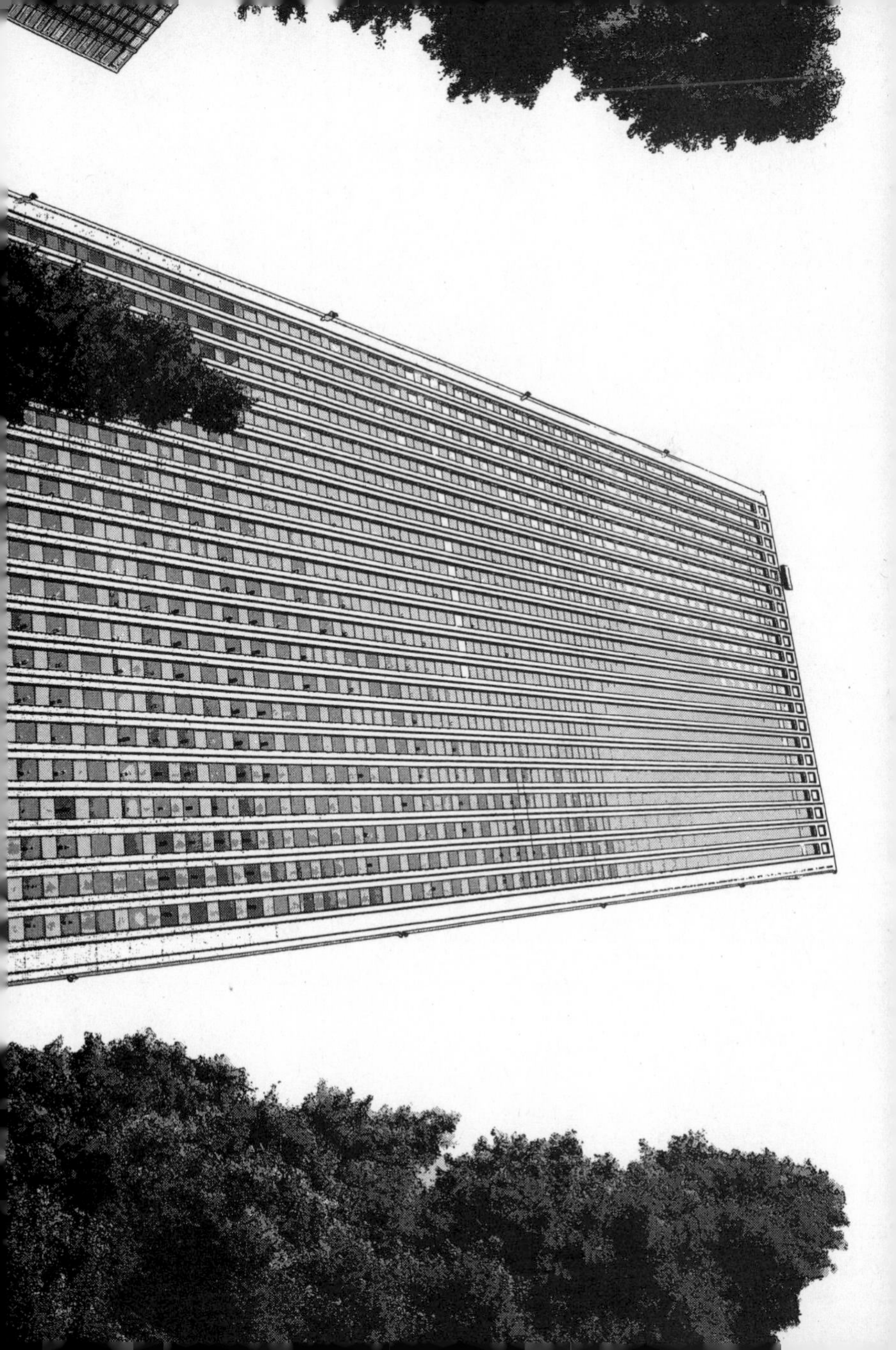

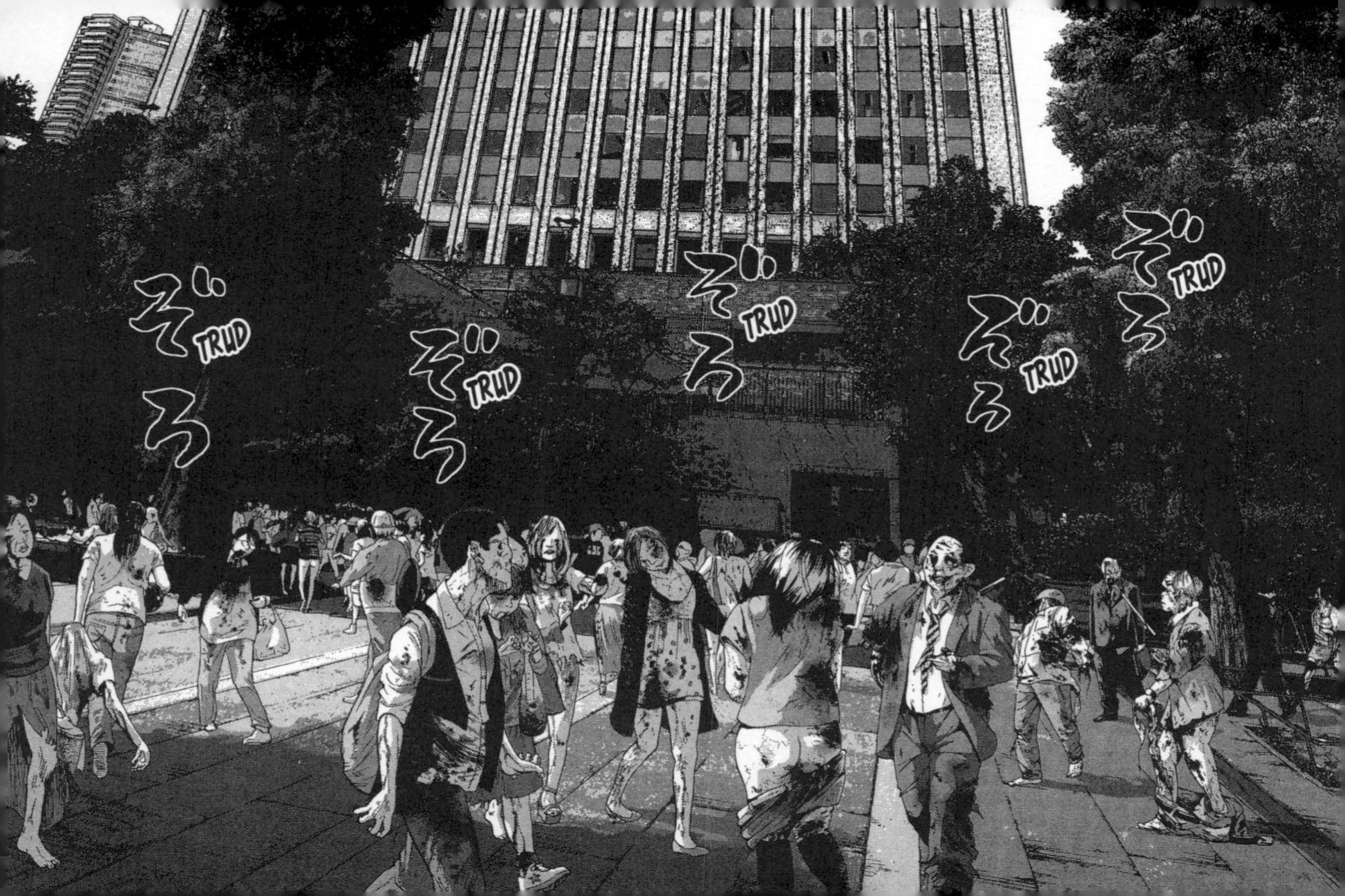
ぞろ TRUD
ぞろ TRUD
ぞろ TRUD
ぞろ TRUD
ぞろ TRUD

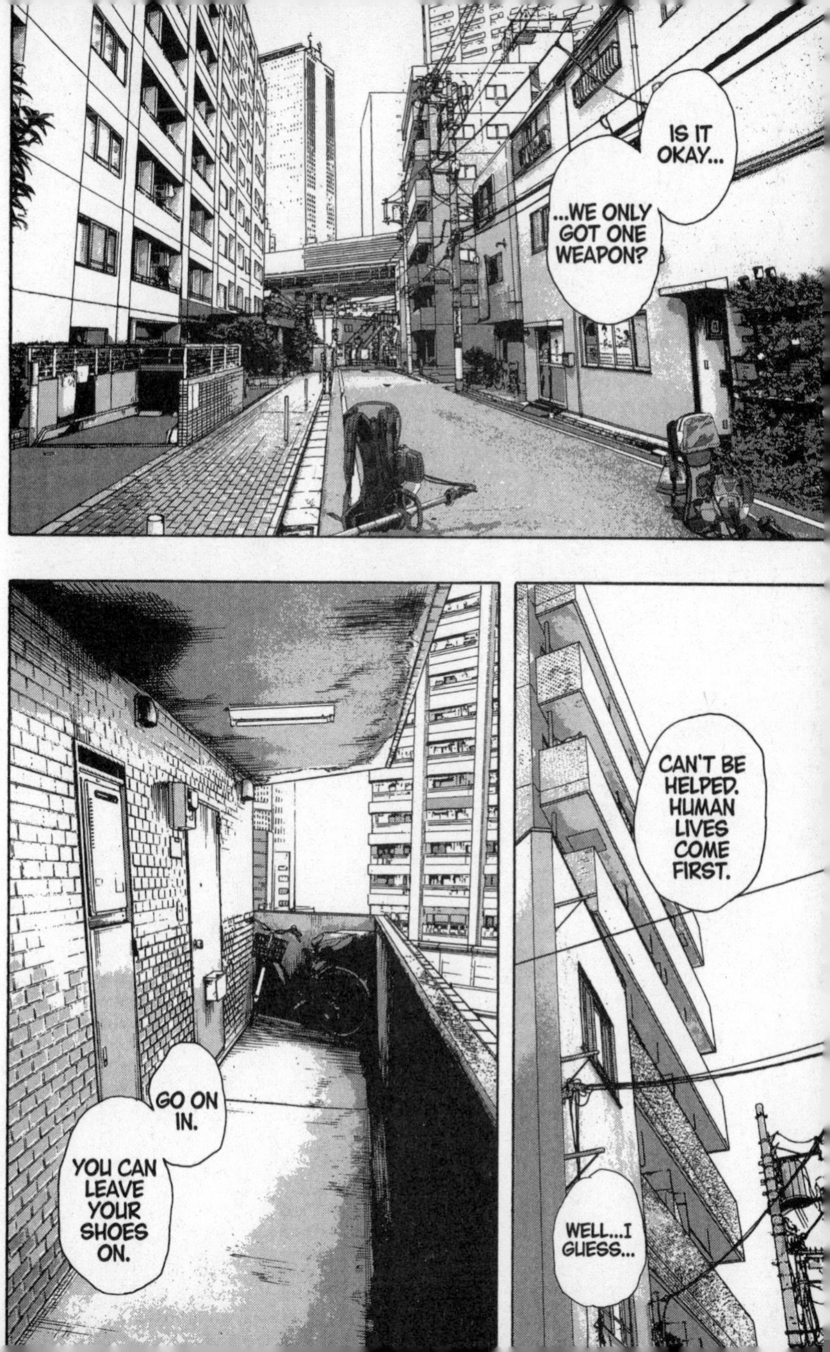
IS IT OKAY...
...WE ONLY GOT ONE WEAPON?
CAN'T BE HELPED. HUMAN LIVES COME FIRST.
WELL...I GUESS...
GO ON IN.
YOU CAN LEAVE YOUR SHOES ON.

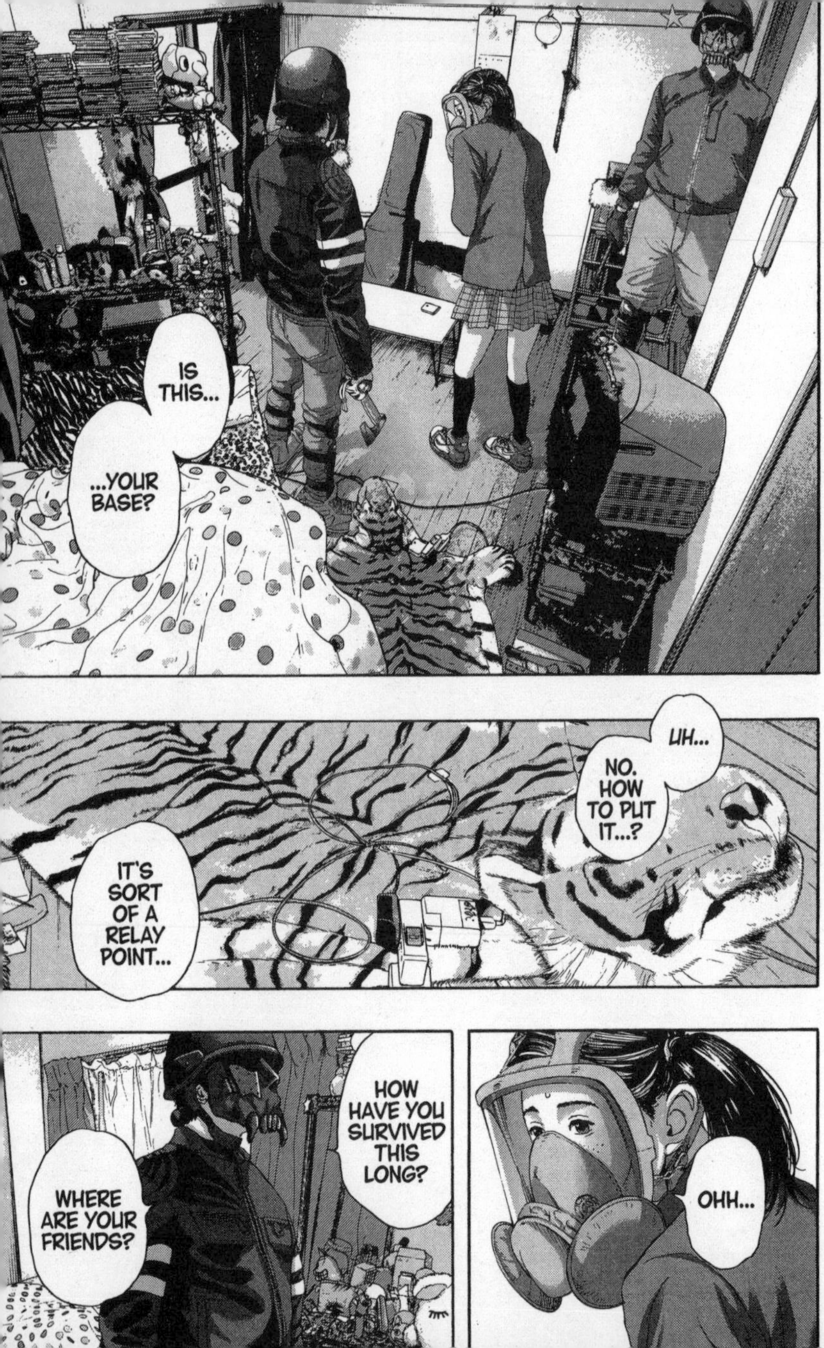
IS THIS...
...YOUR BASE?
UH...
NO. HOW TO PUT IT...?
IT'S SORT OF A RELAY POINT...
OHH...
HOW HAVE YOU SURVIVED THIS LONG?
WHERE ARE YOUR FRIENDS?

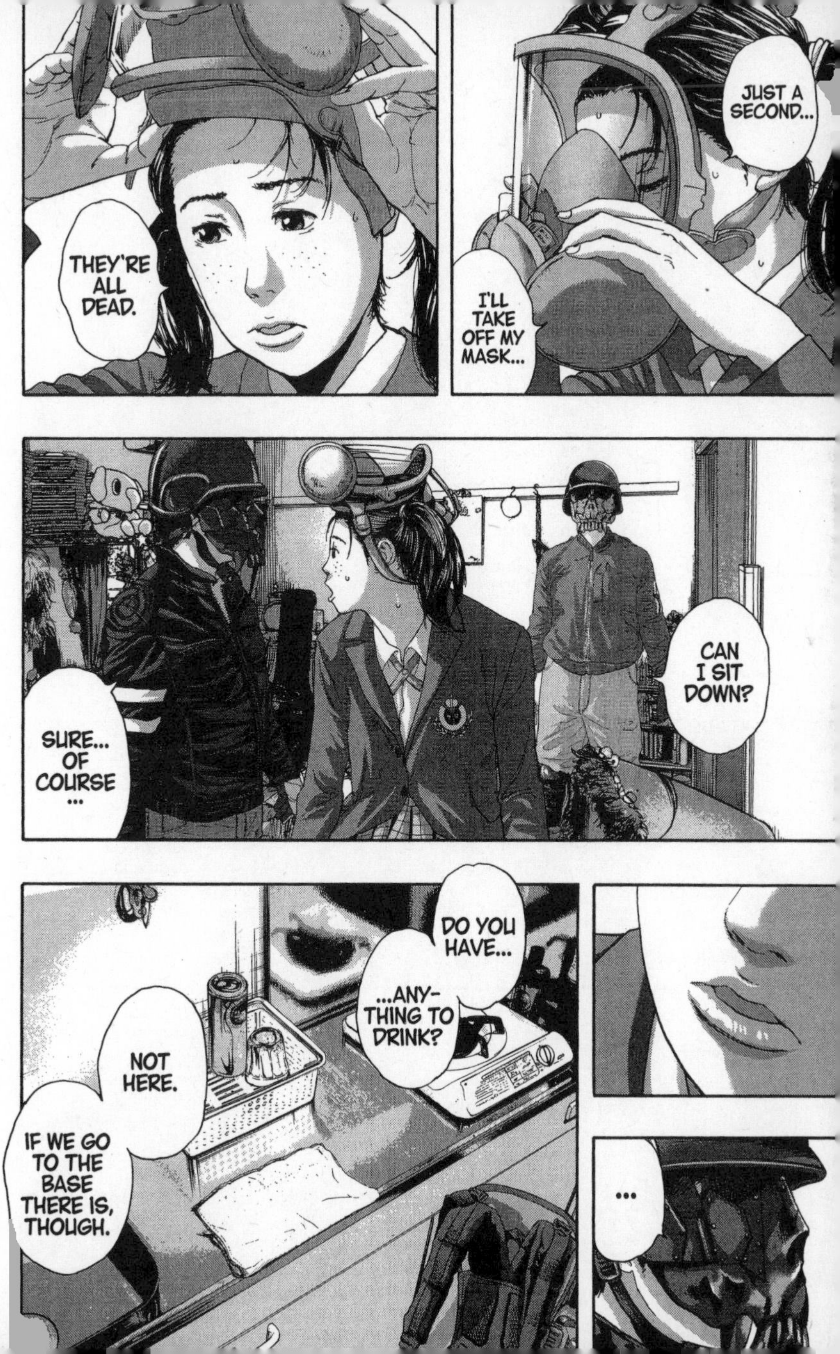
JUST A SECOND...
I'LL TAKE OFF MY MASK...
THEY'RE ALL DEAD.
CAN I SIT DOWN?
SURE... OF COURSE ...
...
DO YOU HAVE...
...ANY-THING TO DRINK?
NOT HERE.
IF WE GO TO THE BASE THERE IS, THOUGH.

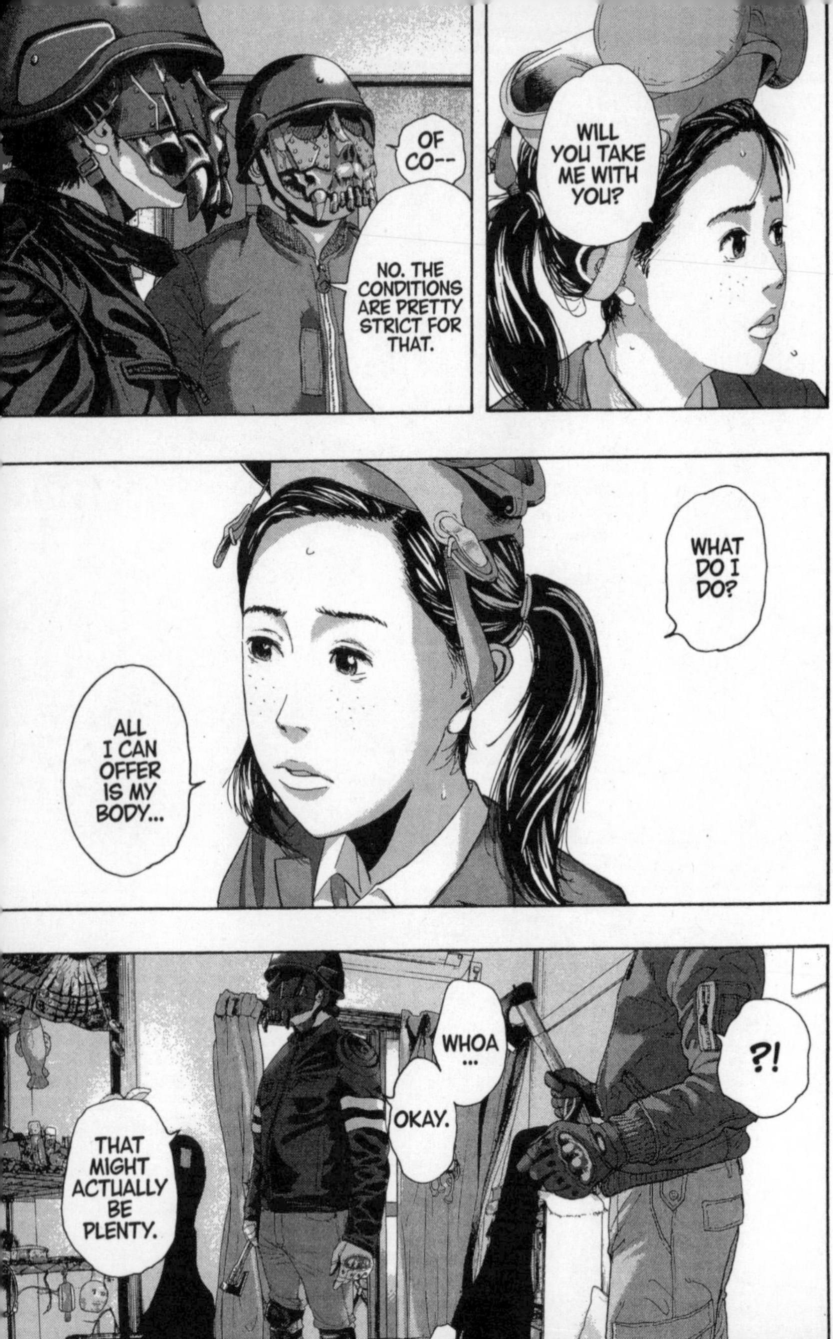

WILL YOU TAKE ME WITH YOU?
OF CO--
NO. THE CONDITIONS ARE PRETTY STRICT FOR THAT.
WHAT DO I DO?
ALL I CAN OFFER IS MY BODY...
?!
WHOA ...
OKAY.
THAT MIGHT ACTUALLY BE PLENTY.

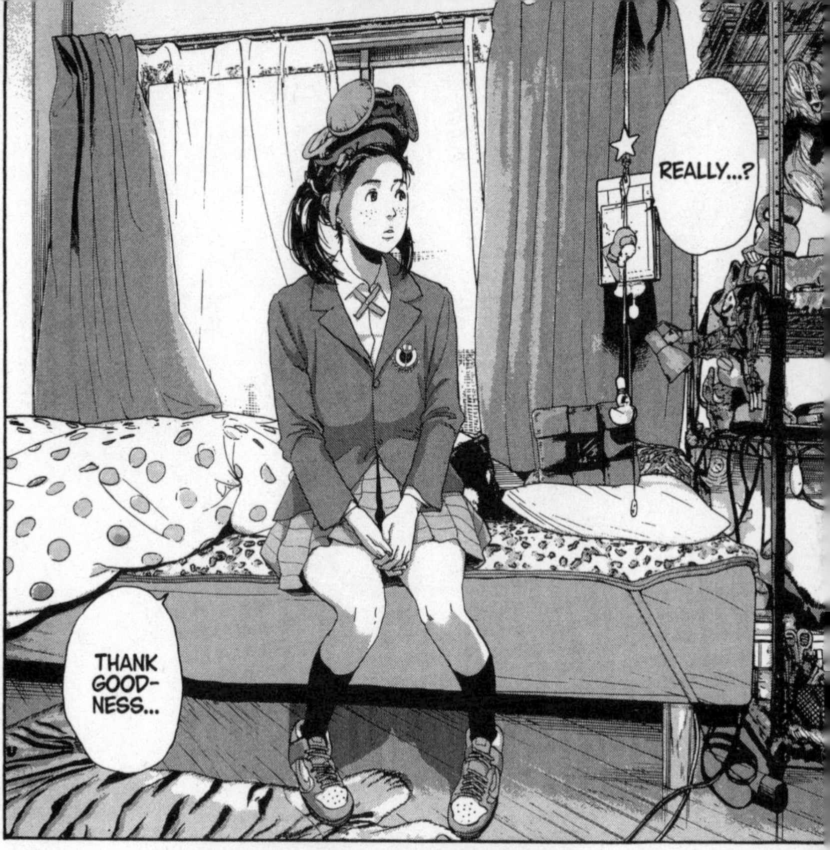
REALLY...?
THANK GOOD-NESS...
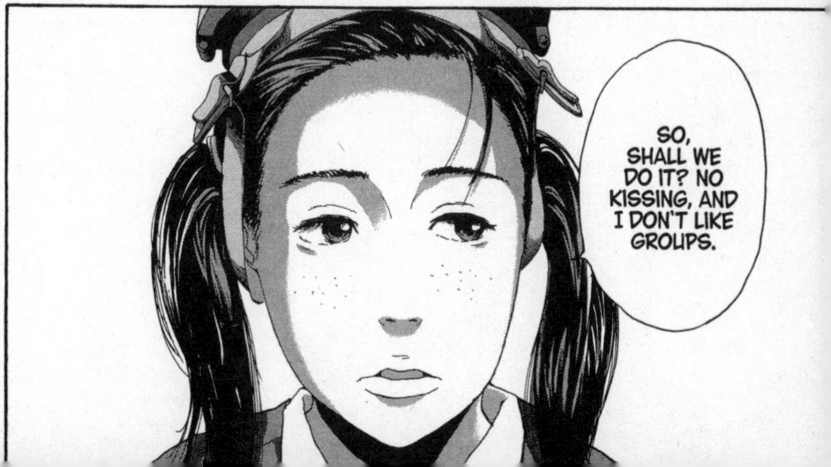
SO, SHALL WE DO IT? NO KISSING, AND I DON'T LIKE GROUPS.

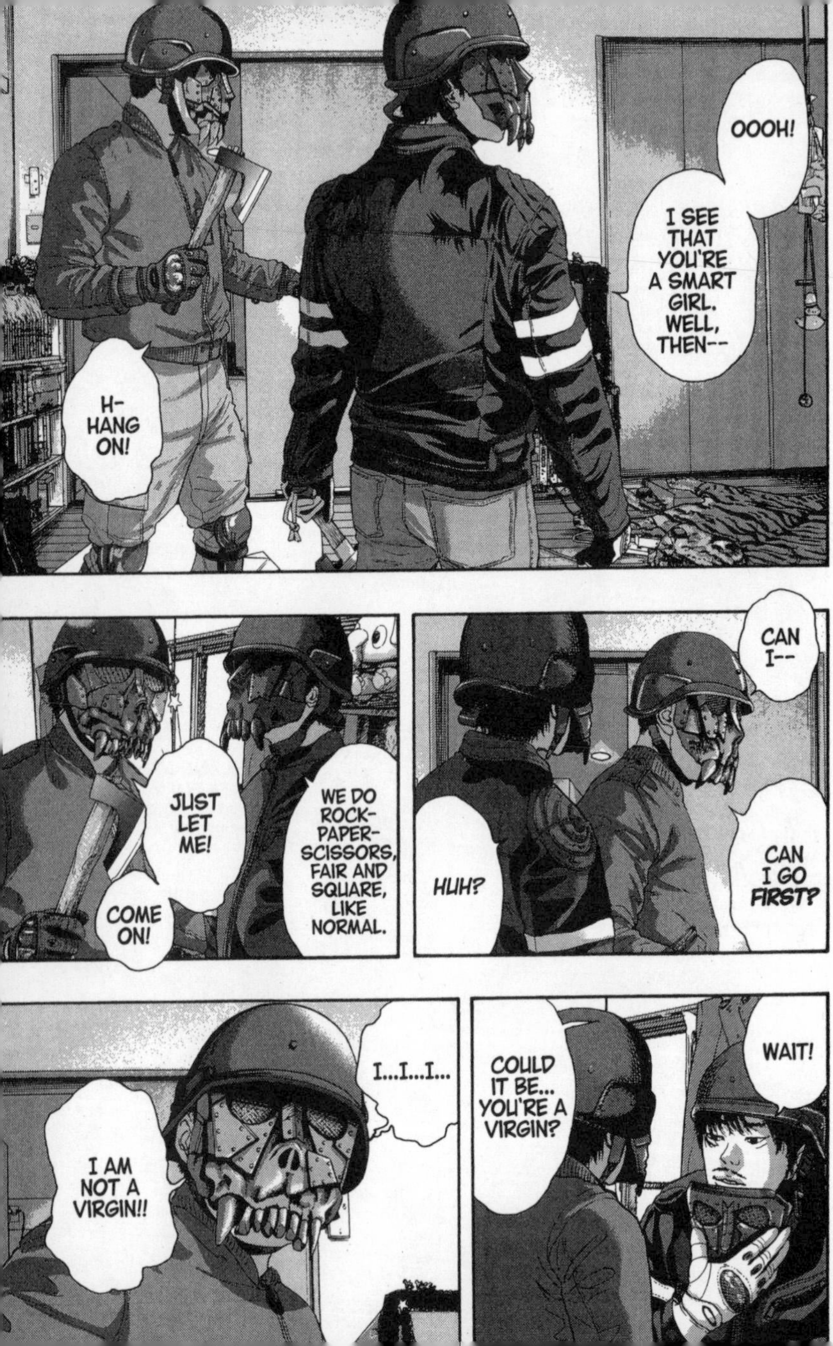
OOOH!
I SEE THAT YOU'RE A SMART GIRL. WELL, THEN--
H-HANG ON!
CAN I--
CAN I GO *FIRST?*
HUH?
WE DO ROCK-PAPER-SCISSORS, FAIR AND SQUARE, LIKE NORMAL.
JUST LET ME!
COME ON!
WAIT!
COULD IT BE... YOU'RE A VIRGIN?
I...I...I...
I AM NOT A VIRGIN!!

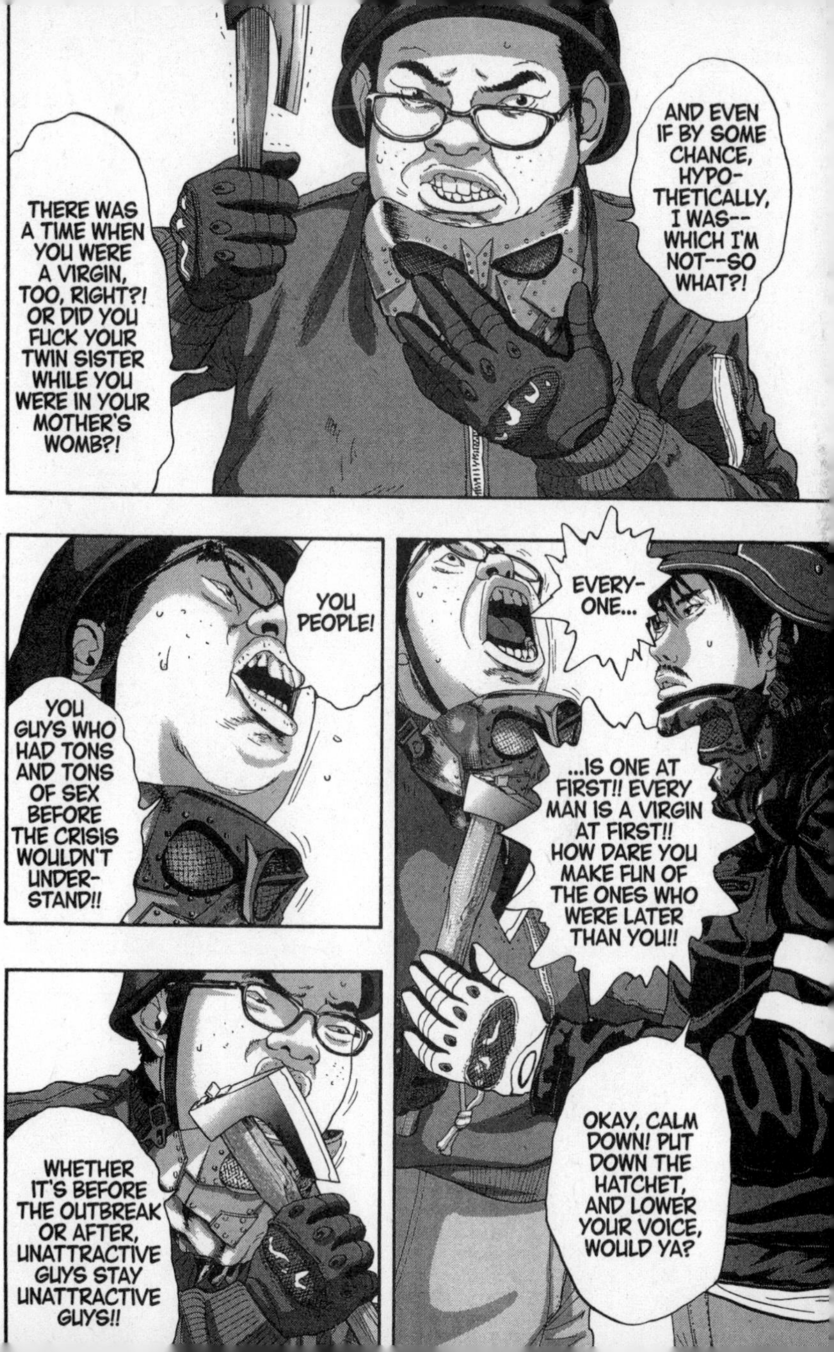
AND EVEN IF BY SOME CHANCE, HYPO-THETICALLY, I WAS-- WHICH I'M NOT--SO WHAT?!
THERE WAS A TIME WHEN YOU WERE A VIRGIN, TOO, RIGHT?! OR DID YOU FUCK YOUR TWIN SISTER WHILE YOU WERE IN YOUR MOTHER'S WOMB?!
EVERY-ONE...
...IS ONE AT FIRST!! EVERY MAN IS A VIRGIN AT FIRST!! HOW DARE YOU MAKE FUN OF THE ONES WHO WERE LATER THAN YOU!!
OKAY, CALM DOWN! PUT DOWN THE HATCHET, AND LOWER YOUR VOICE, WOULD YA?
YOU PEOPLE!
YOU GUYS WHO HAD TONS AND TONS OF SEX BEFORE THE CRISIS WOULDN'T UNDER-STAND!!
WHETHER IT'S BEFORE THE OUTBREAK OR AFTER, UNATTRACTIVE GUYS STAY UNATTRACTIVE GUYS!!

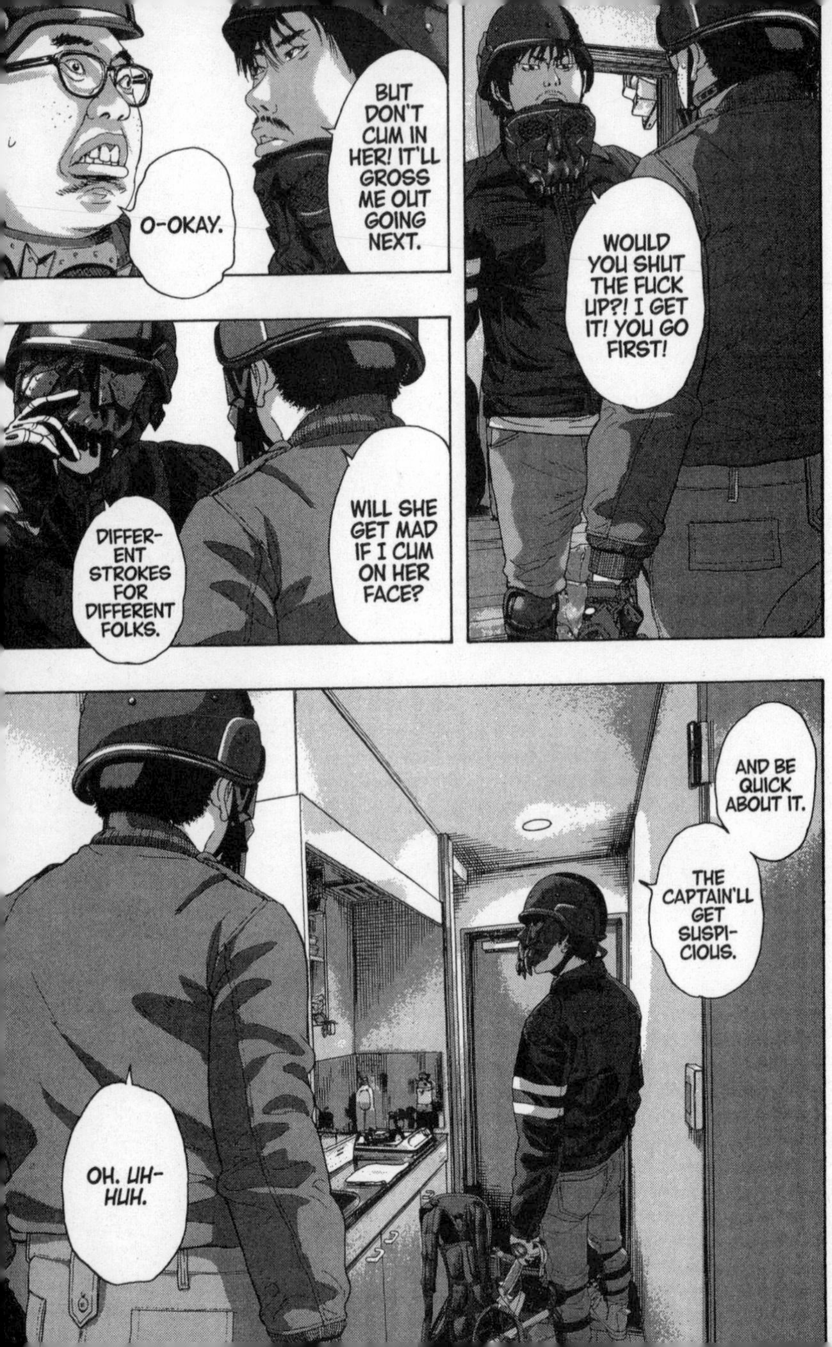
WOULD YOU SHUT THE FUCK UP?! I GET IT! YOU GO FIRST!
BUT DON'T CUM IN HER! IT'LL GROSS ME OUT GOING NEXT.
O-OKAY.
WILL SHE GET MAD IF I CUM ON HER FACE?
DIFFER-ENT STROKES FOR DIFFERENT FOLKS.
AND BE QUICK ABOUT IT.
THE CAPTAIN'LL GET SUSPI-CIOUS.
OH. UH-HUH.

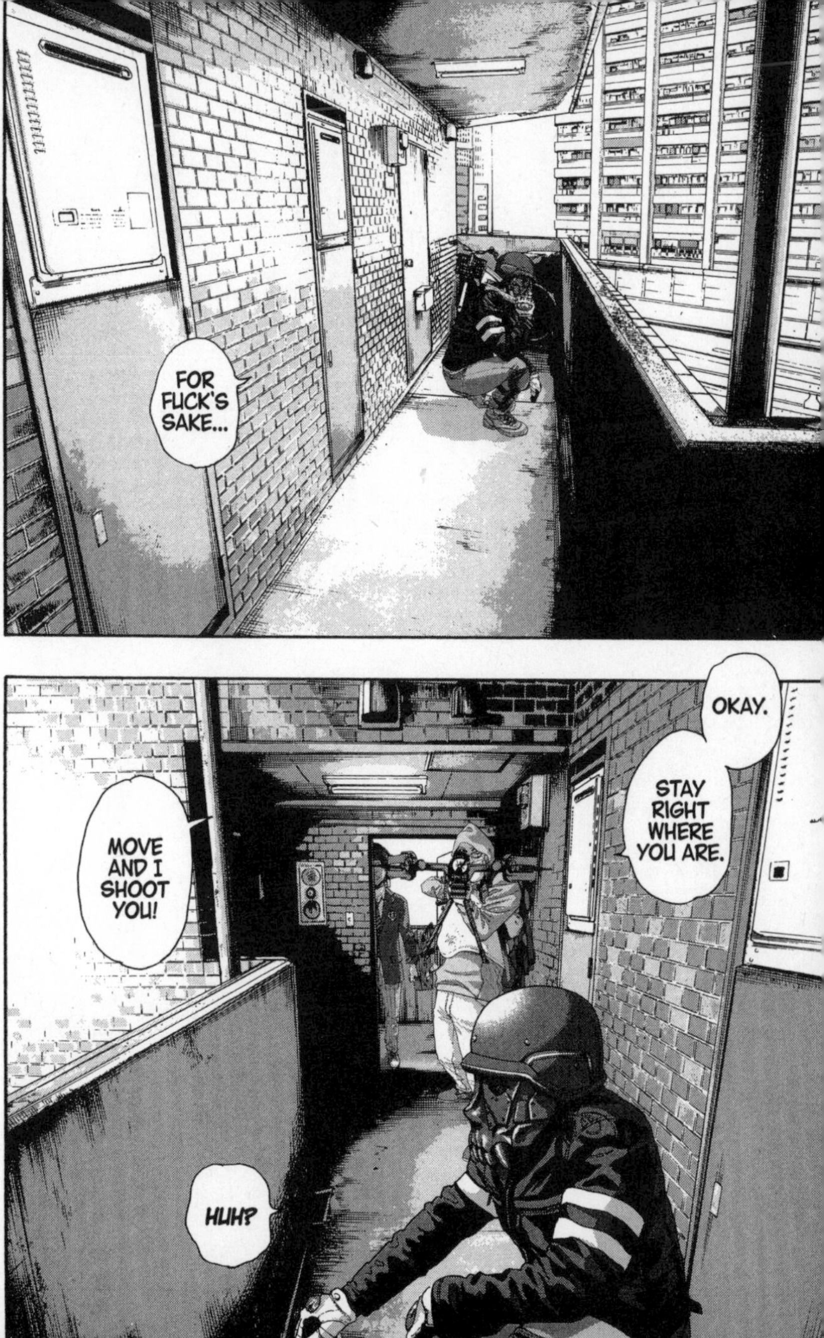
FOR FUCK'S SAKE...
OKAY.
STAY RIGHT WHERE YOU ARE.
MOVE AND I SHOOT YOU!
HUH?

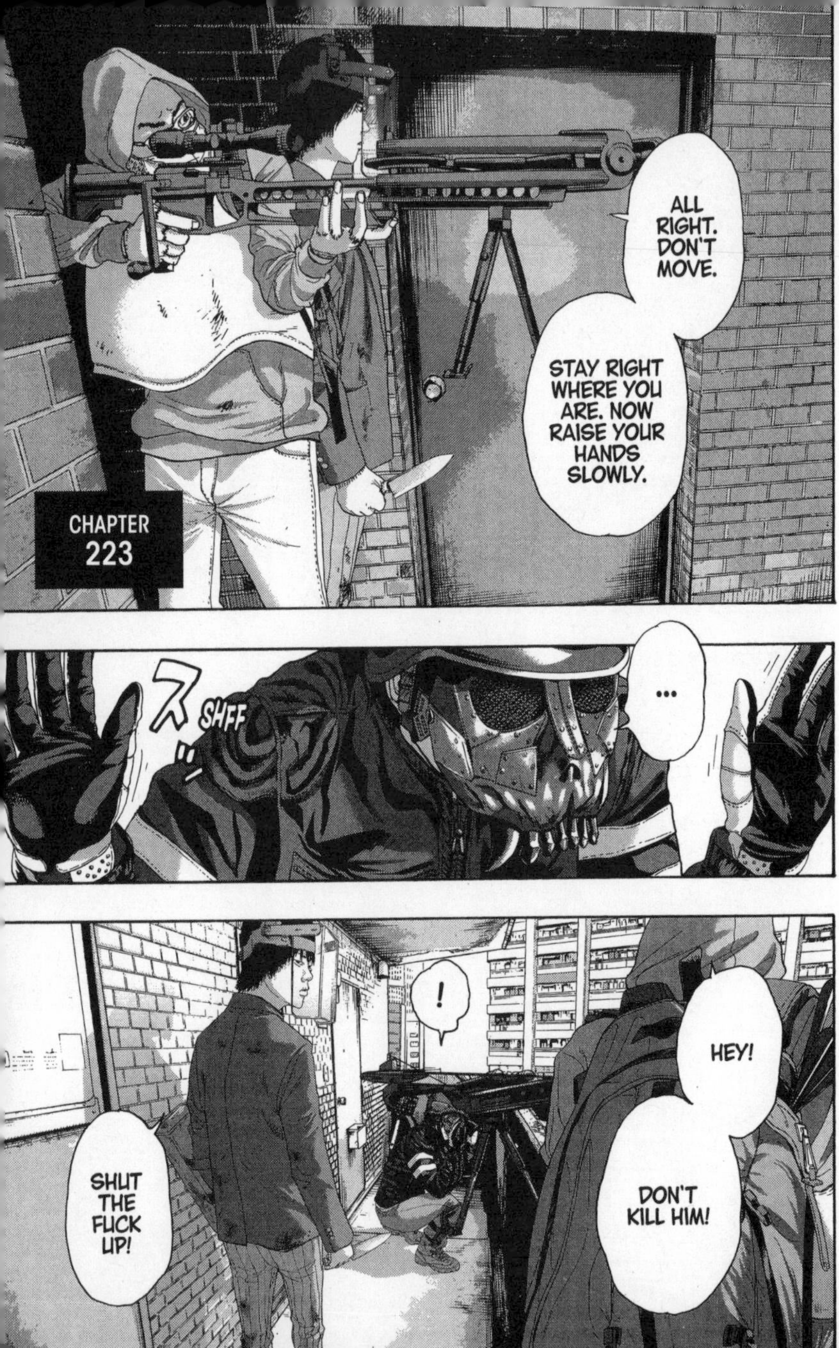
ALL RIGHT. DON'T MOVE.
STAY RIGHT WHERE YOU ARE. NOW RAISE YOUR HANDS SLOWLY.
CHAPTER 223
...
スッ
SHFF
HEY!
DON'T KILL HIM!
!
SHUT THE FUCK UP!

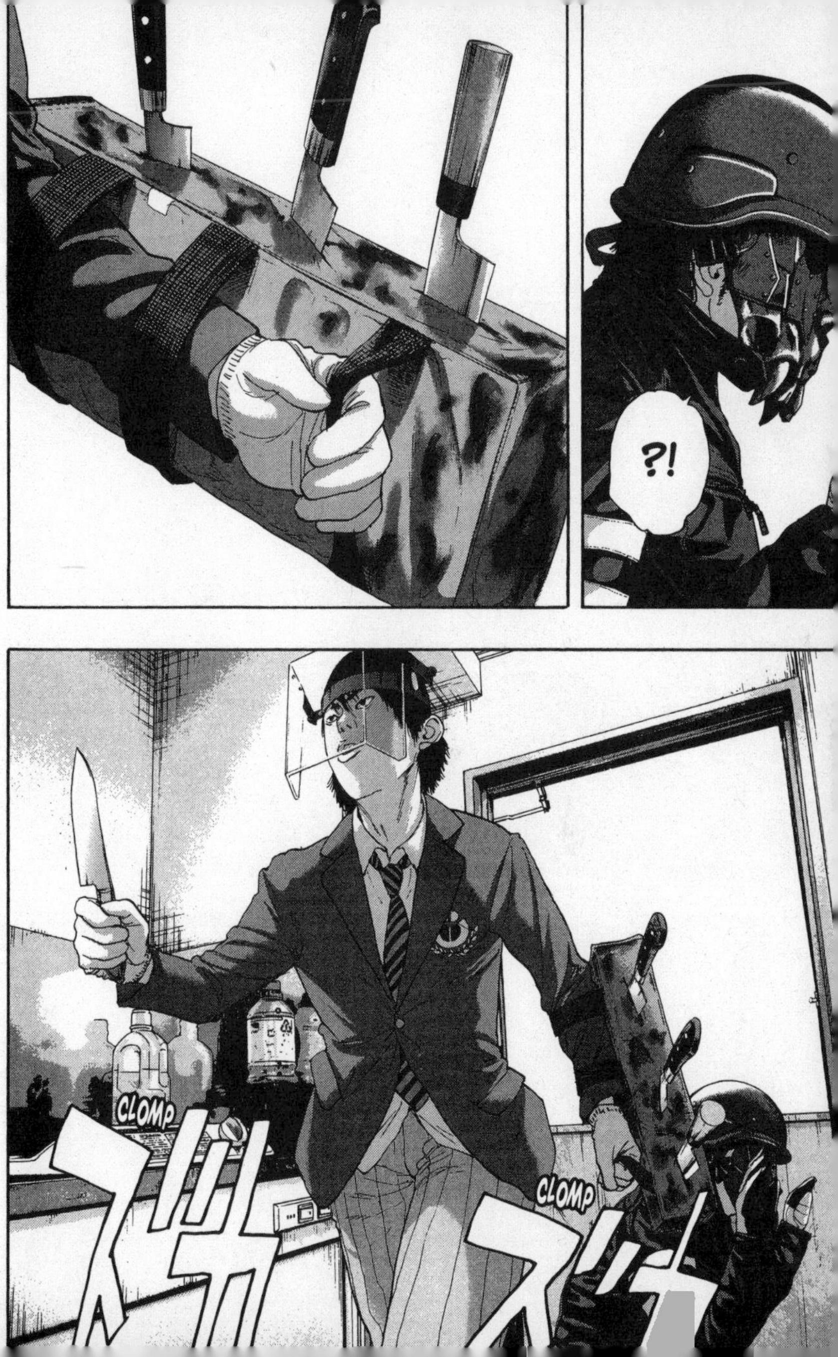
?!
CLOMP
CLOMP

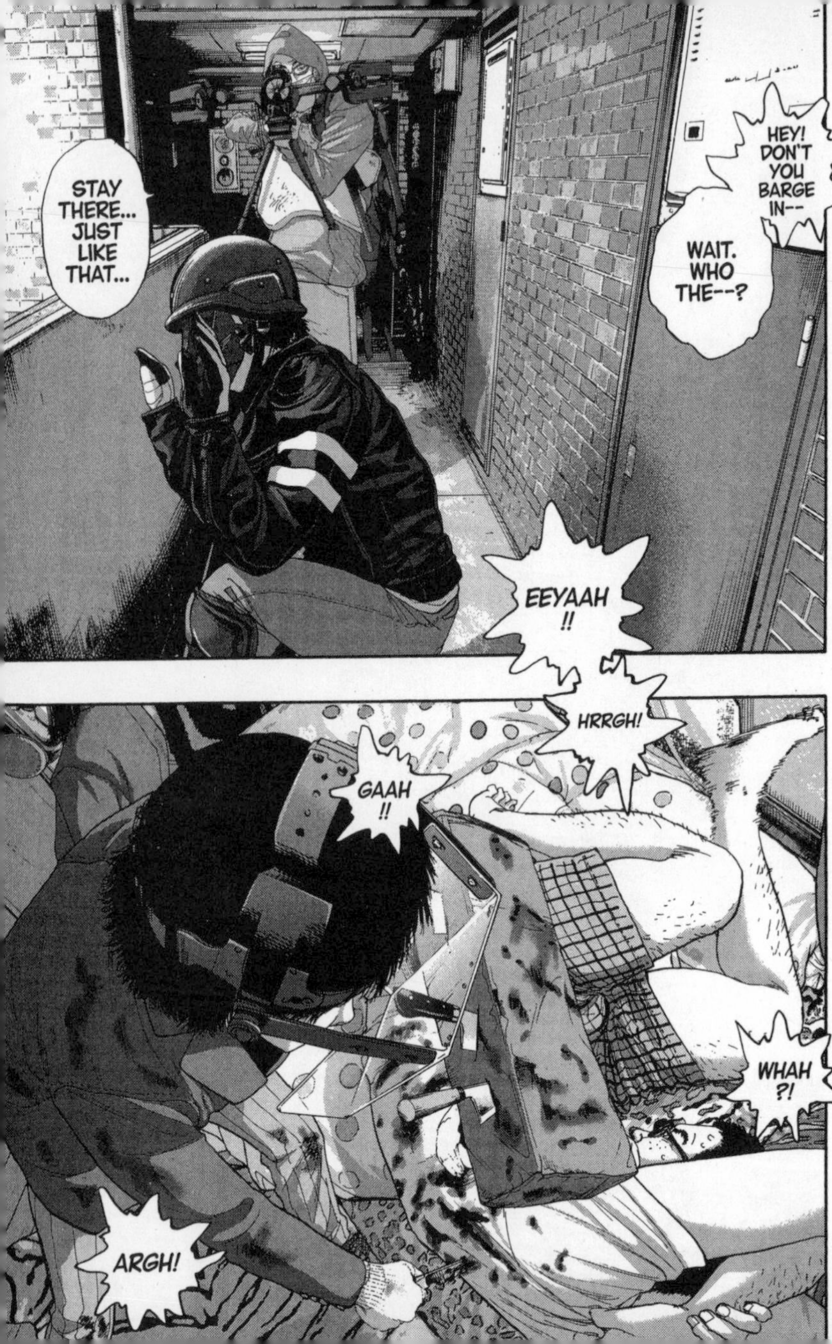
HEY! DON'T YOU BARGE IN--
WAIT. WHO THE--?
STAY THERE... JUST LIKE THAT...
EEYAAH!!
HRRGH!
GAAH!!
WHAH?!
ARGH!

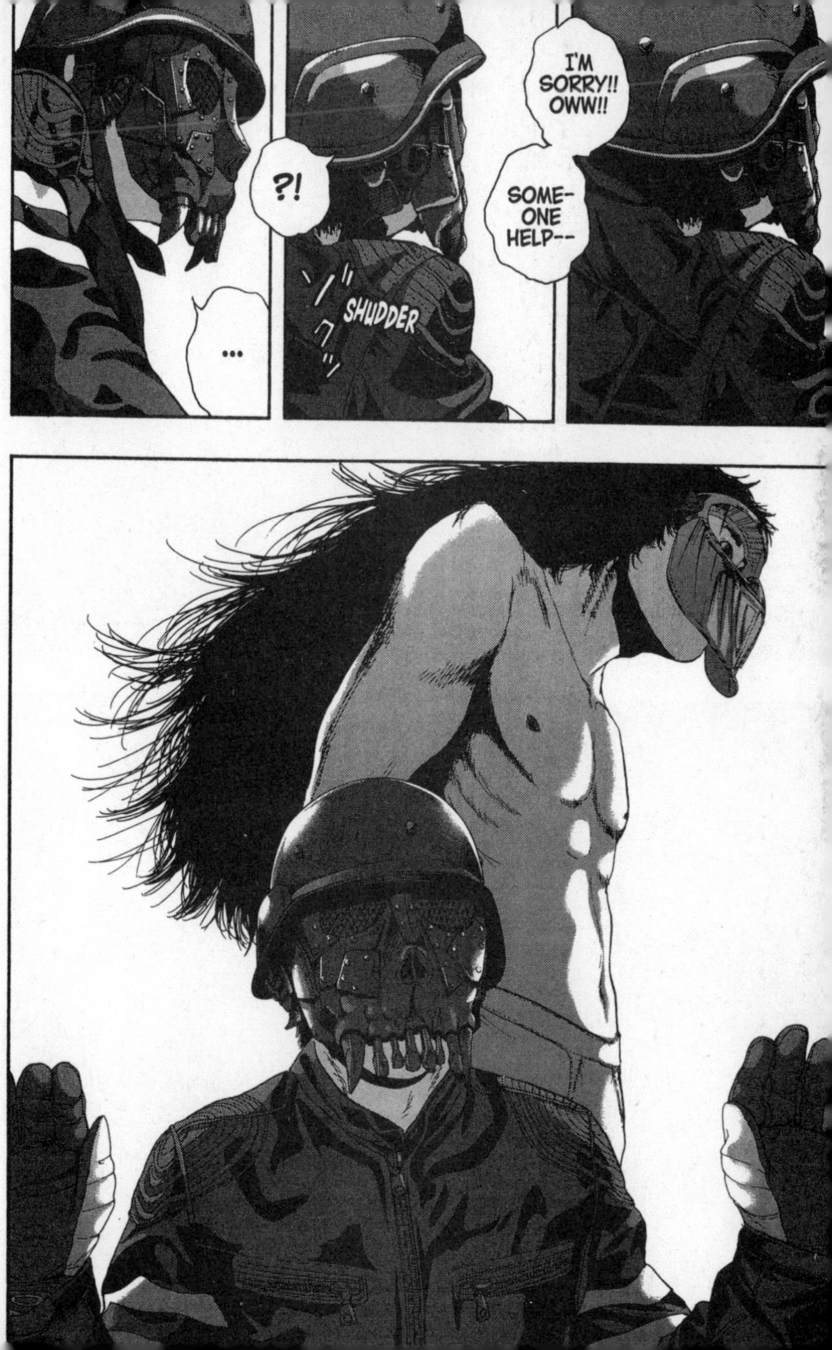
I'M SORRY!! OWW!!
SOME-ONE HELP--
?!
SHUDDER
...

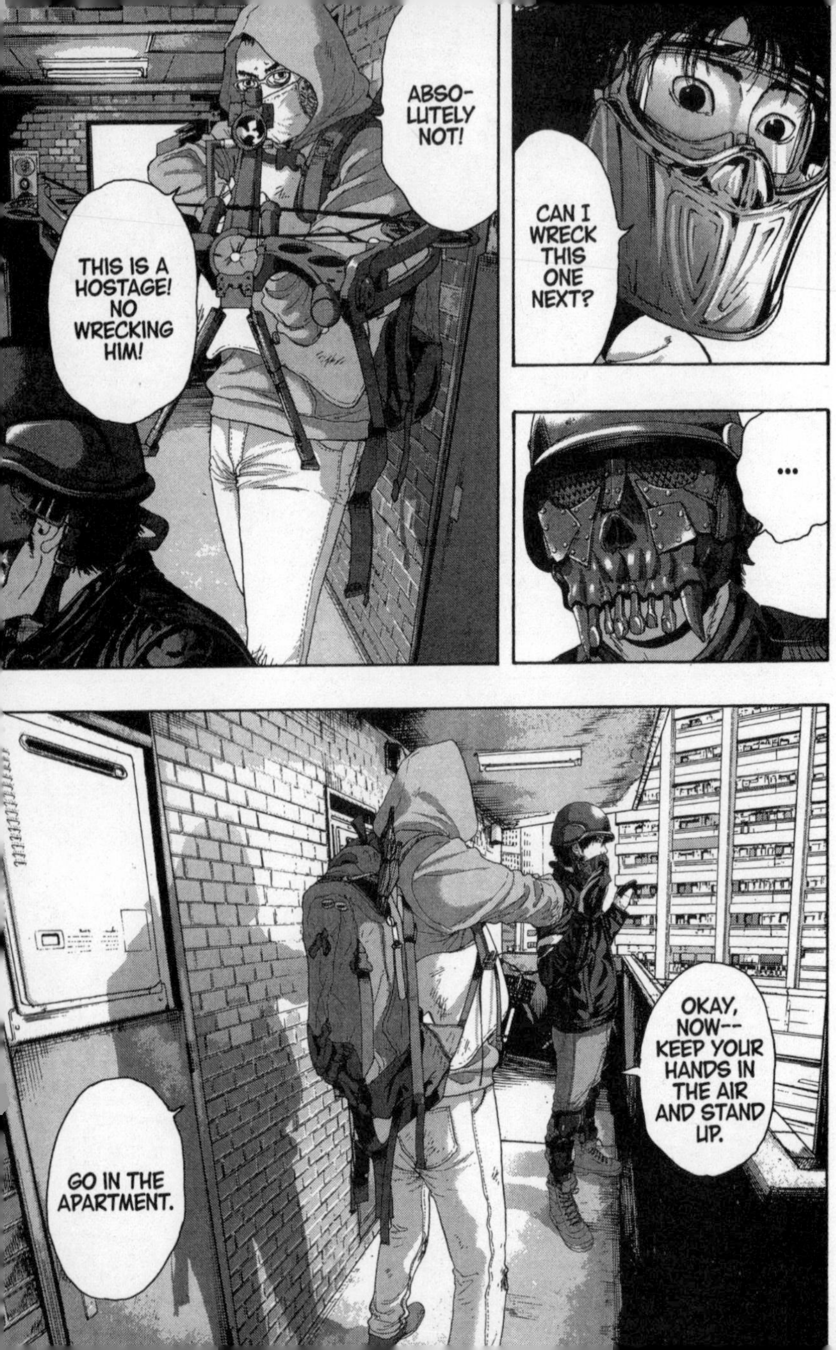
CAN I WRECK THIS ONE NEXT?
...
ABSO-LUTELY NOT!
THIS IS A HOSTAGE! NO WRECKING HIM!
OKAY, NOW-- KEEP YOUR HANDS IN THE AIR AND STAND UP.
GO IN THE APARTMENT.

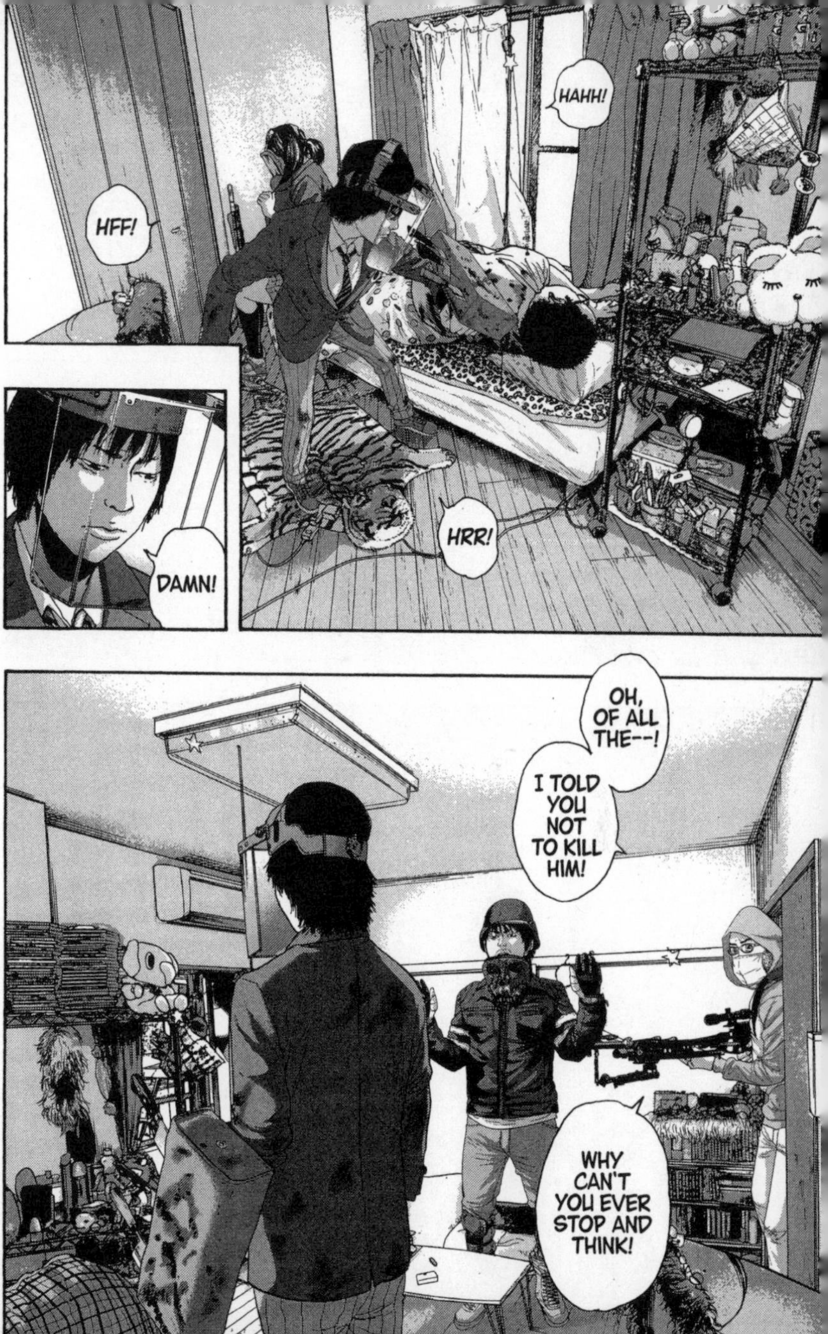
HAHH!
HFF!
HRR!
DAMN!
OH, OF ALL THE--!
I TOLD YOU NOT TO KILL HIM!
WHY CAN'T YOU EVER STOP AND THINK!

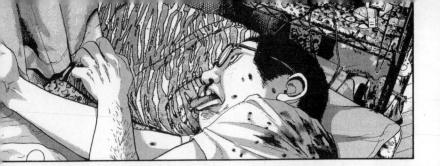

ONE'S ALIVE, RIGHT? THAT'S ENOUGH, ISN'T IT?

LISTEN TO ME-- IF WE HAD *TWO OF THEM,* WE'D GET DIFFERENT INFORMATION FROM THEM DEPENDING ON WHO HAD THE HIGHER RANK...

...AND IF WE HAD *TWO,* WE'D'VE BEEN ABLE TO WATCH FOR ANY DISCREPANCIES WHEN WE INTERROGATED THEM!

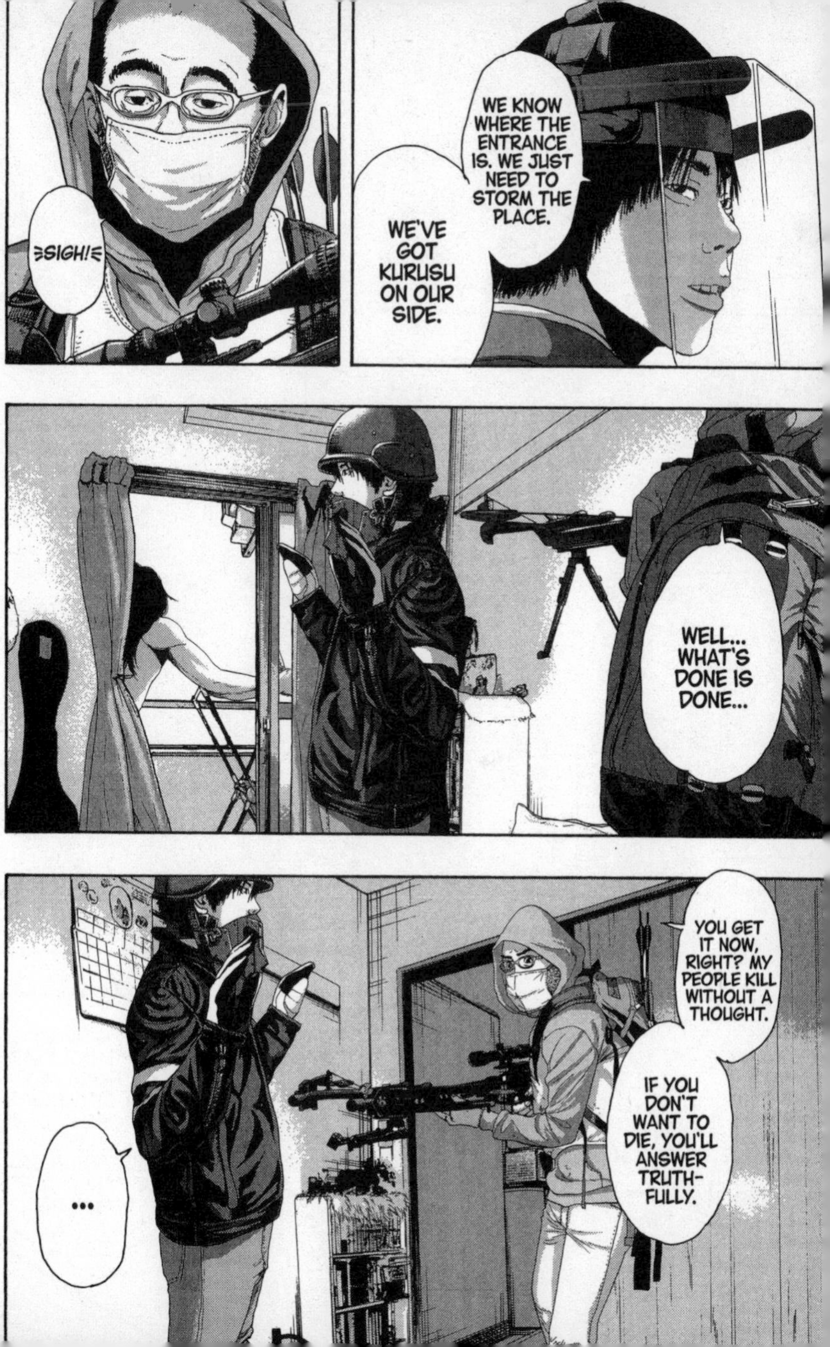
WE KNOW WHERE THE ENTRANCE IS. WE JUST NEED TO STORM THE PLACE.
WE'VE GOT KURUSU ON OUR SIDE.
≥SIGH!≤
WELL... WHAT'S DONE IS DONE...
YOU GET IT NOW, RIGHT? MY PEOPLE KILL WITHOUT A THOUGHT.
IF YOU DON'T WANT TO DIE, YOU'LL ANSWER TRUTH-FULLY.
...

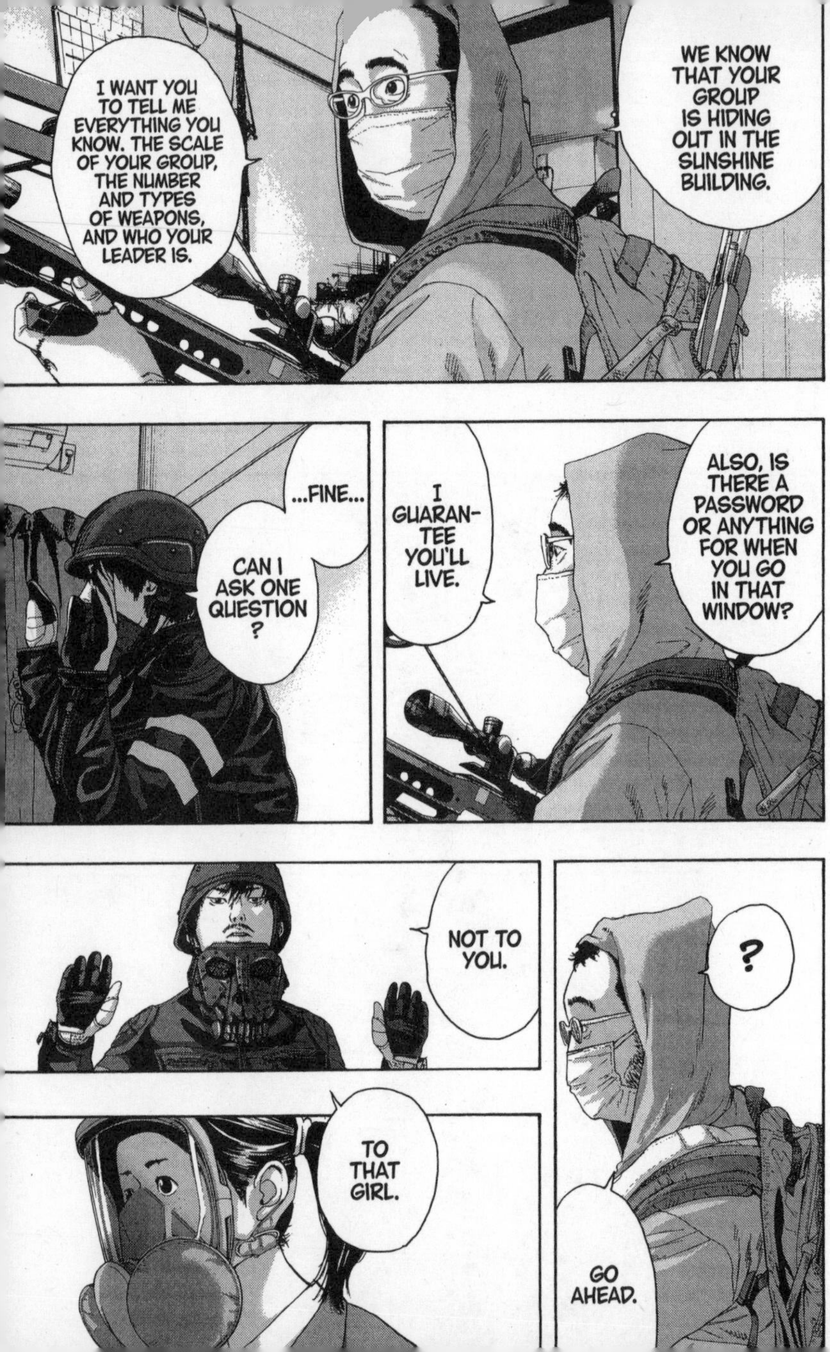
WE KNOW THAT YOUR GROUP IS HIDING OUT IN THE SUNSHINE BUILDING.
I WANT YOU TO TELL ME EVERYTHING YOU KNOW. THE SCALE OF YOUR GROUP, THE NUMBER AND TYPES OF WEAPONS, AND WHO YOUR LEADER IS.
ALSO, IS THERE A PASSWORD OR ANYTHING FOR WHEN YOU GO IN THAT WINDOW?
I GUARAN-TEE YOU'LL LIVE.
...FINE...
CAN I ASK ONE QUESTION?
?
GO AHEAD.
NOT TO YOU.
TO THAT GIRL.

HUH?

WHAT IS IT?

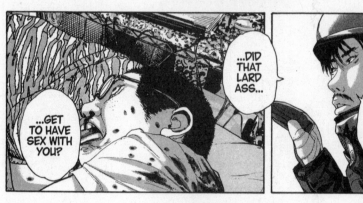

...DID THAT LARD ASS...

...GET TO HAVE SEX WITH YOU?

DID HE...

OF COURSE NOT.

HE WAS GROSS.

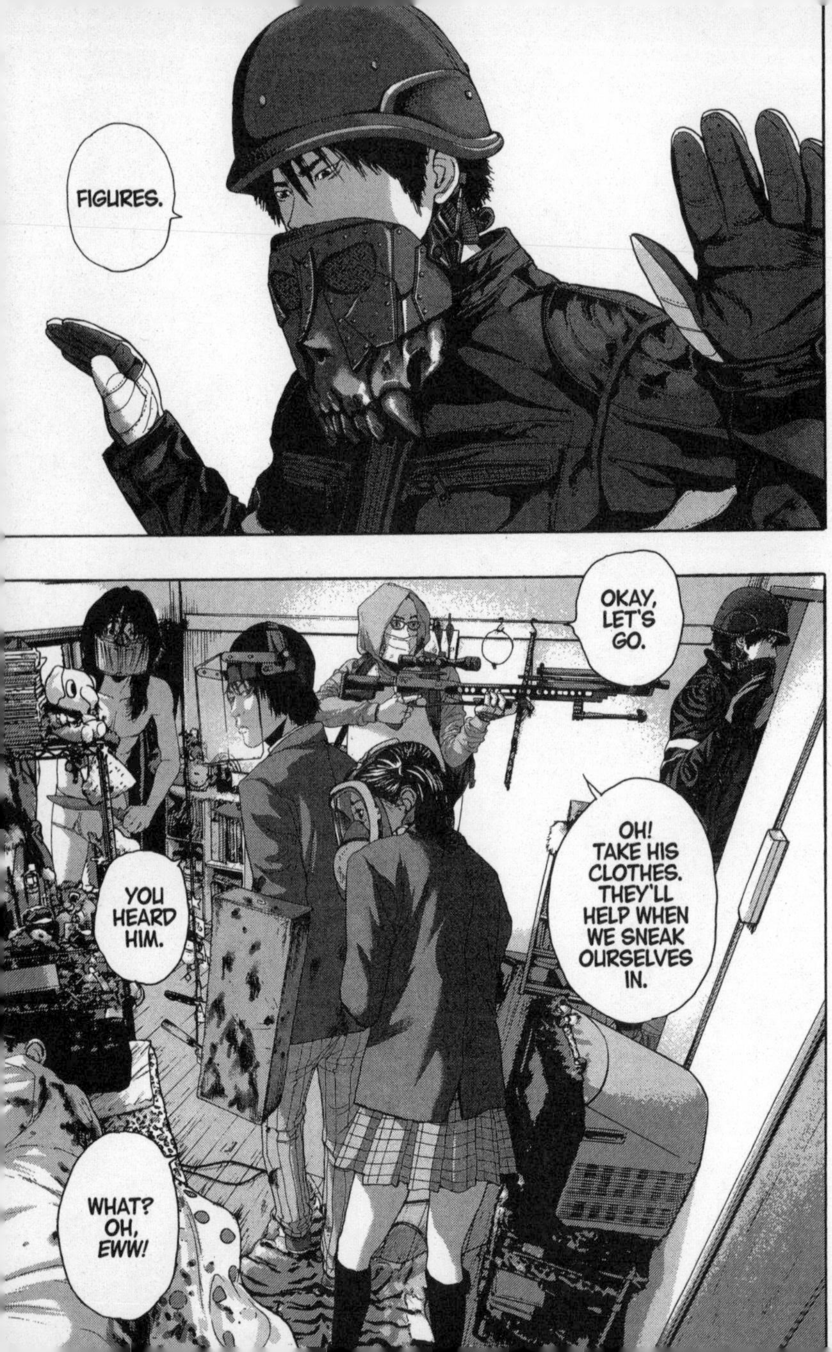
FIGURES.
OKAY, LET'S GO.
OH! TAKE HIS CLOTHES. THEY'LL HELP WHEN WE SNEAK OURSELVES IN.
YOU HEARD HIM.
WHAT? OH, EWW!

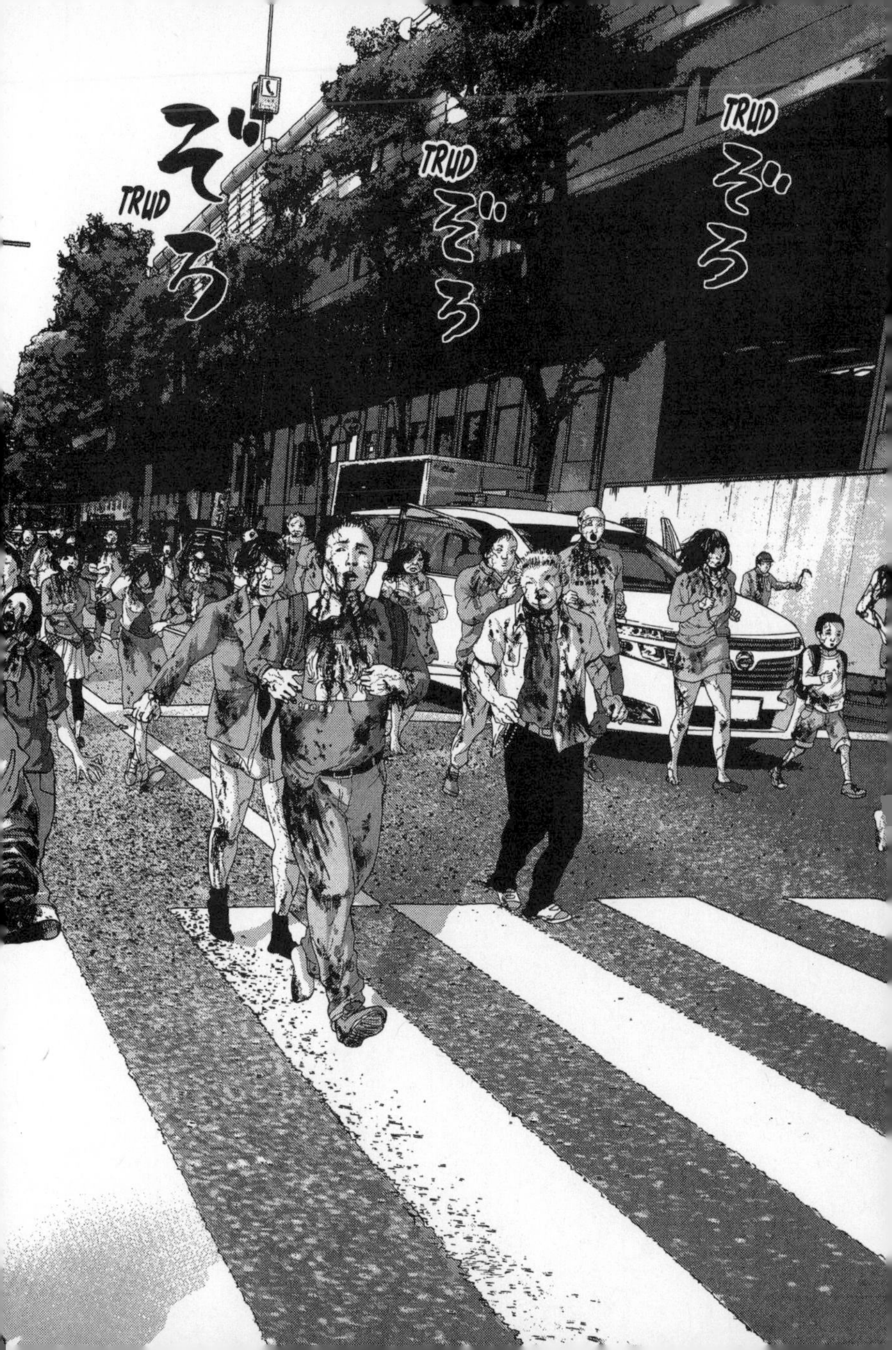
TRUD
ぞろ
TRUD
ぞろ
ぞろ
TRUD

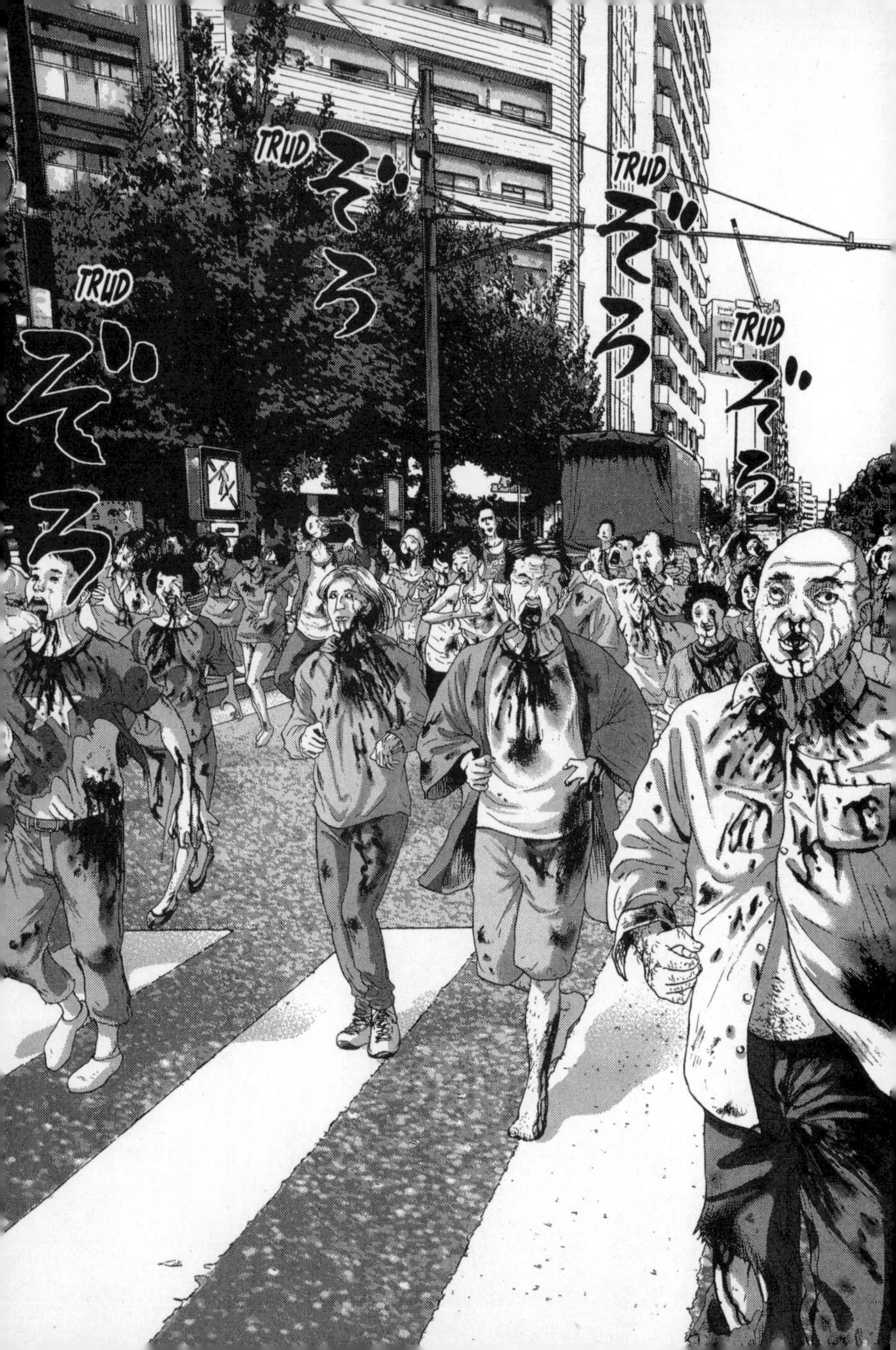
TRUD
ぞろ
TRUD
ぞろ
TRUD
ぞろ
TRUD
ぞろ

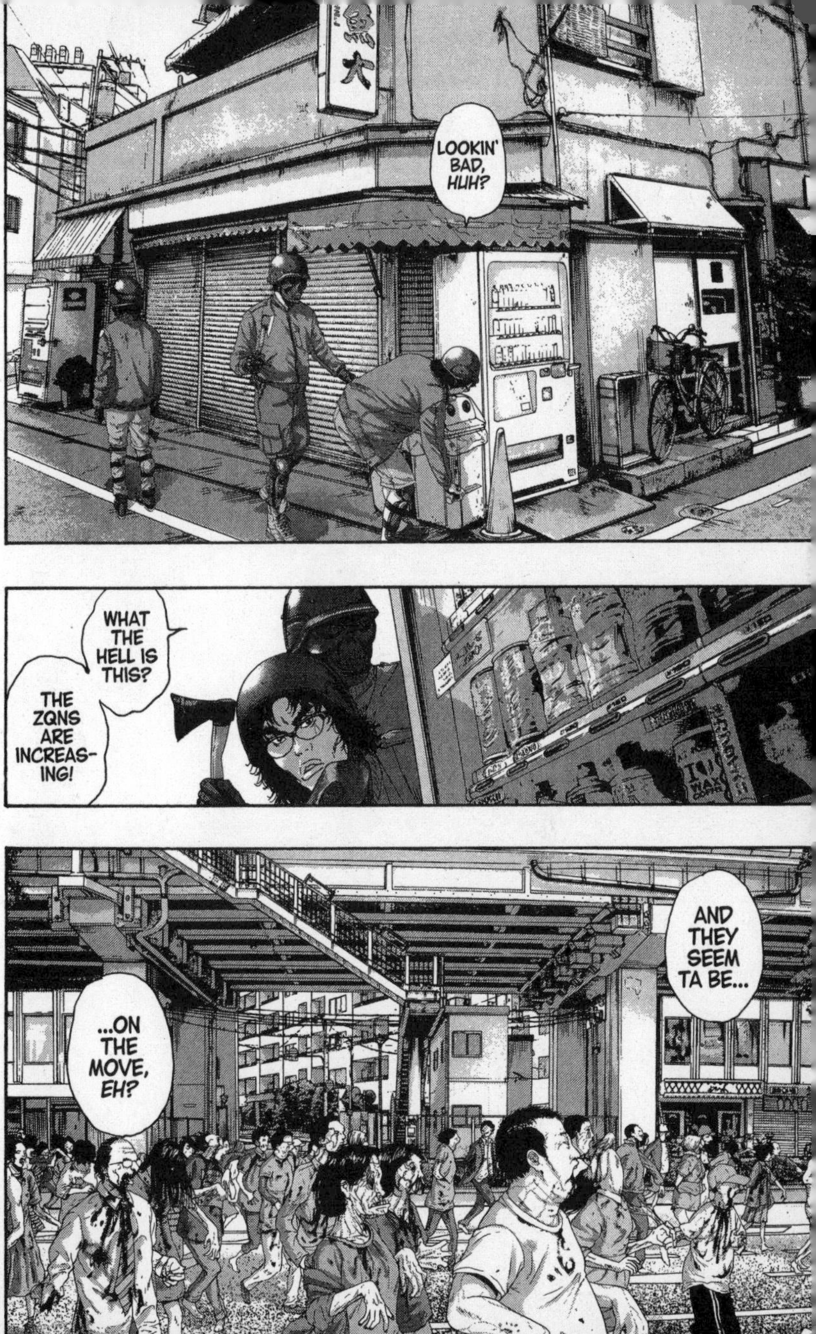
LOOKIN' BAD, HUH?
WHAT THE HELL IS THIS?
THE ZQNS ARE INCREAS-ING!
AND THEY SEEM TA BE...
...ON THE MOVE, EH?

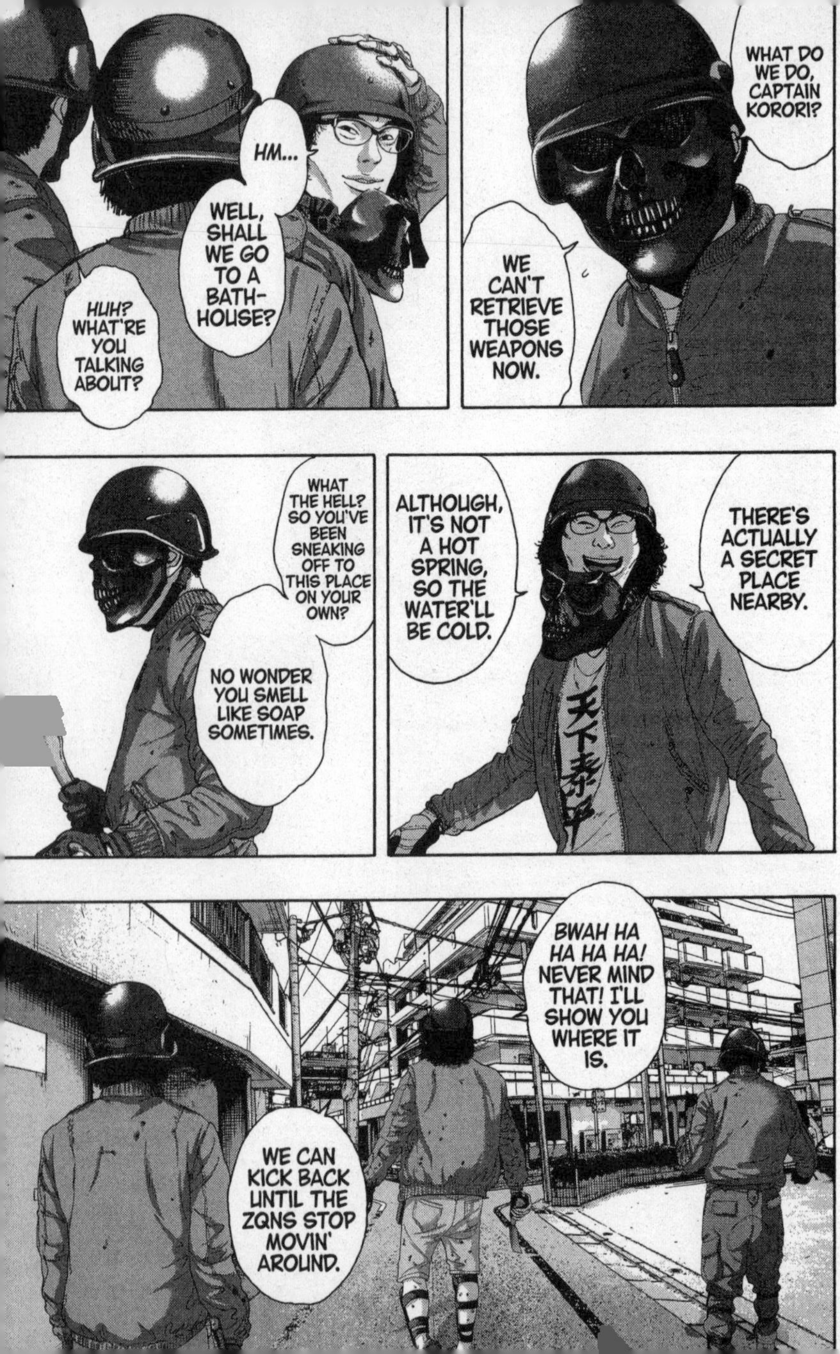

WHAT DO WE DO, CAPTAIN KORORI?
WE CAN'T RETRIEVE THOSE WEAPONS NOW.
HM...
WELL, SHALL WE GO TO A BATH-HOUSE?
HUH? WHAT'RE YOU TALKING ABOUT?
THERE'S ACTUALLY A SECRET PLACE NEARBY.
ALTHOUGH, IT'S NOT A HOT SPRING, SO THE WATER'LL BE COLD.
WHAT THE HELL? SO YOU'VE BEEN SNEAKING OFF TO THIS PLACE ON YOUR OWN?
NO WONDER YOU SMELL LIKE SOAP SOMETIMES.
BWAH HA HA HA HA! NEVER MIND THAT! I'LL SHOW YOU WHERE IT IS.
WE CAN KICK BACK UNTIL THE ZQNS STOP MOVIN' AROUND.

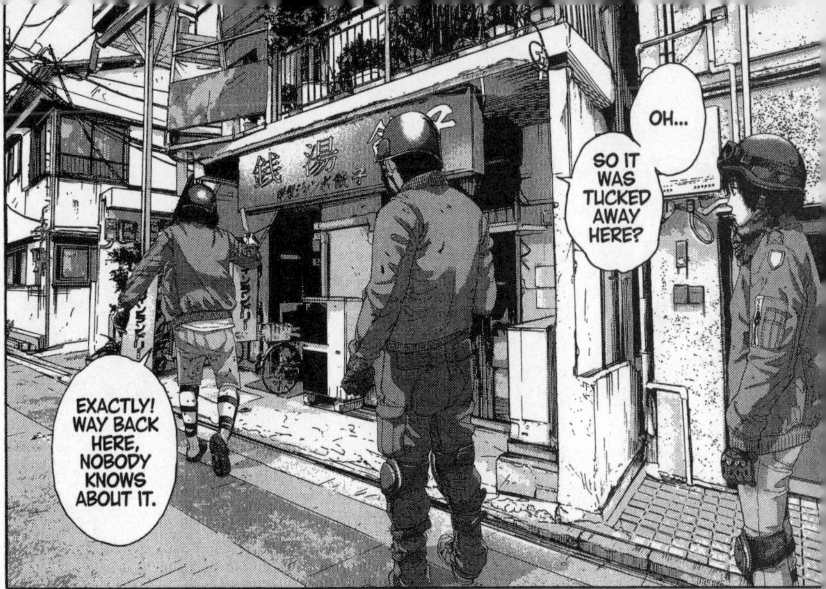
OH...
SO IT WAS TUCKED AWAY HERE?
EXACTLY! WAY BACK HERE, NOBODY KNOWS ABOUT IT.
SIGN ON BUILDING: BATHHOUSE

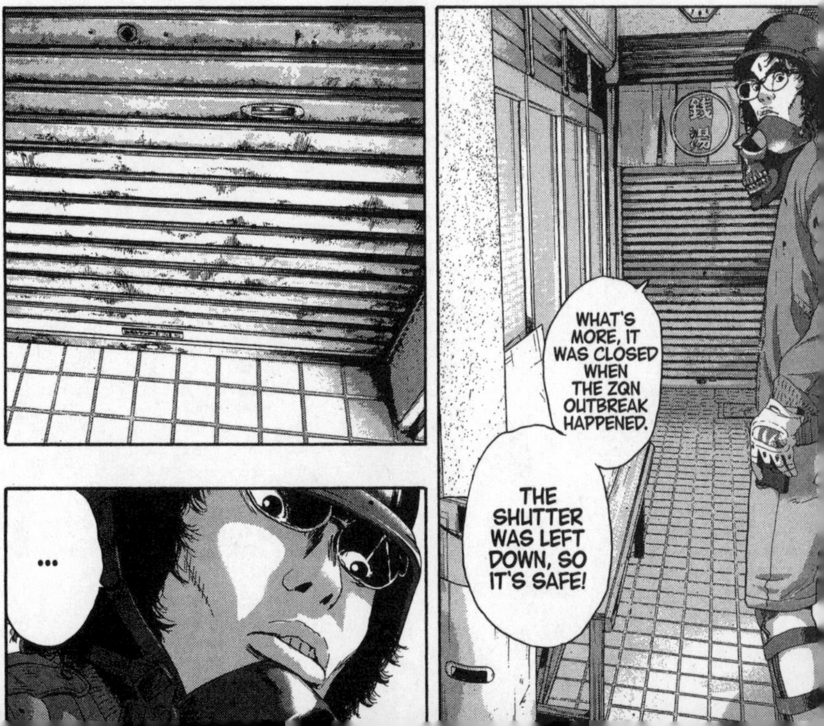
WHAT'S MORE, IT WAS CLOSED WHEN THE ZQN OUTBREAK HAPPENED.
THE SHUTTER WAS LEFT DOWN, SO IT'S SAFE!
...

CHAPTER
224

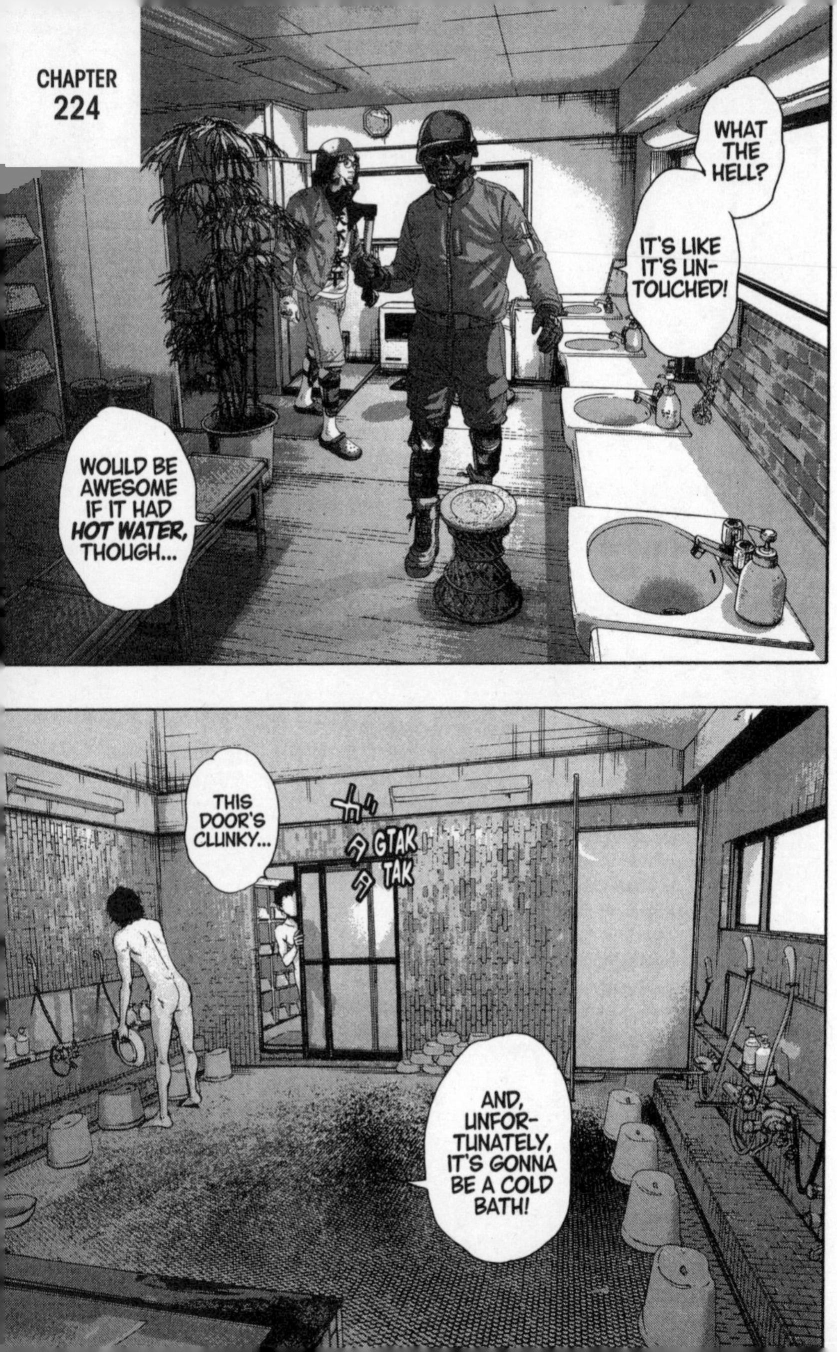
WHAT THE HELL?
IT'S LIKE IT'S UN-TOUCHED!
WOULD BE AWESOME IF IT HAD HOT WATER, THOUGH...
THIS DOOR'S CLUNKY...
GTAK TAK
AND, UNFOR-TUNATELY, IT'S GONNA BE A COLD BATH!

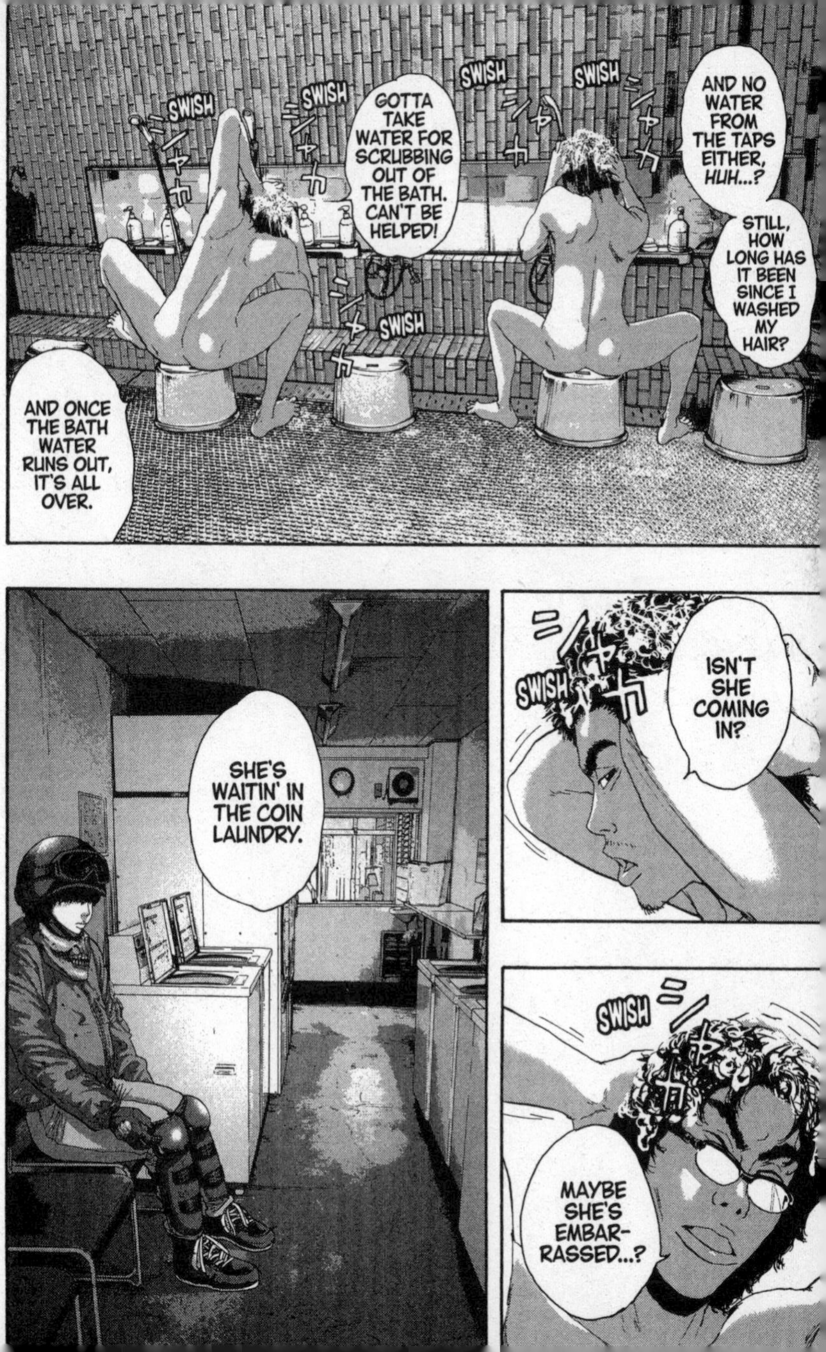
SWISH
SWISH
AND NO WATER FROM THE TAPS EITHER, HUH...?
STILL, HOW LONG HAS IT BEEN SINCE I WASHED MY HAIR?
SWISH
SWISH
GOTTA TAKE WATER FOR SCRUBBING OUT OF THE BATH. CAN'T BE HELPED!
SWISH
AND ONCE THE BATH WATER RUNS OUT, IT'S ALL OVER.
SWISH
ISN'T SHE COMING IN?
SWISH
MAYBE SHE'S EMBAR-RASSED...?
SHE'S WAITIN' IN THE COIN LAUNDRY.

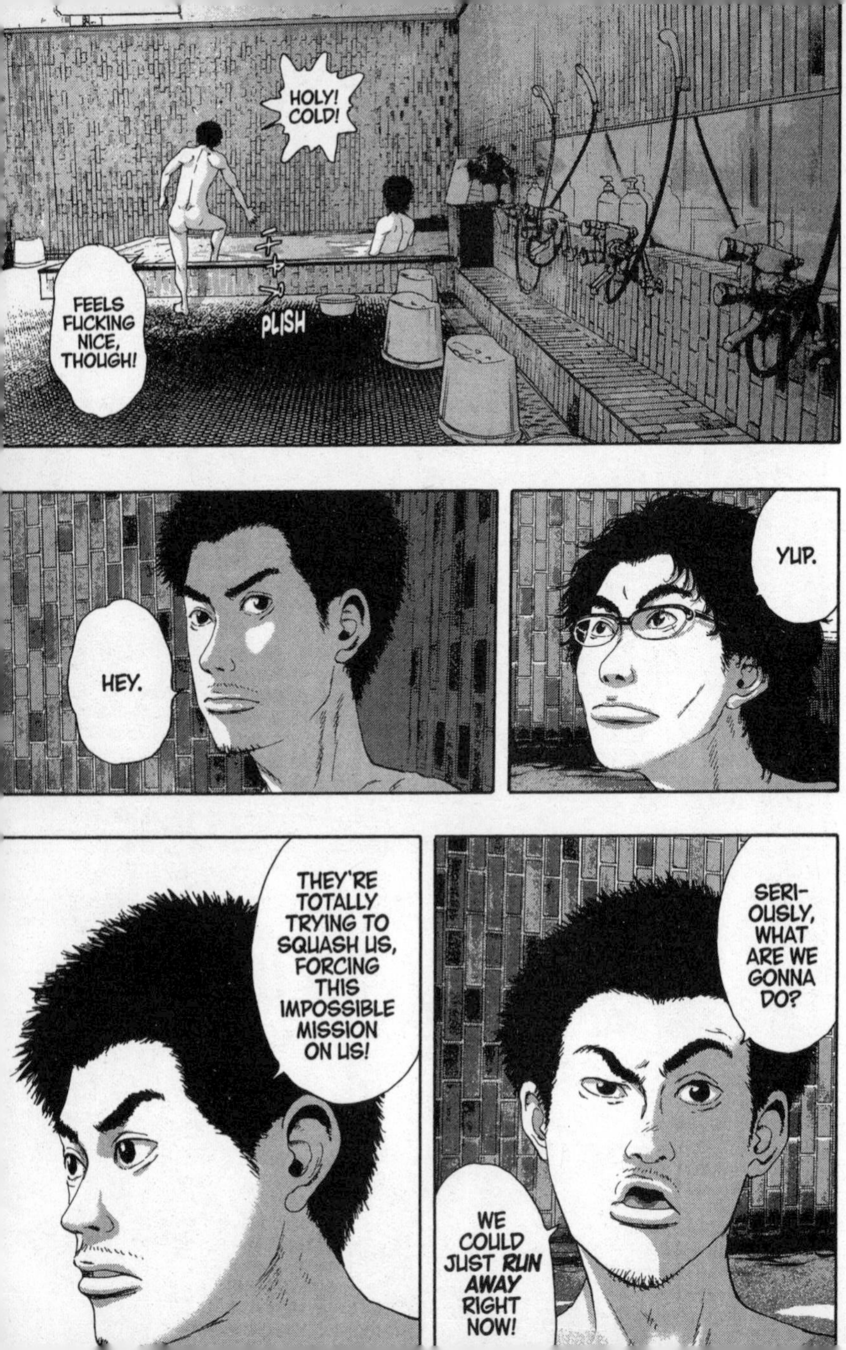
HOLY! COLD!
PLISH
FEELS FUCKING NICE, THOUGH!
YUP.
HEY.
SERI-OUSLY, WHAT ARE WE GONNA DO?
WE COULD JUST RUN AWAY RIGHT NOW!
THEY'RE TOTALLY TRYING TO SQUASH US, FORCING THIS IMPOSSIBLE MISSION ON US!

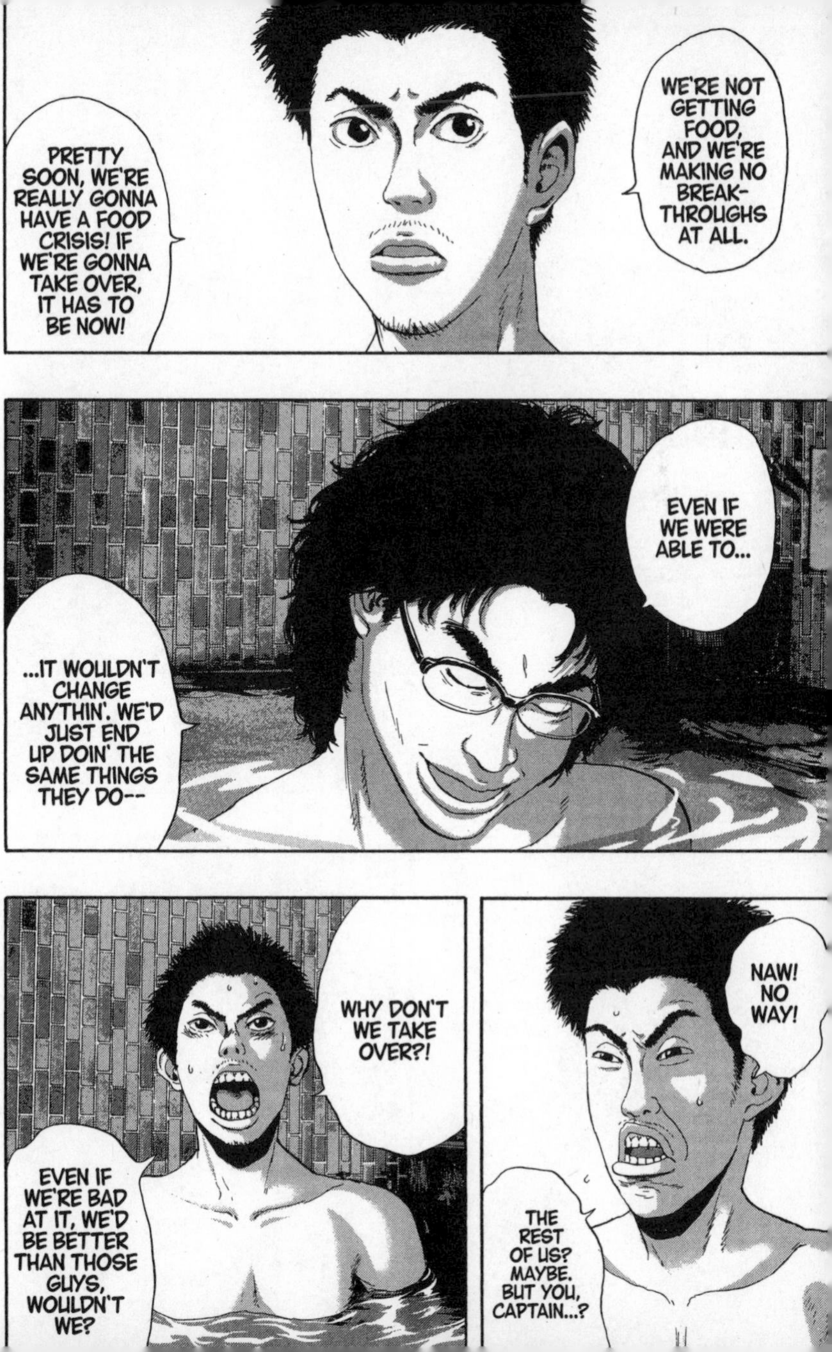
WE'RE NOT GETTING FOOD, AND WE'RE MAKING NO BREAK-THROUGHS AT ALL.
PRETTY SOON, WE'RE REALLY GONNA HAVE A FOOD CRISIS! IF WE'RE GONNA TAKE OVER, IT HAS TO BE NOW!
EVEN IF WE WERE ABLE TO...
...IT WOULDN'T CHANGE ANYTHIN'. WE'D JUST END UP DOIN' THE SAME THINGS THEY DO--
NAW! NO WAY!
THE REST OF US? MAYBE. BUT YOU, CAPTAIN...?
WHY DON'T WE TAKE OVER?!
EVEN IF WE'RE BAD AT IT, WE'D BE BETTER THAN THOSE GUYS, WOULDN'T WE?

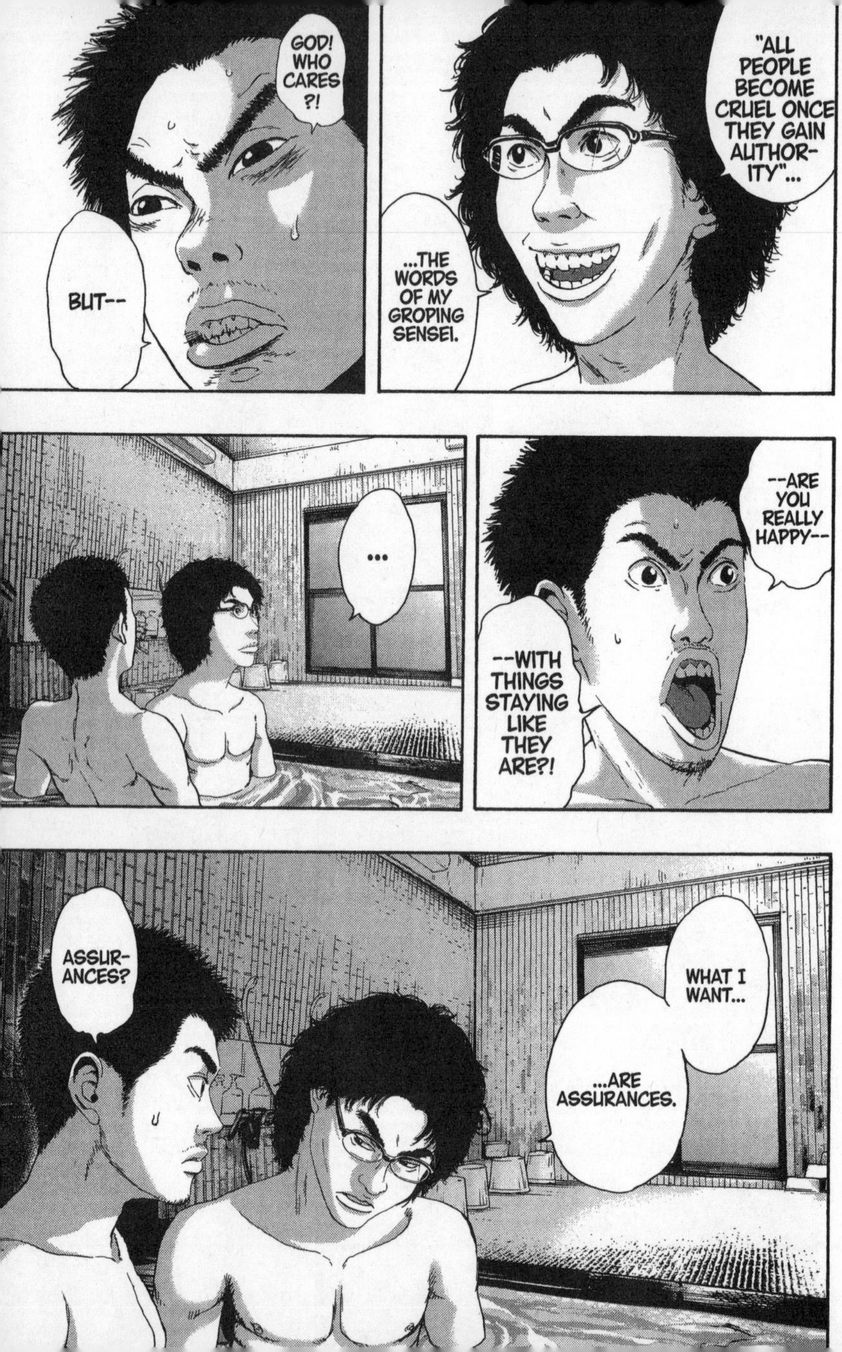
"ALL PEOPLE BECOME CRUEL ONCE THEY GAIN AUTHORITY"...
...THE WORDS OF MY GROPING SENSEI.
GOD! WHO CARES?!
BUT--
--ARE YOU REALLY HAPPY--
--WITH THINGS STAYING LIKE THEY ARE?!
...
WHAT I WANT...
...ARE ASSURANCES.
ASSURANCES?

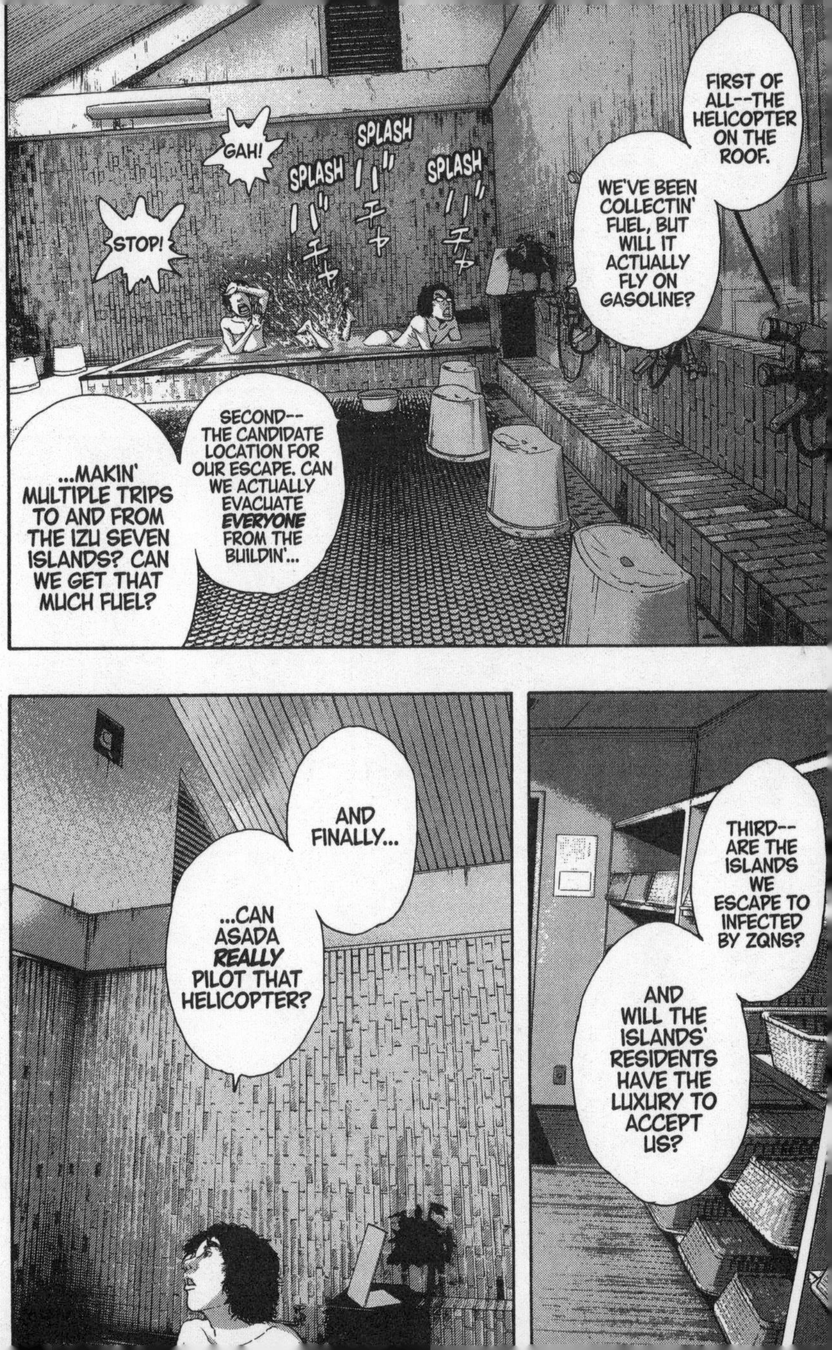
FIRST OF ALL--THE HELICOPTER ON THE ROOF.
WE'VE BEEN COLLECTIN' FUEL, BUT WILL IT ACTUALLY FLY ON GASOLINE?
SPLASH
バチャ
SPLASH
バチャ
GAH!
SPLASH
バチャ
STOP!
SECOND--THE CANDIDATE LOCATION FOR OUR ESCAPE. CAN WE ACTUALLY EVACUATE **EVERYONE** FROM THE BUILDIN'...
...MAKIN' MULTIPLE TRIPS TO AND FROM THE IZU SEVEN ISLANDS? CAN WE GET THAT MUCH FUEL?
THIRD--ARE THE ISLANDS WE ESCAPE TO INFECTED BY ZQNS?
AND WILL THE ISLANDS' RESIDENTS HAVE THE LUXURY TO ACCEPT US?
AND FINALLY...
...CAN ASADA **REALLY** PILOT THAT HELICOPTER?

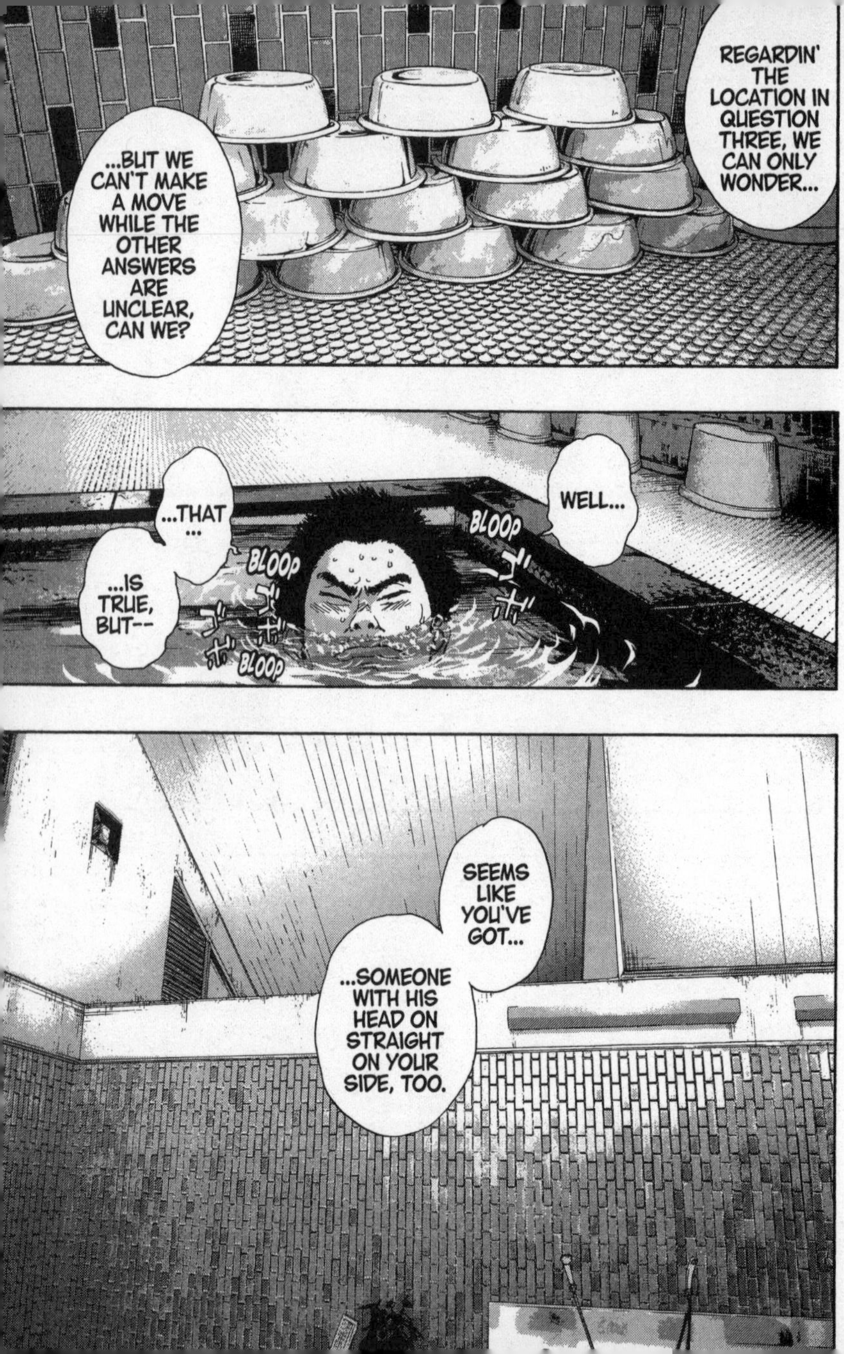
REGARDIN' THE LOCATION IN QUESTION THREE, WE CAN ONLY WONDER...
...BUT WE CAN'T MAKE A MOVE WHILE THE OTHER ANSWERS ARE UNCLEAR, CAN WE?
WELL...
BLOOP
ゴボ
BLOOP
ゴボ
BLOOP
...THAT ...
...IS TRUE, BUT--
SEEMS LIKE YOU'VE GOT...
...SOMEONE WITH HIS HEAD ON STRAIGHT ON YOUR SIDE, TOO.

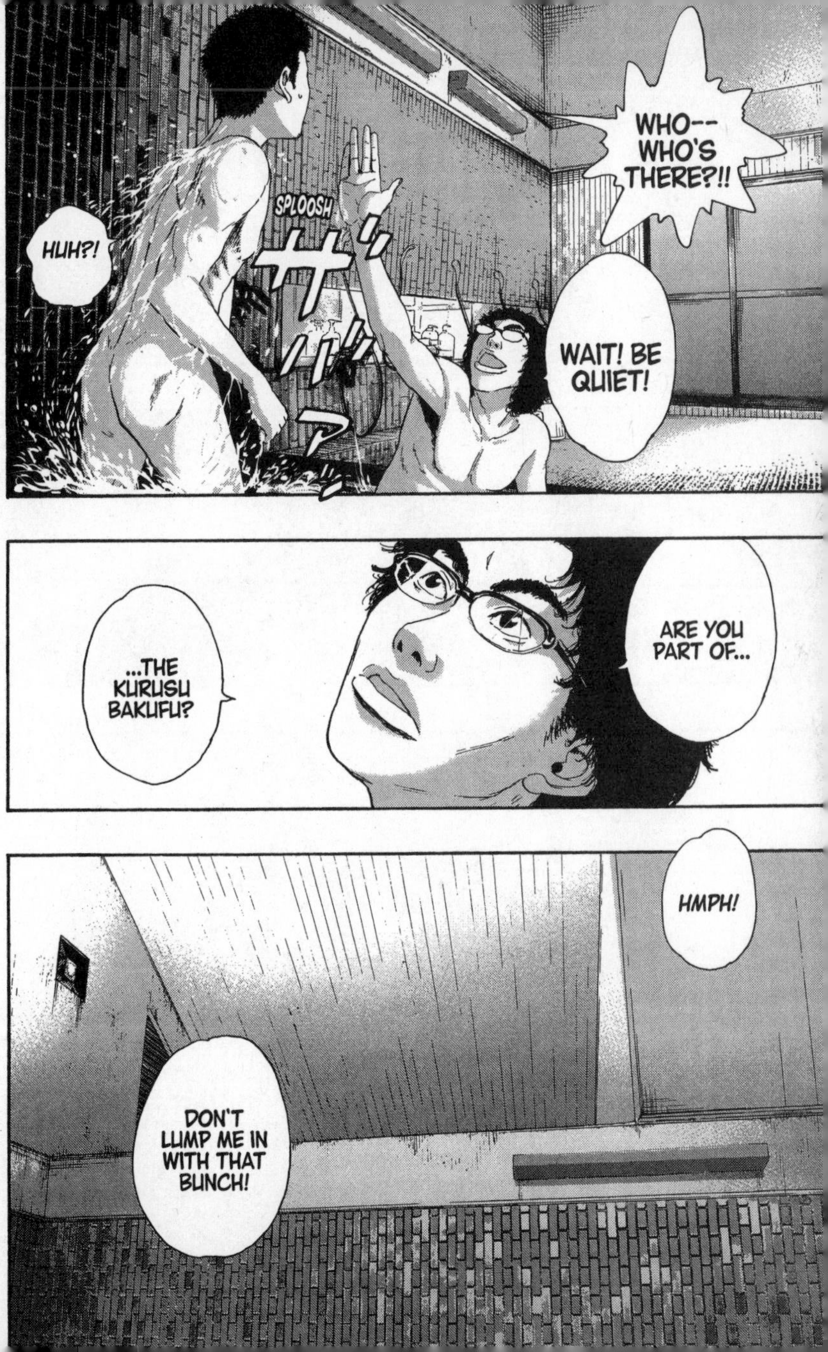
WHO-- WHO'S THERE?!!
WAIT! BE QUIET!
SPLOOSH
HUH?!
ARE YOU PART OF...
...THE KURUSU BAKUFU?
HMPH!
DON'T LUMP ME IN WITH THAT BUNCH!

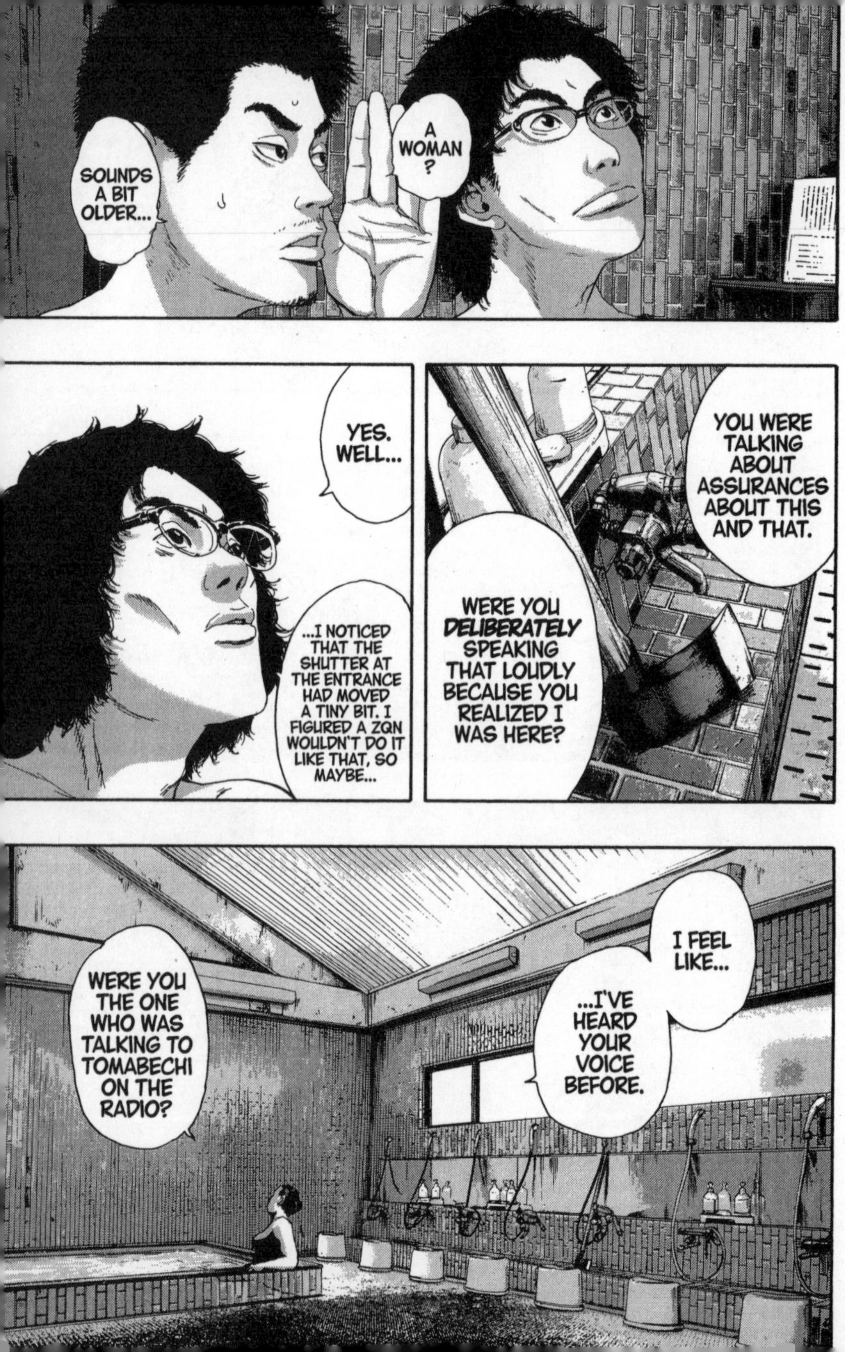
A WOMAN?
SOUNDS A BIT OLDER...
YOU WERE TALKING ABOUT ASSURANCES ABOUT THIS AND THAT.
WERE YOU *DELIBERATELY* SPEAKING THAT LOUDLY BECAUSE YOU REALIZED I WAS HERE?
YES. WELL...
...I NOTICED THAT THE SHUTTER AT THE ENTRANCE HAD MOVED A TINY BIT. I FIGURED A ZQN WOULDN'T DO IT LIKE THAT, SO MAYBE...
I FEEL LIKE...
...I'VE HEARD YOUR VOICE BEFORE.
WERE YOU THE ONE WHO WAS TALKING TO TOMABECHI ON THE RADIO?

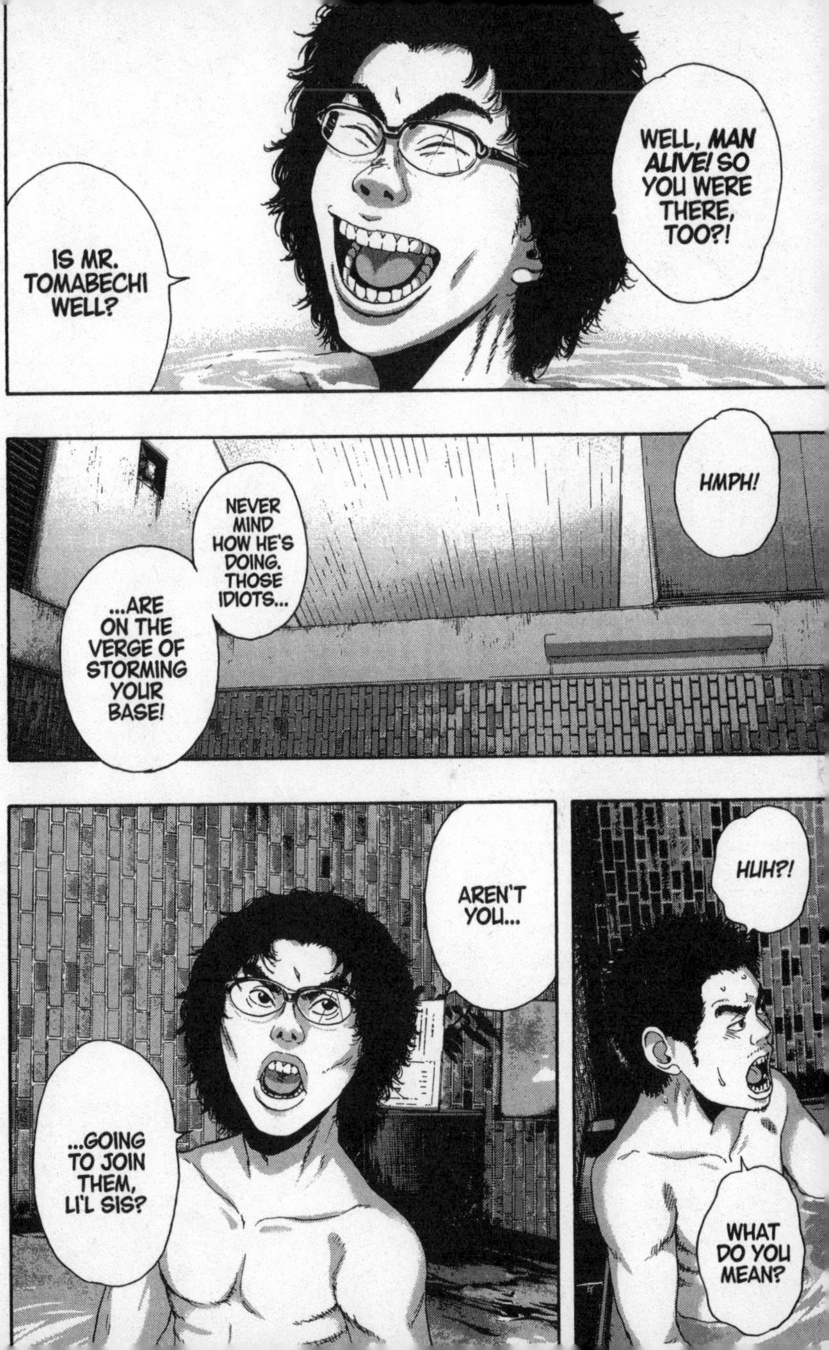
WELL, *MAN ALIVE!* SO YOU WERE THERE, TOO?!
IS MR. TOMABECHI WELL?
HMPH!
NEVER MIND HOW HE'S DOING. THOSE IDIOTS...
...ARE ON THE VERGE OF STORMING YOUR BASE!
HUH?!
WHAT DO YOU MEAN?
AREN'T YOU...
...GOING TO JOIN THEM, LI'L SIS?

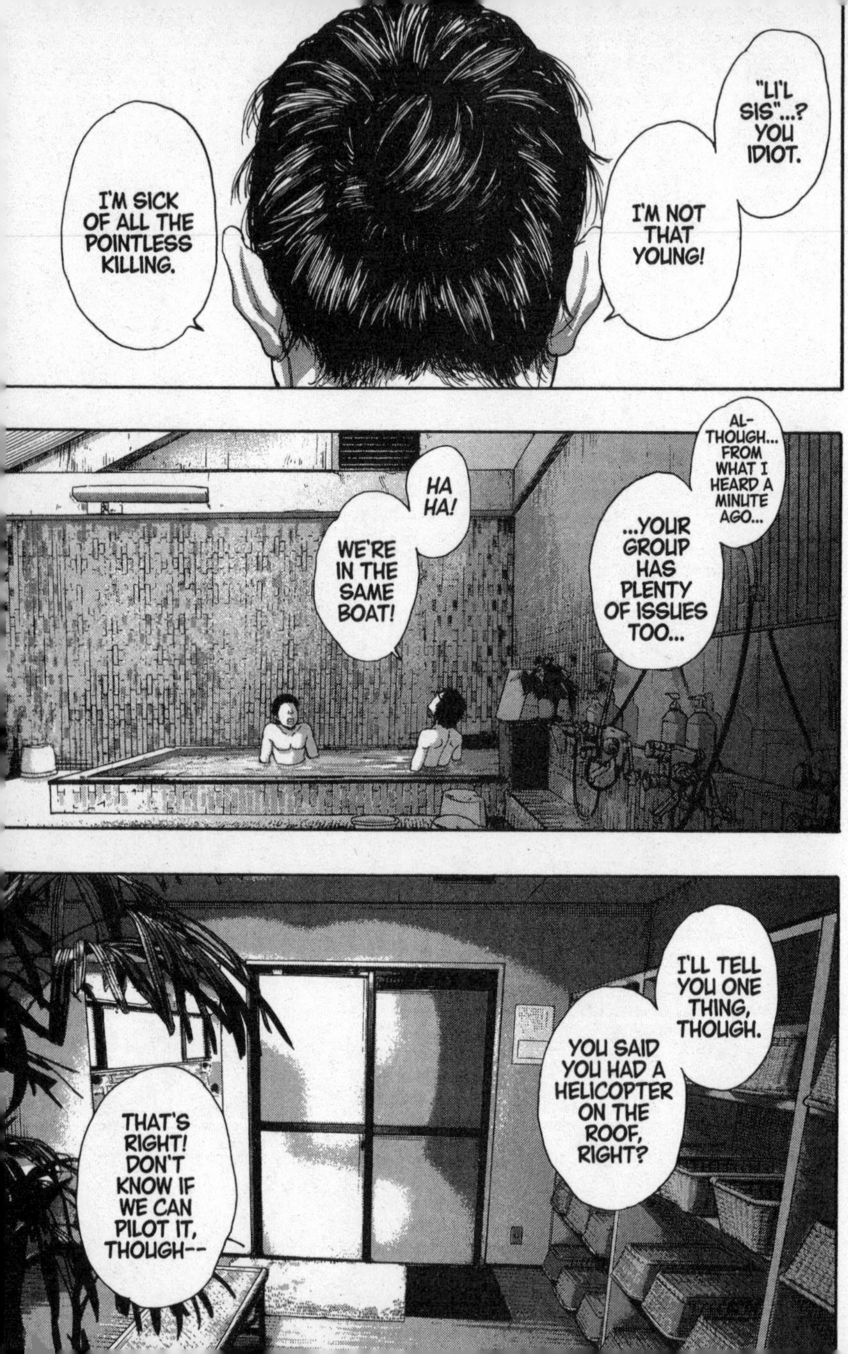
"LI'L SIS"...? YOU IDIOT.
I'M NOT THAT YOUNG!
I'M SICK OF ALL THE POINTLESS KILLING.
AL-THOUGH... FROM WHAT I HEARD A MINUTE AGO...
...YOUR GROUP HAS PLENTY OF ISSUES TOO...
HA HA!
WE'RE IN THE SAME BOAT!
I'LL TELL YOU ONE THING, THOUGH.
YOU SAID YOU HAD A HELICOPTER ON THE ROOF, RIGHT?
THAT'S RIGHT! DON'T KNOW IF WE CAN PILOT IT, THOUGH--

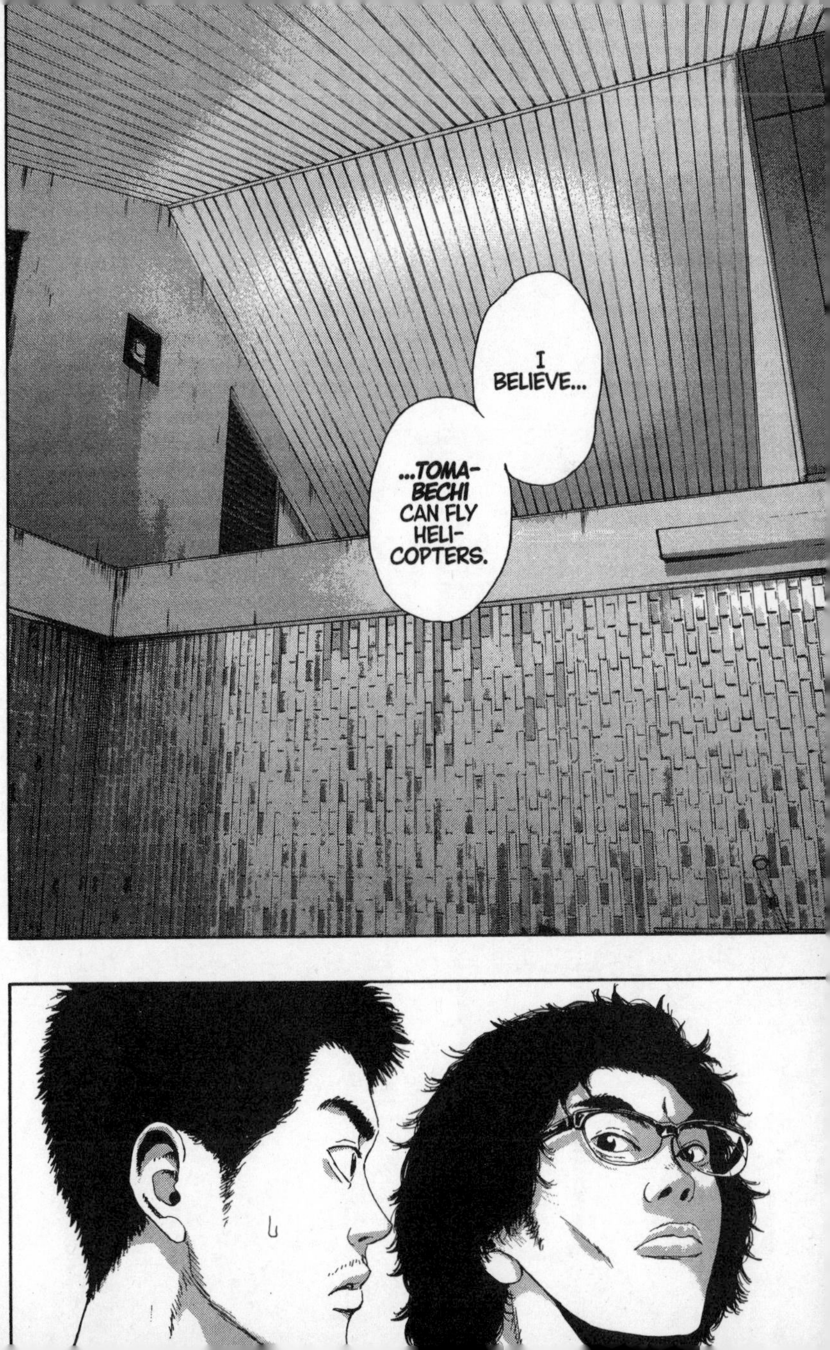
I BELIEVE...
...TOMA-BECHI CAN FLY HELI-COPTERS.

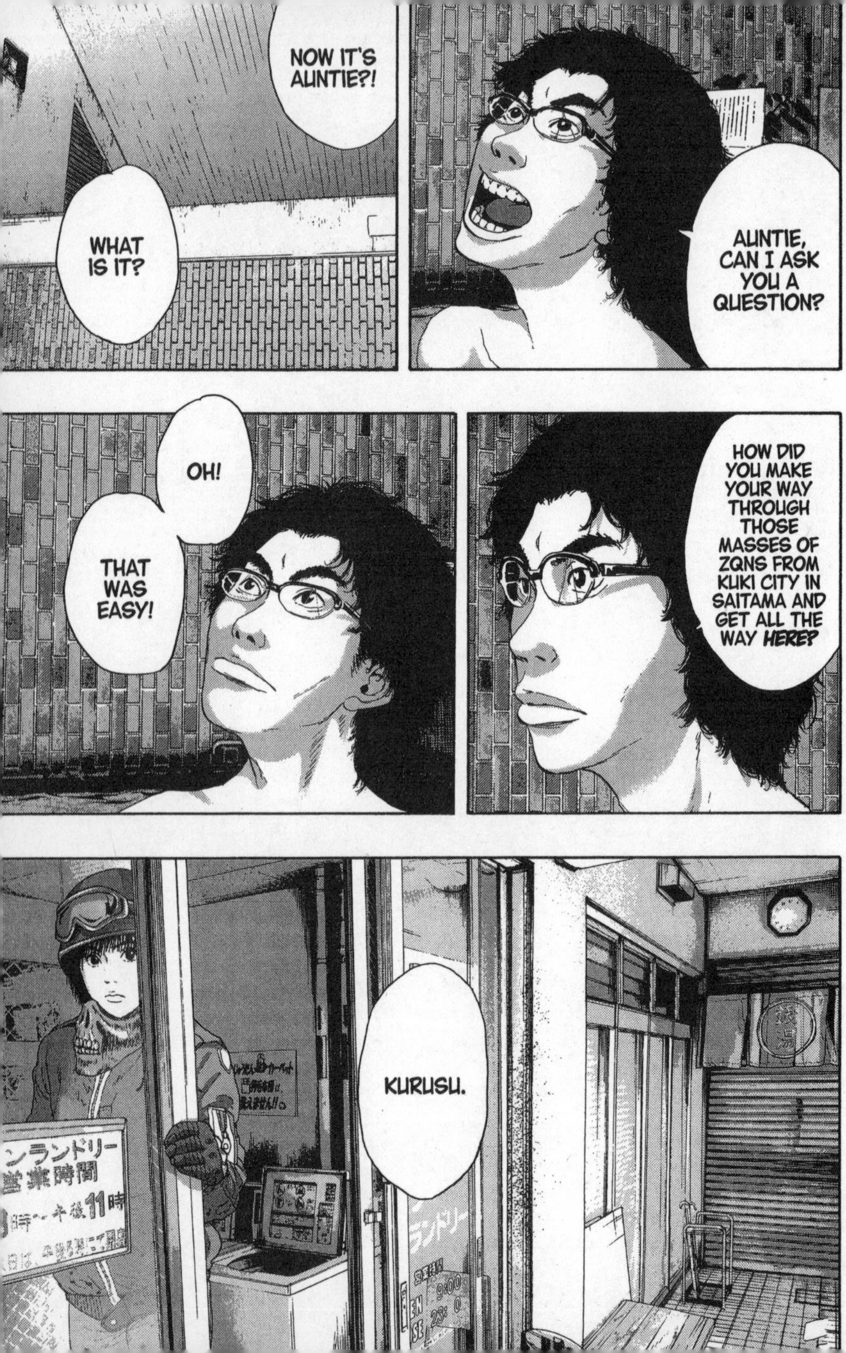
AUNTIE, CAN I ASK YOU A QUESTION?
NOW IT'S AUNTIE?!
WHAT IS IT?
HOW DID YOU MAKE YOUR WAY THROUGH THOSE MASSES OF ZQNS FROM KUKI CITY IN SAITAMA AND GET ALL THE WAY *HERE?*
OH!
THAT WAS EASY!
KURUSU.

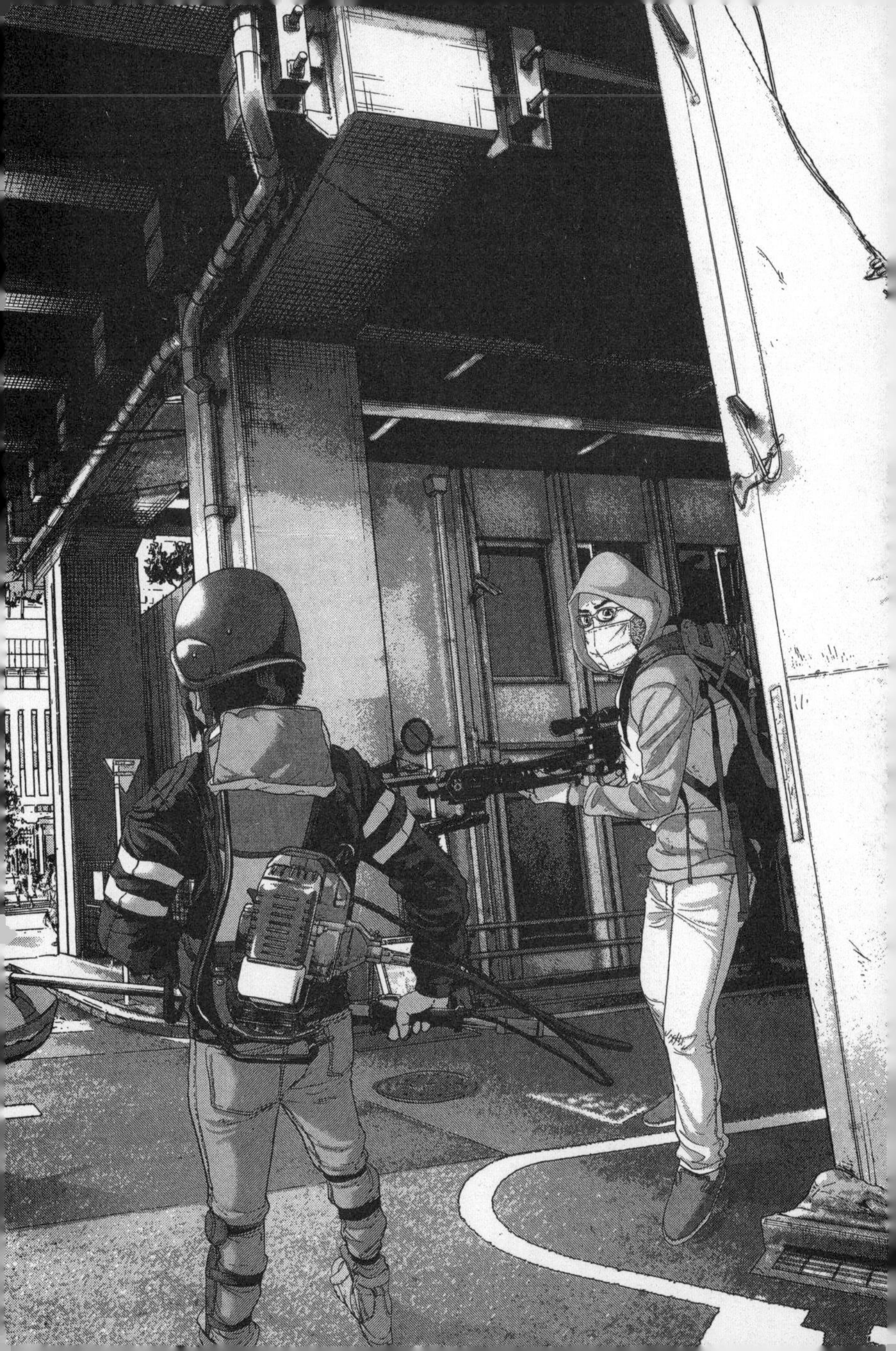

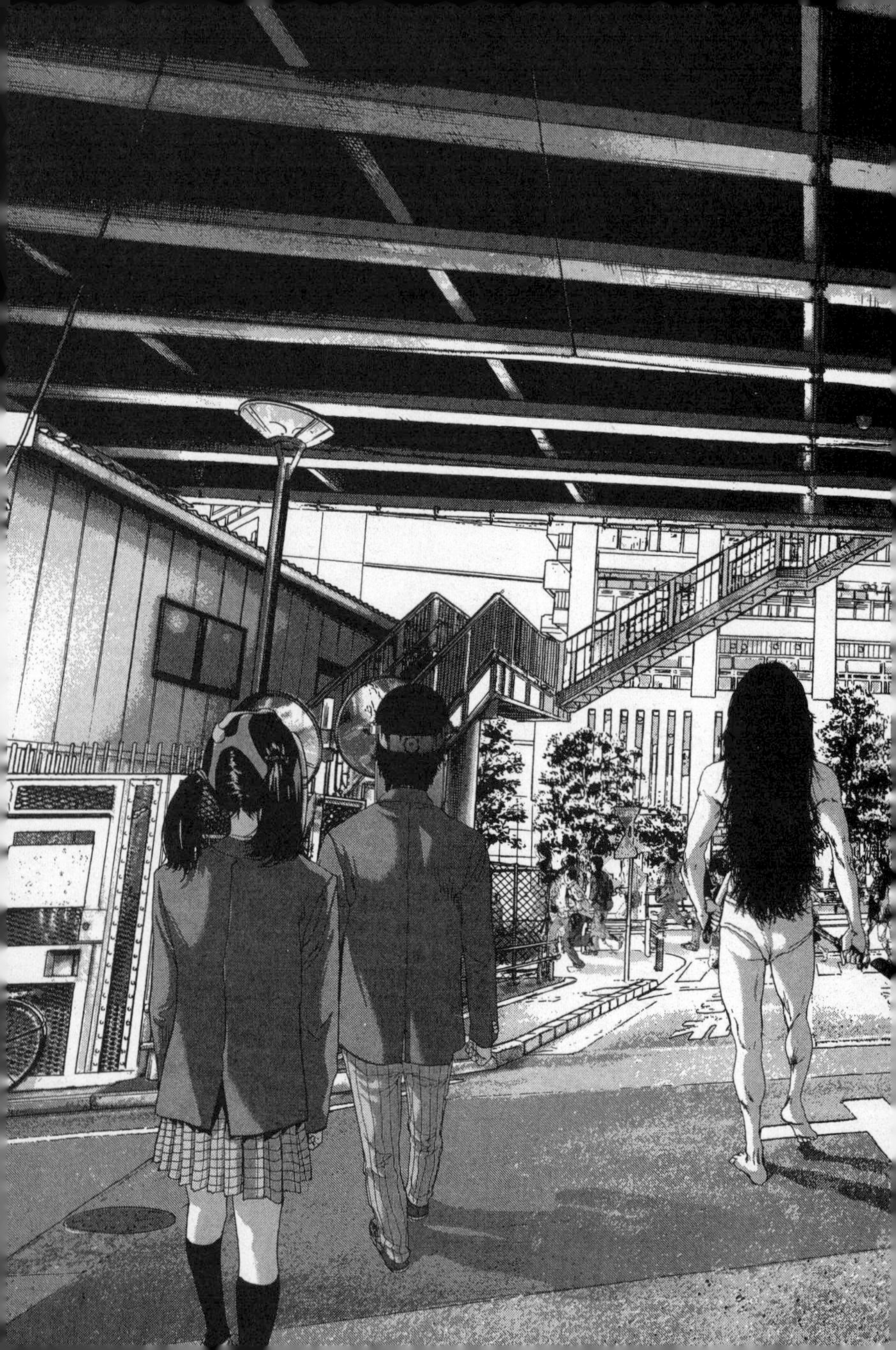

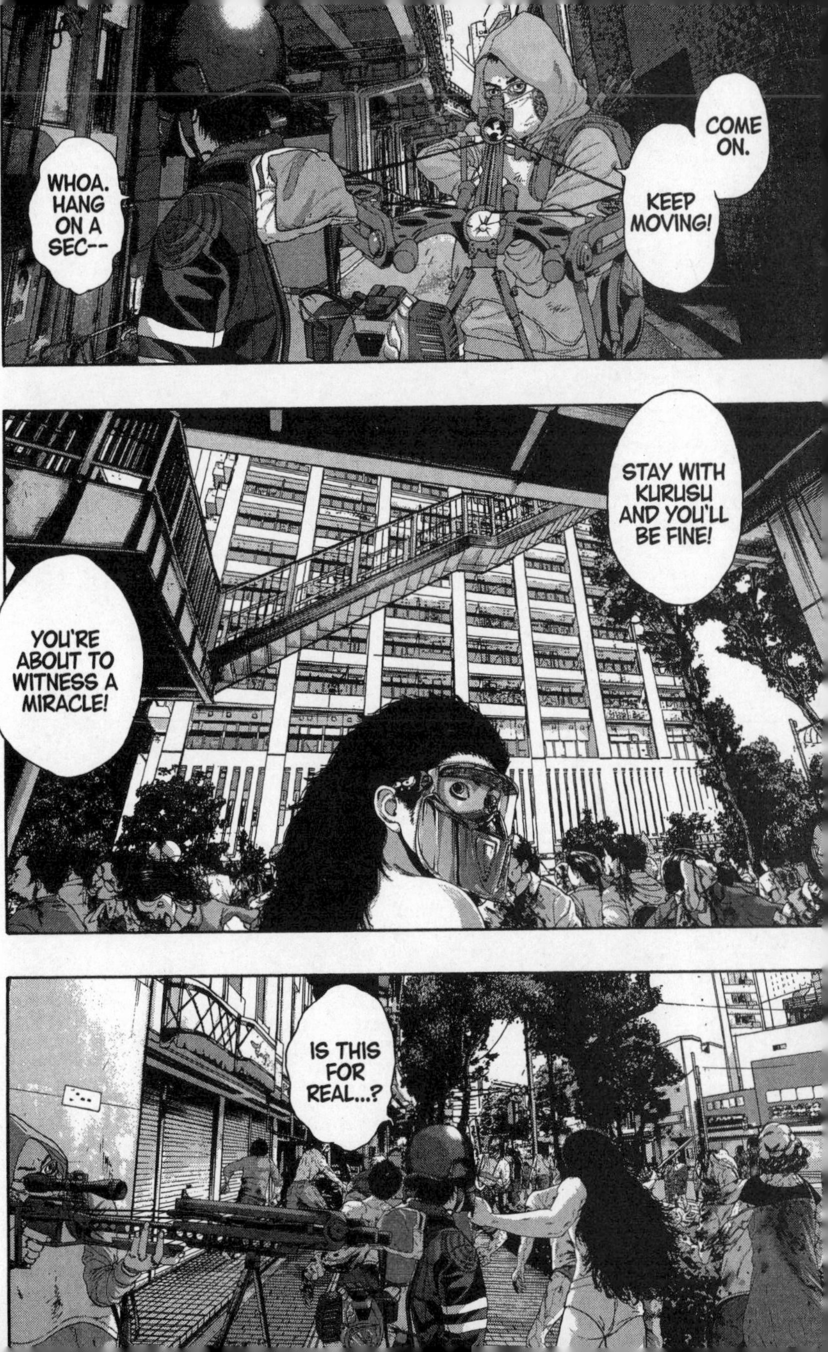
COME ON.
KEEP MOVING!
WHOA. HANG ON A SEC--
STAY WITH KURUSU AND YOU'LL BE FINE!
YOU'RE ABOUT TO WITNESS A MIRACLE!
IS THIS FOR REAL...?

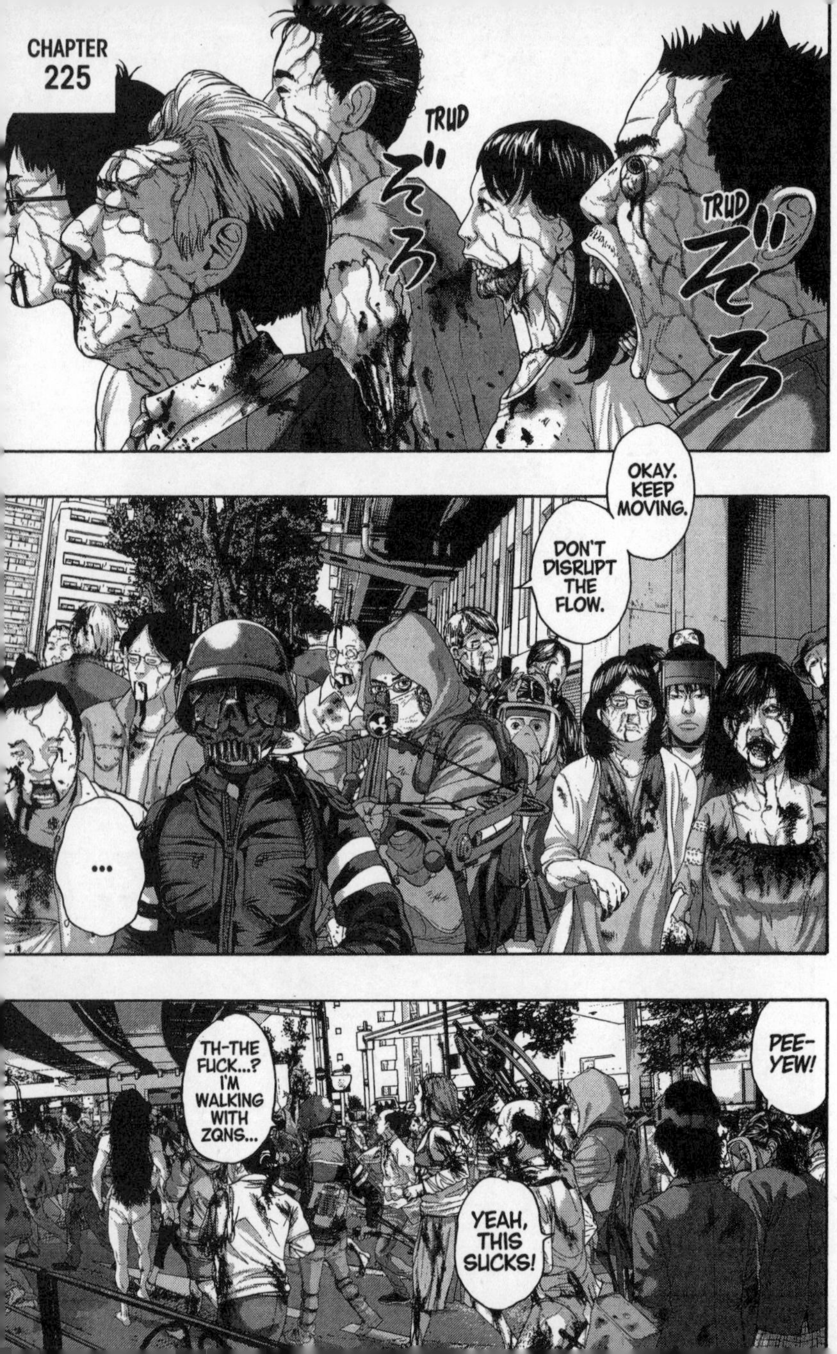
CHAPTER 225
TRUD
ぞろ
TRUD
ぞろ
OKAY. KEEP MOVING.
DON'T DISRUPT THE FLOW.
...
PEE-YEW!
TH-THE FUCK...? I'M WALKING WITH ZQNS...
YEAH, THIS SUCKS!

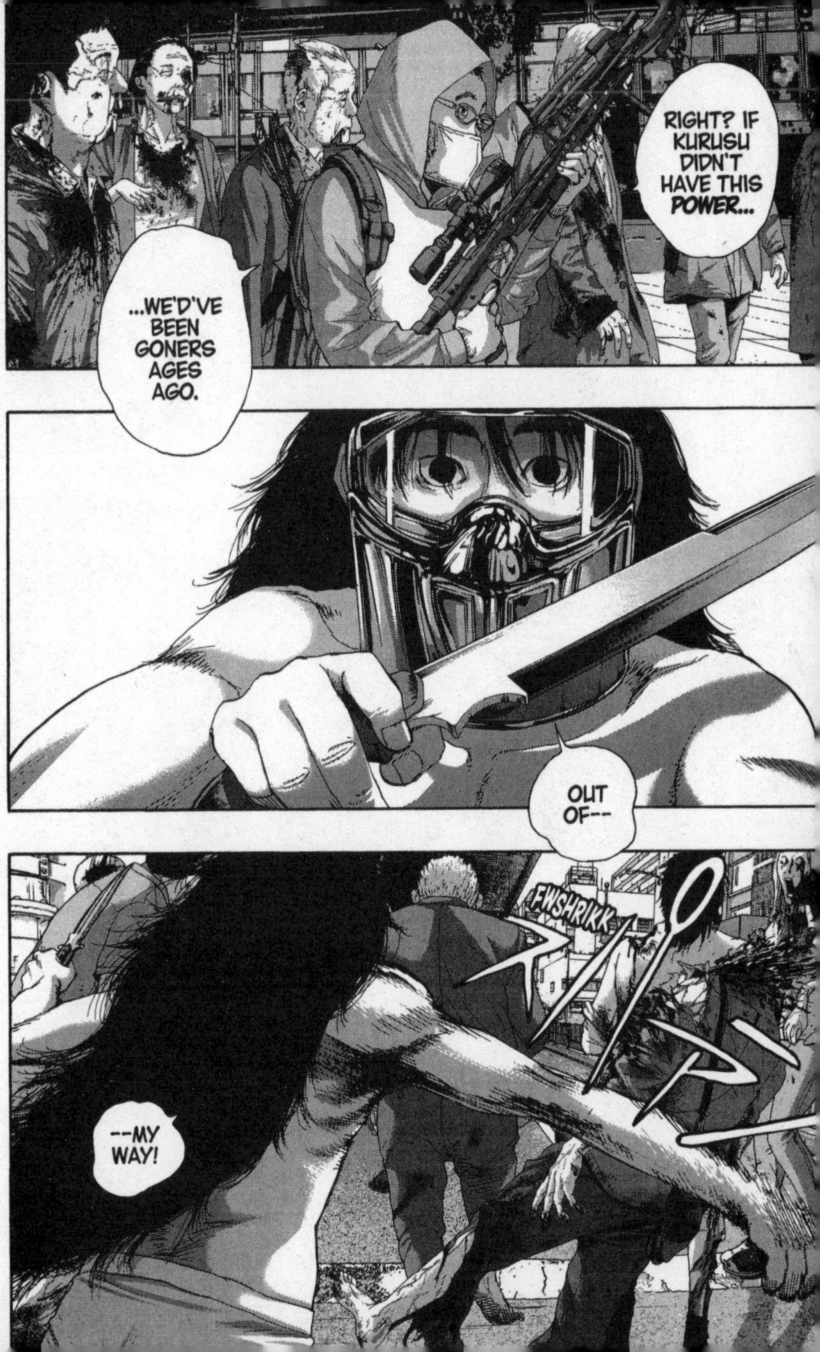
RIGHT? IF KURUSU DIDN'T HAVE THIS POWER...
...WE'D'VE BEEN GONERS AGES AGO.
OUT OF--
FWSHRIKK
--MY WAY!

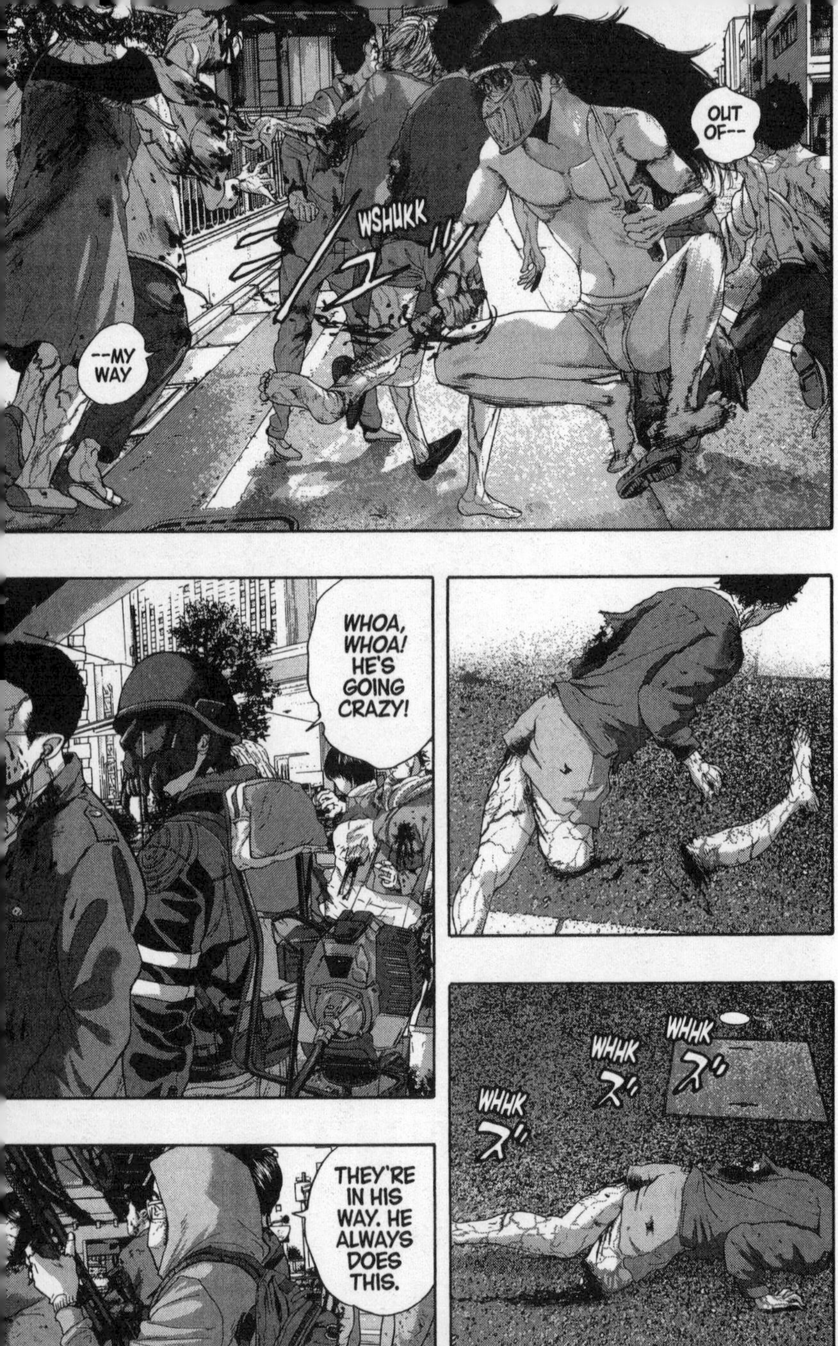
OUT OF--
WSHUKK
--MY WAY
WHOA, WHOA! HE'S GOING CRAZY!
WHHK
WHHK
WHHK
THEY'RE IN HIS WAY. HE ALWAYS DOES THIS.

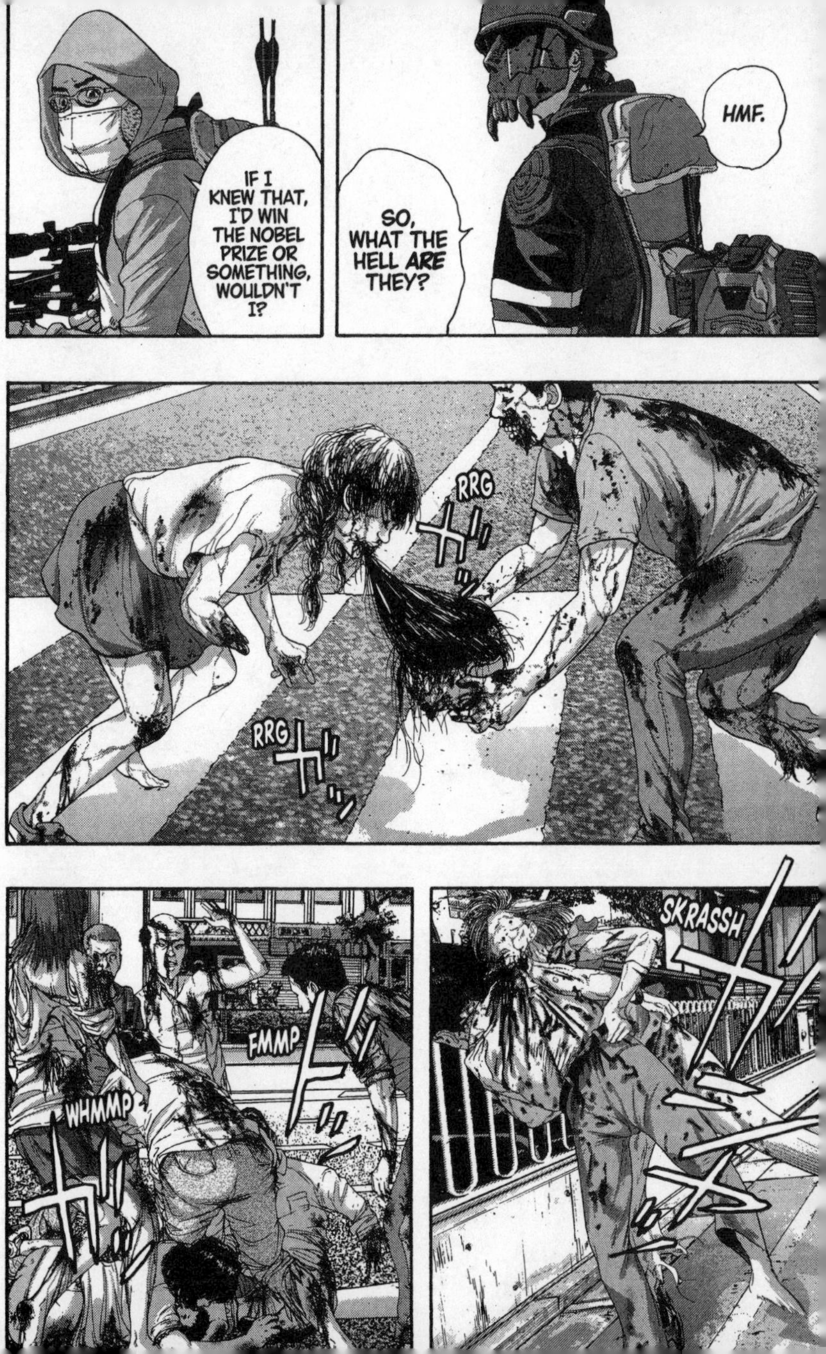
HMF.
SO, WHAT THE HELL ARE THEY?
IF I KNEW THAT, I'D WIN THE NOBEL PRIZE OR SOMETHING, WOULDN'T I?
RRG
RRG
SKRASSH
FMMP
WHMMP

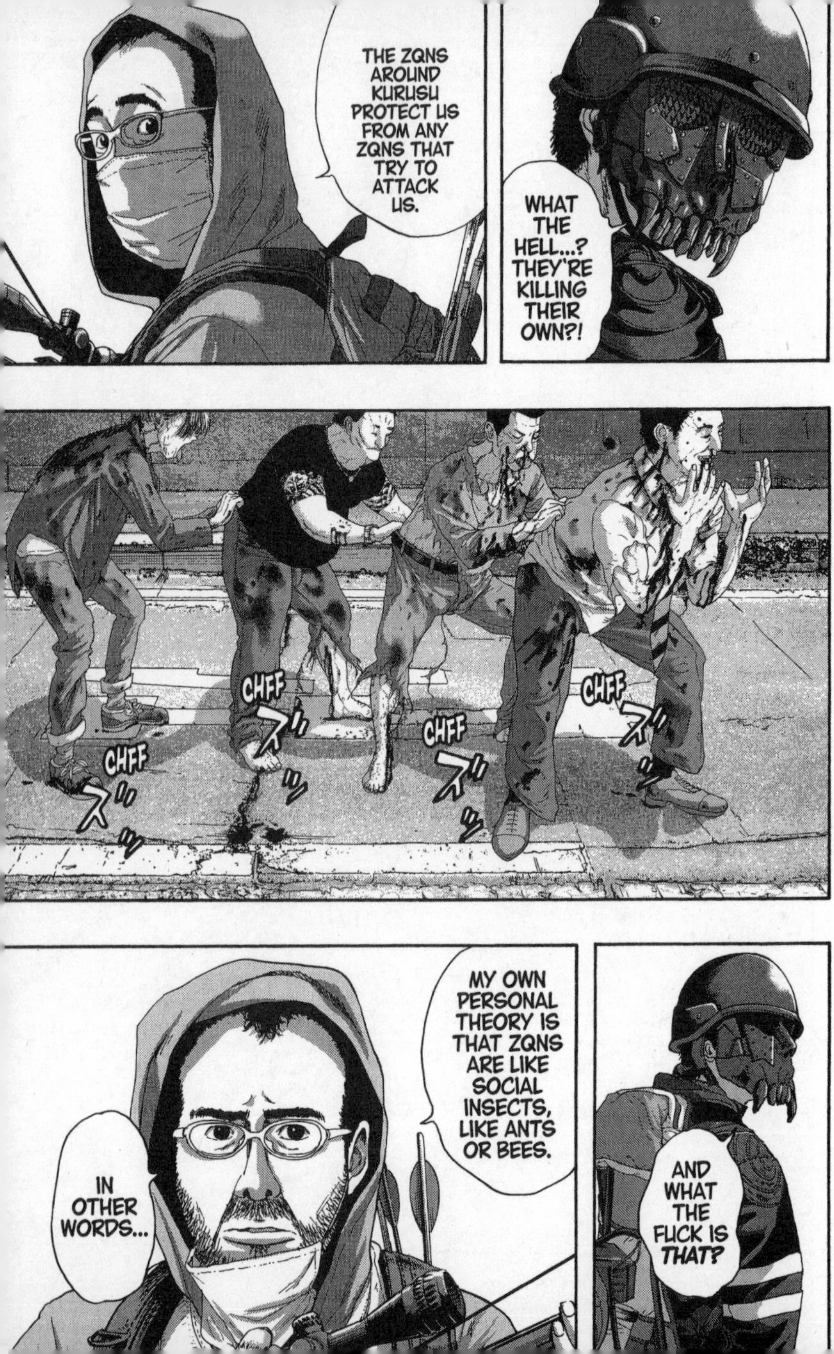
WHAT THE HELL...? THEY'RE KILLING THEIR OWN?!
THE ZQNS AROUND KURUSU PROTECT US FROM ANY ZQNS THAT TRY TO ATTACK US.
CHFF
CHFF
CHFF
CHFF
AND WHAT THE FUCK IS *THAT?*
MY OWN PERSONAL THEORY IS THAT ZQNS ARE LIKE SOCIAL INSECTS, LIKE ANTS OR BEES.
IN OTHER WORDS...

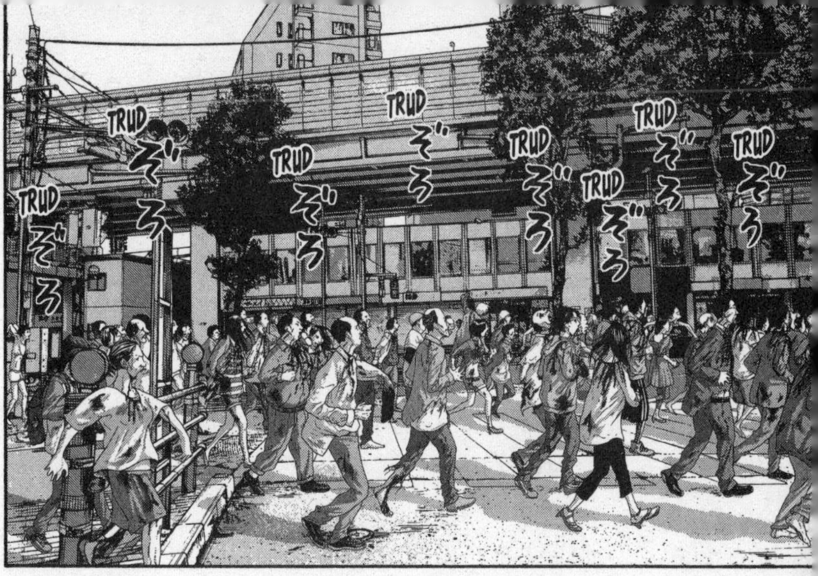
TRUD ぞろ
TRUD ぞろ
TRUD ぞろ
TRUD ぞろ
TRUD ぞろ
TRUD ぞろ
TRUD ぞろ
TRUD ぞろ

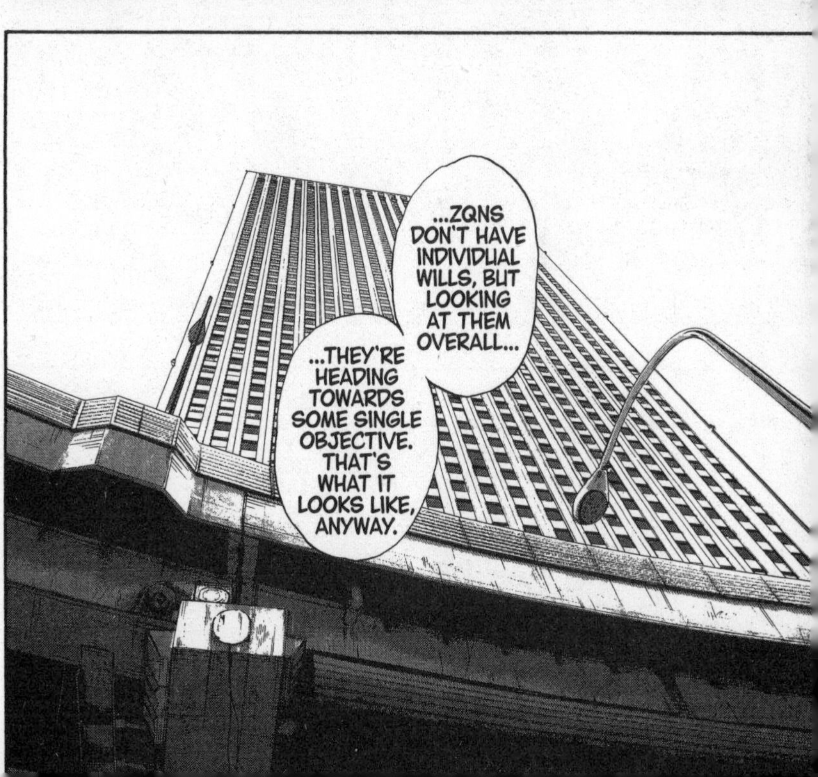
...ZQNS DON'T HAVE INDIVIDUAL WILLS, BUT LOOKING AT THEM OVERALL...
...THEY'RE HEADING TOWARDS SOME SINGLE OBJECTIVE. THAT'S WHAT IT LOOKS LIKE, ANYWAY.

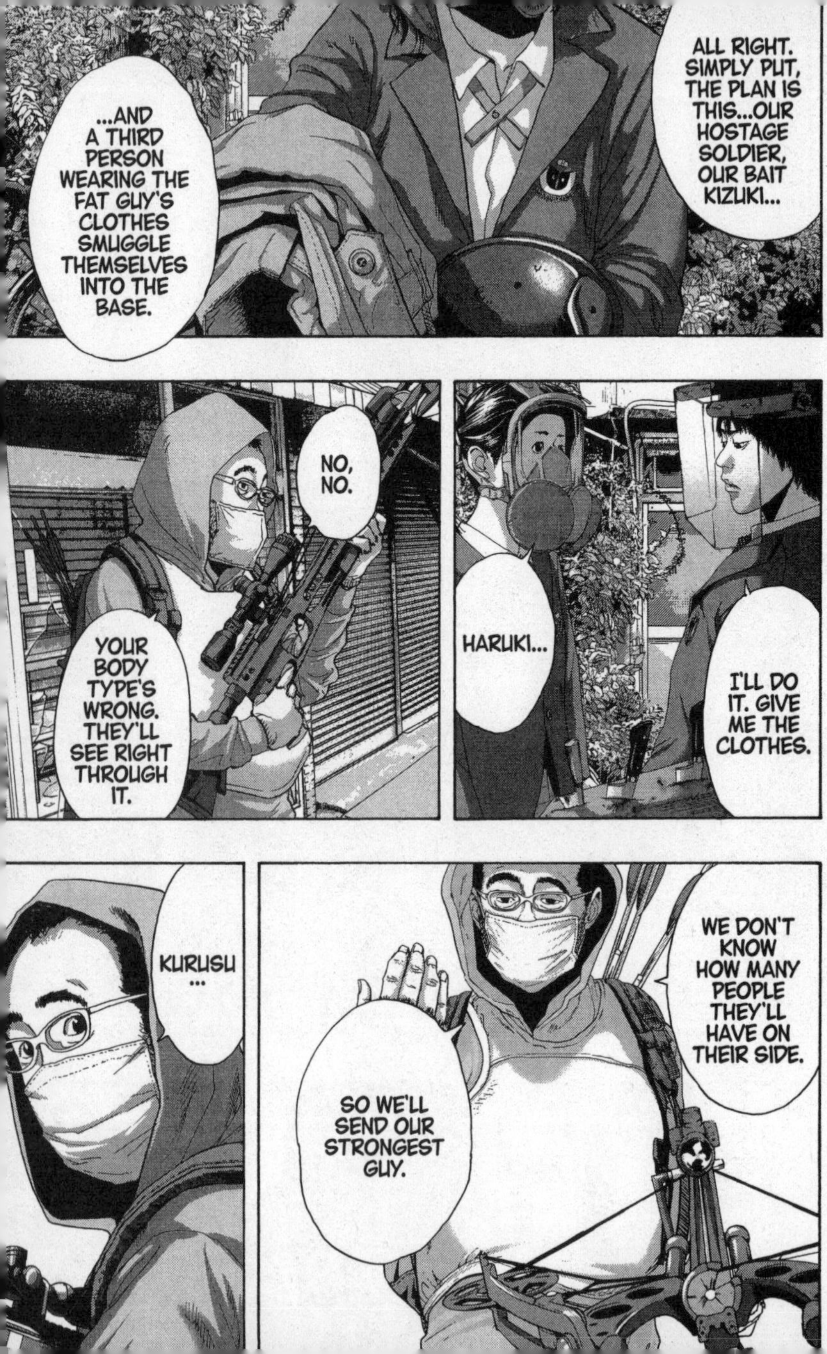
ALL RIGHT. SIMPLY PUT, THE PLAN IS THIS...OUR HOSTAGE SOLDIER, OUR BAIT KIZUKI...
...AND A THIRD PERSON WEARING THE FAT GUY'S CLOTHES SMUGGLE THEMSELVES INTO THE BASE.
I'LL DO IT. GIVE ME THE CLOTHES.
HARUKI...
NO, NO.
YOUR BODY TYPE'S WRONG. THEY'LL SEE RIGHT THROUGH IT.
WE DON'T KNOW HOW MANY PEOPLE THEY'LL HAVE ON THEIR SIDE.
SO WE'LL SEND OUR STRONGEST GUY.
KURUSU ...

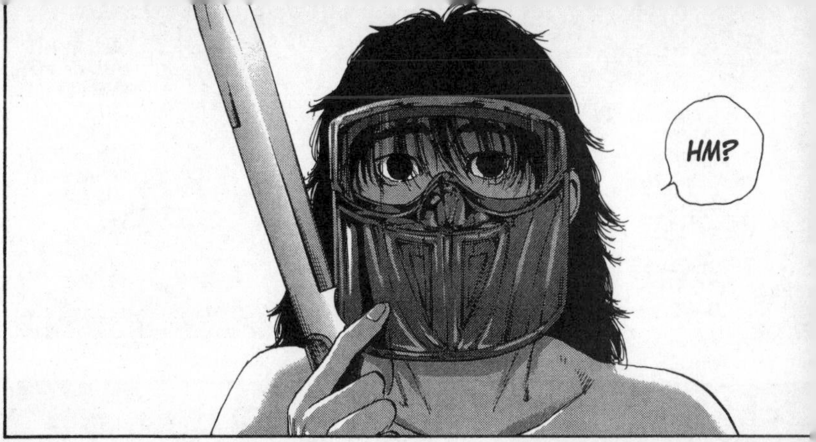
HM?

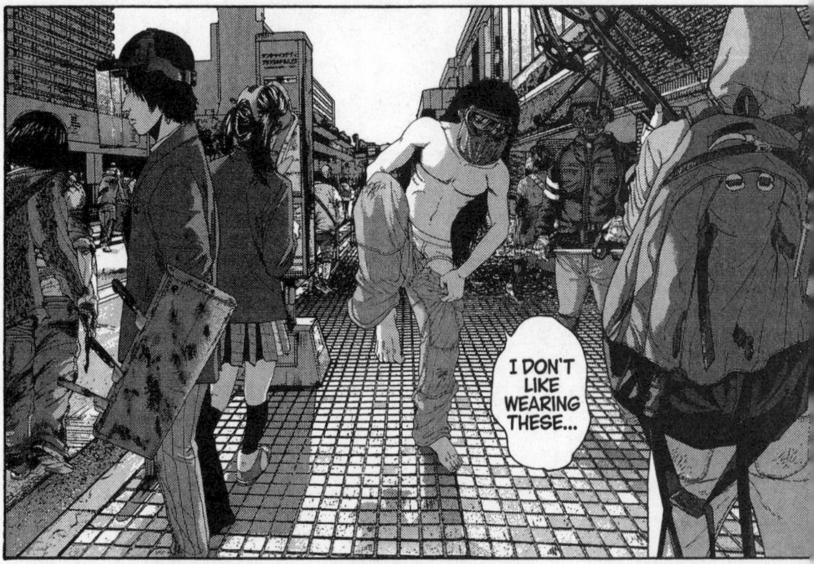
I DON'T LIKE WEARING THESE...

SIGN: COIN LAUNDRY

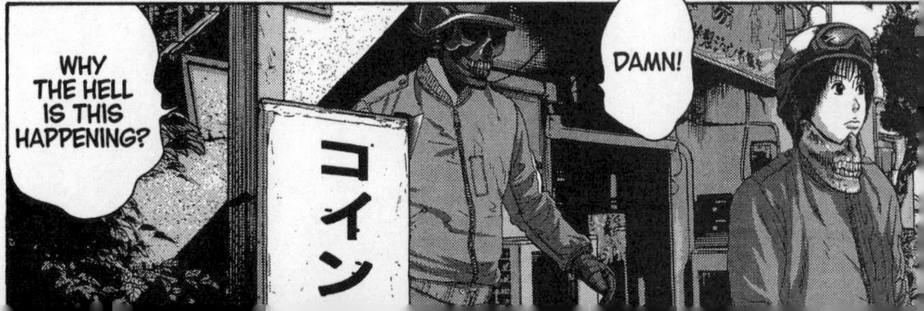
DAMN!
WHY THE HELL IS THIS HAPPENING?
コイン

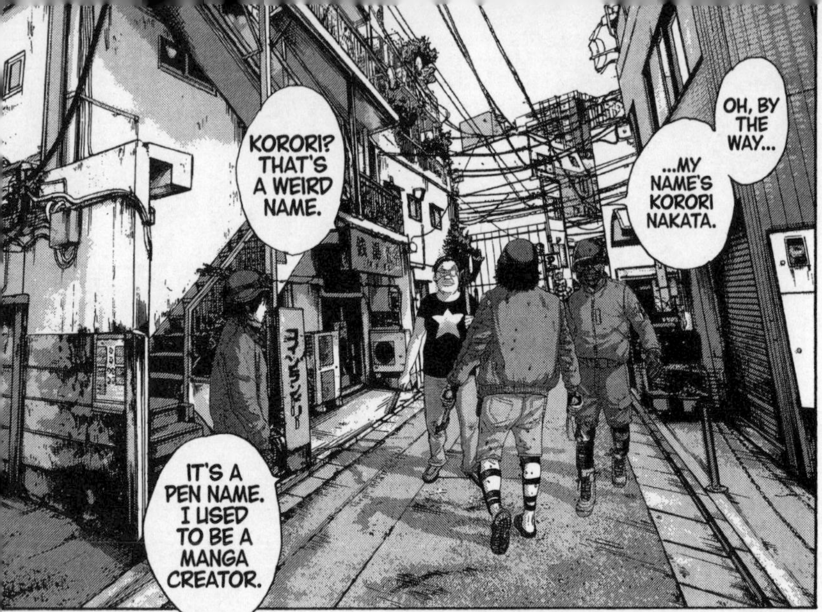
OH, BY THE WAY...
...MY NAME'S KORORI NAKATA.
KORORI? THAT'S A WEIRD NAME.
IT'S A PEN NAME. I USED TO BE A MANGA CREATOR.

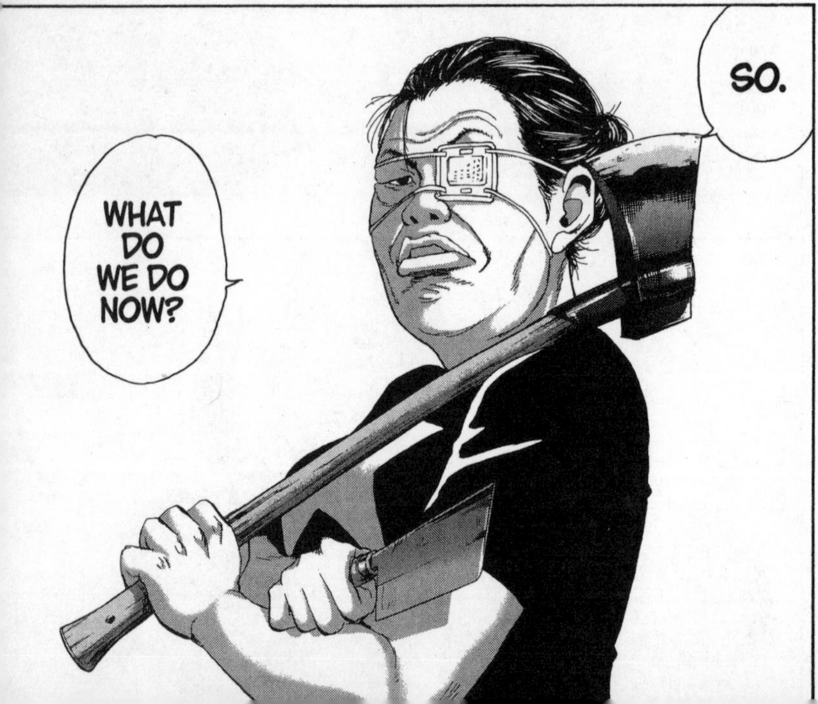
SO.
WHAT DO WE DO NOW?

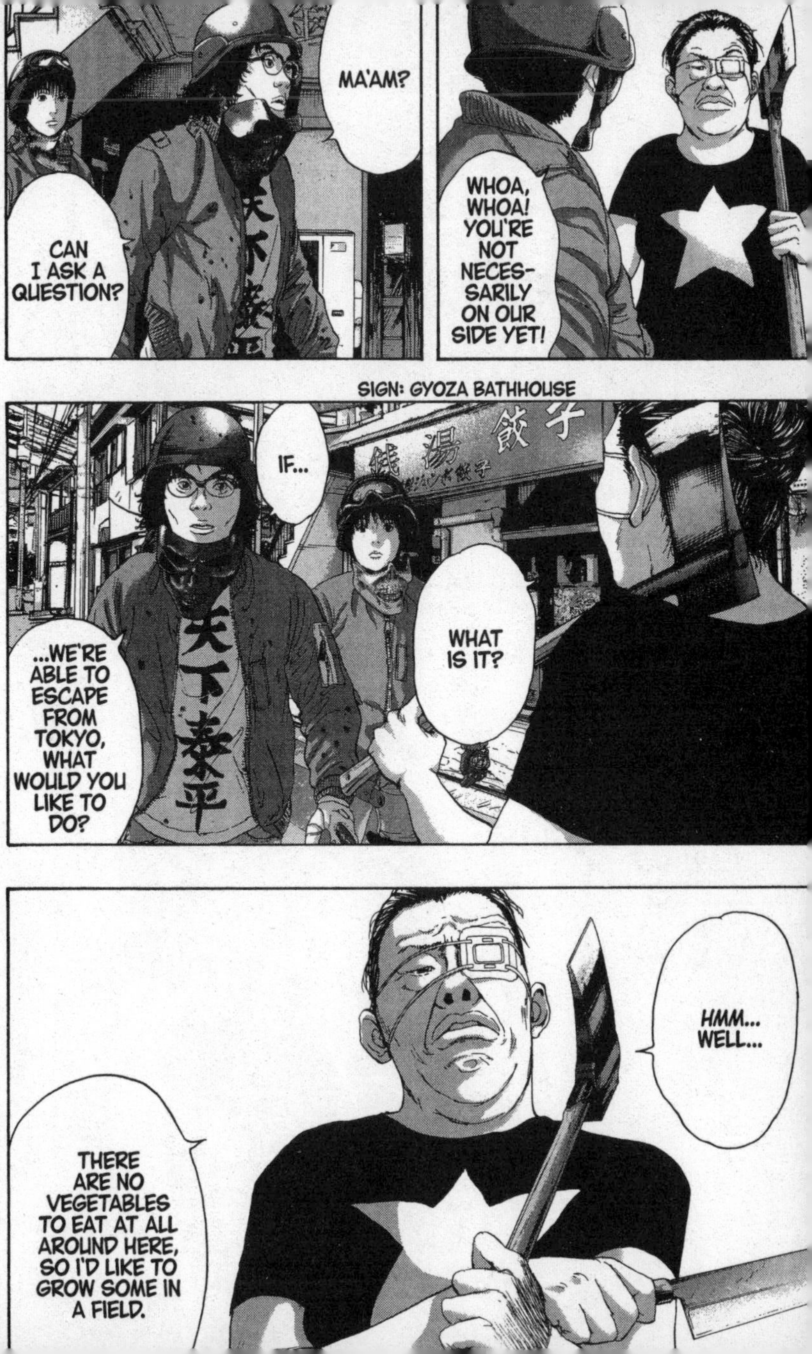
WHOA, WHOA! YOU'RE NOT NECES-SARILY ON OUR SIDE YET!
MA'AM?
CAN I ASK A QUESTION?
SIGN: GYOZA BATHHOUSE
銭湯 餃子
WHAT IS IT?
IF...
...WE'RE ABLE TO ESCAPE FROM TOKYO, WHAT WOULD YOU LIKE TO DO?
HMM... WELL...
THERE ARE NO VEGETABLES TO EAT AT ALL AROUND HERE, SO I'D LIKE TO GROW SOME IN A FIELD.

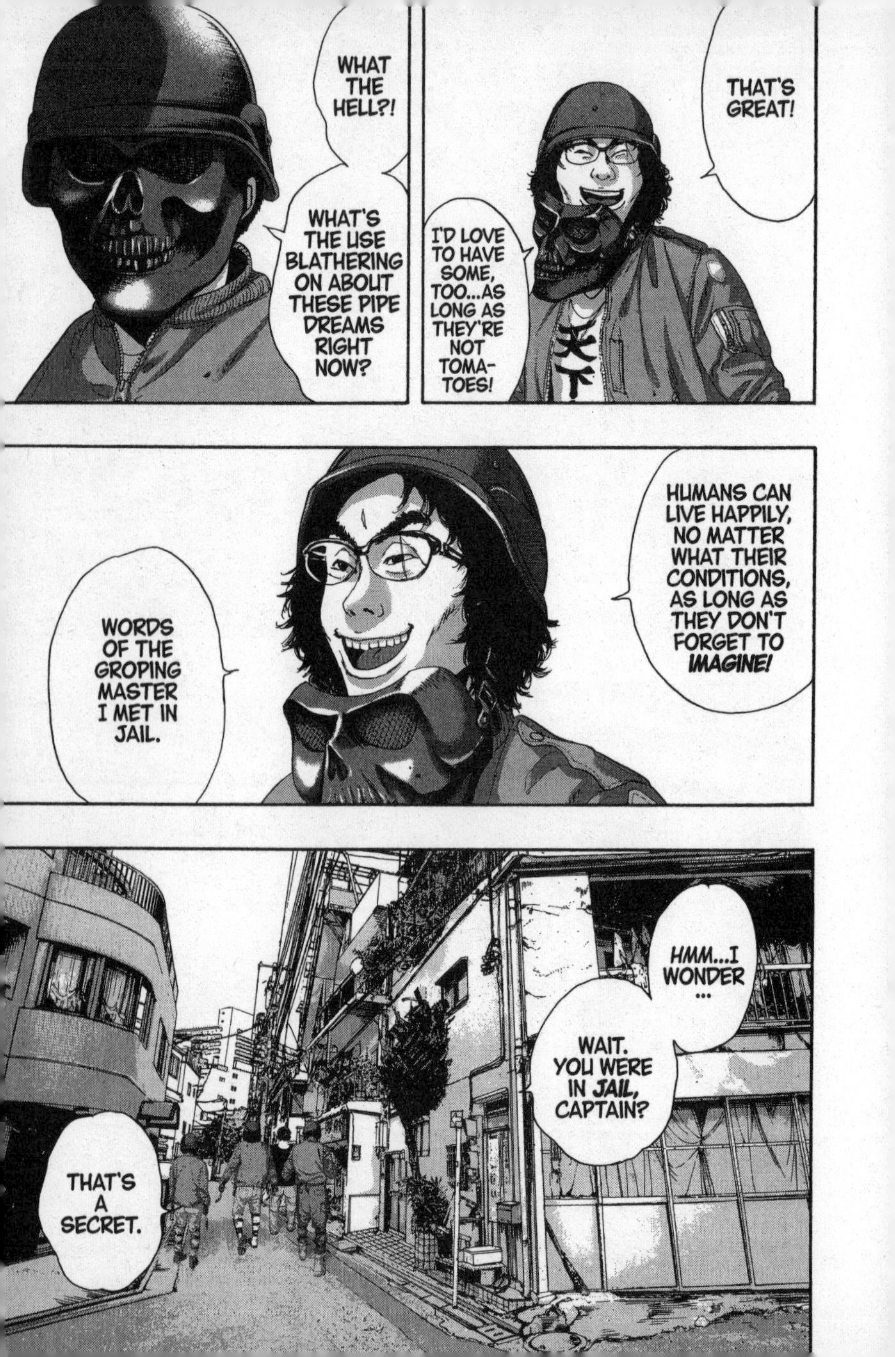
THAT'S GREAT!
I'D LOVE TO HAVE SOME, TOO...AS LONG AS THEY'RE NOT TOMA-TOES!
WHAT THE HELL?!
WHAT'S THE USE BLATHERING ON ABOUT THESE PIPE DREAMS RIGHT NOW?
HUMANS CAN LIVE HAPPILY, NO MATTER WHAT THEIR CONDITIONS, AS LONG AS THEY DON'T FORGET TO *IMAGINE!*
WORDS OF THE GROPING MASTER I MET IN JAIL.
HMM...I WONDER ...
WAIT. YOU WERE IN *JAIL,* CAPTAIN?
THAT'S A SECRET.

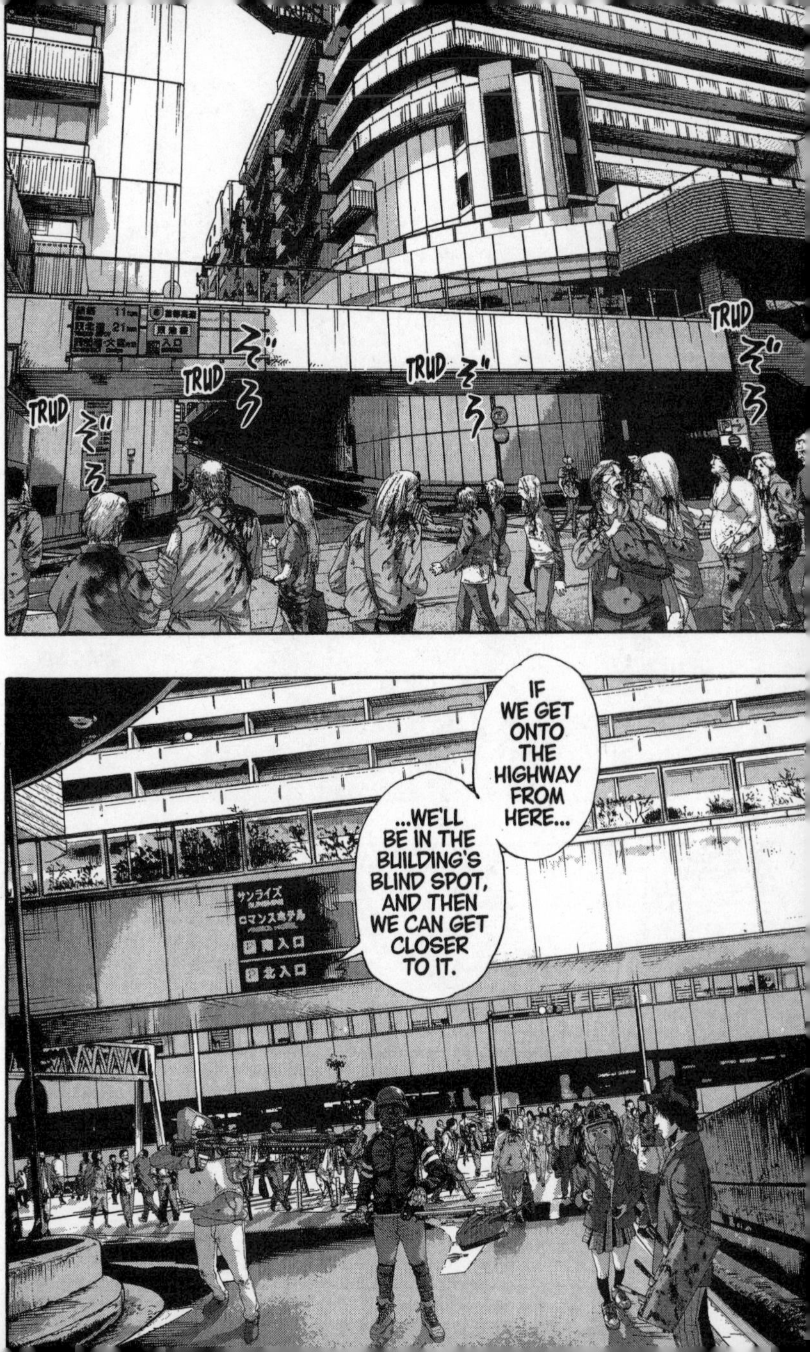
TRUD
ぞろ
TRUD
ぞろ
TRUD
ぞろ
TRUD
ぞろ
IF WE GET ONTO THE HIGHWAY FROM HERE...
...WE'LL BE IN THE BUILDING'S BLIND SPOT, AND THEN WE CAN GET CLOSER TO IT.

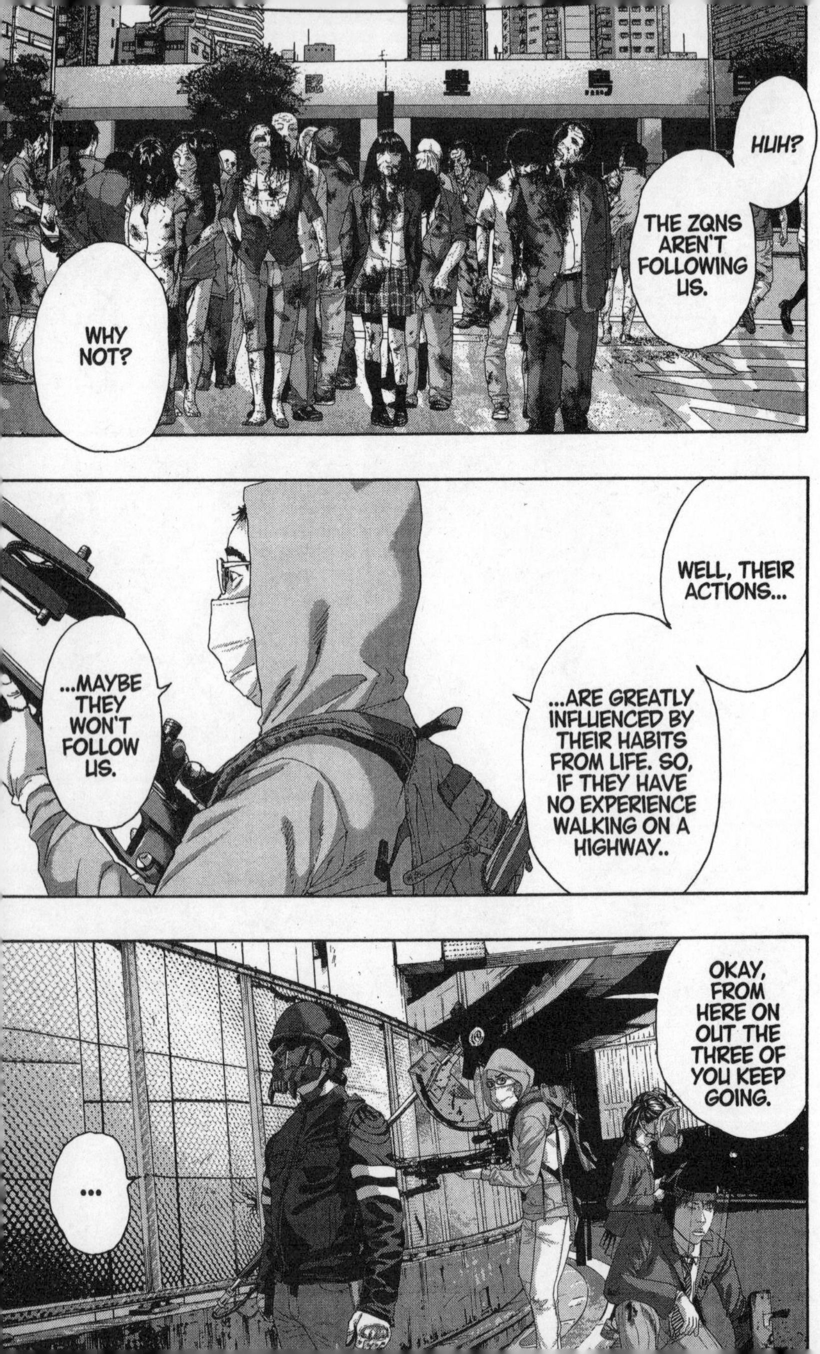
HUH?
THE ZQNS AREN'T FOLLOWING US.
WHY NOT?
WELL, THEIR ACTIONS...
...ARE GREATLY INFLUENCED BY THEIR HABITS FROM LIFE. SO, IF THEY HAVE NO EXPERIENCE WALKING ON A HIGHWAY..
...MAYBE THEY WON'T FOLLOW US.
OKAY, FROM HERE ON OUT THE THREE OF YOU KEEP GOING.
...

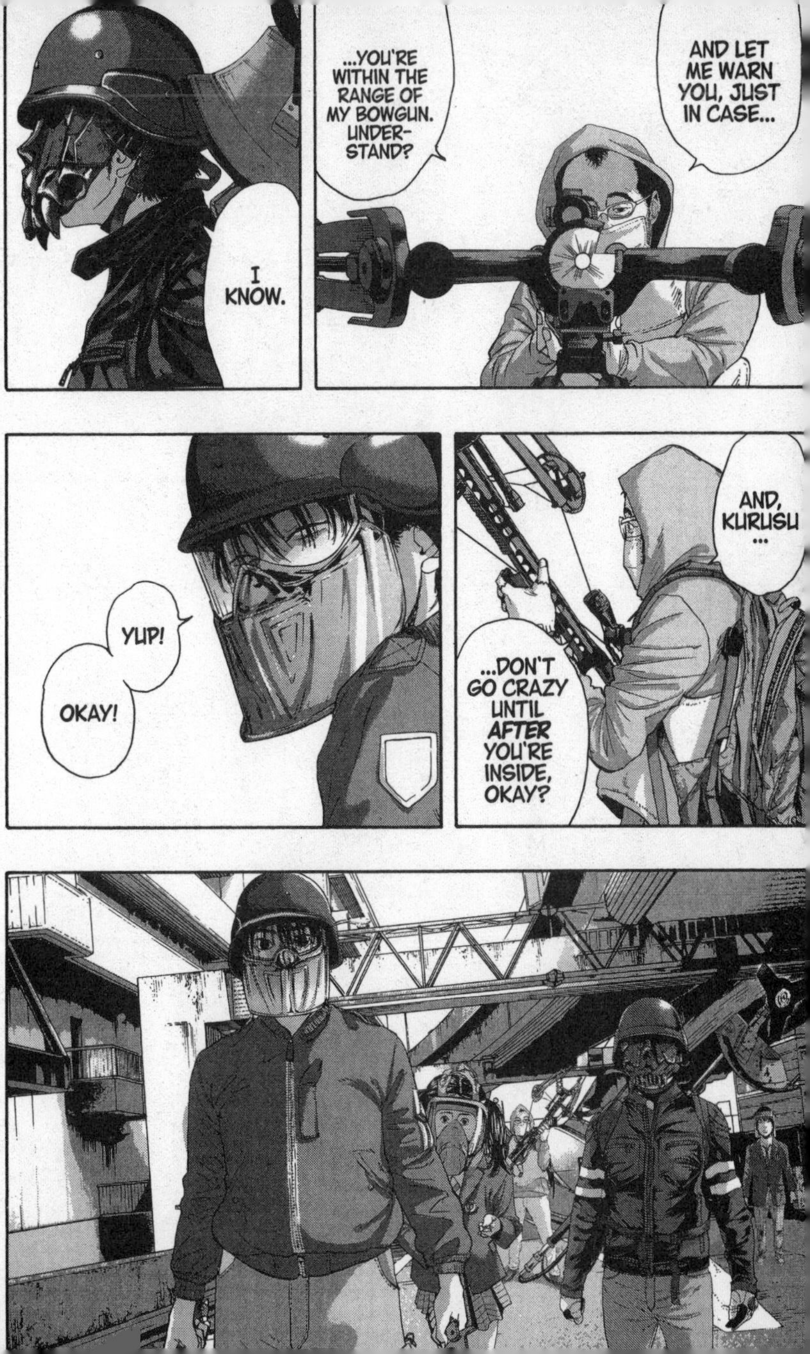
AND LET ME WARN YOU, JUST IN CASE...
...YOU'RE WITHIN THE RANGE OF MY BOWGUN. UNDER-STAND?
I KNOW.
AND, KURUSU...
...DON'T GO CRAZY UNTIL AFTER YOU'RE INSIDE, OKAY?
YUP!
OKAY!

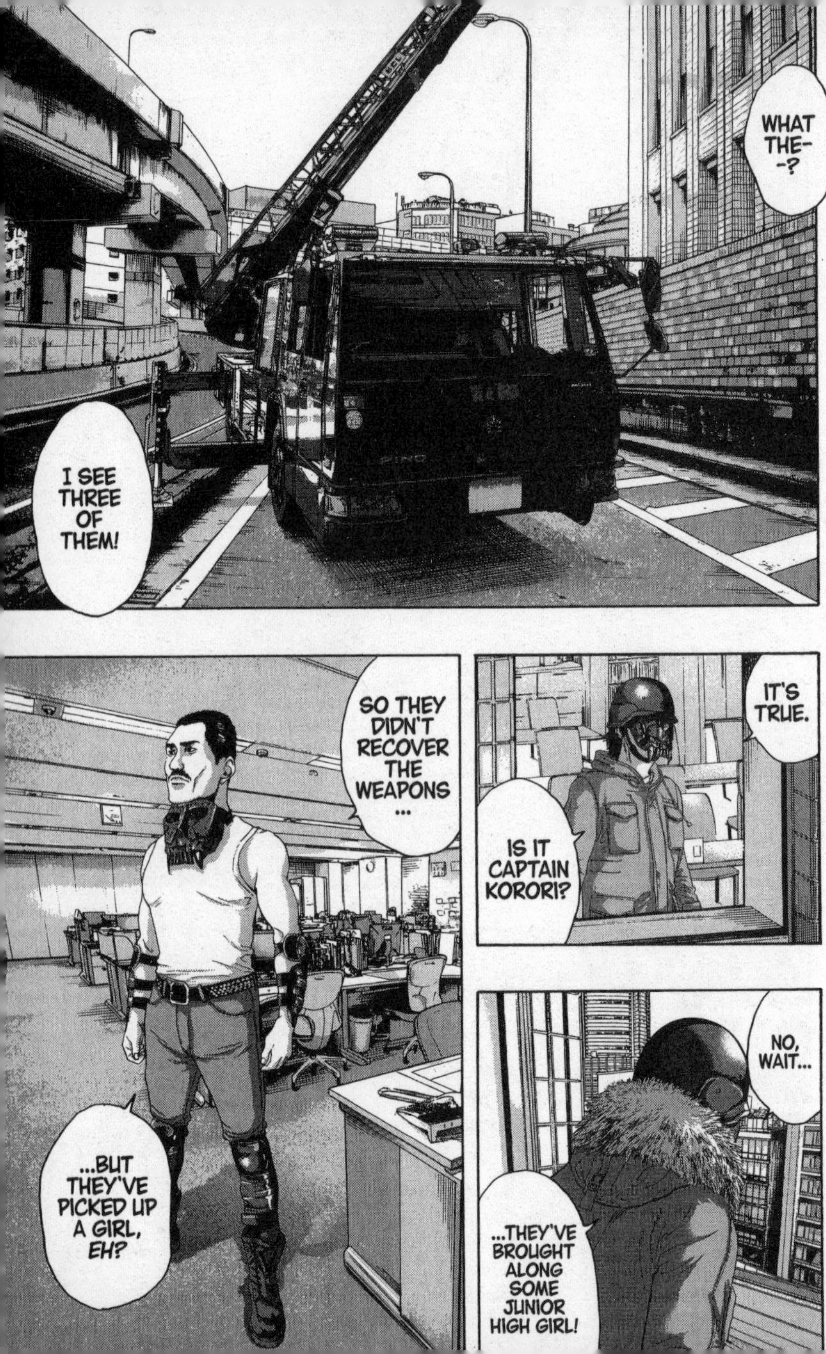
WHAT THE--?
I SEE THREE OF THEM!
IT'S TRUE.
IS IT CAPTAIN KORORI?
NO, WAIT...
...THEY'VE BROUGHT ALONG SOME JUNIOR HIGH GIRL!
SO THEY DIDN'T RECOVER THE WEAPONS...
...BUT THEY'VE PICKED UP A GIRL, EH?

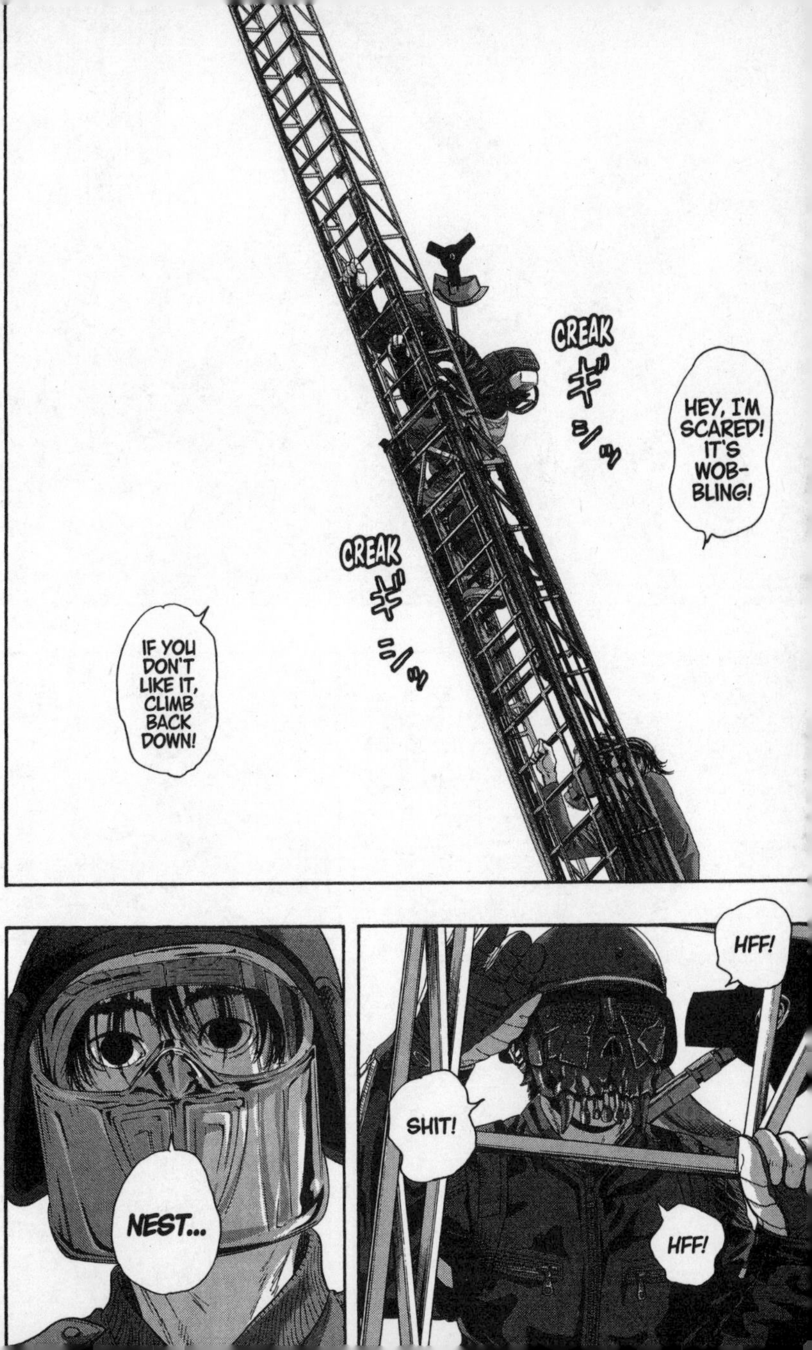
HEY, I'M SCARED! IT'S WOB-BLING!
CREAK
ギシッ
CREAK
ギシッ
IF YOU DON'T LIKE IT, CLIMB BACK DOWN!
HFF!
SHIT!
HFF!
NEST...

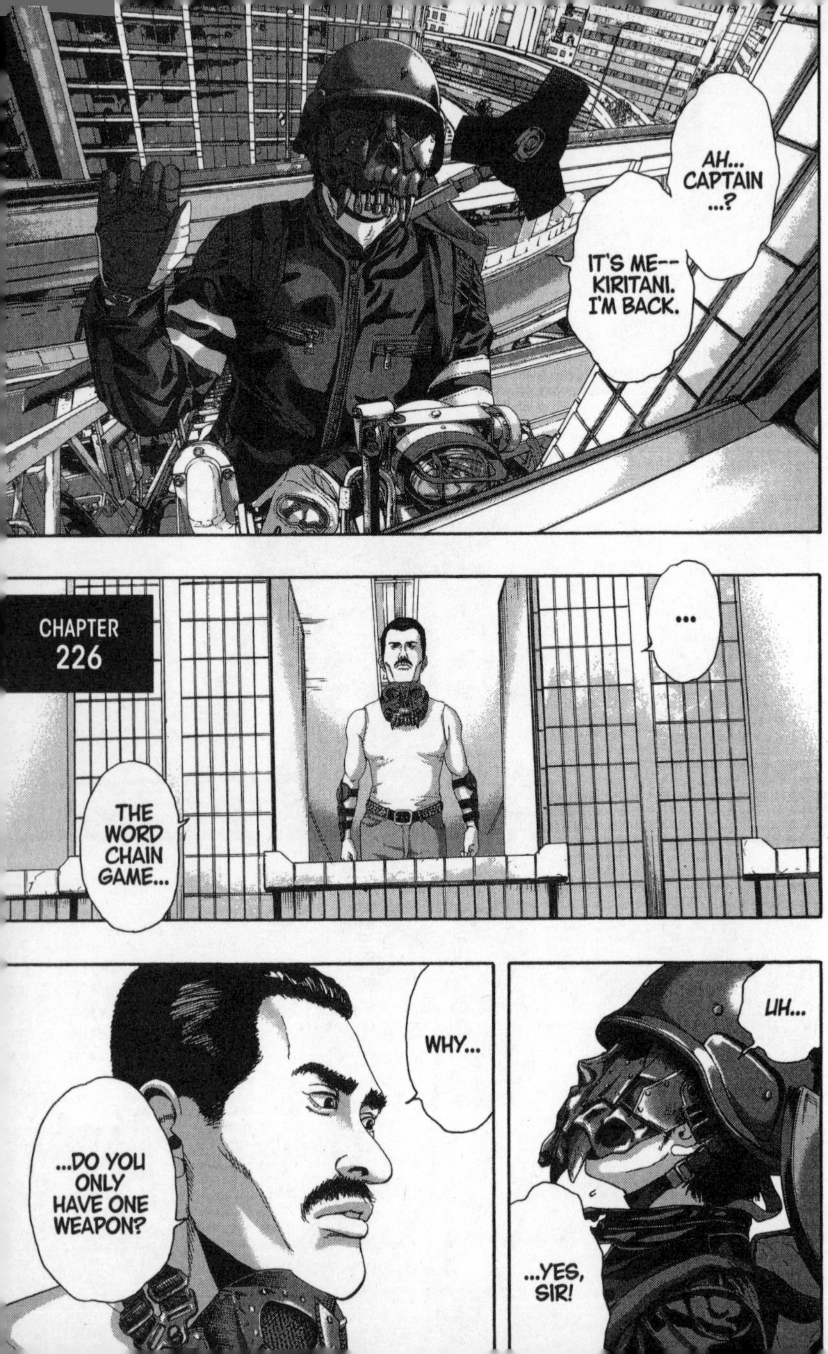
AH... CAPTAIN ...?
IT'S ME-- KIRITANI. I'M BACK.
...
THE WORD CHAIN GAME...
CHAPTER 226
UH...
...YES, SIR!
WHY...
...DO YOU ONLY HAVE ONE WEAPON?

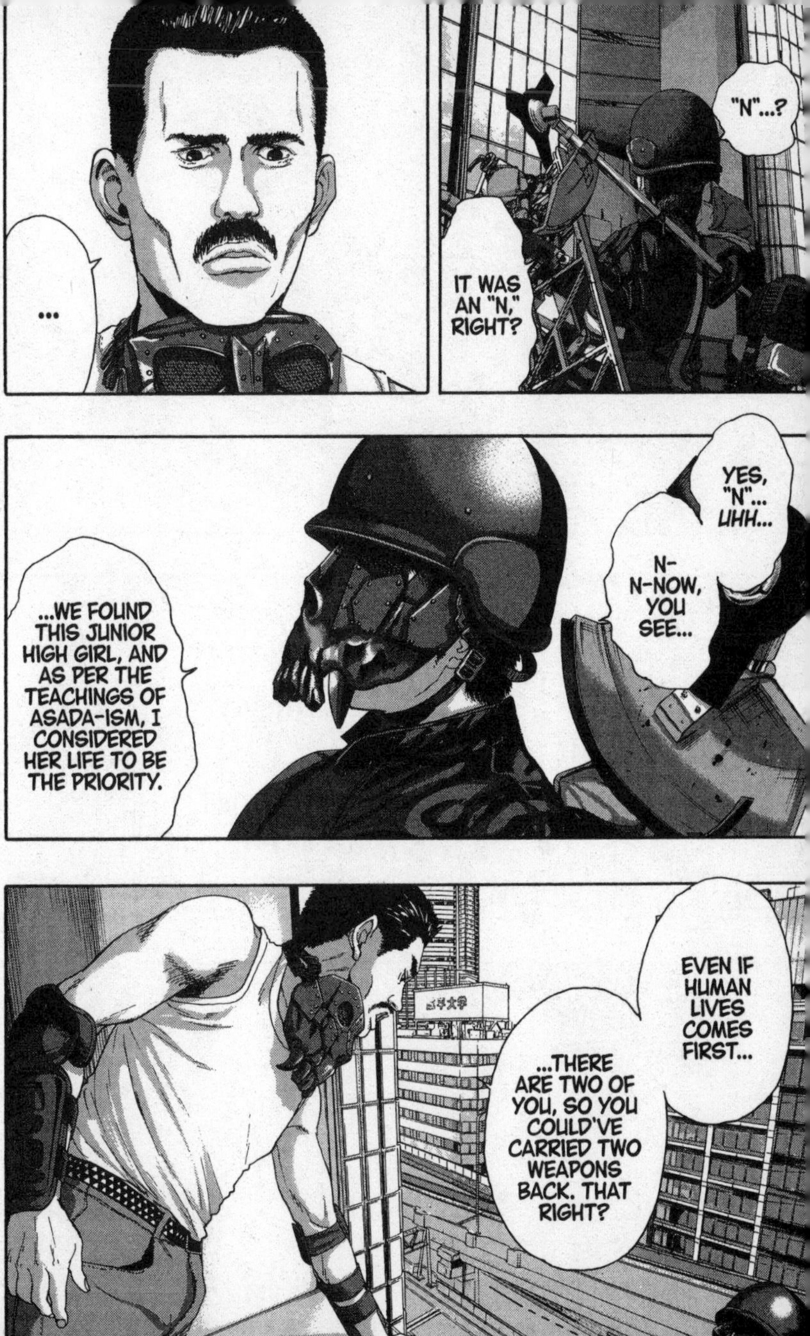
"N"...?
IT WAS AN "N," RIGHT?
...
YES, "N"... UHH...
N- N-NOW, YOU SEE...
...WE FOUND THIS JUNIOR HIGH GIRL, AND AS PER THE TEACHINGS OF ASADA-ISM, I CONSIDERED HER LIFE TO BE THE PRIORITY.
EVEN IF HUMAN LIVES COMES FIRST...
...THERE ARE TWO OF YOU, SO YOU COULD'VE CARRIED TWO WEAPONS BACK. THAT RIGHT?

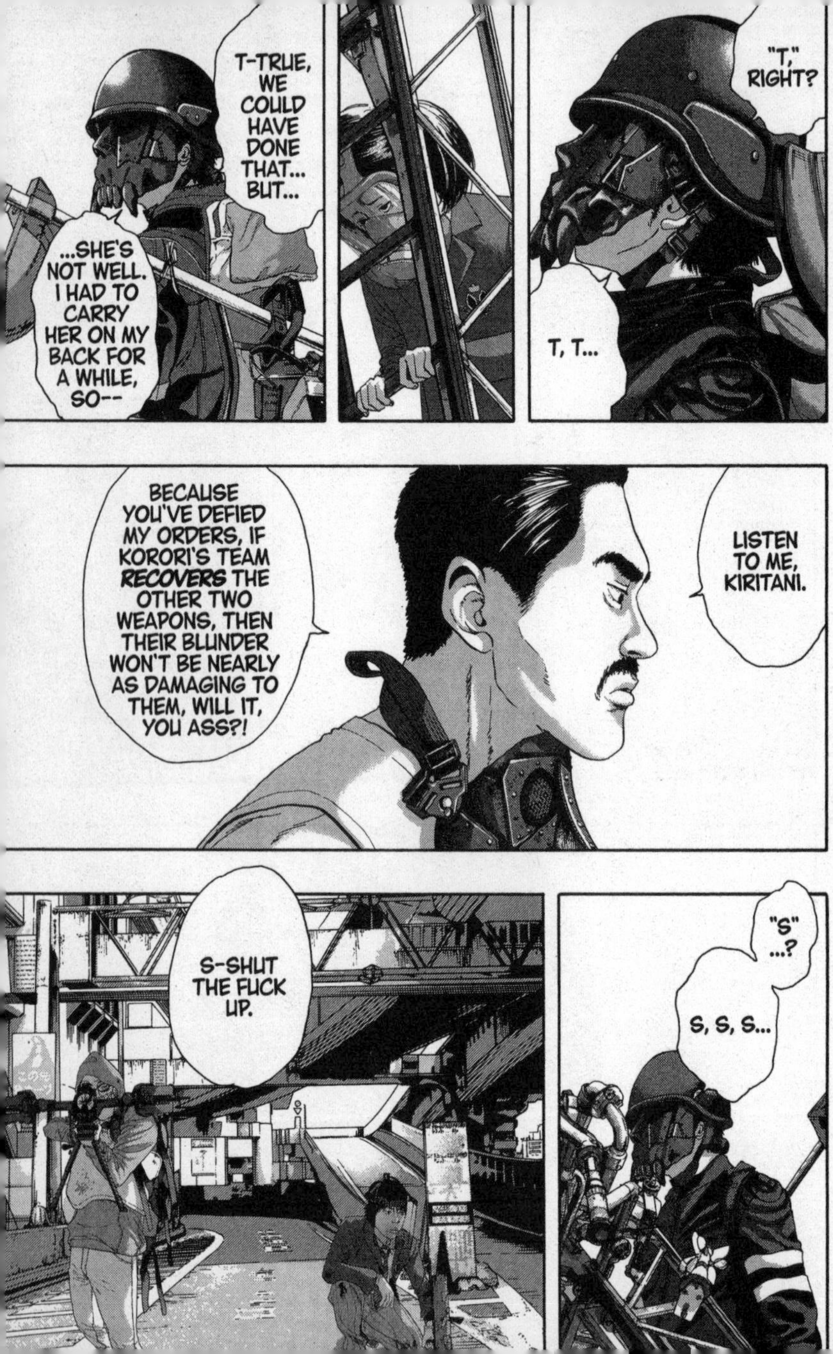
"T," RIGHT?
T, T...
T-TRUE, WE COULD HAVE DONE THAT... BUT...
...SHE'S NOT WELL. I HAD TO CARRY HER ON MY BACK FOR A WHILE, SO--
LISTEN TO ME, KIRITANI.
BECAUSE YOU'VE DEFIED MY ORDERS, IF KORORI'S TEAM *RECOVERS* THE OTHER TWO WEAPONS, THEN THEIR BLUNDER WON'T BE NEARLY AS DAMAGING TO THEM, WILL IT, YOU ASS?!
"S" ...?
S, S, S...
S-SHUT THE FUCK UP.

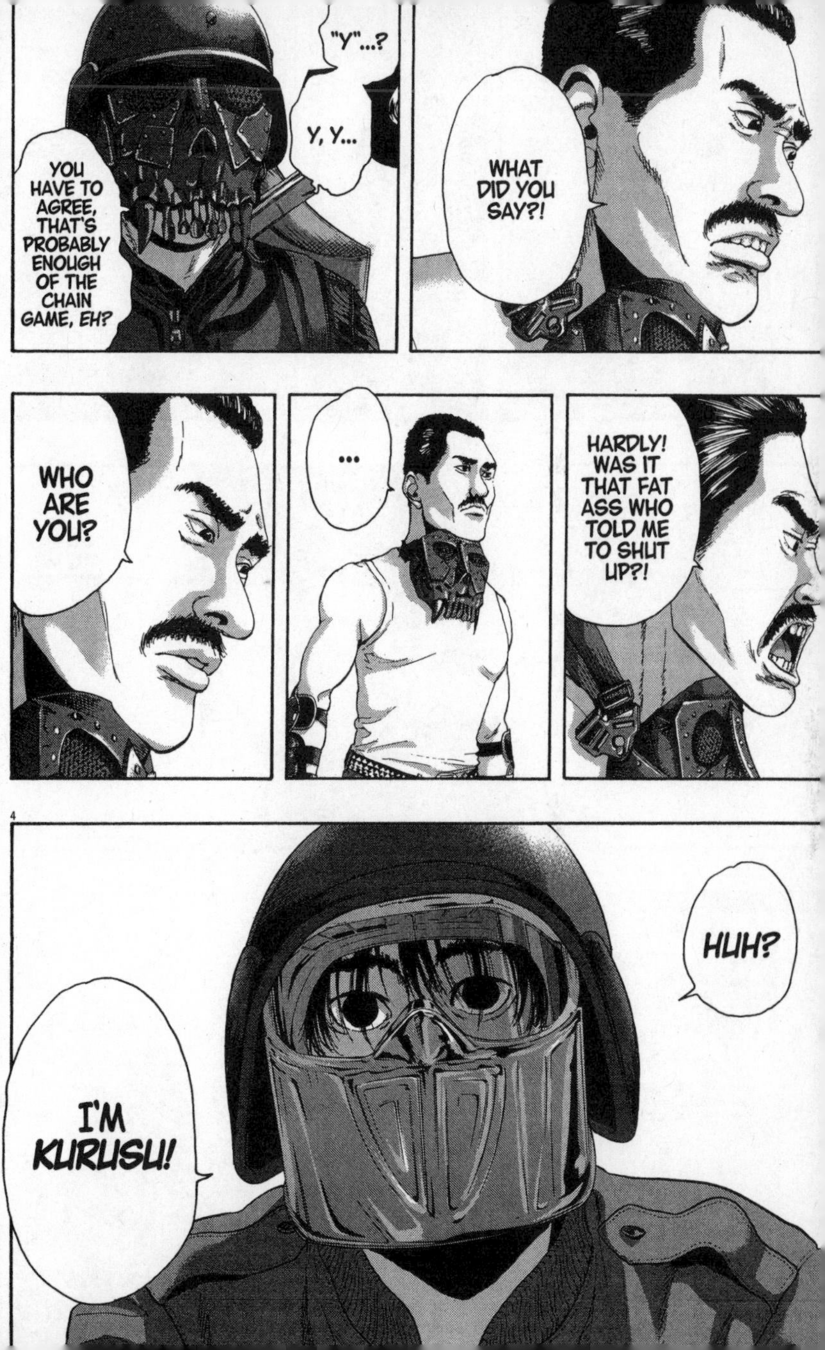
WHAT DID YOU SAY?!
"Y"...?
Y, Y...
YOU HAVE TO AGREE, THAT'S PROBABLY ENOUGH OF THE CHAIN GAME, EH?
HARDLY! WAS IT THAT FAT ASS WHO TOLD ME TO SHUT UP?!
...
WHO ARE YOU?
HUH?
I'M KURUSU!

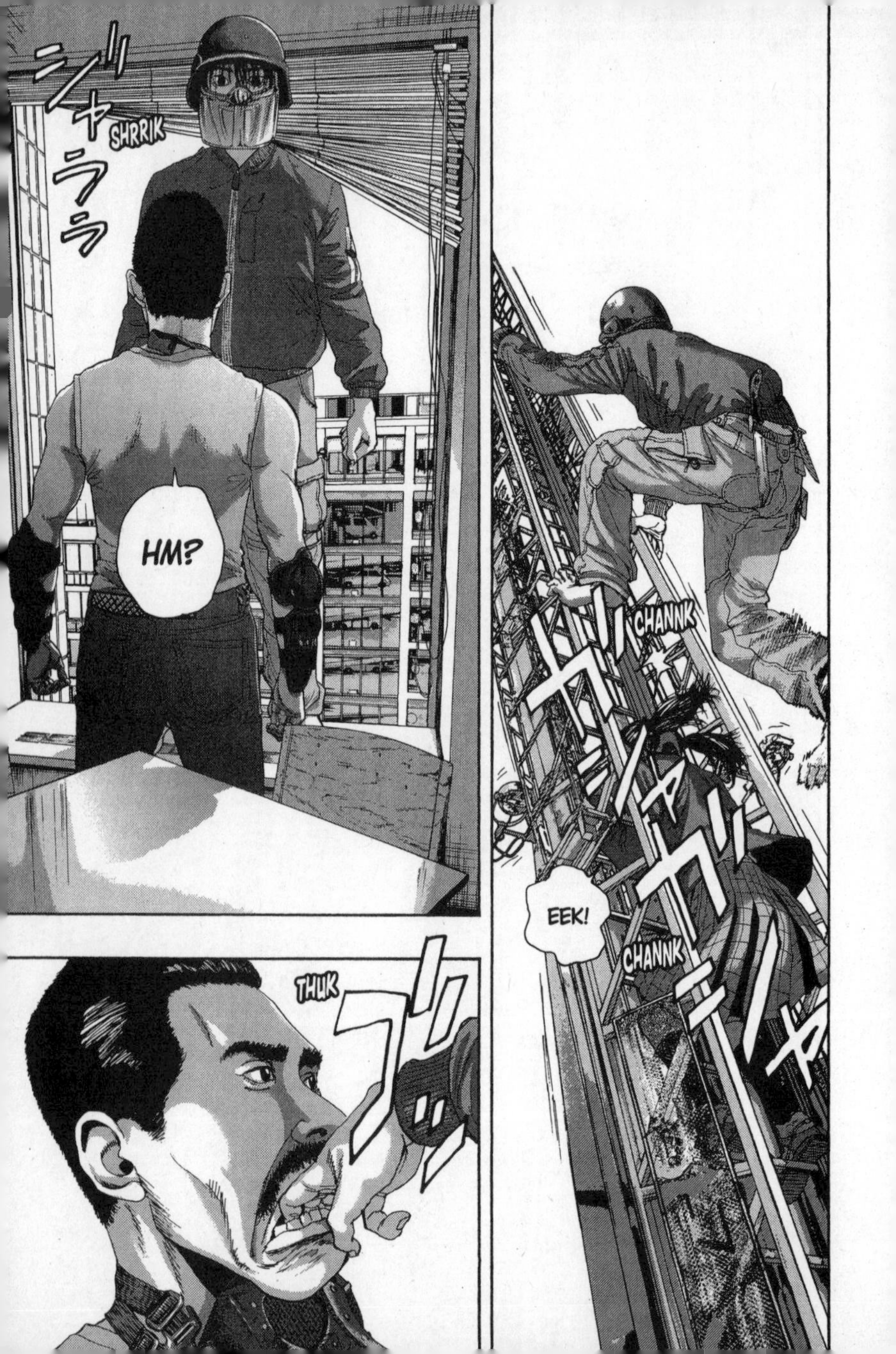
CHANNK
EEK!
CHANNK
SHRRIK
HM?
THUK

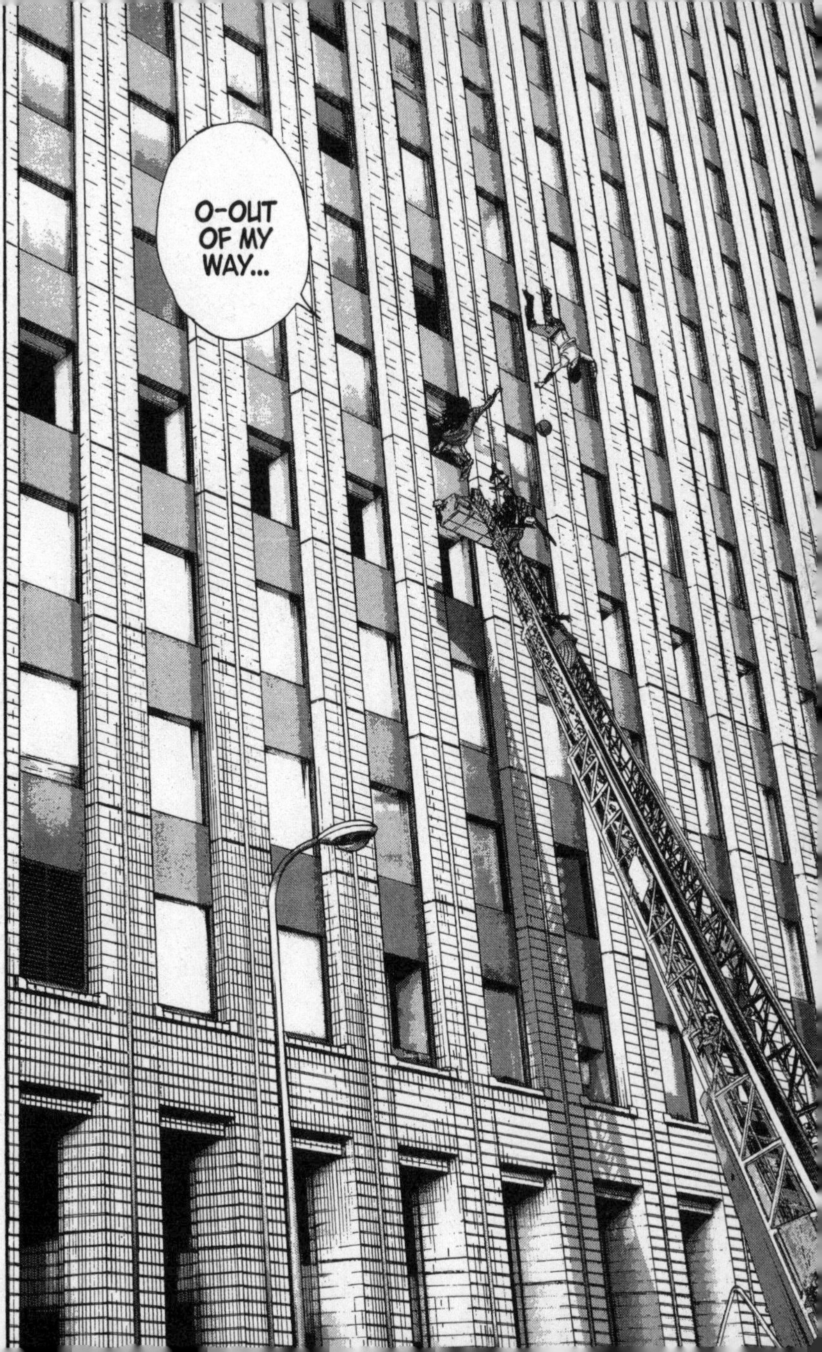
O-OUT OF MY WAY...

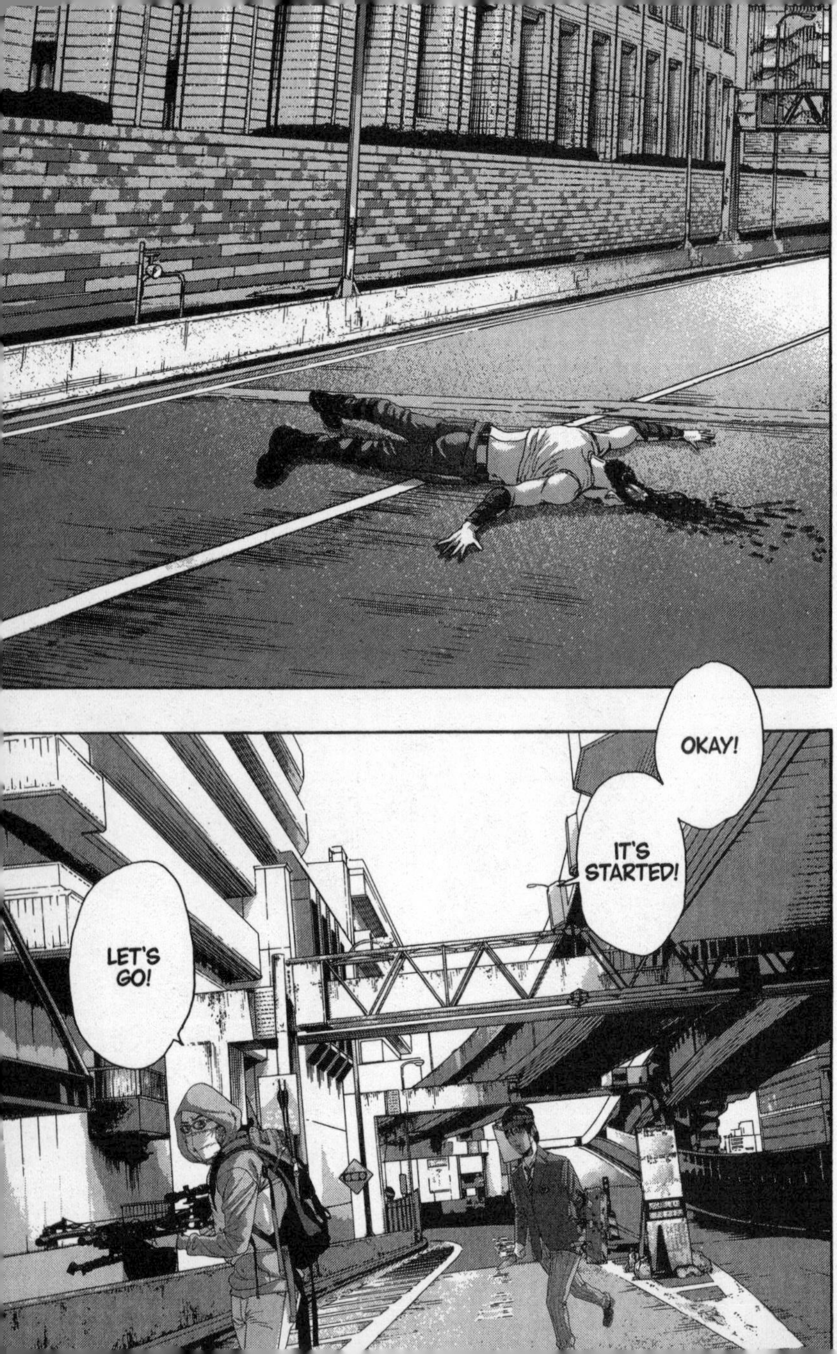
OKAY!
IT'S STARTED!
LET'S GO!

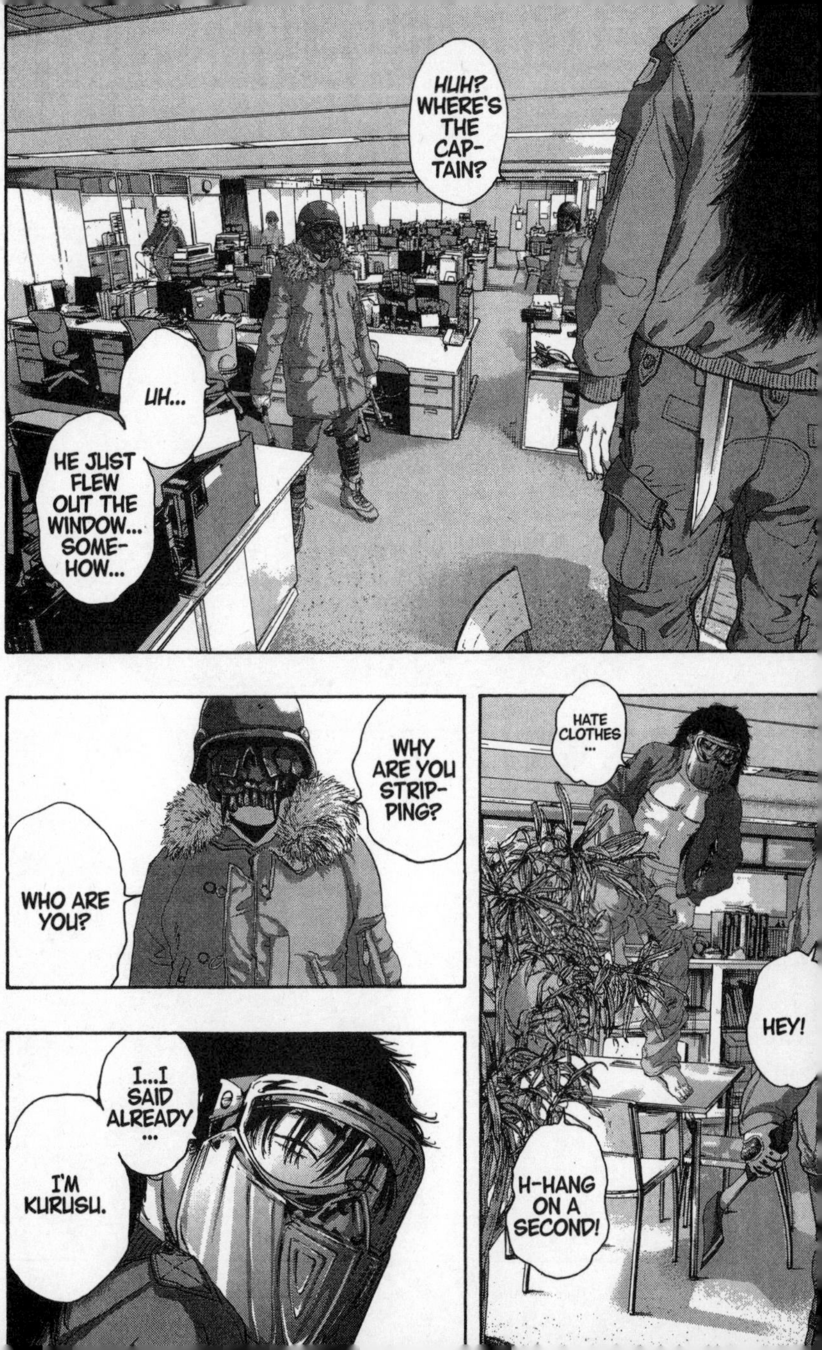
HUH? WHERE'S THE CAP-TAIN?
UH...
HE JUST FLEW OUT THE WINDOW... SOME-HOW...
HATE CLOTHES ...
HEY!
H-HANG ON A SECOND!
WHY ARE YOU STRIP-PING?
WHO ARE YOU?
I...I SAID ALREADY ...
I'M KURUSU.

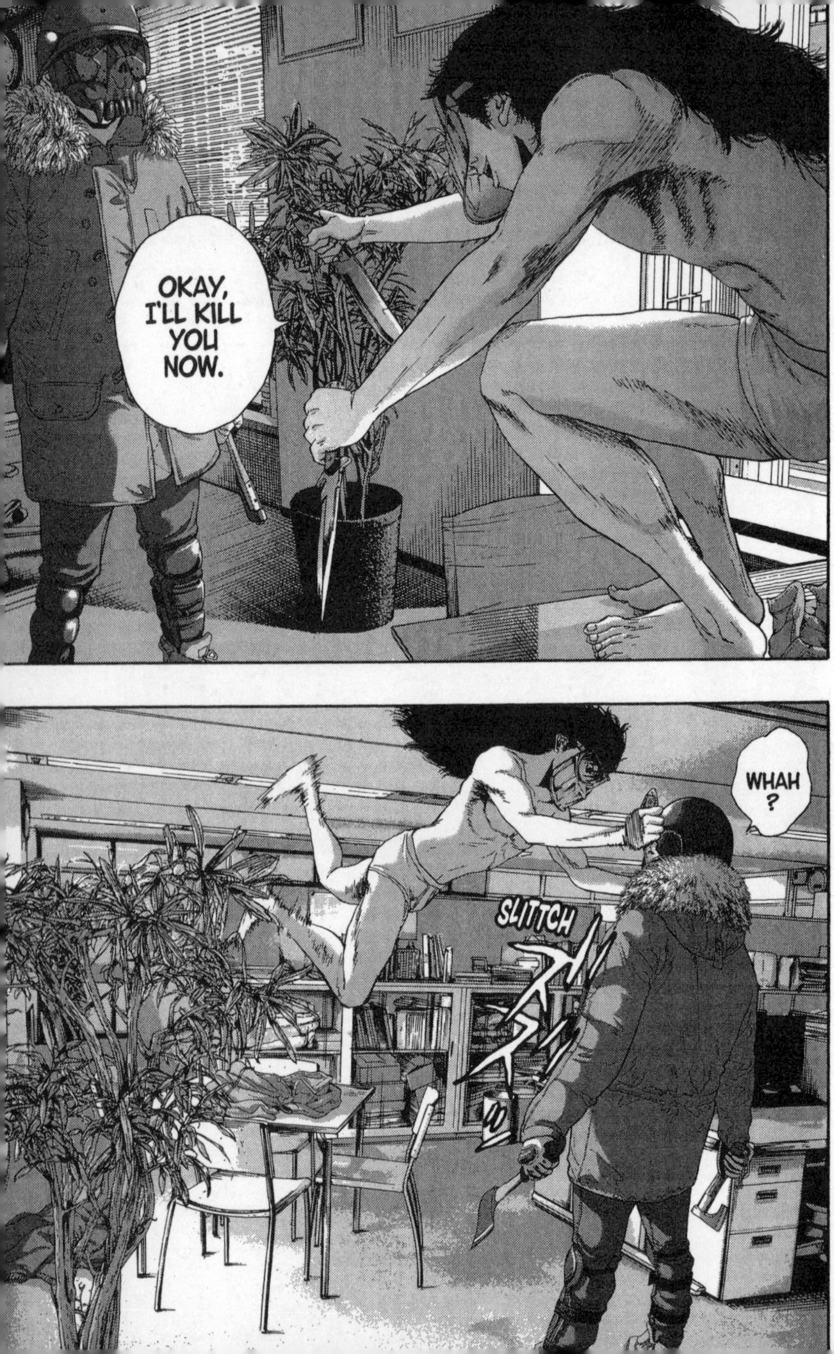
OKAY, I'LL KILL YOU NOW.
WHAH ?
SLITTCH

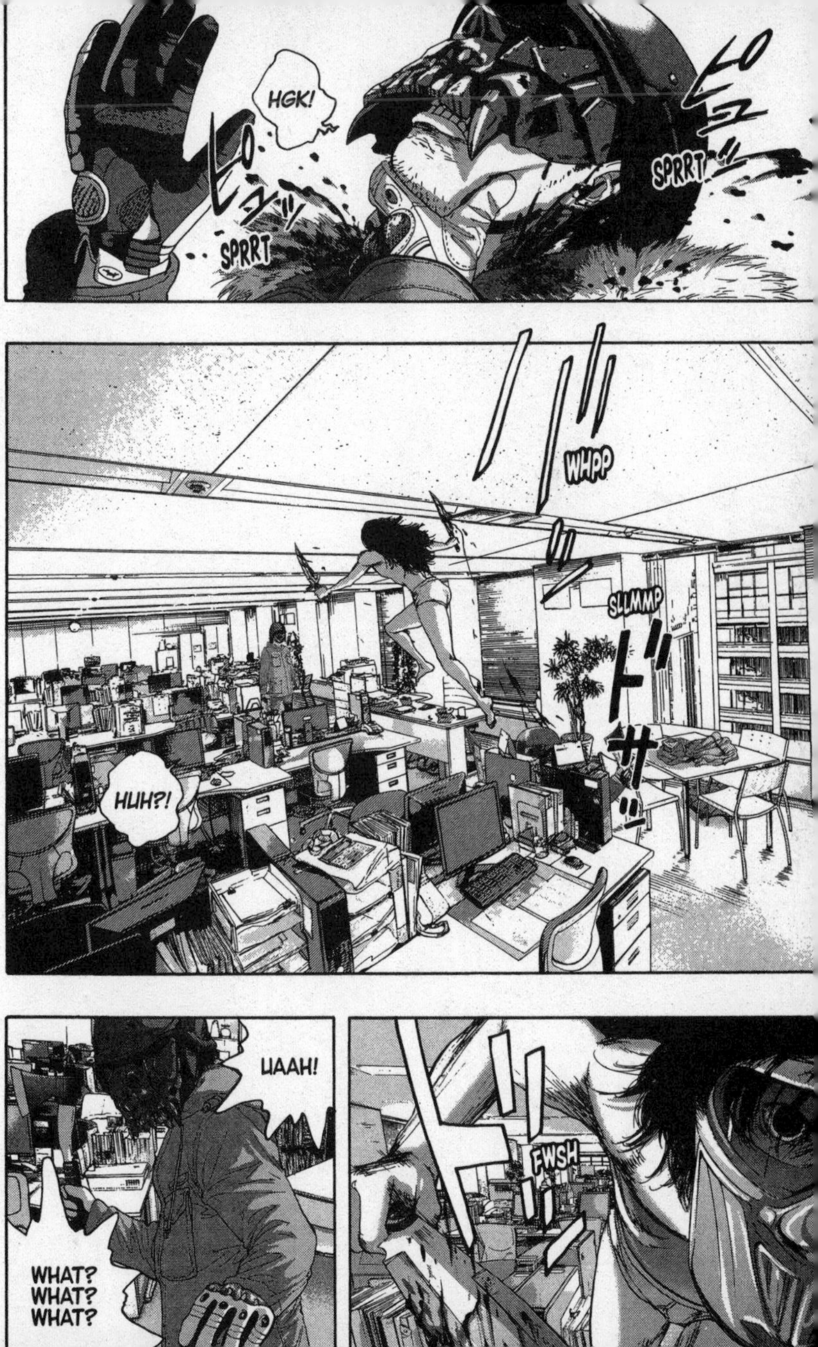
HGK!
SPRRT
SPRRT
WHPP
SLLMMP
HUH?!
FWSH
UAAH!
WHAT?
WHAT?
WHAT?

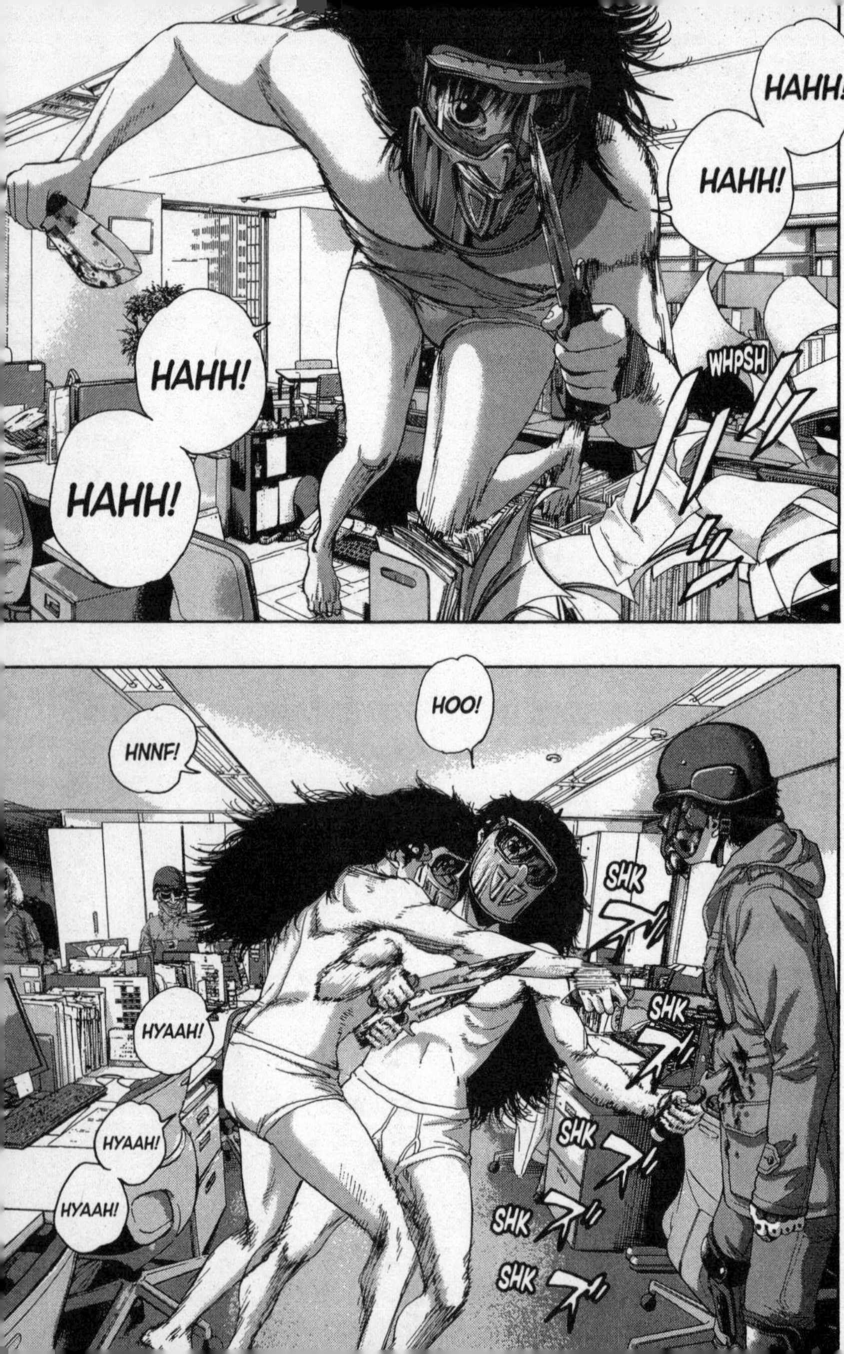
HAHH!
HAHH!
WHPSH
HAHH!
HAHH!
HOO!
HNNF!
SHK
SHK
HYAAH!
SHK
HYAAH!
SHK
HYAAH!
SHK

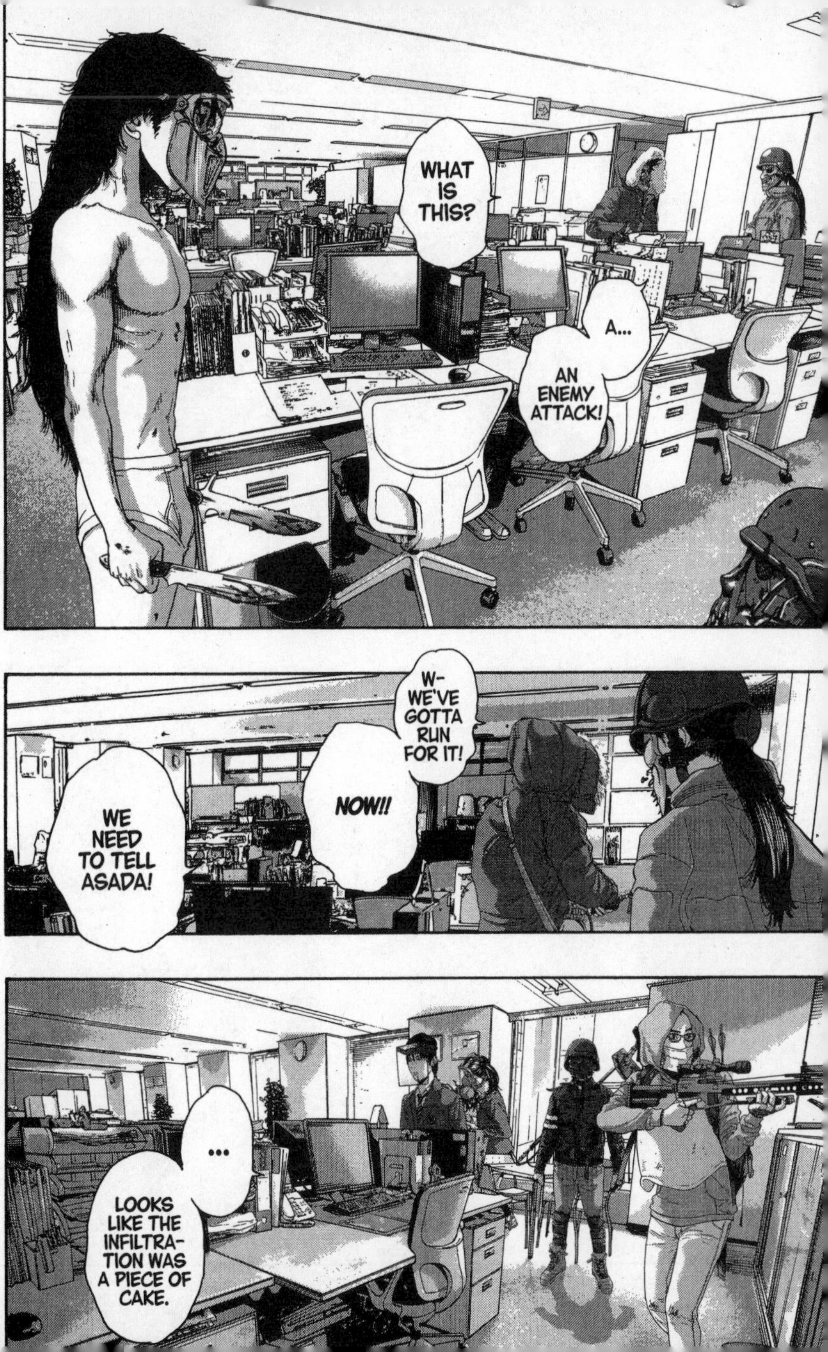
WHAT IS THIS?
A...
AN ENEMY ATTACK!
W- WE'VE GOTTA RUN FOR IT!
NOW!!
WE NEED TO TELL ASADA!
...
LOOKS LIKE THE INFILTRA-TION WAS A PIECE OF CAKE.

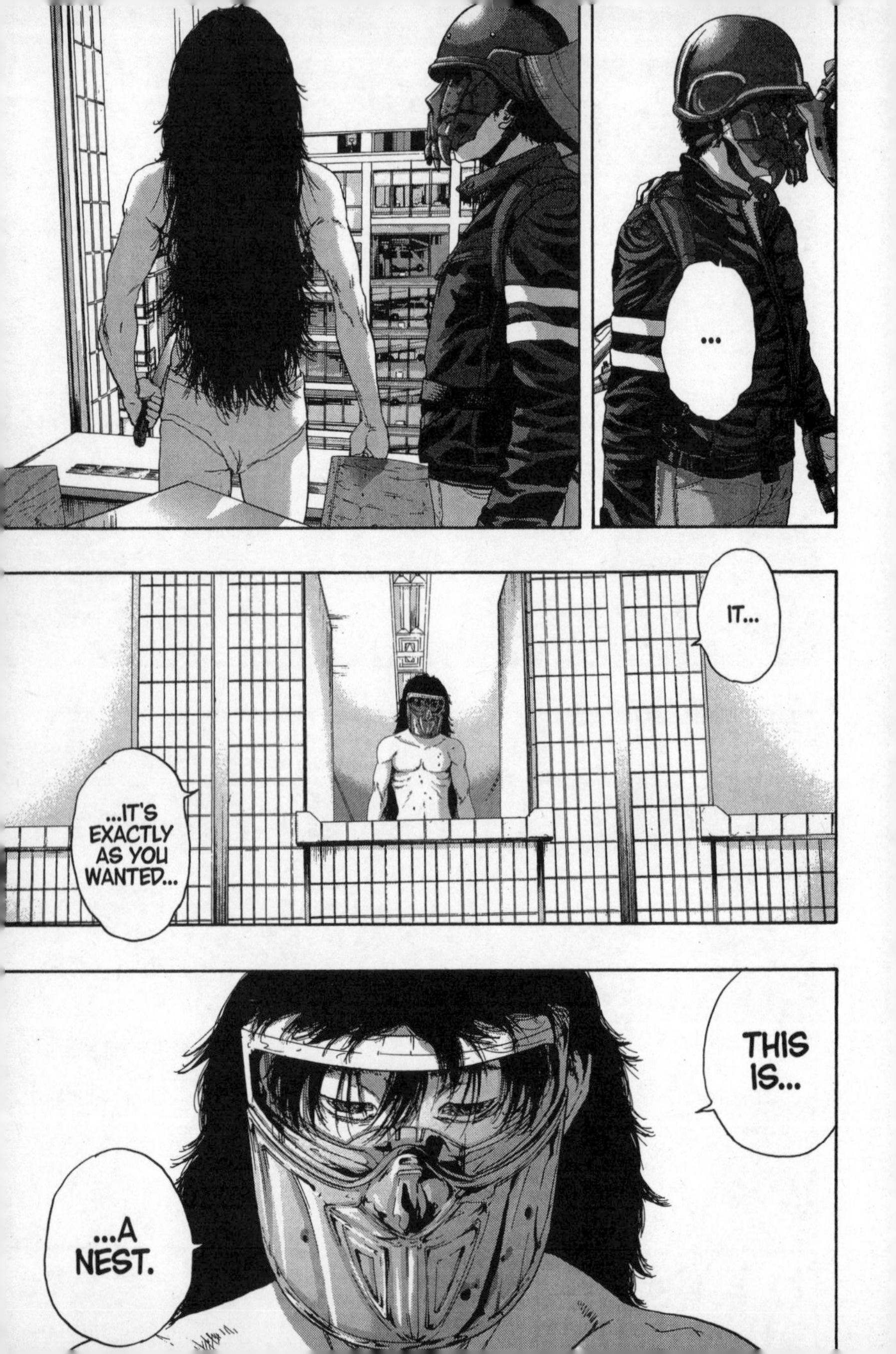
...
IT...
...IT'S EXACTLY AS YOU WANTED...
THIS IS...
...A NEST.

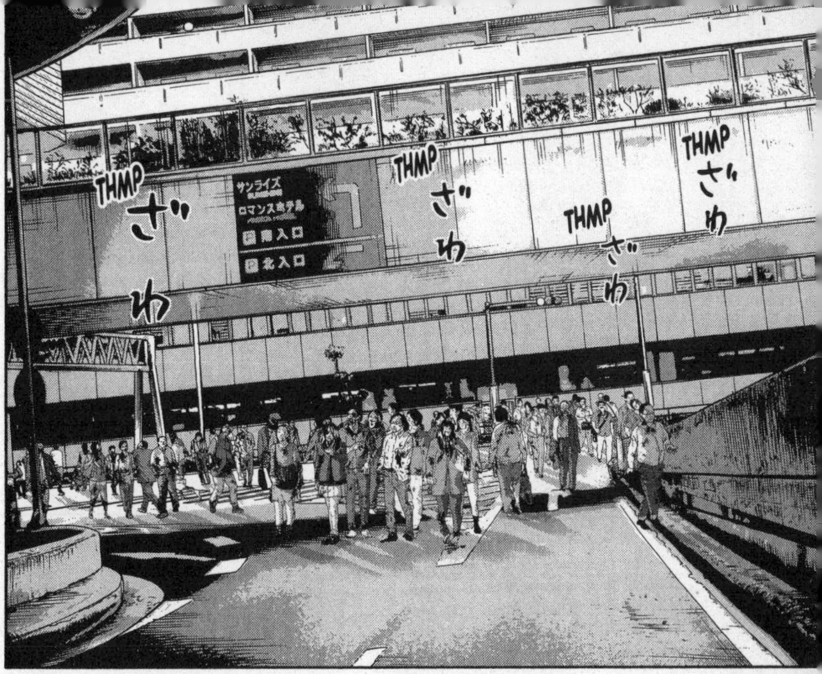
THMP
ざわ
THMP
ざわ
THMP
ざわ
サンライズ
南入口
北入口
THMP
ざわ
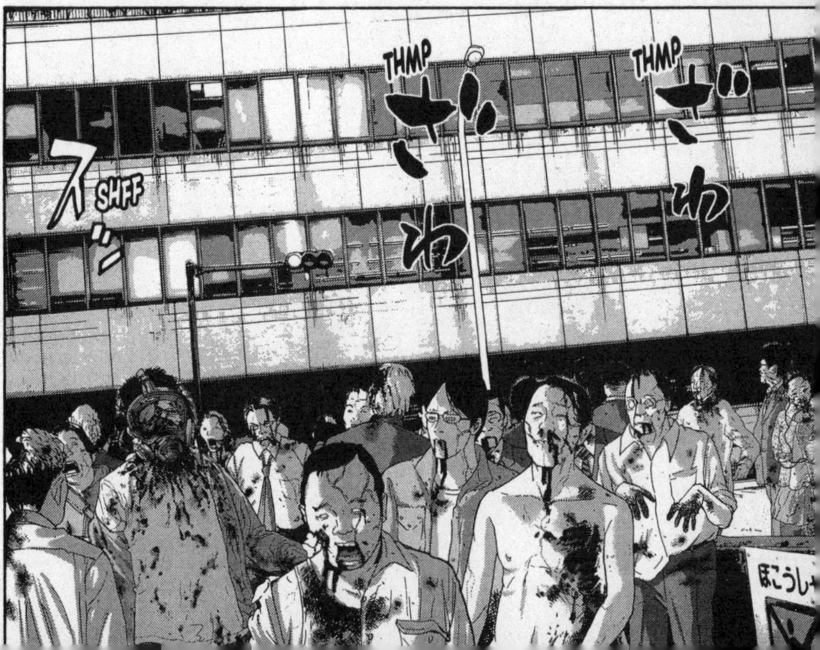
THMP
ざわ
THMP
ざわ
SHFF
ズ

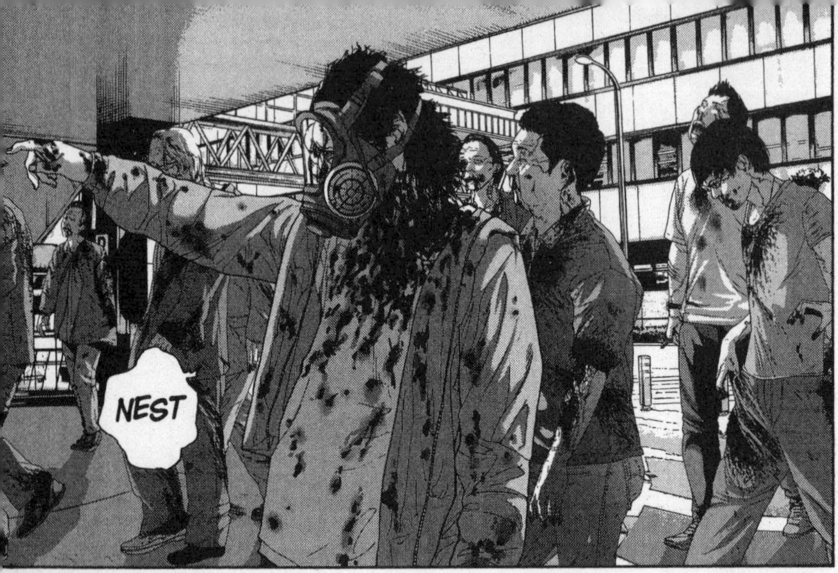
NEST

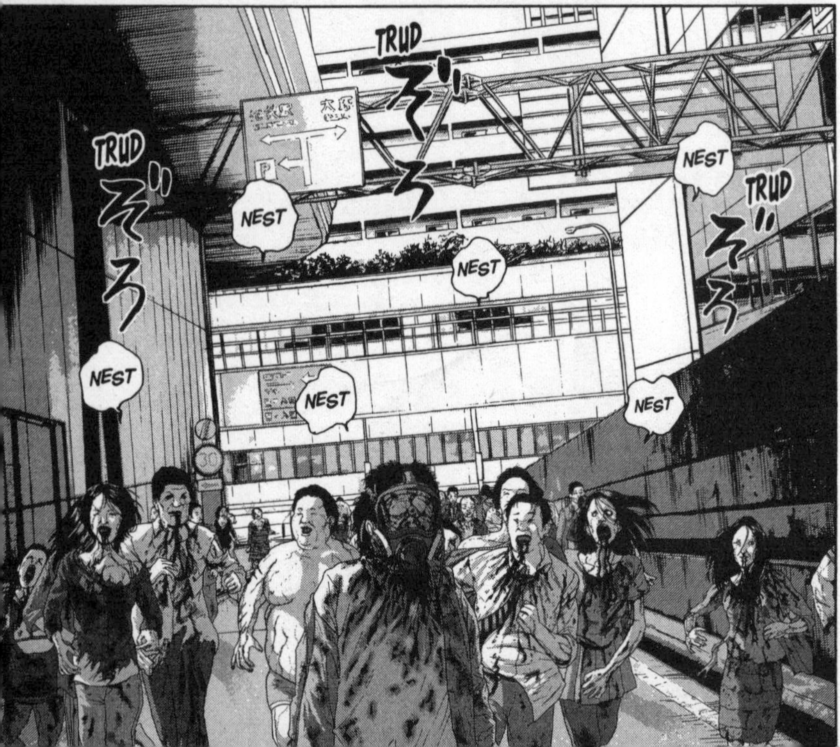
NEST
TRUD
ぞろ
TRUD
ぞろ
NEST
NEST
TRUD
ぞろ
NEST
NEST
NEST

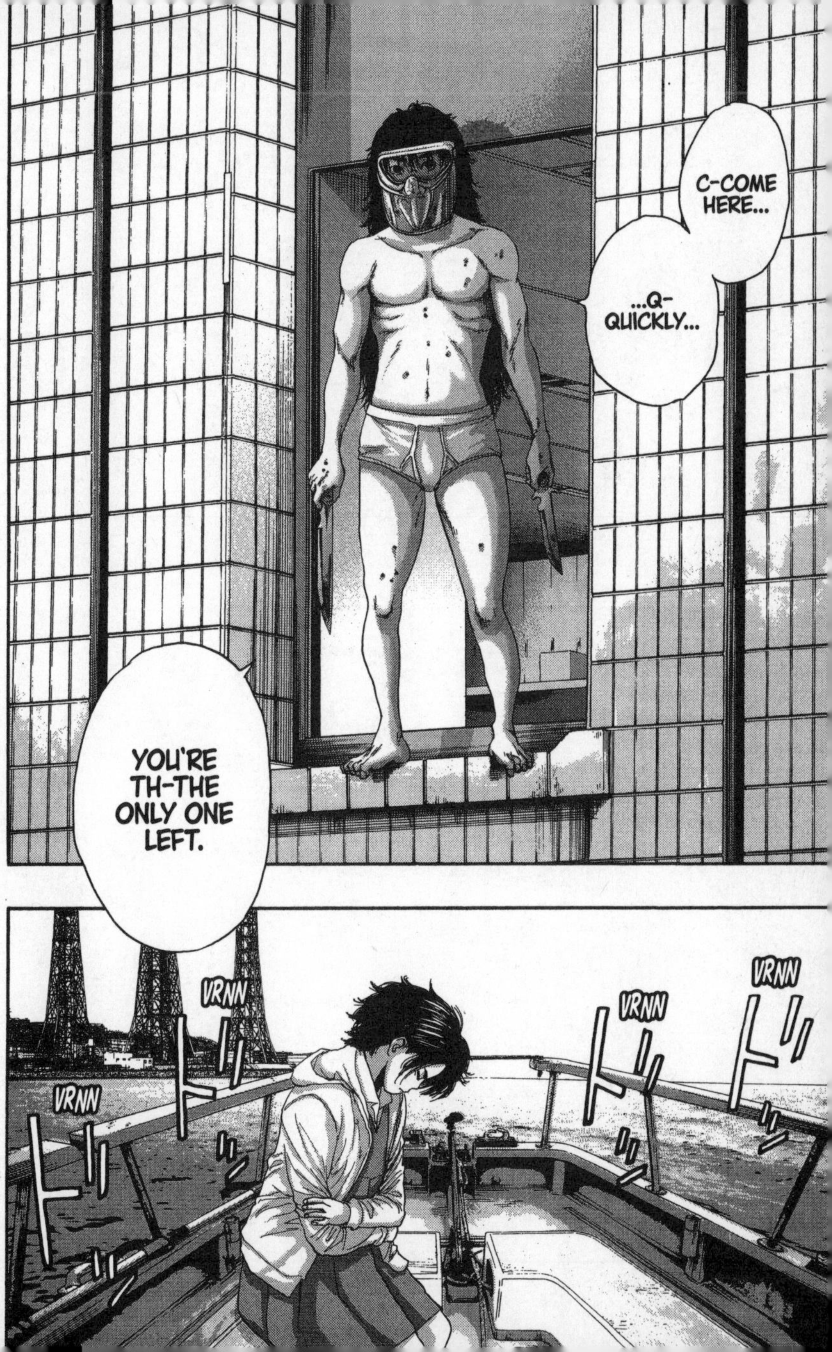
C-COME HERE...
...Q-QUICKLY...
YOU'RE TH-THE ONLY ONE LEFT.
VRNN
VRNN
VRNN
VRNN

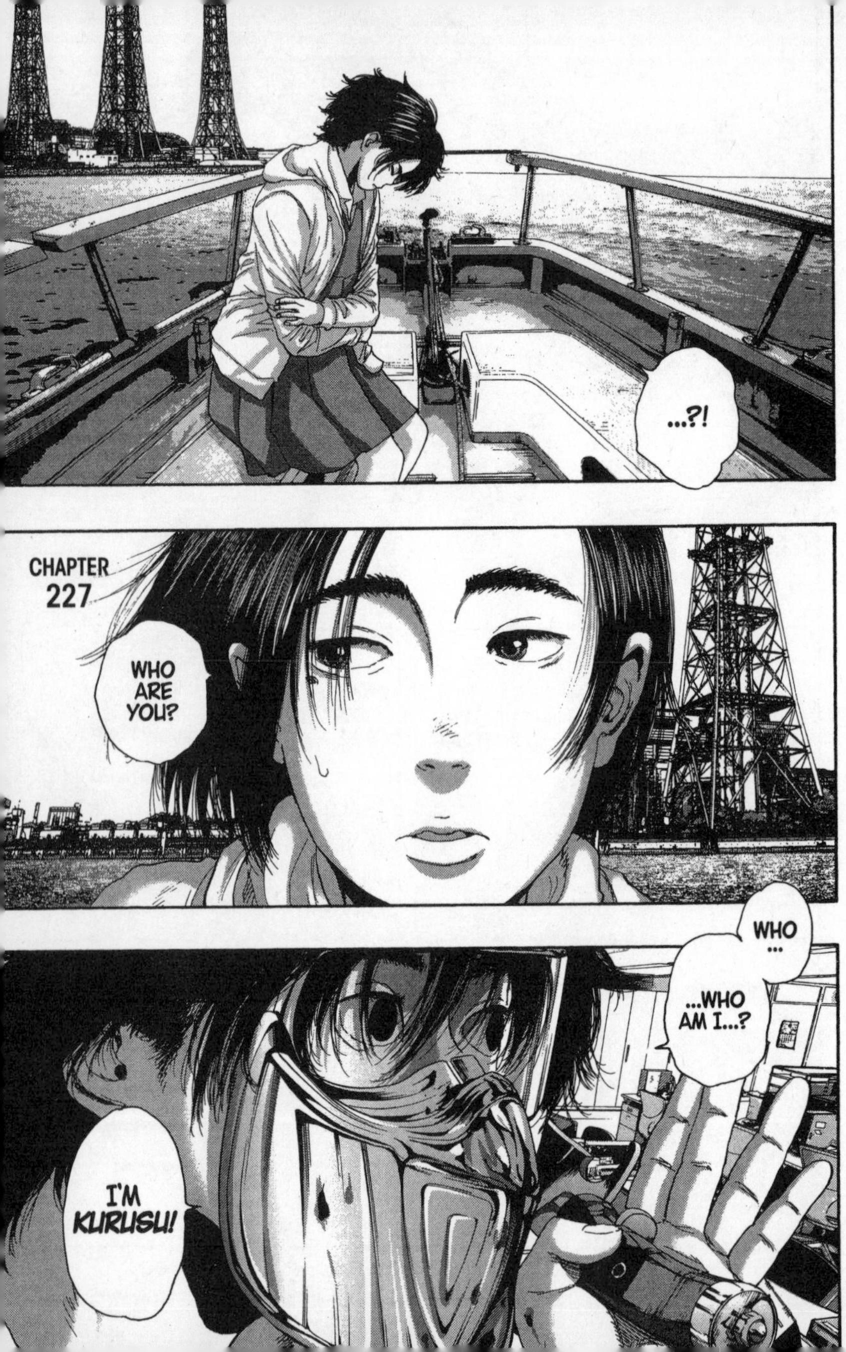
...?!
CHAPTER 227
WHO ARE YOU?
WHO ...
...WHO AM I...?
I'M KURUSU!

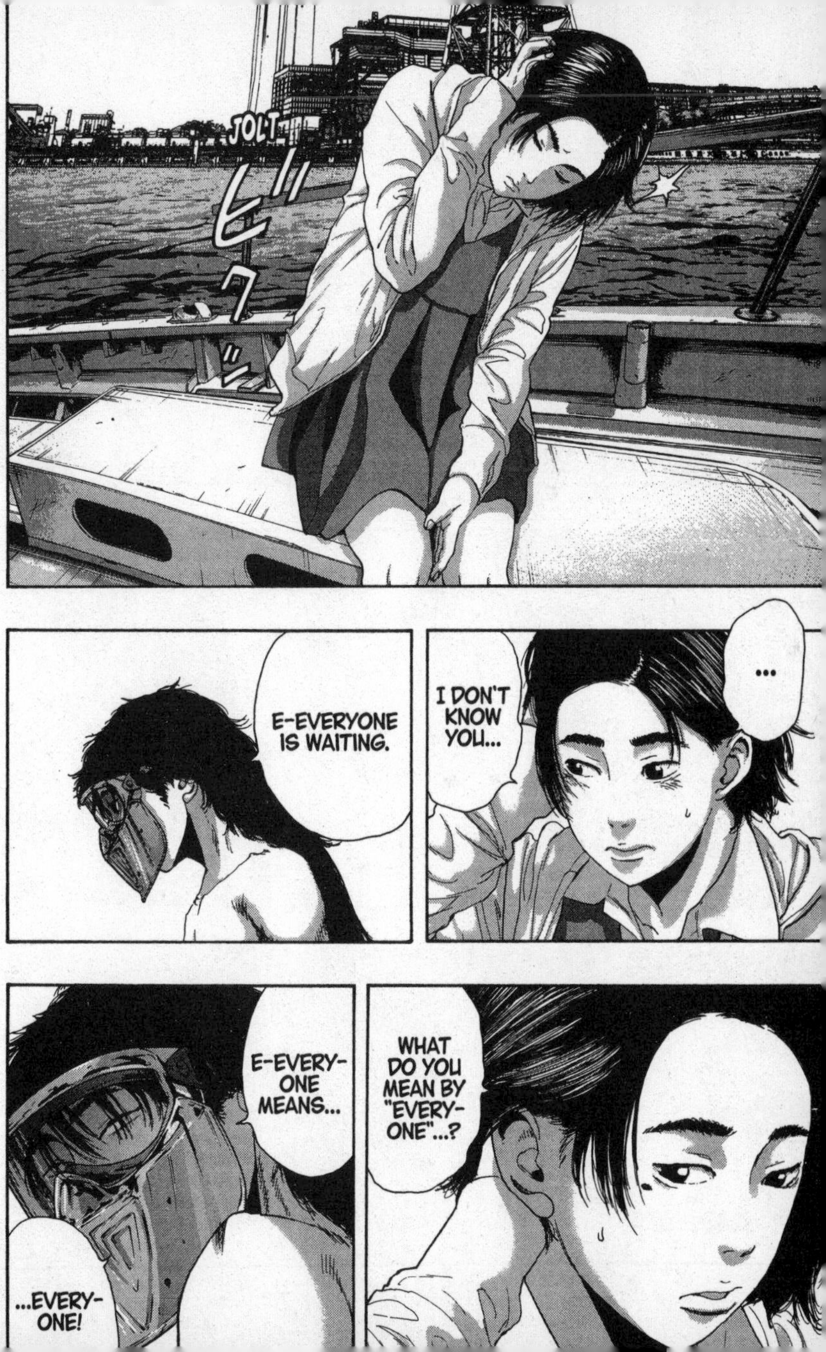
JOLT
ビクッ
...
I DON'T KNOW YOU...
E-EVERYONE IS WAITING.
WHAT DO YOU MEAN BY "EVERY-ONE"...?
E-EVERY-ONE MEANS...
...EVERY-ONE!

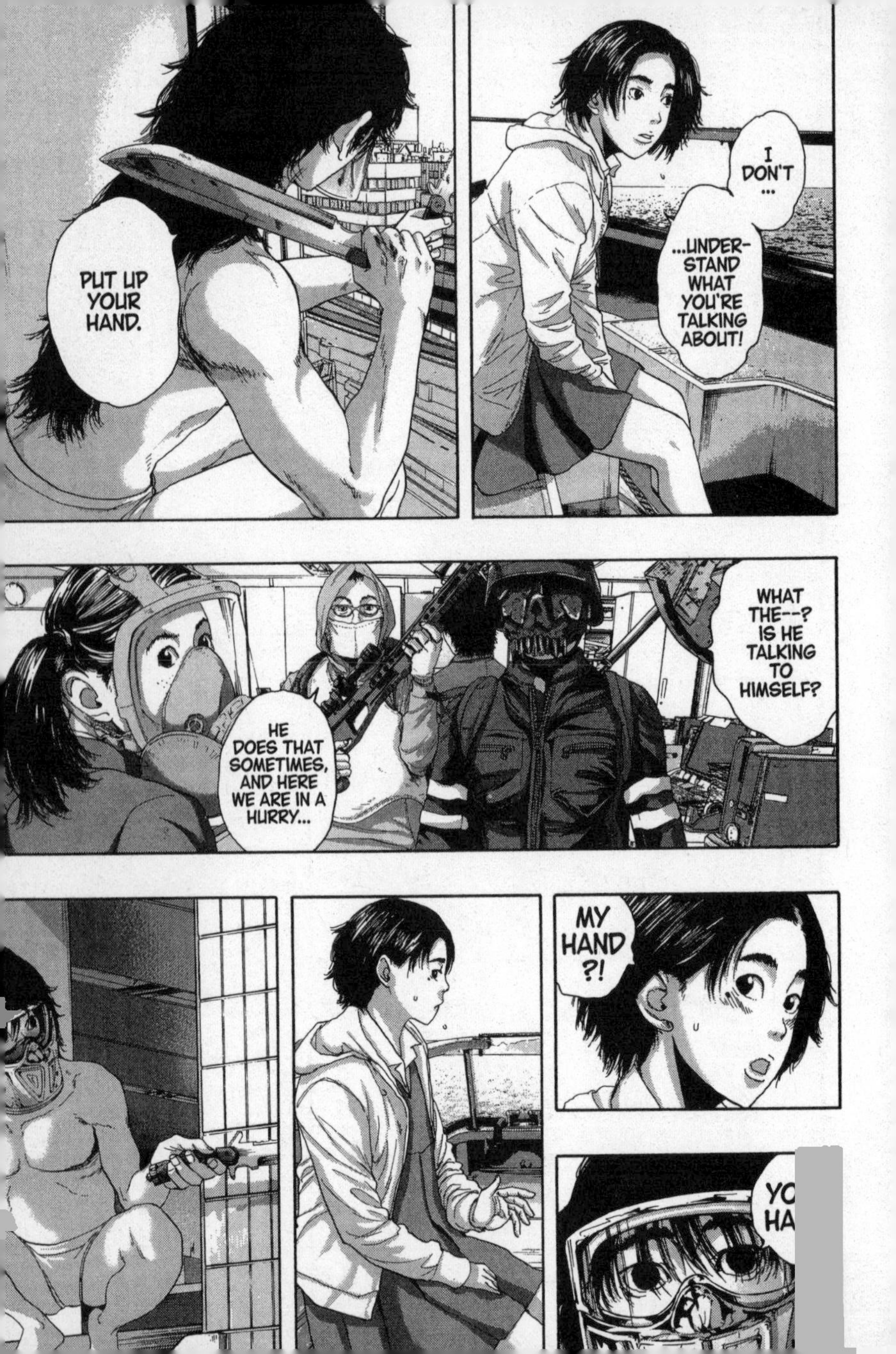
I DON'T ...
...UNDER-STAND WHAT YOU'RE TALKING ABOUT!
PUT UP YOUR HAND.
WHAT THE--? IS HE TALKING TO HIMSELF?
HE DOES THAT SOMETIMES, AND HERE WE ARE IN A HURRY...
MY HAND ?!
YO HA

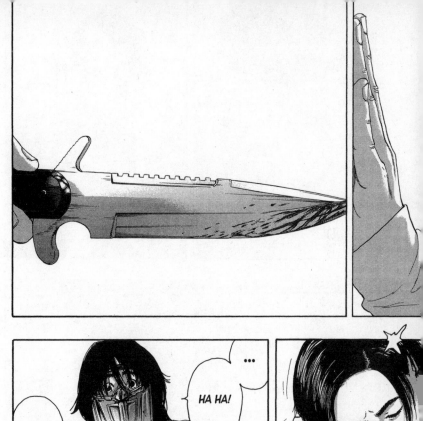

DID THAT HURT?

HA HA!

...

WHAT...

...DID YOU DO?

PANNG

OW?!

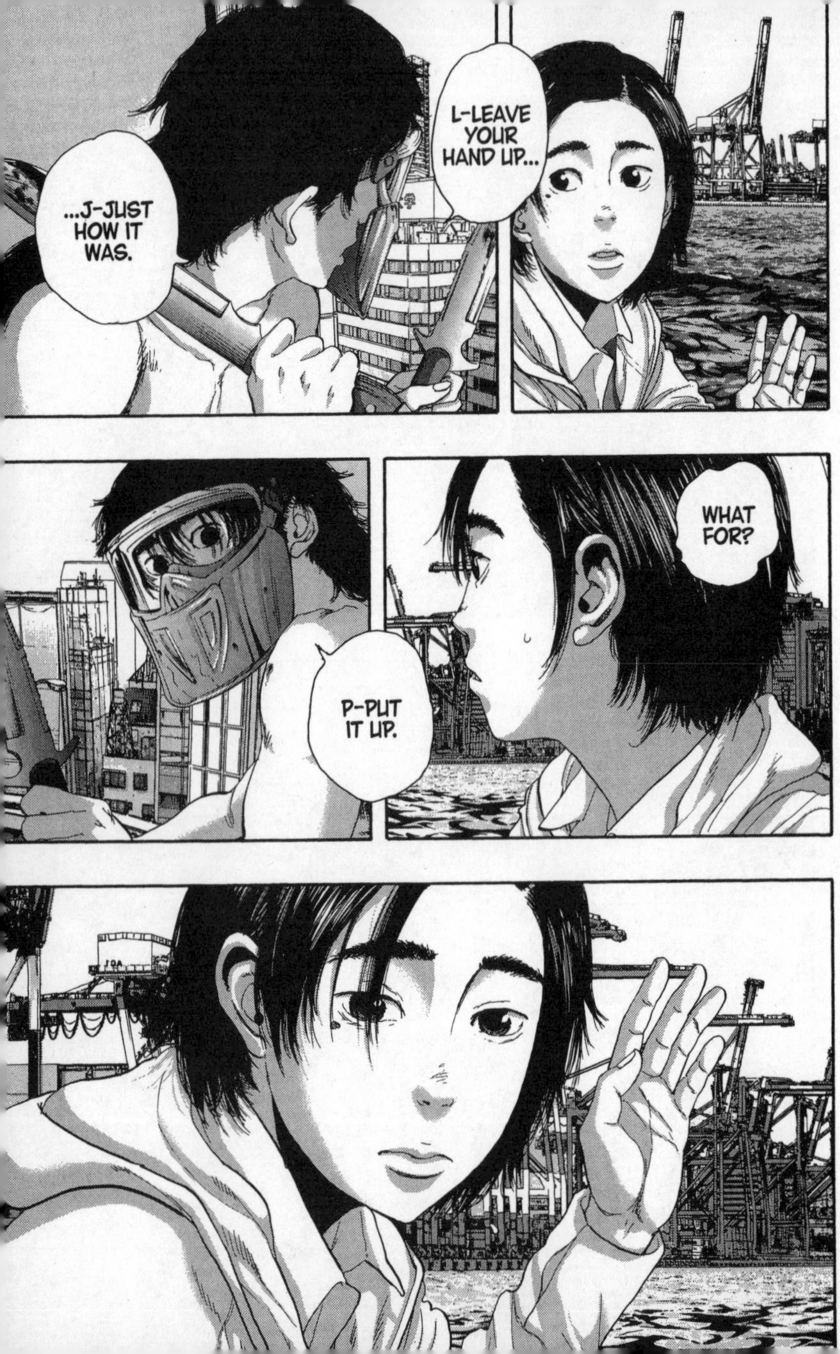
L-LEAVE YOUR HAND UP...
...J-JUST HOW IT WAS.
WHAT FOR?
P-PUT IT UP.

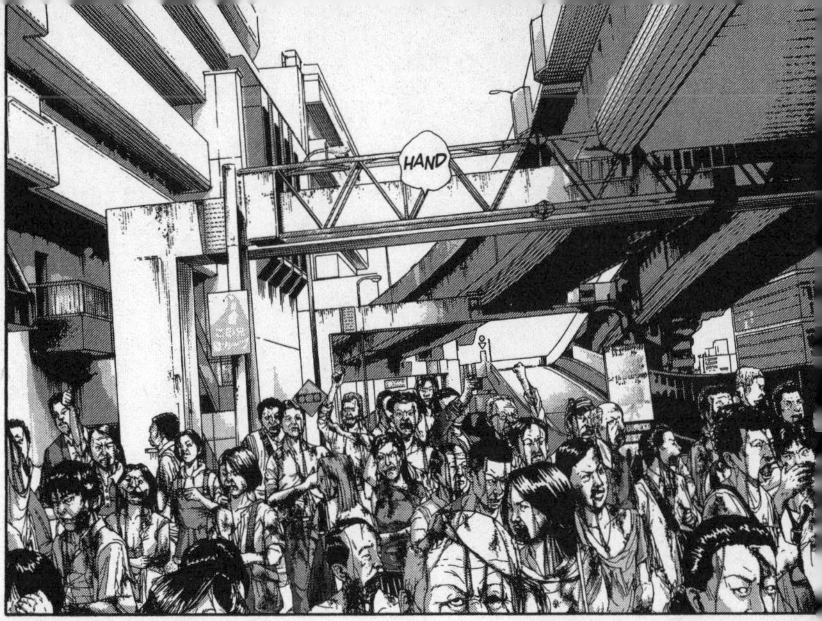
HAND

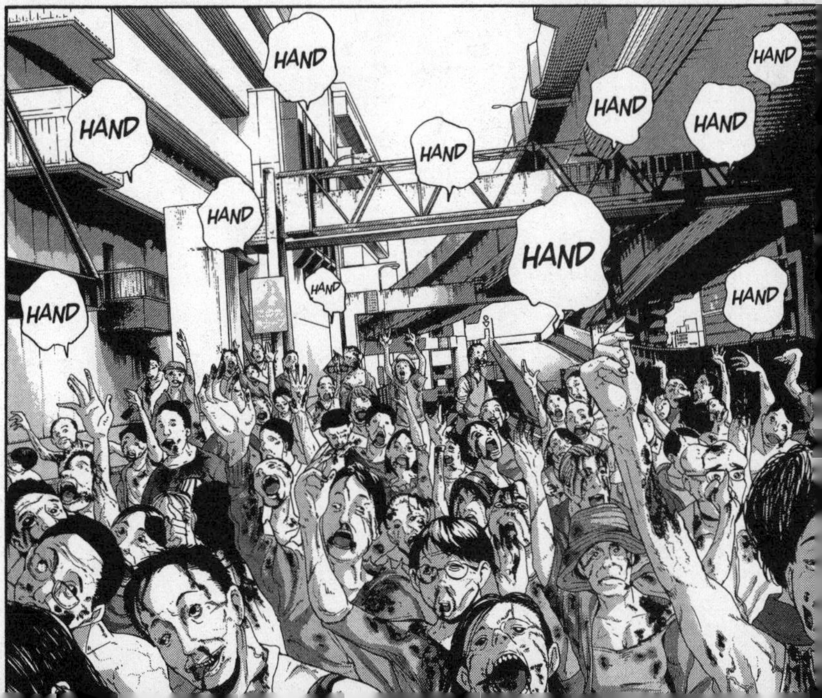
HAND
HAND
HAND
HAND
HAND
HAND
HAND
HAND
HAND
HAND
HAND

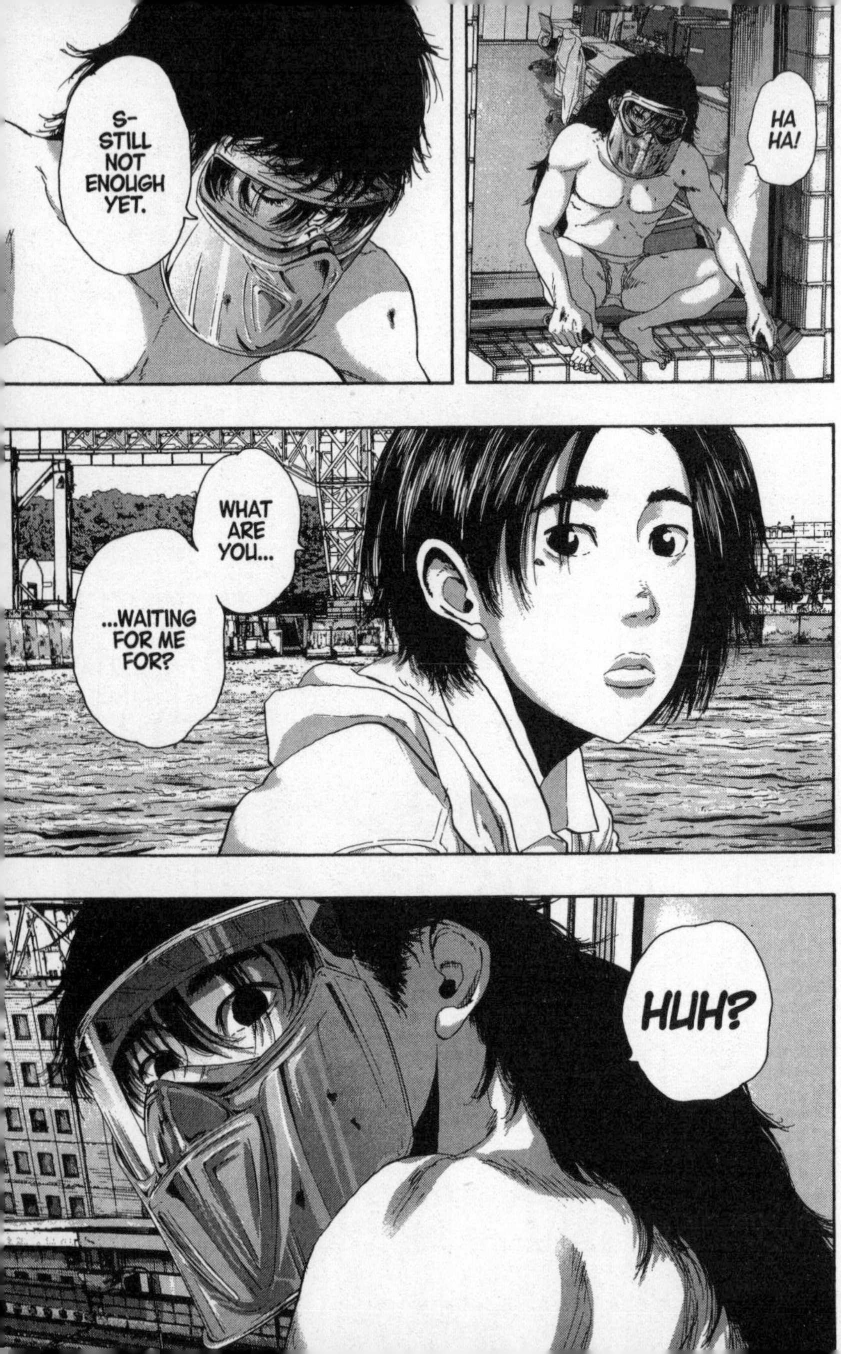
HA HA!
S- STILL NOT ENOUGH YET.
WHAT ARE YOU...
...WAITING FOR ME FOR?
HUH?

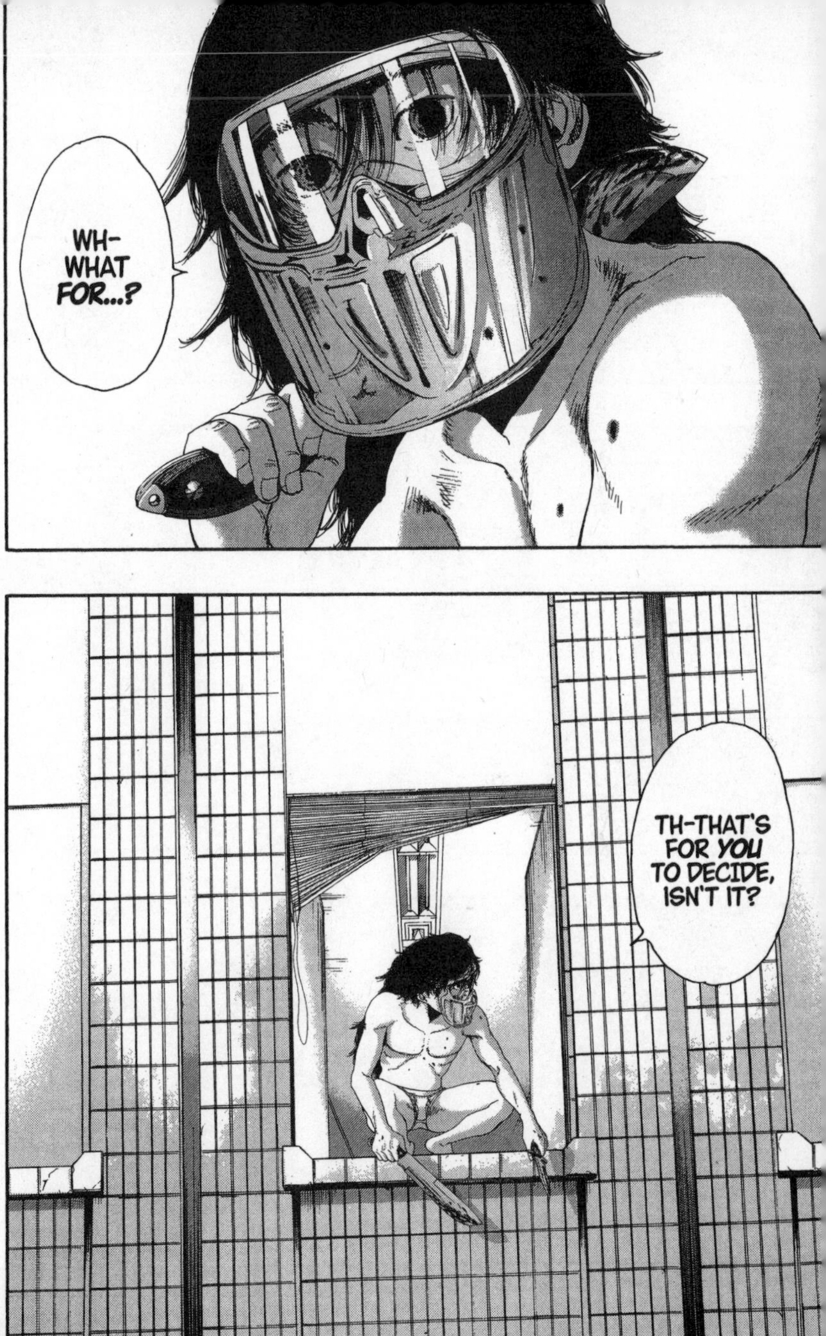
WH-WHAT FOR...?
TH-THAT'S FOR *YOU* TO DECIDE, ISN'T IT?

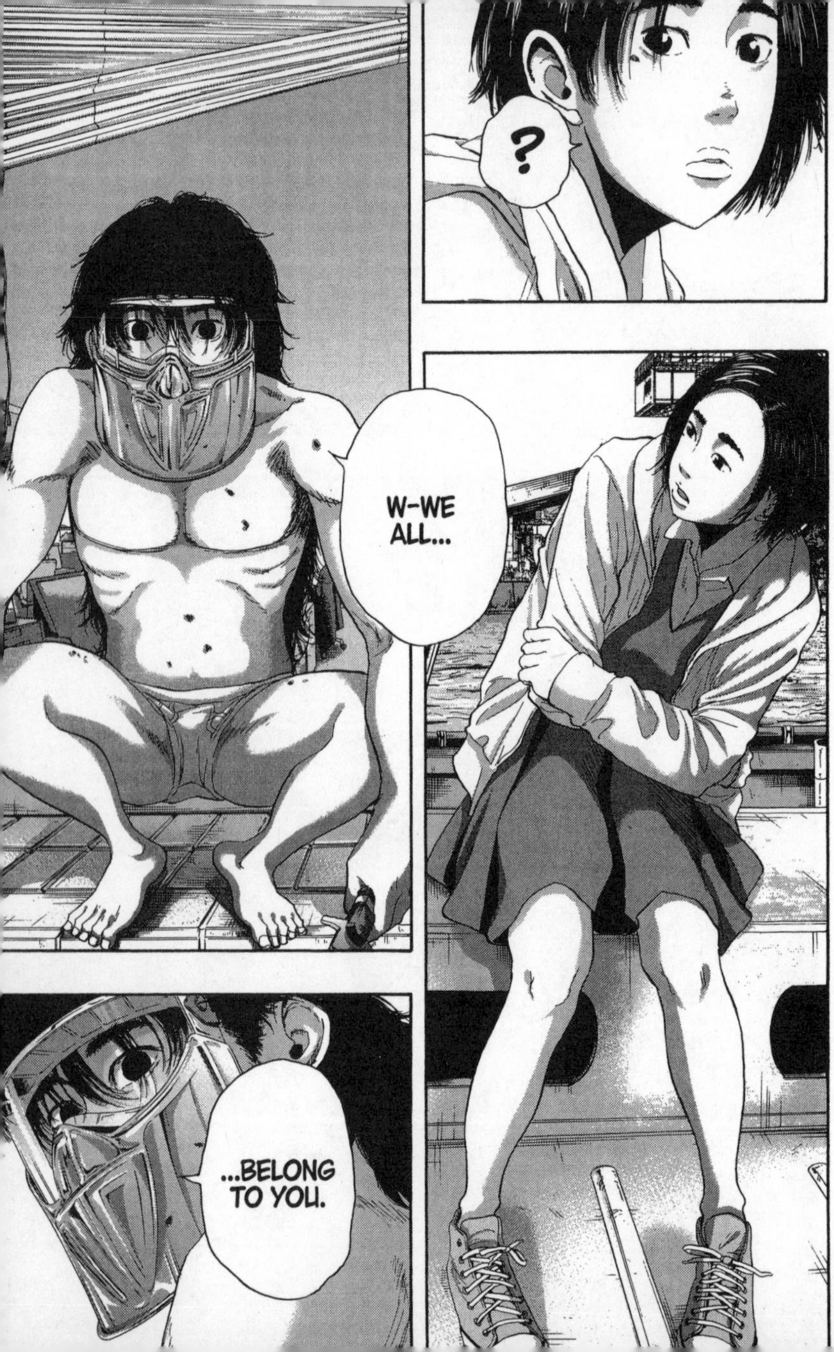
?
W-WE ALL...
...BELONG TO YOU.

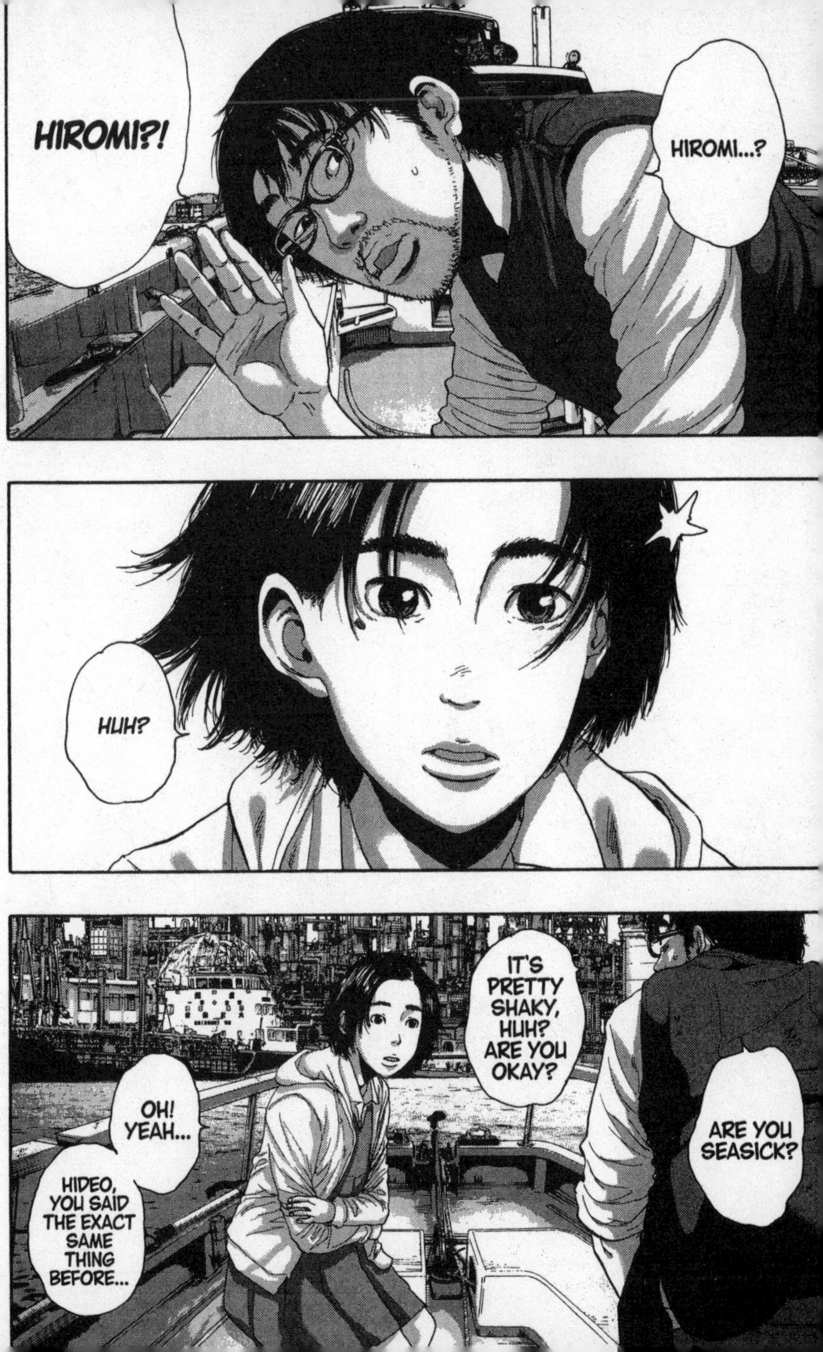
HIROMI...?
HIROMI?!
HUH?
ARE YOU SEASICK?
IT'S PRETTY SHAKY, HUH? ARE YOU OKAY?
OH! YEAH...
HIDEO, YOU SAID THE EXACT SAME THING BEFORE...

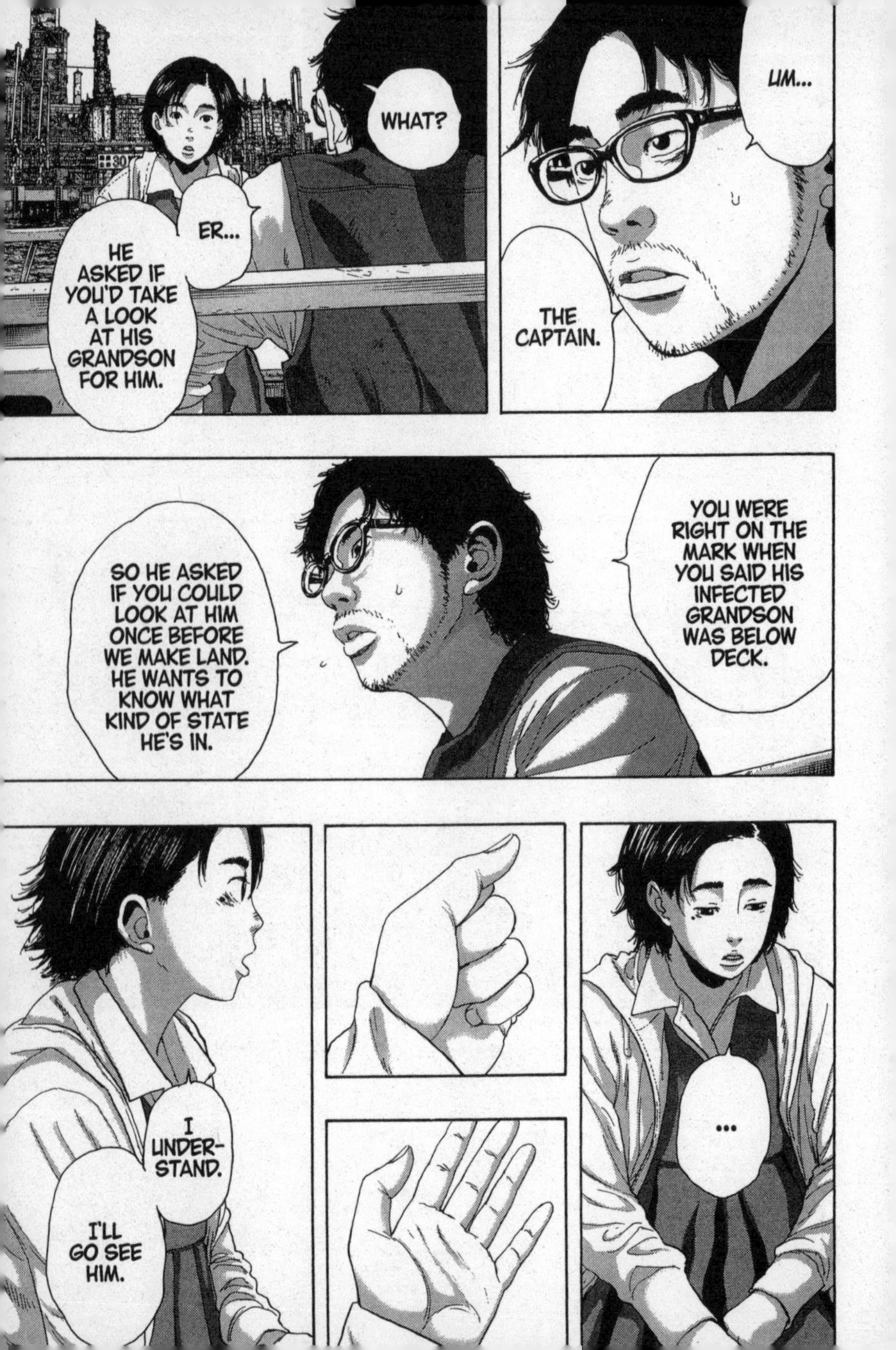
UM...
THE CAPTAIN.
WHAT?
ER...
HE ASKED IF YOU'D TAKE A LOOK AT HIS GRANDSON FOR HIM.
YOU WERE RIGHT ON THE MARK WHEN YOU SAID HIS INFECTED GRANDSON WAS BELOW DECK.
SO HE ASKED IF YOU COULD LOOK AT HIM ONCE BEFORE WE MAKE LAND. HE WANTS TO KNOW WHAT KIND OF STATE HE'S IN.
...
I UNDER-STAND.
I'LL GO SEE HIM.

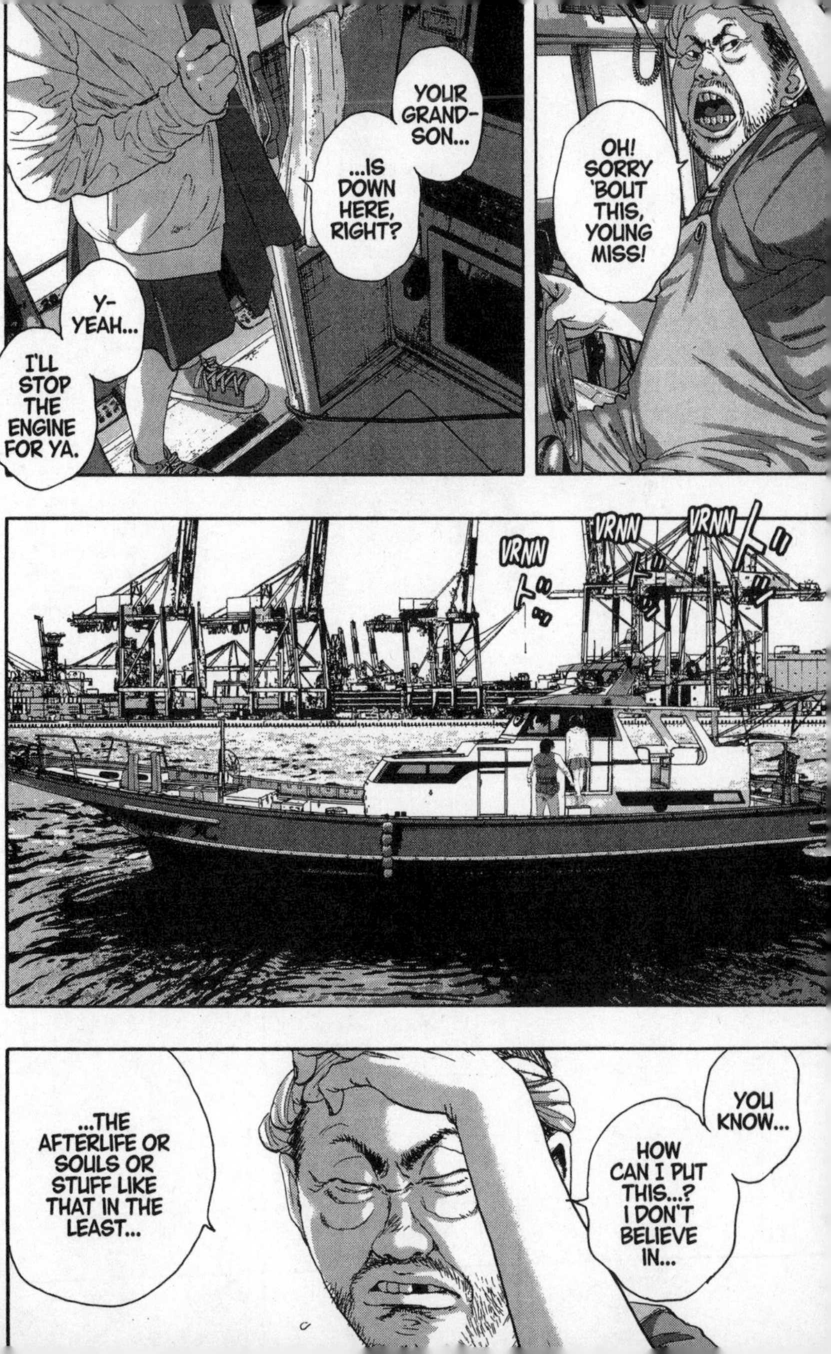
OH! SORRY 'BOUT THIS, YOUNG MISS!
YOUR GRAND-SON...
...IS DOWN HERE, RIGHT?
Y-YEAH...
I'LL STOP THE ENGINE FOR YA.
VRNN
VRNN
VRNN
YOU KNOW...
HOW CAN I PUT THIS...? I DON'T BELIEVE IN...
...THE AFTERLIFE OR SOULS OR STUFF LIKE THAT IN THE LEAST...

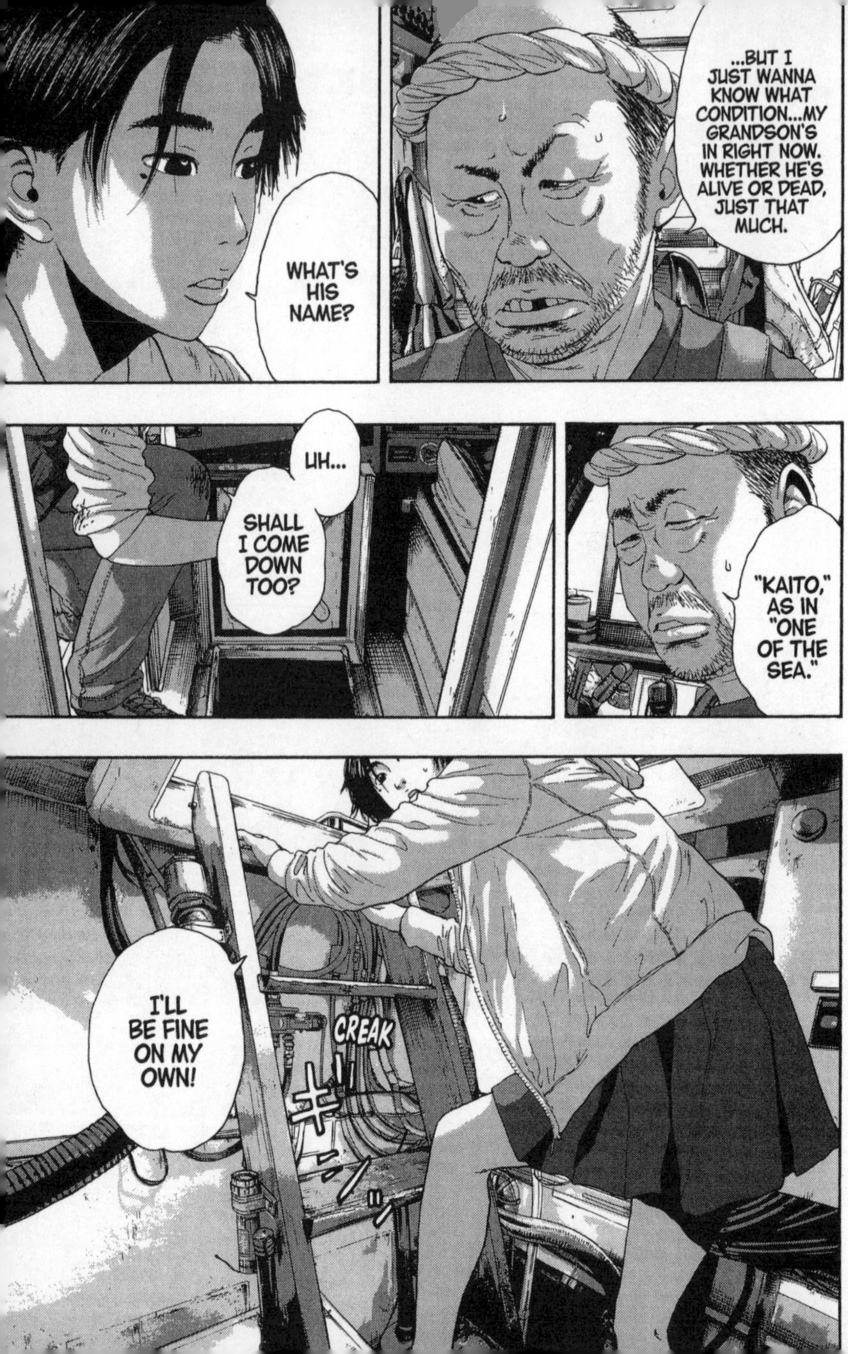
...BUT I JUST WANNA KNOW WHAT CONDITION...MY GRANDSON'S IN RIGHT NOW. WHETHER HE'S ALIVE OR DEAD, JUST THAT MUCH.
WHAT'S HIS NAME?
"KAITO," AS IN "ONE OF THE SEA."
UH...
SHALL I COME DOWN TOO?
I'LL BE FINE ON MY OWN!
CREAK

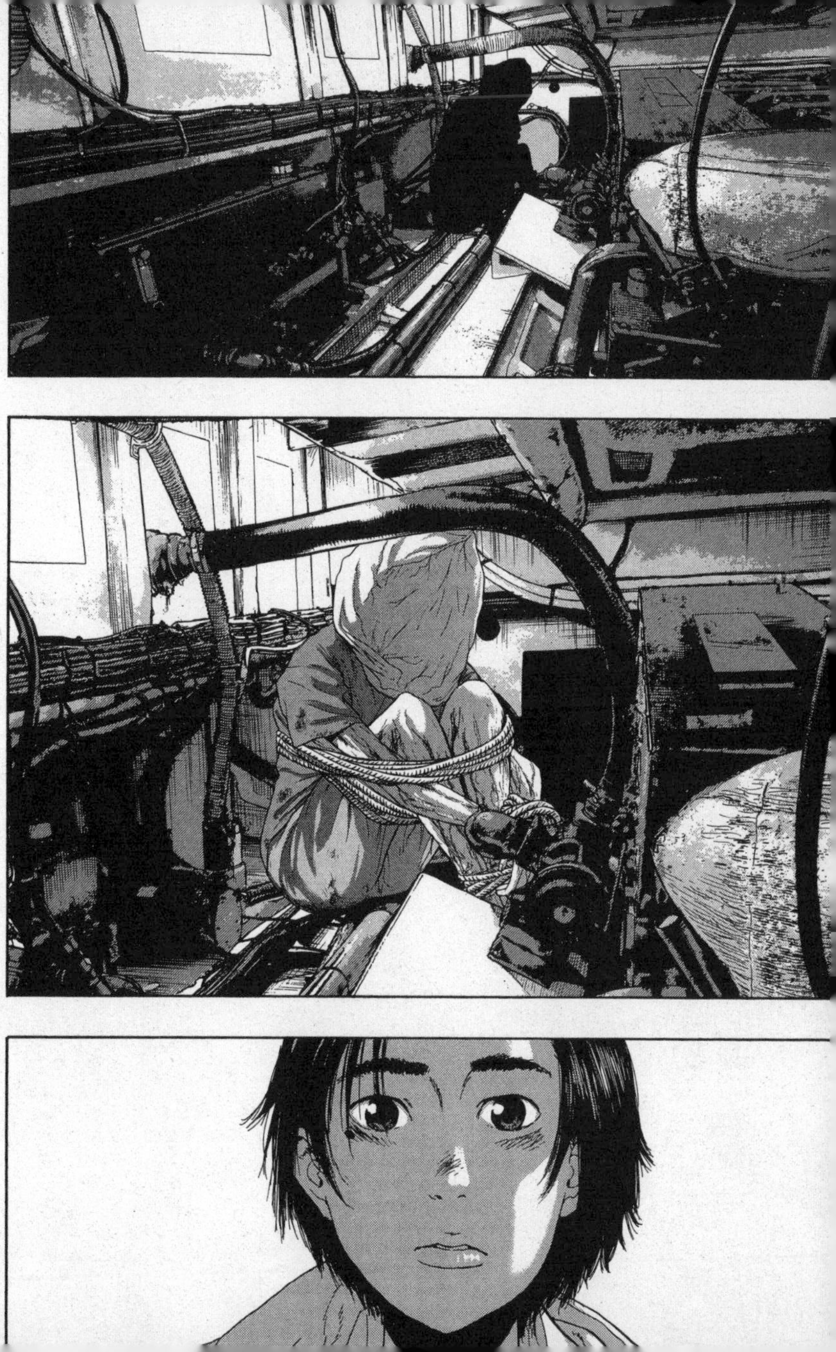

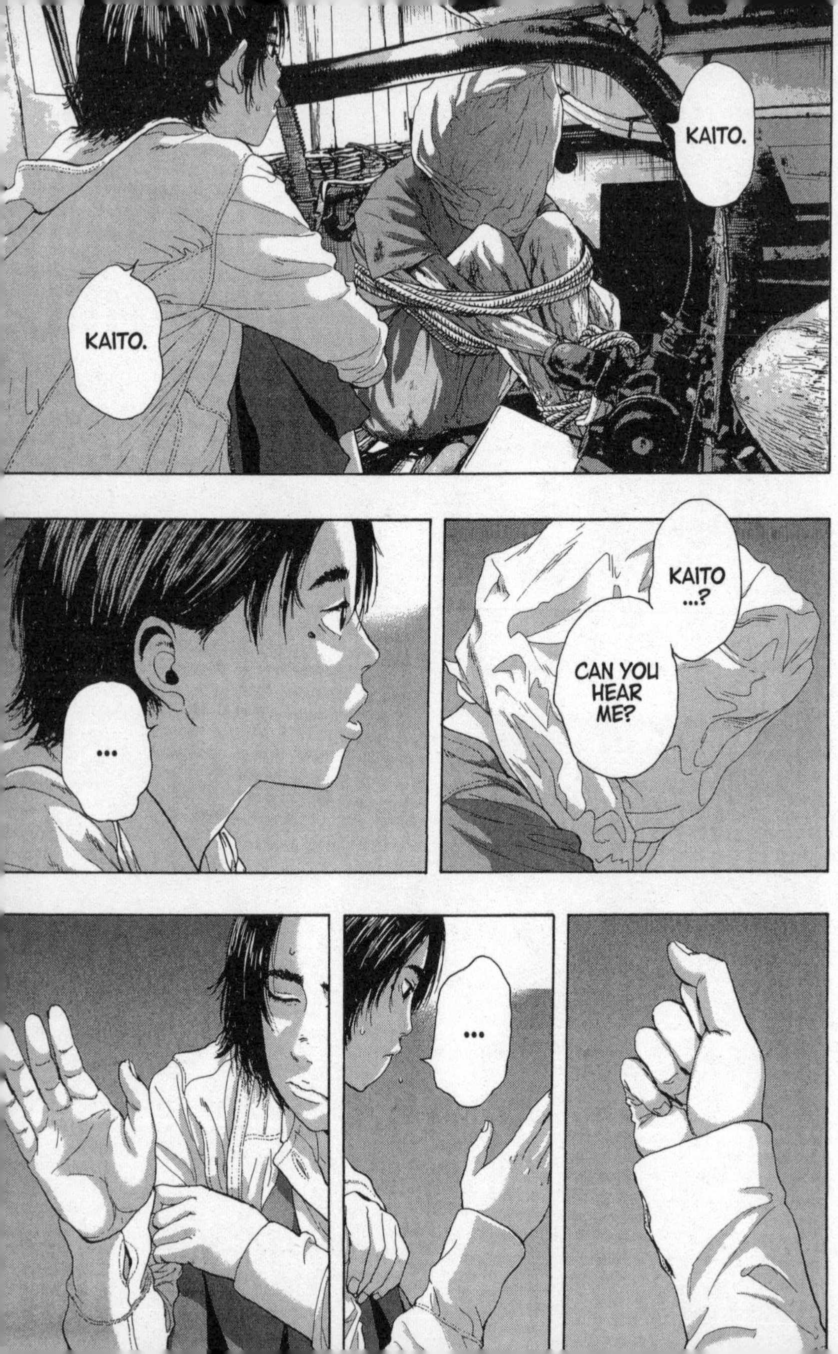
KAITO.
KAITO.
KAITO ...?
CAN YOU HEAR ME?
...
...

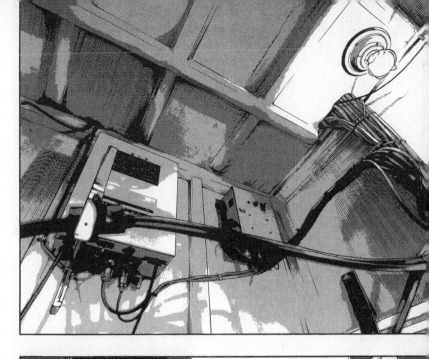

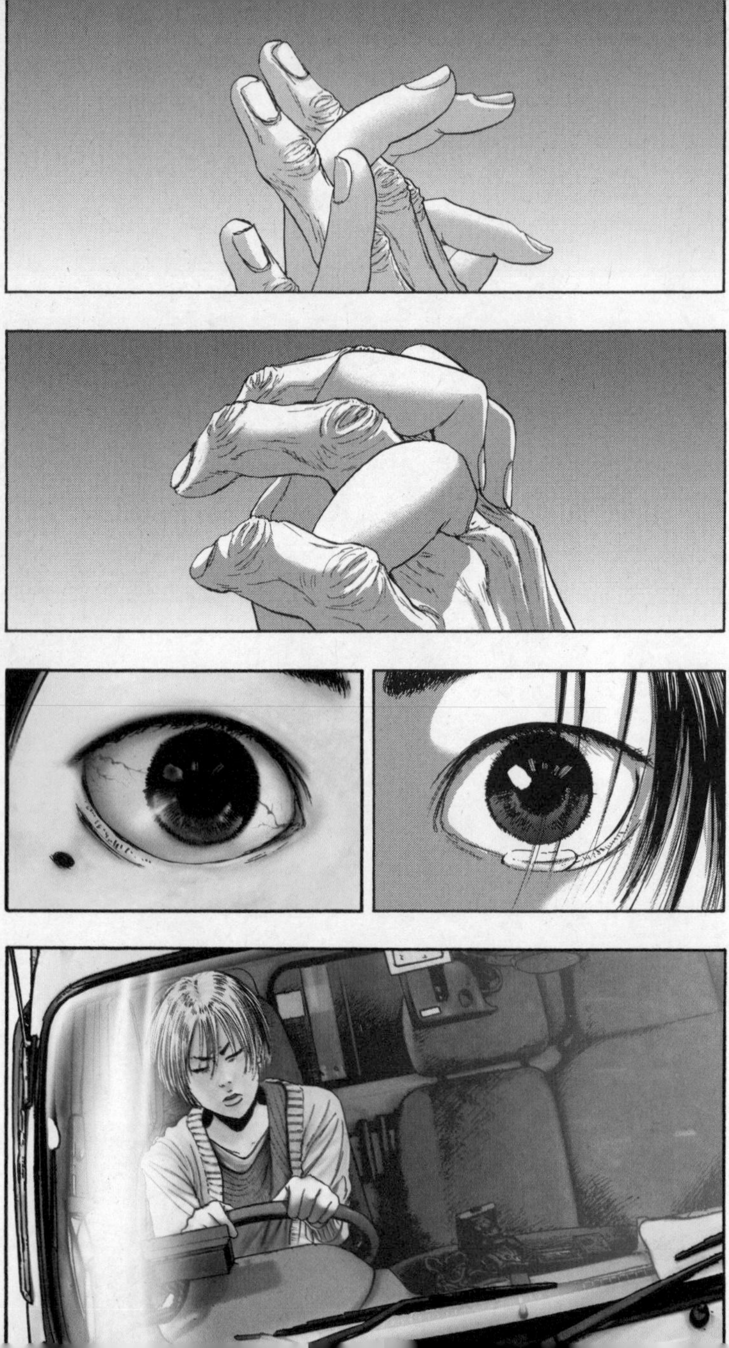

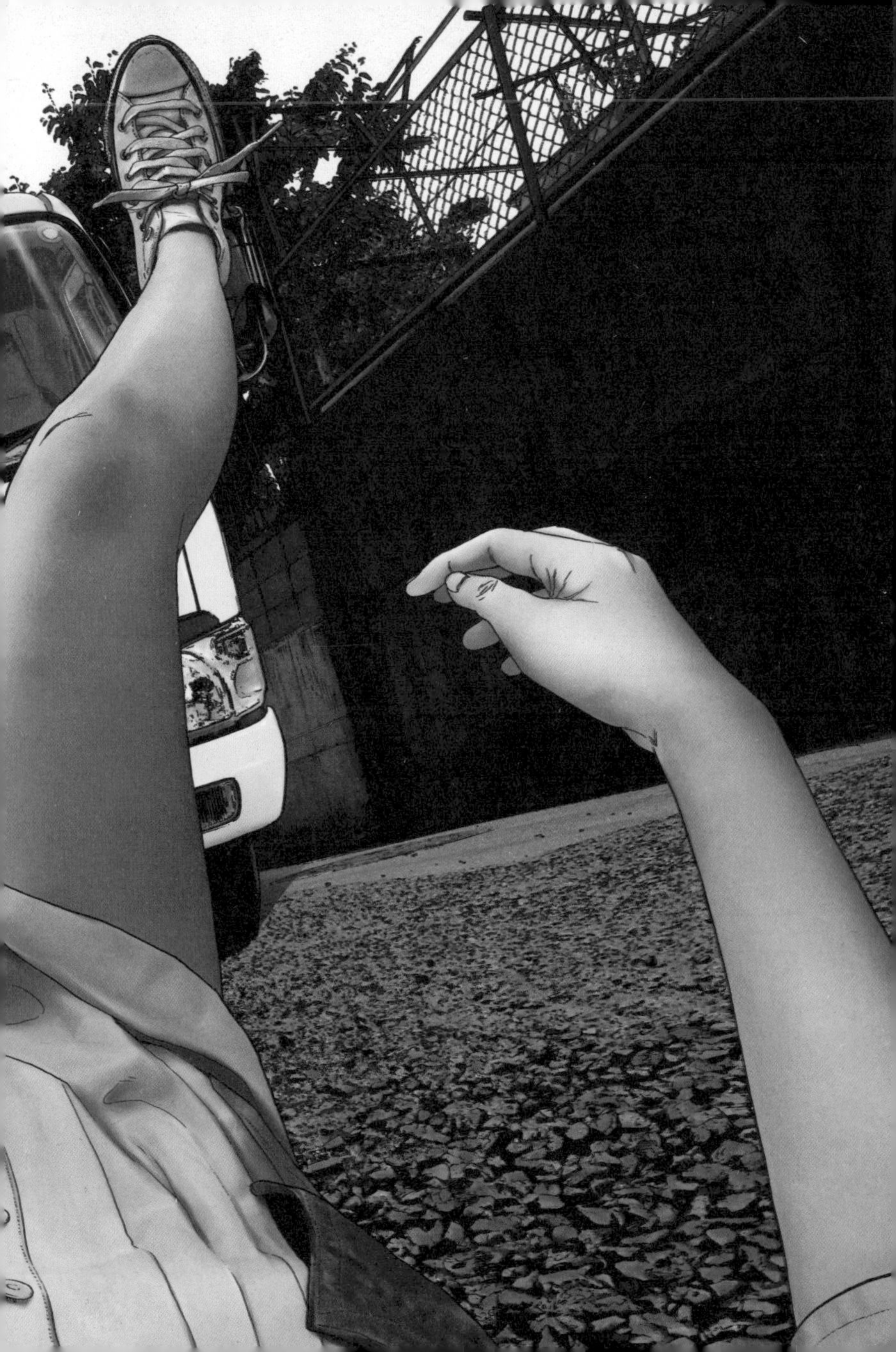

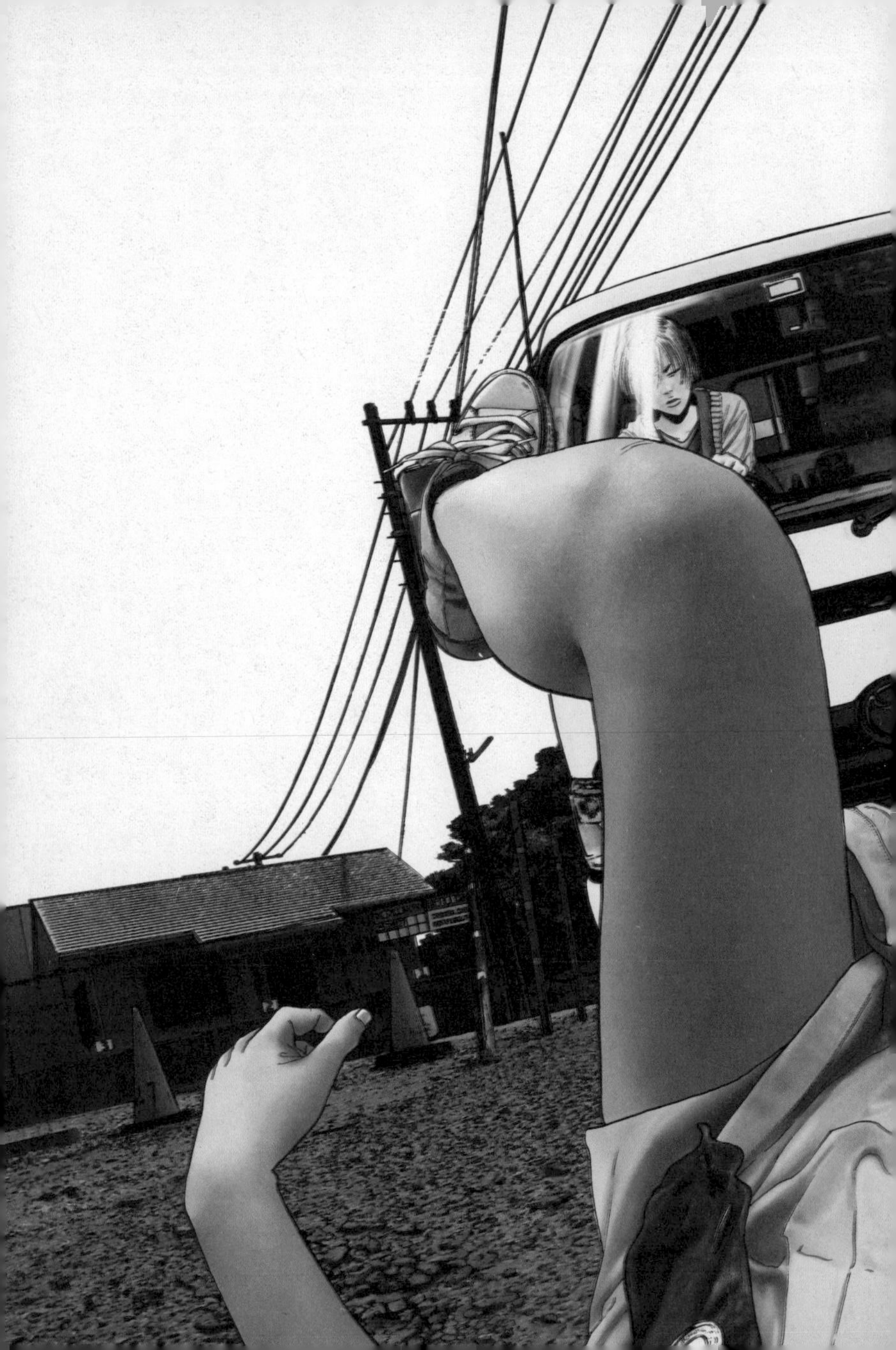

CHAPTER
228

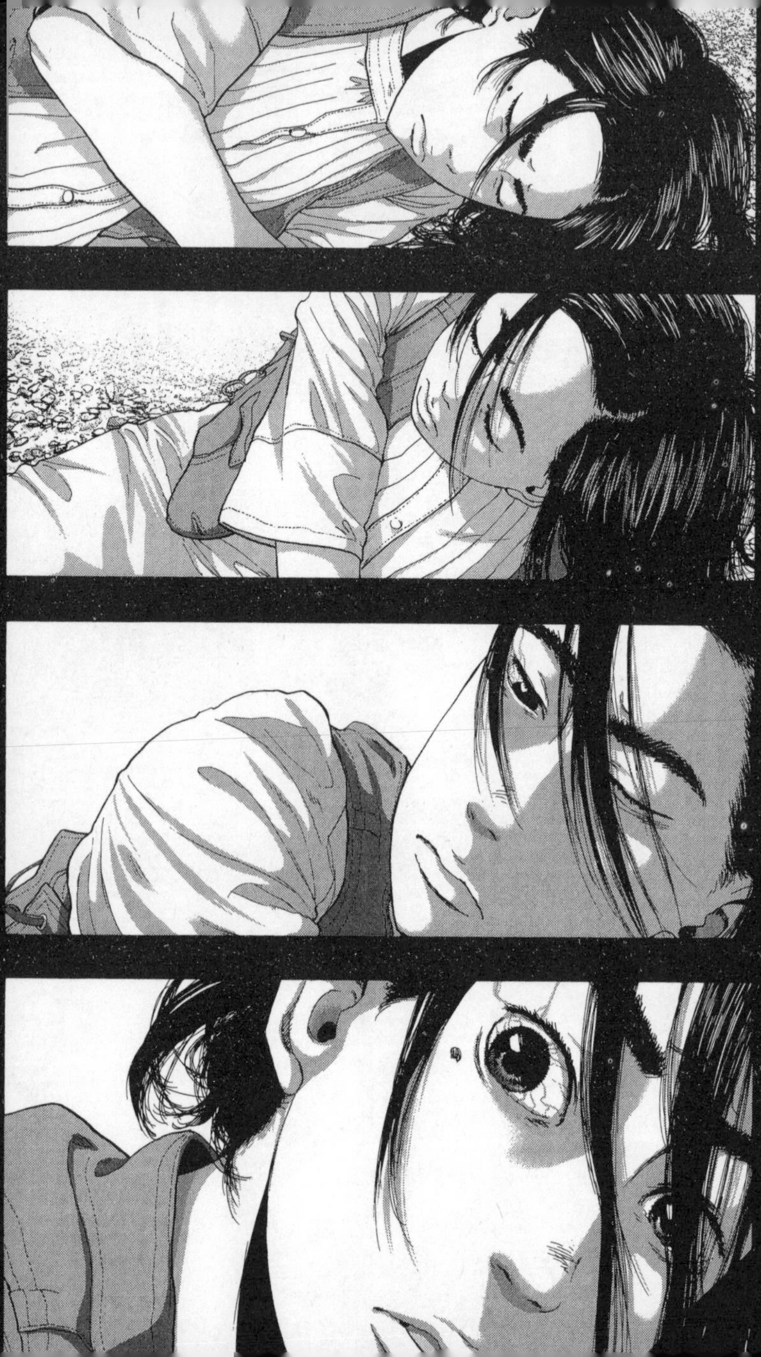

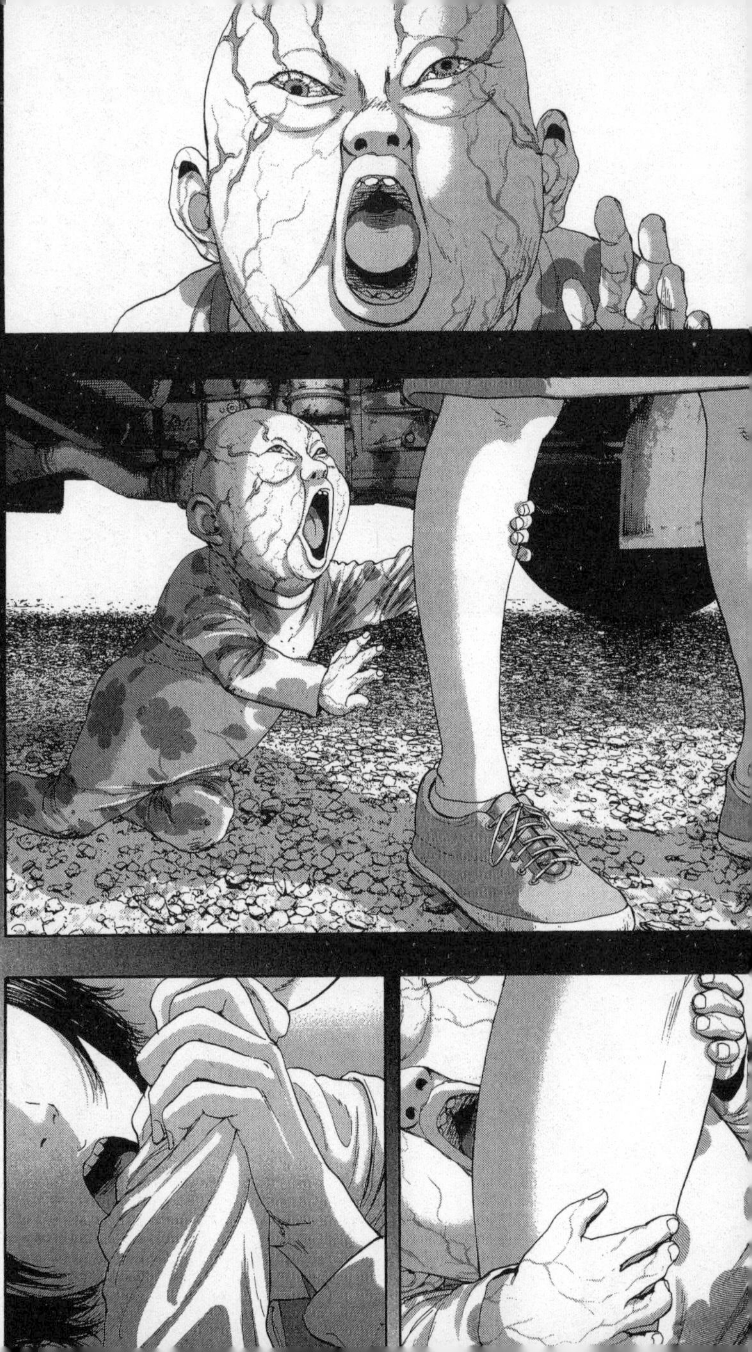

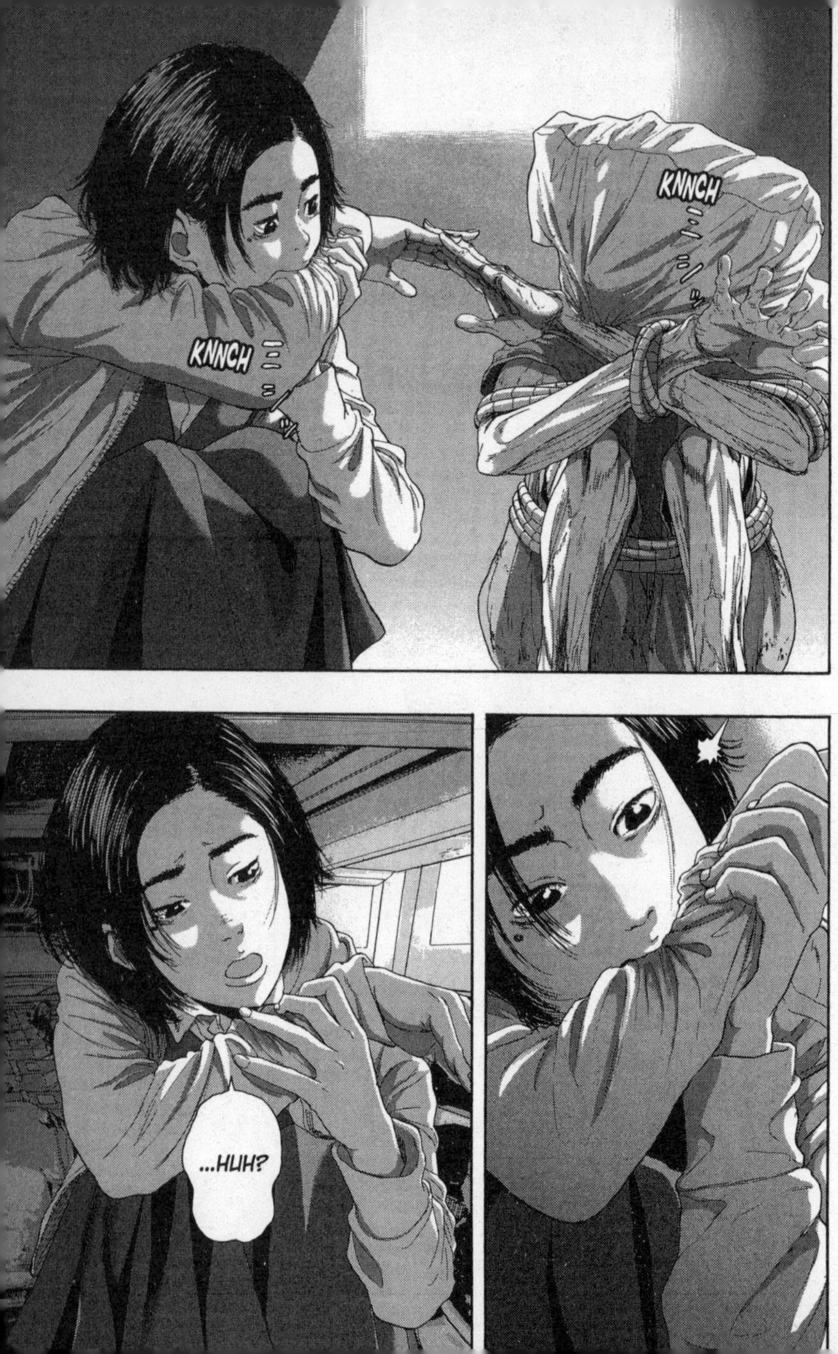
KNNCH
KNNCH
...HUH?

WHPP

KRRIK

KRRIK

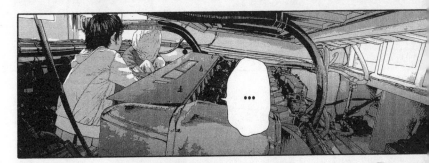

...

...

HUH?
WHAT'S
WRONG
?

HIROMI...

CREAK

...HOW
WAS HE?

I'M SORRY...

...BUT I DON'T KNOW...

IS KAITO...

...BEYOND HOPE?

WE'LL GO TO TOKYO.

NO. THAT'S ALL RIGHT.

HIROMI!

I'M...

...A MURDER-ER.

THE BLOOD ON YOUR ARM!

DID HE BITE YOU?

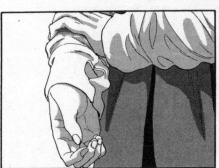

WHAT?

I WAS THE ONE...

...WHO KILLED MISS ODA...

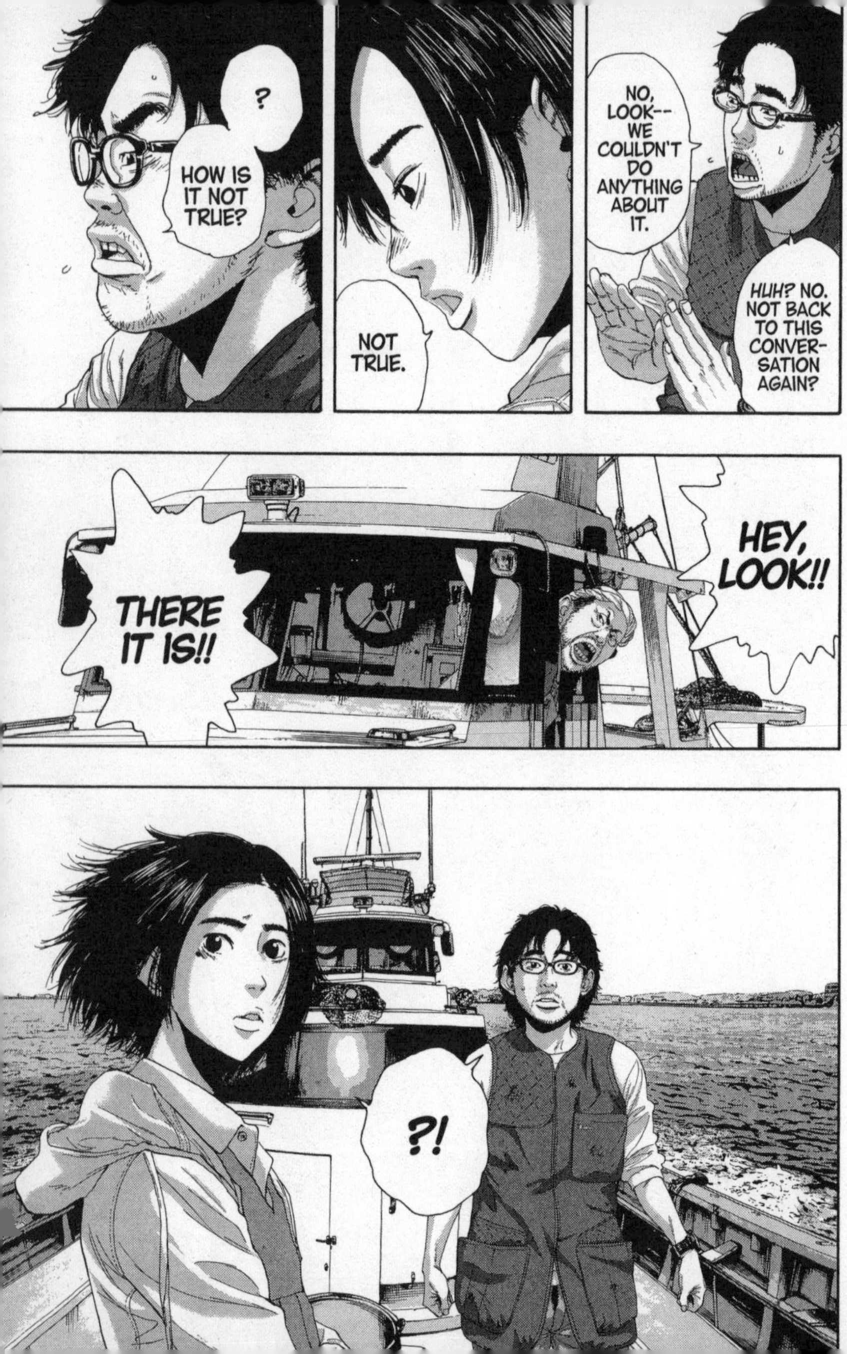
NO, LOOK-- WE COULDN'T DO ANYTHING ABOUT IT.
HUH? NO. NOT BACK TO THIS CONVER-SATION AGAIN?
NOT TRUE.
?
HOW IS IT NOT TRUE?
HEY, LOOK!!
THERE IT IS!!
?!

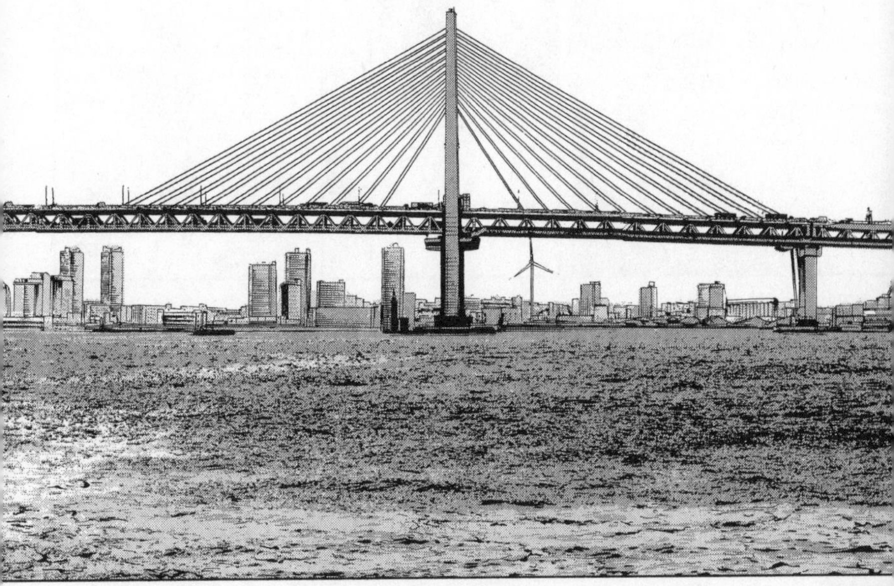

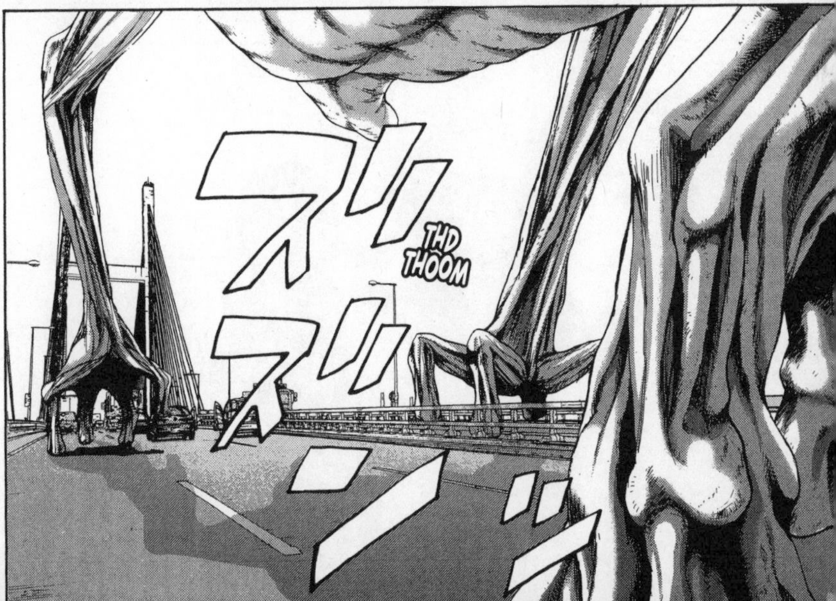
THD
THOOM

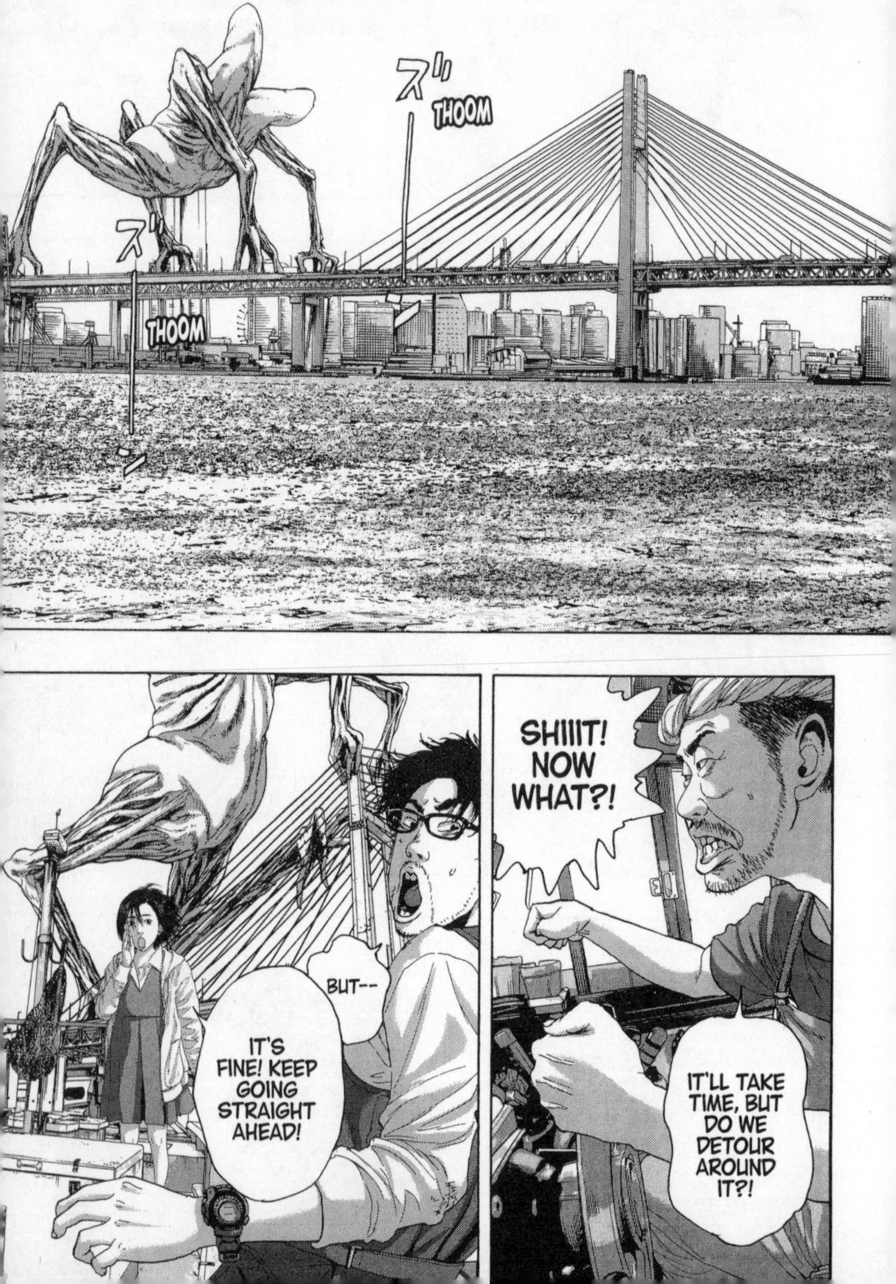
ズ
THOOM
ズ
THOOM
SHIIIT! NOW WHAT?!
IT'LL TAKE TIME, BUT DO WE DETOUR AROUND IT?!
BUT--
IT'S FINE! KEEP GOING STRAIGHT AHEAD!

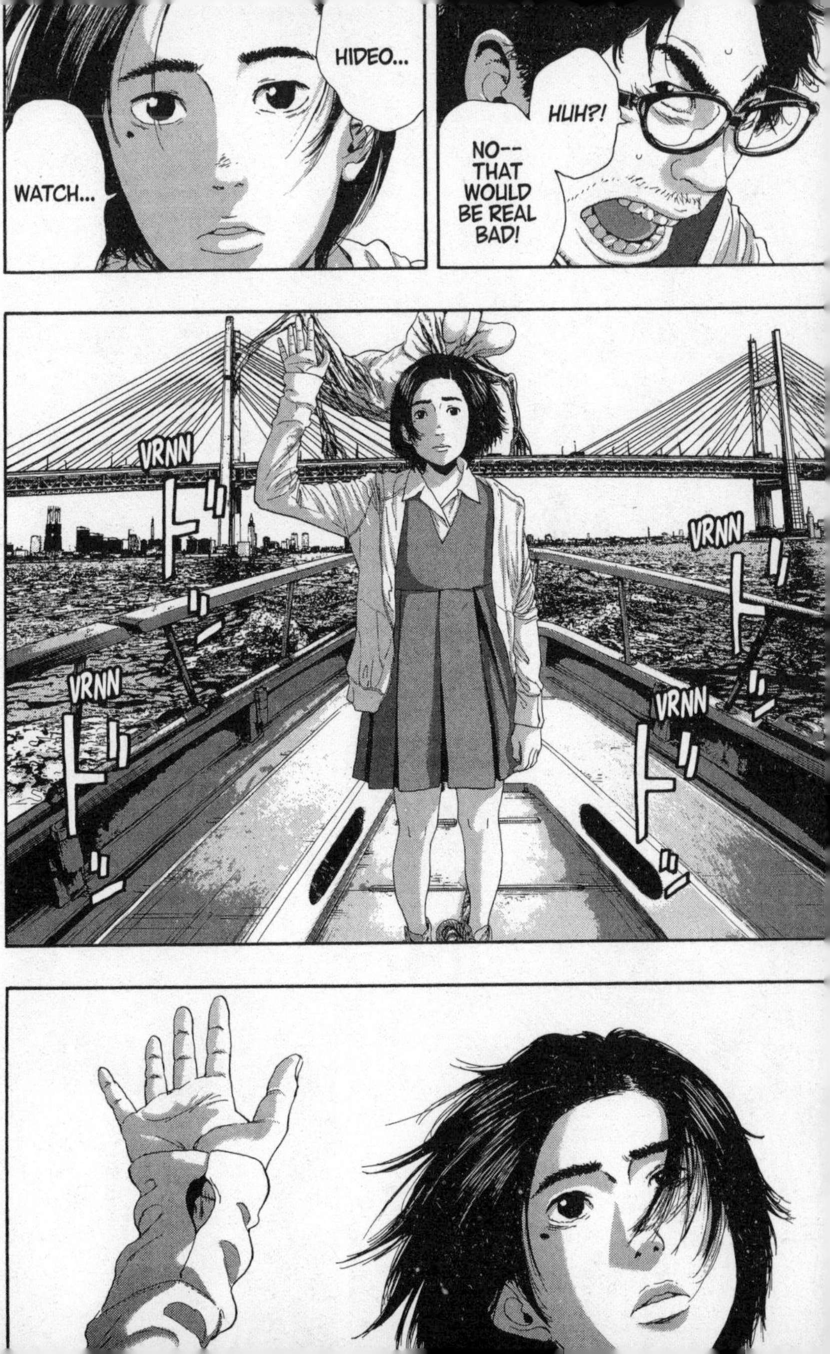
HUH?!
NO-- THAT WOULD BE REAL BAD!
HIDEO...
WATCH...
VRNN
VRNN
VRNN
VRNN

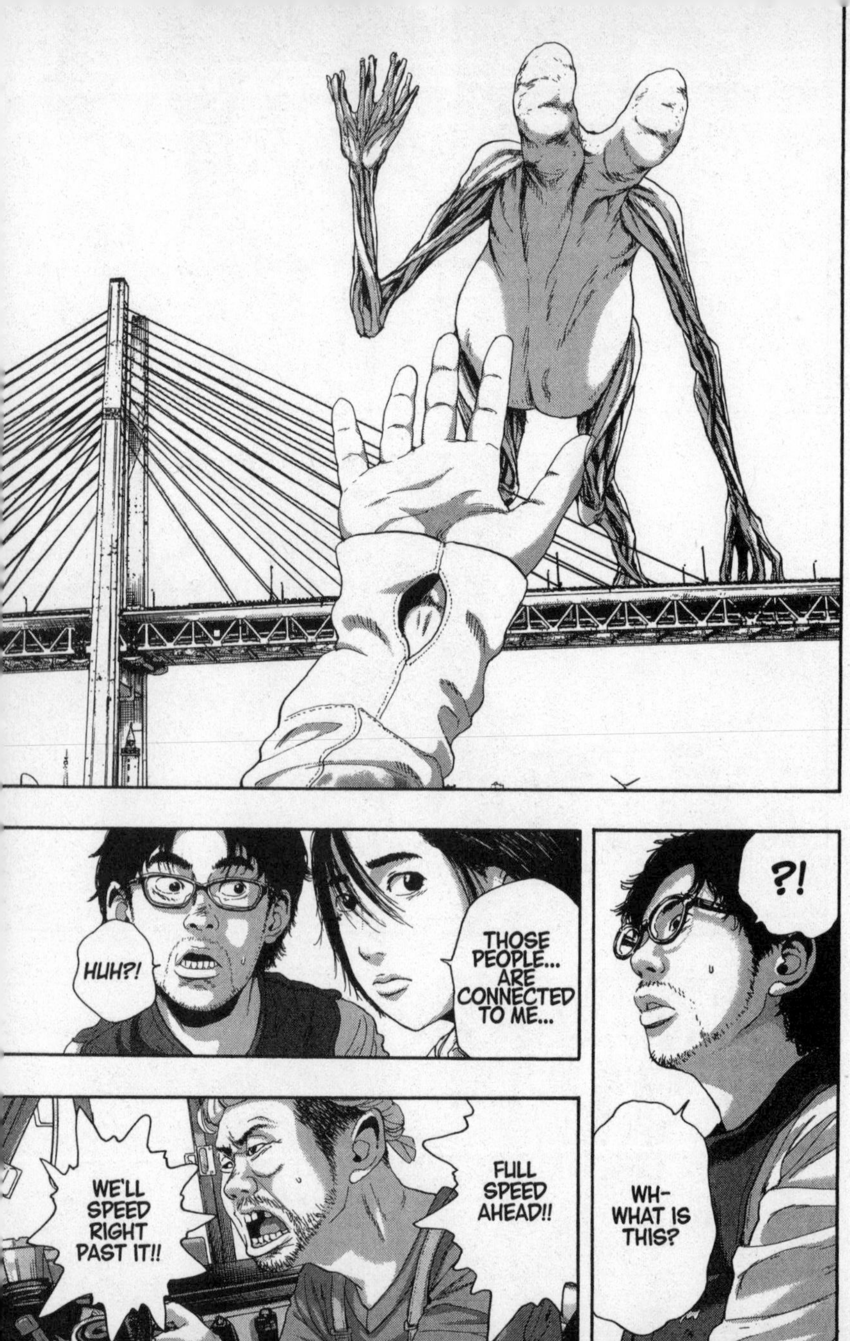
?!
WH- WHAT IS THIS?
THOSE PEOPLE... ARE CONNECTED TO ME...
HUH?!
FULL SPEED AHEAD!!
WE'LL SPEED RIGHT PAST IT!!

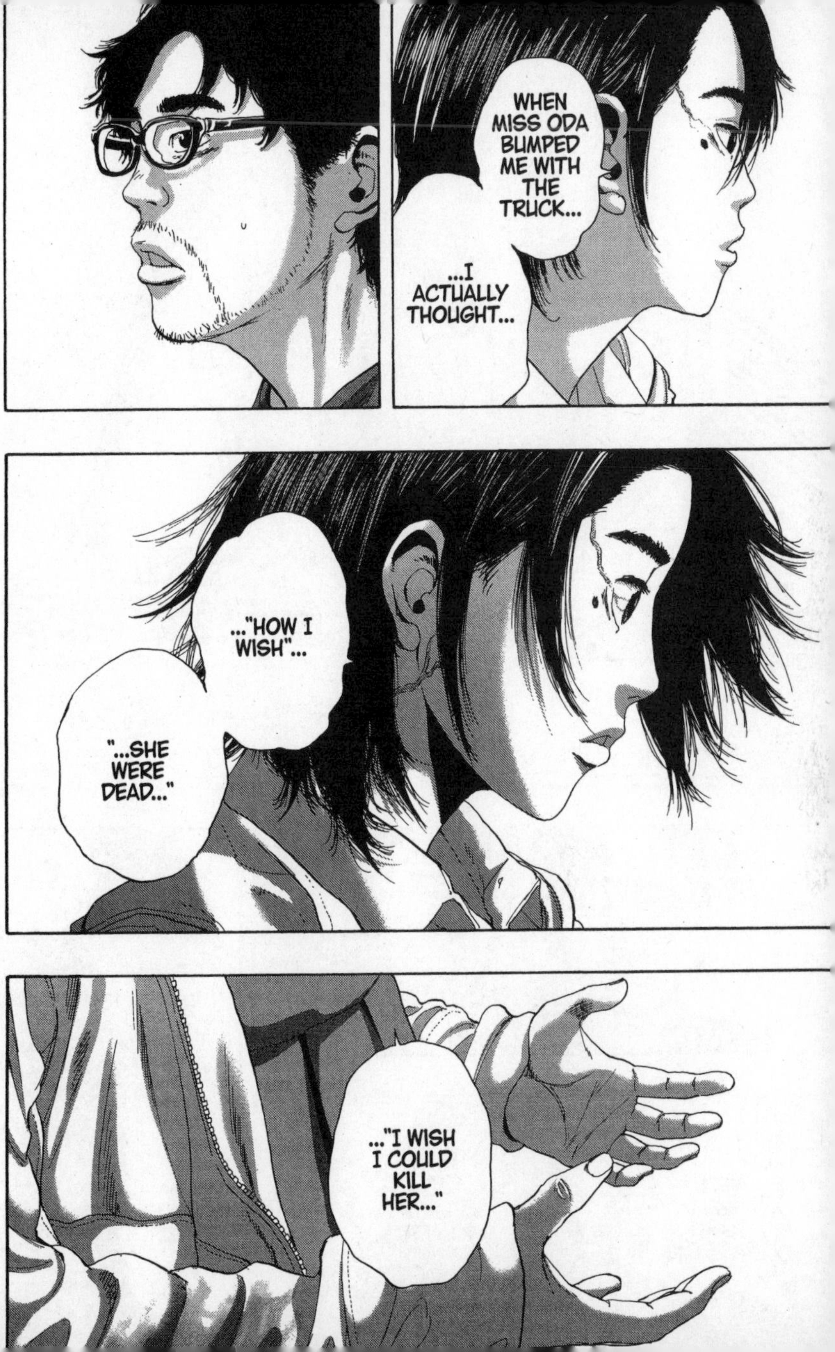
WHEN MISS ODA BUMPED ME WITH THE TRUCK...
...I ACTUALLY THOUGHT...
..."HOW I WISH"...
"...SHE WERE DEAD..."
..."I WISH I COULD KILL HER..."

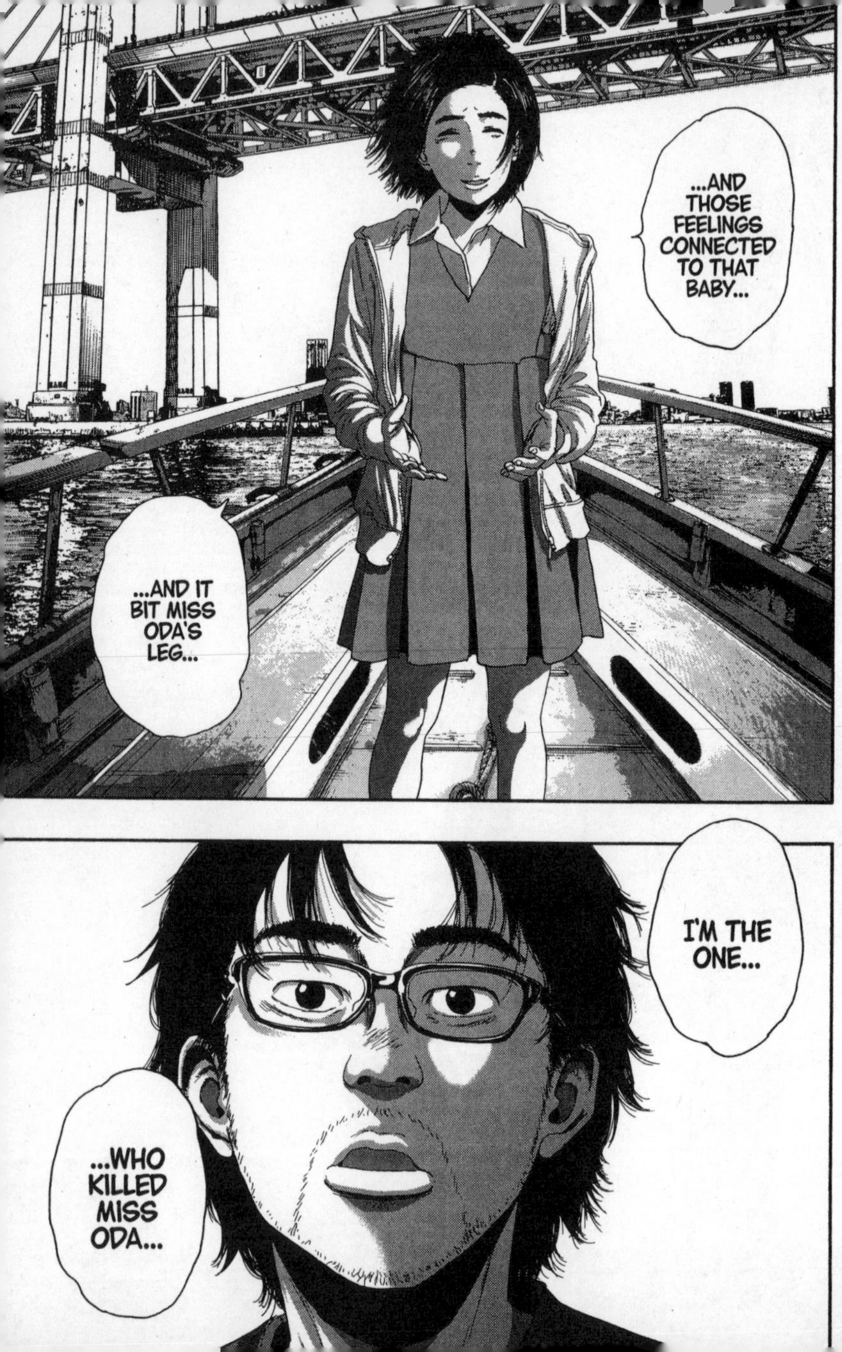
...AND THOSE FEELINGS CONNECTED TO THAT BABY...
...AND IT BIT MISS ODA'S LEG...
I'M THE ONE...
...WHO KILLED MISS ODA...

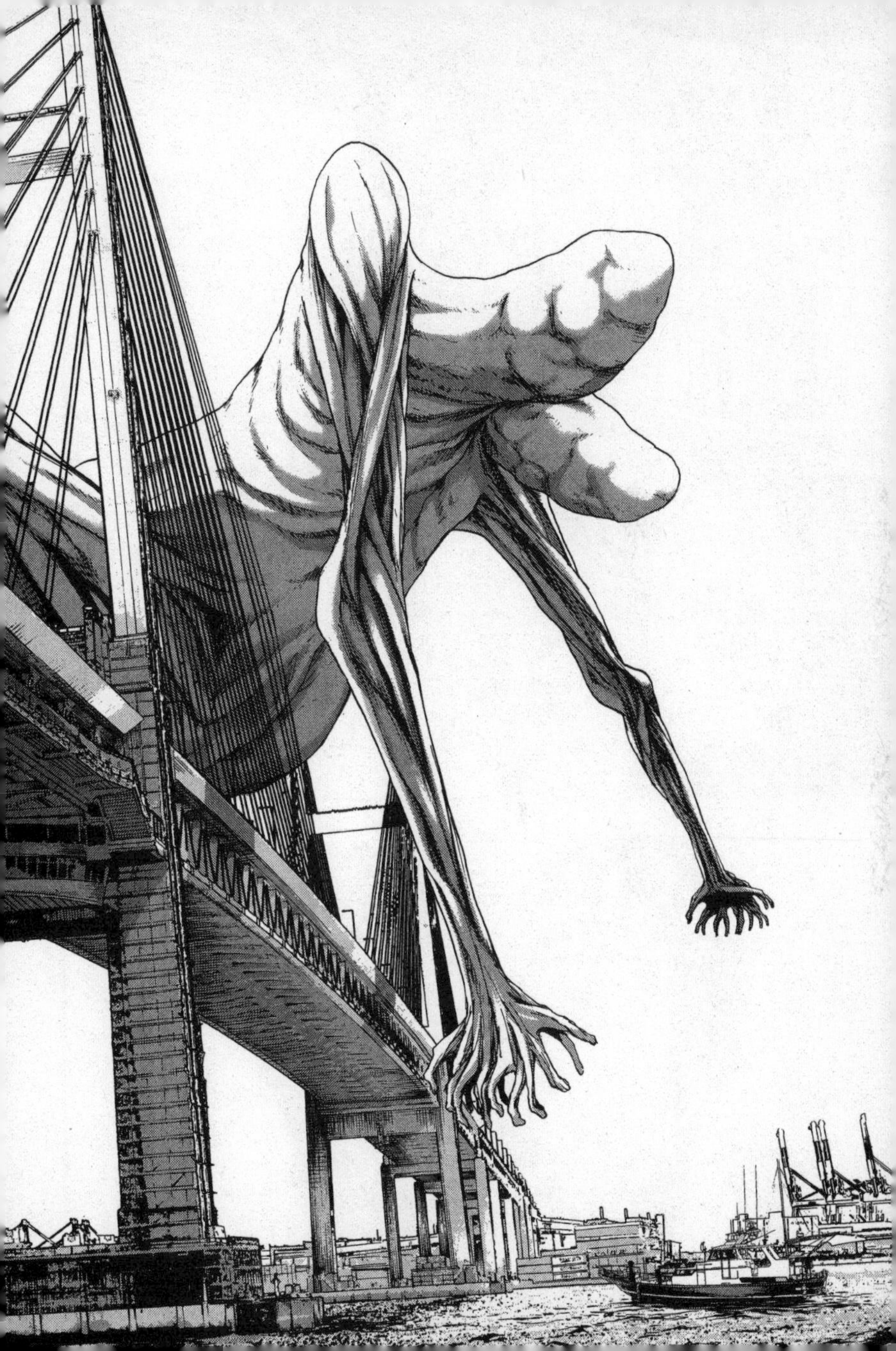

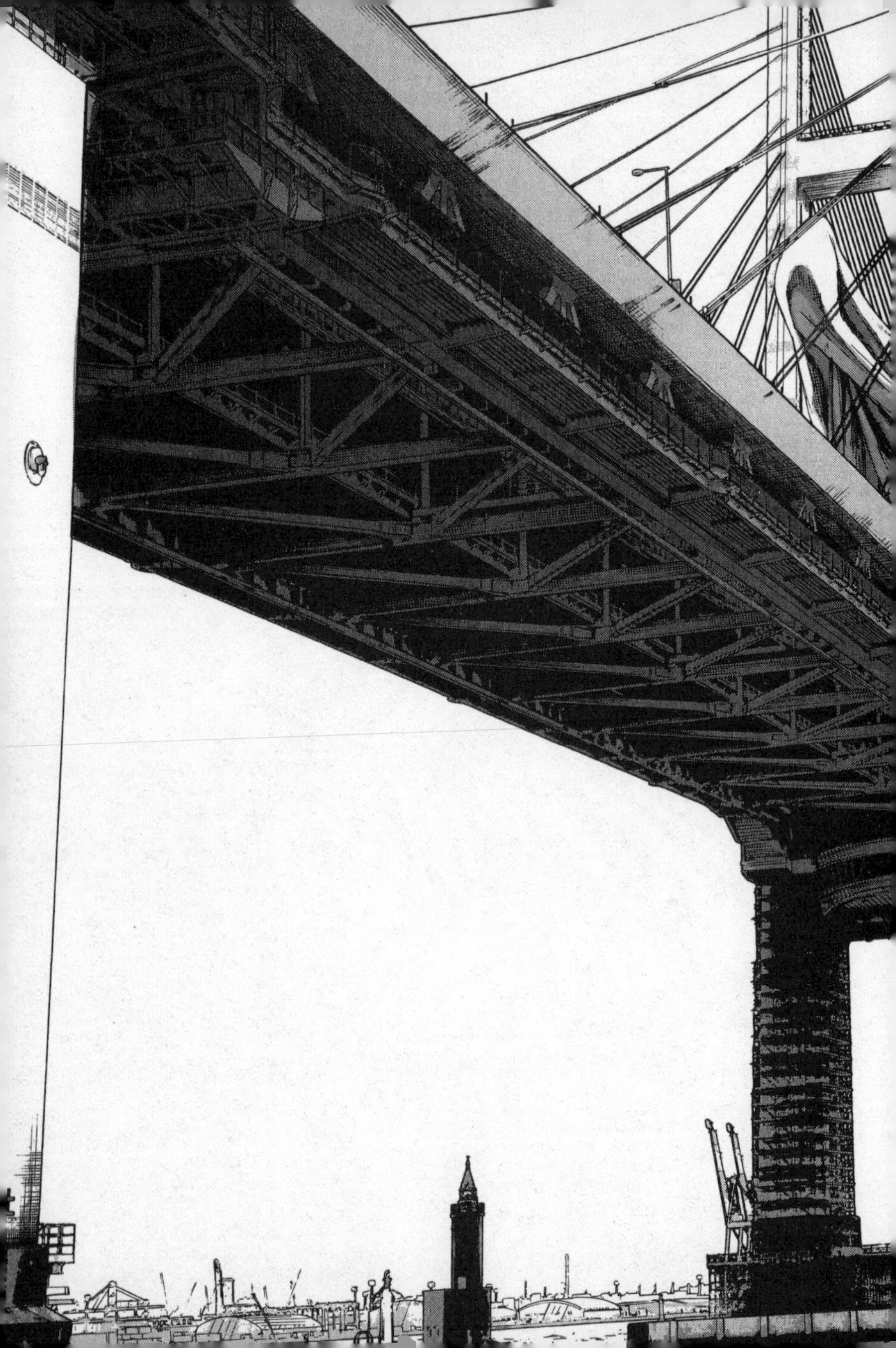

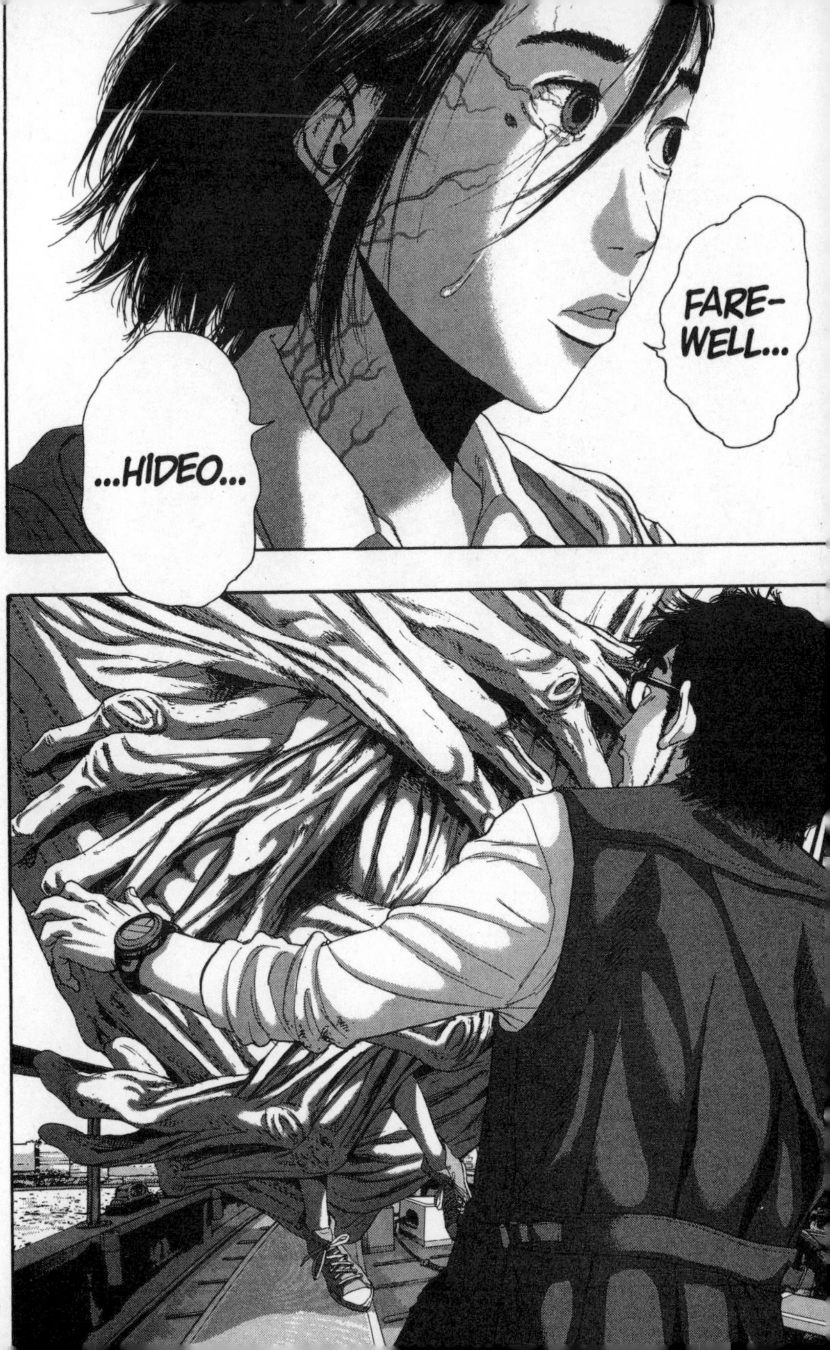
FARE-WELL...
...HIDEO...

I AM
A HERO

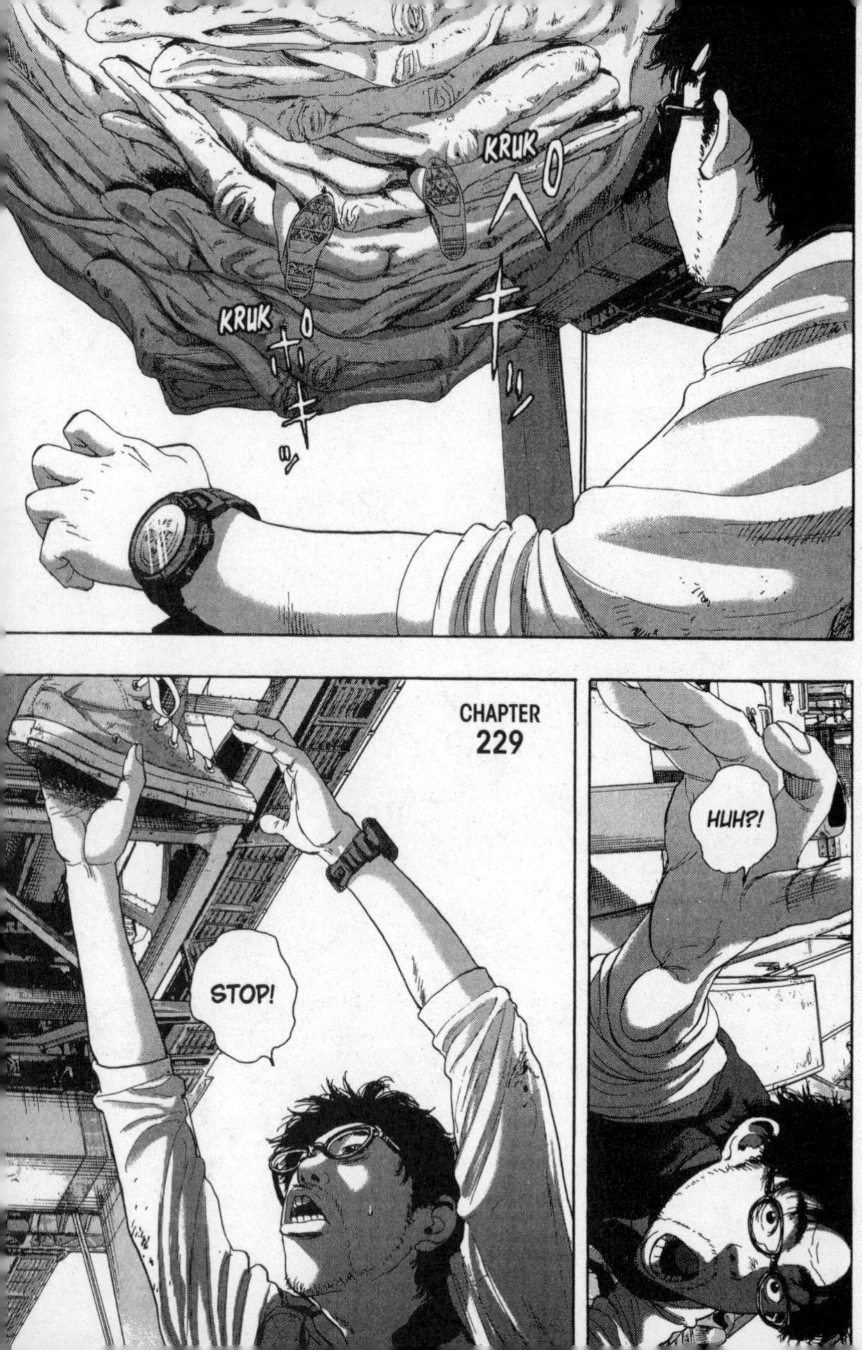
KRUK
KRUK
HUH?!
CHAPTER 229
STOP!

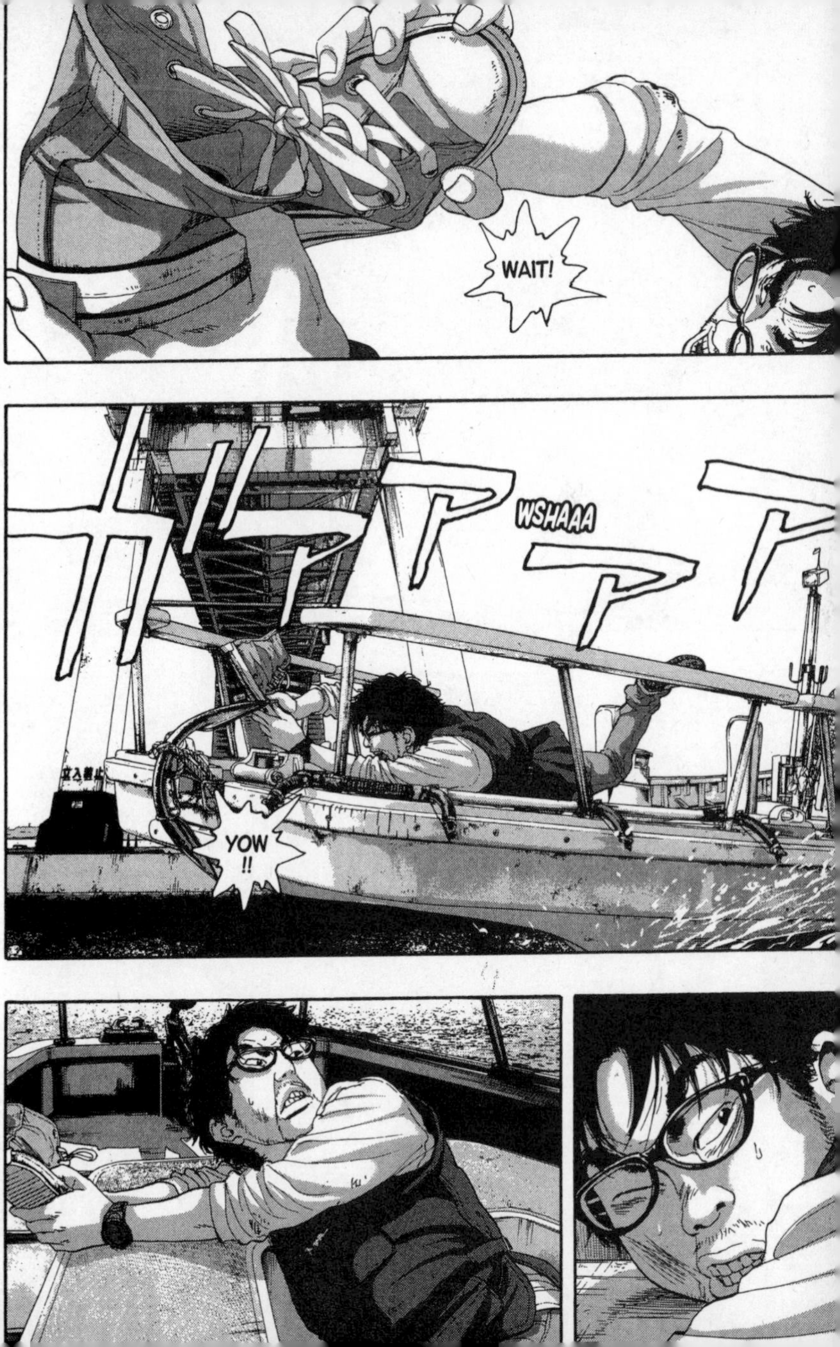
WAIT!
WSHAAA
YOW !!

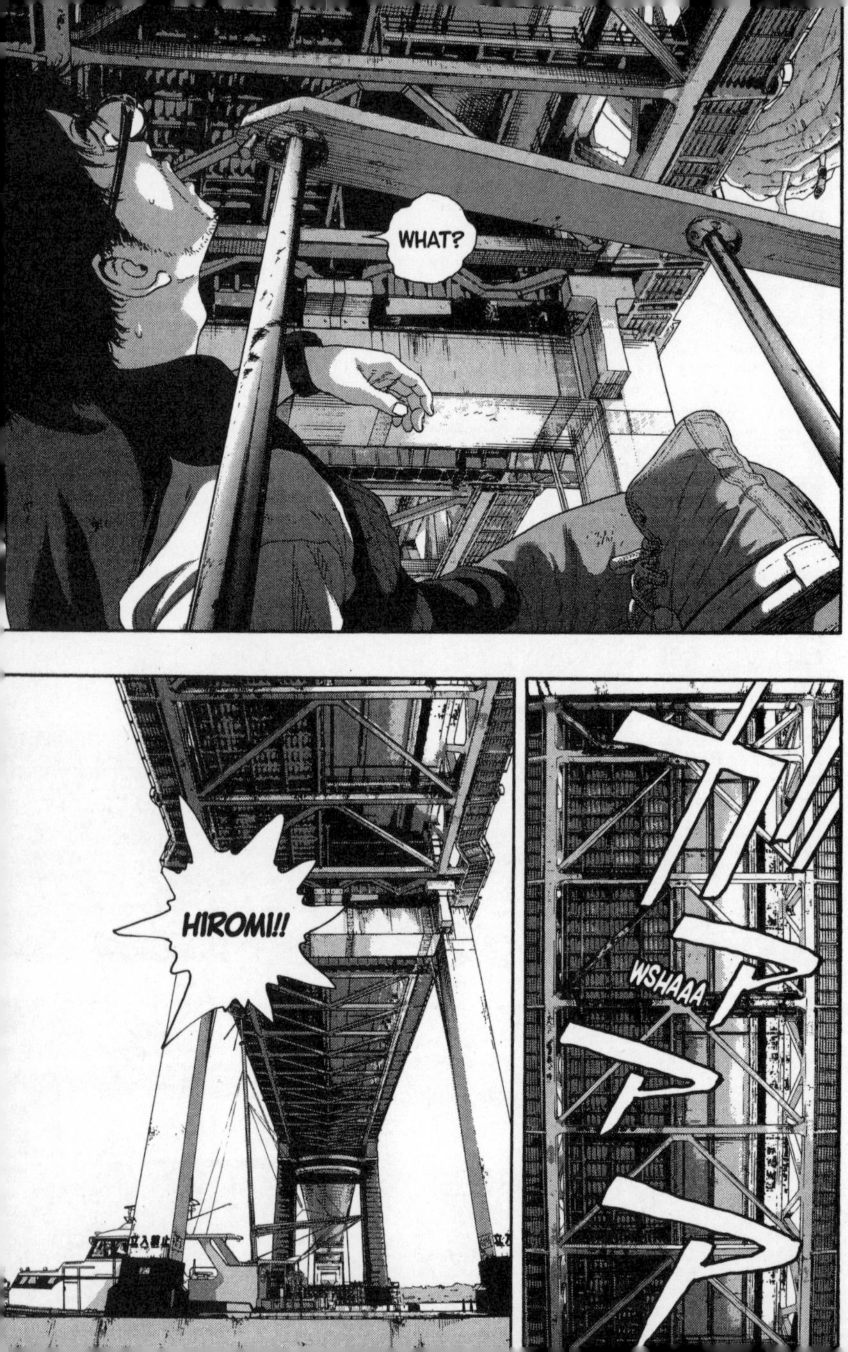
WHAT?
WSHAAA
HIROMI!!

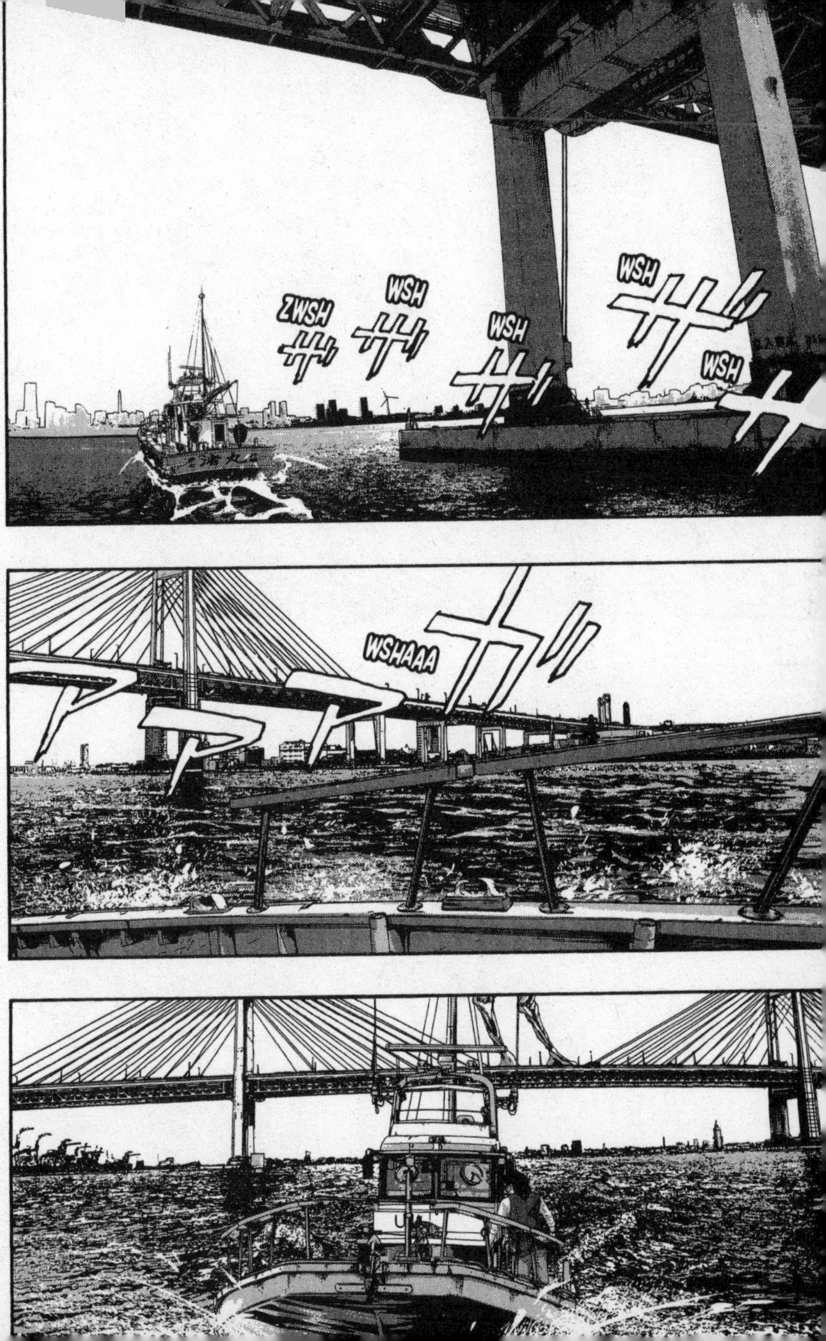
WSH
WSH
WSH
WSH
ZWSH
WSHAAA

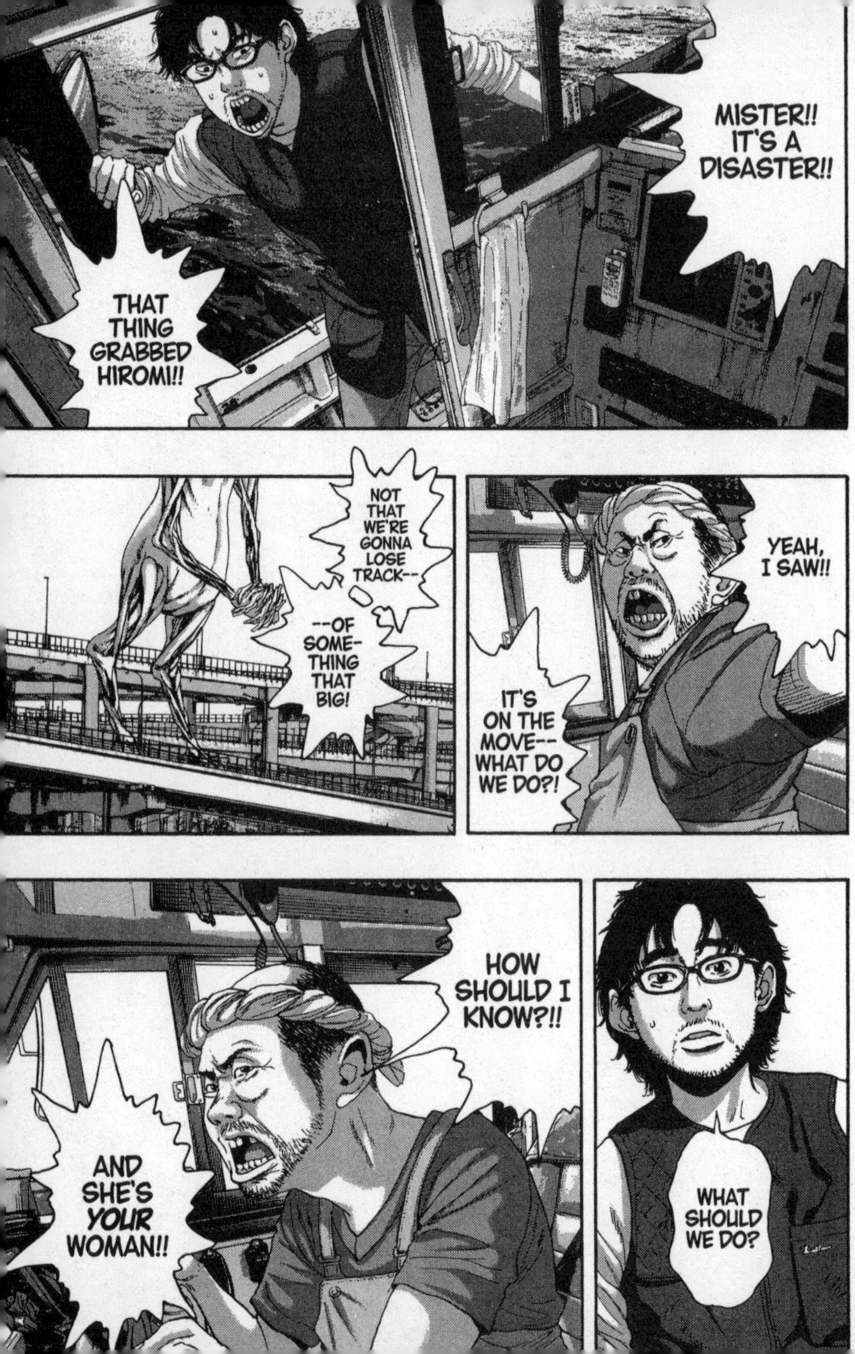
MISTER!! IT'S A DISASTER!!
THAT THING GRABBED HIROMI!!
YEAH, I SAW!!
IT'S ON THE MOVE-- WHAT DO WE DO?!
NOT THAT WE'RE GONNA LOSE TRACK--
--OF SOME-THING THAT BIG!
WHAT SHOULD WE DO?
HOW SHOULD I KNOW?!!
AND SHE'S *YOUR* WOMAN!!

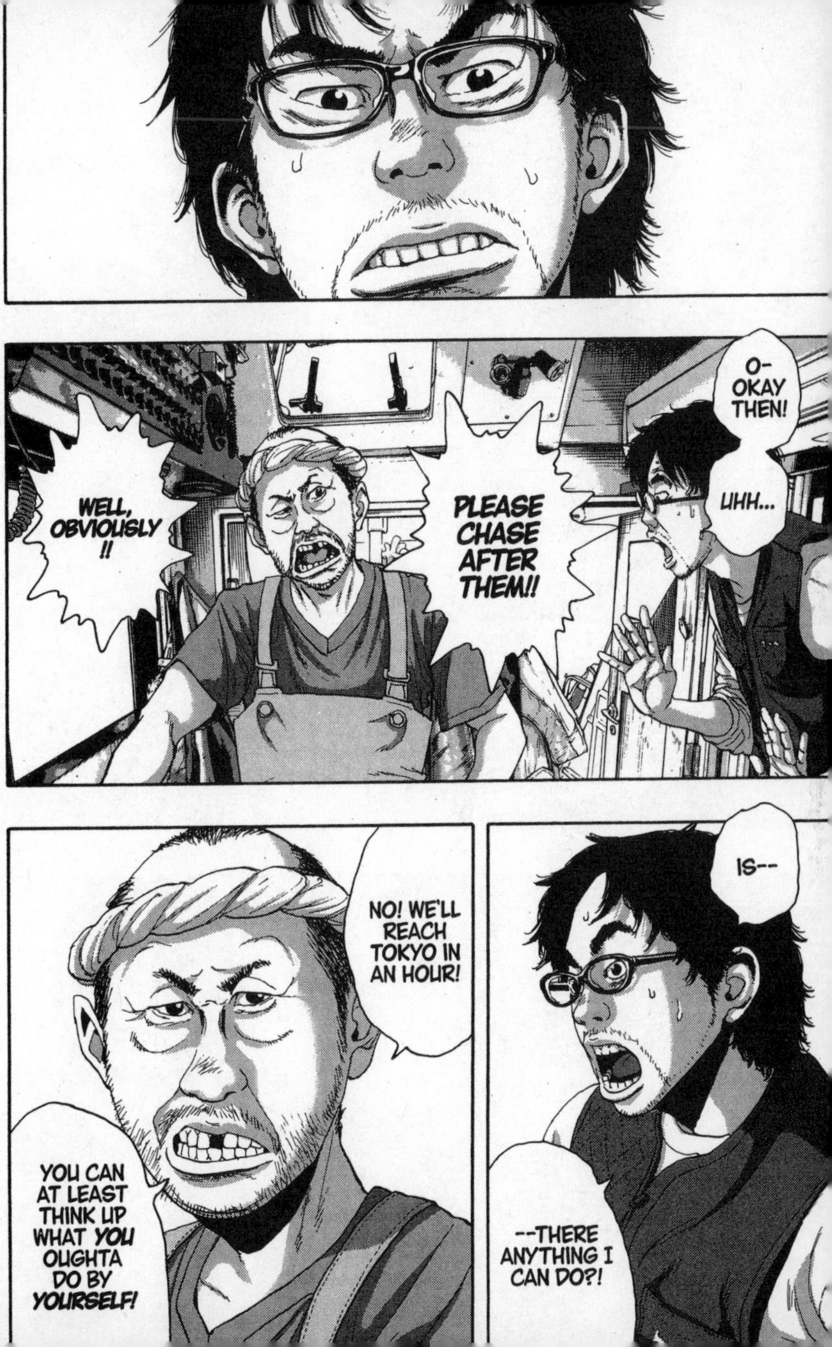
O-OKAY THEN!
UHH...
PLEASE CHASE AFTER THEM!!
WELL, OBVIOUSLY!!
IS--
--THERE ANYTHING I CAN DO?!
NO! WE'LL REACH TOKYO IN AN HOUR!
YOU CAN AT LEAST THINK UP WHAT *YOU* OUGHTA DO BY *YOURSELF!*

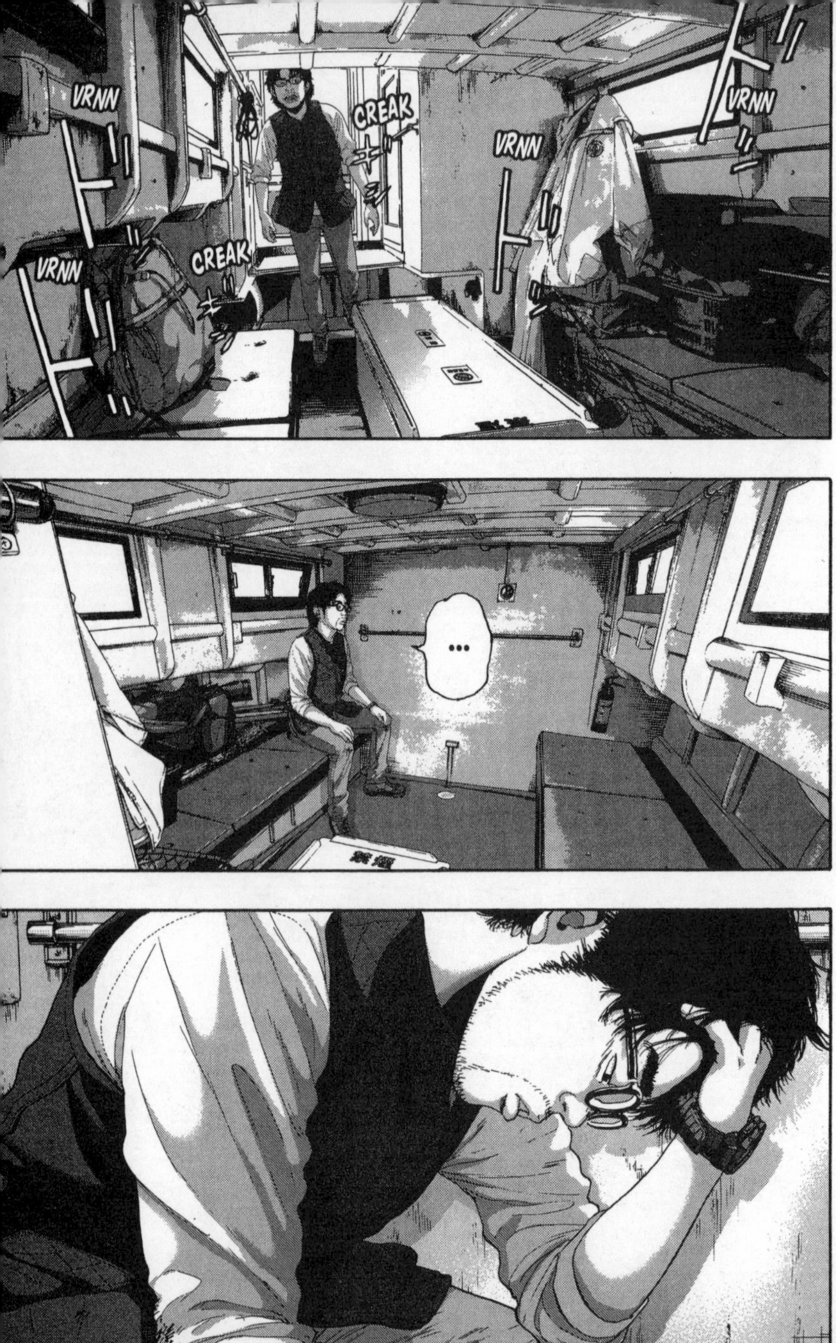
VRNN
CREAK
VRNN
VRNN
CREAK
VRNN
...

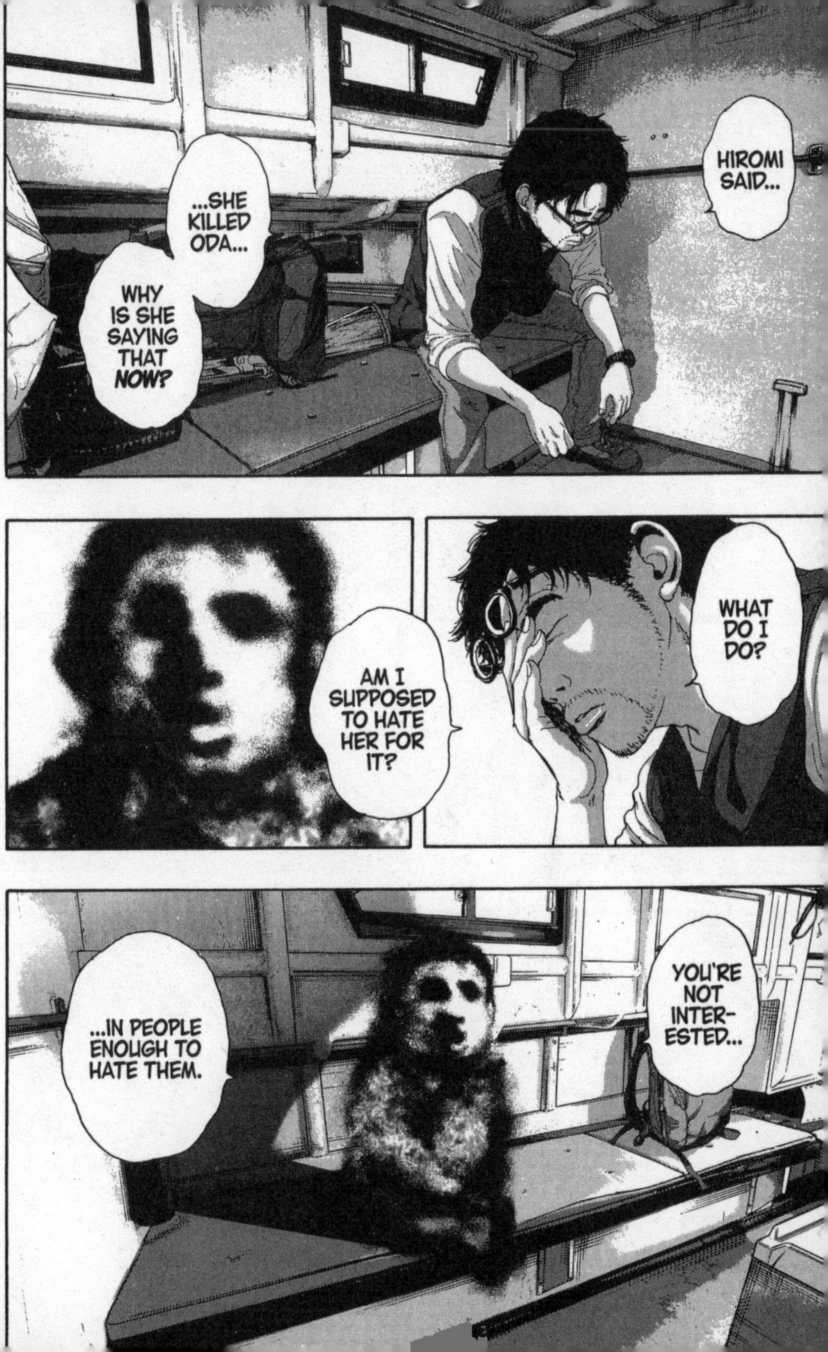
HIROMI SAID...
...SHE KILLED ODA...
WHY IS SHE SAYING THAT NOW?
WHAT DO I DO?
AM I SUPPOSED TO HATE HER FOR IT?
YOU'RE NOT INTER-ESTED...
...IN PEOPLE ENOUGH TO HATE THEM.

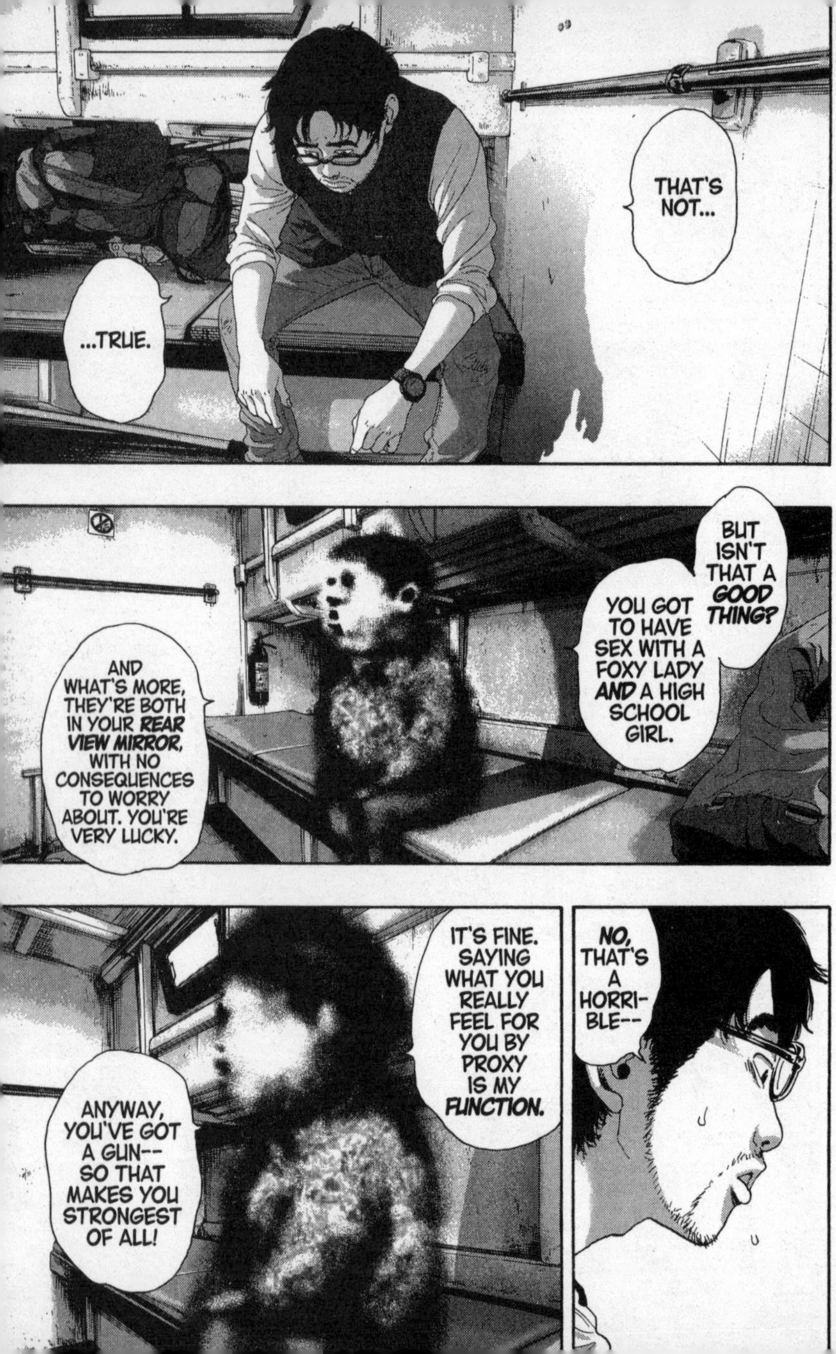
THAT'S NOT...
...TRUE.
BUT ISN'T THAT A GOOD THING?
YOU GOT TO HAVE SEX WITH A FOXY LADY AND A HIGH SCHOOL GIRL.
AND WHAT'S MORE, THEY'RE BOTH IN YOUR REAR VIEW MIRROR, WITH NO CONSEQUENCES TO WORRY ABOUT. YOU'RE VERY LUCKY.
NO, THAT'S A HORRI-BLE--
IT'S FINE. SAYING WHAT YOU REALLY FEEL FOR YOU BY PROXY IS MY FUNCTION.
ANYWAY, YOU'VE GOT A GUN-- SO THAT MAKES YOU STRONGEST OF ALL!

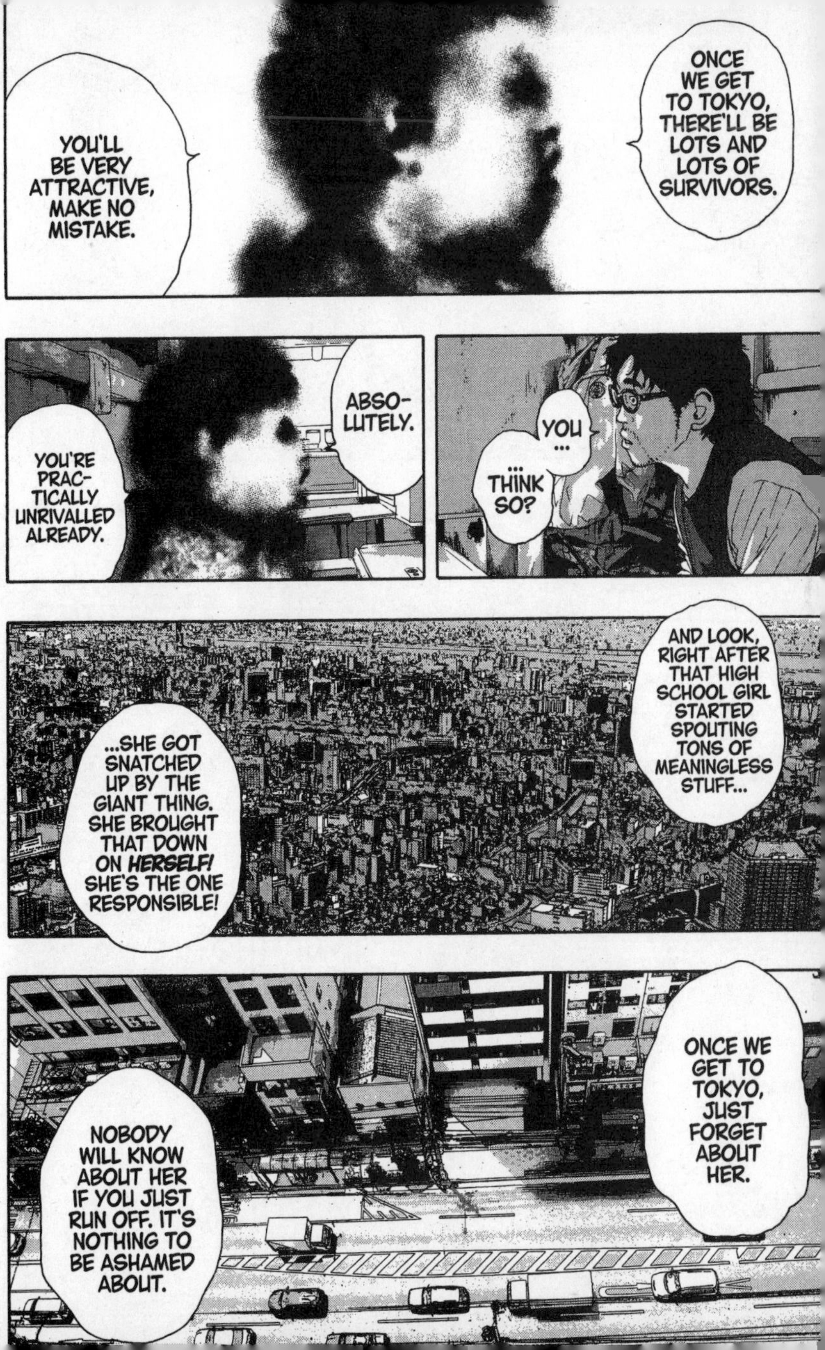
ONCE WE GET TO TOKYO, THERE'LL BE LOTS AND LOTS OF SURVIVORS.
YOU'LL BE VERY ATTRACTIVE, MAKE NO MISTAKE.
YOU...
...THINK SO?
ABSO-LUTELY.
YOU'RE PRAC-TICALLY UNRIVALLED ALREADY.
AND LOOK, RIGHT AFTER THAT HIGH SCHOOL GIRL STARTED SPOUTING TONS OF MEANINGLESS STUFF...
...SHE GOT SNATCHED UP BY THE GIANT THING. SHE BROUGHT THAT DOWN ON *HERSELF!* SHE'S THE ONE RESPONSIBLE!
ONCE WE GET TO TOKYO, JUST FORGET ABOUT HER.
NOBODY WILL KNOW ABOUT HER IF YOU JUST RUN OFF. IT'S NOTHING TO BE ASHAMED ABOUT.

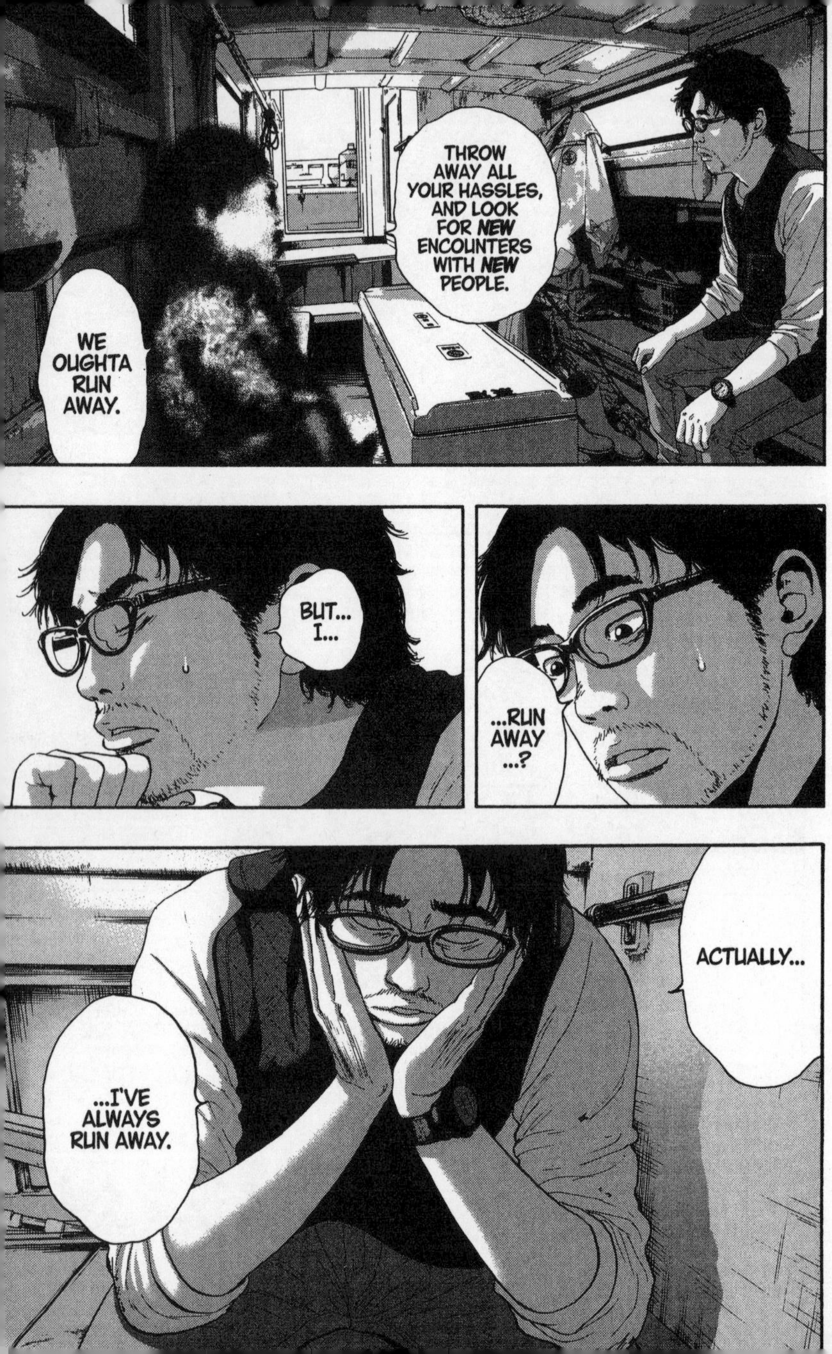
THROW AWAY ALL YOUR HASSLES, AND LOOK FOR NEW ENCOUNTERS WITH NEW PEOPLE.
WE OUGHTA RUN AWAY.
...RUN AWAY ...?
BUT... I...
ACTUALLY...
...I'VE ALWAYS RUN AWAY.

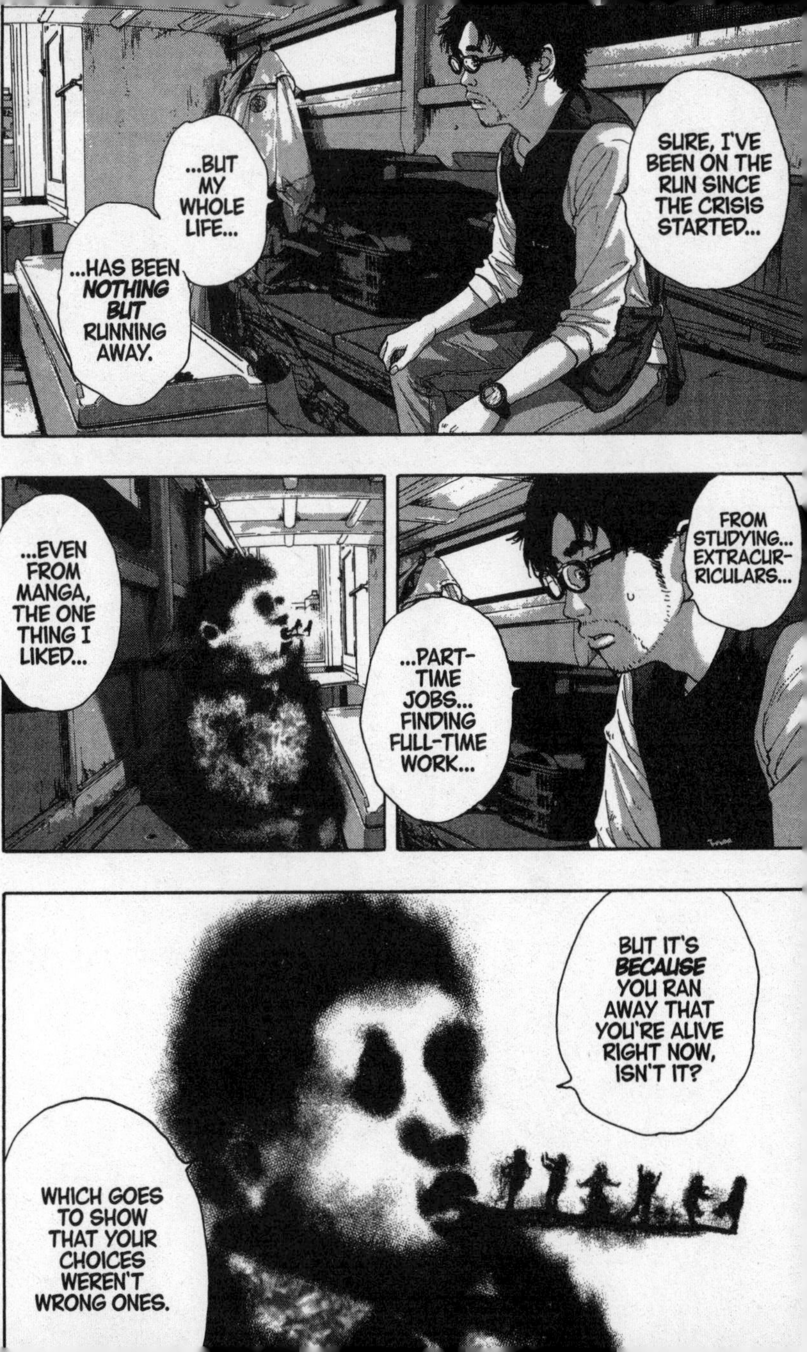
SURE, I'VE BEEN ON THE RUN SINCE THE CRISIS STARTED...
...BUT MY WHOLE LIFE...
...HAS BEEN *NOTHING BUT* RUNNING AWAY.
FROM STUDYING... EXTRACURRICULARS...
...PART-TIME JOBS... FINDING FULL-TIME WORK...
...EVEN FROM MANGA, THE ONE THING I LIKED...
BUT IT'S *BECAUSE* YOU RAN AWAY THAT YOU'RE ALIVE RIGHT NOW, ISN'T IT?
WHICH GOES TO SHOW THAT YOUR CHOICES WEREN'T WRONG ONES.

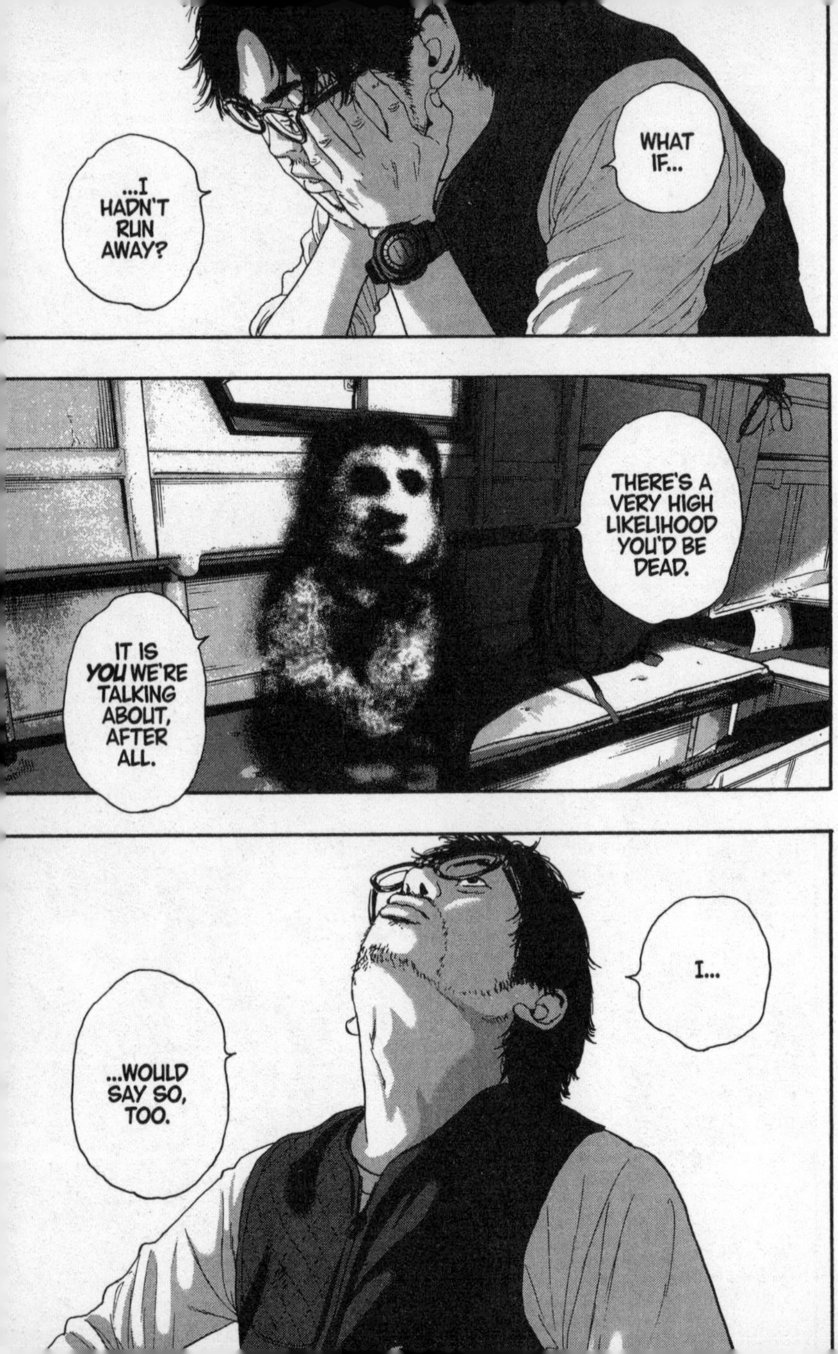
WHAT IF...
...I HADN'T RUN AWAY?
THERE'S A VERY HIGH LIKELIHOOD YOU'D BE DEAD.
IT IS *YOU* WE'RE TALKING ABOUT, AFTER ALL.
I...
...WOULD SAY SO, TOO.

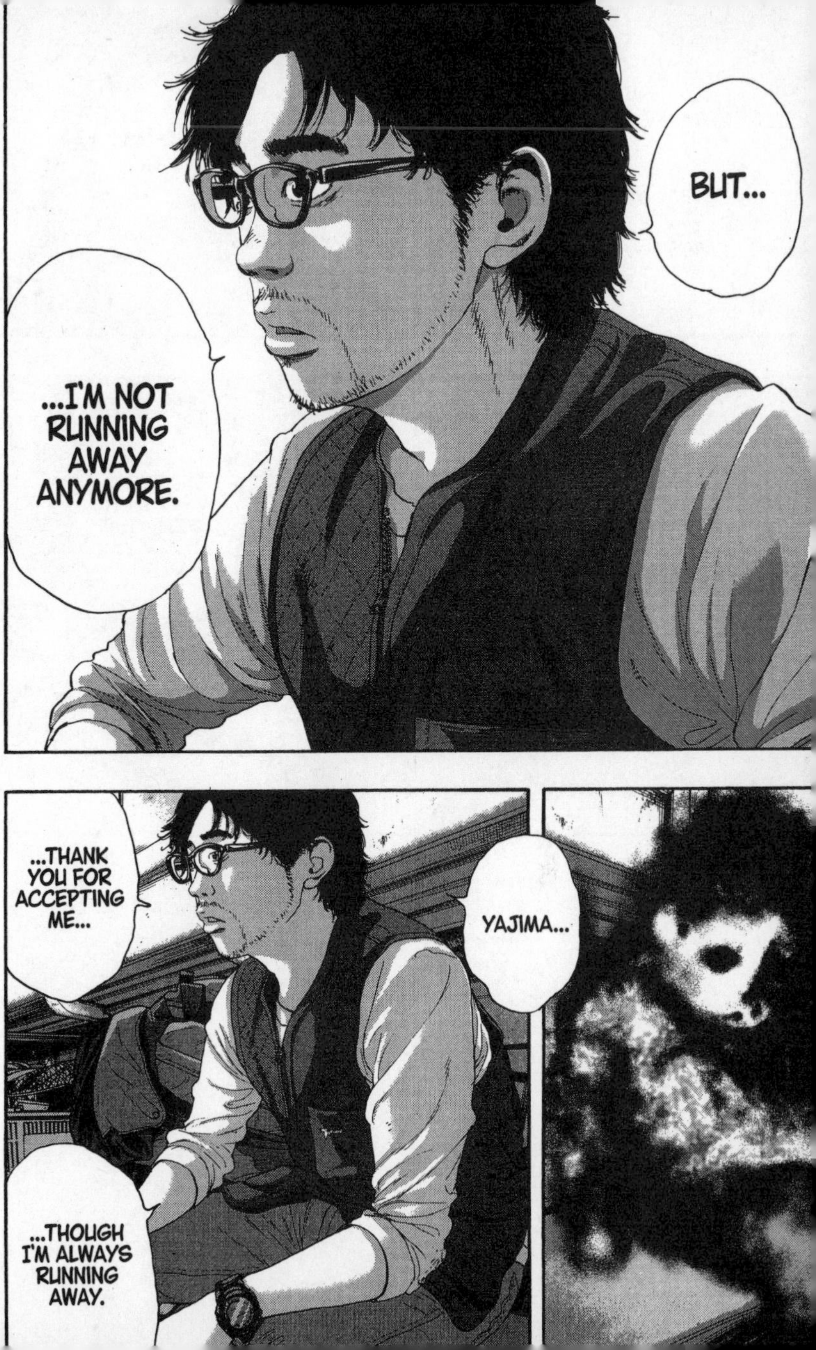
BUT...
...I'M NOT RUNNING AWAY ANYMORE.
YAJIMA...
...THANK YOU FOR ACCEPTING ME...
...THOUGH I'M ALWAYS RUNNING AWAY.

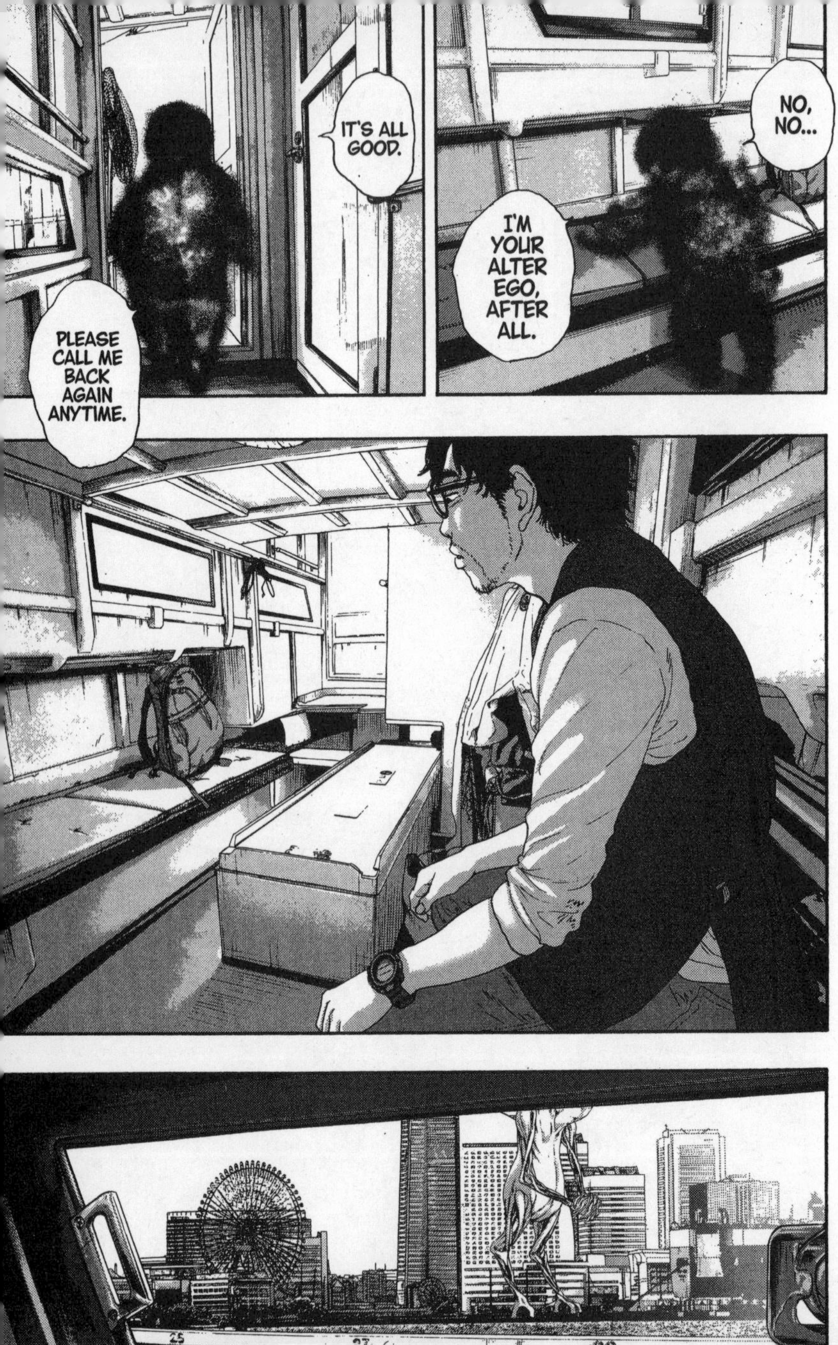
NO, NO...
I'M YOUR ALTER EGO, AFTER ALL.
IT'S ALL GOOD.
PLEASE CALL ME BACK AGAIN ANYTIME.

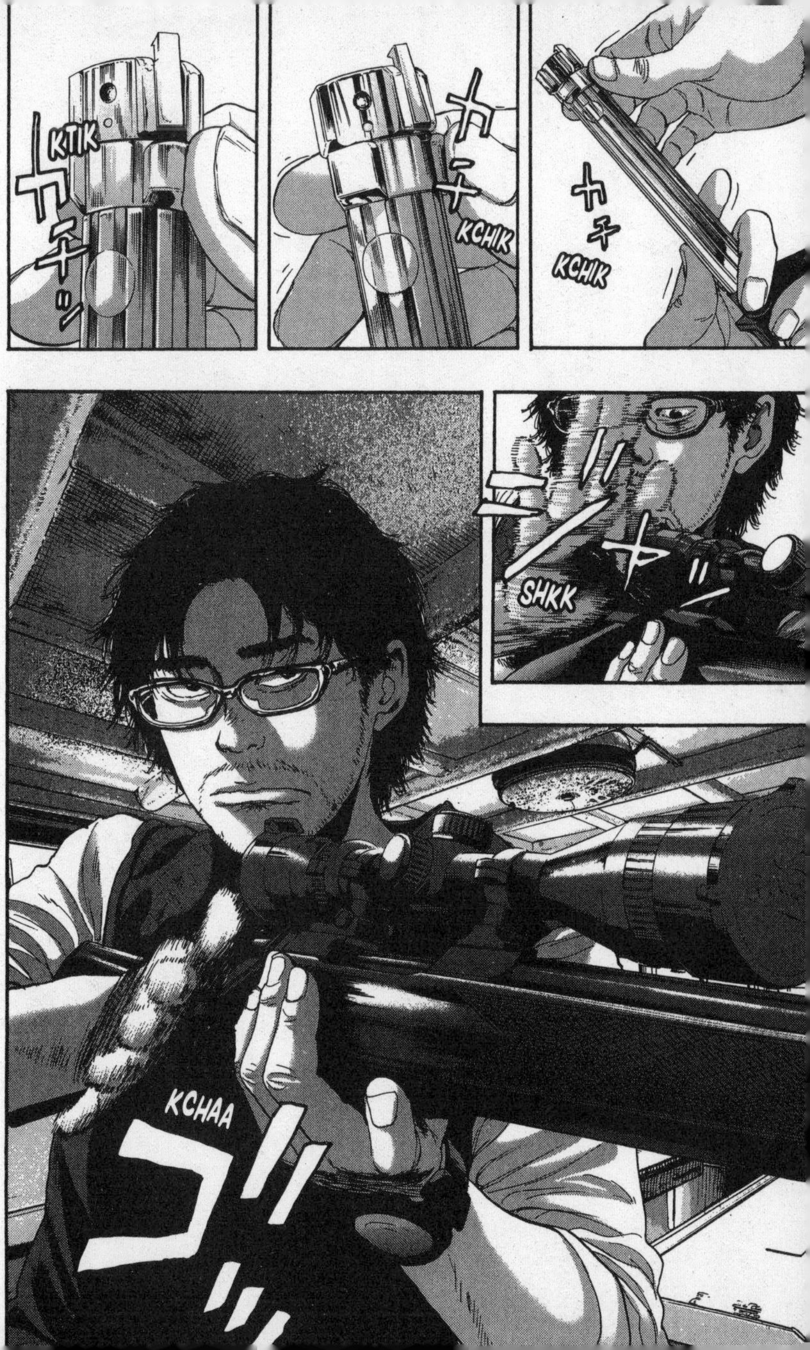
KCHIK
KCHIK
KTIK
SHKK
KCHAA

CHAPTER 230

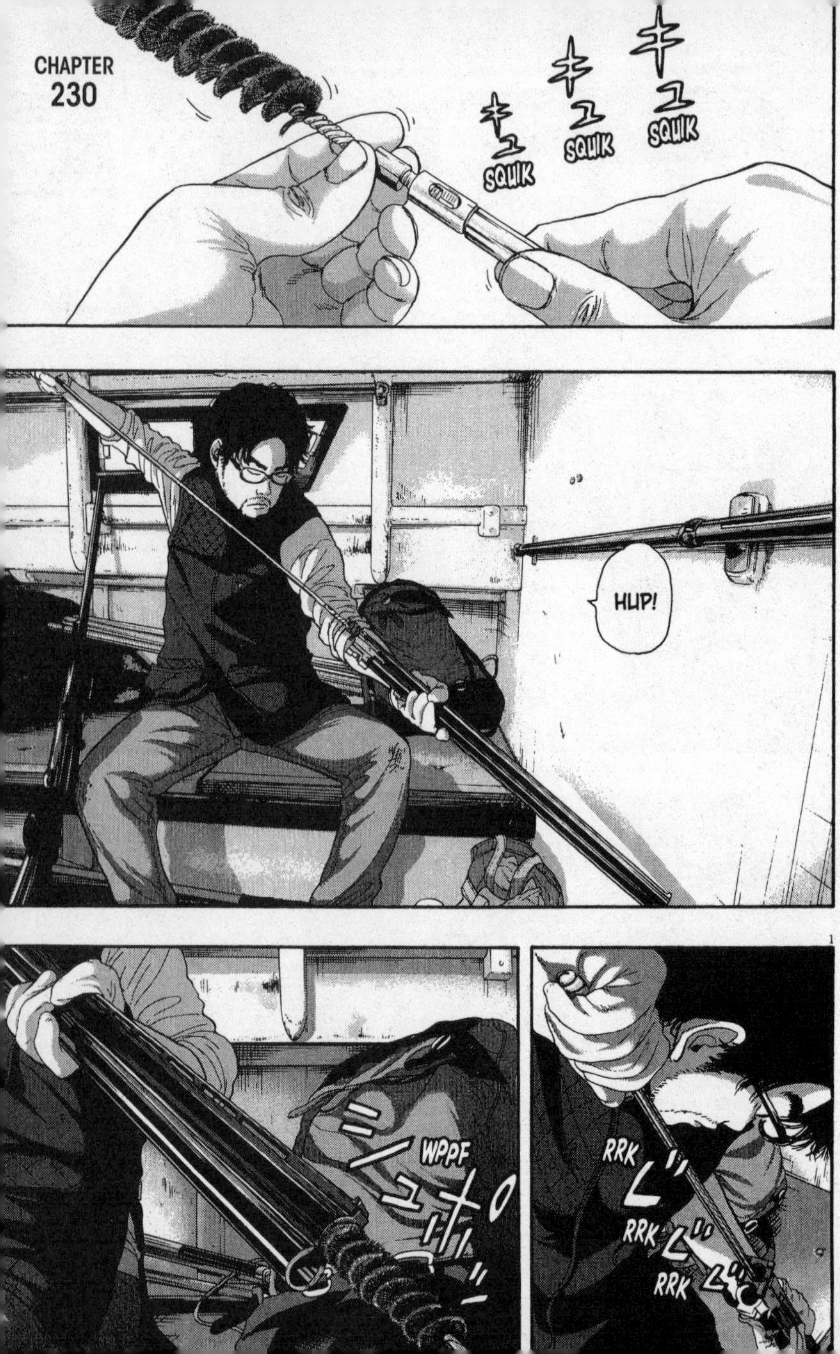
キュ
SQUIK
キュ
SQUIK
キュ
SQUIK
HUP!
RRK
RRK
RRK
WPPF

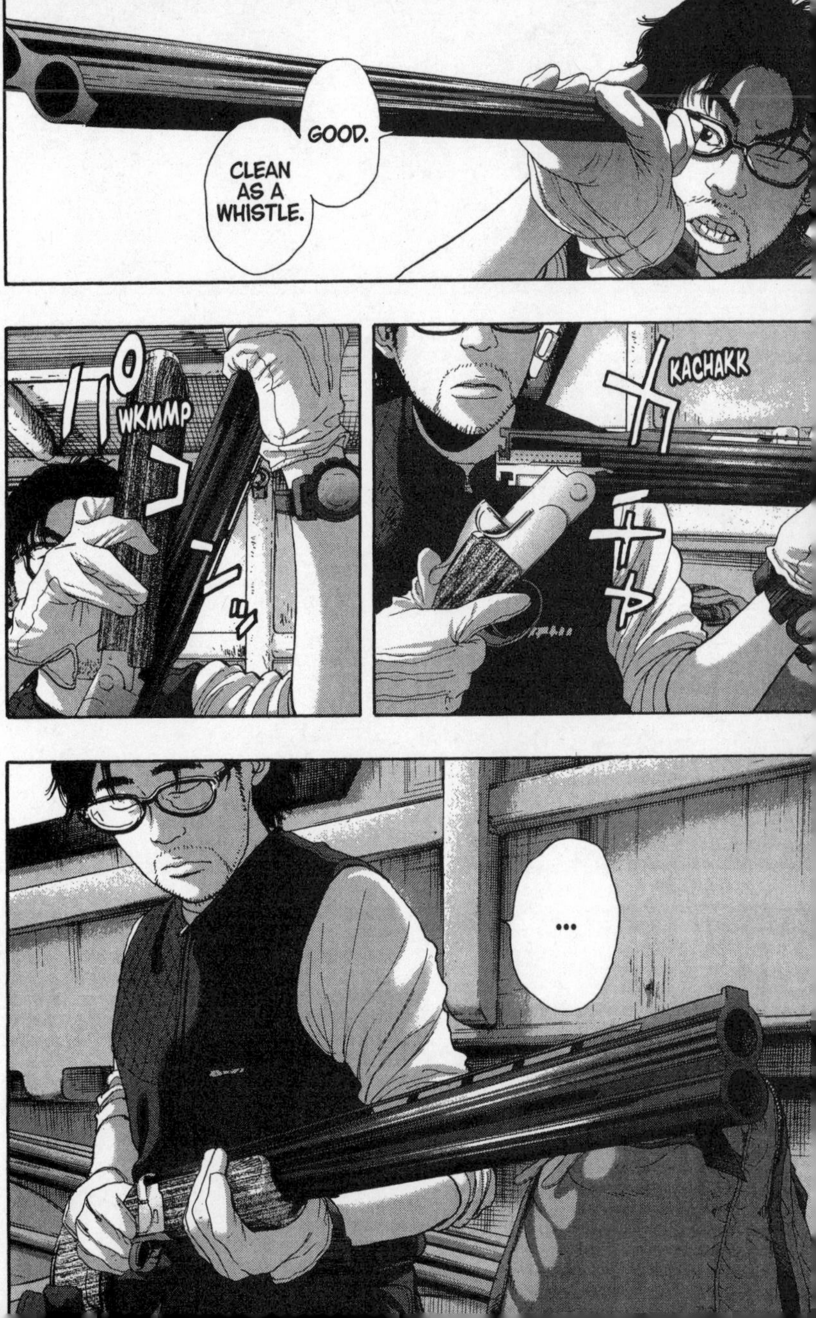
GOOD.
CLEAN AS A WHISTLE.
KACHAKK
WKMMP
...

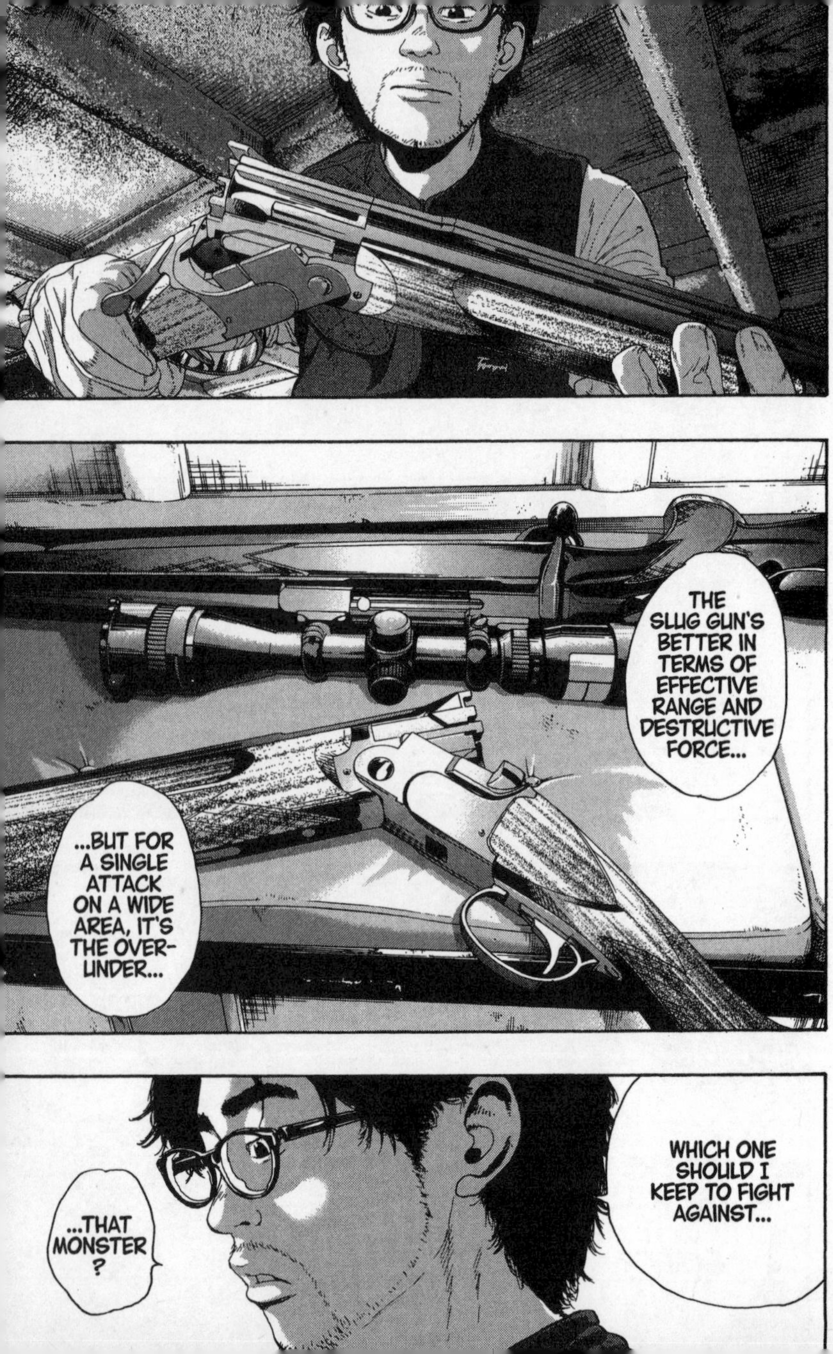
THE SLUG GUN'S BETTER IN TERMS OF EFFECTIVE RANGE AND DESTRUCTIVE FORCE...
...BUT FOR A SINGLE ATTACK ON A WIDE AREA, IT'S THE OVER-UNDER...
WHICH ONE SHOULD I KEEP TO FIGHT AGAINST...
...THAT MONSTER ?

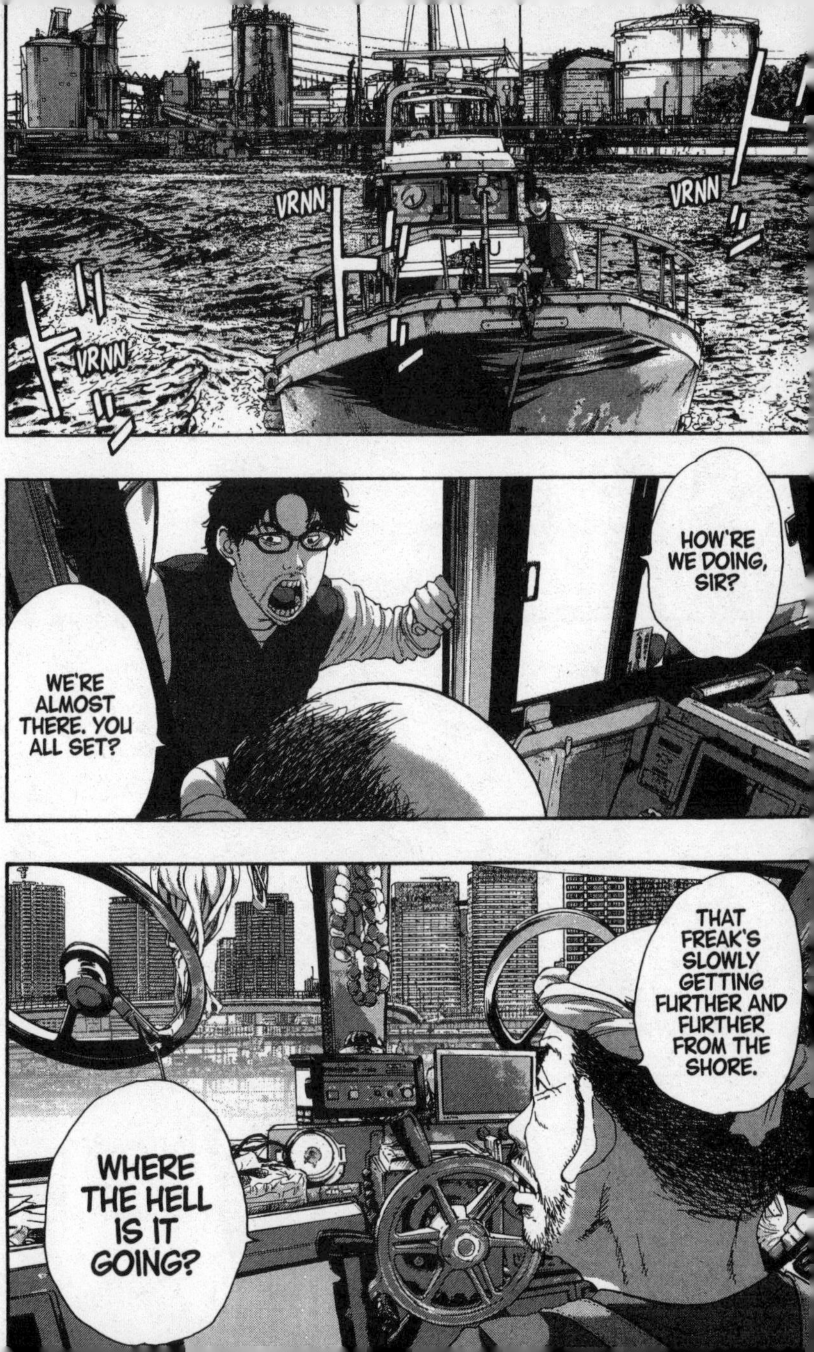
VRNN
VRNN
VRNN
HOW'RE WE DOING, SIR?
WE'RE ALMOST THERE. YOU ALL SET?
THAT FREAK'S SLOWLY GETTING FURTHER AND FURTHER FROM THE SHORE.
WHERE THE HELL IS IT GOING?

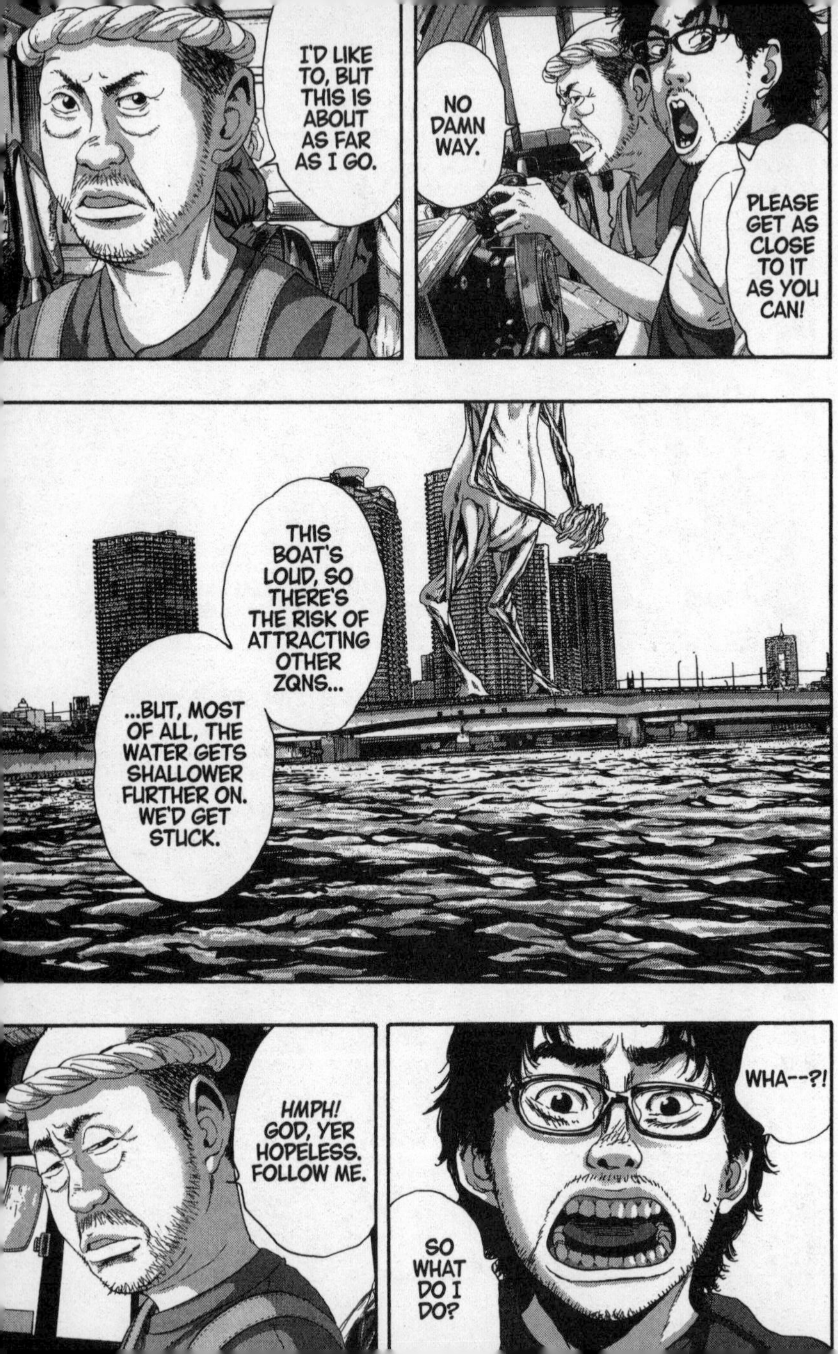
PLEASE GET AS CLOSE TO IT AS YOU CAN!
NO DAMN WAY.
I'D LIKE TO, BUT THIS IS ABOUT AS FAR AS I GO.
THIS BOAT'S LOUD, SO THERE'S THE RISK OF ATTRACTING OTHER ZQNS...
...BUT, MOST OF ALL, THE WATER GETS SHALLOWER FURTHER ON. WE'D GET STUCK.
WHA--?!
SO WHAT DO I DO?
HMPH! GOD, YER HOPELESS. FOLLOW ME.

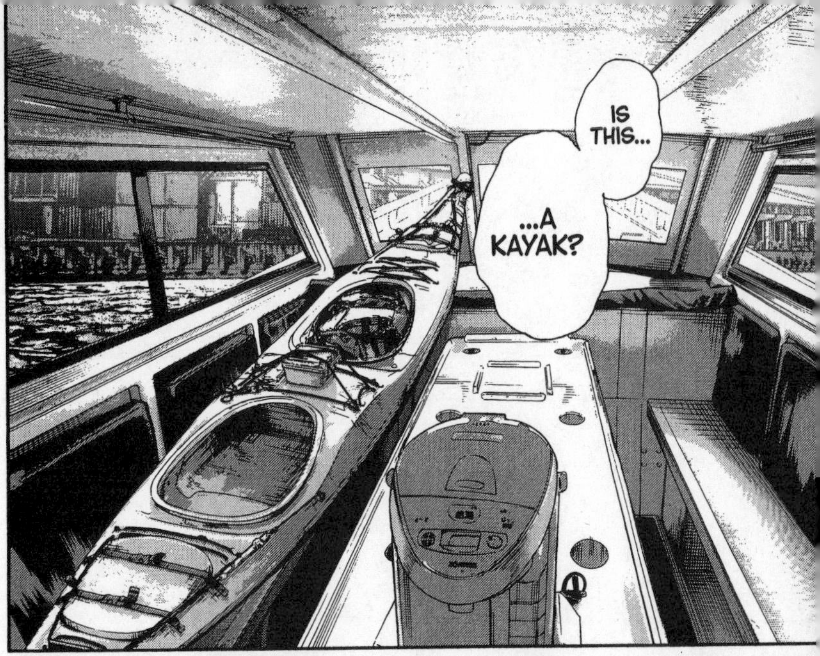
IS THIS...
...A KAYAK?

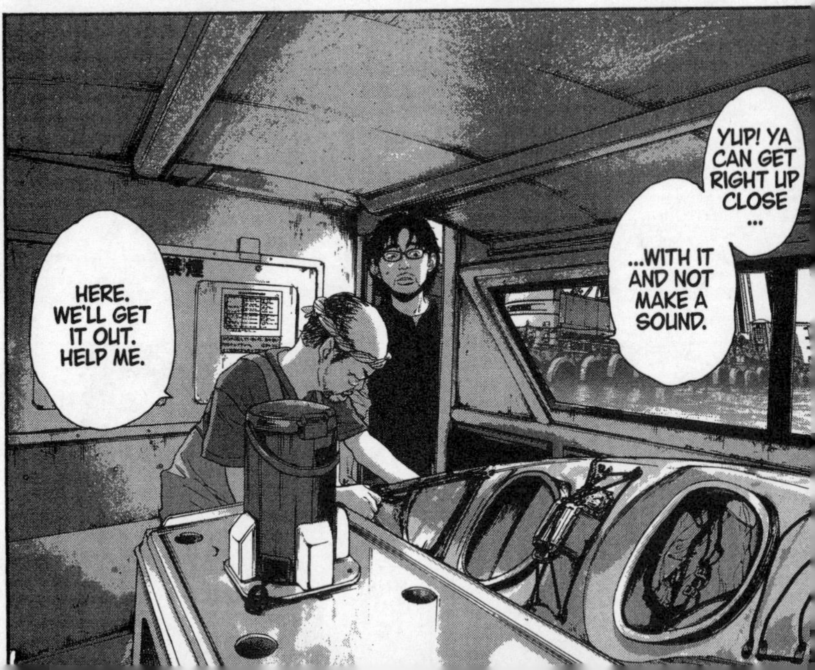
YUP! YA CAN GET RIGHT UP CLOSE ...
...WITH IT AND NOT MAKE A SOUND.
HERE. WE'LL GET IT OUT. HELP ME.

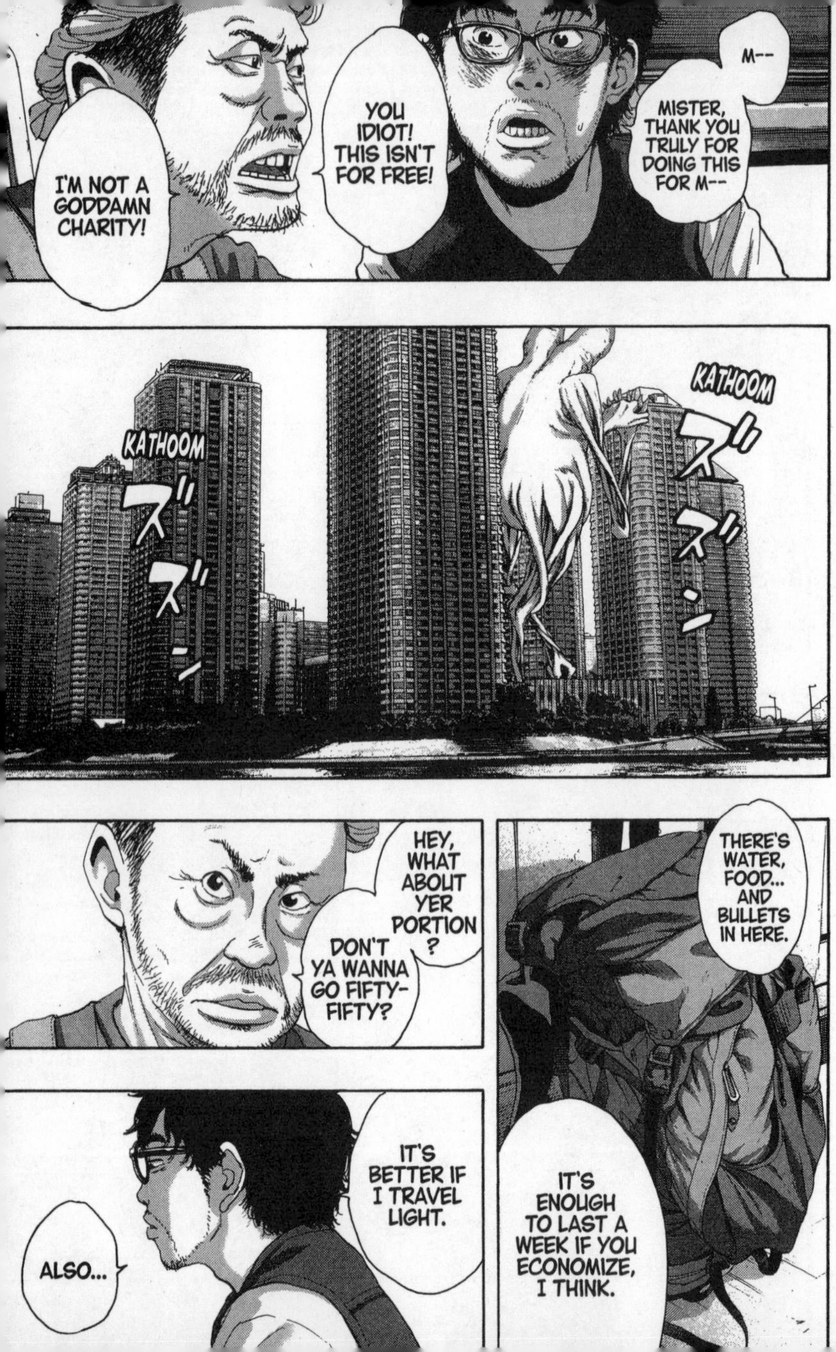
M--
MISTER, THANK YOU TRULY FOR DOING THIS FOR M--
YOU IDIOT! THIS ISN'T FOR FREE!
I'M NOT A GODDAMN CHARITY!
KATHOOM
ズズズ…
KATHOOM
ズズズ…
THERE'S WATER, FOOD... AND BULLETS IN HERE.
IT'S ENOUGH TO LAST A WEEK IF YOU ECONOMIZE, I THINK.
HEY, WHAT ABOUT YER PORTION?
DON'T YA WANNA GO FIFTY-FIFTY?
IT'S BETTER IF I TRAVEL LIGHT.
ALSO...

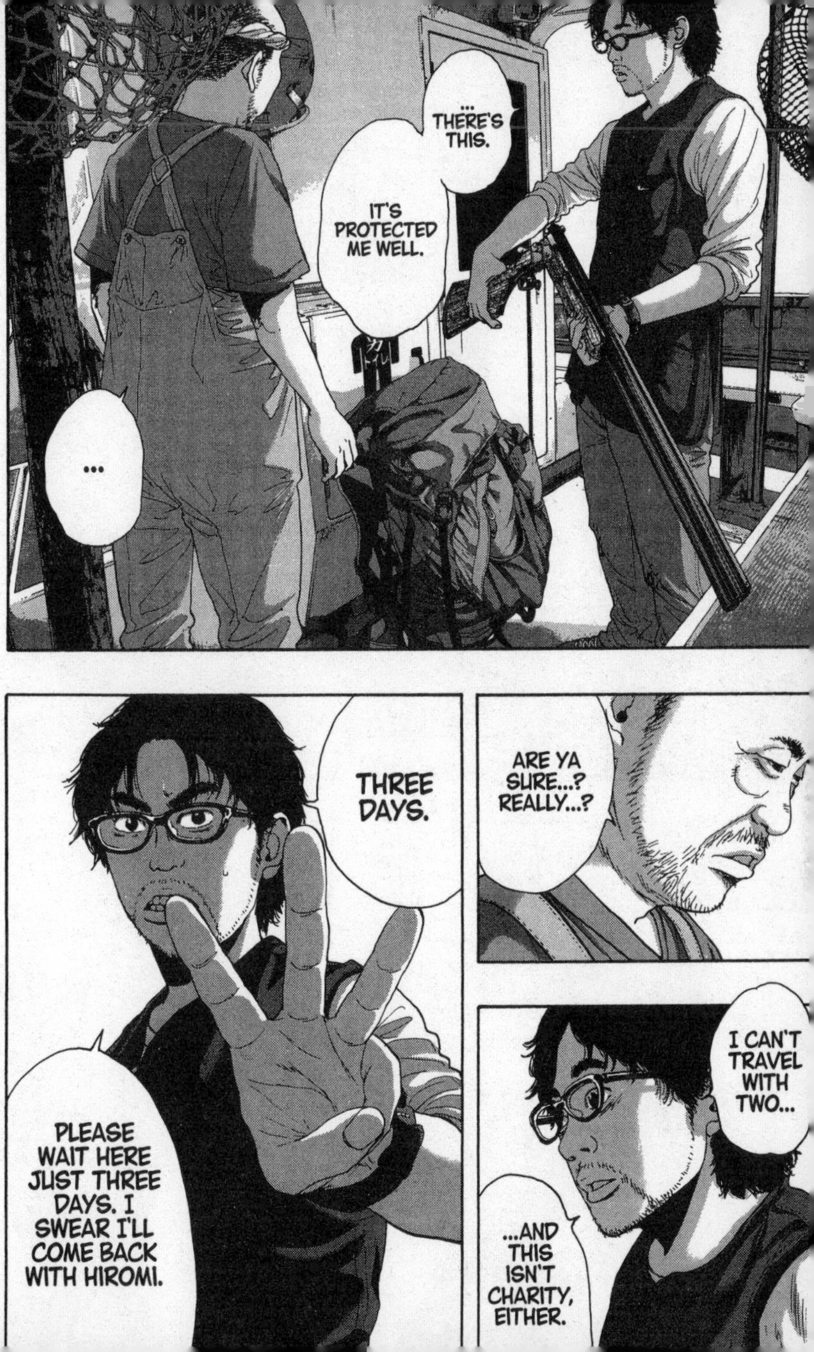
... THERE'S THIS.
IT'S PROTECTED ME WELL.
...
ARE YA SURE...? REALLY...?
I CAN'T TRAVEL WITH TWO...
...AND THIS ISN'T CHARITY, EITHER.
THREE DAYS.
PLEASE WAIT HERE JUST THREE DAYS. I SWEAR I'LL COME BACK WITH HIROMI.

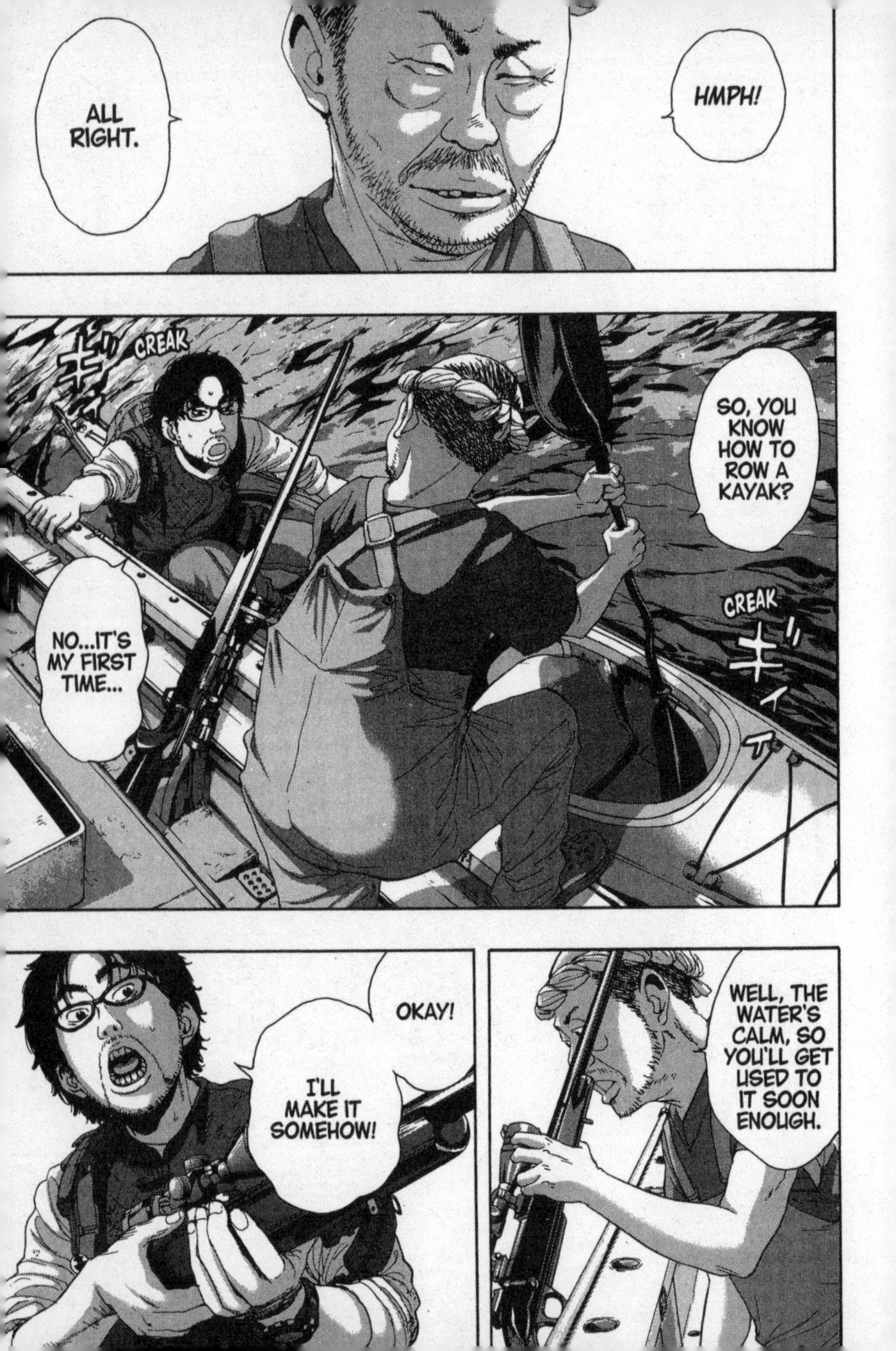
HMPH!
ALL RIGHT.
SO, YOU KNOW HOW TO ROW A KAYAK?
CREAK
CREAK
NO...IT'S MY FIRST TIME...
WELL, THE WATER'S CALM, SO YOU'LL GET USED TO IT SOON ENOUGH.
OKAY!
I'LL MAKE IT SOMEHOW!

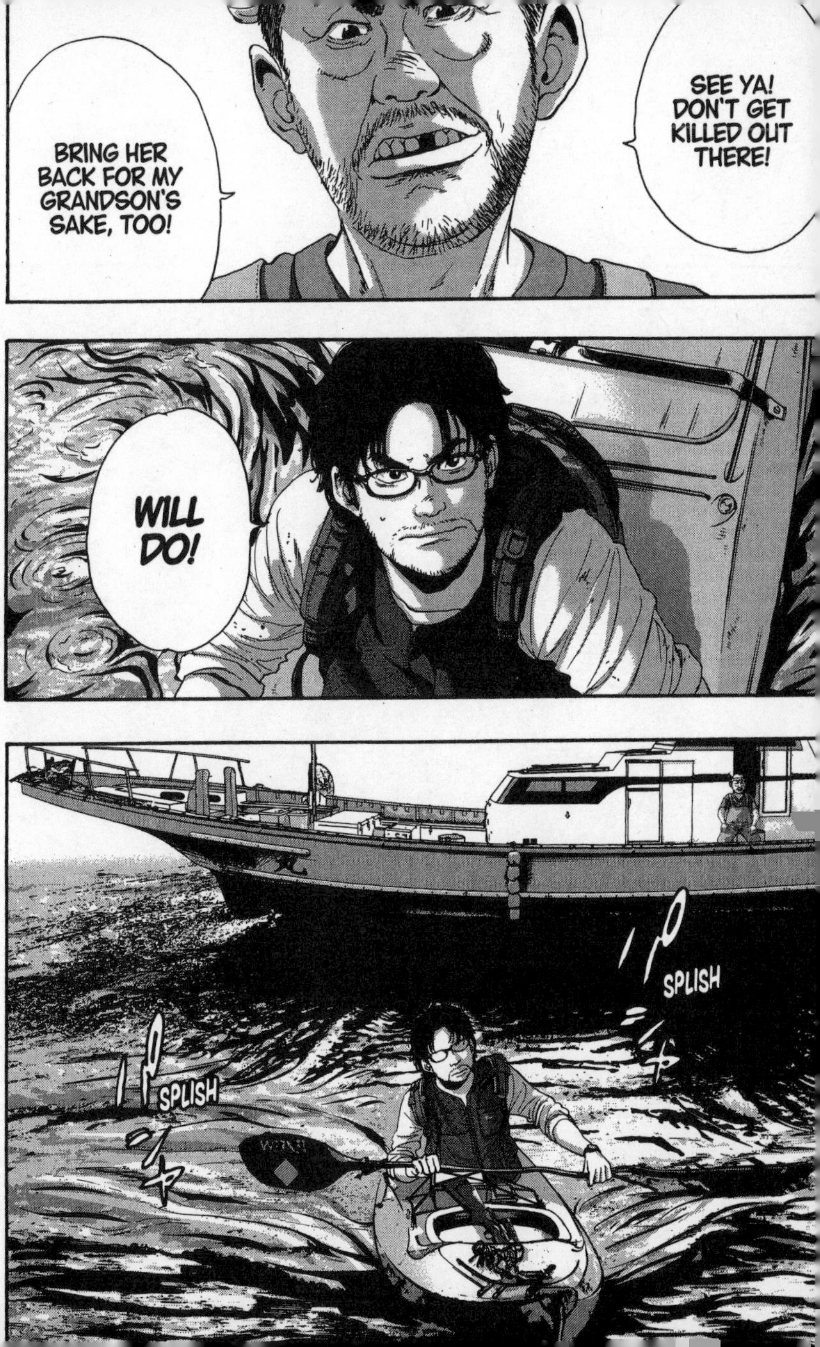
SEE YA! DON'T GET KILLED OUT THERE!
BRING HER BACK FOR MY GRANDSON'S SAKE, TOO!
WILL DO!
SPLISH
SPLISH

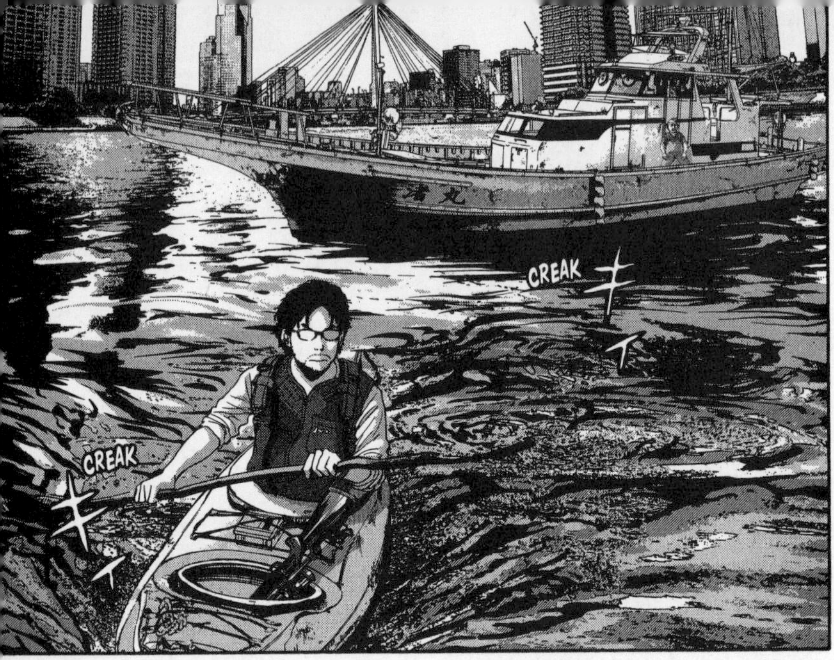
CREAK
CREAK

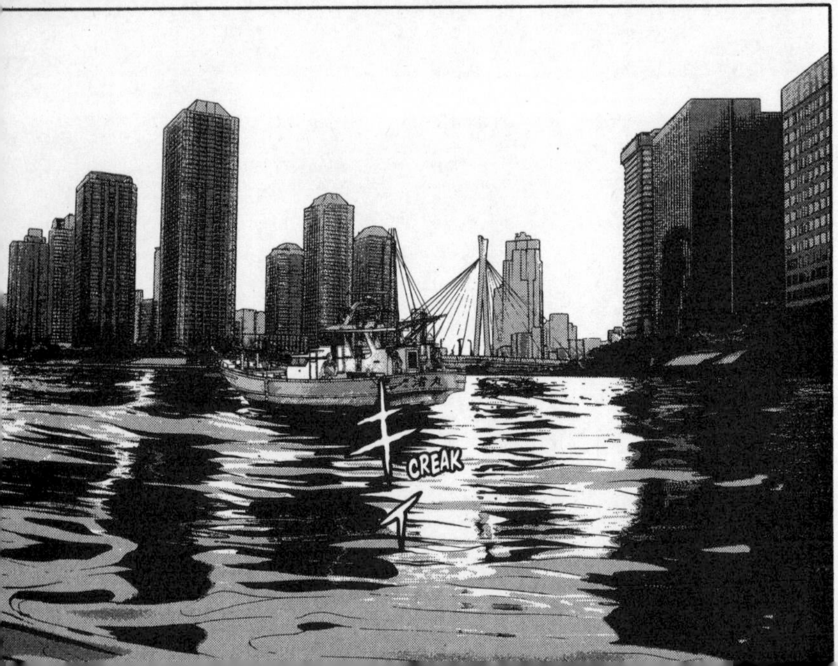
CREAK

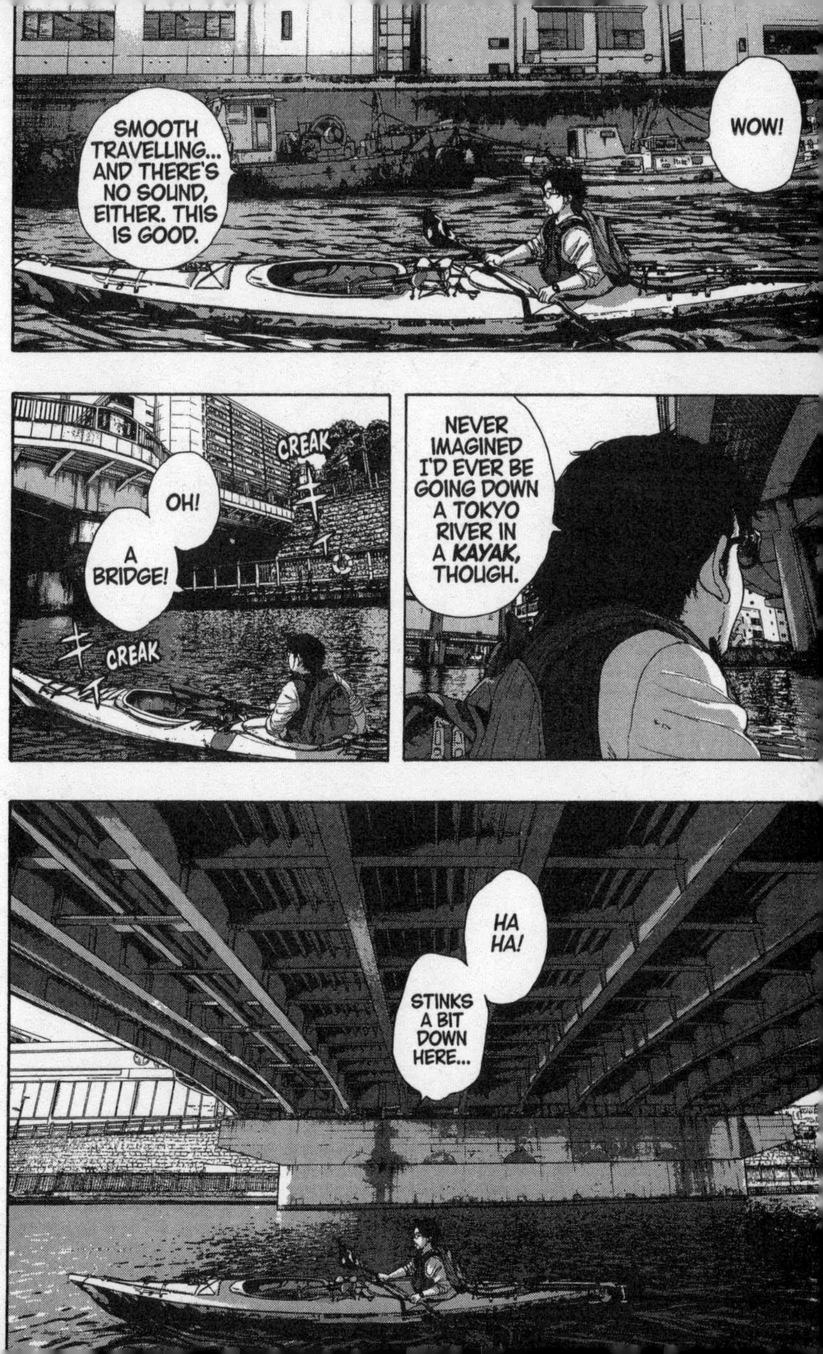
WOW!
SMOOTH TRAVELLING... AND THERE'S NO SOUND, EITHER. THIS IS GOOD.
NEVER IMAGINED I'D EVER BE GOING DOWN A TOKYO RIVER IN A KAYAK, THOUGH.
CREAK
OH!
A BRIDGE!
CREAK
HA HA!
STINKS A BIT DOWN HERE...

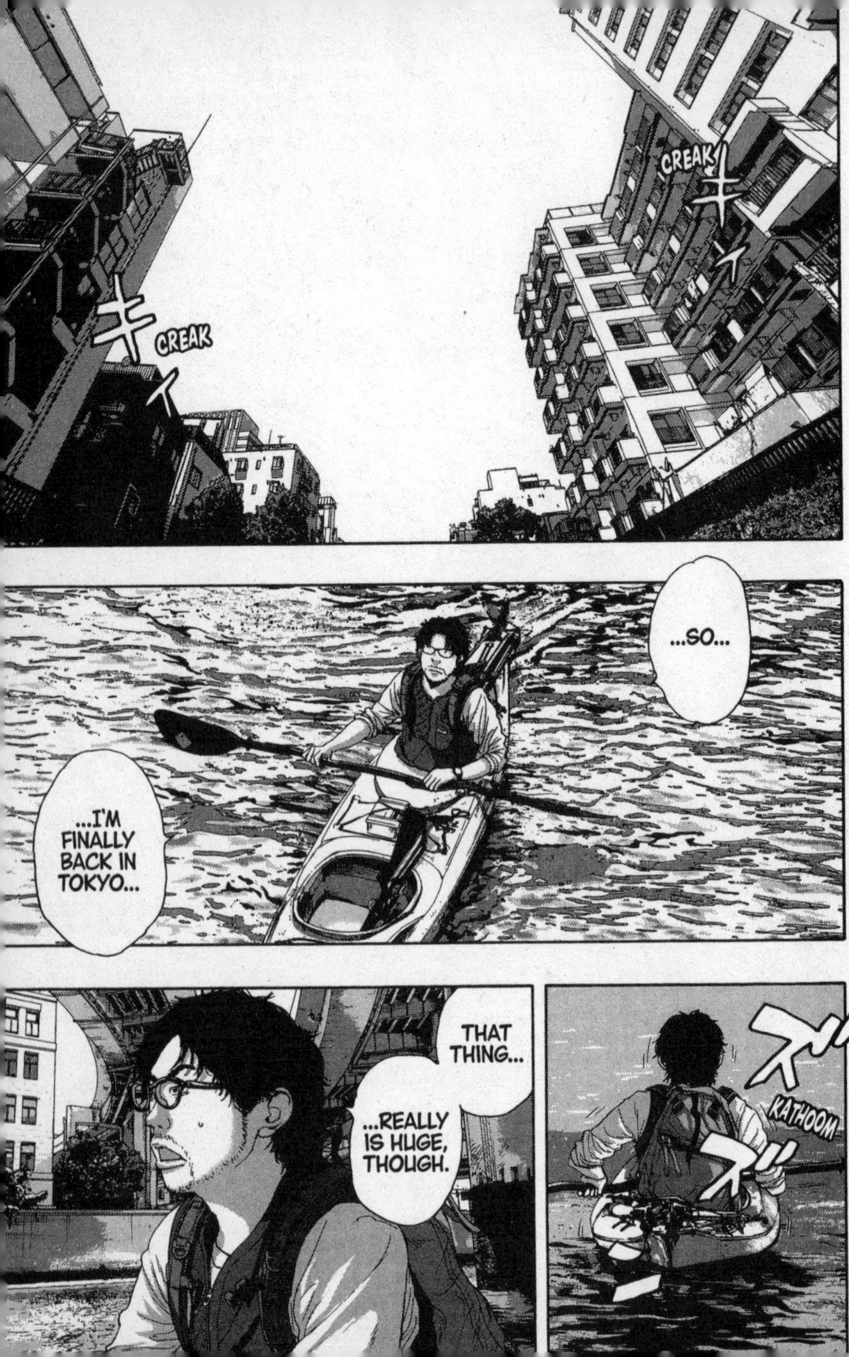
CREAK
CREAK
...SO...
...I'M FINALLY BACK IN TOKYO...
KATHOOM
THAT THING...
...REALLY IS HUGE, THOUGH.

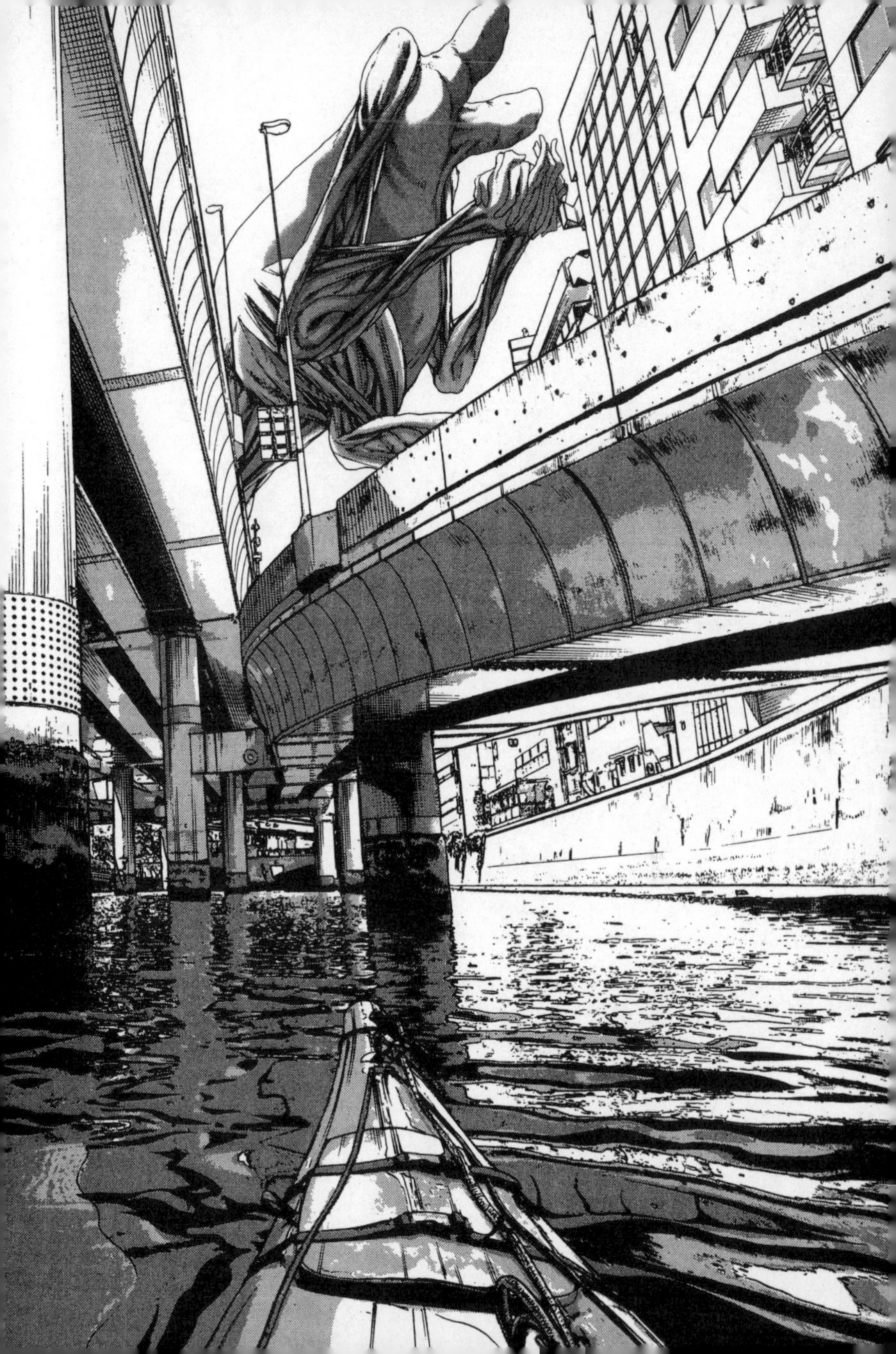

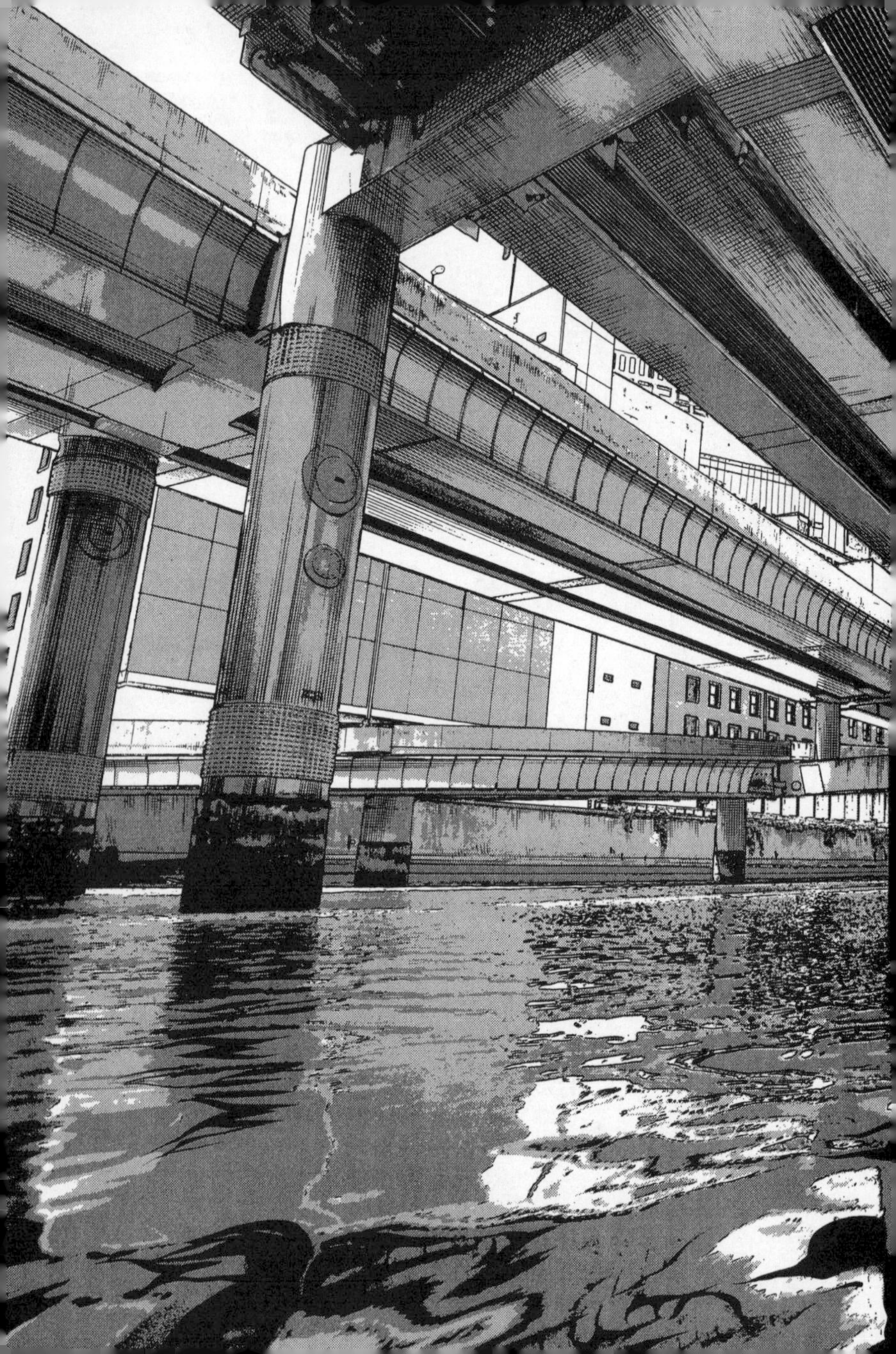

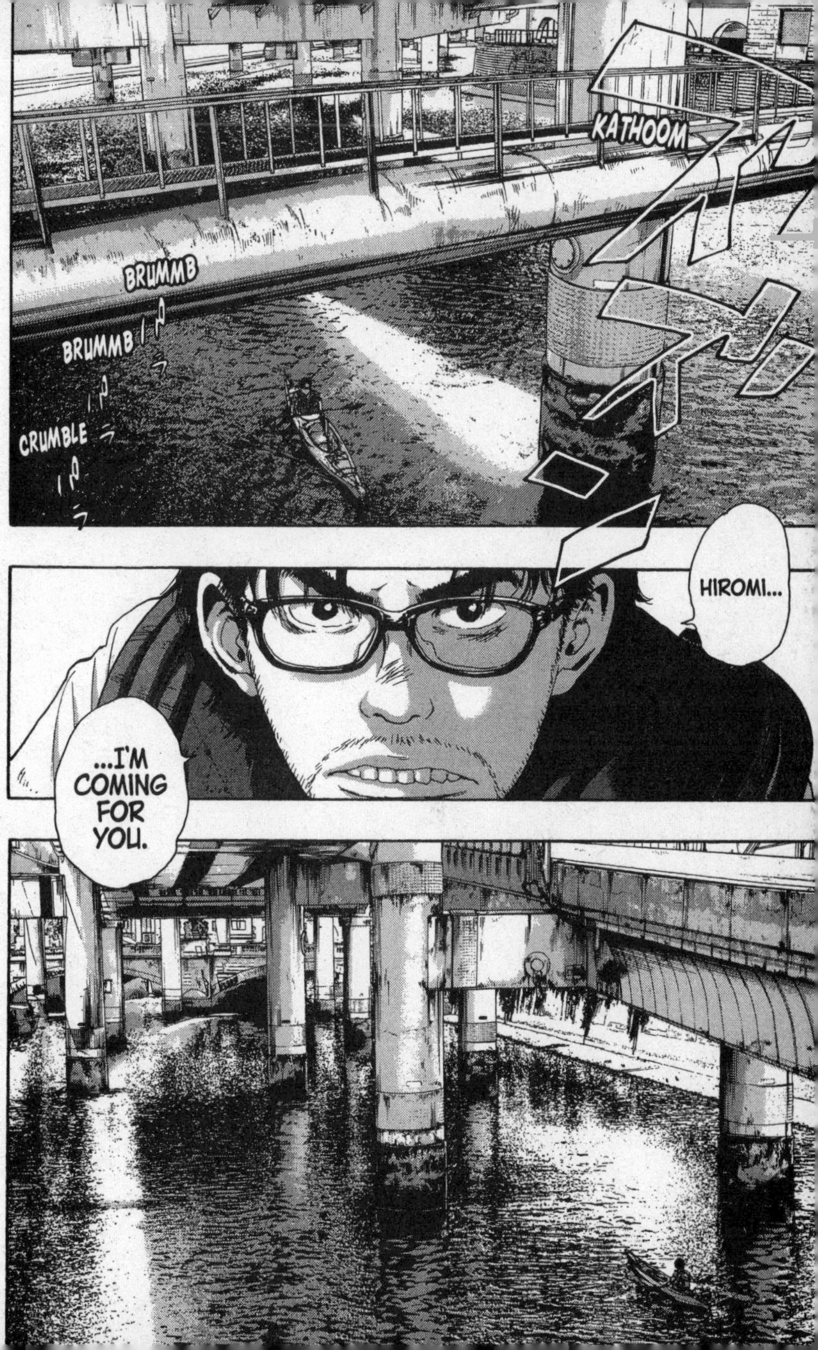
KATHOOM
BRUMMB
BRUMMB
CRUMBLE
HIROMI...
...I'M COMING FOR YOU.

CHAPTER
231

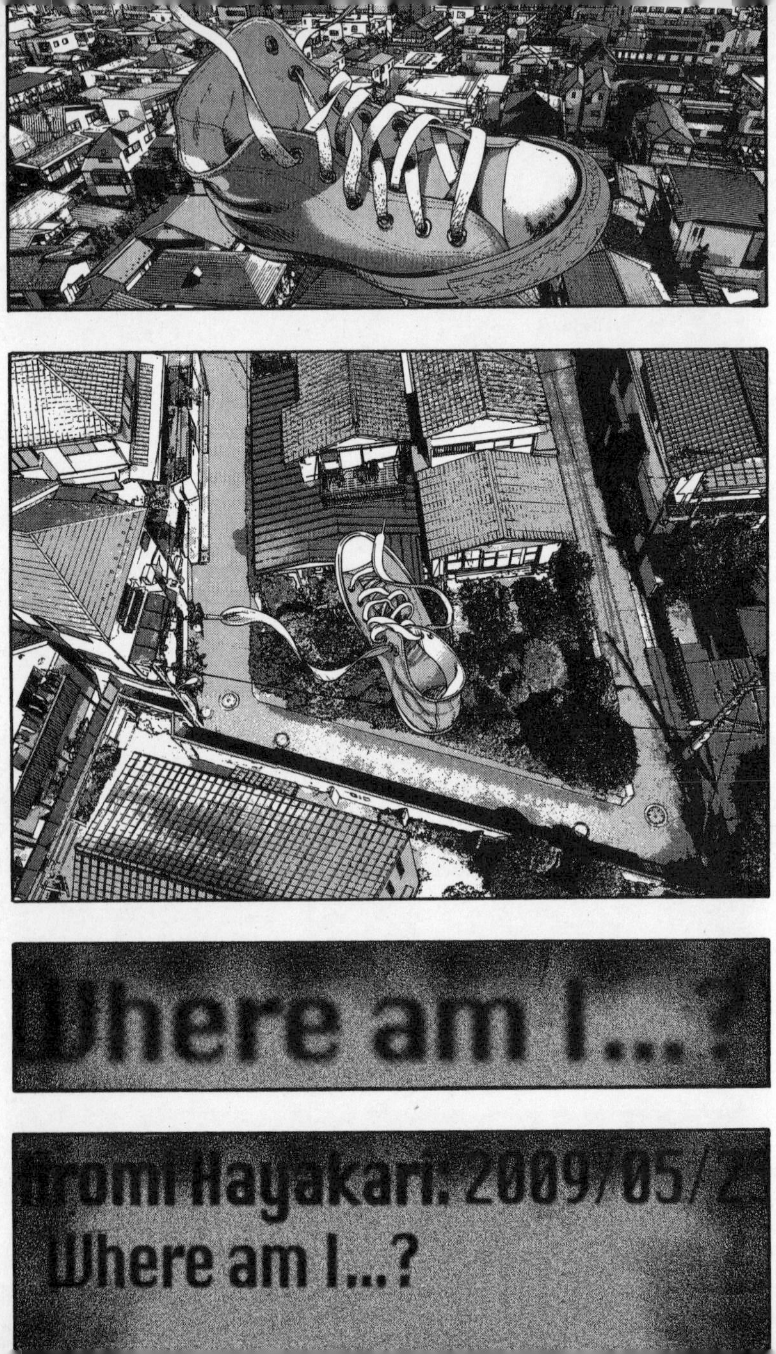
Where am I...?
romi Hayakari: 2009/05/2
Where am I...?

08: Hiromi Hayakari: 2009/05/23 (Sat) 16:30:05 ID: hirohay
Where am I...?

108: Hiromi Hayakari: 2009/05/23 (Sat) 16:30:05 ID: hirohaya
Where am I...?

638: Anonymous Integrated Mind: 2009/05/23 (Sat) 16:30:12 ID: brain
Oh, you can see this?
I wonder if we've connected?

107: Hiromi Hayakari: 2008/07/18 (Fri) 13:55:22 ID: hirohaya
???
I can see it...but where am I?

197: Hiromi Hayakari: 2008/07/18 (Fri) 13:55:22 ID: hirohaya
???
I can see it...but where am I?

228: Anonymous Brain: 2009/05/23 (Sat) 16:31:57 ID: spirit
>>108
Google it, dork

639: Anonymous Integrated Mind: 2009/05/23 (Sat) 16:30:55 ID: brain
>>107
Hmm. This is a mental world that's something like a gigantic BBS messa...
Does that make sense to you?

Hmm. This is a mental world that's something like a gigantic BBS me...
Does that make sense to you?

106: Hiromi Hayakari: 2001/02/07 (Wed) 07:05:59 ID: hirohaya
????
Nope...

640: Anonymous Integrated Mind: 2009/05/23 (Sat) 16:31:57 I
>>108
No. It wouldn't.
You may not understand this, but I'll explain anyway.

105: Hiromi Hayakari: 2005/03/07 (Sat) 22:25:48 ID: hirohaya
O...kay

641: Anonymous Integrated Mind: 2009/05/23 (Sat) 16
Hmm. Do you remember being taken into the ZQN?

104: Hiromi Hayakari: 2006/09/02 (Sat) 09:27:10 ID: hiro
Uh...yes....

104: Hiromi Hayakari: 2006/09/02 (Sat) 09:27:10 ID: hirohaya
Uh...yes....

642: Anonymous Integrated Mind: 2009/05/23 (Sat) 16:32:51 ID: brain
You're at the stage right now in which your body has just
been sucked into the ZQN aggregate.
And at the same time, you are in physical contact with the
ZQN Integrated Mind, so two-way communication is possible
between us.

ZQN Integrated Mind, so two-way communication is possible
between us.

103: Hiromi Hayakari: 2002/11/24 (Sat) 13:09:06 ID: hirohaya
?

843: Anonymous Integrated Mind: 2009/05/23 (Sat) 16:33:45 ID: brain
>>103
Well...I don't suppose you understand what I mean.

102: Hiromi Hayakari: 2007/10/09 (Sat) 02:54:51 ID: hiromi
...I don't.

> **843: Anonymous Brain:** 2009/05/23 (Sat) 16:32:35 ID: mind
> So Google it, dork

844: Anonymous Integrated Mind: 2009/05/23 (Sat) 16:35:11 ID: brain
>>102
Well, then, let me change the subject.
What comes to mind when I say the word "red"...?

360: Forever with My Sister: 2009/05/23 (Sat) 16:32:40 ID: sister
I'm not sad about being literally psychically connected to my sister.

101: Hiromi Hayakari: 1999/12/31/ (Sat) 14:27:2
...???
Uh, blood?

844: Anonymous Integrated Mind: 2009/05/23 (Sat) 16:35:11 ID: brain
>>102
Well, then, let me change the subject.
What comes to mind when I say the word "red"?

360: Forever with My Sister: 2009/05/23 (Sat) 16:32:40 ID: sister
I'm not sad about being literally psychically connected to my sister.

101: Hiromi Hayakari: 1999/12/31/ (Sat) 14:27:2
...???
Uh, blood?

Anonymous Integrated Mind: 2009/05/23 (Sat) 16:36:14 ID: brain
>>101
For some people "blood" is what pops into their heads, and some people think of "apples."
There are as many answers as there are people. There's no limit to the associations that
come up, and if you just slap it all together, you get chaos. So, to cushion that and allow for
smooth unification of consciousnesses for those who are willing, some of us created this
city-like mental space.

100: Hiromi Hayakari: 2003/08/01 (Sat) 04:49:00 ID: hirohaya
Those who are willing?

446: Anonymous Integrated Mind: 2009/05/23 (Sat) 16:37:35 ID:

100: Hiromi Hayakari: 2003/08/01 (Sat) 04:49:00 ID: hirohaya
those who are willing?

446: Anonymous Integrated Mind: 2009/05/23 (Sat) 16:37:35 ID: brain
>>100
Well, it's hard to create a world which all people can agree to.
It was concluded that a gigantic internet message board would be
the thing with the greatest affinity for us.
Your being able to understand this space, means that you've seen
something like this before, right?

367: Anonymous Brain: 2009/05/23 (Sat) 16:32:51 ID: soul
It's creepy, but it's a good thing...

99: Hiromi Hayakari: 1998/04/29 (Sat) 19:09:18 ID hirohaya
Well...
What happens to people who haven't seen one before?

647: Anonymous Integrated Mind: 2009/05/23 (Sat) 16:87:03 ID:
>>99
That's different for everybody, too.

What happens to people who haven't seen one before?

647: Anonymous Integrated Mind: 2009/05/23 (Sat) 16:37:03 ID: bra
>>99
That's different for everybody, too.
Some people quickly dismantle their "individuality" and
melt into the "all."
Some people remain isolated as "individuals" and sink to the
bottom of the "all."

912: Anonymous Brain: 2009/05/23 (Sat) 16:33:23 ID: synapse (maybe
>>360
Do you ever give up?

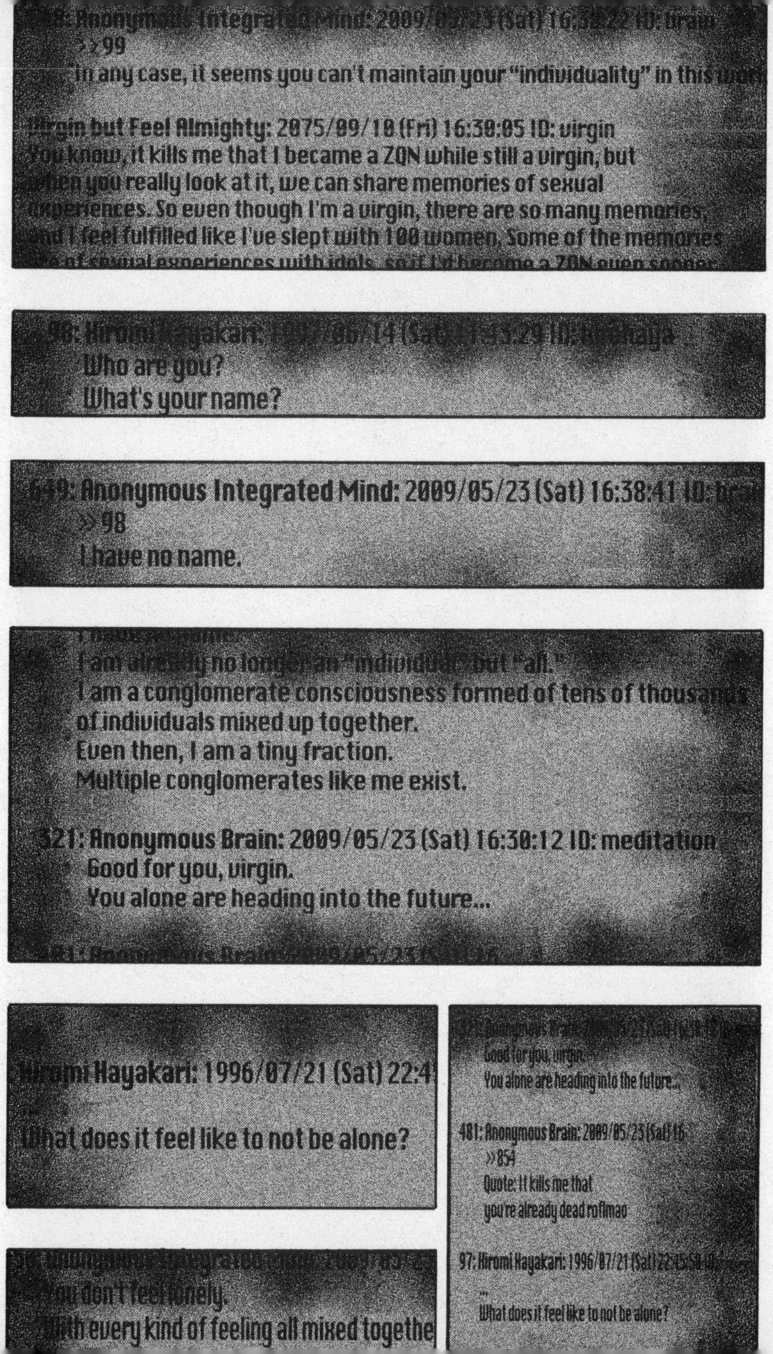

648: Anonymous Integrated Mind: 2009/05/23 (Sat) 16:38:22 ID: brain
≥99
in any case, it seems you can't maintain your "individuality" in this world

Virgin but Feel Almighty: 2075/09/10 (Fri) 16:30:05 ID: virgin
You know, it kills me that I became a ZQN while still a virgin, but
when you really look at it, we can share memories of sexual
experiences. So even though I'm a virgin, there are so many memories,
and I feel fulfilled like I've slept with 100 women. Some of the memories
are of sexual experiences with idols, so if I'd become a ZQN even sooner,

98: Hiromi Hayakari: 1997/06/14 (Sat) 13:29 ID: hayakaya
Who are you?
What's your name?

649: Anonymous Integrated Mind: 2009/05/23 (Sat) 16:38:41 ID: brain
≥98
I have no name.

I have no name.
I am already no longer an "individual" but "all."
I am a conglomerate consciousness formed of tens of thousands
of individuals mixed up together.
Even then, I am a tiny fraction.
Multiple conglomerates like me exist.

321: Anonymous Brain: 2009/05/23 (Sat) 16:30:12 ID: meditation
Good for you, virgin.
You alone are heading into the future...

Hiromi Hayakari: 1996/07/21 (Sat) 22:4

What does it feel like to not be alone?

Good for you, virgin.
You alone are heading into the future...

481: Anonymous Brain: 2009/05/23 (Sat) 16
≥854
Quote: It kills me that
you're already dead roflmao

97: Hiromi Hayakari: 1996/07/21 (Sat) 22:45:50 ID:

What does it feel like to not be alone?

You don't feel lonely.
With every kind of feeling all mixed togethe

95: Anonymous Integrated Mind: 2009/05/23 16:40:00 ID: brain
You don't feel lonely.
With every kind of feeling all mixed together, it's like it makes
things peaceful and very settled.

96: Hiromi Hayakari: 1995/01/05 (Thu) 03:57:13 ID hirohaya
I see...That sounds nice.

Anonymous Integrated Mind: 2009/05/23
>>96
You, too, will slowly mix in and become "all."
We all share our pain and suffering together and eventually a tranquil
peace comes over your mind.

That makes me happy.
I'm so tired..

652: Anonymous Integrated Mind: 2009/05/23 16:40:00 ID: brain
>>95
You can rest all you like.
There's plenty of time.

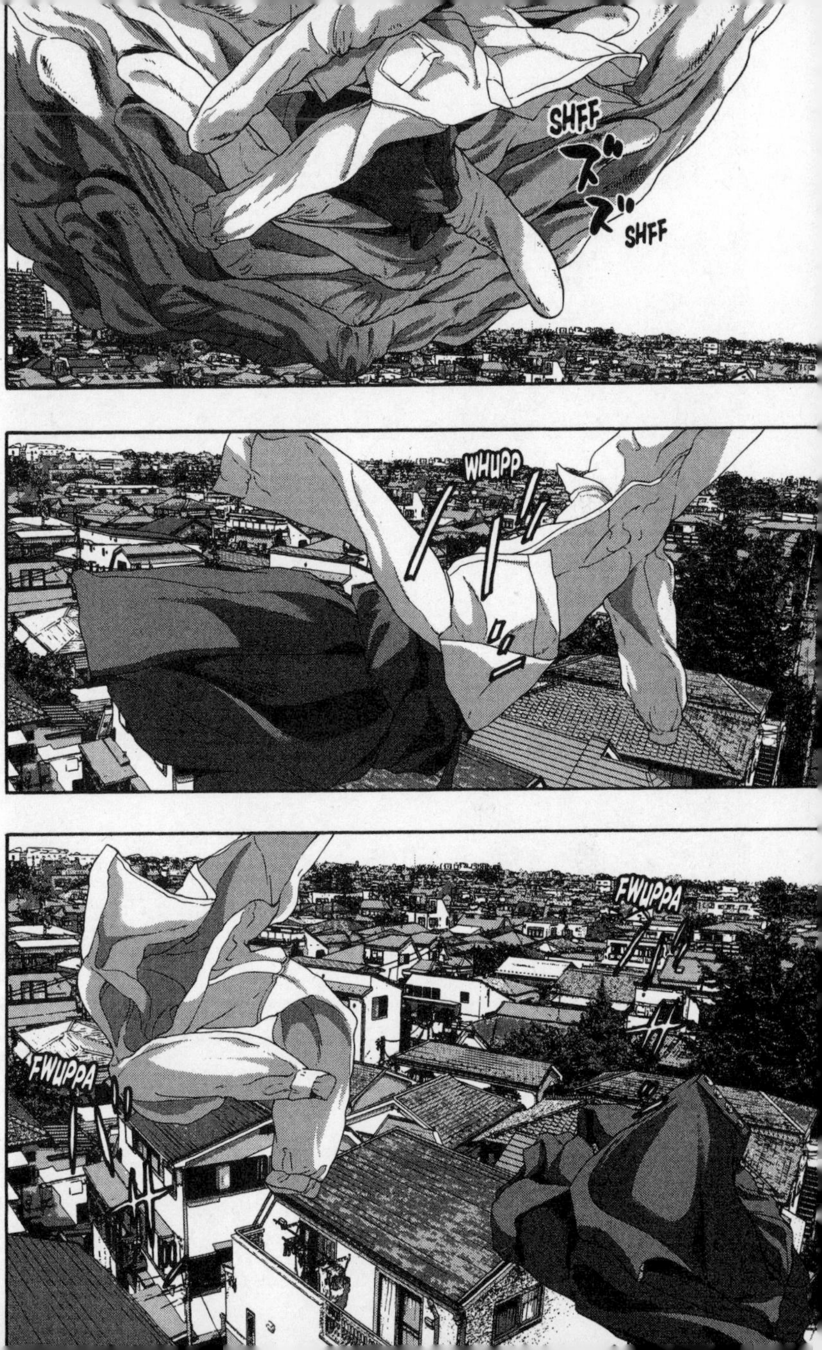
SHFF
ズズ
SHFF
WHUPP
FWUPPA
FWUPPA

94: Hiromi Hayakari: 1993/02/0
Can I...see the outside world?

Can I...see the outside world?

653: Anonymous Integrated Mind: 2009/05/23 16:40:35 ID: brain
>>94
I think you can.
If you connect the optic nerves...
Why don't you try it?

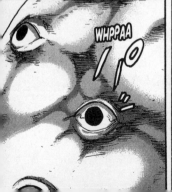

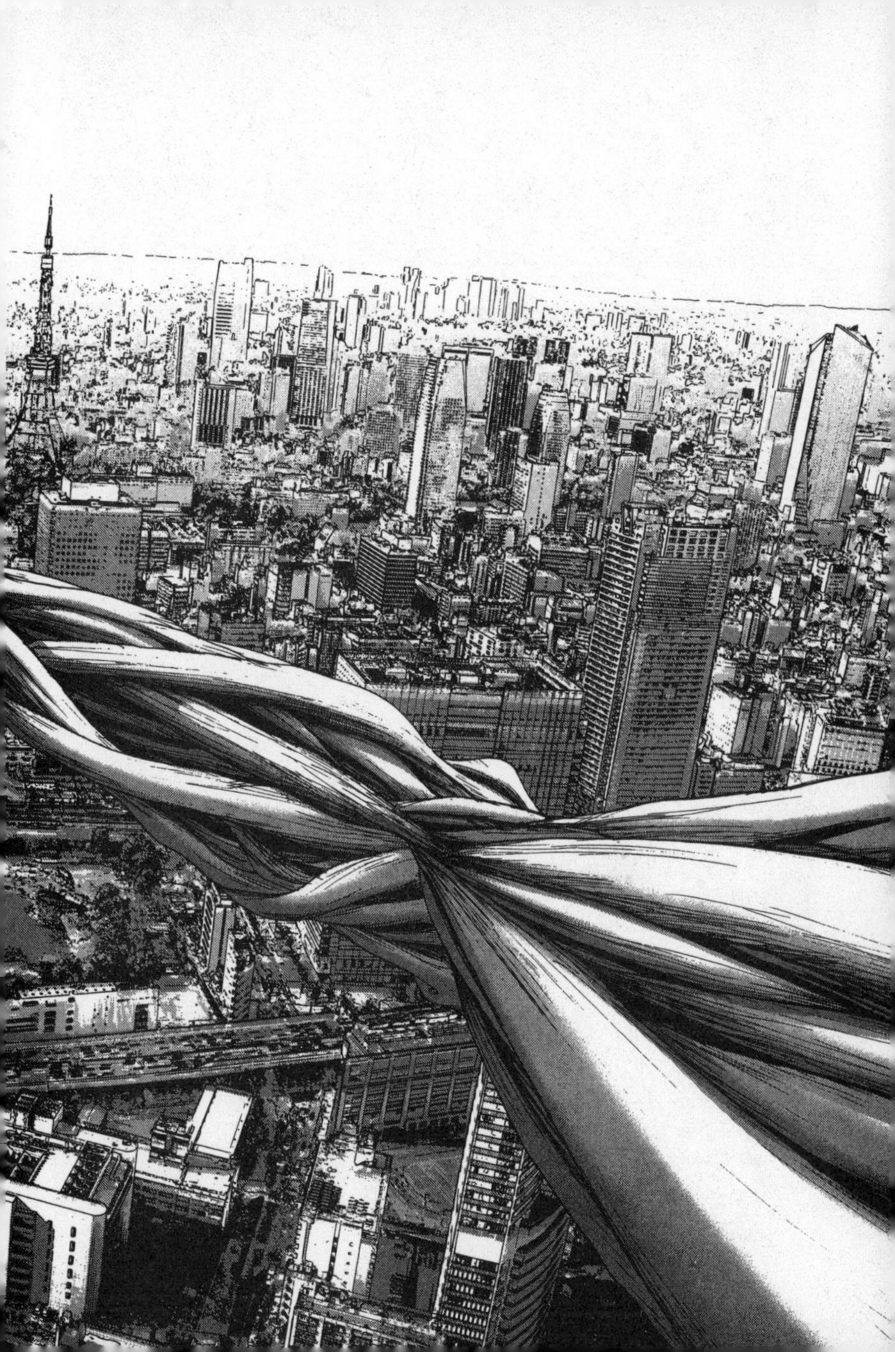

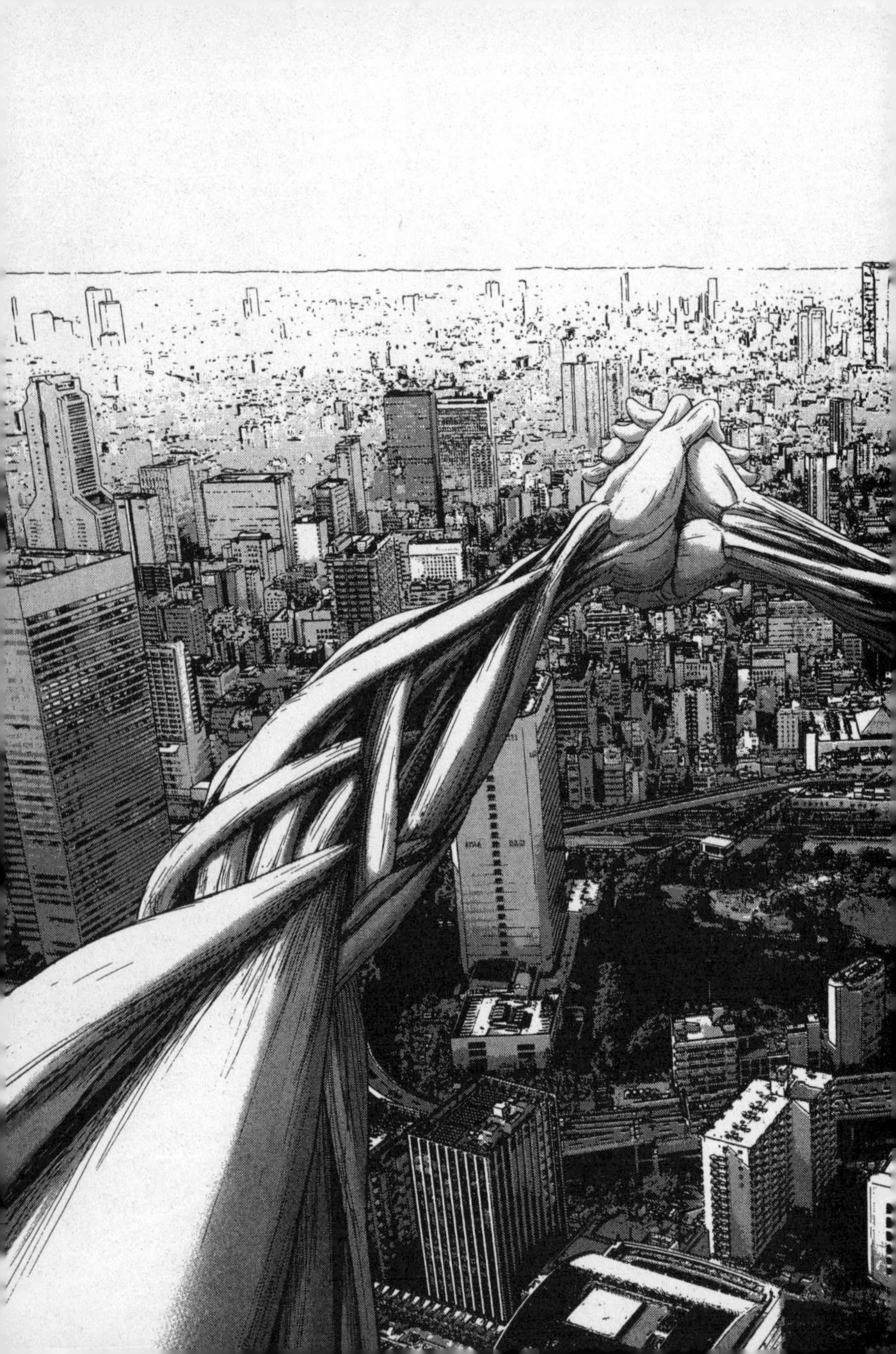

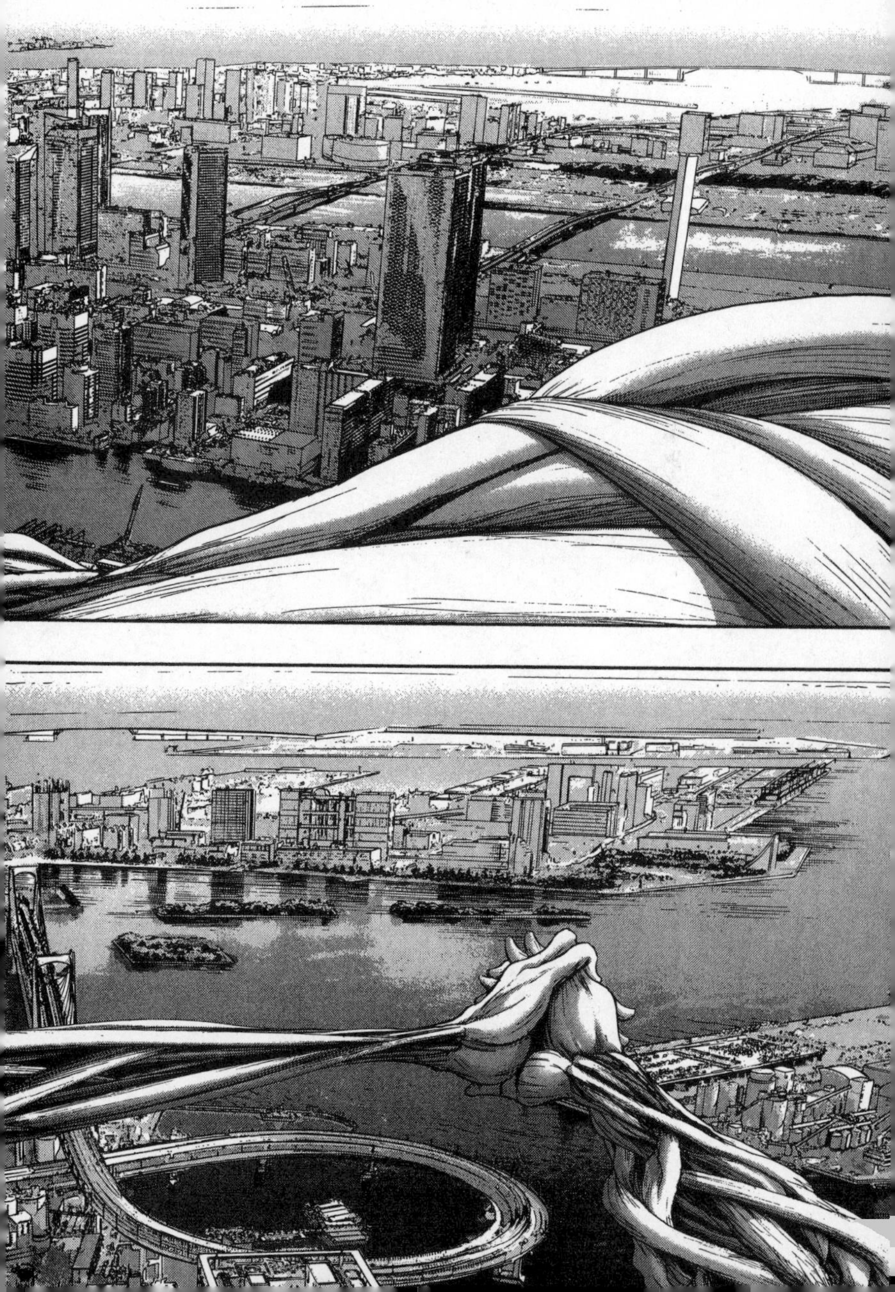

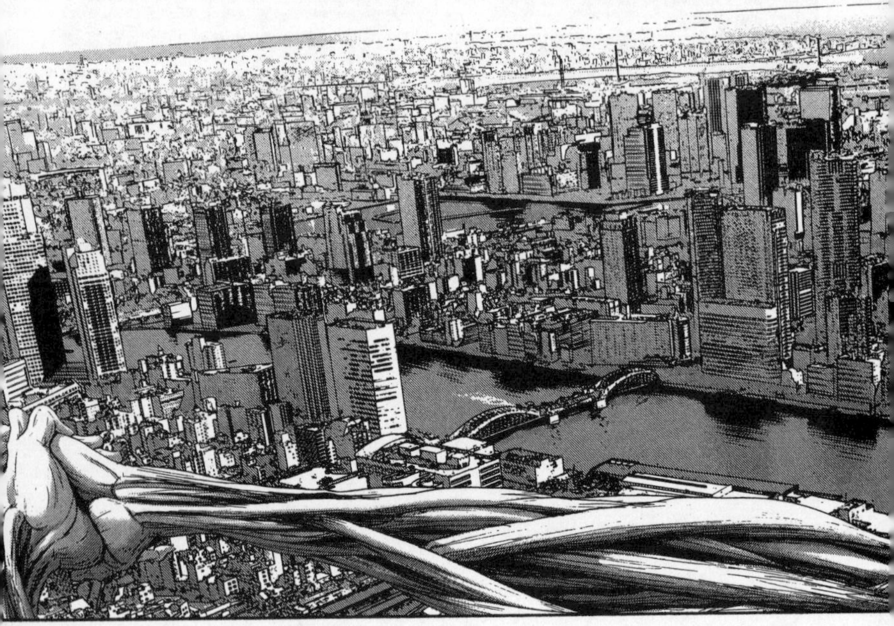
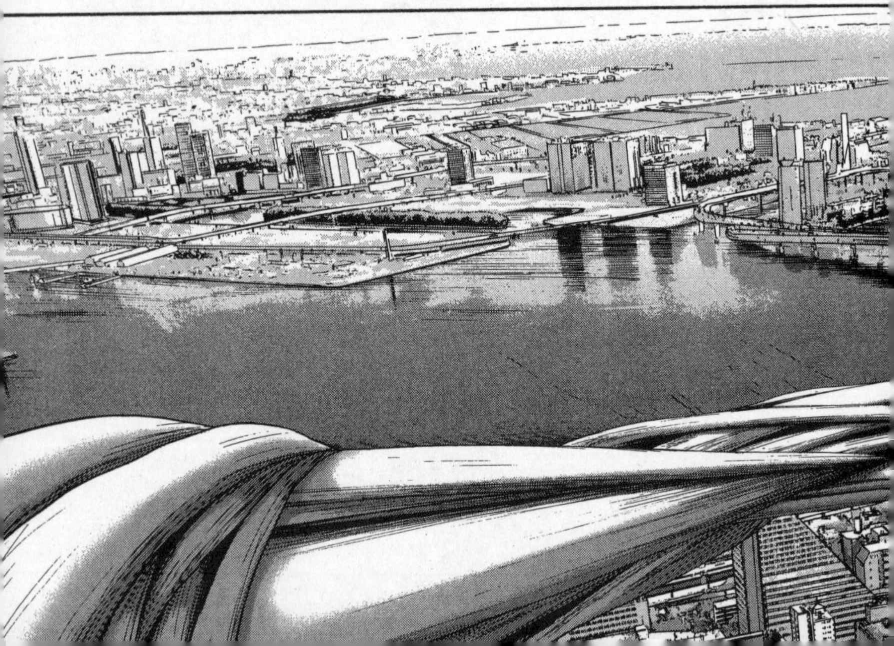

93: Hiromi Hayakari: 1992/12/2
Incredible! I can see!!
It's so high up!!!

Hiromi Hayakari: 1992/10/18 (Sun) 20:47:09 ID:shirohaya
Are we destroying houses though?
Is this okay?

54: Anonymous Integrated Mind: 2009/05/23 16:41:15 ID: brain
》92
You don't need to worry. We're walking around them.
I don't know what the objective for ZQNs is, but they don't
seem to have any desire to destroy the existing infrastructure

91: Hiromi Hayakari: 1992/08/13 (Thu) 14:31:39
Hm...

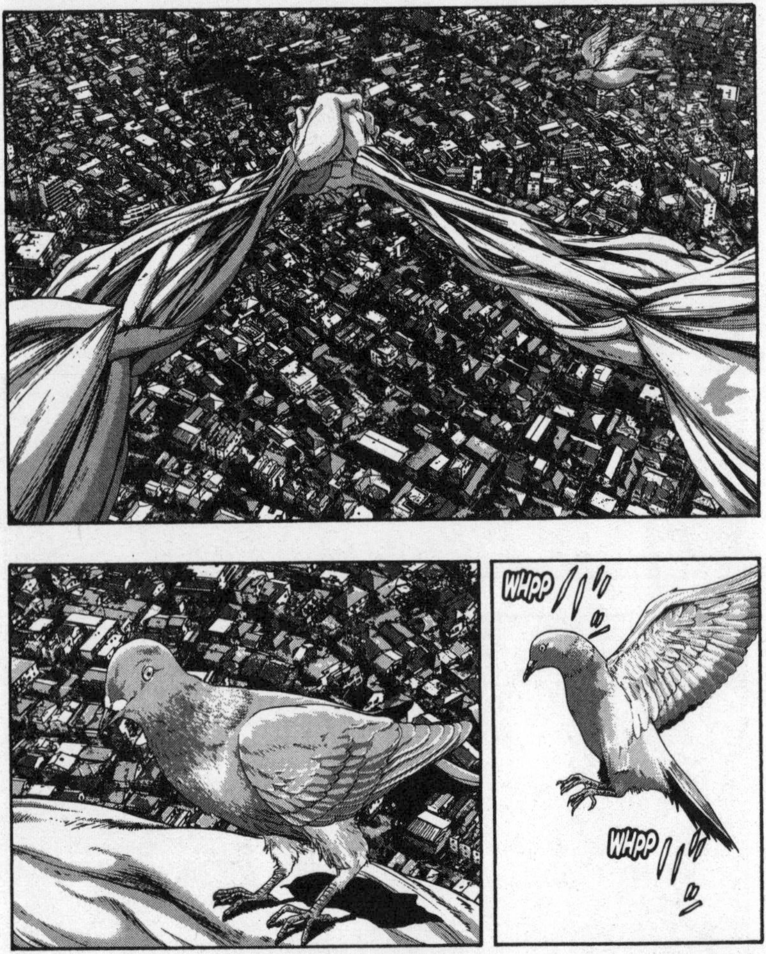
WHPP
WHPP

98: Hiromi Hayakari: 1992/08/10 (Wed) 12:12:12 ID: hirohaya
A pigeon!
Ha ha ha...

654: Anonymous Integrated Mind: 2009/05/23 16:42:01 ID: bra
>>90

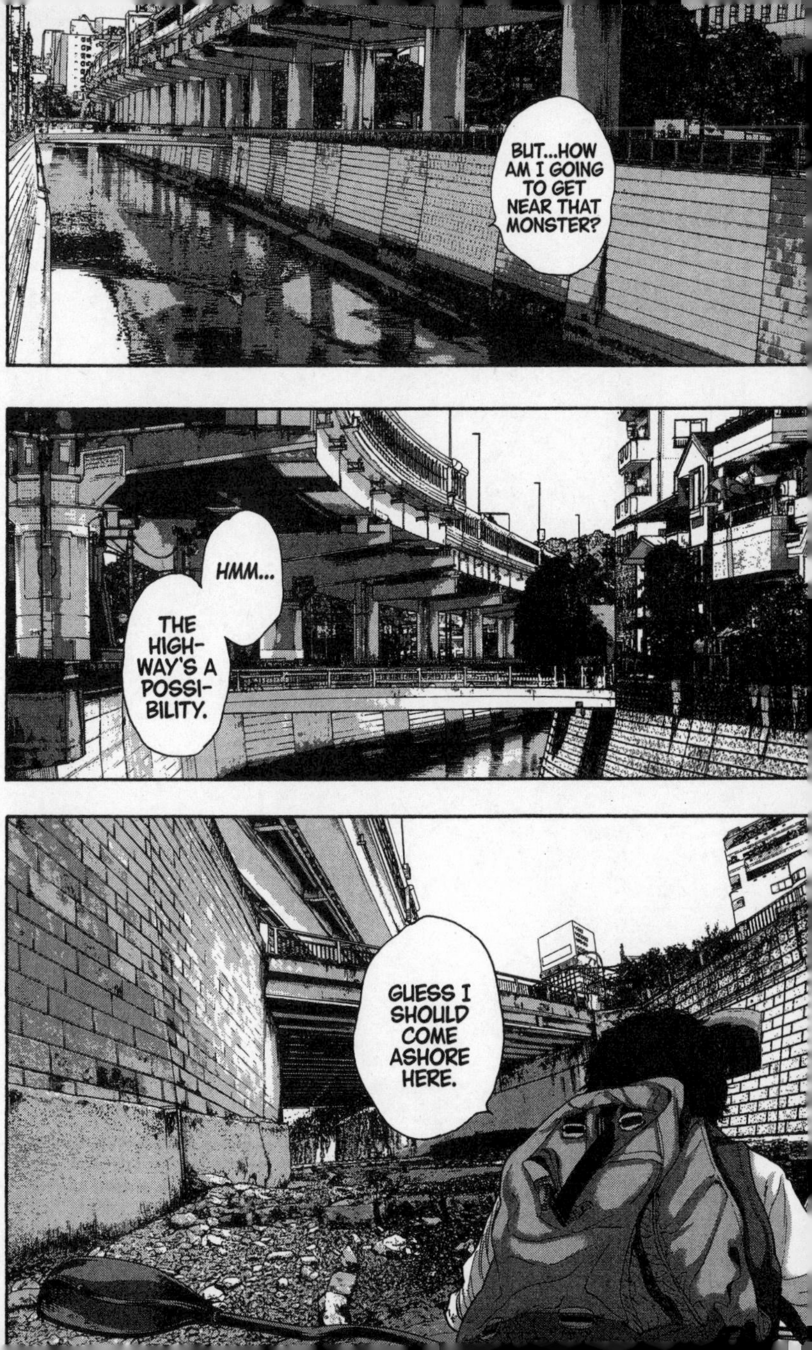
BUT...HOW AM I GOING TO GET NEAR THAT MONSTER?
HMM...
THE HIGH-WAY'S A POSSI-BILITY.
GUESS I SHOULD COME ASHORE HERE.

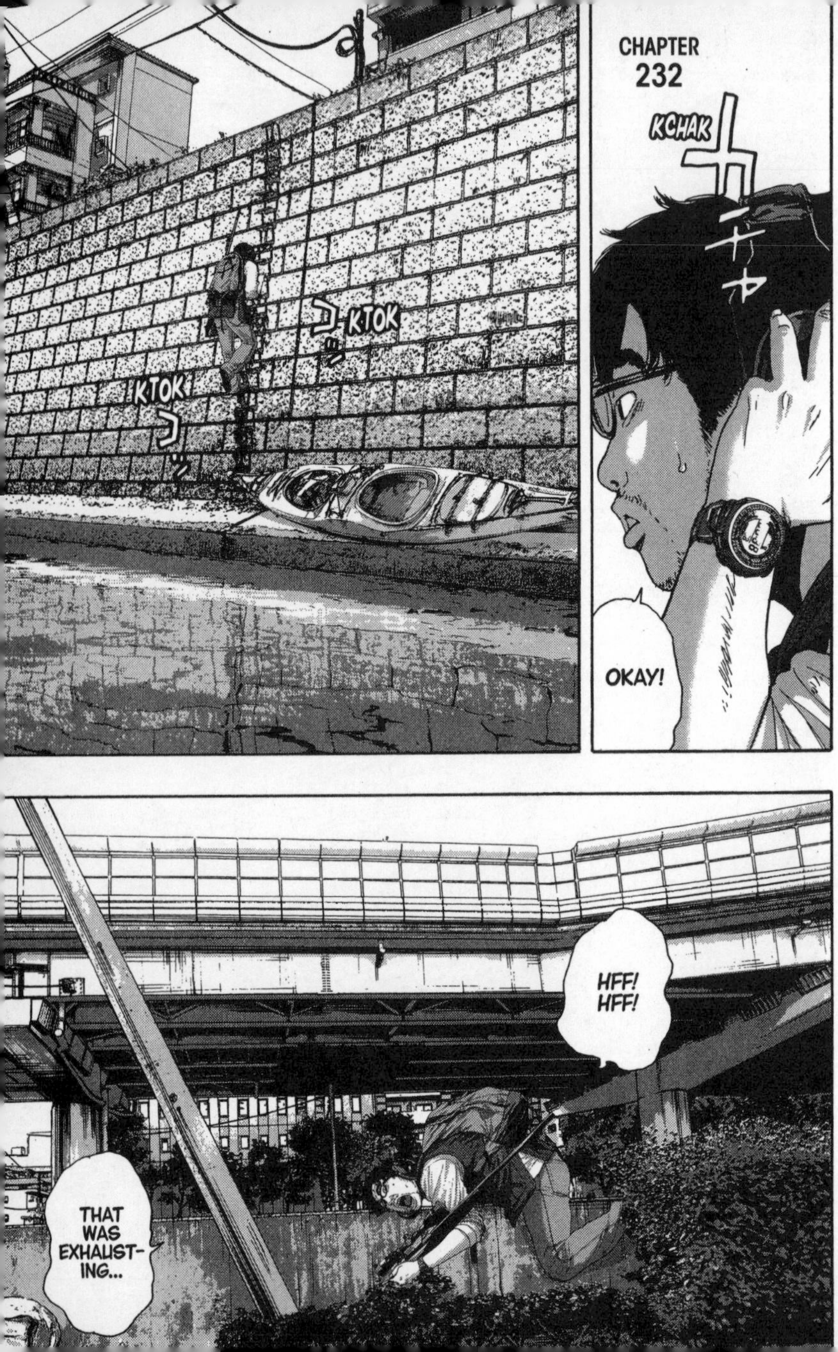
CHAPTER 232
KCHAK
OKAY!
KTOK
KTOK
HFF! HFF!
THAT WAS EXHAUST-ING...

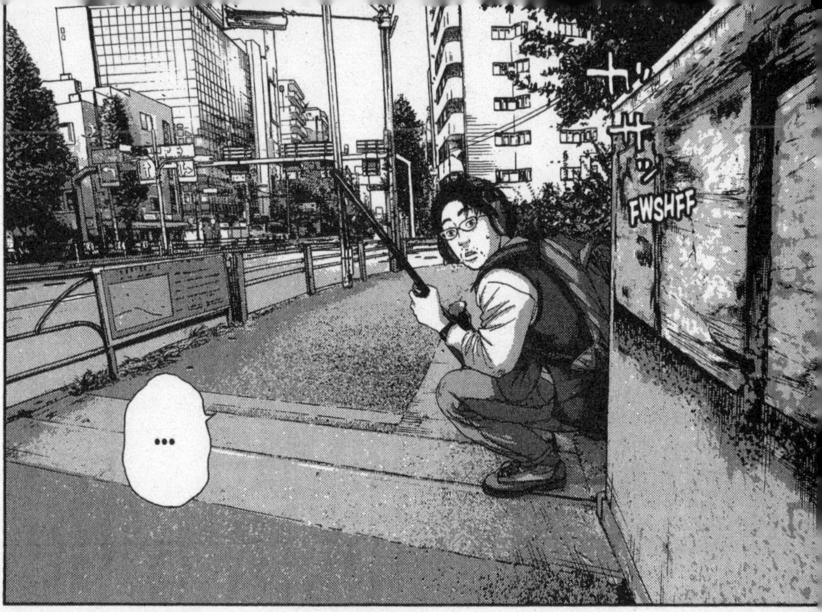
FWSHFF
...

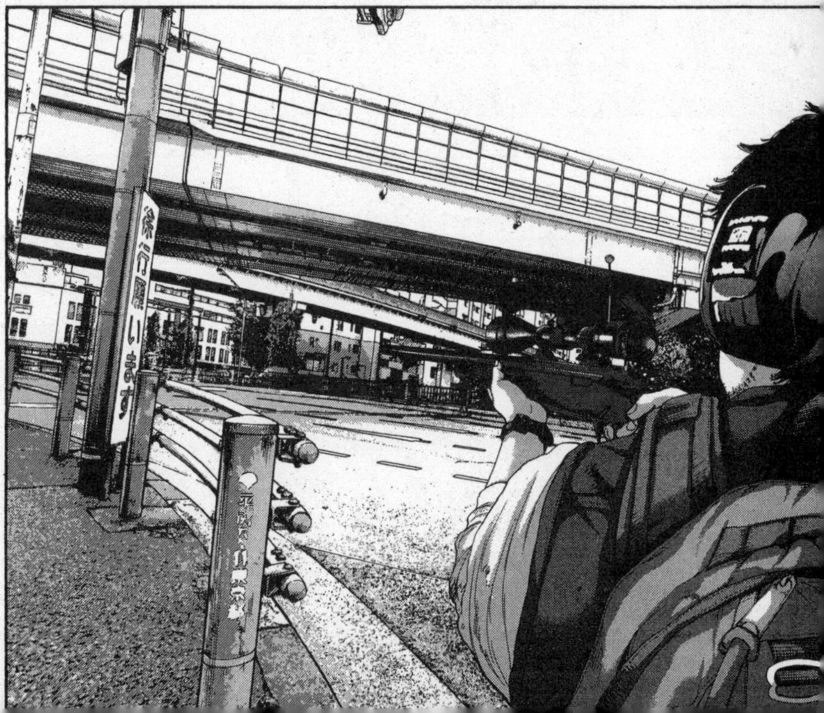
徐行願います

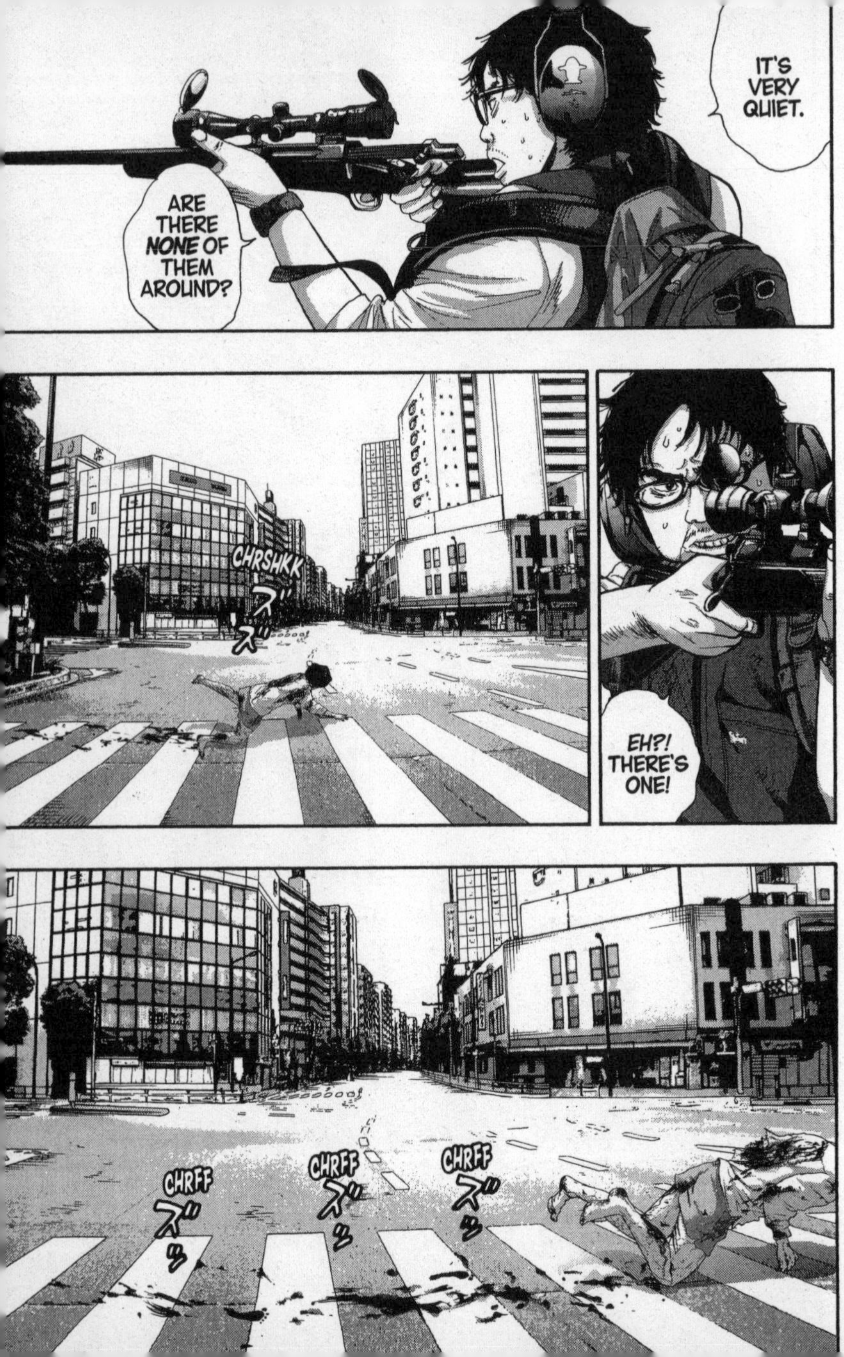
IT'S VERY QUIET.
ARE THERE *NONE* OF THEM AROUND?
EH?! THERE'S ONE!
CHRSHKK
ズズ
CHRFF
ズッ
CHRFF
ズッ
CHRFF
ズッ

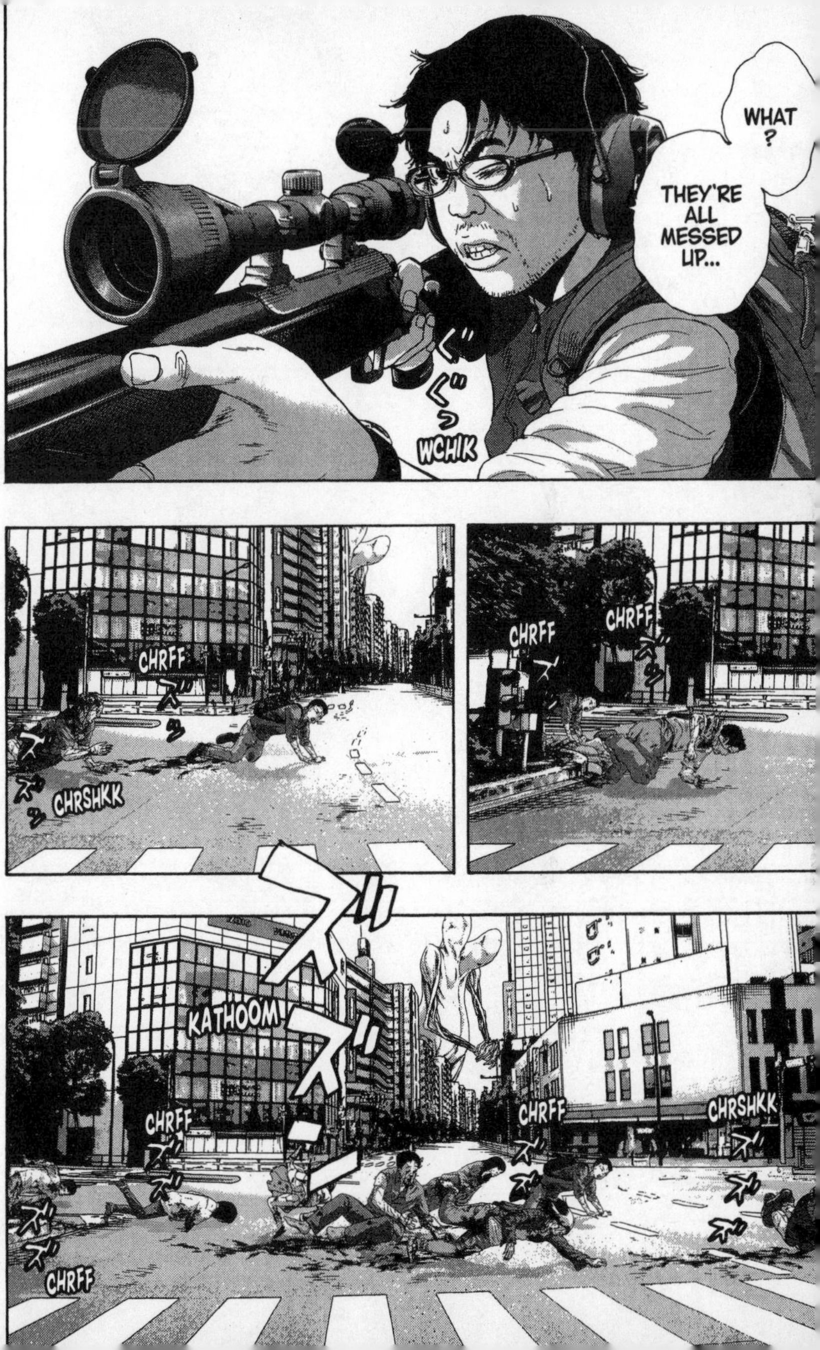
WHAT?
THEY'RE ALL MESSED UP...
WCHIK
CHRFF
CHRFF
CHRFF
CHRSHKK
CHRSHKK
CHRFF
KATHOOM
CHRFF
CHRFF

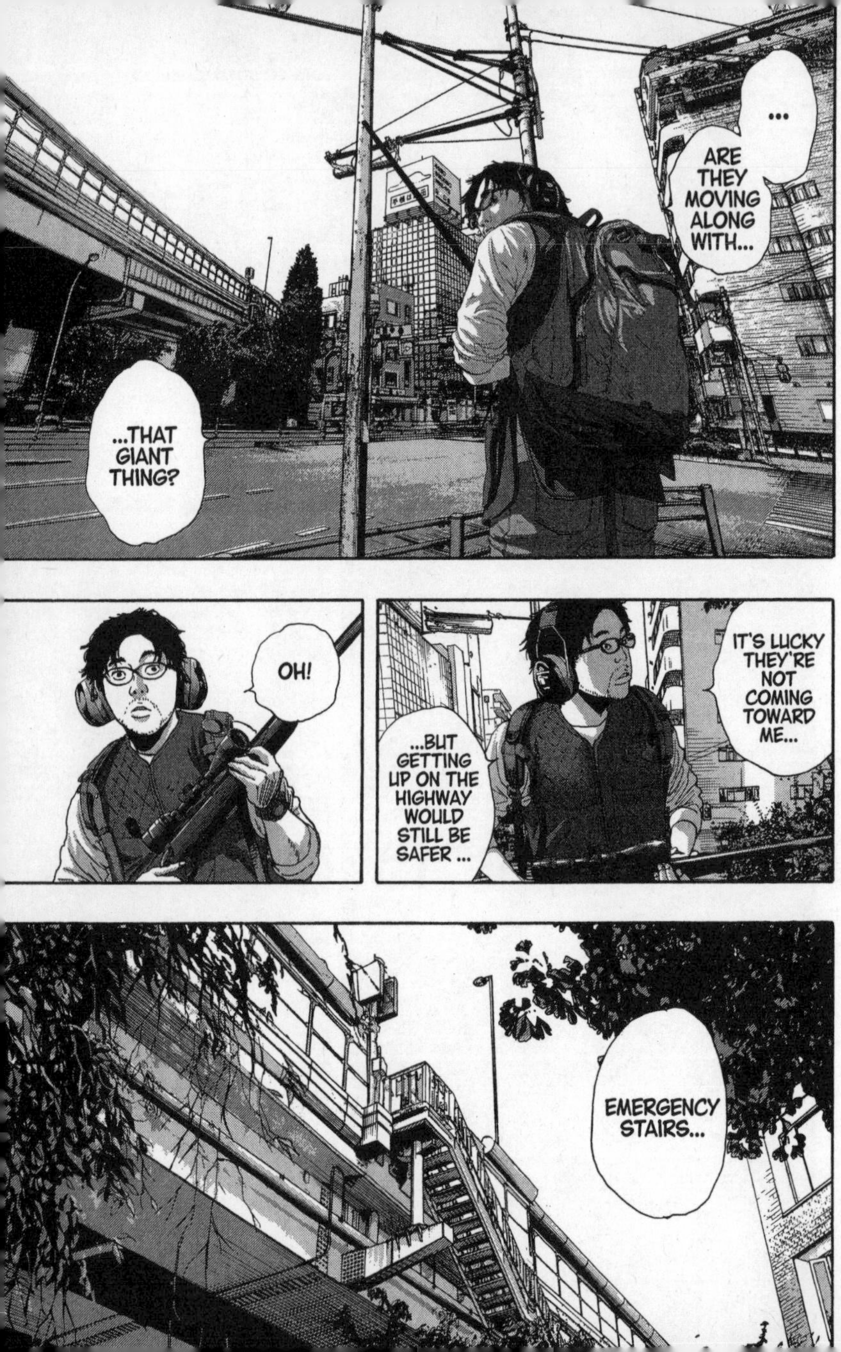
...
ARE THEY MOVING ALONG WITH...
...THAT GIANT THING?
IT'S LUCKY THEY'RE NOT COMING TOWARD ME...
...BUT GETTING UP ON THE HIGHWAY WOULD STILL BE SAFER ...
OH!
EMERGENCY STAIRS...

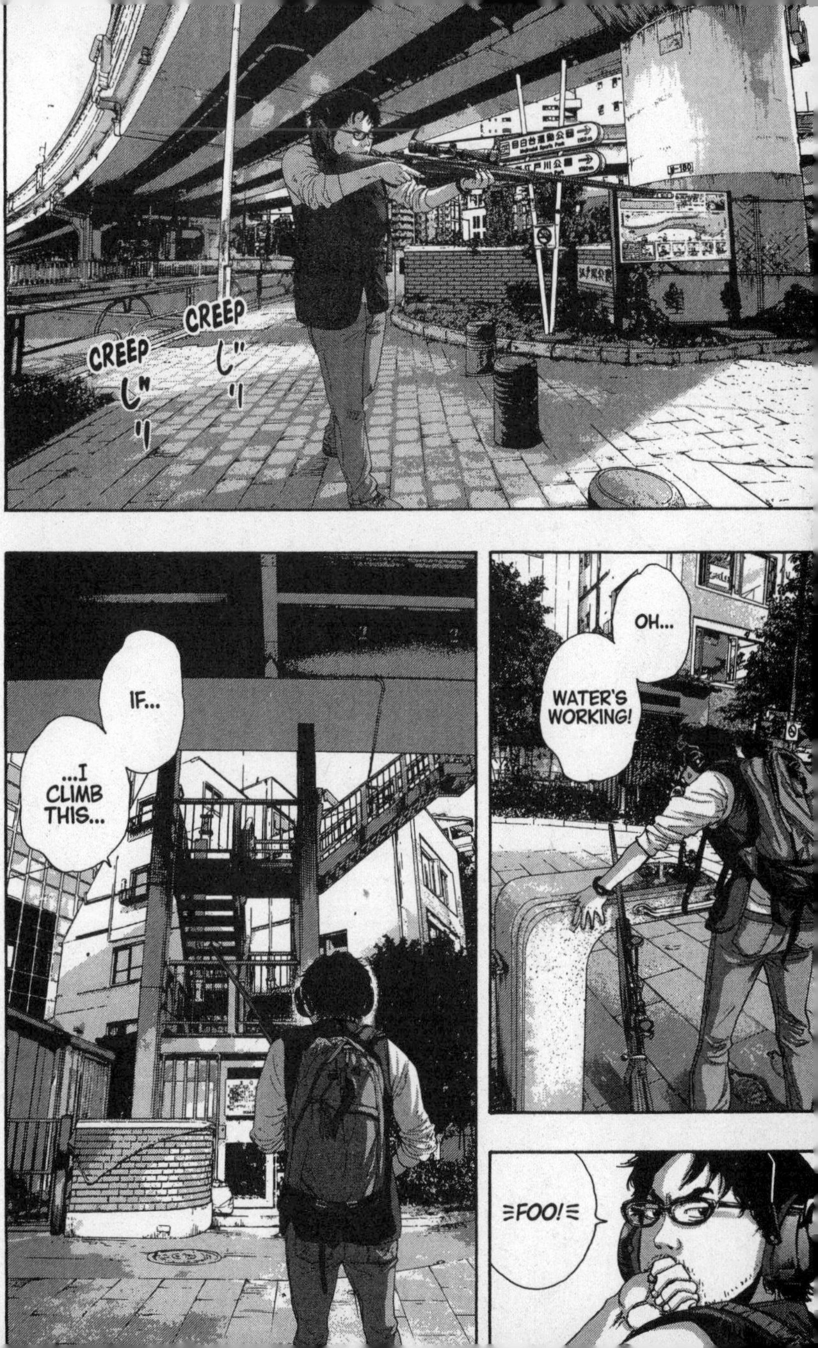
CREEP
じり
CREEP
じり
OH...
WATER'S WORKING!
≡FOO!≡
IF...
...I CLIMB THIS...

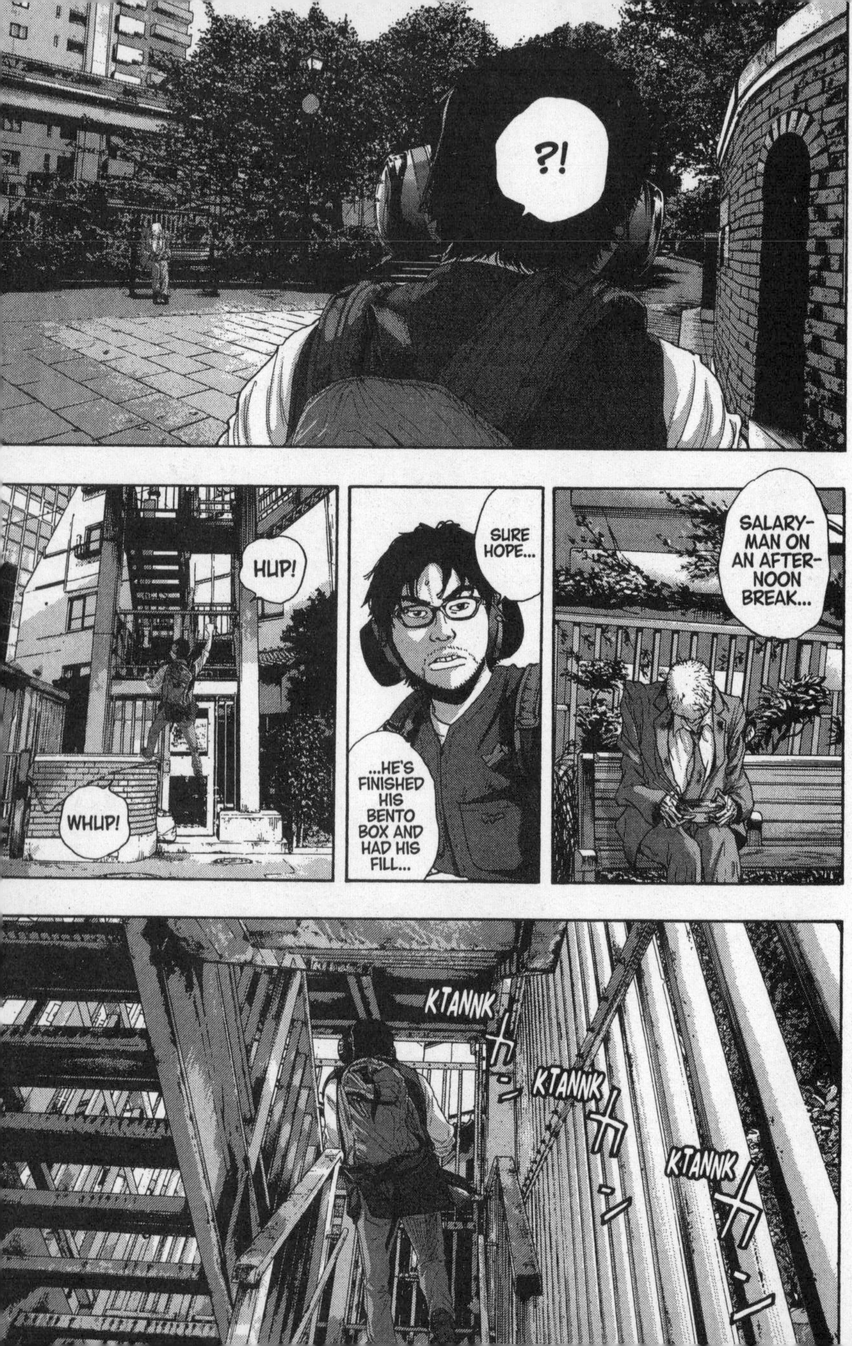
?!
SALARY-MAN ON AN AFTER-NOON BREAK...
SURE HOPE...
...HE'S FINISHED HIS BENTO BOX AND HAD HIS FILL...
HUP!
WHUP!
KTANNK
KTANNK
KTANNK

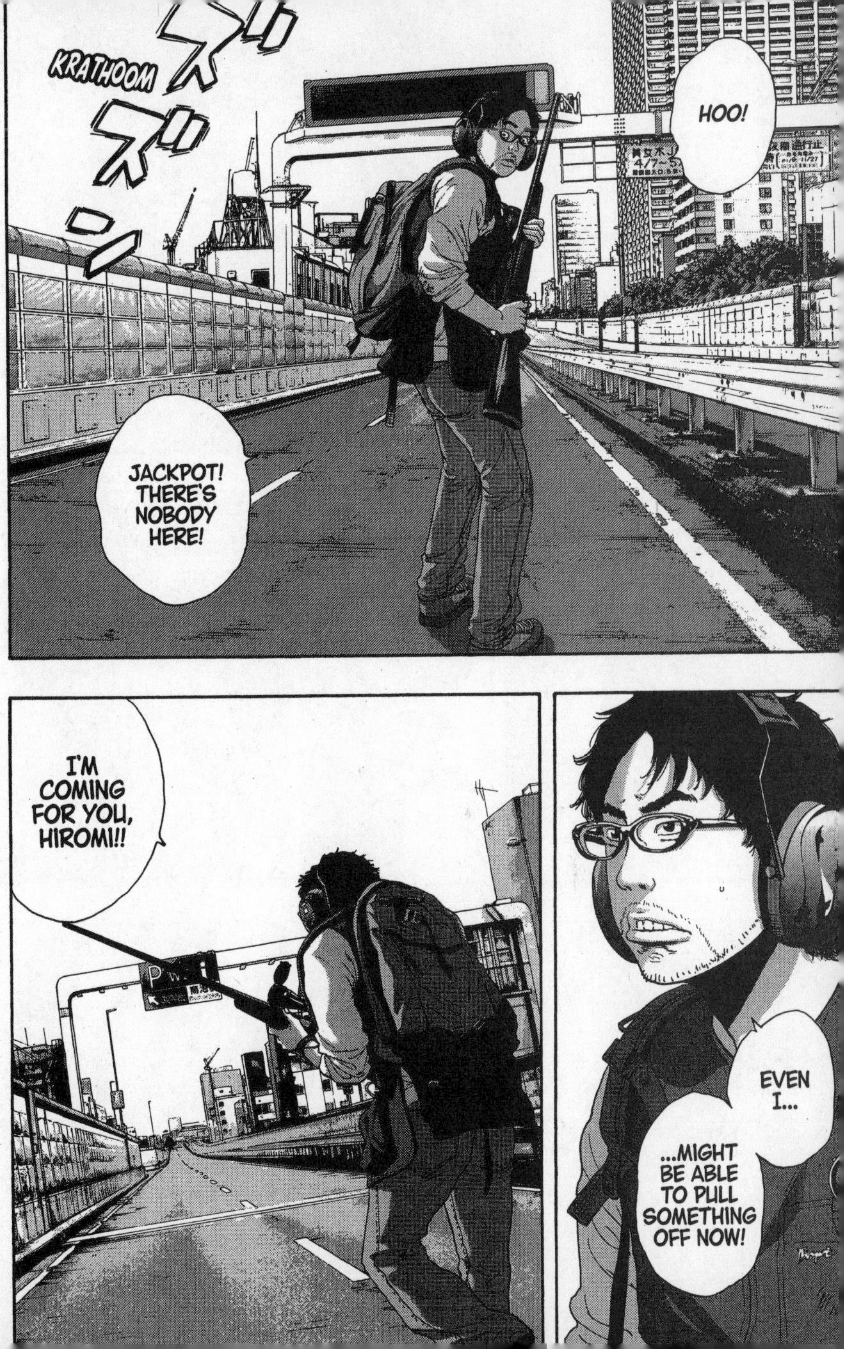
KRATHOOM
HOO!
JACKPOT! THERE'S NOBODY HERE!
EVEN I...
...MIGHT BE ABLE TO PULL SOMETHING OFF NOW!
I'M COMING FOR YOU, HIROMI!!

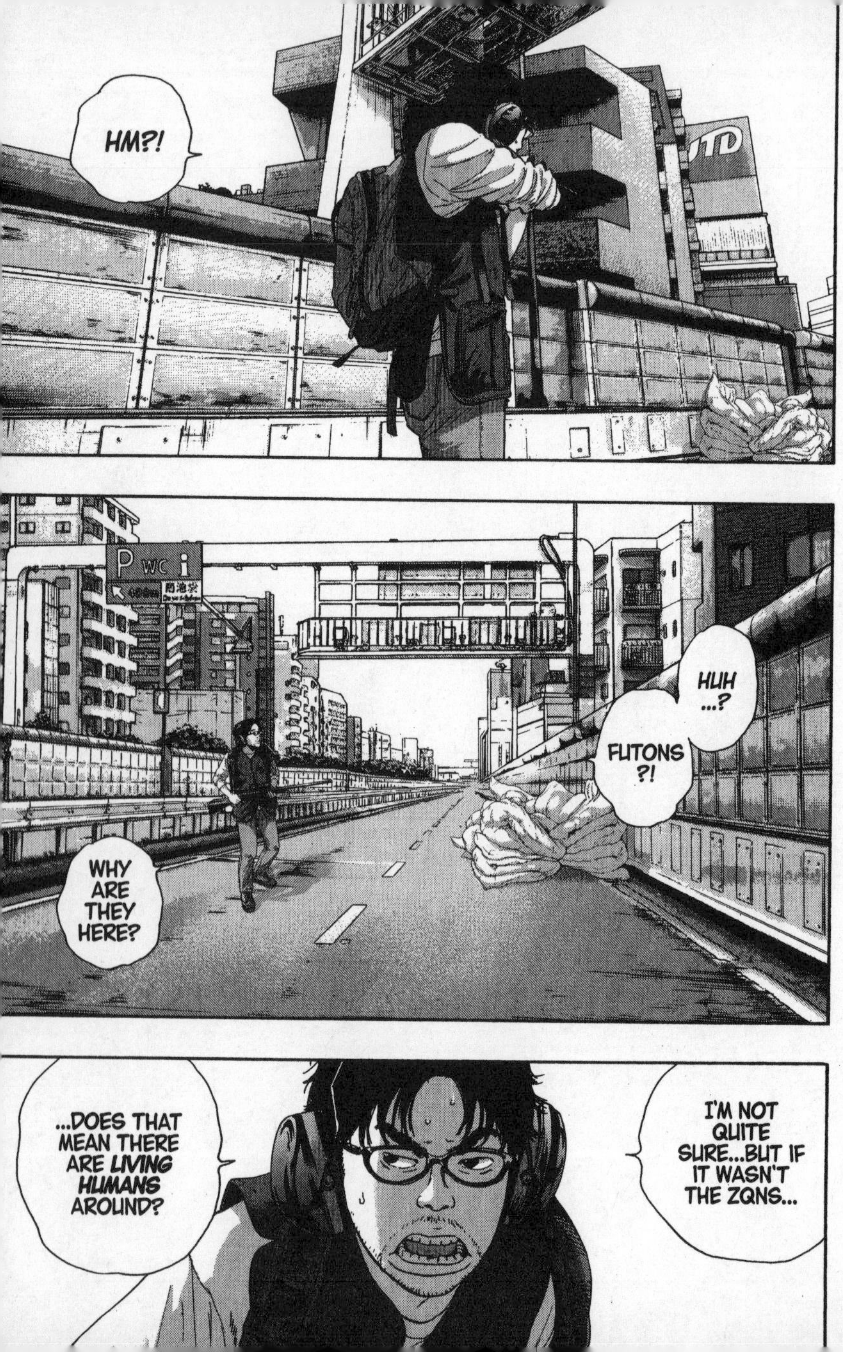
HM?!
HUH ...?
FUTONS ?!
WHY ARE THEY HERE?
I'M NOT QUITE SURE...BUT IF IT WASN'T THE ZQNS...
...DOES THAT MEAN THERE ARE LIVING HUMANS AROUND?

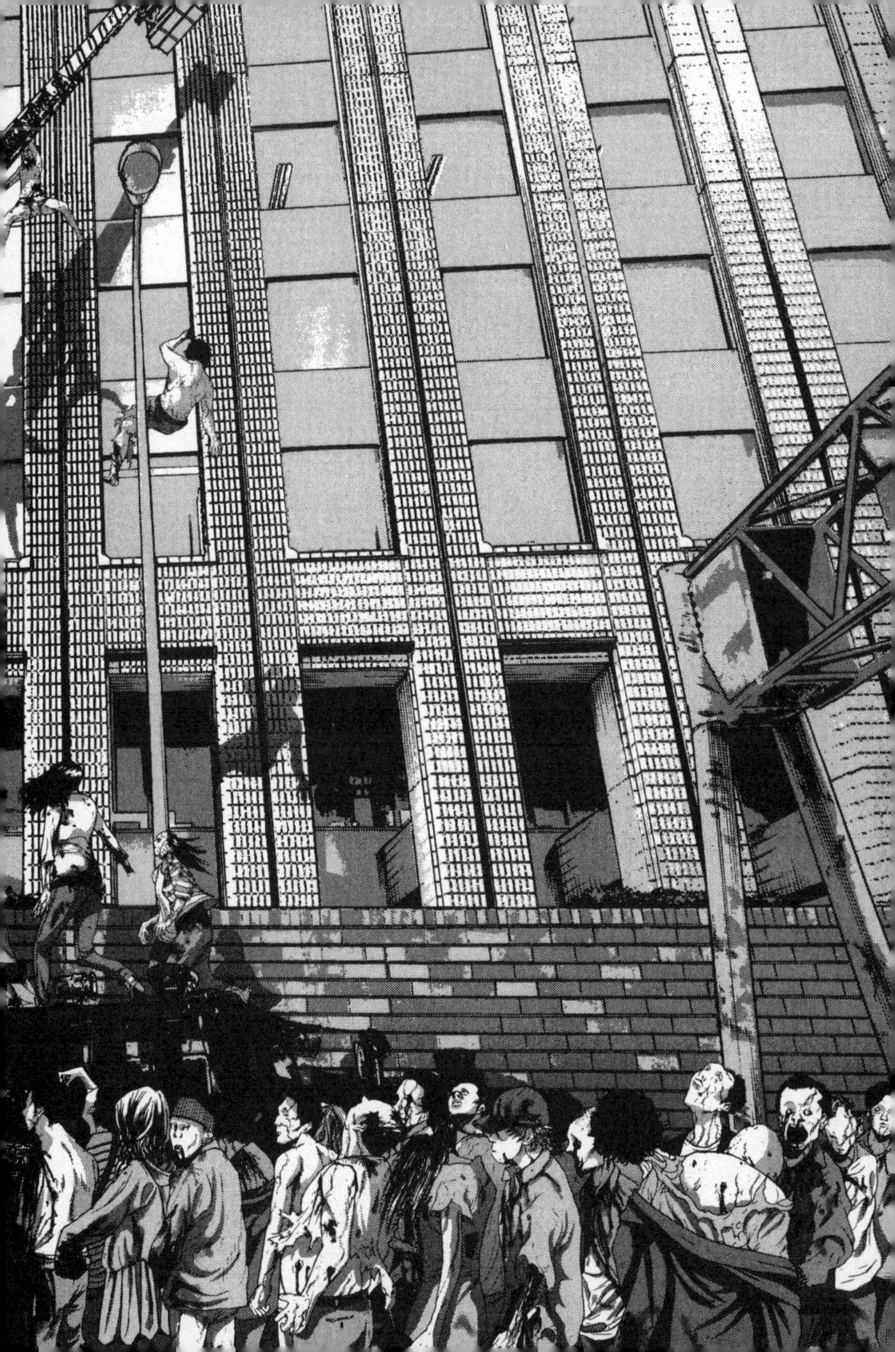

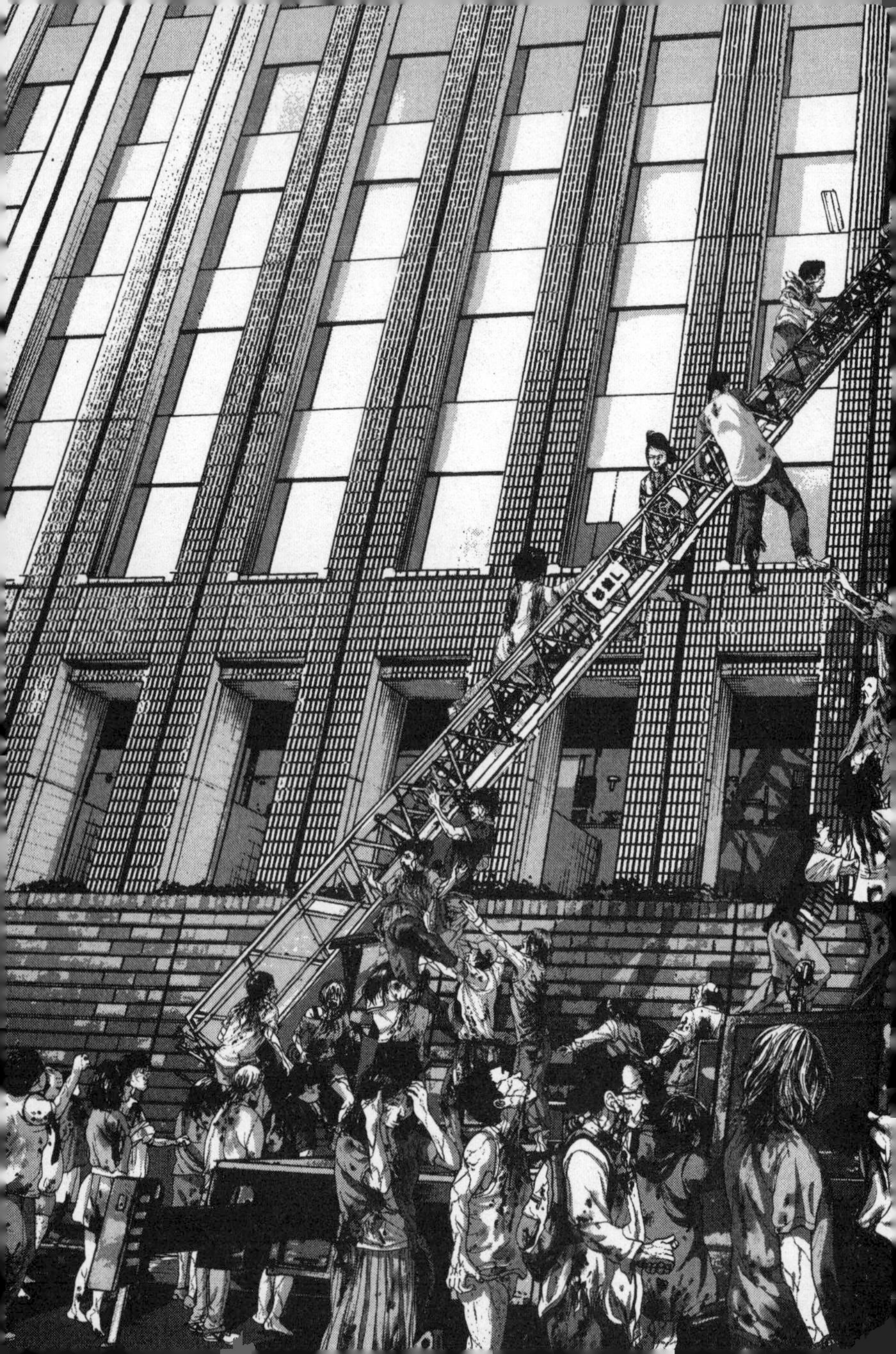

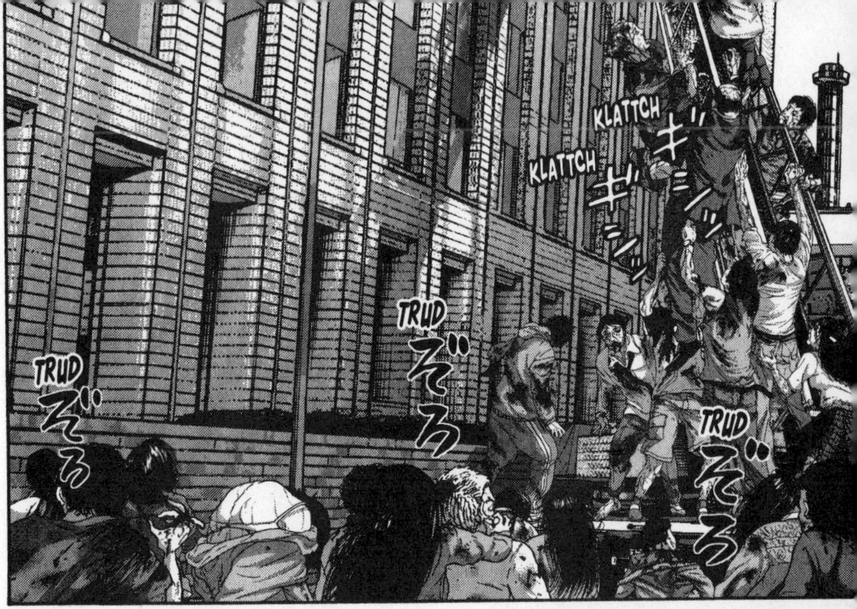
KLATTCH
KLATTCH
TRUD
ぞろ
TRUD
ぞろ
TRUD
ぞろ
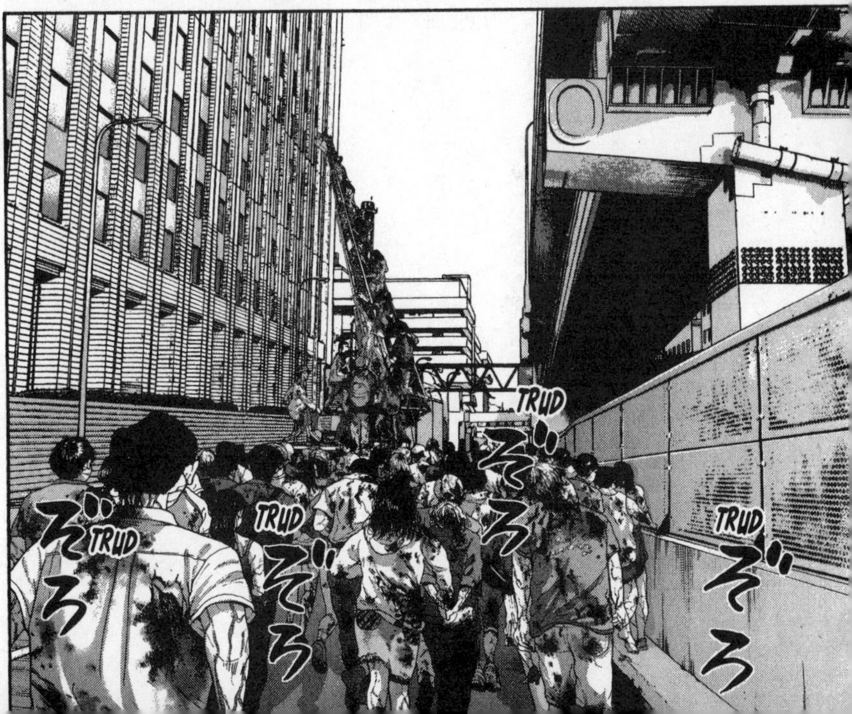
TRUD
ぞろ
TRUD
ぞろ
TRUD
ぞろ
TRUD
ぞろ

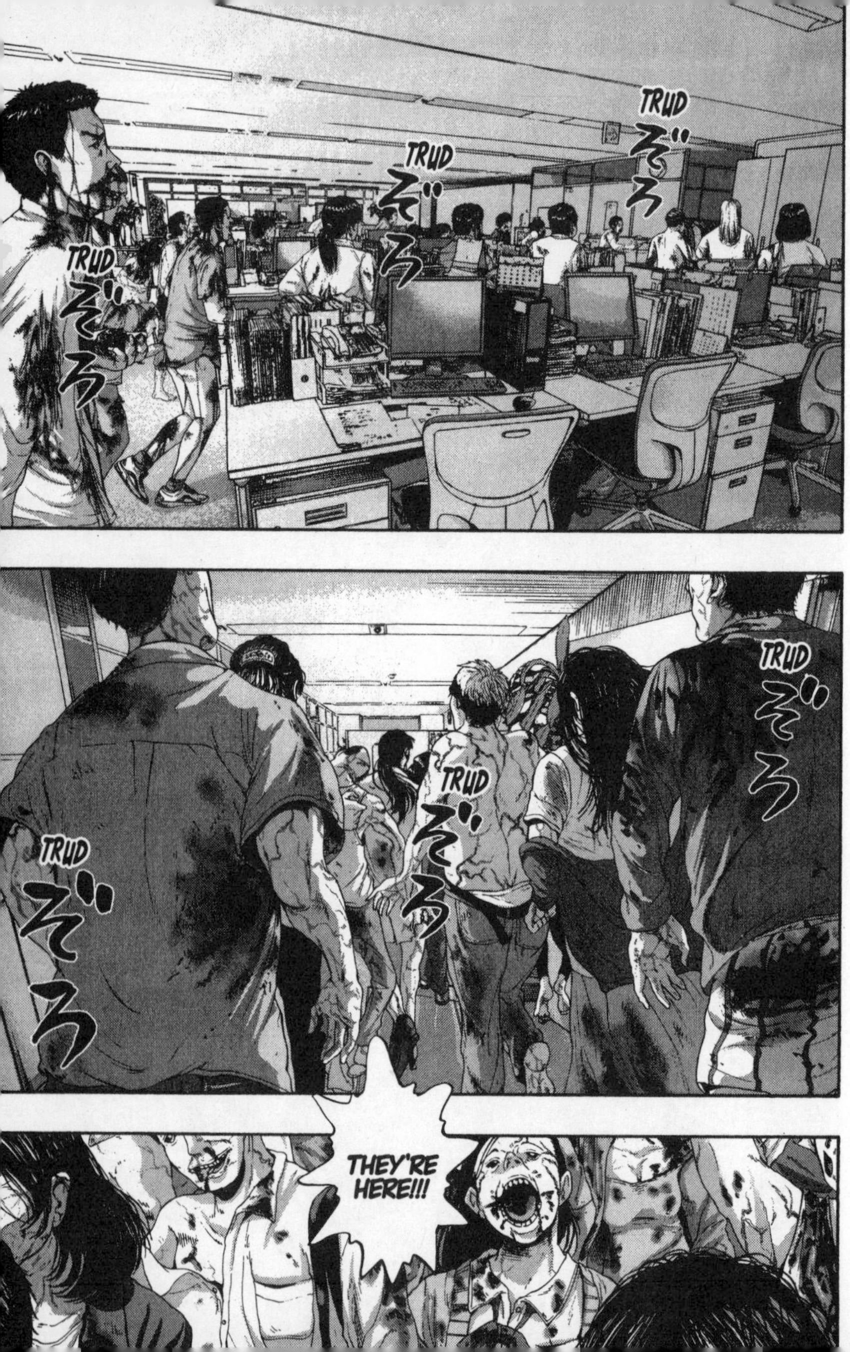
TRUD
ぞろ
TRUD
ぞろ
TRUD
ぞろ
TRUD
ぞろ
TRUD
ぞろ
TRUD
ぞろ
THEY'RE HERE!!!

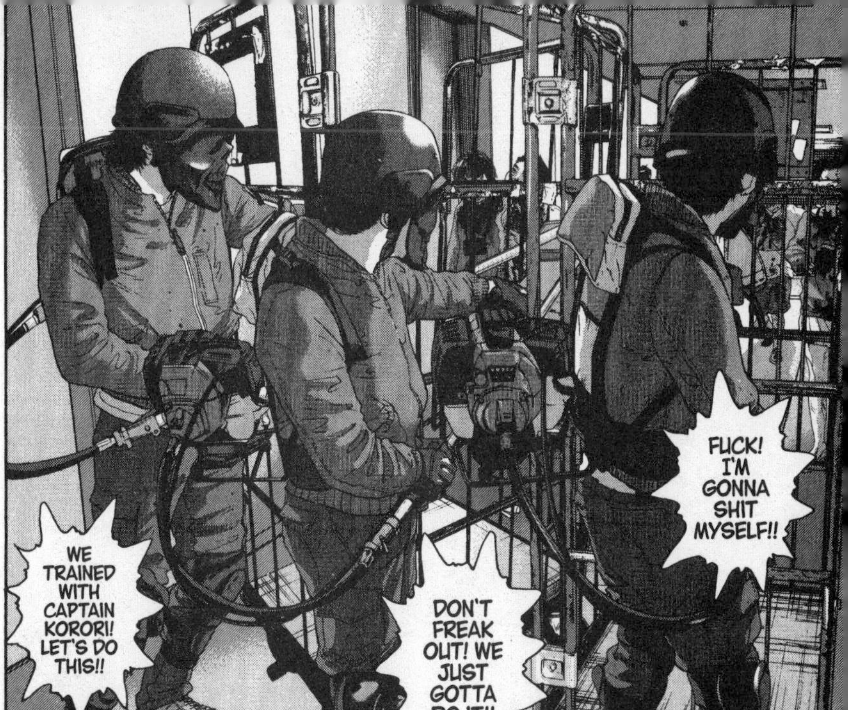

FUCK! I'M GONNA SHIT MYSELF!!
DON'T FREAK OUT! WE JUST GOTTA DO IT!!
WE TRAINED WITH CAPTAIN KORORI! LET'S DO THIS!!

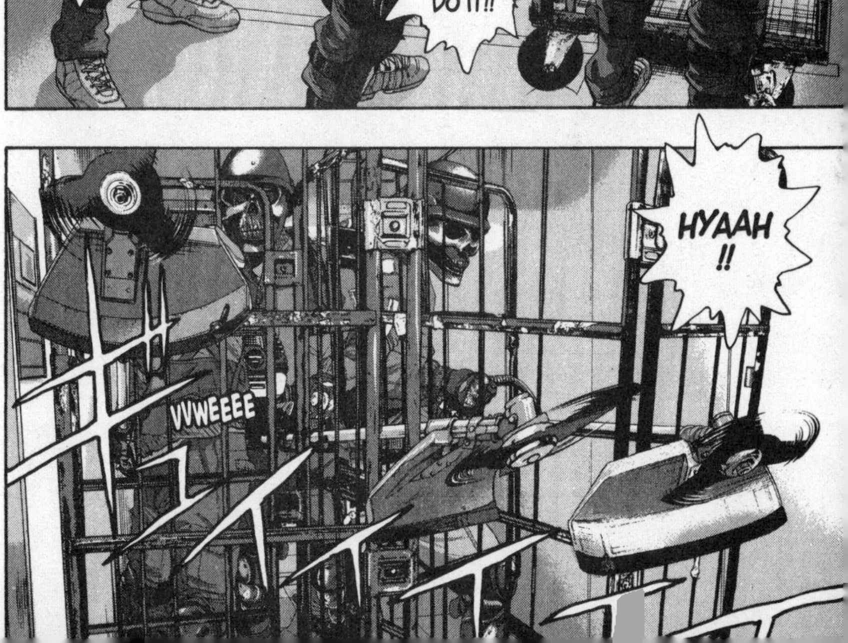

HYAAH !!
VVWEEEE

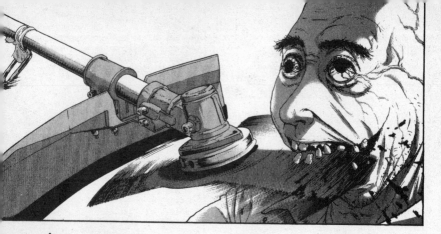

ZZKKEEENN

ZTCHWEEE

VVWEEEE

VVWEEEE

SWAP IN TEN MINUTES!! DON'T FORGET TO REFUEL!!

MAKE SURE YOU AIM FOR THE HEADS! DON'T FALL BACK!

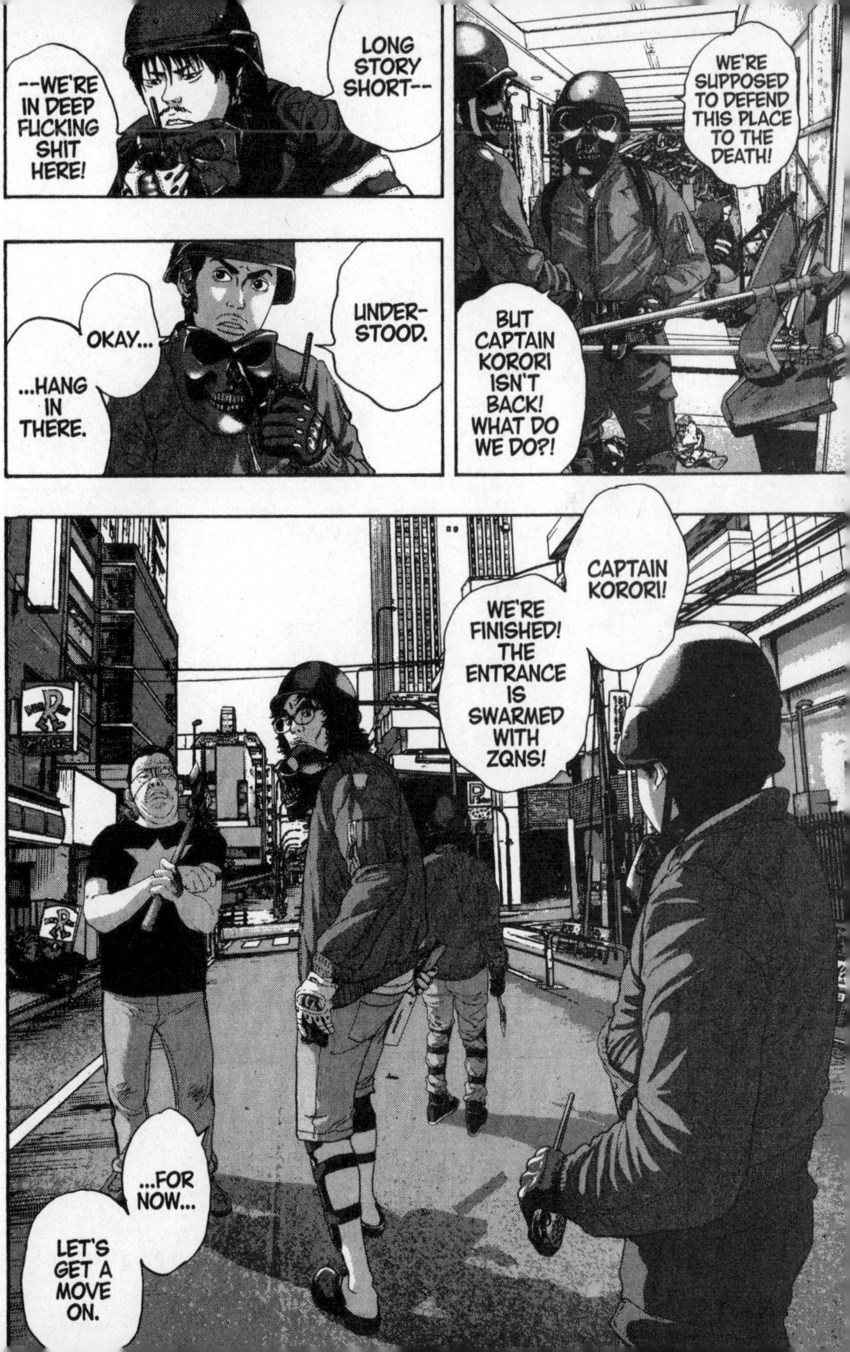
WE'RE SUPPOSED TO DEFEND THIS PLACE TO THE DEATH!
BUT CAPTAIN KORORI ISN'T BACK! WHAT DO WE DO?!
LONG STORY SHORT--
--WE'RE IN DEEP FUCKING SHIT HERE!
UNDER-STOOD.
OKAY...
...HANG IN THERE.
CAPTAIN KORORI!
WE'RE FINISHED! THE ENTRANCE IS SWARMED WITH ZQNS!
...FOR NOW...
LET'S GET A MOVE ON.

CHAPTER
233

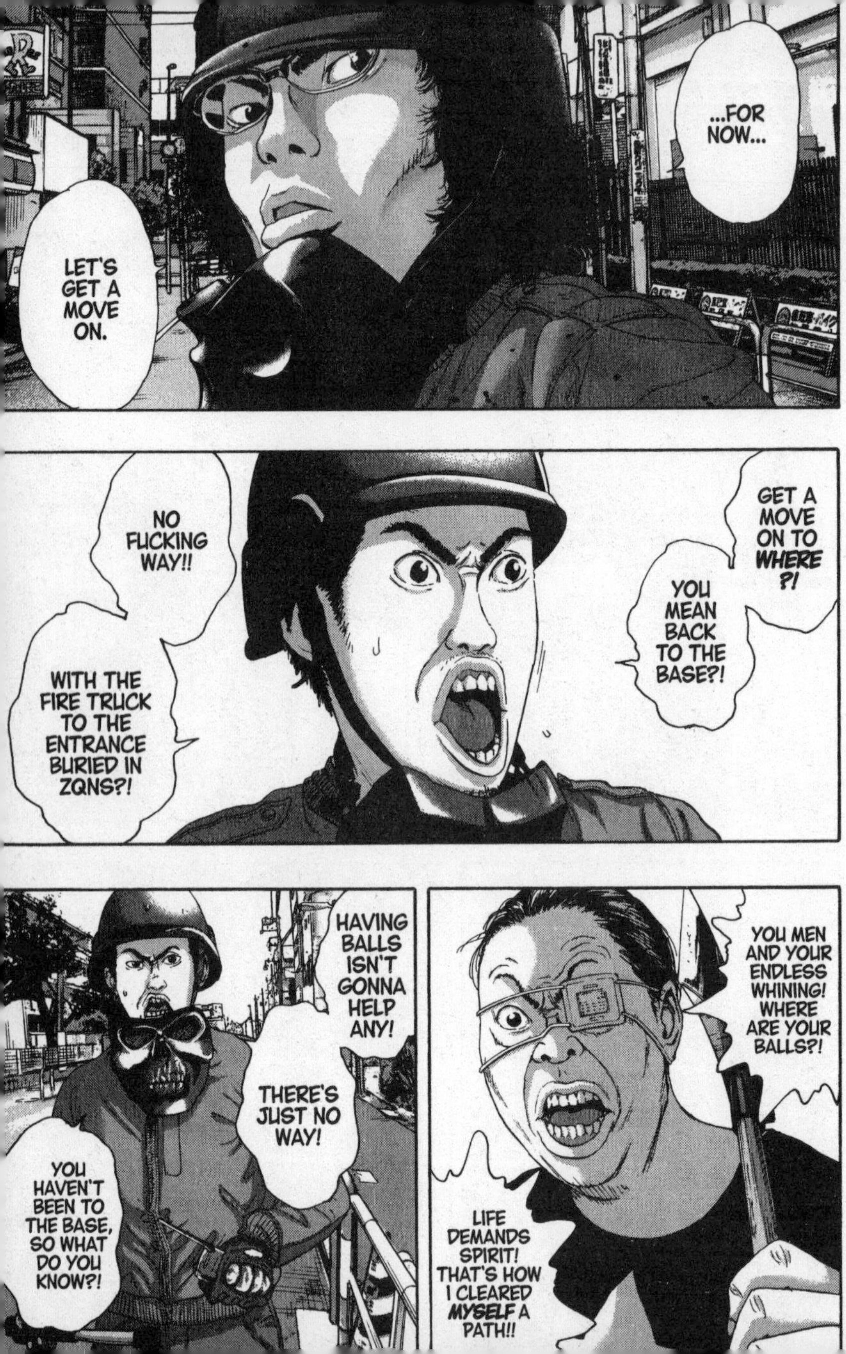
...FOR NOW...
LET'S GET A MOVE ON.
GET A MOVE ON TO WHERE?!
YOU MEAN BACK TO THE BASE?!
NO FUCKING WAY!!
WITH THE FIRE TRUCK TO THE ENTRANCE BURIED IN ZQNS?!
YOU MEN AND YOUR ENDLESS WHINING! WHERE ARE YOUR BALLS?!
LIFE DEMANDS SPIRIT! THAT'S HOW I CLEARED MYSELF A PATH!!
HAVING BALLS ISN'T GONNA HELP ANY!
THERE'S JUST NO WAY!
YOU HAVEN'T BEEN TO THE BASE, SO WHAT DO YOU KNOW?!

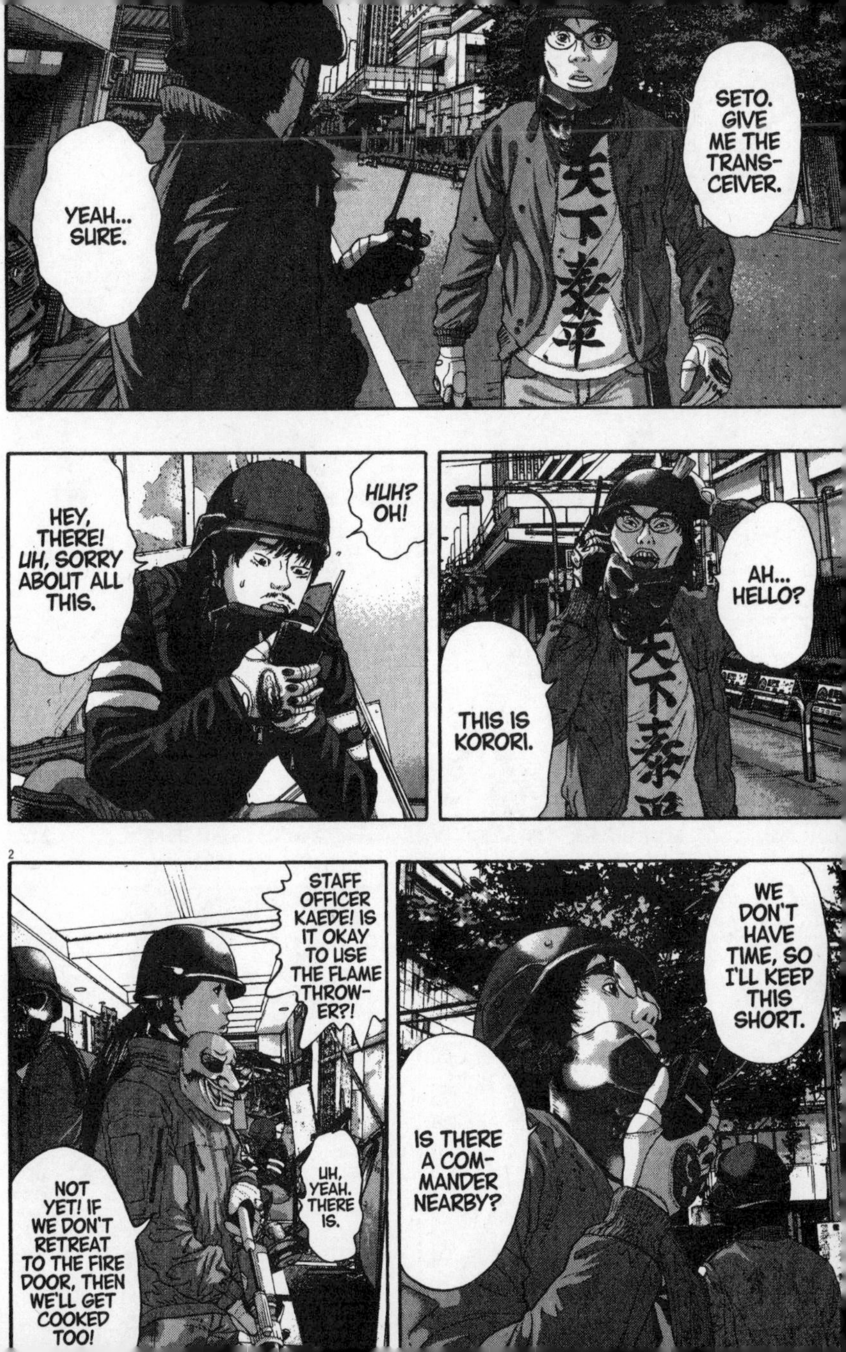
SETO. GIVE ME THE TRANS-CEIVER.
YEAH... SURE.
AH... HELLO?
THIS IS KORORI.
HUH? OH!
HEY, THERE! UH, SORRY ABOUT ALL THIS.
WE DON'T HAVE TIME, SO I'LL KEEP THIS SHORT.
IS THERE A COMMANDER NEARBY?
STAFF OFFICER KAEDE! IS IT OKAY TO USE THE FLAME THROWER?!
UH, YEAH. THERE IS.
NOT YET! IF WE DON'T RETREAT TO THE FIRE DOOR, THEN WE'LL GET COOKED TOO!

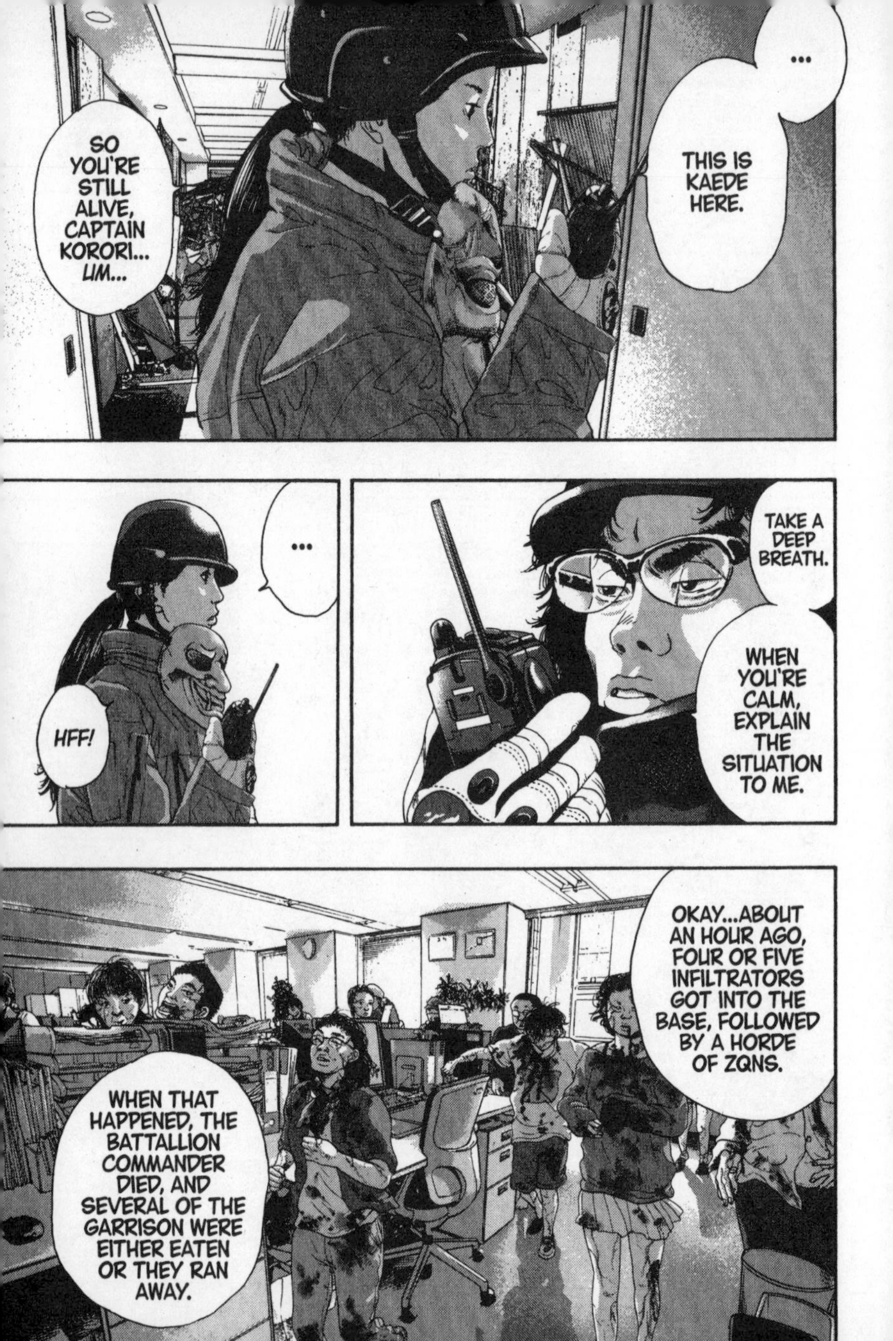
...
THIS IS KAEDE HERE.
SO YOU'RE STILL ALIVE, CAPTAIN KORORI... UM...
TAKE A DEEP BREATH.
WHEN YOU'RE CALM, EXPLAIN THE SITUATION TO ME.
...
HFF!
OKAY...ABOUT AN HOUR AGO, FOUR OR FIVE INFILTRATORS GOT INTO THE BASE, FOLLOWED BY A HORDE OF ZQNS.
WHEN THAT HAPPENED, THE BATTALLION COMMANDER DIED, AND SEVERAL OF THE GARRISON WERE EITHER EATEN OR THEY RAN AWAY.

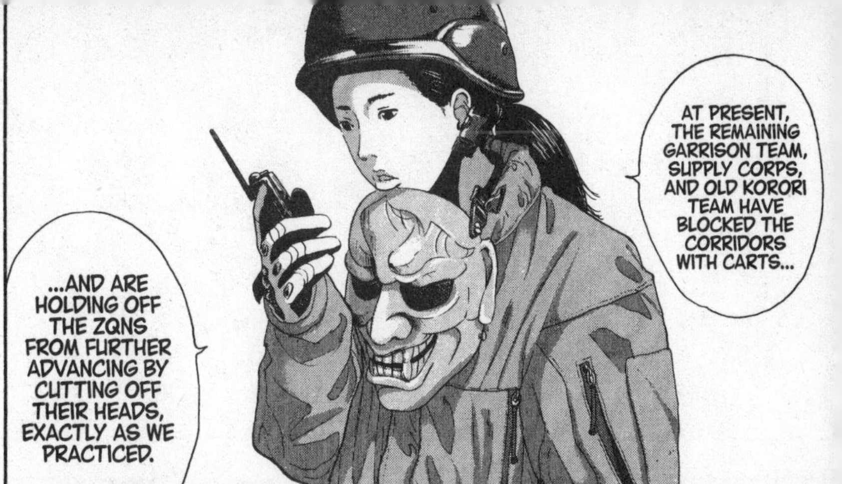
AT PRESENT, THE REMAINING GARRISON TEAM, SUPPLY CORPS, AND OLD KORORI TEAM HAVE BLOCKED THE CORRIDORS WITH CARTS...
...AND ARE HOLDING OFF THE ZQNS FROM FURTHER ADVANCING BY CUTTING OFF THEIR HEADS, EXACTLY AS WE PRACTICED.

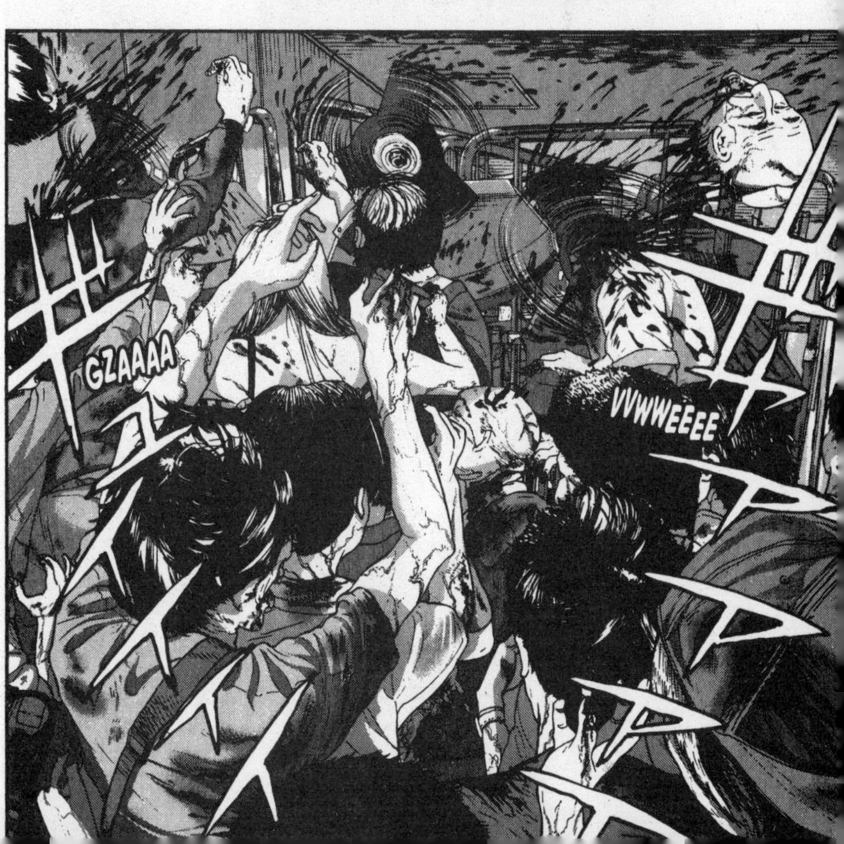
VVWWEEEE
GZAAAA

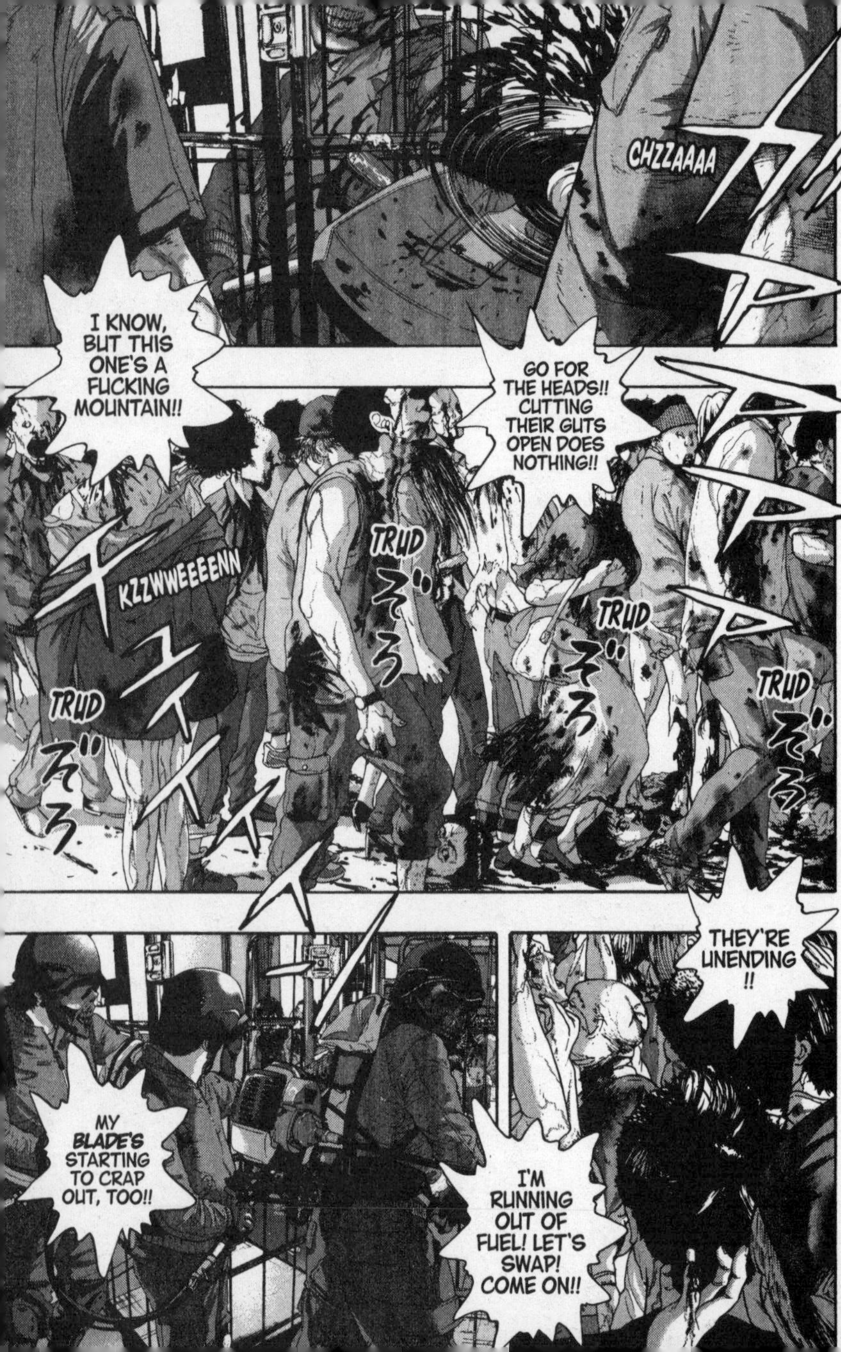
CHZZAAAA
I KNOW, BUT THIS ONE'S A FUCKING MOUNTAIN!!
GO FOR THE HEADS!! CUTTING THEIR GUTS OPEN DOES NOTHING!!
TRUD
ぞろ
TRUD
ぞろ
TRUD
ぞろ
KZZWWEEEENN
TRUD
ぞろ
THEY'RE UNENDING!!
I'M RUNNING OUT OF FUEL! LET'S SWAP! COME ON!!
MY BLADE'S STARTING TO CRAP OUT, TOO!!

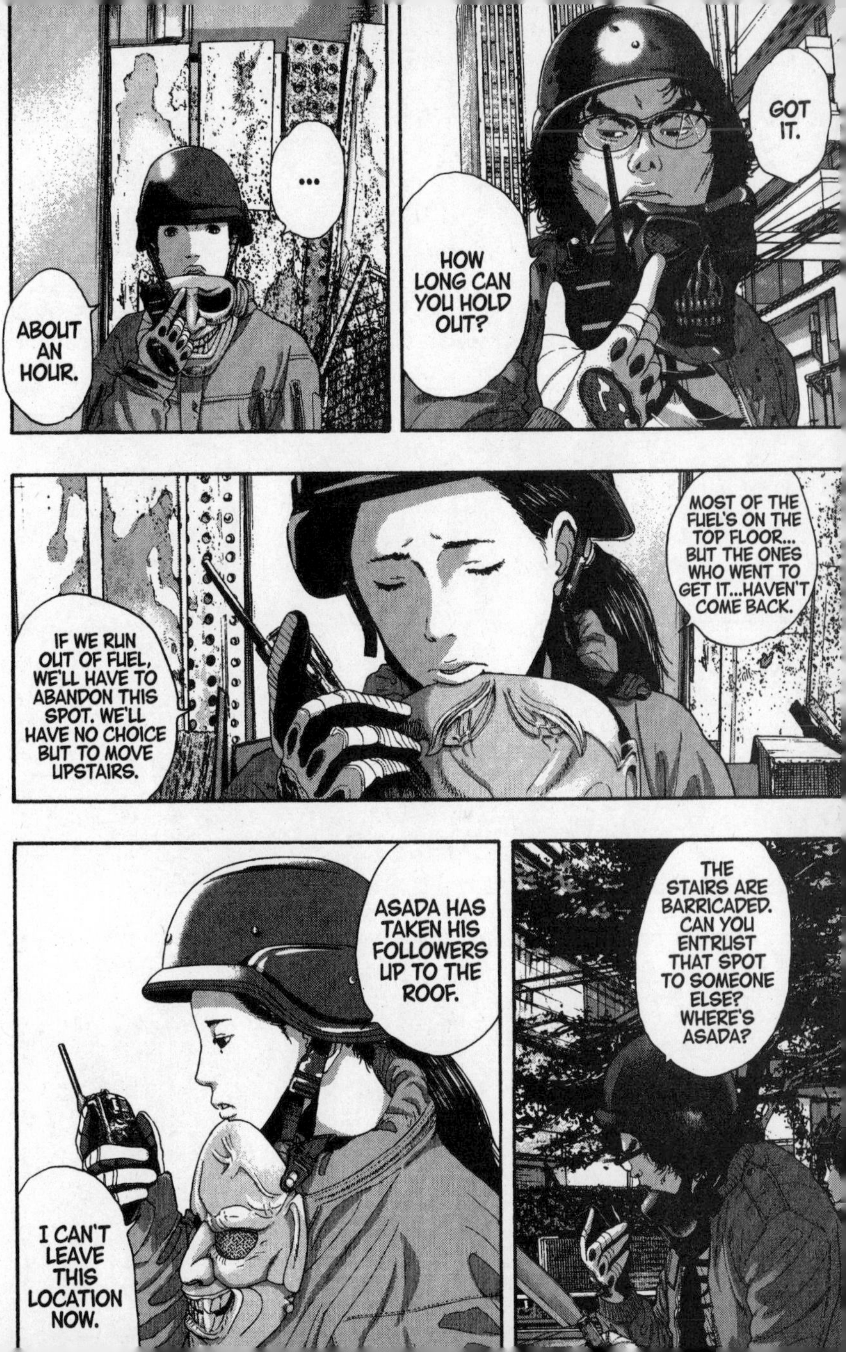
GOT IT.
HOW LONG CAN YOU HOLD OUT?
...
ABOUT AN HOUR.
MOST OF THE FUEL'S ON THE TOP FLOOR... BUT THE ONES WHO WENT TO GET IT...HAVEN'T COME BACK.
IF WE RUN OUT OF FUEL, WE'LL HAVE TO ABANDON THIS SPOT. WE'LL HAVE NO CHOICE BUT TO MOVE UPSTAIRS.
THE STAIRS ARE BARRICADED. CAN YOU ENTRUST THAT SPOT TO SOMEONE ELSE? WHERE'S ASADA?
ASADA HAS TAKEN HIS FOLLOWERS UP TO THE ROOF.
I CAN'T LEAVE THIS LOCATION NOW.

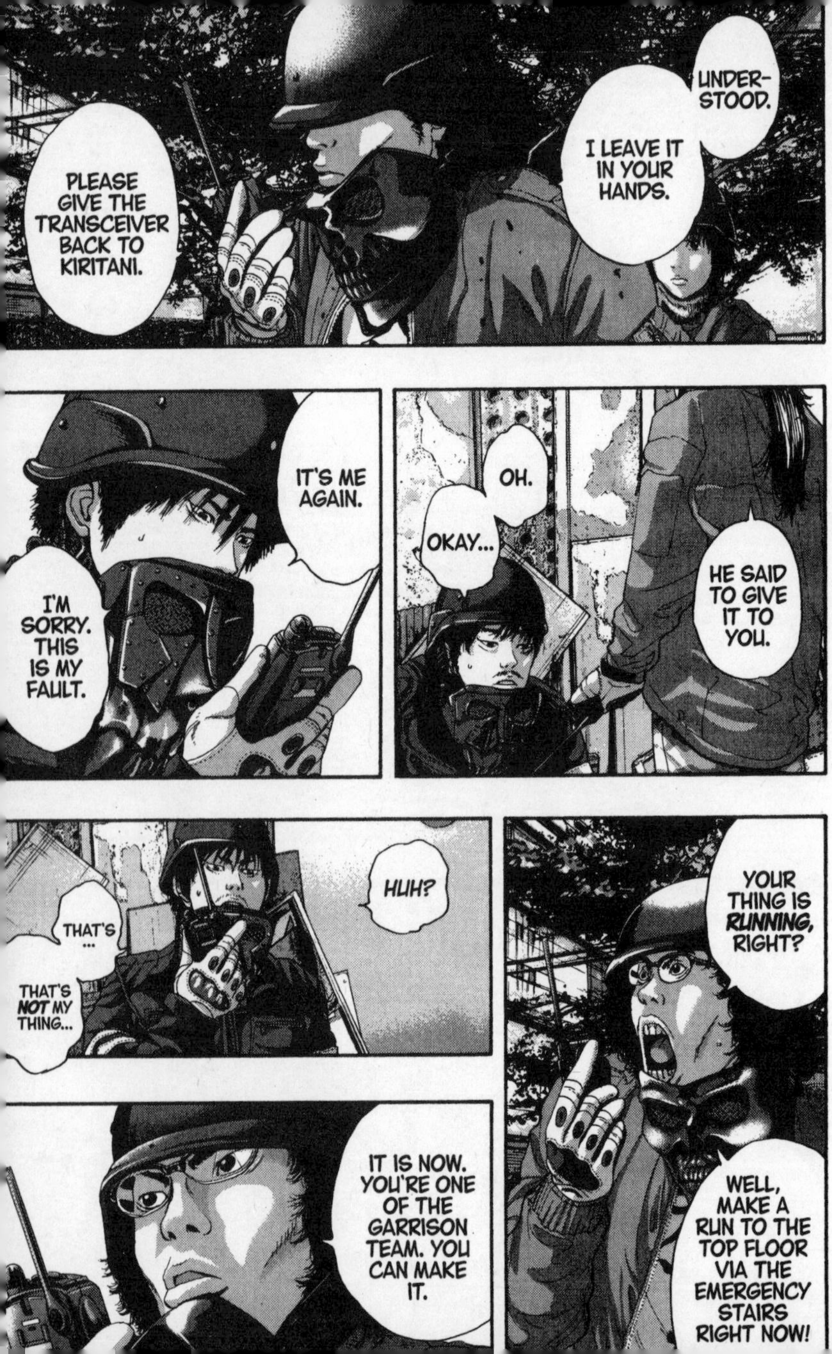
UNDER-STOOD.
I LEAVE IT IN YOUR HANDS.
PLEASE GIVE THE TRANSCEIVER BACK TO KIRITANI.
HE SAID TO GIVE IT TO YOU.
OH.
OKAY...
IT'S ME AGAIN.
I'M SORRY. THIS IS MY FAULT.
YOUR THING IS *RUNNING*, RIGHT?
HUH?
THAT'S...
THAT'S *NOT* MY THING...
IT IS NOW. YOU'RE ONE OF THE GARRISON TEAM. YOU CAN MAKE IT.
WELL, MAKE A RUN TO THE TOP FLOOR VIA THE EMERGENCY STAIRS RIGHT NOW!

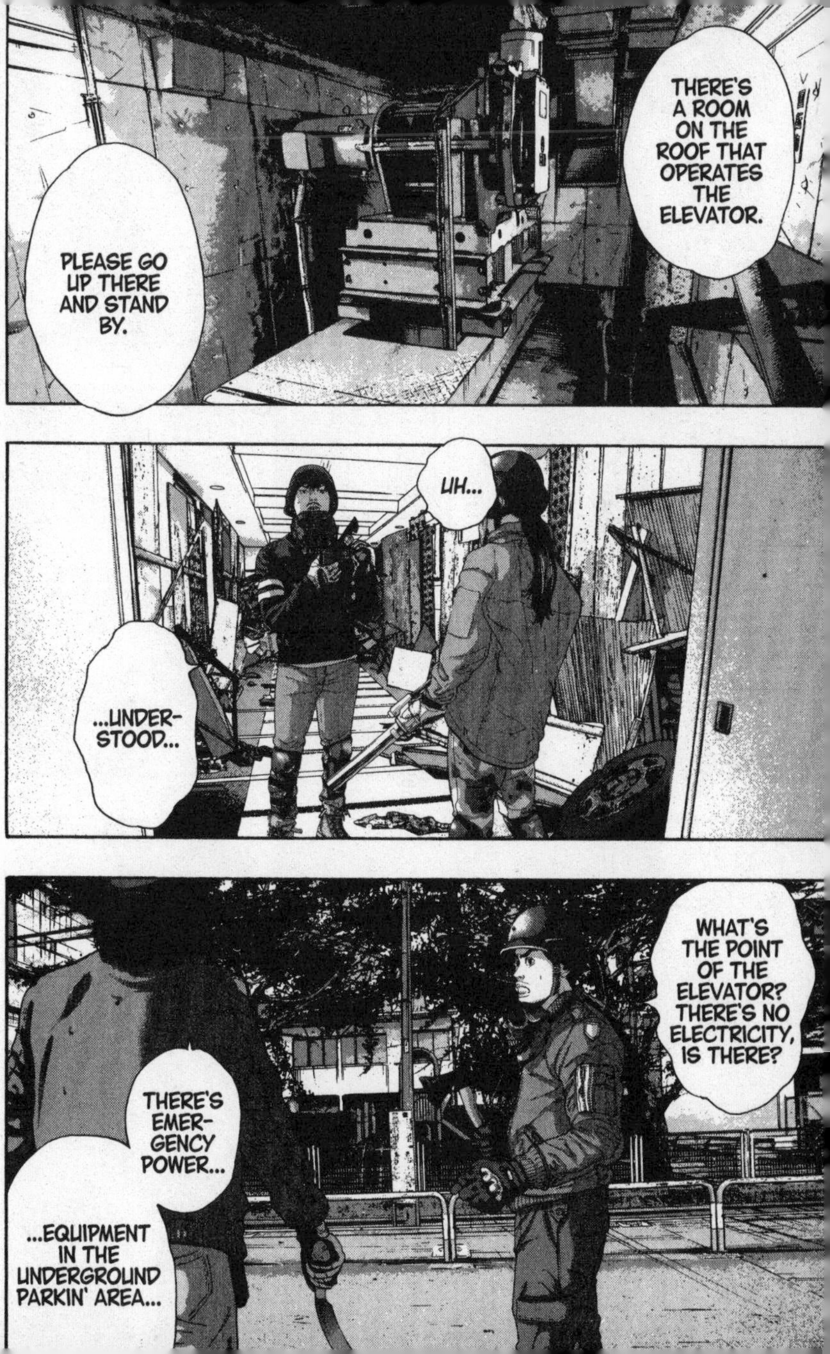
THERE'S A ROOM ON THE ROOF THAT OPERATES THE ELEVATOR.
PLEASE GO UP THERE AND STAND BY.
UH...
...UNDER-STOOD...
WHAT'S THE POINT OF THE ELEVATOR? THERE'S NO ELECTRICITY, IS THERE?
THERE'S EMER-GENCY POWER...
...EQUIPMENT IN THE UNDERGROUND PARKIN' AREA...

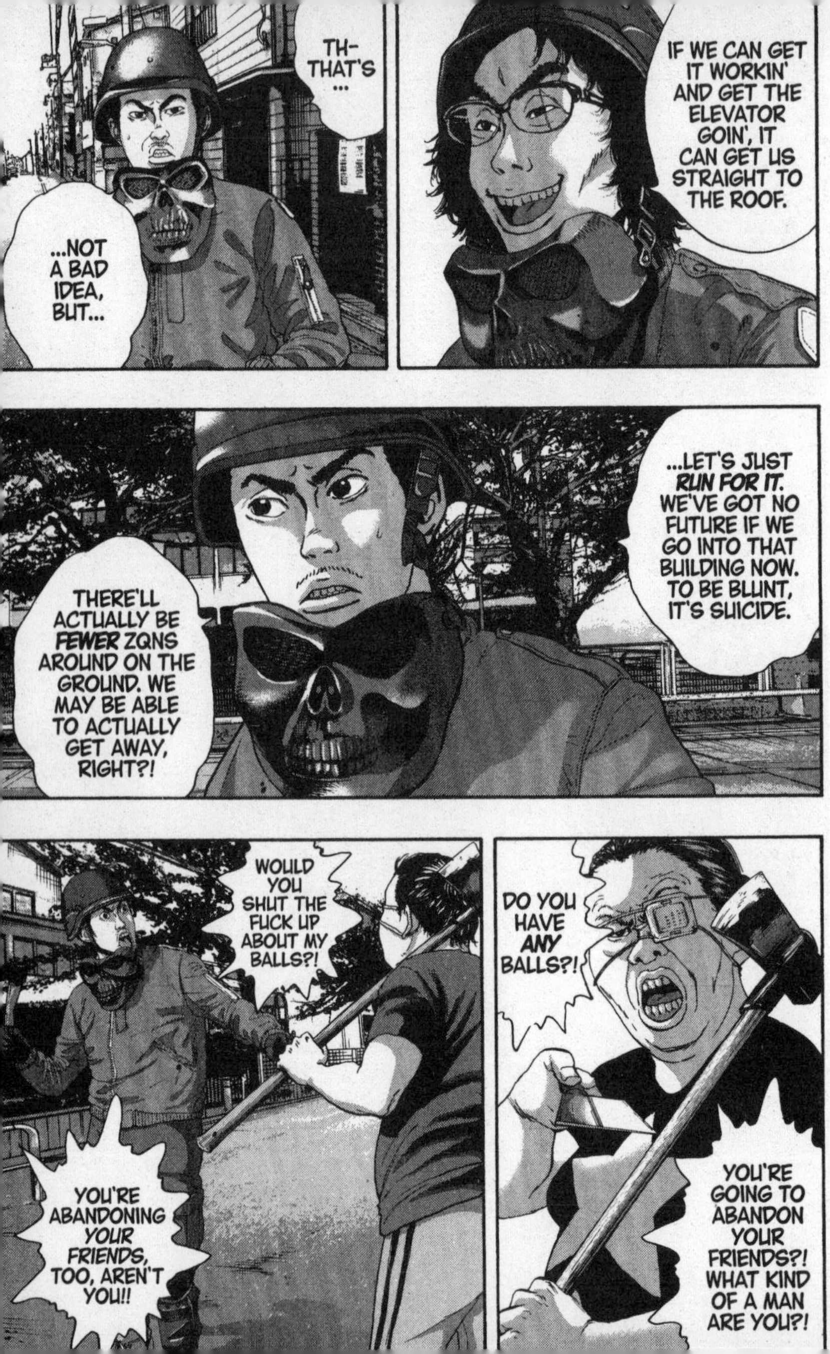
IF WE CAN GET IT WORKIN' AND GET THE ELEVATOR GOIN', IT CAN GET US STRAIGHT TO THE ROOF.
TH- THAT'S ...
...NOT A BAD IDEA, BUT...
...LET'S JUST *RUN FOR IT.* WE'VE GOT NO FUTURE IF WE GO INTO THAT BUILDING NOW. TO BE BLUNT, IT'S SUICIDE.
THERE'LL ACTUALLY BE *FEWER* ZQNS AROUND ON THE GROUND. WE MAY BE ABLE TO ACTUALLY GET AWAY, RIGHT?!
DO YOU HAVE *ANY* BALLS?!
YOU'RE GOING TO ABANDON YOUR FRIENDS?! WHAT KIND OF A MAN ARE YOU?!
WOULD YOU SHUT THE FUCK UP ABOUT MY BALLS?!
YOU'RE ABANDONING *YOUR* FRIENDS, TOO, AREN'T YOU!!

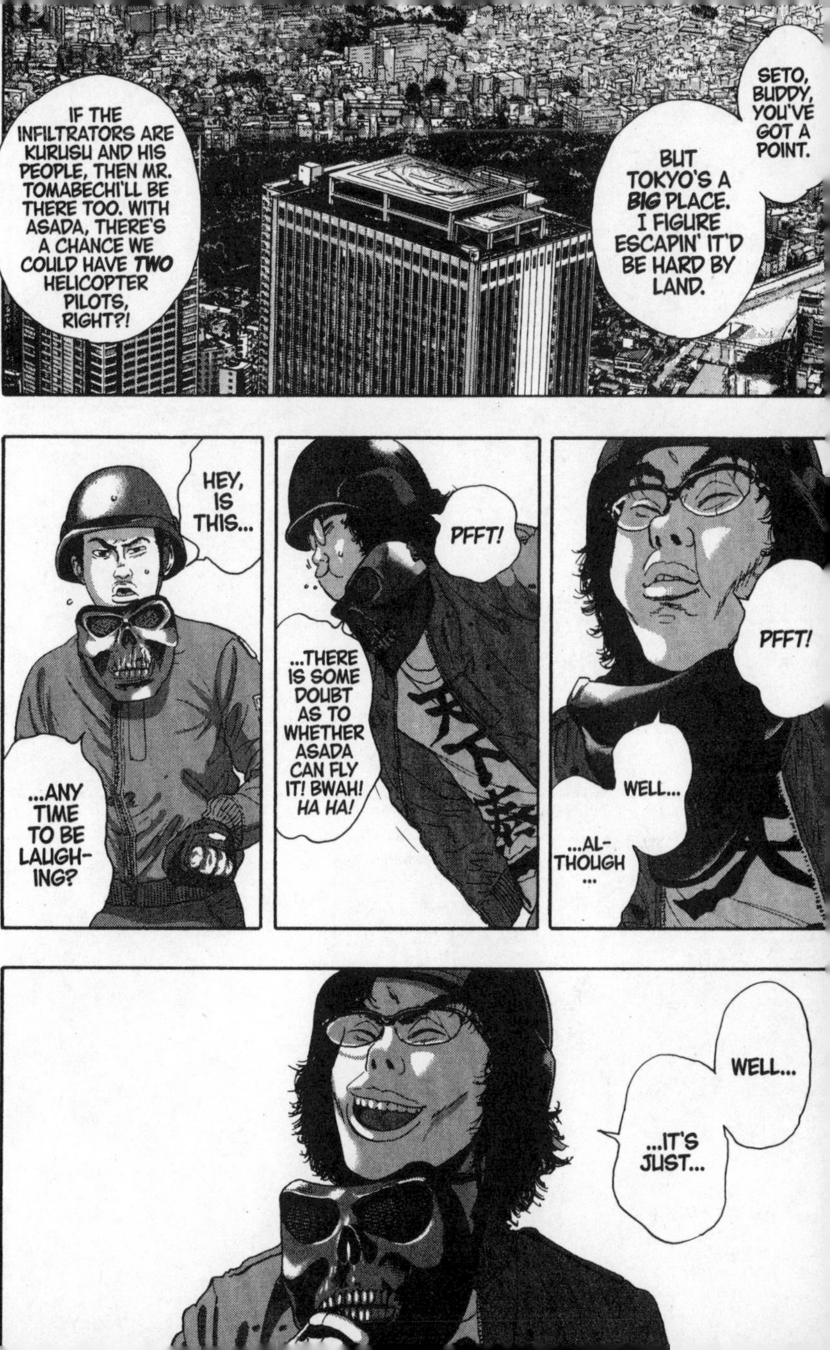
SETO, BUDDY, YOU'VE GOT A POINT.
BUT TOKYO'S A BIG PLACE. I FIGURE ESCAPIN' IT'D BE HARD BY LAND.
IF THE INFILTRATORS ARE KURUSU AND HIS PEOPLE, THEN MR. TOMABECHI'LL BE THERE TOO. WITH ASADA, THERE'S A CHANCE WE COULD HAVE TWO HELICOPTER PILOTS, RIGHT?!
PFFT!
WELL...
...AL-THOUGH...
PFFT!
...THERE IS SOME DOUBT AS TO WHETHER ASADA CAN FLY IT! BWAH! HA HA!
HEY, IS THIS...
...ANY TIME TO BE LAUGH-ING?
WELL...
...IT'S JUST...

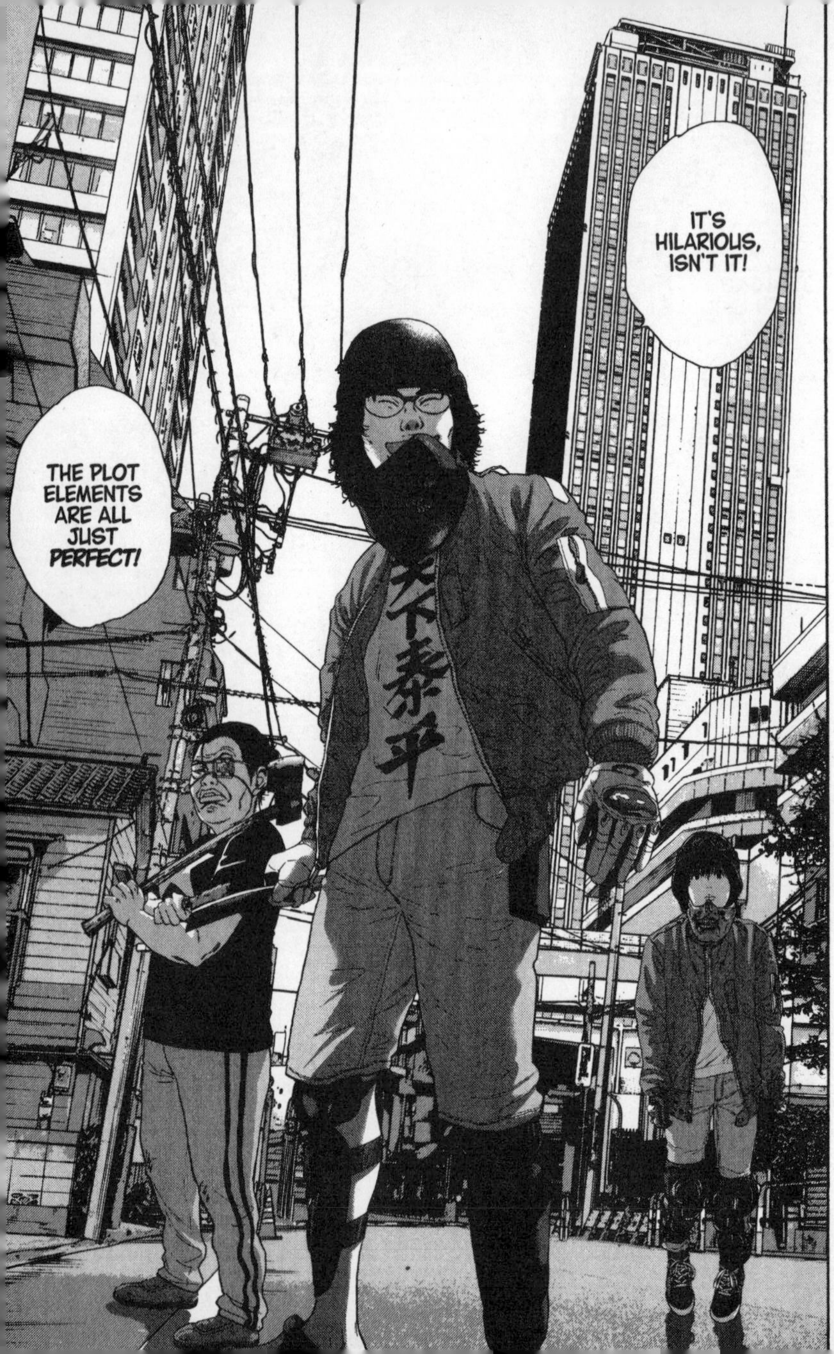
IT'S HILARIOUS, ISN'T IT!
THE PLOT ELEMENTS ARE ALL JUST PERFECT!

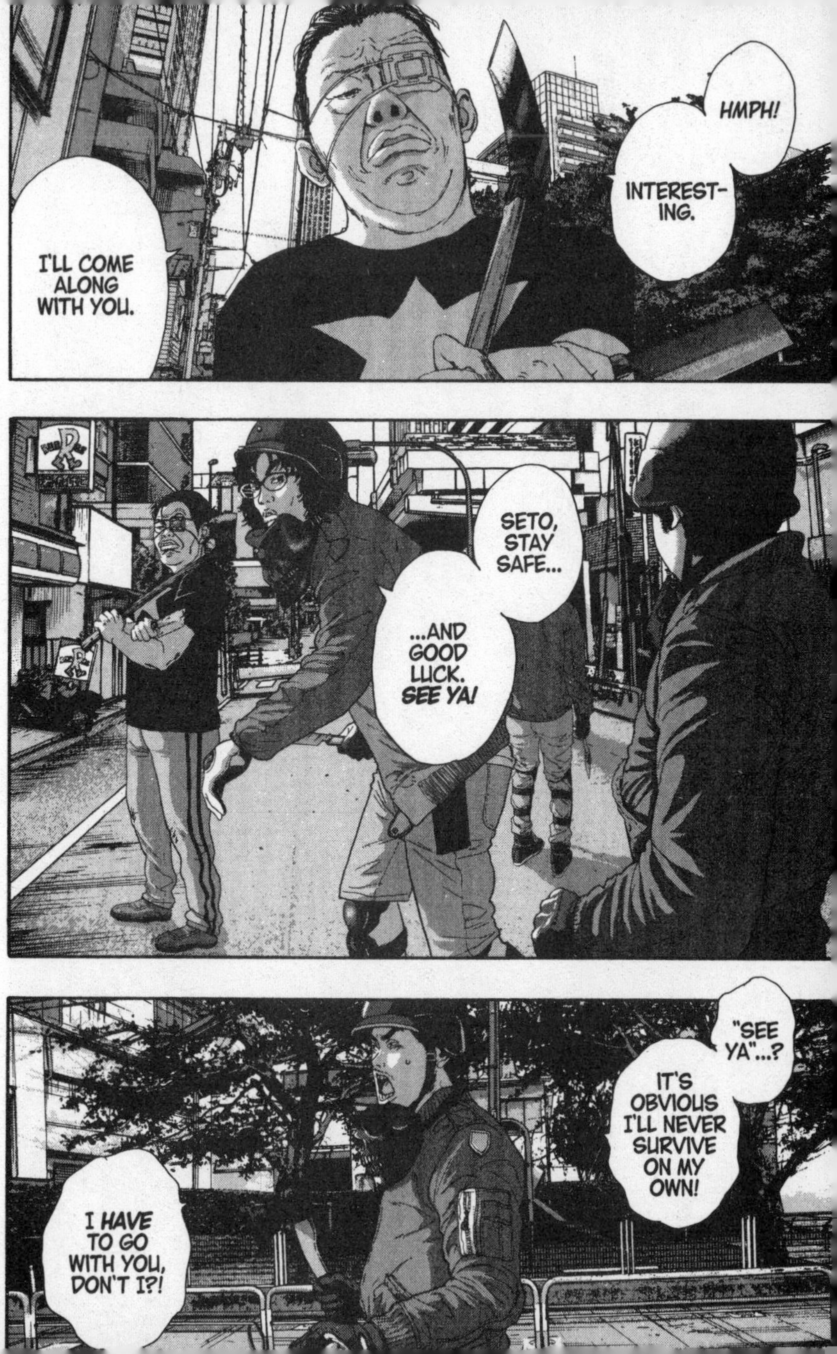
HMPH!
INTERESTING-ING.
I'LL COME ALONG WITH YOU.
SETO, STAY SAFE...
...AND GOOD LUCK. SEE YA!
"SEE YA"...?
IT'S OBVIOUS I'LL NEVER SURVIVE ON MY OWN!
I HAVE TO GO WITH YOU, DON'T I?!

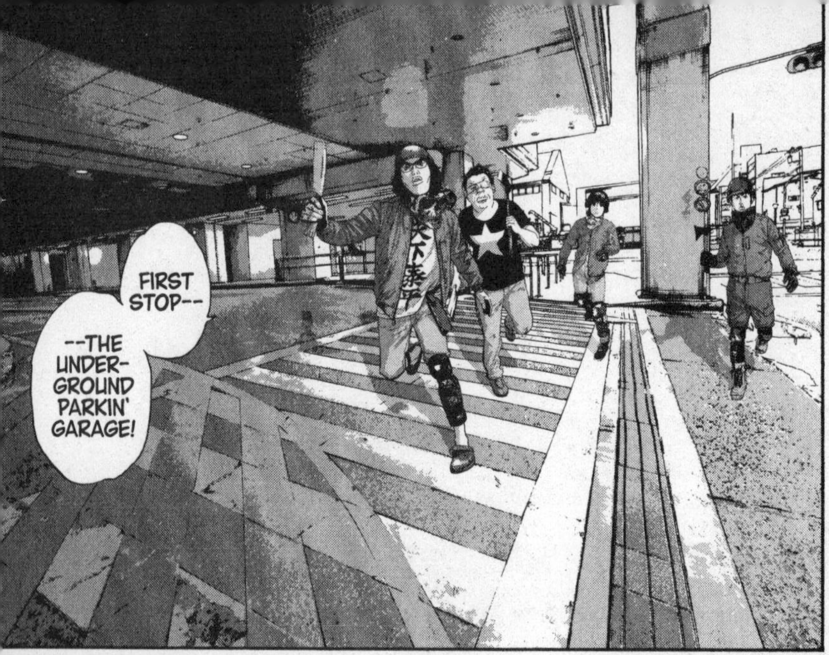
FIRST STOP--
--THE UNDER-GROUND PARKIN' GARAGE!

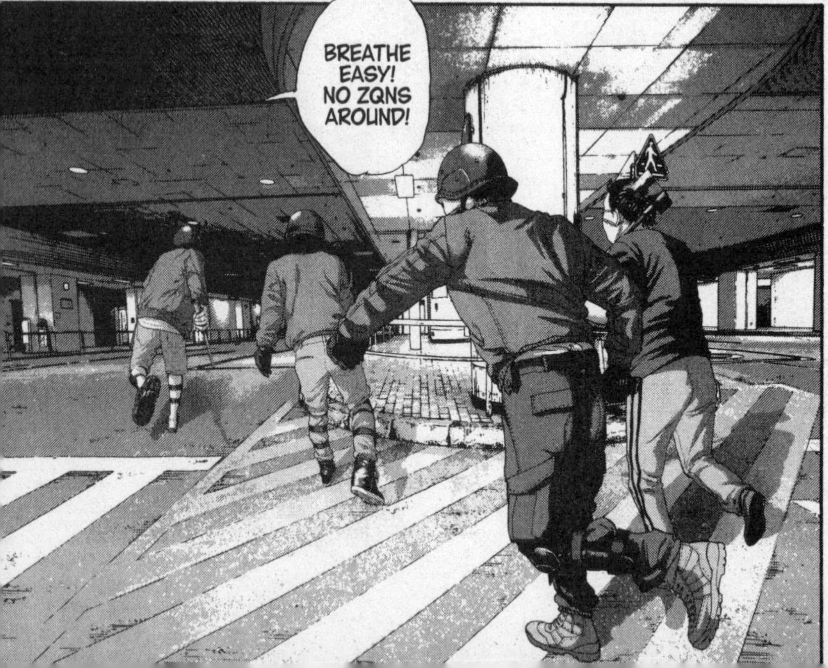
BREATHE EASY! NO ZQNS AROUND!

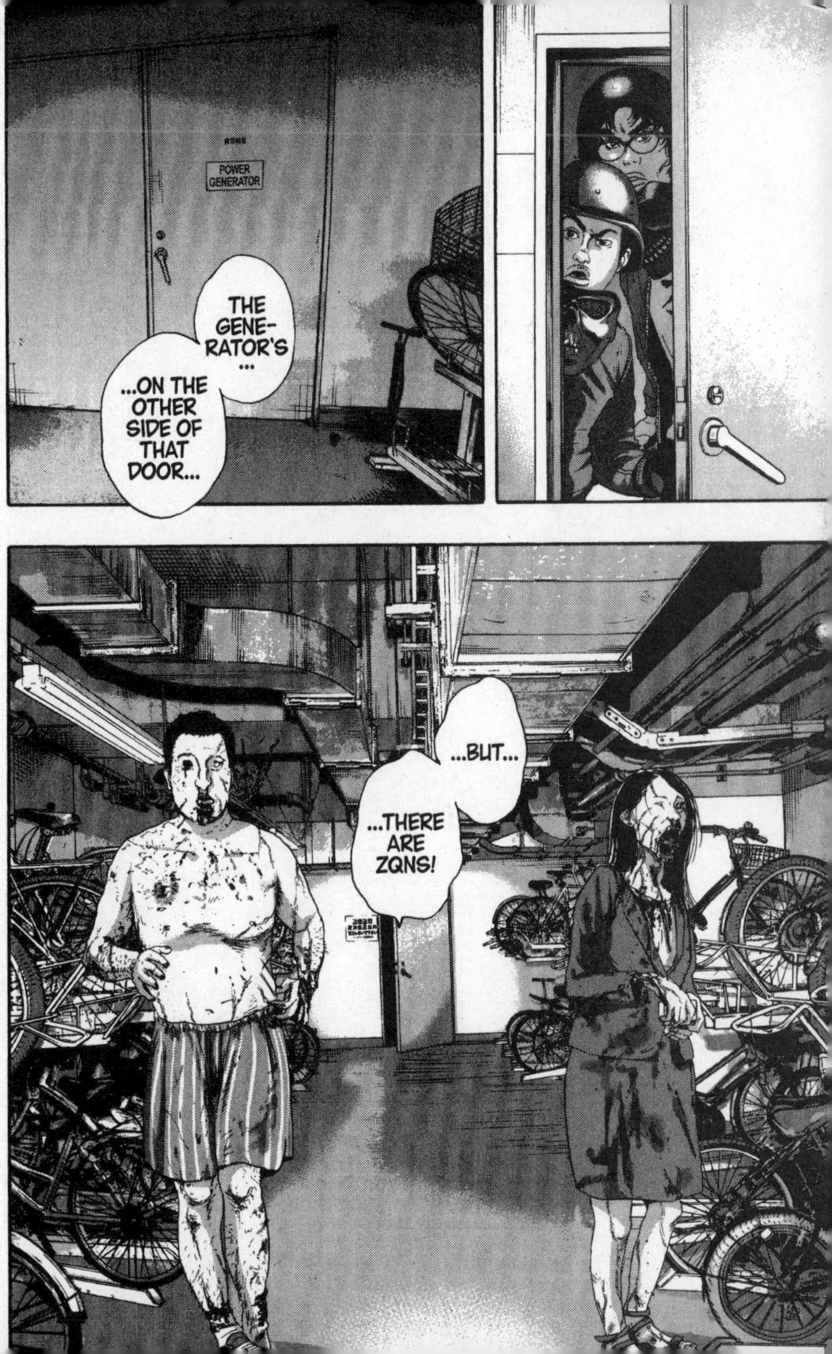
POWER GENERATOR
THE GENE-RATOR'S...
...ON THE OTHER SIDE OF THAT DOOR...
...BUT...
...THERE ARE ZQNS!

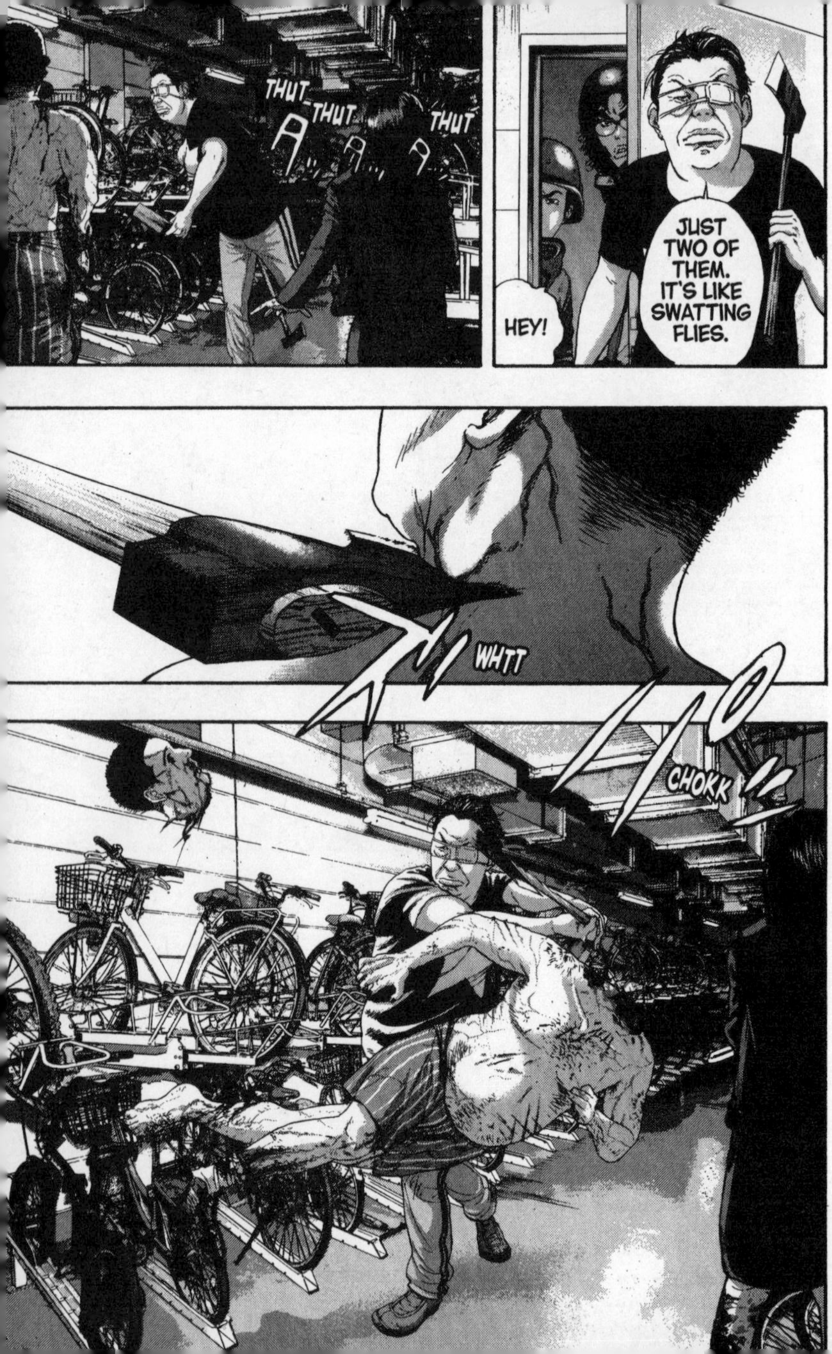
JUST TWO OF THEM. IT'S LIKE SWATTING FLIES.
HEY!
THUT
THUT
THUT
WHTT
CHOKK

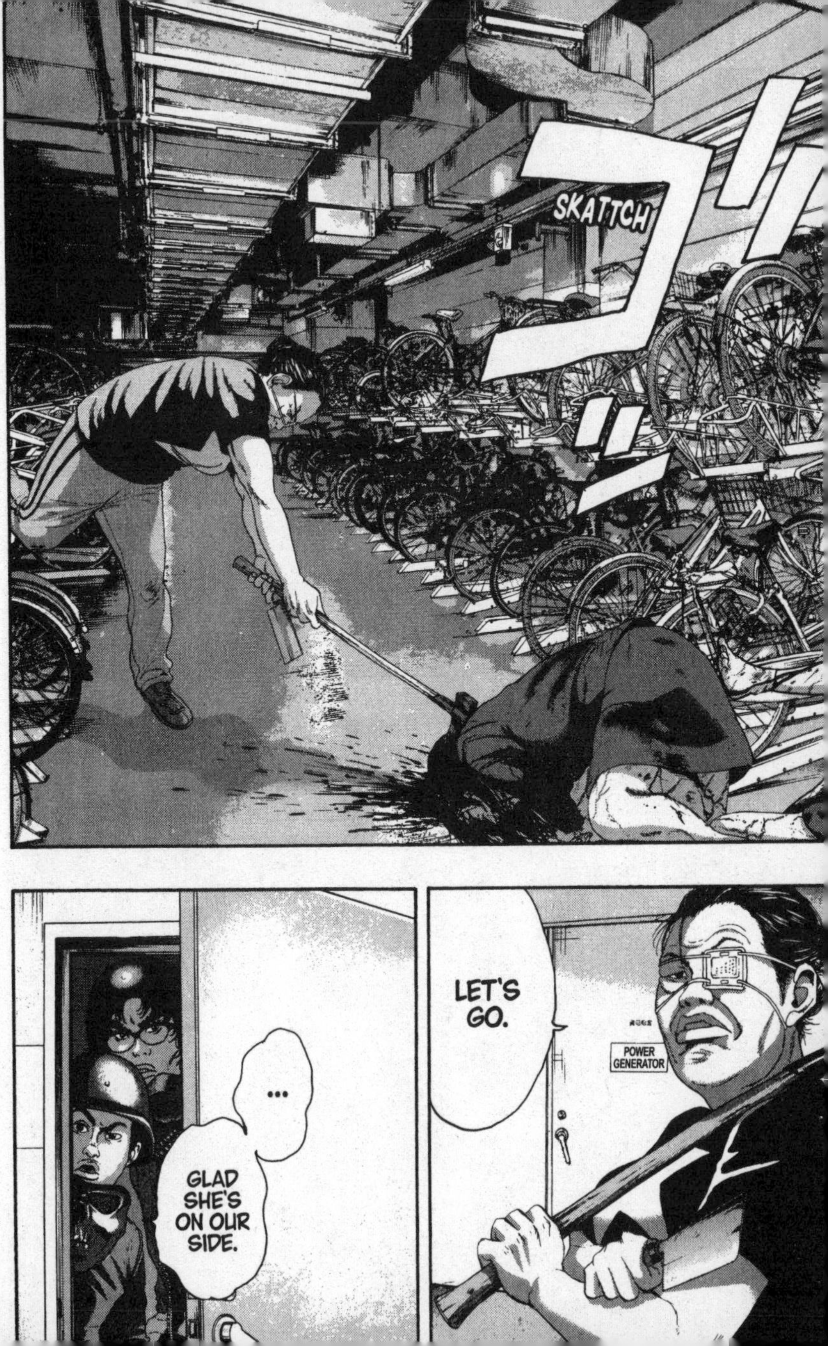
SKATTCH
LET'S GO.
POWER GENERATOR
...
GLAD SHE'S ON OUR SIDE.

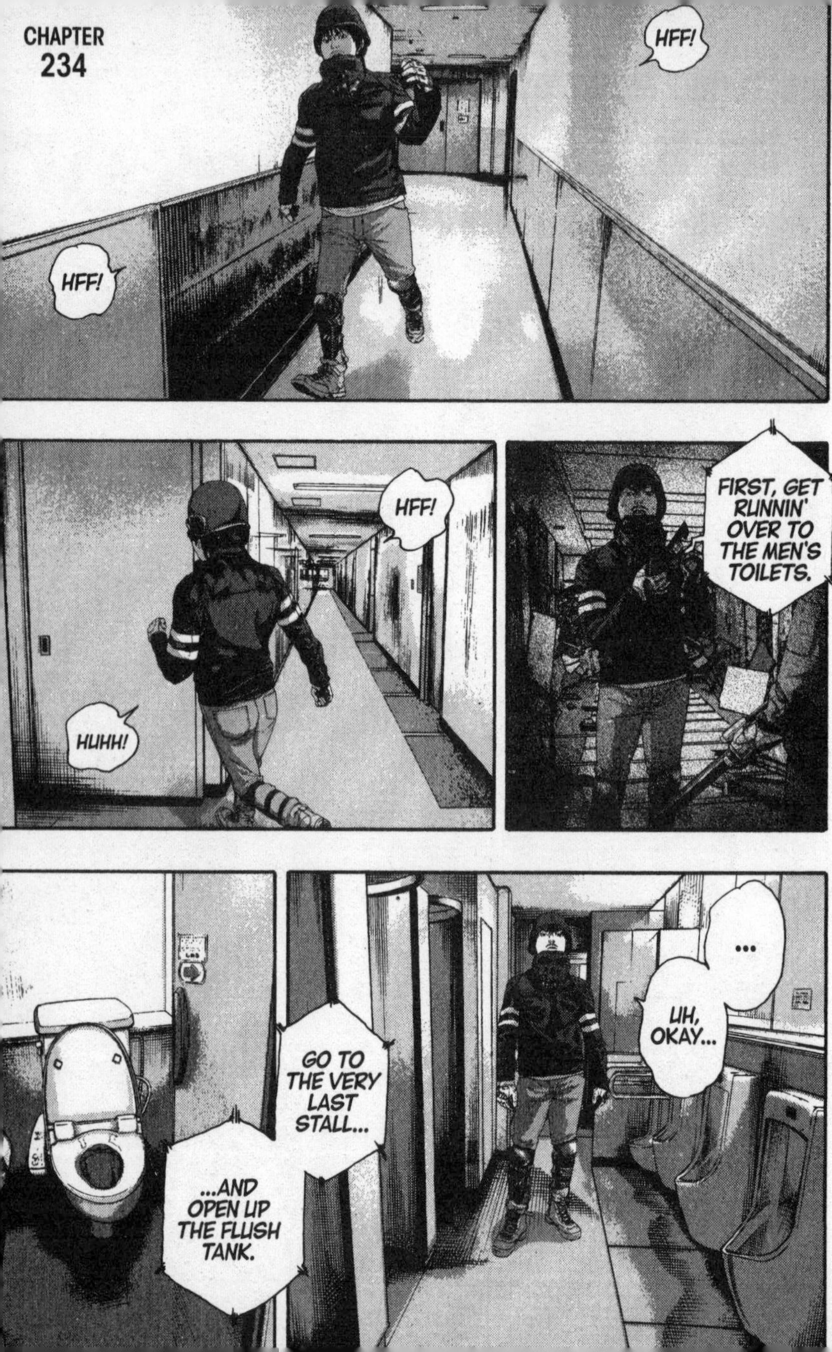
CHAPTER 234
HFF!
HFF!
FIRST, GET RUNNIN' OVER TO THE MEN'S TOILETS.
HFF!
HUHH!
...
UH, OKAY...
GO TO THE VERY LAST STALL...
...AND OPEN UP THE FLUSH TANK.

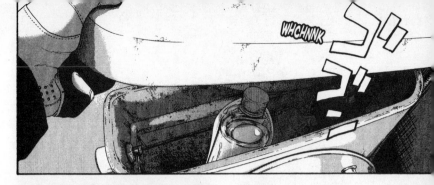

WHCHNNK

THAT'S THE SCRIPTURAL MANGA OF ASADA-ISM IN THAT BOTTLE.

TAKE IT AND HEAD ON UP TO THE TOP FLOOR.

FUCK!

ARE YOU SERIOUS?

DASH

THIS THING'S GONNA HELP ME GET BY?

WHY WASTE BRAIN CELLS THINKING ABOUT IT?!

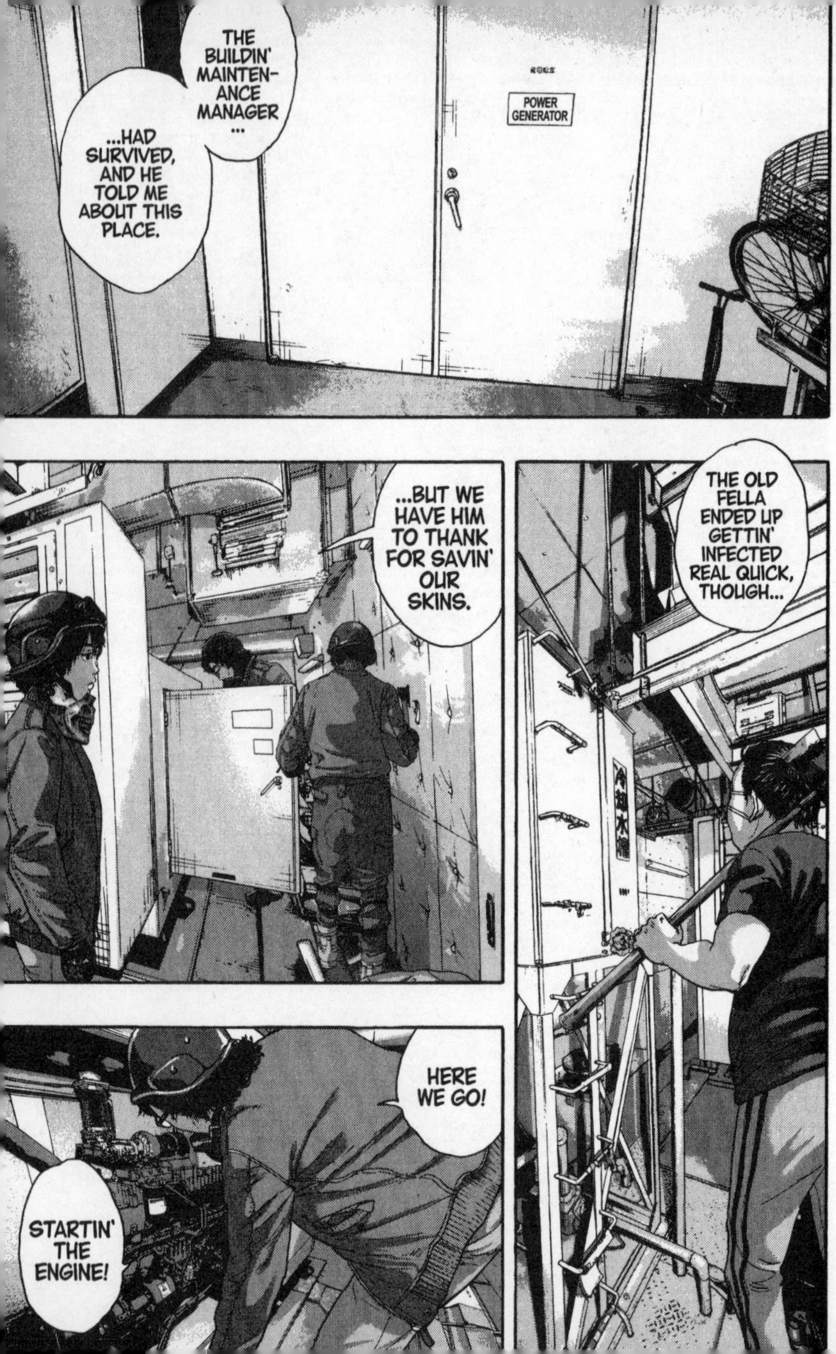
THE BUILDIN' MAINTENANCE MANAGER...
POWER GENERATOR
...HAD SURVIVED, AND HE TOLD ME ABOUT THIS PLACE.
THE OLD FELLA ENDED UP GETTIN' INFECTED REAL QUICK, THOUGH...
...BUT WE HAVE HIM TO THANK FOR SAVIN' OUR SKINS.
HERE WE GO!
STARTIN' THE ENGINE!

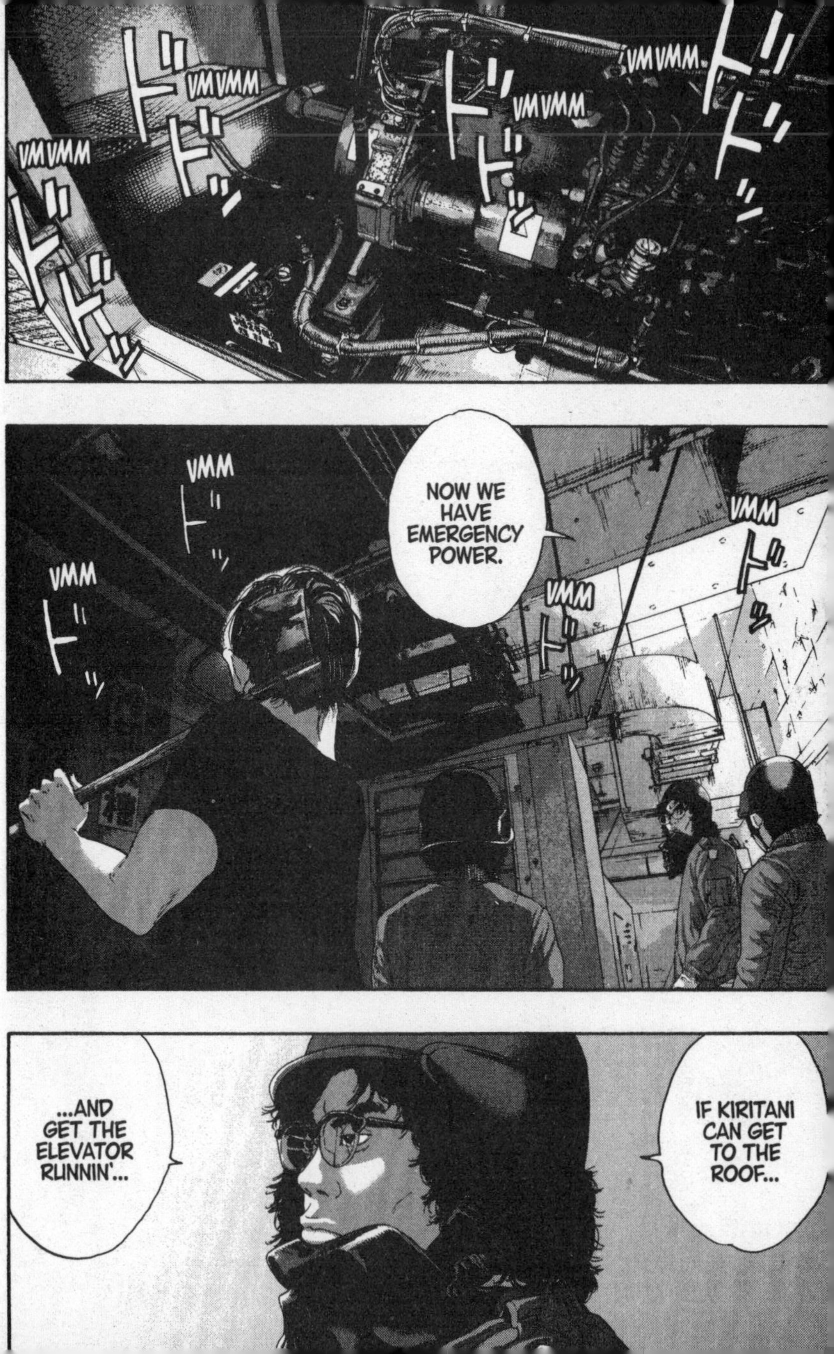
VMVMM
VMVMM
VMVMM
VMVMM
VMM
VMM
NOW WE HAVE EMERGENCY POWER.
VMM
VMM
IF KIRITANI CAN GET TO THE ROOF...
...AND GET THE ELEVATOR RUNNIN'...

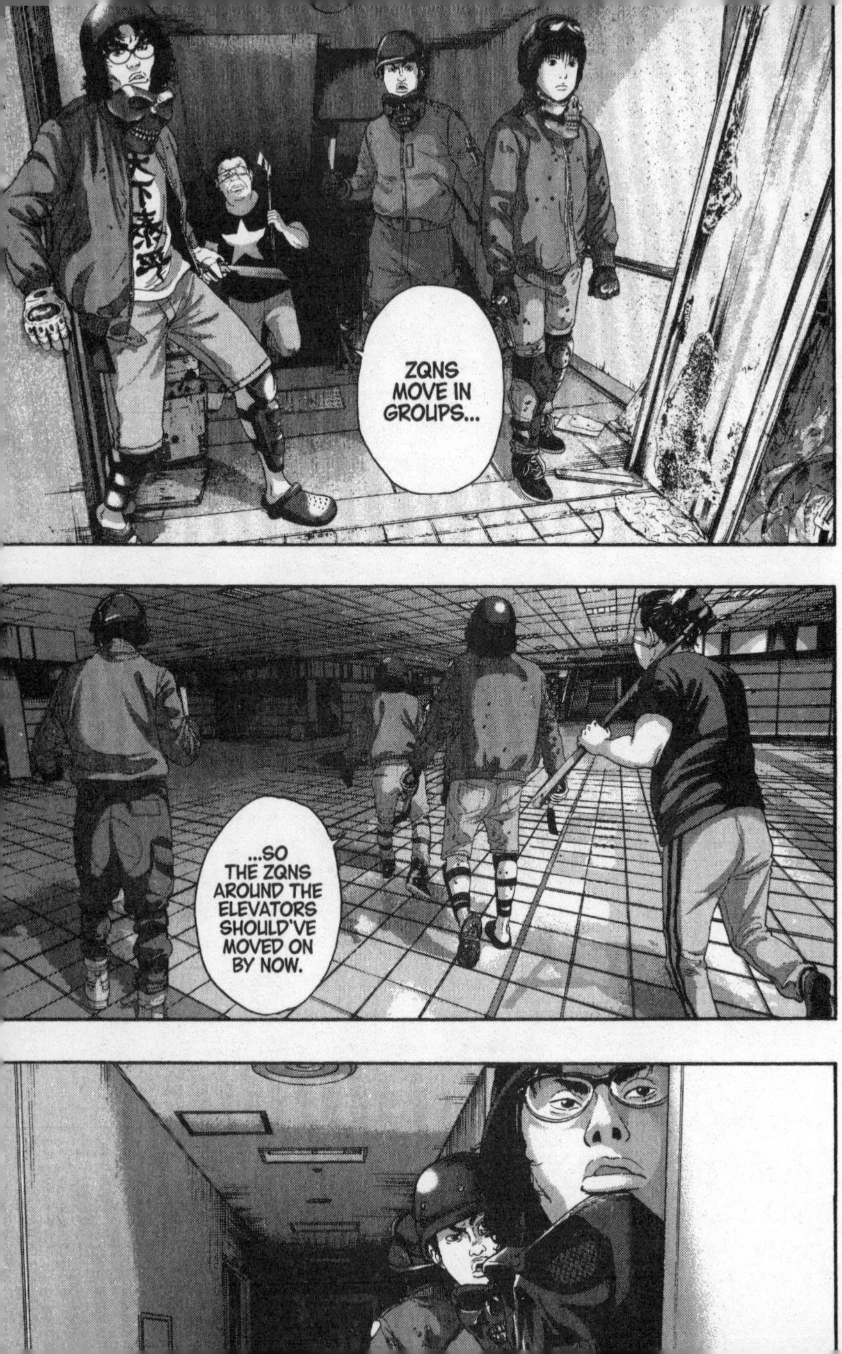
ZQNS MOVE IN GROUPS...
...SO THE ZQNS AROUND THE ELEVATORS SHOULD'VE MOVED ON BY NOW.

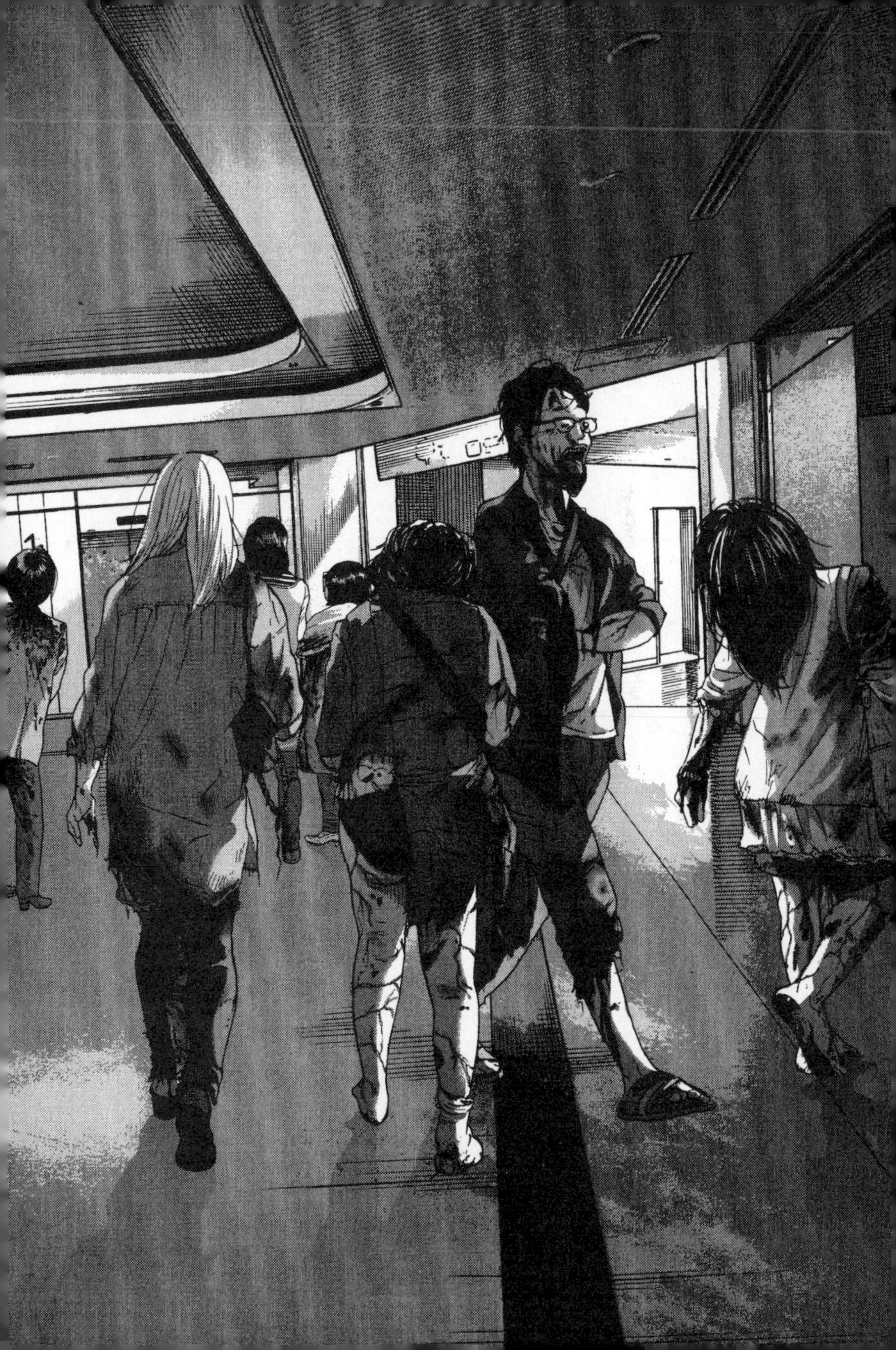

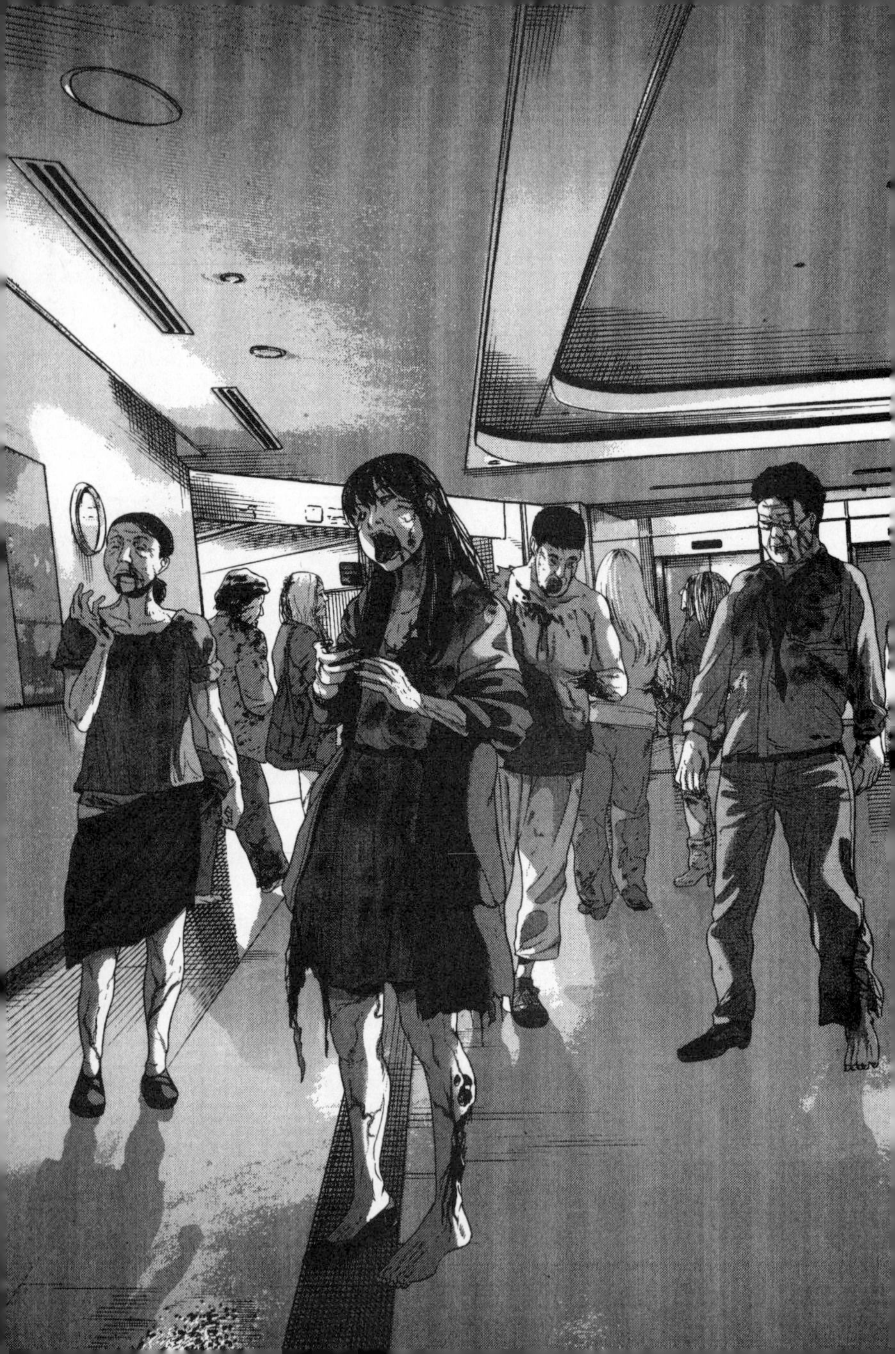

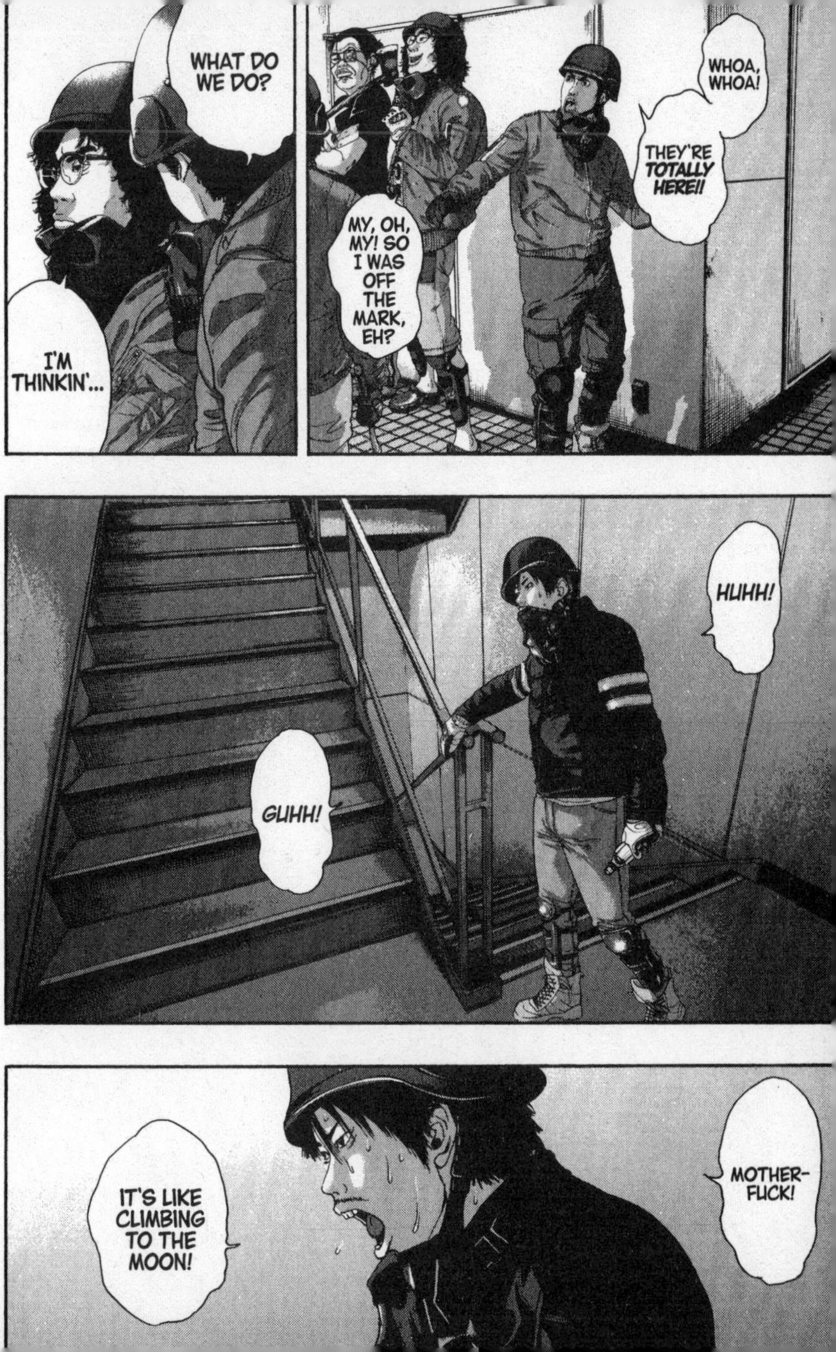
WHOA, WHOA!
THEY'RE *TOTALLY* HERE!!
MY, OH, MY! SO I WAS OFF THE MARK, EH?
WHAT DO WE DO?
I'M THINKIN'...
HUHH!
GUHH!
MOTHER-FUCK!
IT'S LIKE CLIMBING TO THE MOON!

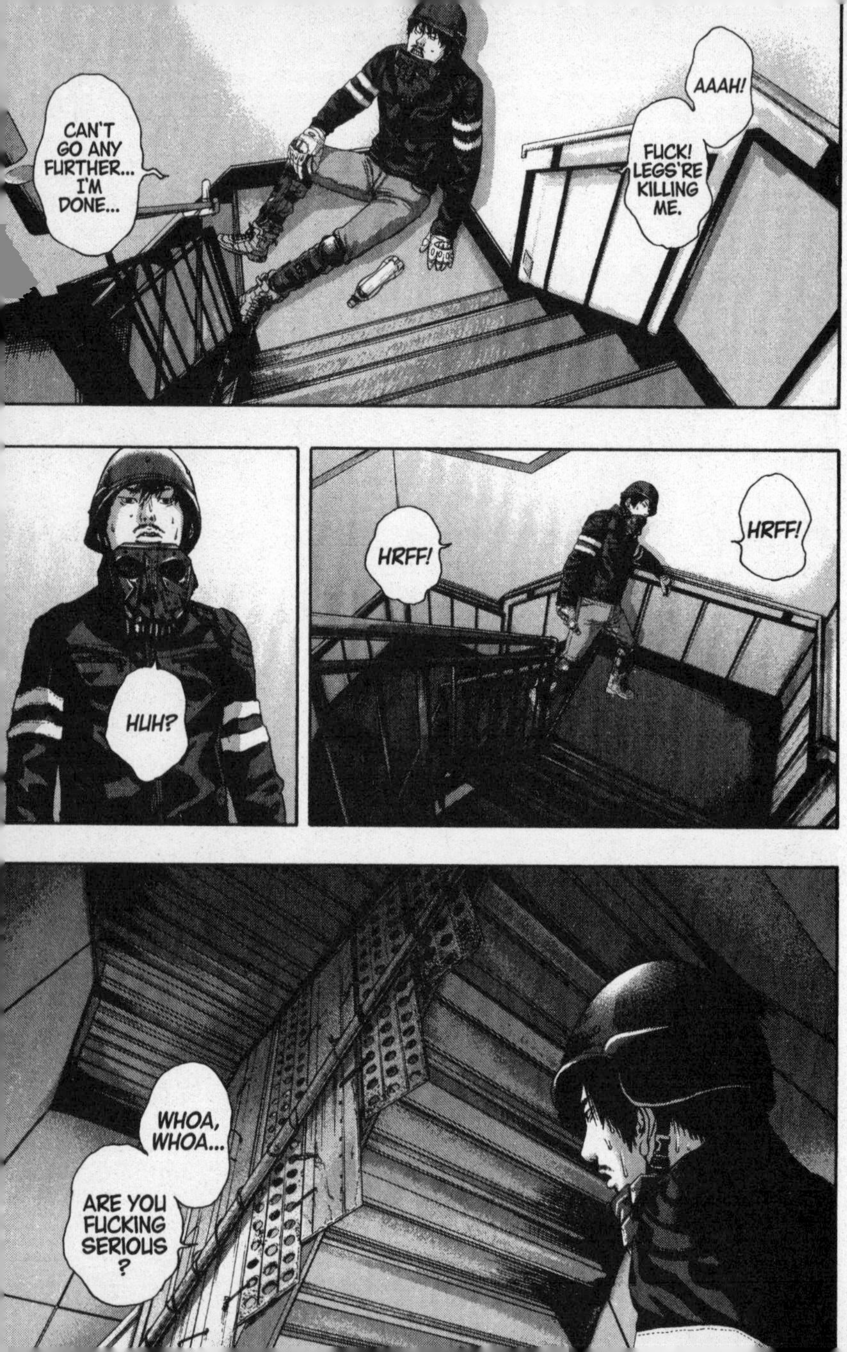
AAAH!
FUCK! LEGS'RE KILLING ME.
CAN'T GO ANY FURTHER... I'M DONE...
HRFF!
HRFF!
HUH?
WHOA, WHOA...
ARE YOU FUCKING SERIOUS?

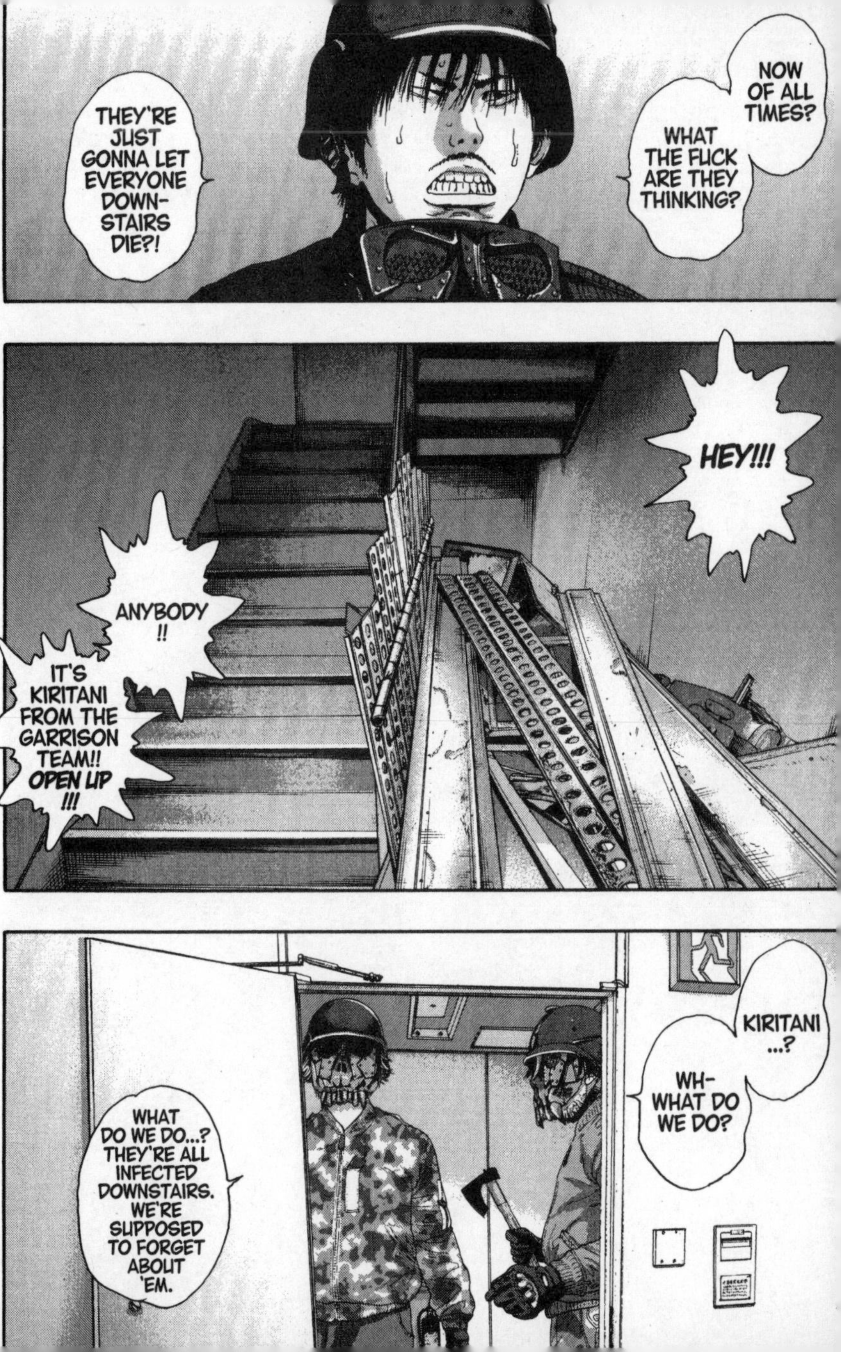
NOW OF ALL TIMES?
WHAT THE FUCK ARE THEY THINKING?
THEY'RE JUST GONNA LET EVERYONE DOWN-STAIRS DIE?!
HEY!!!
ANYBODY !!
IT'S KIRITANI FROM THE GARRISON TEAM!! OPEN UP !!!
KIRITANI ...?
WH- WHAT DO WE DO?
WHAT DO WE DO...? THEY'RE ALL INFECTED DOWNSTAIRS. WE'RE SUPPOSED TO FORGET ABOUT 'EM.

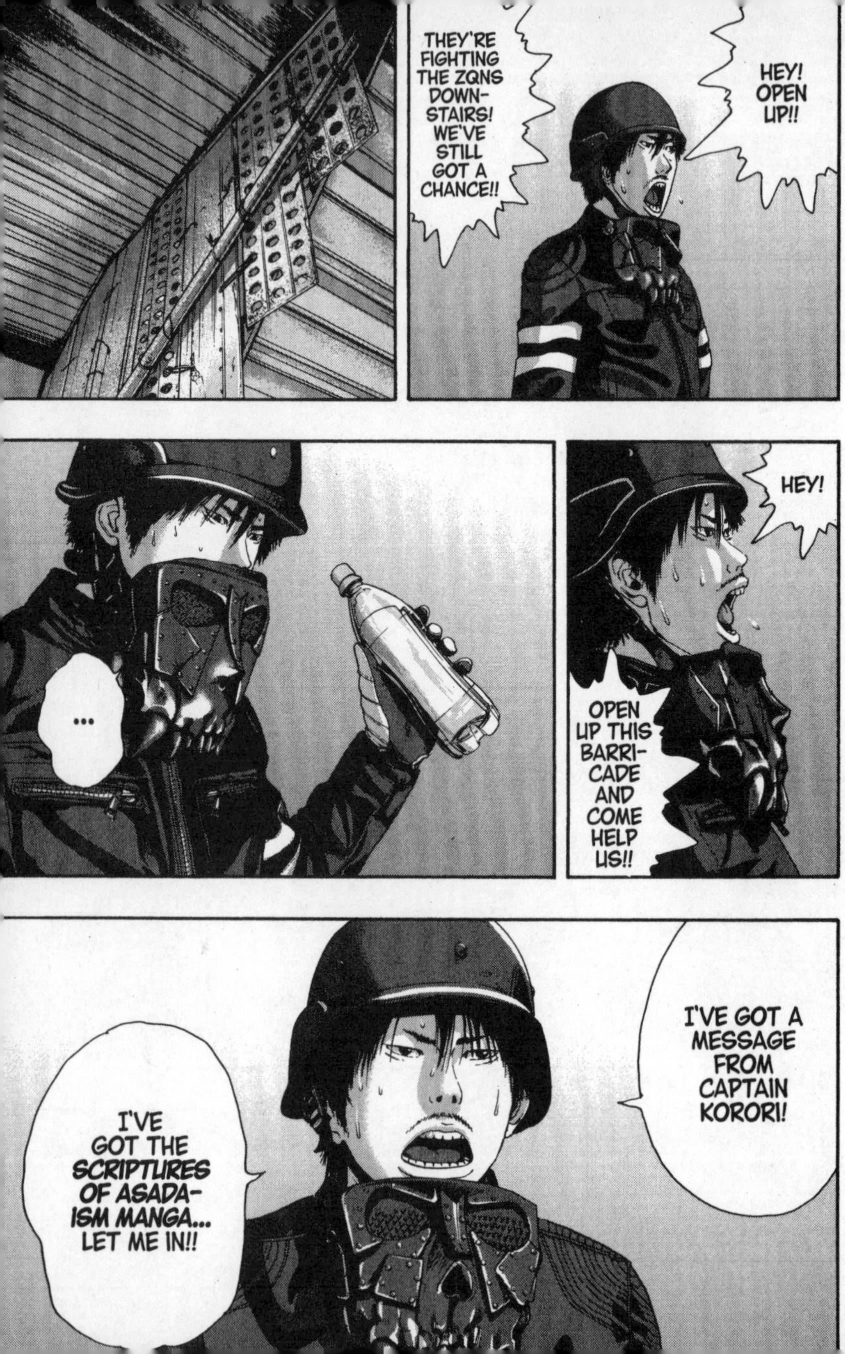
HEY! OPEN UP!!
THEY'RE FIGHTING THE ZQNS DOWN-STAIRS! WE'VE STILL GOT A CHANCE!!
HEY!
OPEN UP THIS BARRI-CADE AND COME HELP US!!
...
I'VE GOT A MESSAGE FROM CAPTAIN KORORI!
I'VE GOT THE SCRIPTURES OF ASADA-ISM MANGA... LET ME IN!!

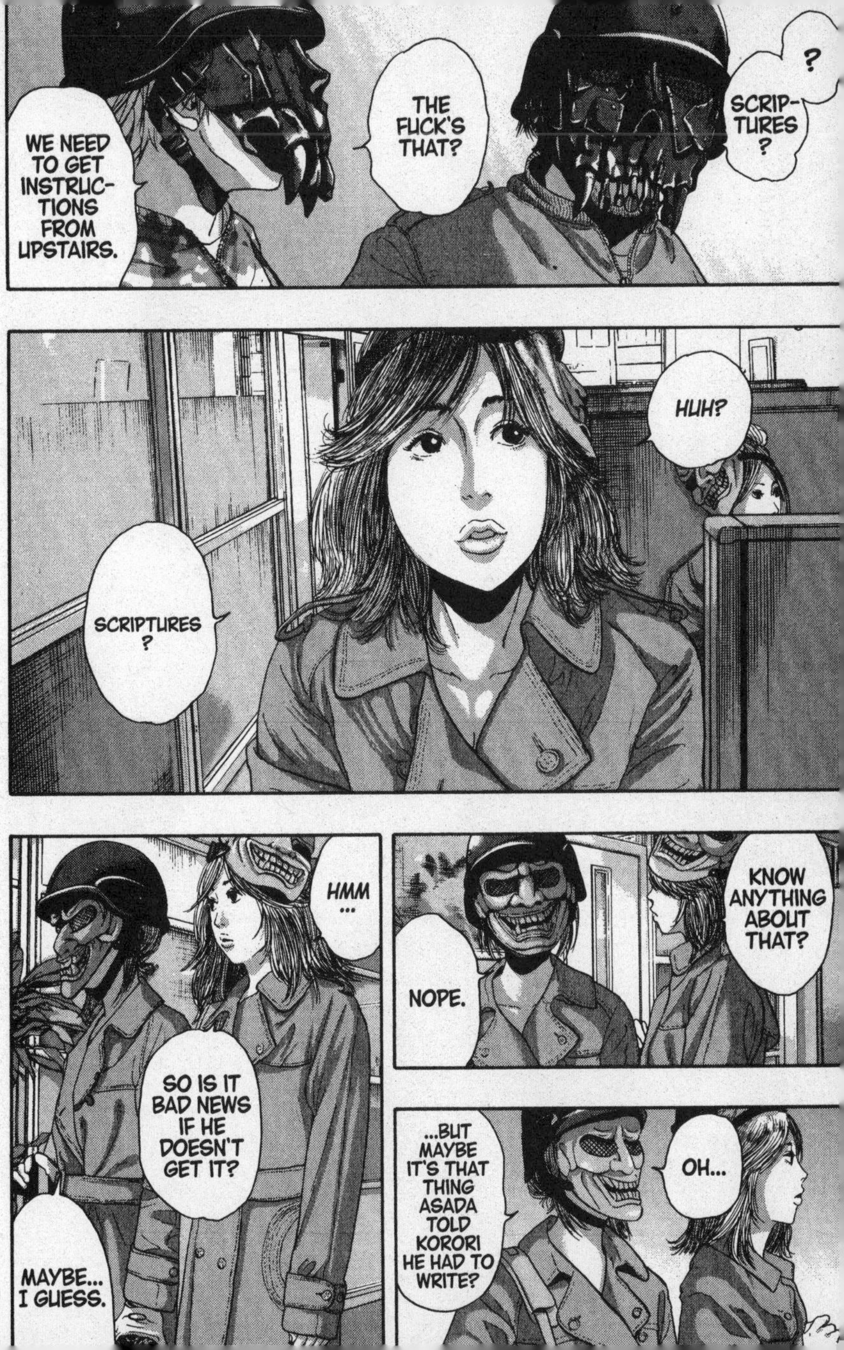
?
SCRIPTURES?
THE FUCK'S THAT?
WE NEED TO GET INSTRUCTIONS FROM UPSTAIRS.
HUH?
SCRIPTURES?
KNOW ANYTHING ABOUT THAT?
NOPE.
OH...
...BUT MAYBE IT'S THAT THING ASADA TOLD KORORI HE HAD TO WRITE?
HMM...
SO IS IT BAD NEWS IF HE DOESN'T GET IT?
MAYBE... I GUESS.

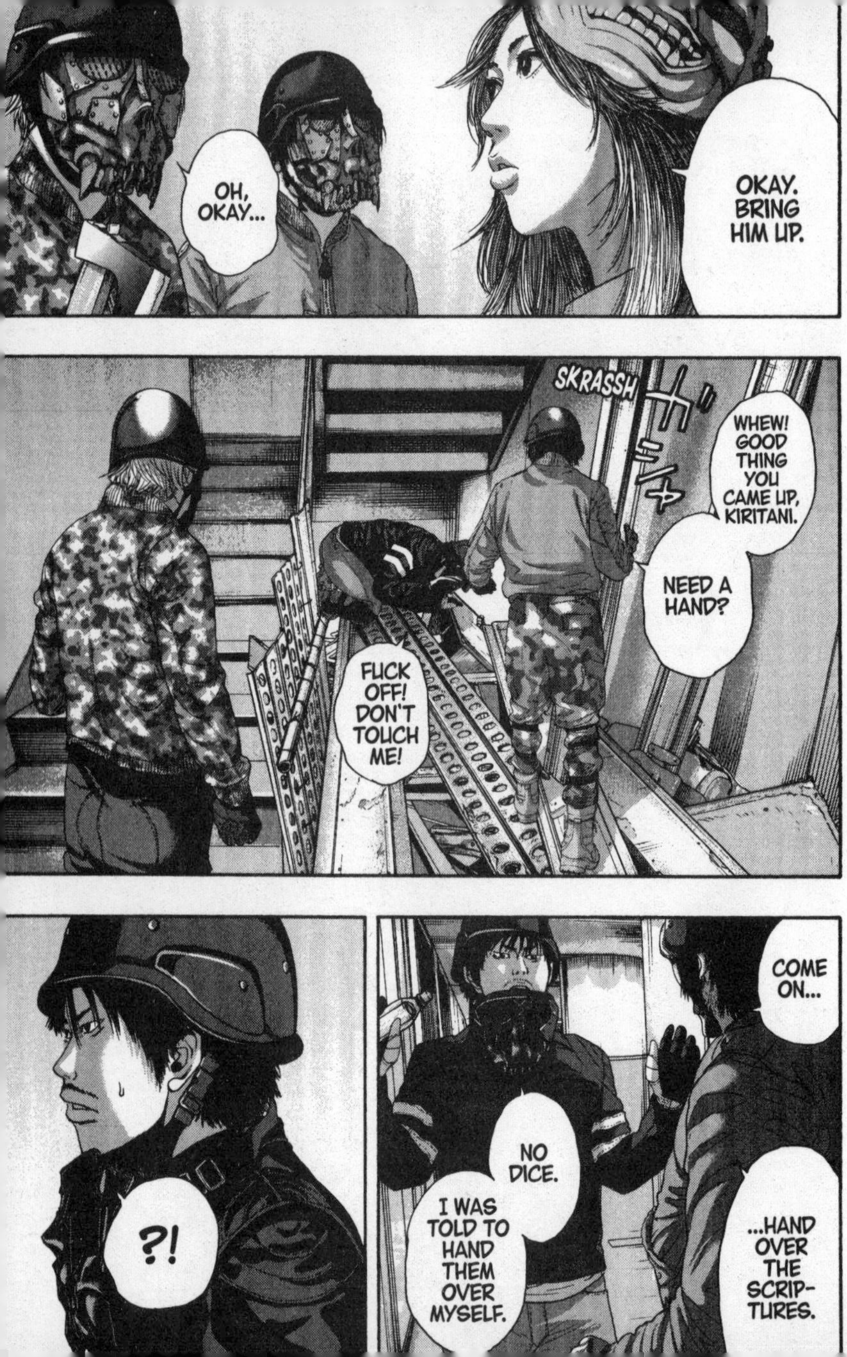
OKAY. BRING HIM UP.
OH, OKAY...
SKRASSH
WHEW! GOOD THING YOU CAME UP, KIRITANI.
NEED A HAND?
FUCK OFF! DON'T TOUCH ME!
COME ON...
...HAND OVER THE SCRIP-TURES.
NO DICE.
I WAS TOLD TO HAND THEM OVER MYSELF.
?!

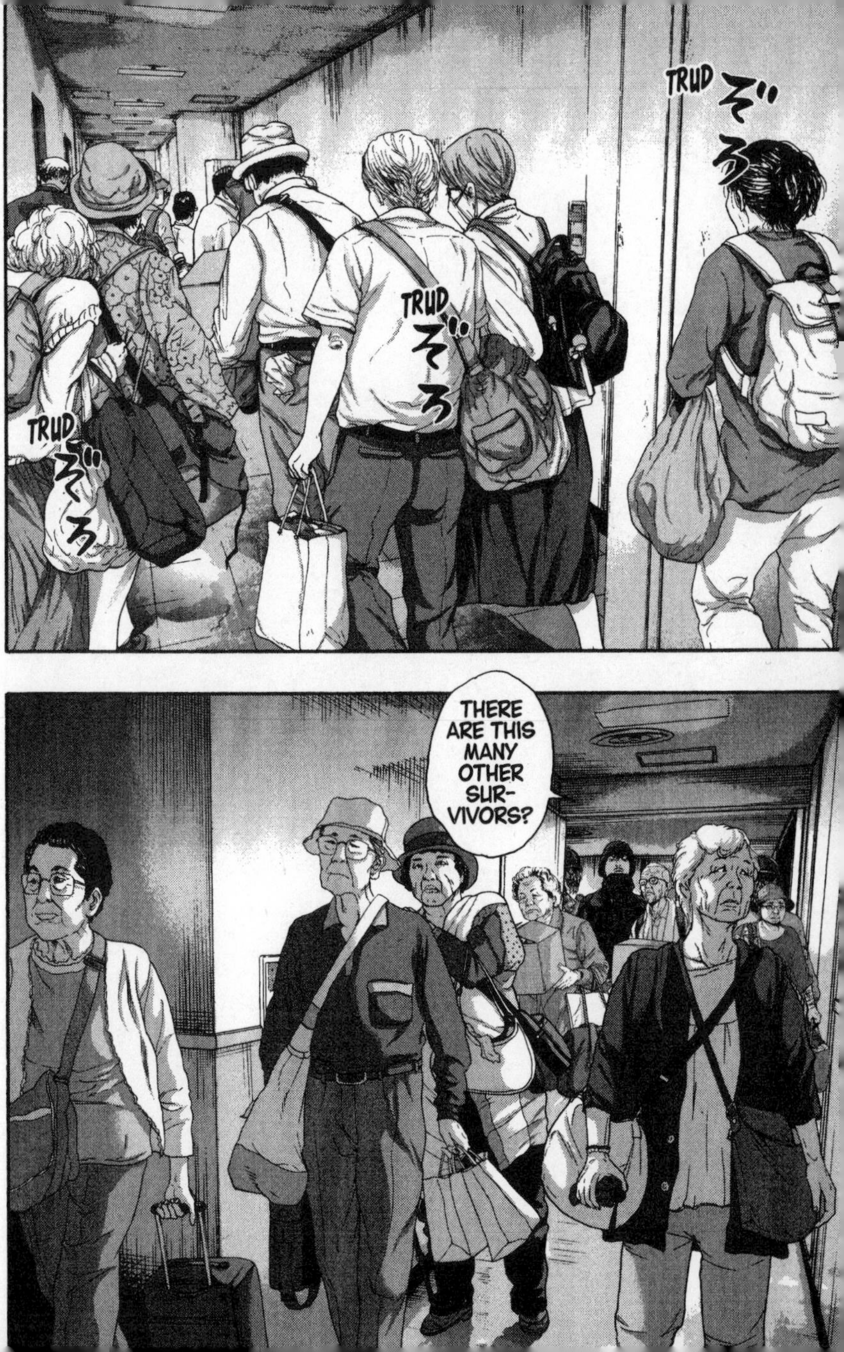
TRUD ぞろ
TRUD ぞろ
TRUD ぞろ
THERE ARE THIS MANY OTHER SUR-VIVORS?

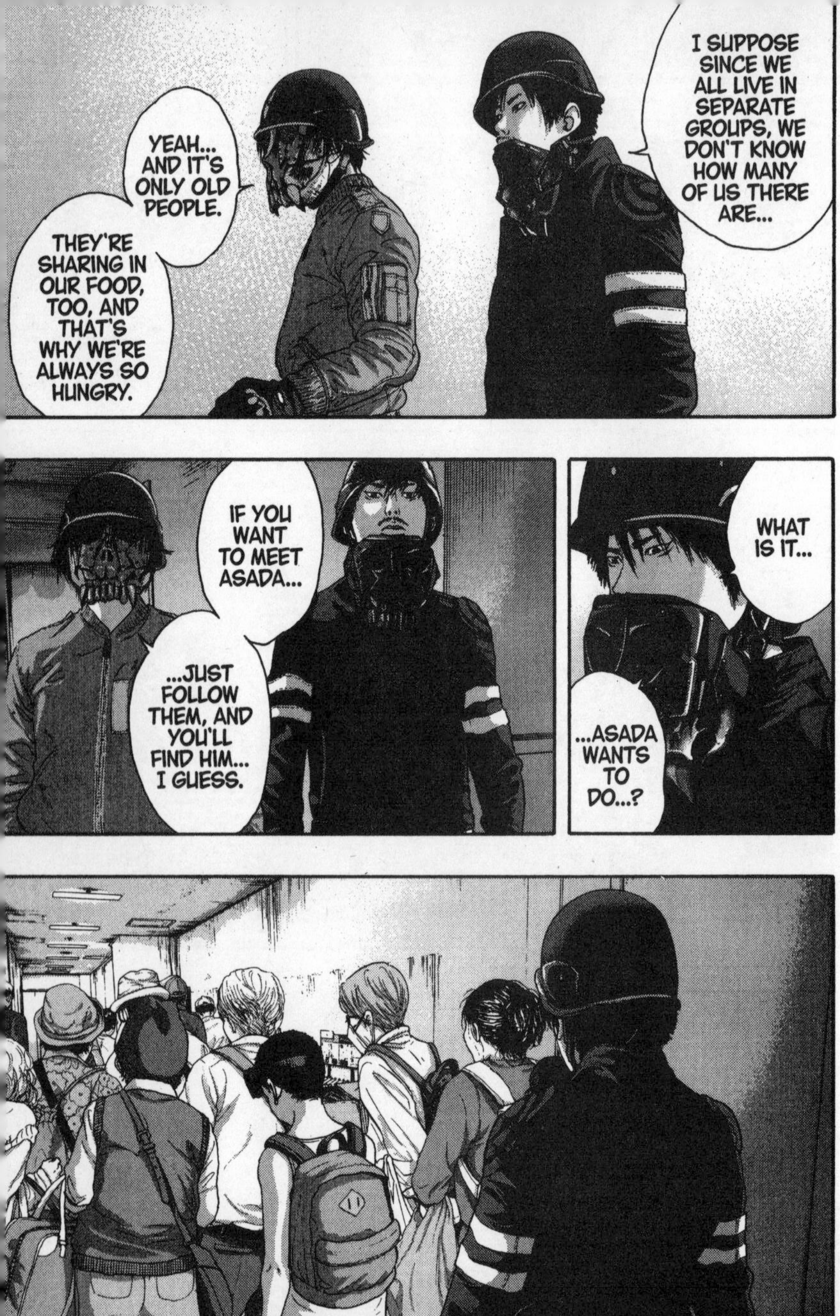
I SUPPOSE SINCE WE ALL LIVE IN SEPARATE GROUPS, WE DON'T KNOW HOW MANY OF US THERE ARE...
YEAH... AND IT'S ONLY OLD PEOPLE.
THEY'RE SHARING IN OUR FOOD, TOO, AND THAT'S WHY WE'RE ALWAYS SO HUNGRY.
WHAT IS IT...
...ASADA WANTS TO DO...?
IF YOU WANT TO MEET ASADA...
...JUST FOLLOW THEM, AND YOU'LL FIND HIM... I GUESS.

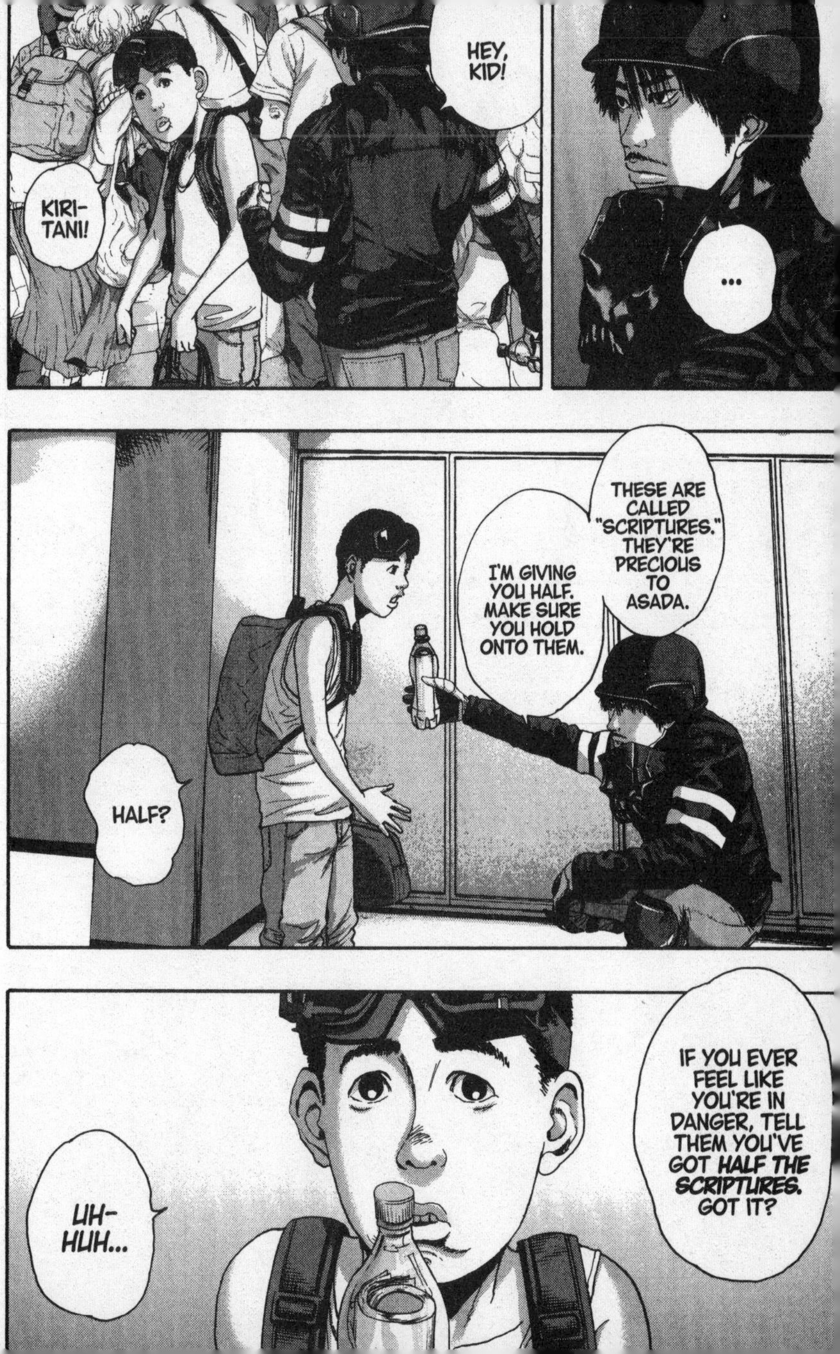
...
HEY, KID!
KIRI-TANI!
THESE ARE CALLED "SCRIPTURES." THEY'RE PRECIOUS TO ASADA.
I'M GIVING YOU HALF. MAKE SURE YOU HOLD ONTO THEM.
HALF?
IF YOU EVER FEEL LIKE YOU'RE IN DANGER, TELL THEM YOU'VE GOT *HALF THE SCRIPTURES.* GOT IT?
UH-HUH...

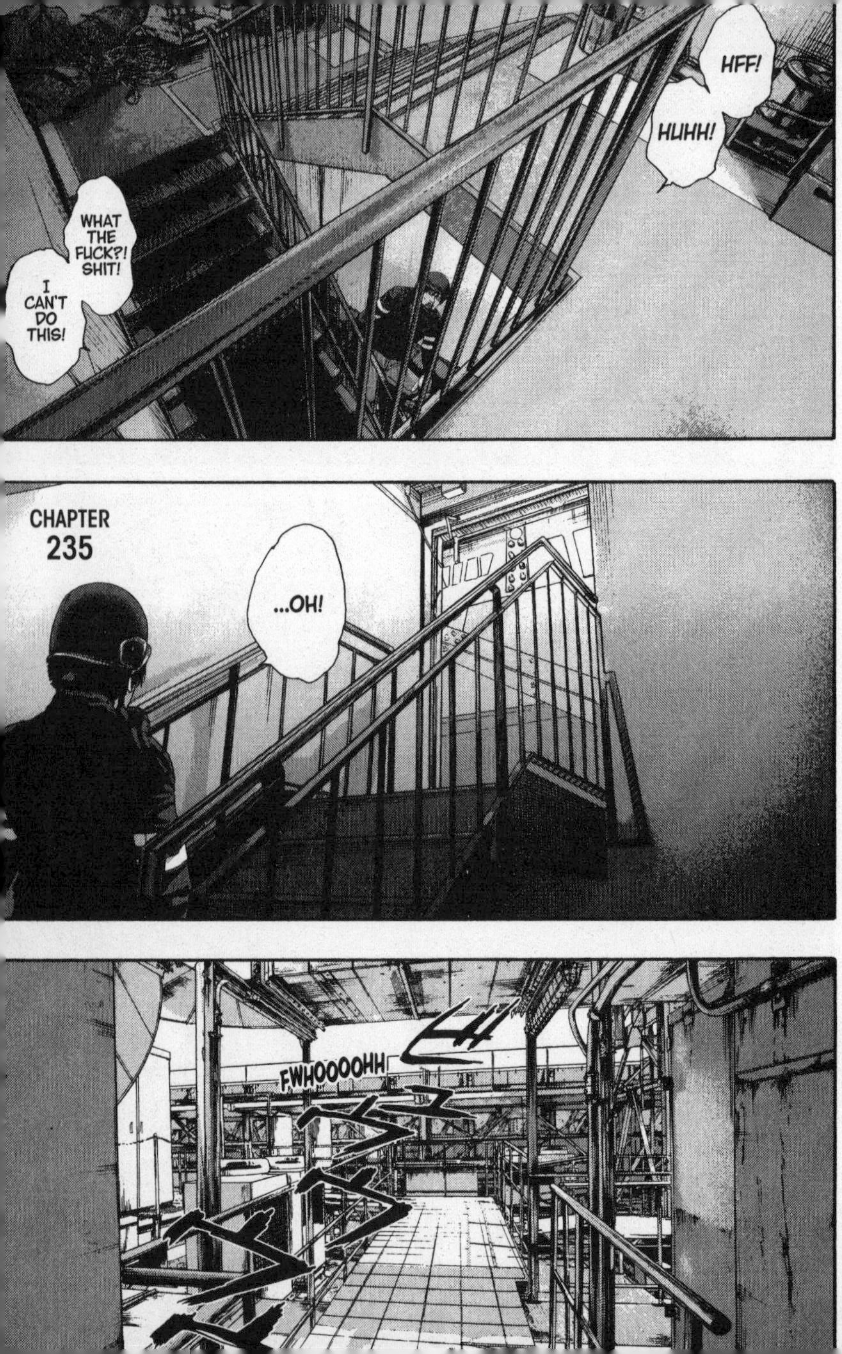
HFF!
HUHH!
WHAT THE FUCK?! SHIT!
I CAN'T DO THIS!
CHAPTER 235
...OH!
FWHOOOOHH

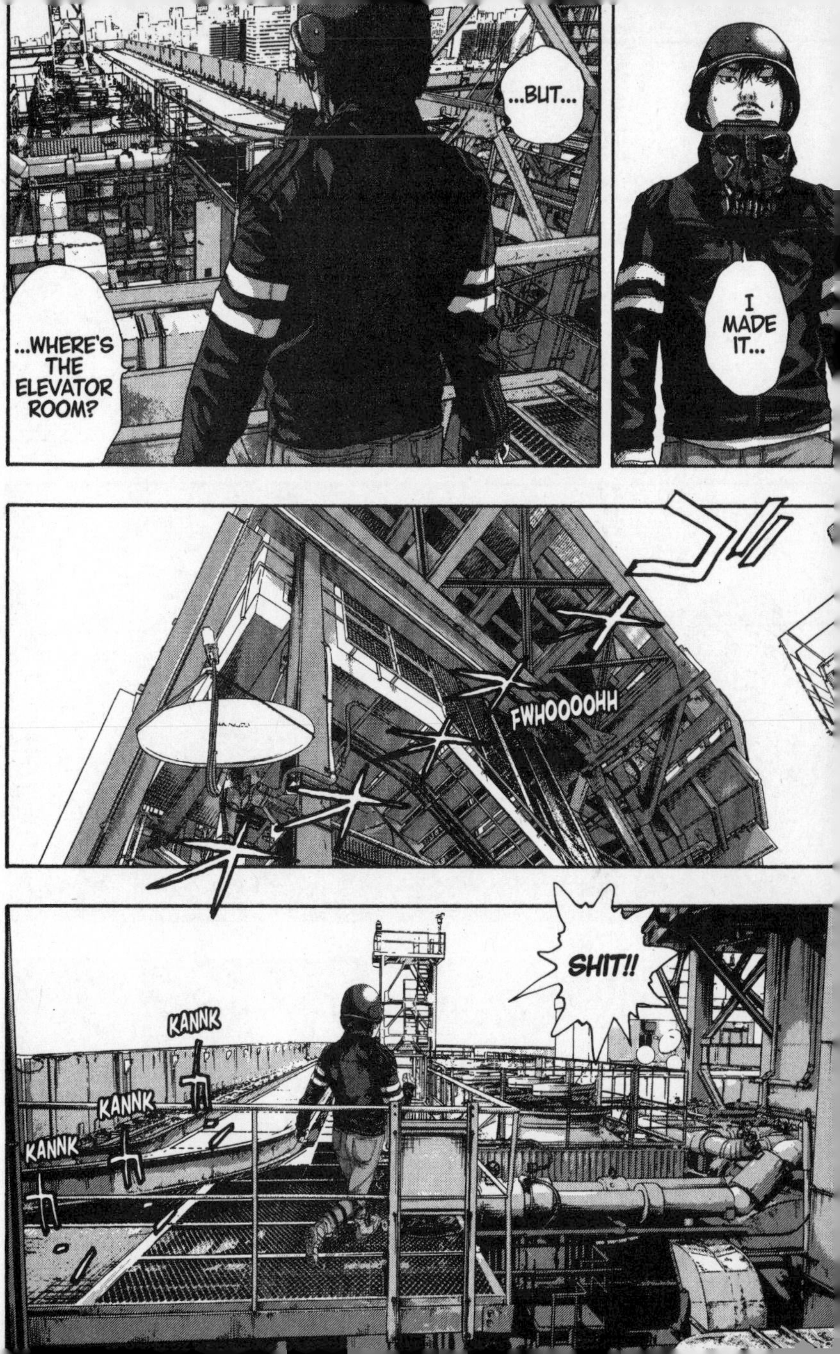
I MADE IT...
...BUT...
...WHERE'S THE ELEVATOR ROOM?
FWHOOOOHH
SHIT!!
KANNK
KANNK
KANNK

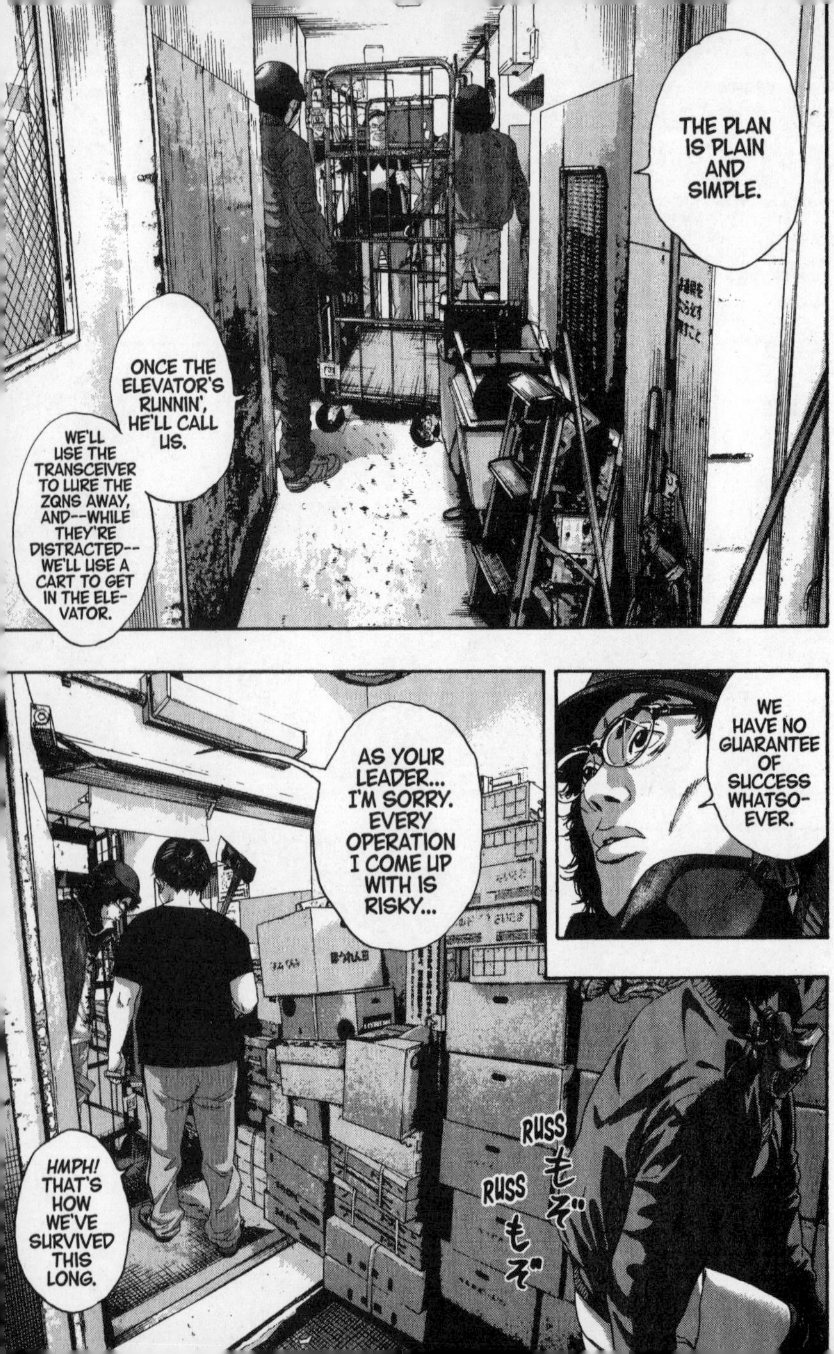

THE PLAN IS PLAIN AND SIMPLE.
ONCE THE ELEVATOR'S RUNNIN', HE'LL CALL US.
WE'LL USE THE TRANSCEIVER TO LURE THE ZQNS AWAY, AND--WHILE THEY'RE DISTRACTED--WE'LL USE A CART TO GET IN THE ELE-VATOR.
WE HAVE NO GUARANTEE OF SUCCESS WHATSO-EVER.
RUSS もぞ
RUSS もぞ
AS YOUR LEADER... I'M SORRY. EVERY OPERATION I COME UP WITH IS RISKY...
HMPH! THAT'S HOW WE'VE SURVIVED THIS LONG.

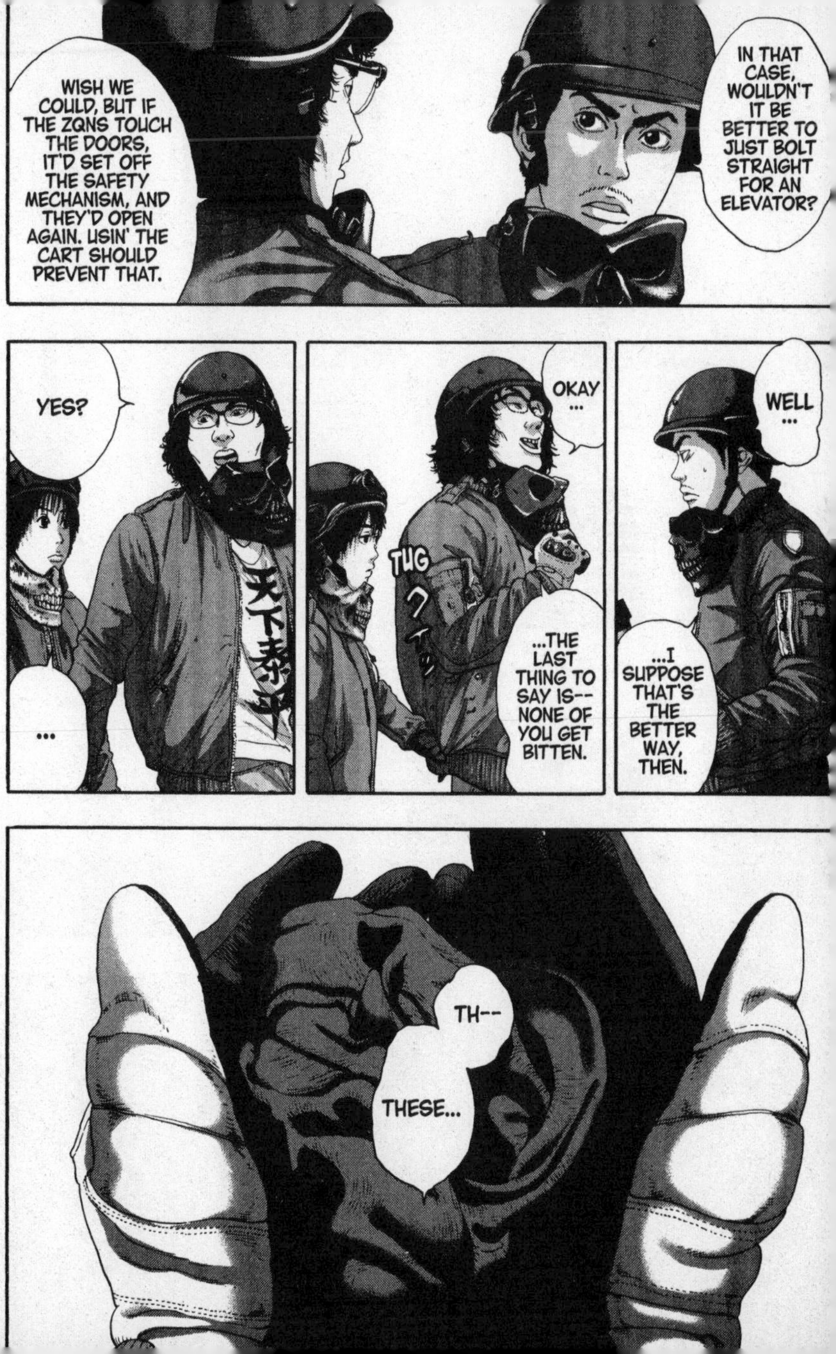
IN THAT CASE, WOULDN'T IT BE BETTER TO JUST BOLT STRAIGHT FOR AN ELEVATOR?
WISH WE COULD, BUT IF THE ZQNS TOUCH THE DOORS, IT'D SET OFF THE SAFETY MECHANISM, AND THEY'D OPEN AGAIN. USIN' THE CART SHOULD PREVENT THAT.
WELL ...
...I SUPPOSE THAT'S THE BETTER WAY, THEN.
OKAY ...
TUG
クイッ
...THE LAST THING TO SAY IS-- NONE OF YOU GET BITTEN.
YES?
天下泰平
...
TH--
THESE...

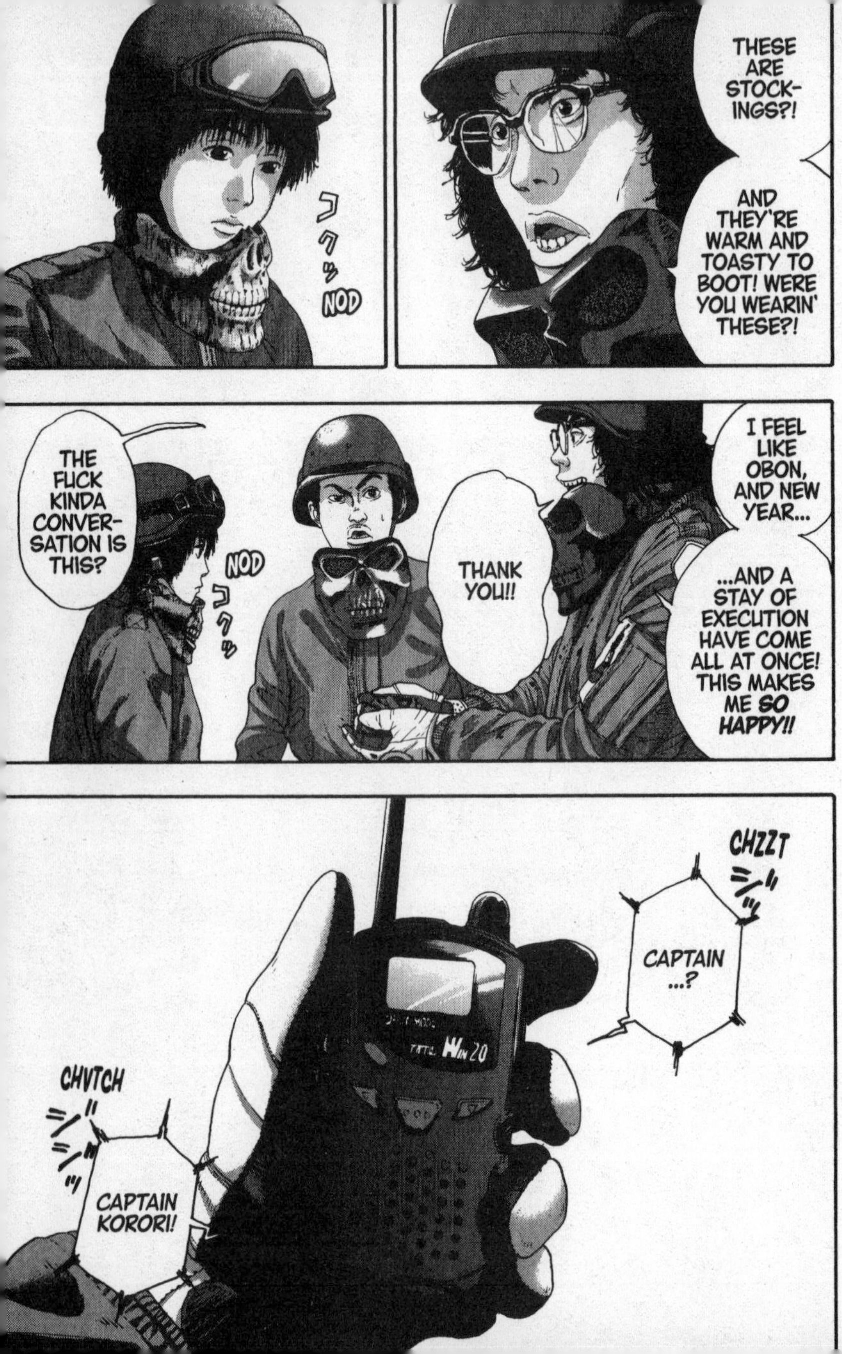
THESE ARE STOCKINGS?!
AND THEY'RE WARM AND TOASTY TO BOOT! WERE YOU WEARIN' THESE?!
コクッ
NOD
I FEEL LIKE OBON, AND NEW YEAR...
...AND A STAY OF EXECUTION HAVE COME ALL AT ONCE! THIS MAKES ME SO HAPPY!!
THANK YOU!!
NOD
コクッ
THE FUCK KINDA CONVERSATION IS THIS?
CHZZT
CAPTAIN ...?
CHVTCH
CAPTAIN KORORI!

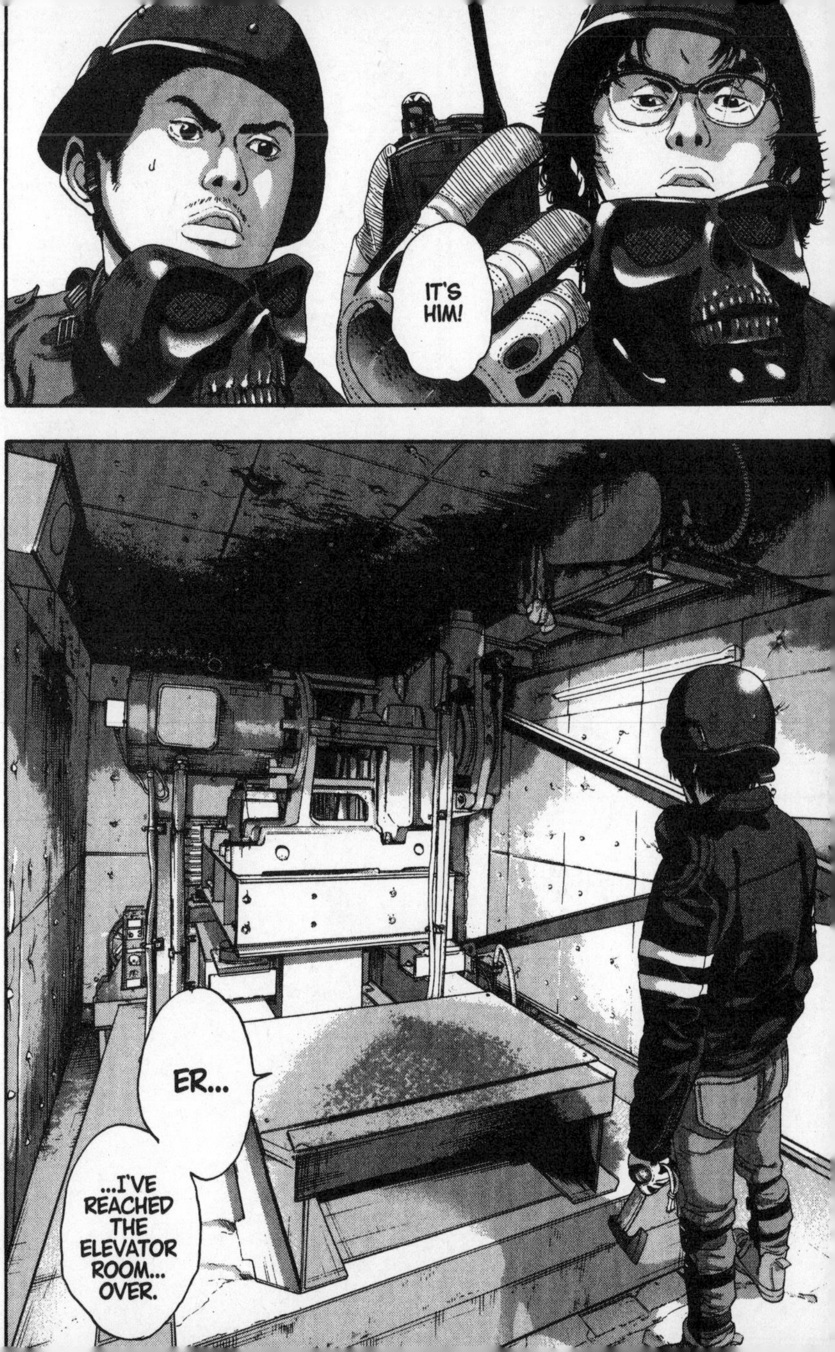
IT'S HIM!
ER...
...I'VE REACHED THE ELEVATOR ROOM... OVER.

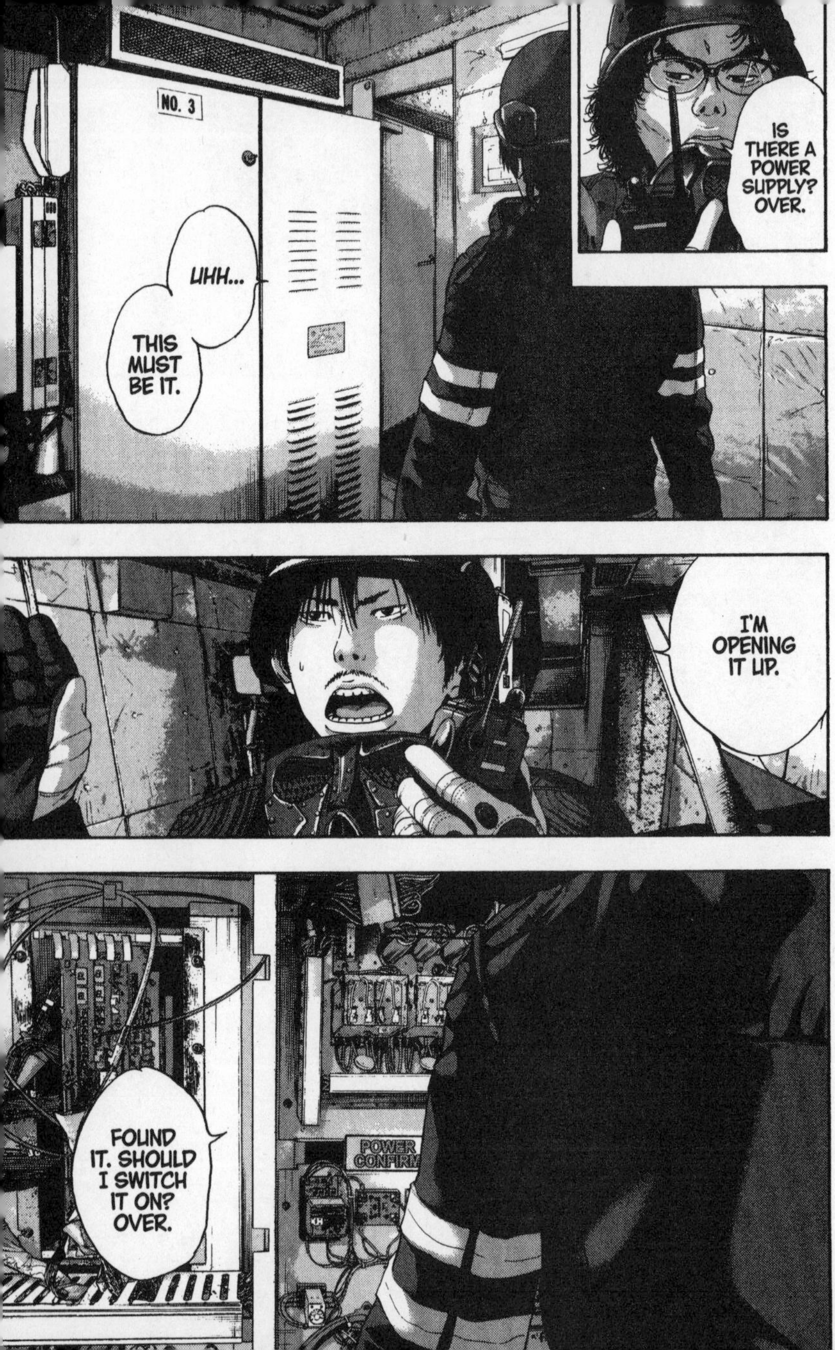
IS THERE A POWER SUPPLY? OVER.
NO. 3
UHH...
THIS MUST BE IT.
I'M OPENING IT UP.
POWER CONFIRM
FOUND IT. SHOULD I SWITCH IT ON? OVER.

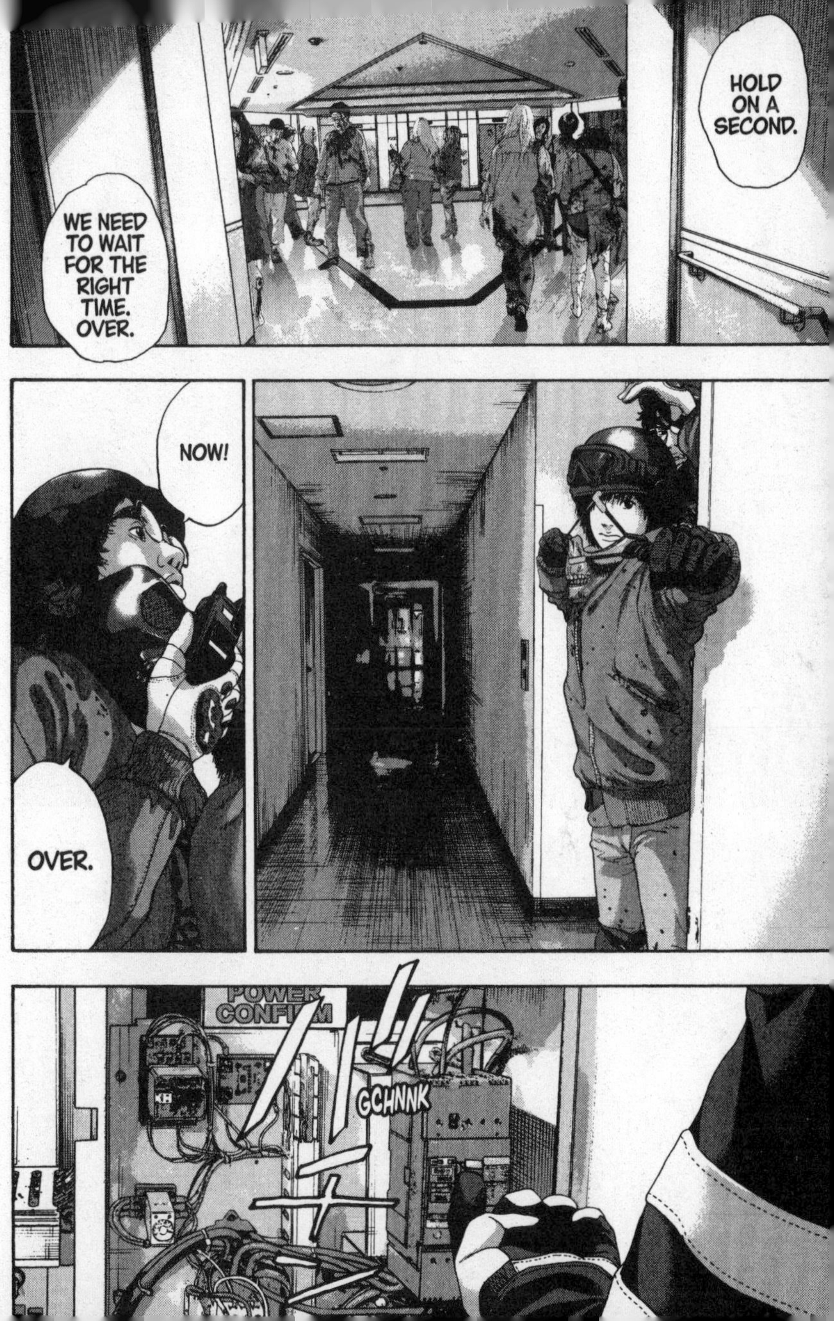
HOLD ON A SECOND.
WE NEED TO WAIT FOR THE RIGHT TIME. OVER.
NOW!
OVER.
POWER
GCHNNK

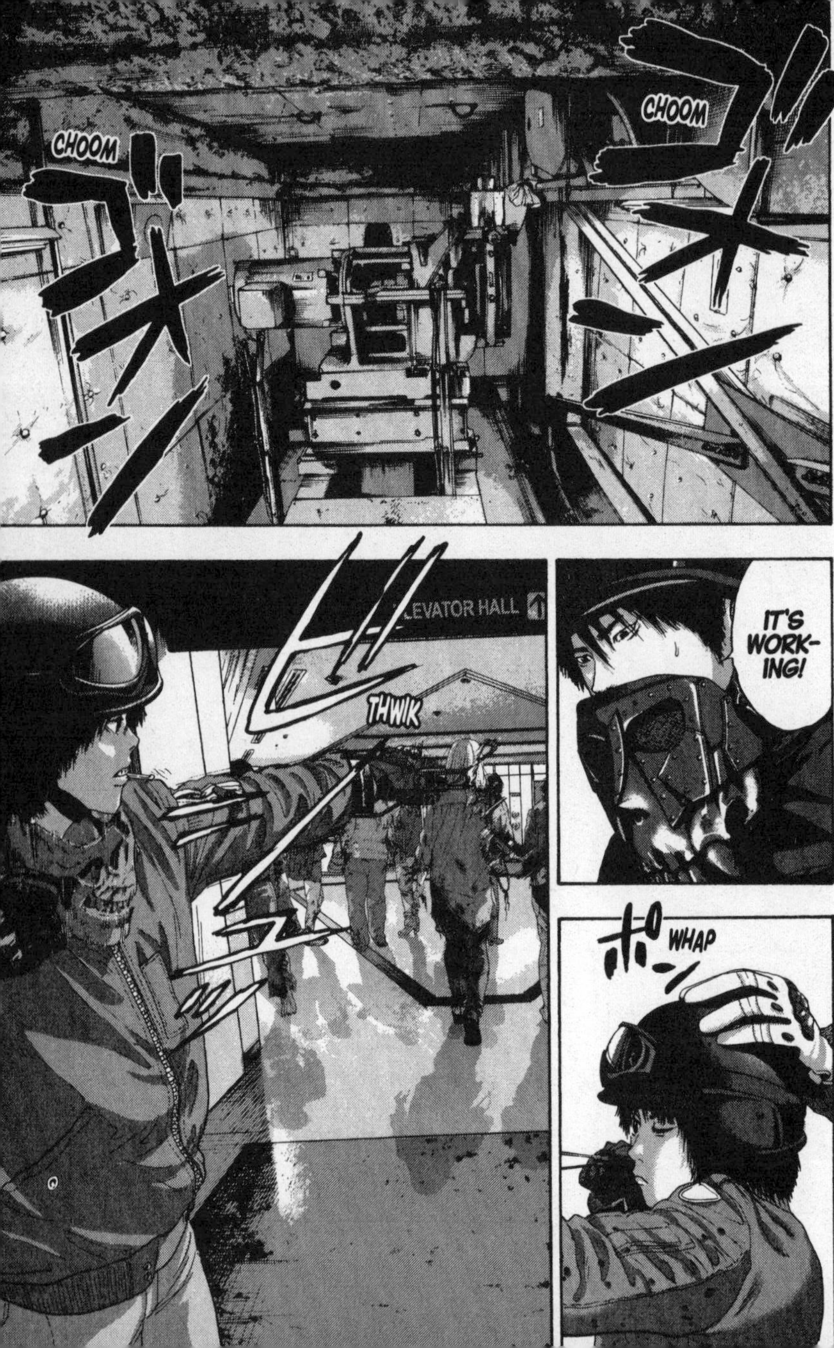
CHOOM
CHOOM
IT'S WORK-ING!
WHAP
LEVATOR HALL
THWIK

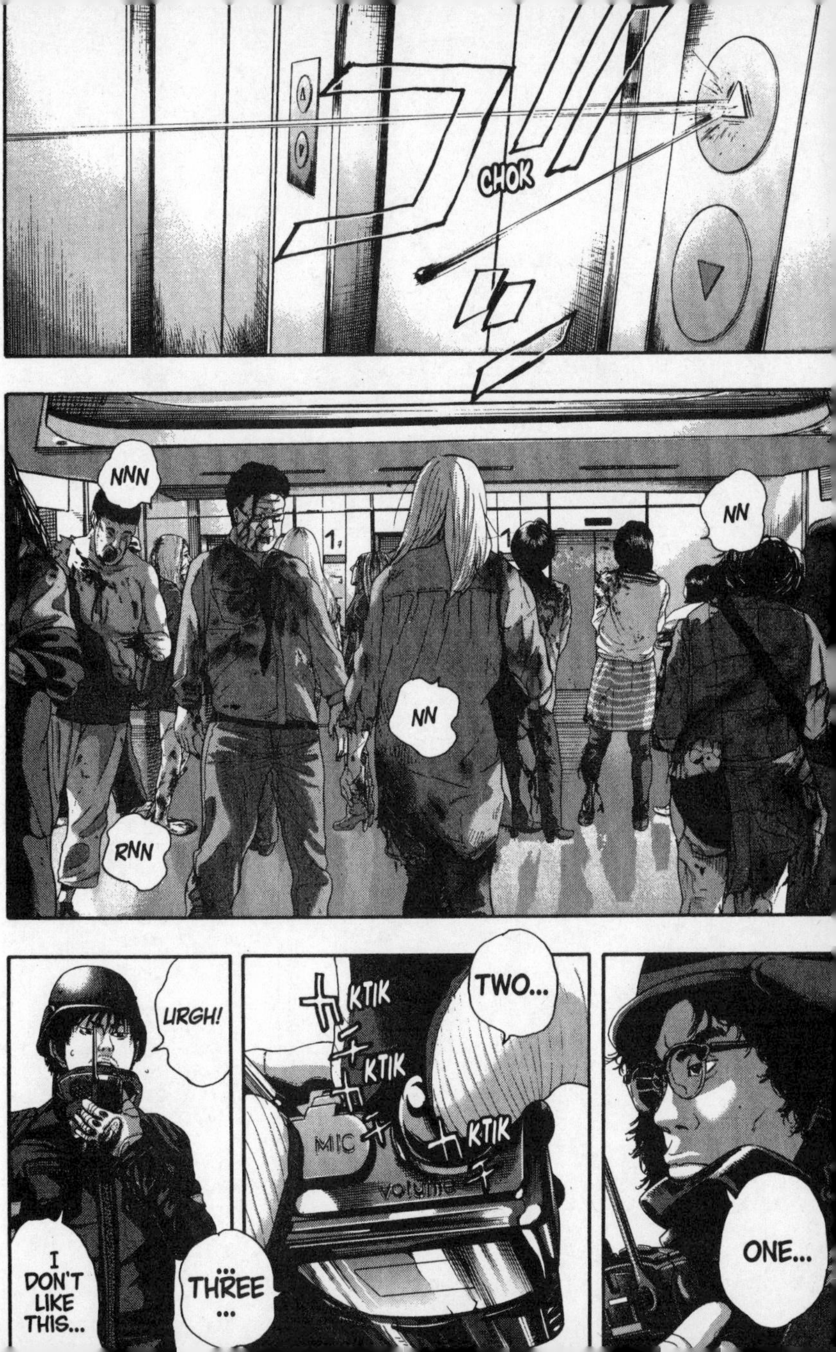
CHOK
NNN
RNN
NN
NN
URGH!
I DON'T LIKE THIS...
...THREE...
KTIK
TWO...
KTIK
KTIK
ONE...

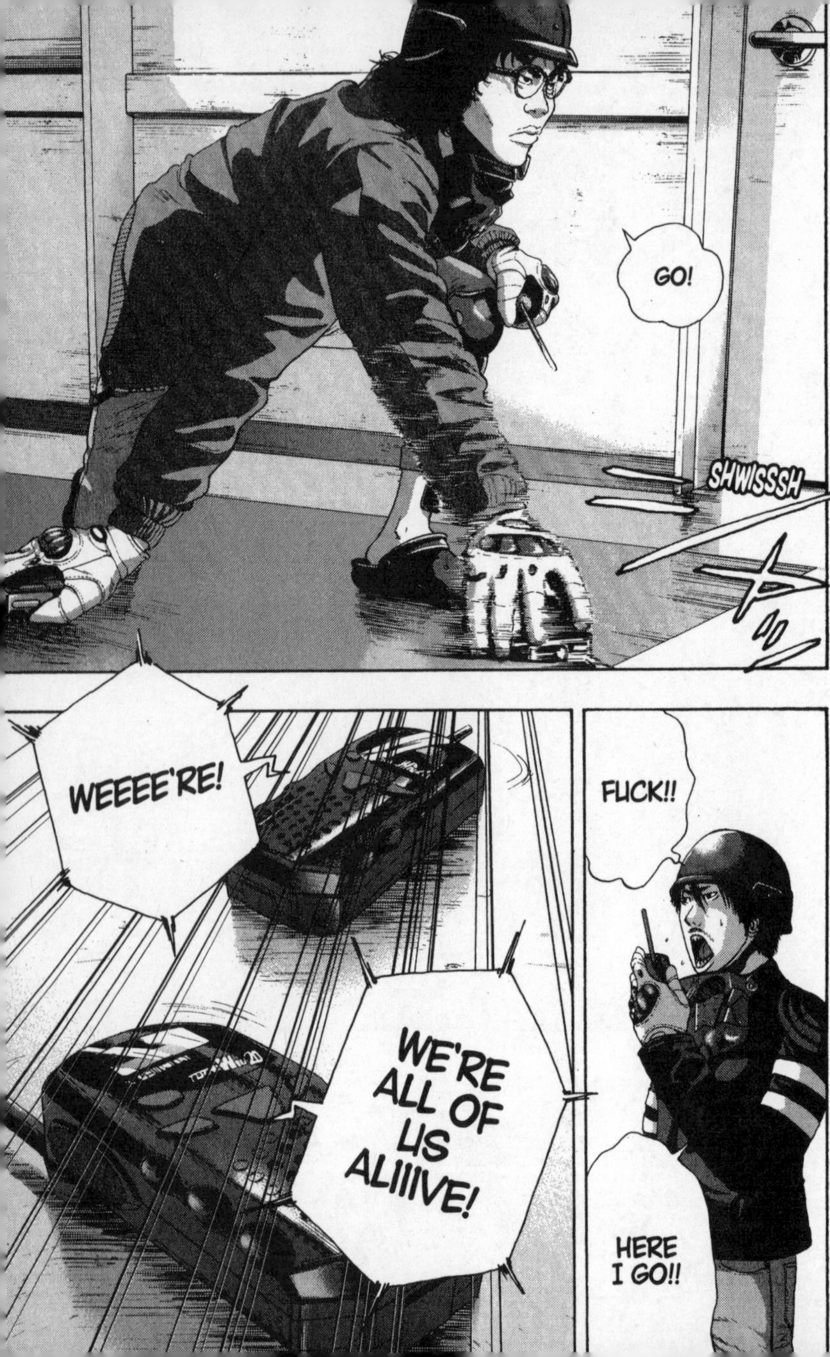
GO!
SHWISSSH
FUCK!!
HERE I GO!!
WEEEE'RE!
WE'RE ALL OF US ALIIIVE!

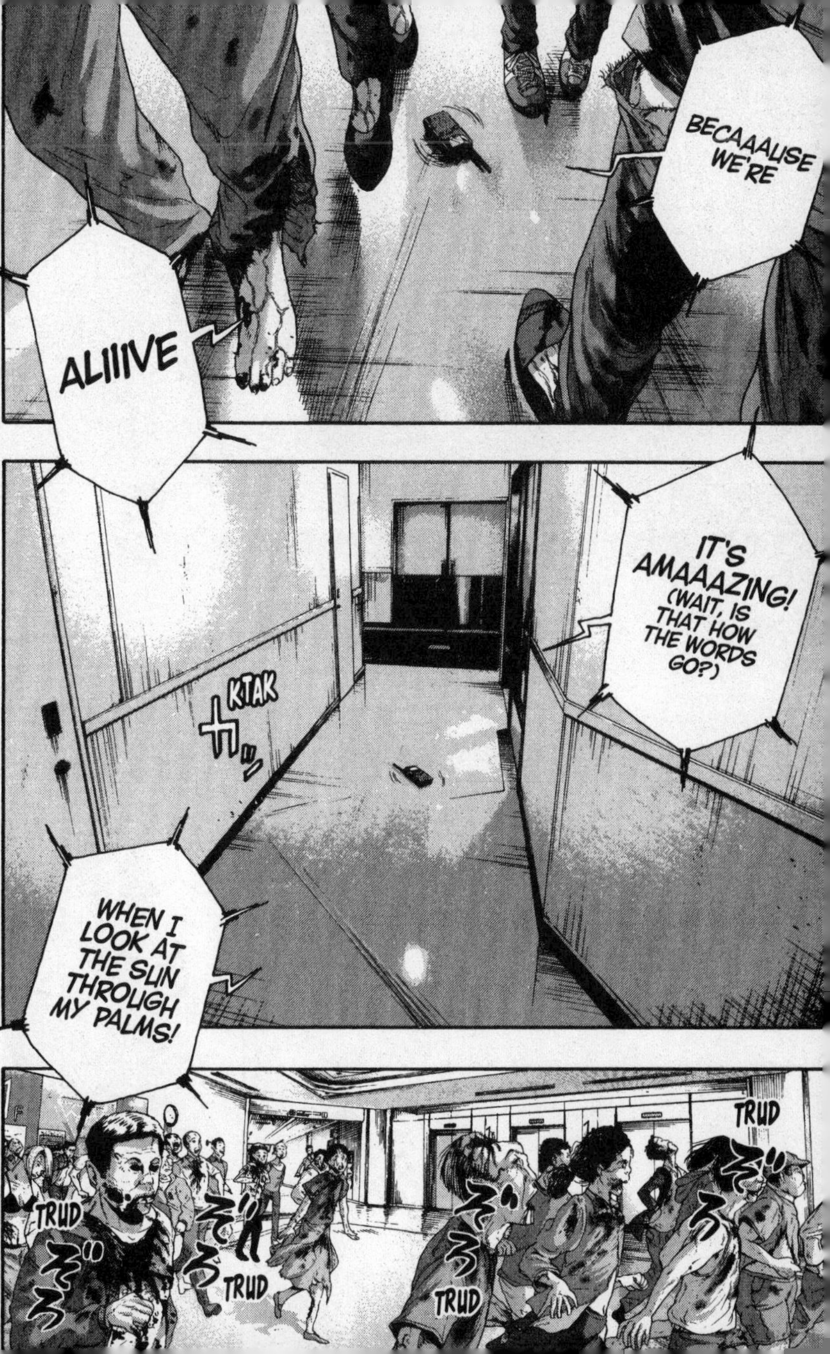
BECAAAUSE WE'RE
ALIIIVE
IT'S AMAAAZING! (WAIT, IS THAT HOW THE WORDS GO?)
KTAK
カッ
WHEN I LOOK AT THE SUN THROUGH MY PALMS!
TRUD
ぞろ
TRUD
ぞろ
TRUD
ぞろ
TRUD
ぞろ

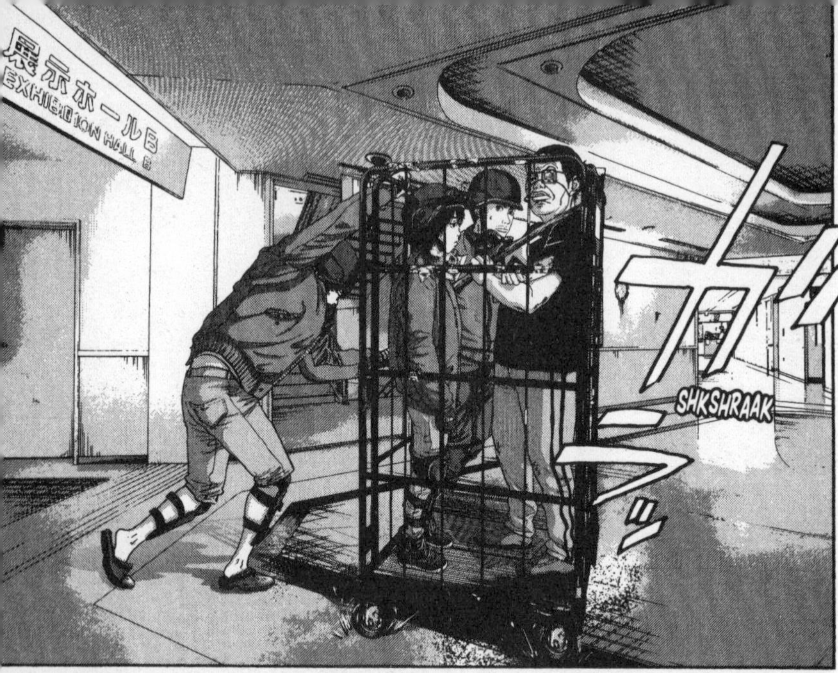
展示ホールB
EXHIBITION HALL B
SHKSHRAAK
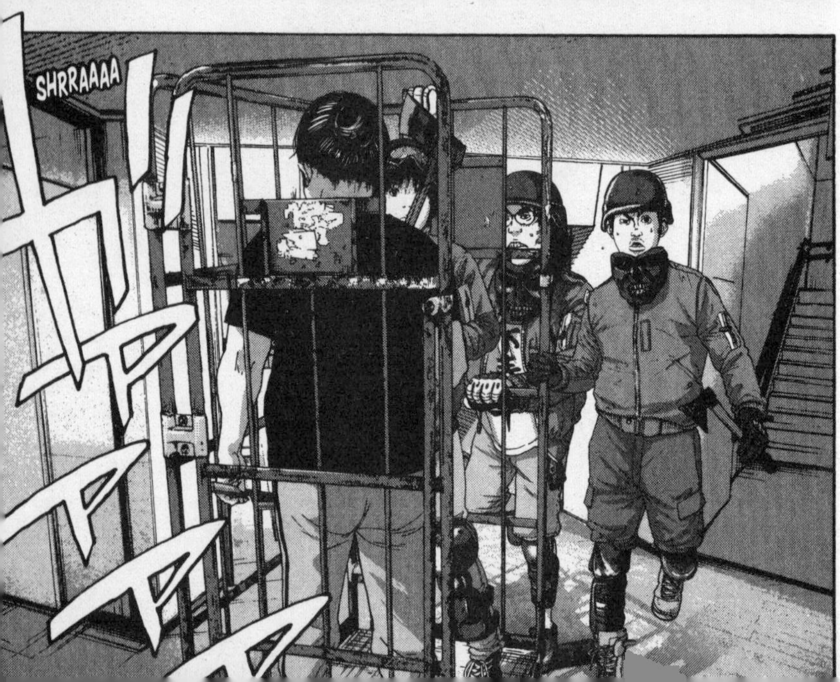
SHRRAAAA

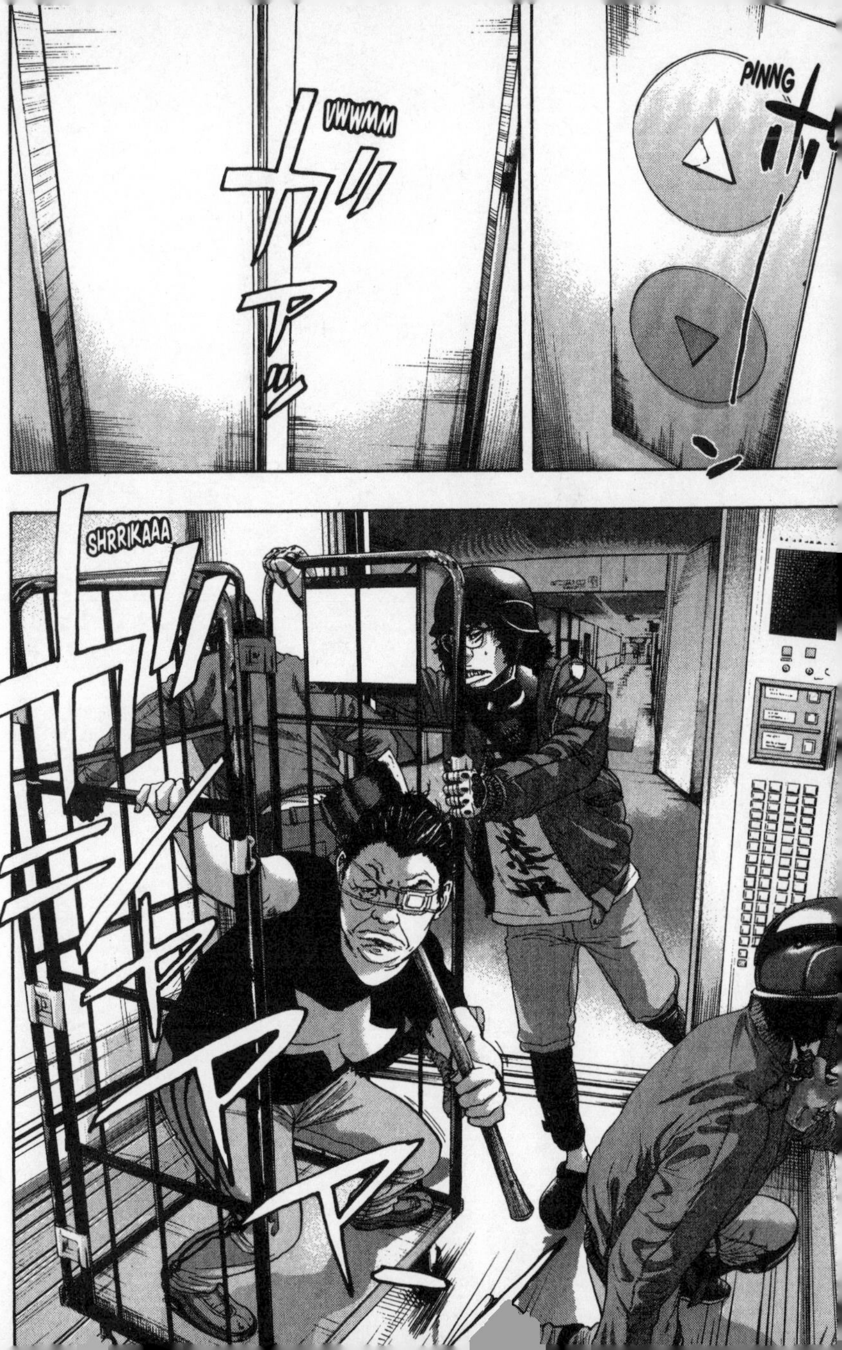
PING
VWWMM
SHRRIKAAA

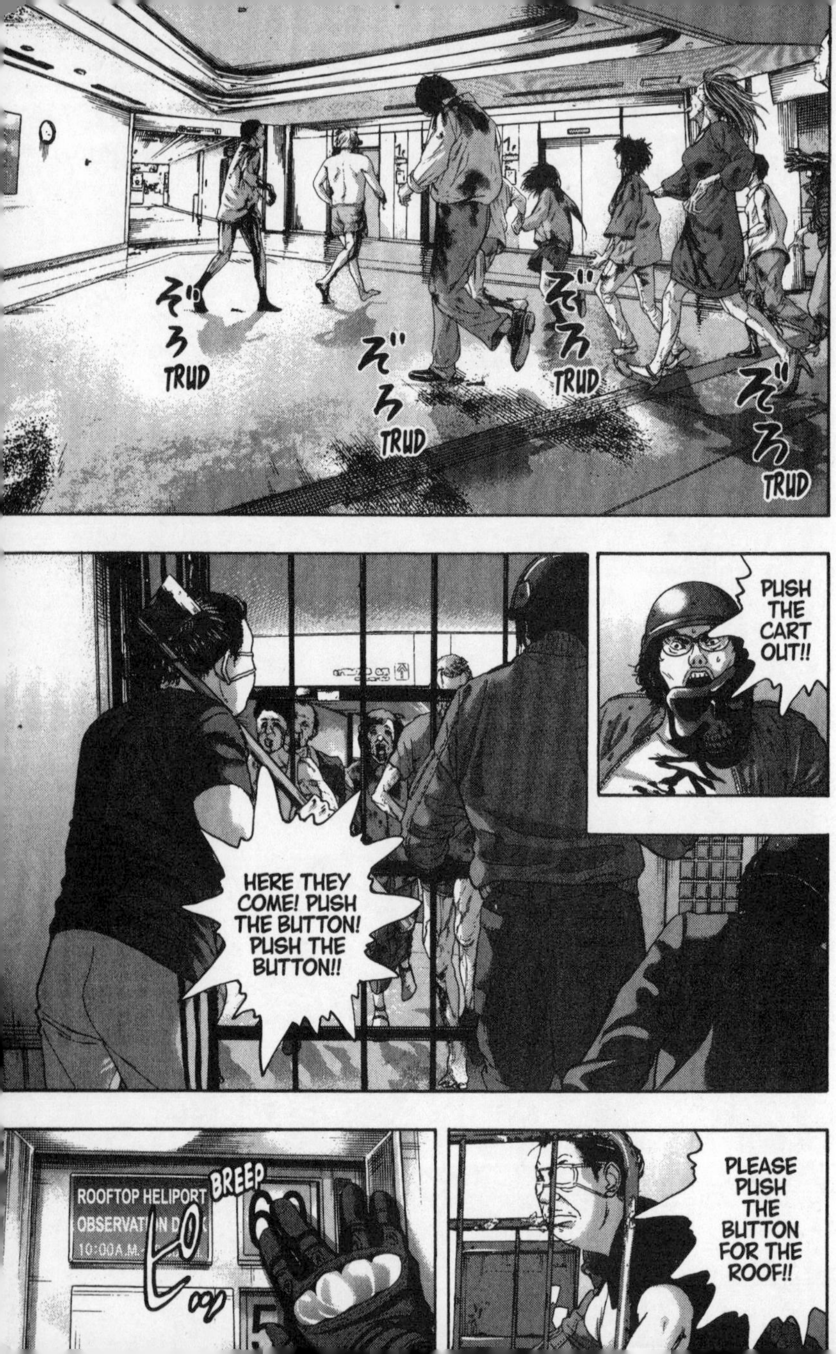
ぞろ
TRUD
ぞろ
TRUD
ぞろ
TRUD
ぞろ
TRUD
PUSH THE CART OUT!!
HERE THEY COME! PUSH THE BUTTON! PUSH THE BUTTON!!
PLEASE PUSH THE BUTTON FOR THE ROOF!!
ROOFTOP HELIPORT
BREEP

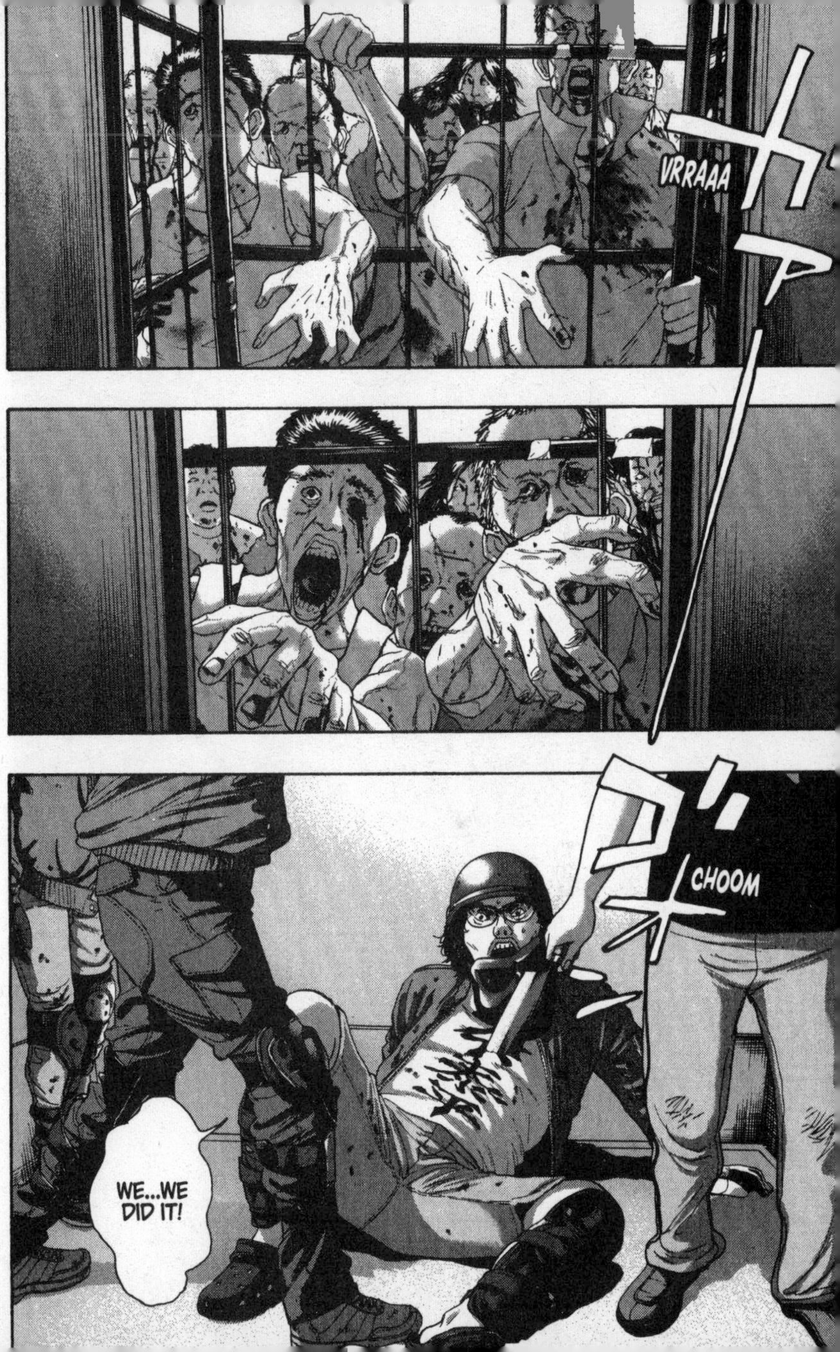
VRRAAA
CHOOM
WE...WE DID IT!

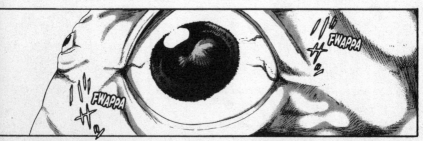

Hiromi Hayakari: 1992/07/07 (Wed) 00:00:00.
Where am I going?

Anonymous Brain: 2009/05/03 (Sun) 06:32:44 ID: tel
>>91
We're heading for the Sunrise 60 building in Ikebukuro.

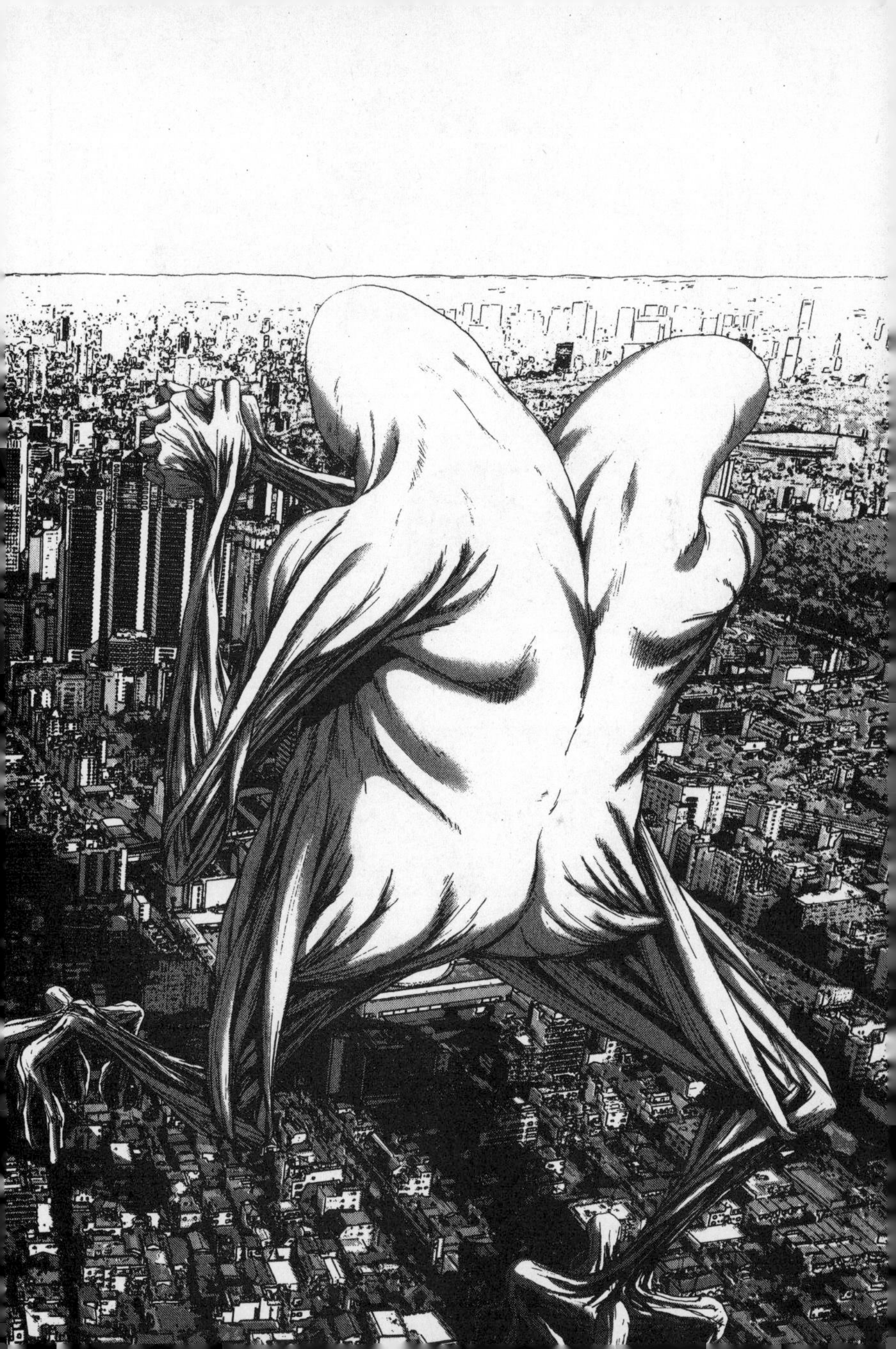

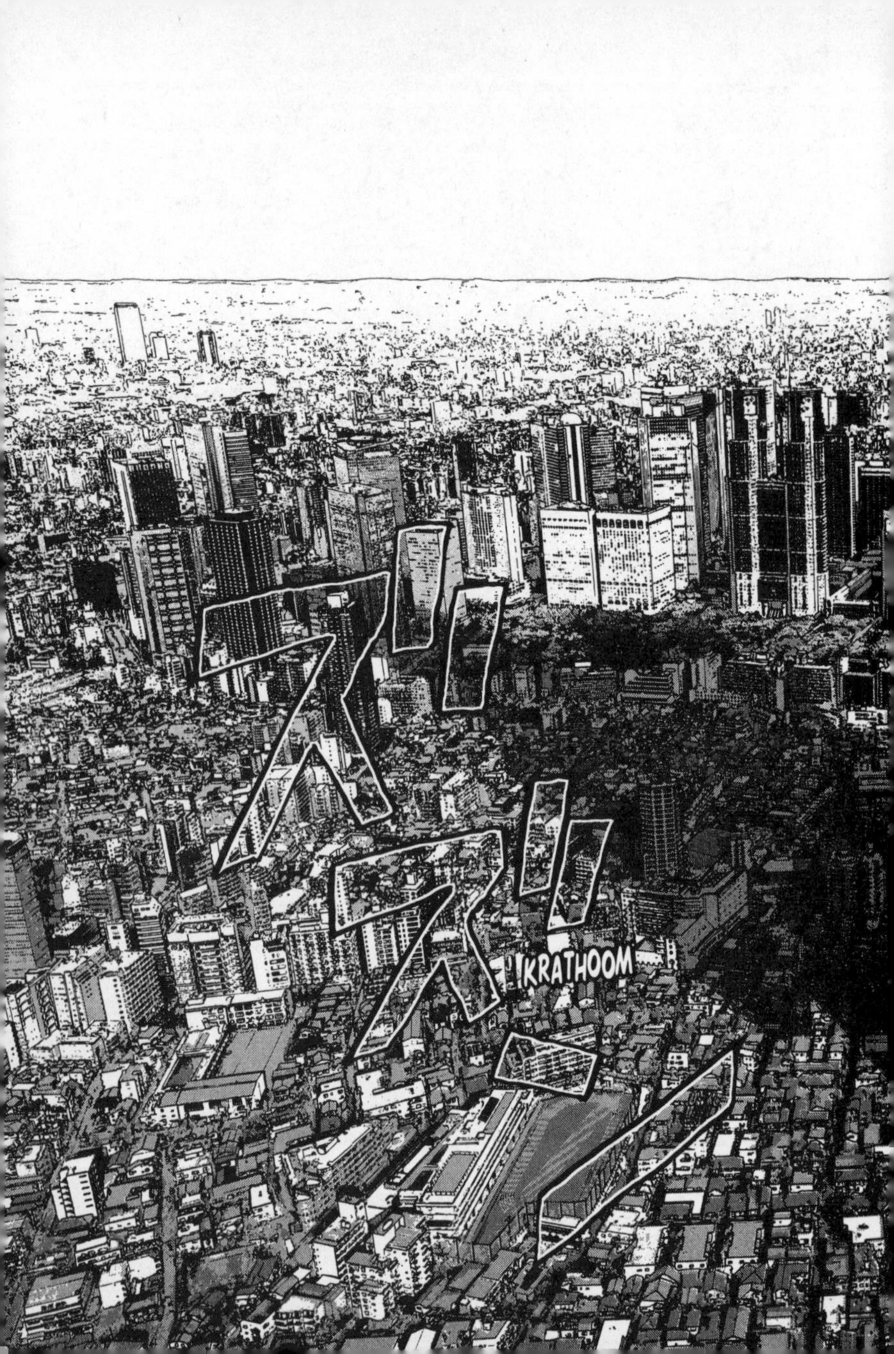
ズズズン
KRATHOOM

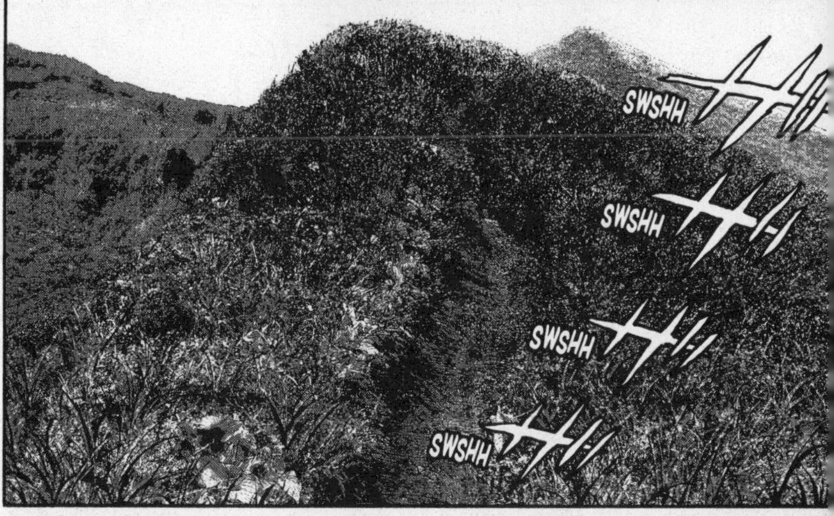
SWSHH
SWSHH
SWSHH
SWSHH

Hiromi Hayakari: 19
What is this place?

66: Anonymous Brain: 2009/0
>>92
What can you see?

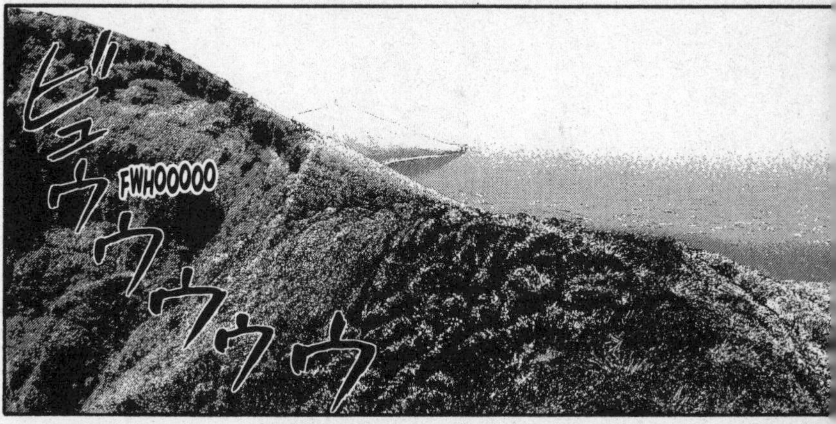
FWHOOOOO
ビュウウウウウ

Mountains...The sea...
Oh! Hachijo-jima Island?

>>93
Bingo!
Hachijo Fuji, I guess they call this?
You must have been there, right?

Hiromi Hayakari: 1999/09/17 (Fri) 03:26:19 ID: hiroba

...I remember climbing it with my mom when
was little, but to remember it this vividly...

Anonymous Beam: 2007/05/02 (We
I climbed it about two years ago with
my boyfriend.
I saw the same view.
So it seems we're able to share our
memories of it.

Hiromi Hayakari: 2009/05/2

?

Anonymous Integrated Mind: 2009/05/23 (Sat
>> 95
We've chosen entities of consciousness of high
affinity which can associate the "red" of which
I spoke before with "blood" and connect with yo
Doing so reduces the chaos as much as possible,
so the unification of consciousnesses can proce
smoothly.
Everything is becoming one.

670: Hiromi Hayakari: 20
Ohh...

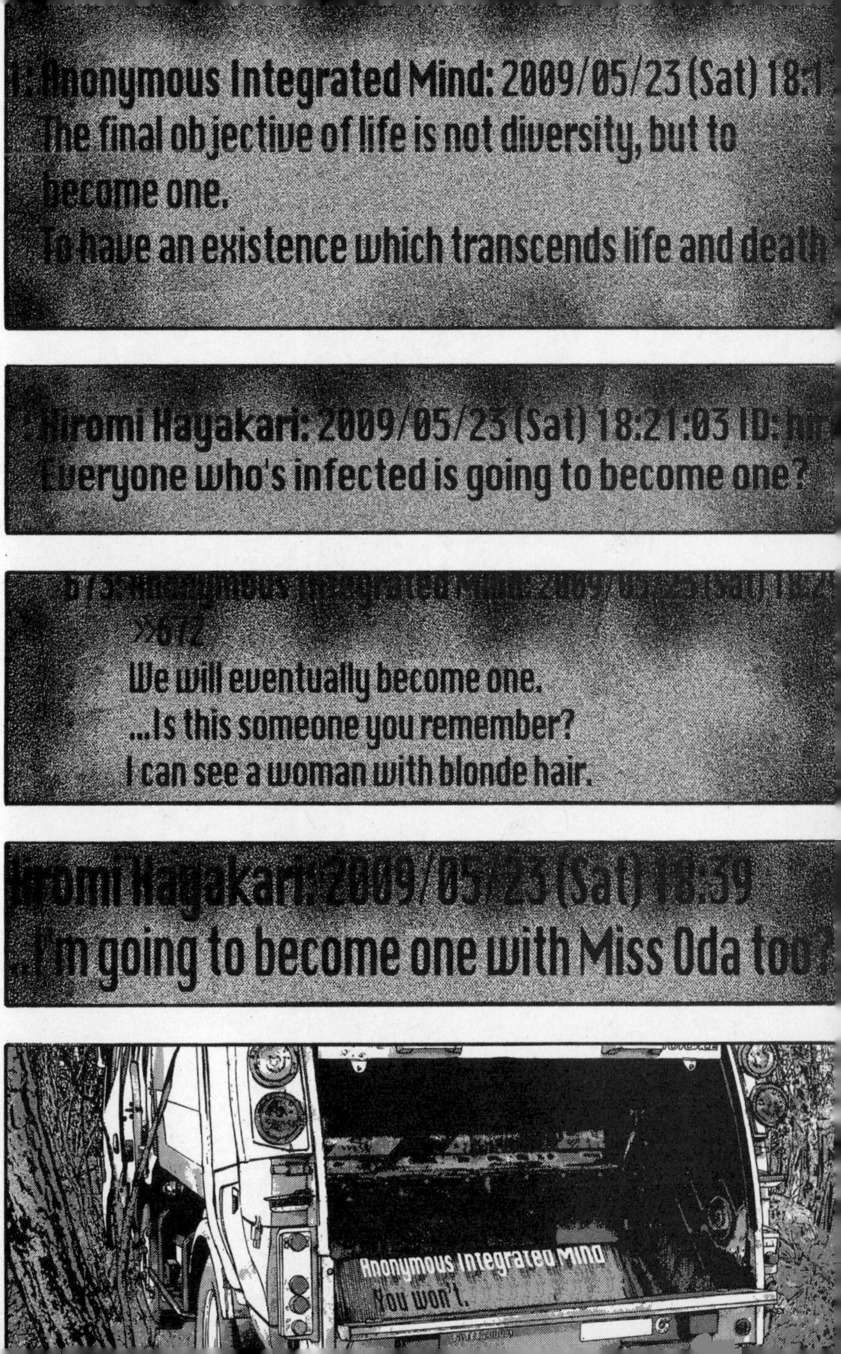

1: Anonymous Integrated Mind: 2009/05/23 (Sat) 18:1

The final objective of life is not diversity, but to become one.
To have an existence which transcends life and death

Hiromi Hayakari: 2009/05/23 (Sat) 18:21:03 ID: hir
Everyone who's infected is going to become one?

673: Anonymous Integrated Mind 2009/05/23 (Sat) 18:2

>672
We will eventually become one.
...Is this someone you remember?
I can see a woman with blonde hair.

Hiromi Hayakari: 2009/05/23 (Sat) 18:39

...I'm going to become one with Miss Oda too?

Anonymous Integrated Mind
You won't.

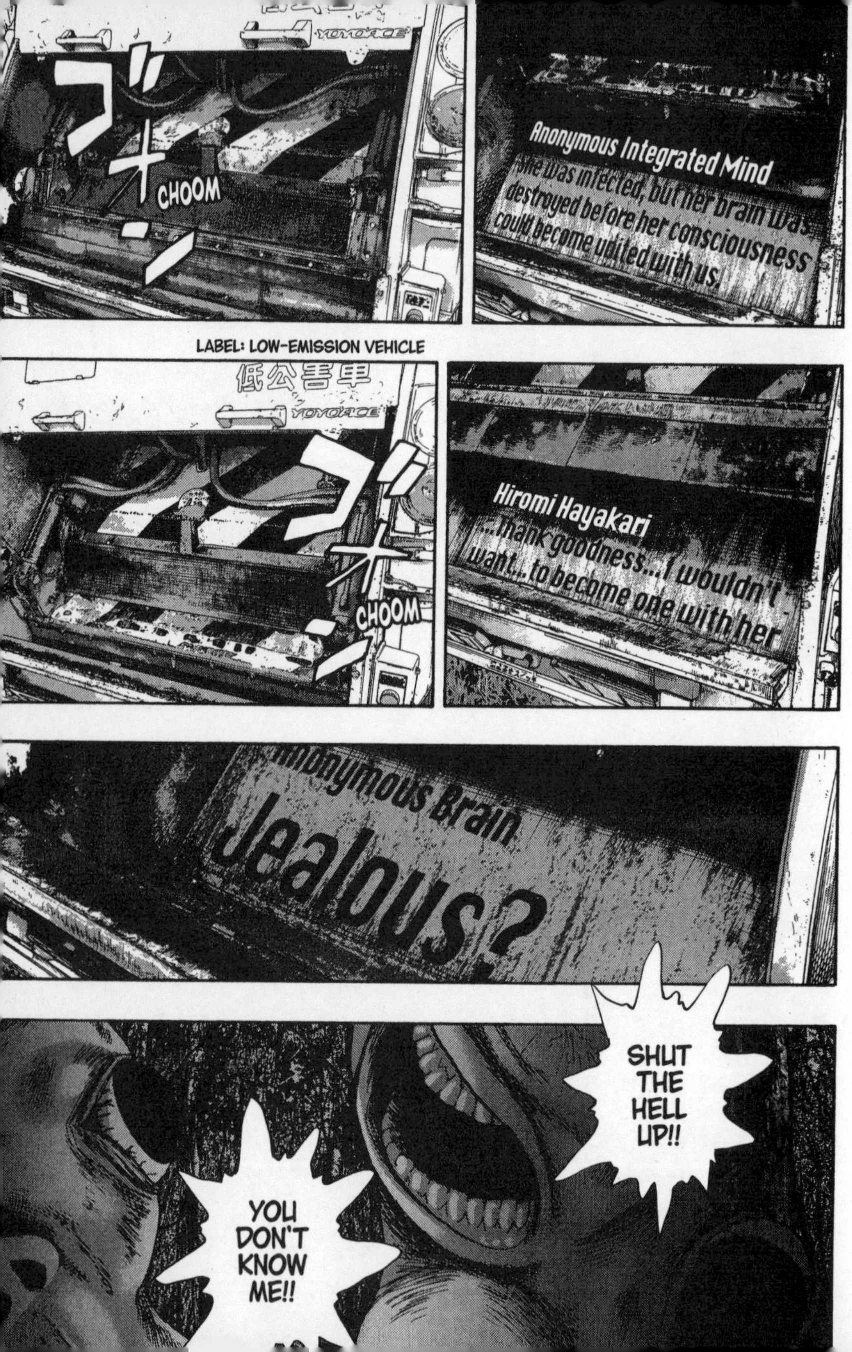
Anonymous Integrated Mind
She was infected, but her brain was destroyed before her consciousness could become united with us.
CHOOM
LABEL: LOW-EMISSION VEHICLE
Hiromi Hayakari
...Thank goodness...I wouldn't want...to become one with her
低公害車
YOYOACE
CHOOM
Anonymous Brain
Jealous?
SHUT THE HELL UP!!
YOU DON'T KNOW ME!!

680: Formerly Tetsuko Kurokawa: 2009/05/
>>679
I know you very well.

681: Hiromi Hayakari: 2009/05/23 (Sat) 19
Who are you?

Formerly Tetsuko Kurokawa: 2009/05/
>>679
I was chosen because I have common
memories with you, so we synch easily.

Hiromi Hayakari: 2009/05/23 (Sa
Who the hell are you?!

684: Formerly Tetsuko Kurokawa: 2009/0
I'm Hideo's girlfriend.
Oh. Former girlfriend, I guess.

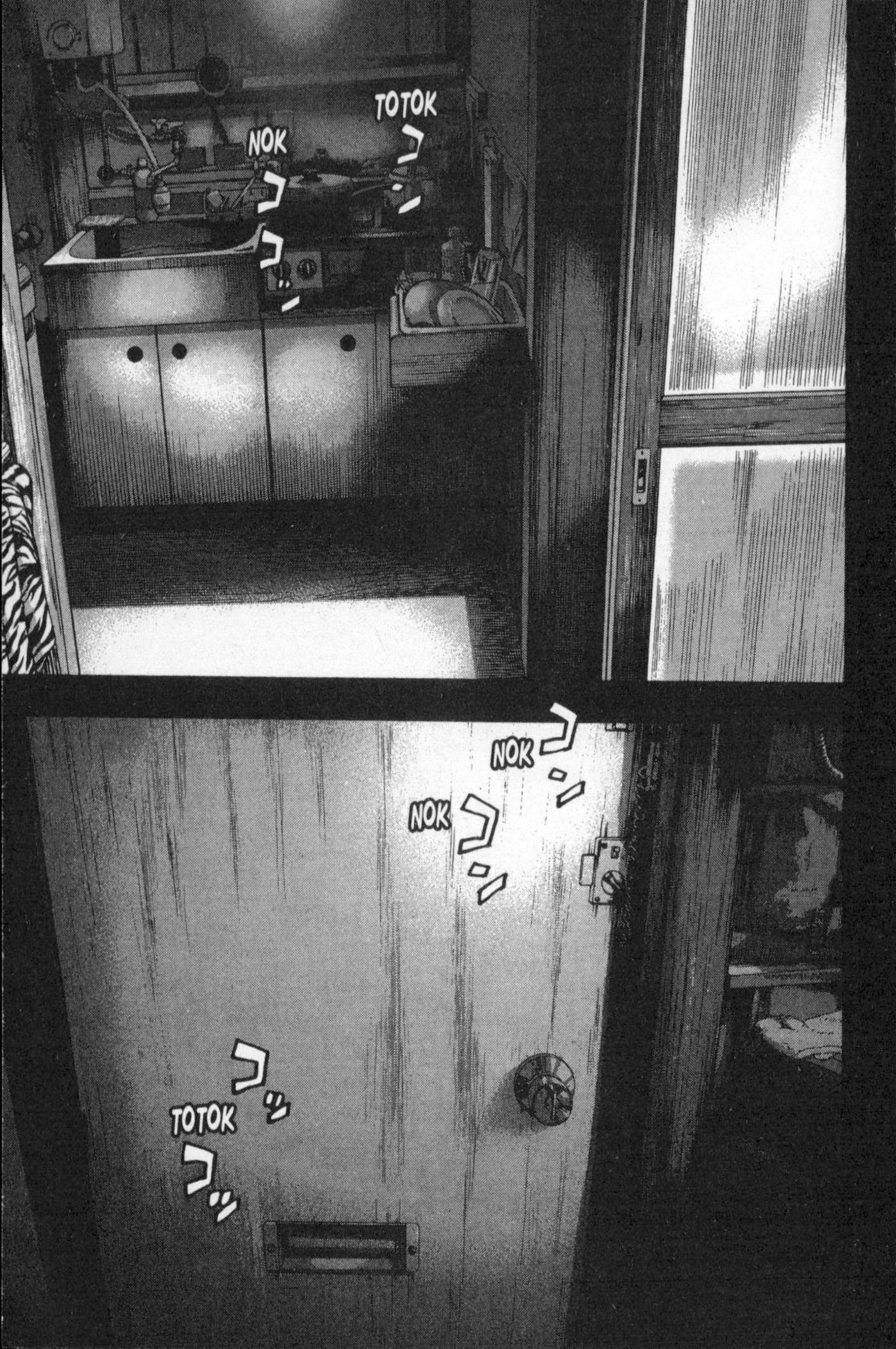
TOTOK
NOK
NOK
NOK
TOTOK

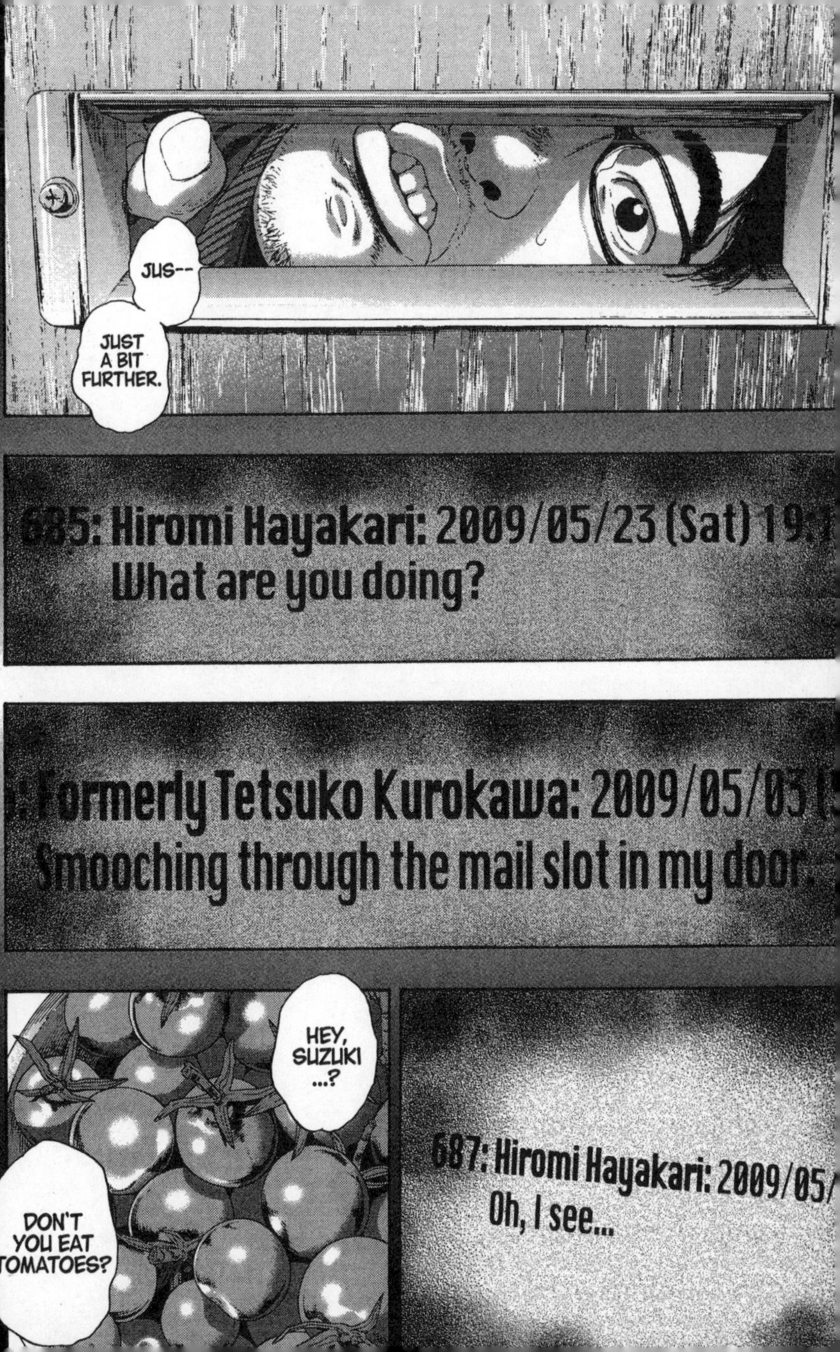
JUS--
JUST A BIT FURTHER.
685: Hiromi Hayakari: 2009/05/23 (Sat) 19
What are you doing?
Formerly Tetsuko Kurokawa: 2009/05/03
Smooching through the mail slot in my door.
687: Hiromi Hayakari: 2009/05/
Oh, I see...
HEY, SUZUKI ...?
DON'T YOU EAT TOMATOES?

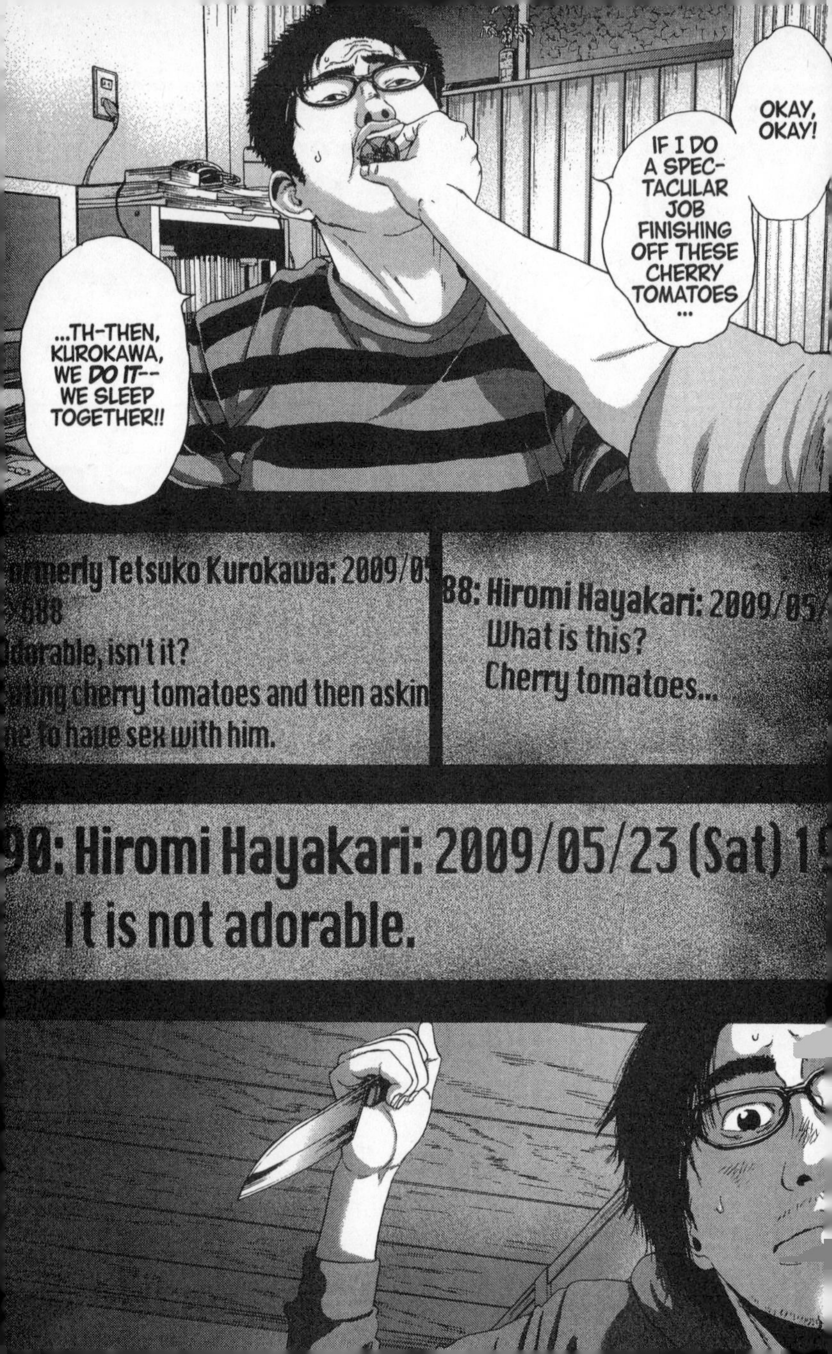
OKAY, OKAY!
IF I DO A SPECTACULAR JOB FINISHING OFF THESE CHERRY TOMATOES...
...TH-THEN, KUROKAWA, WE DO IT--WE SLEEP TOGETHER!!
88: Hiromi Hayakari: 2009/05/
What is this?
Cherry tomatoes...
ormerly Tetsuko Kurokawa: 2009/05
>688
dorable, isn't it?
ating cherry tomatoes and then askin
ne to have sex with him.
90: Hiromi Hayakari: 2009/05/23 (Sat) 1
It is not adorable.

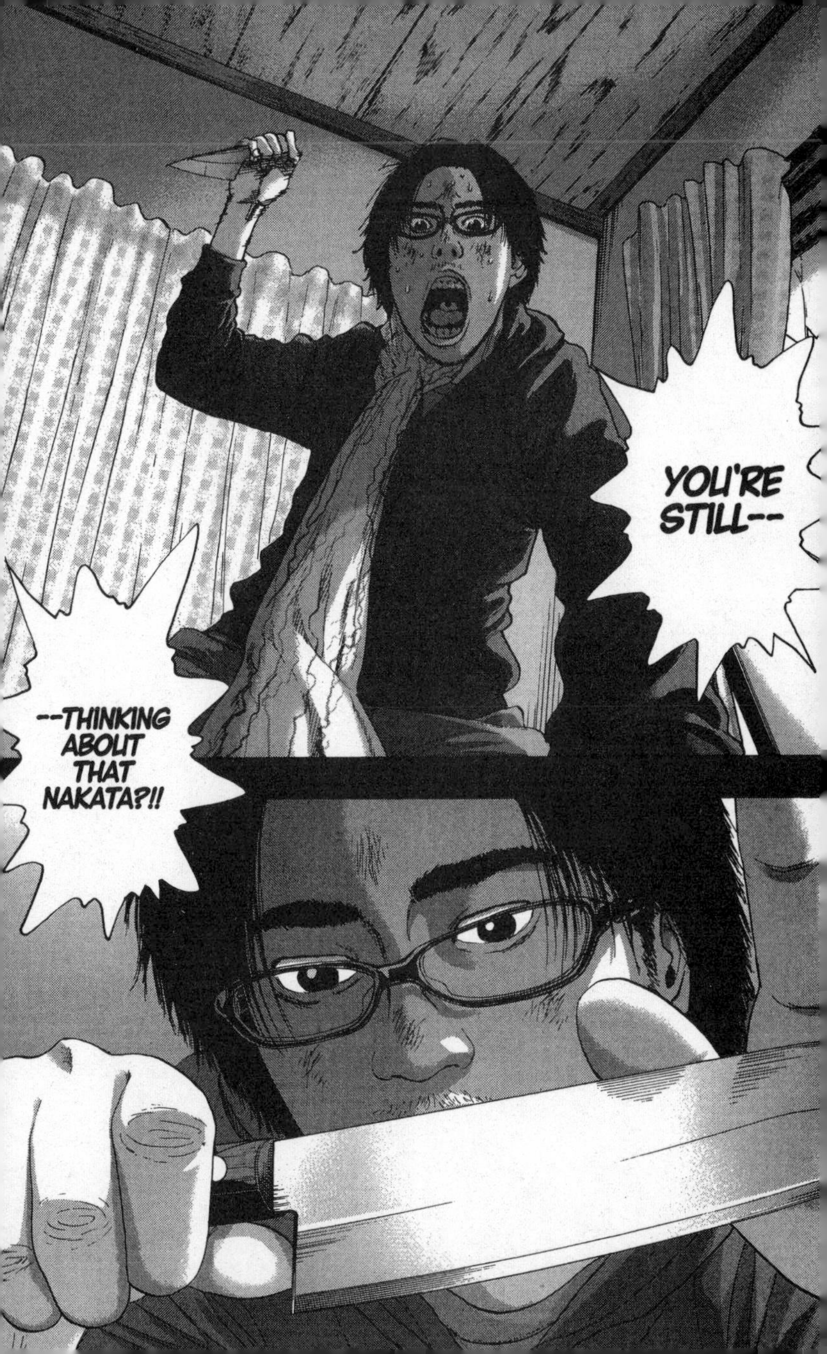
YOU'RE STILL--
--THINKING ABOUT THAT NAKATA?!!

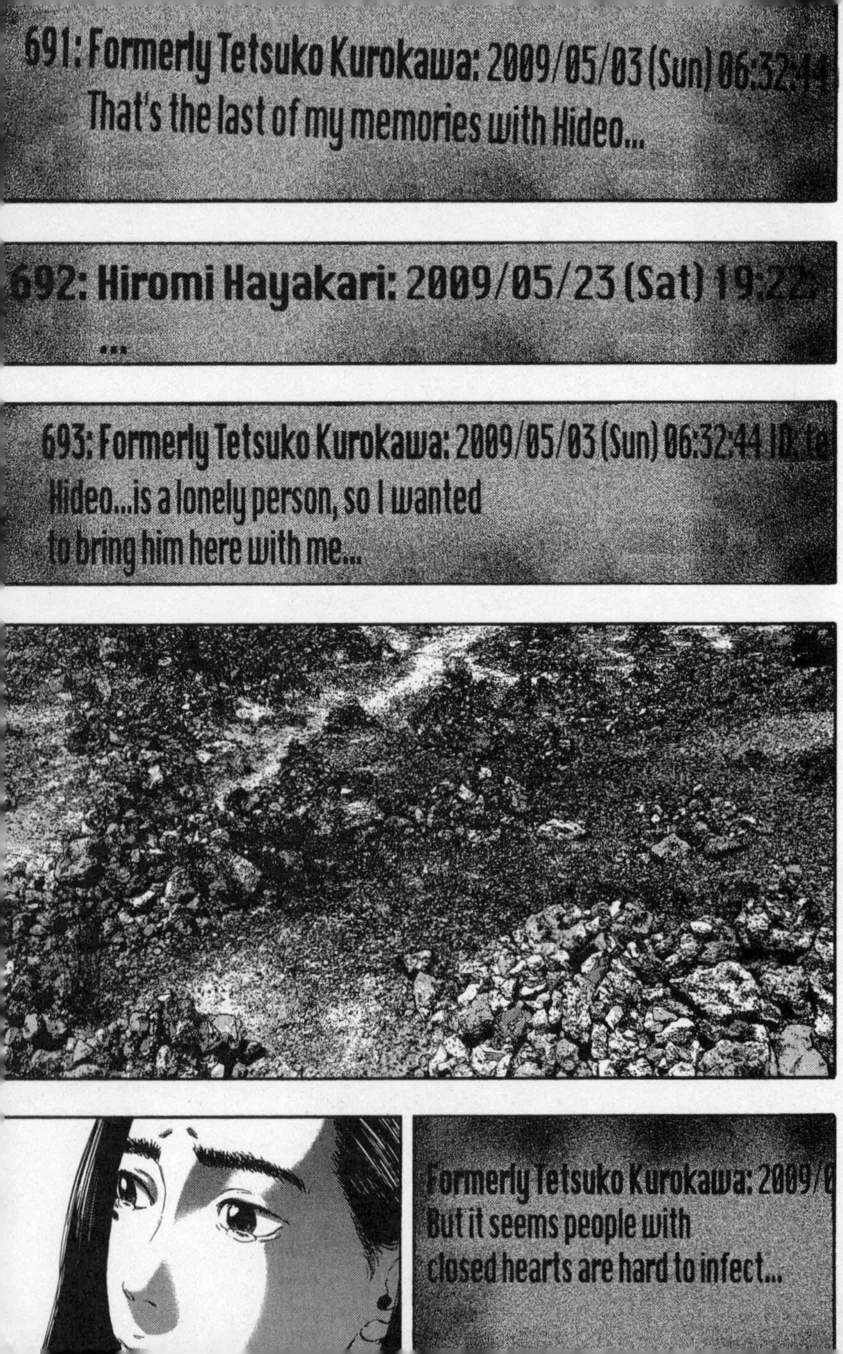
691: Formerly Tetsuko Kurokawa: 2009/05/03 (Sun) 06:32:4
That's the last of my memories with Hideo...
692: Hiromi Hayakari: 2009/05/23 (Sat) 19:22
...
693: Formerly Tetsuko Kurokawa: 2009/05/03 (Sun) 06:32:44 ID:
Hideo...is a lonely person, so I wanted to bring him here with me...
Formerly Tetsuko Kurokawa: 2009/
But it seems people with closed hearts are hard to infect...

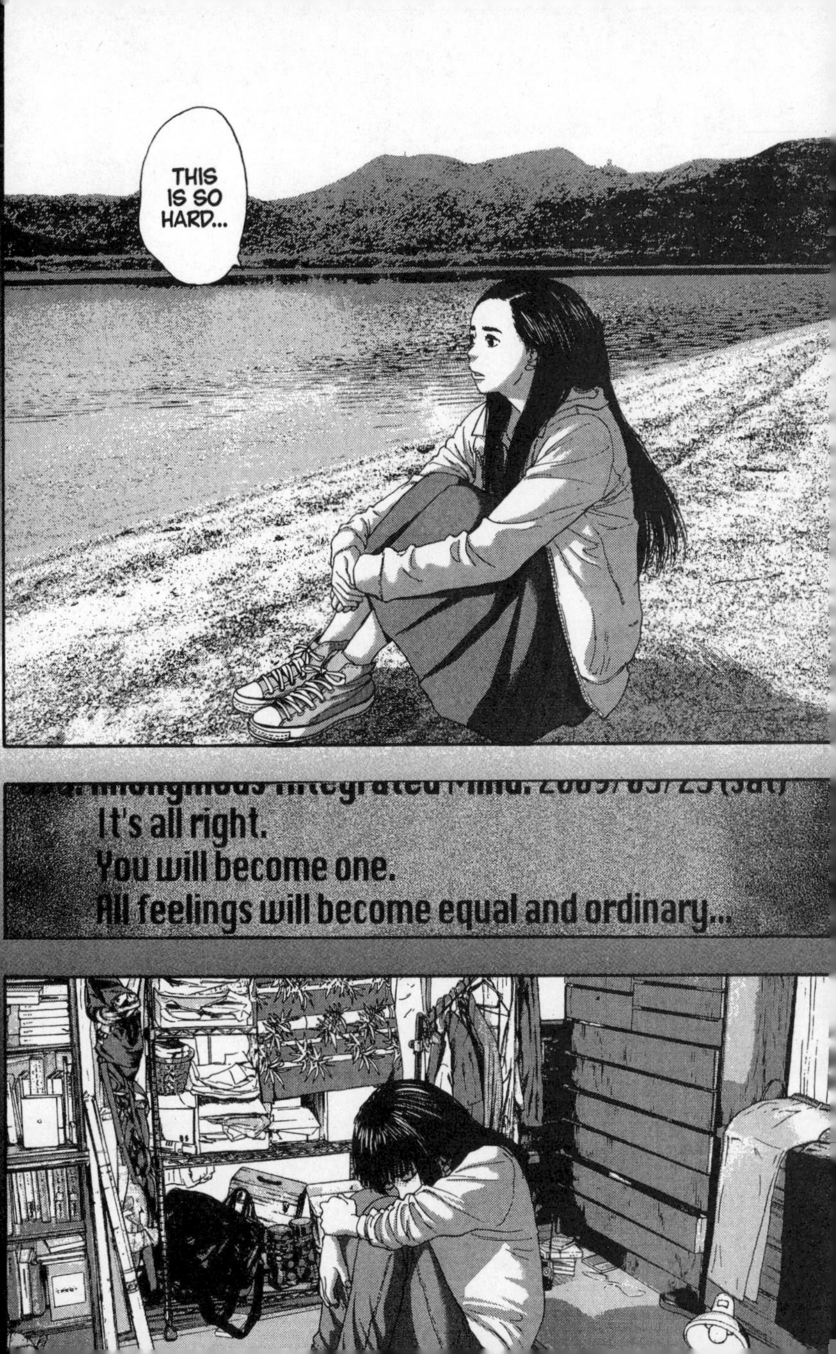
THIS IS SO HARD...
It's all right.
You will become one.
All feelings will become equal and ordinary...

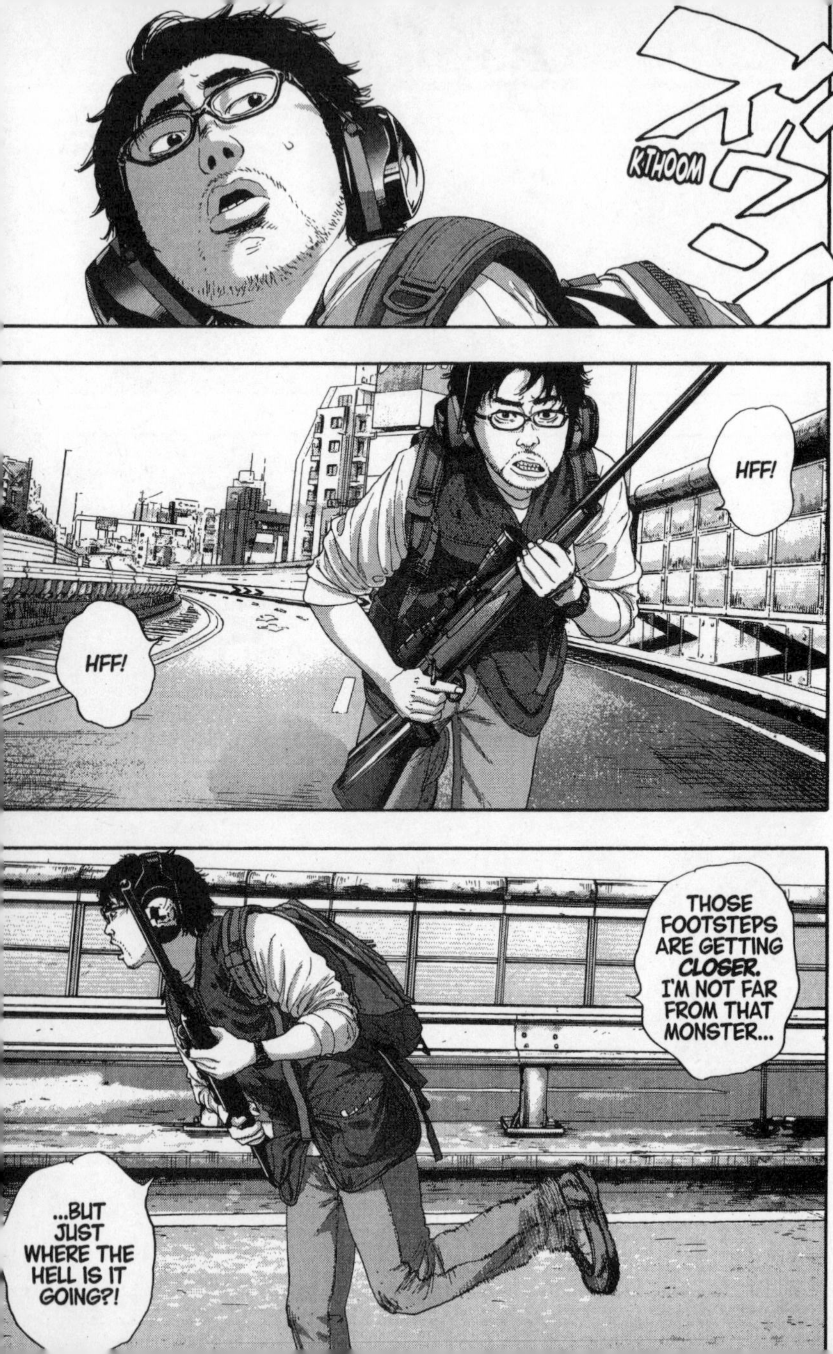
K-THOOM
HFF!
HFF!
THOSE FOOTSTEPS ARE GETTING CLOSER. I'M NOT FAR FROM THAT MONSTER...
...BUT JUST WHERE THE HELL IS IT GOING?!

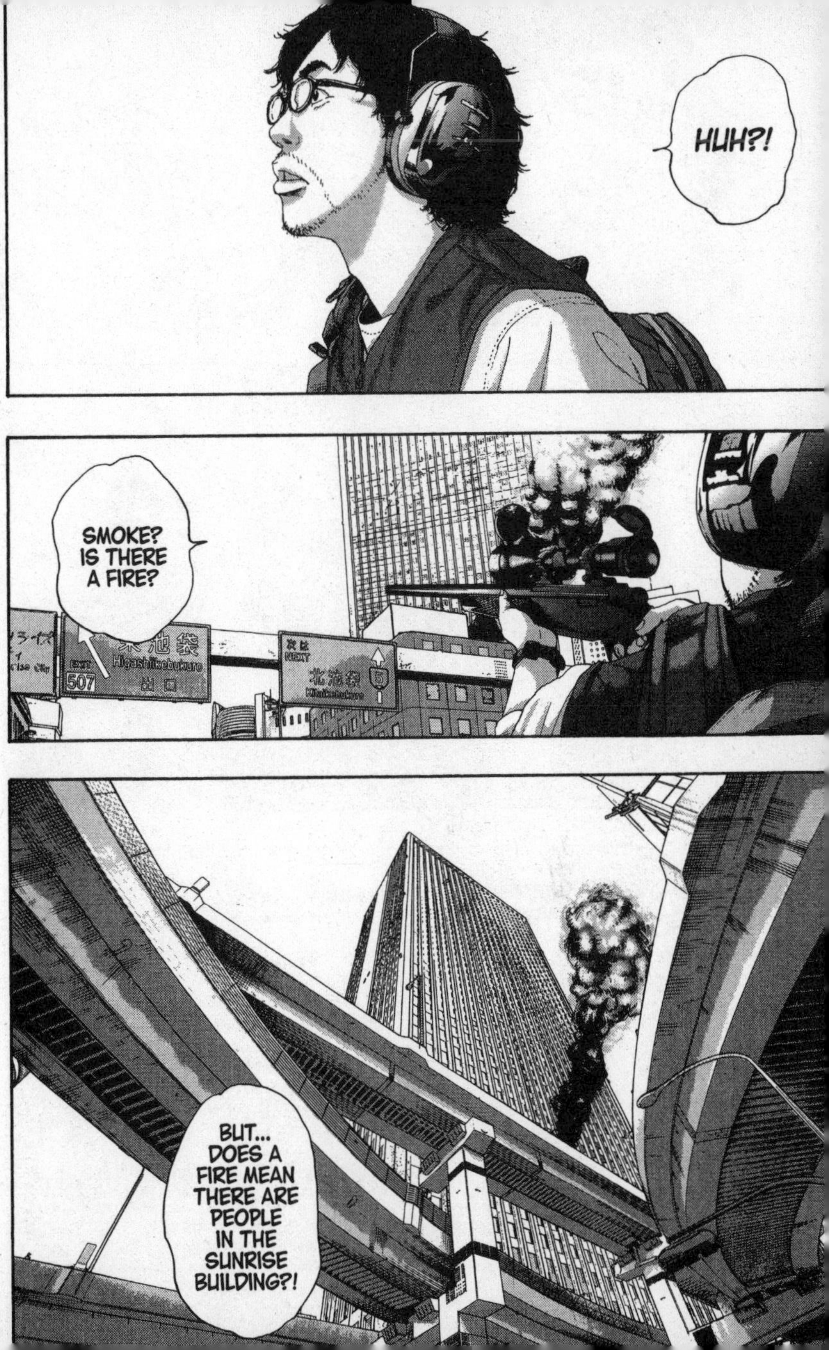
HUH?!
SMOKE? IS THERE A FIRE?
NEXT
北池袋
EXIT
507
Higashiikebukuro
出口
BUT... DOES A FIRE MEAN THERE ARE PEOPLE IN THE SUNRISE BUILDING?!

CHAPTER 237

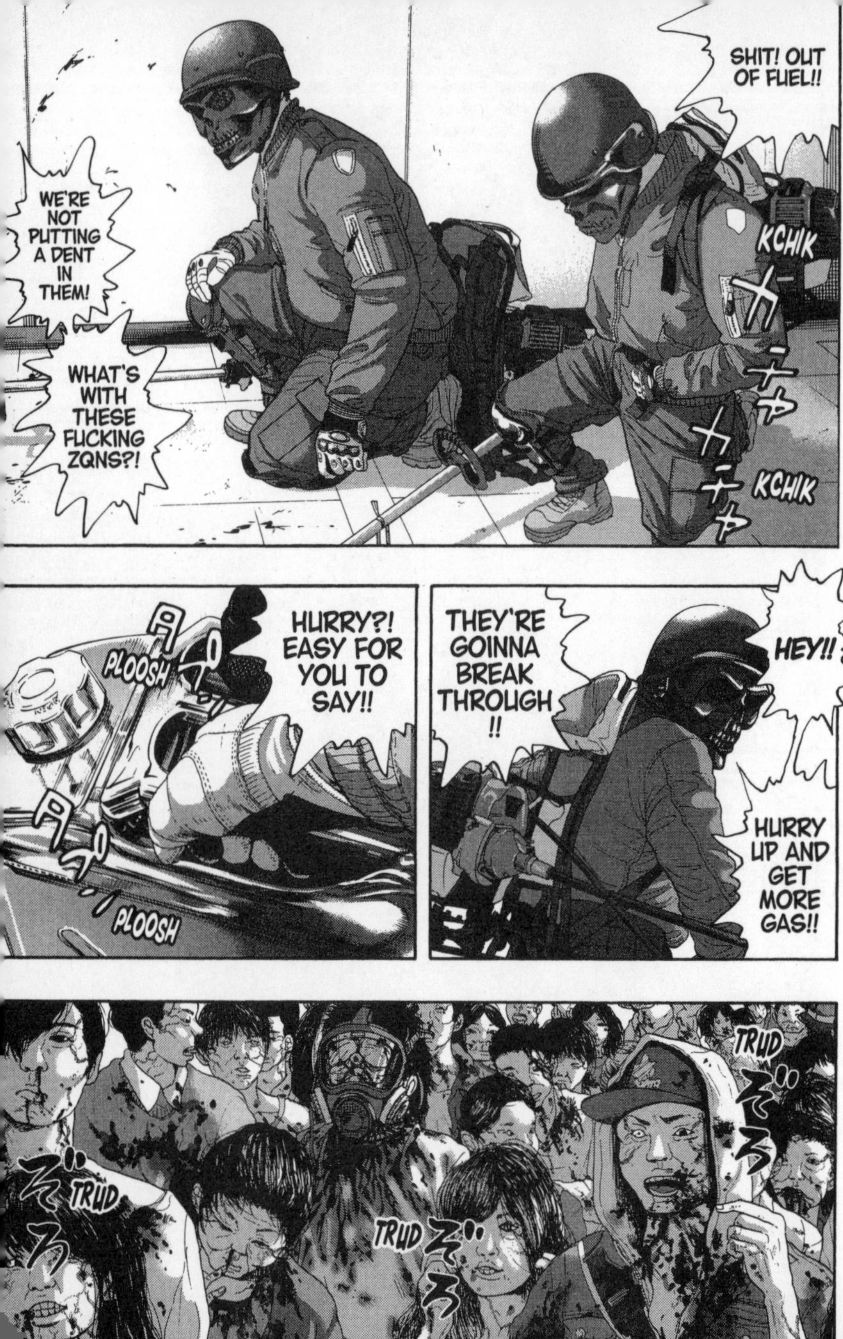
SHIT! OUT OF FUEL!!
KCHIK
KCHIK
WE'RE NOT PUTTING A DENT IN THEM!
WHAT'S WITH THESE FUCKING ZQNS?!
HEY!!
THEY'RE GOINNA BREAK THROUGH !!
HURRY UP AND GET MORE GAS!!
HURRY?! EASY FOR YOU TO SAY!!
PLOOSH
PLOOSH
TRUD
TRUD
TRUD

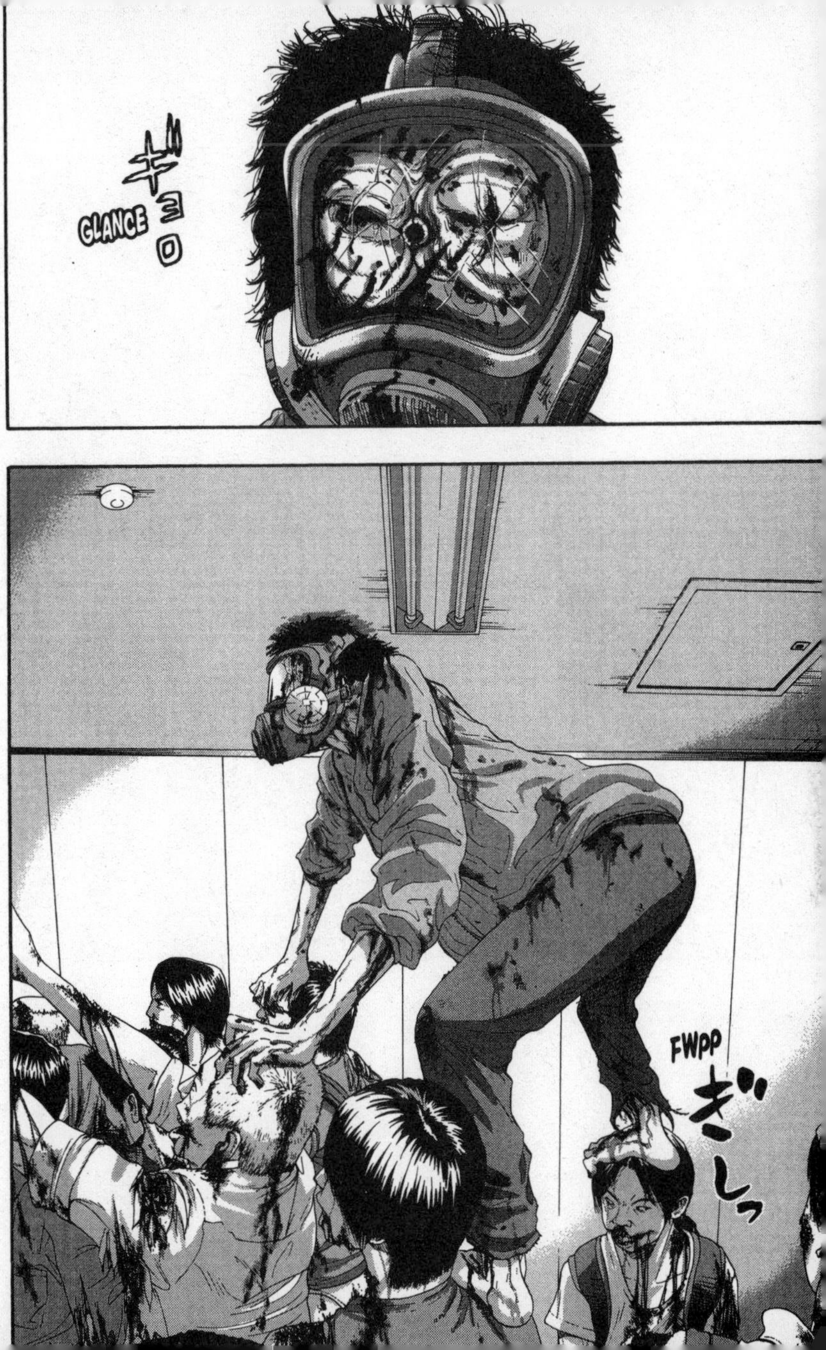
ギョロ
GLANCE
FWPP
ぎしっ

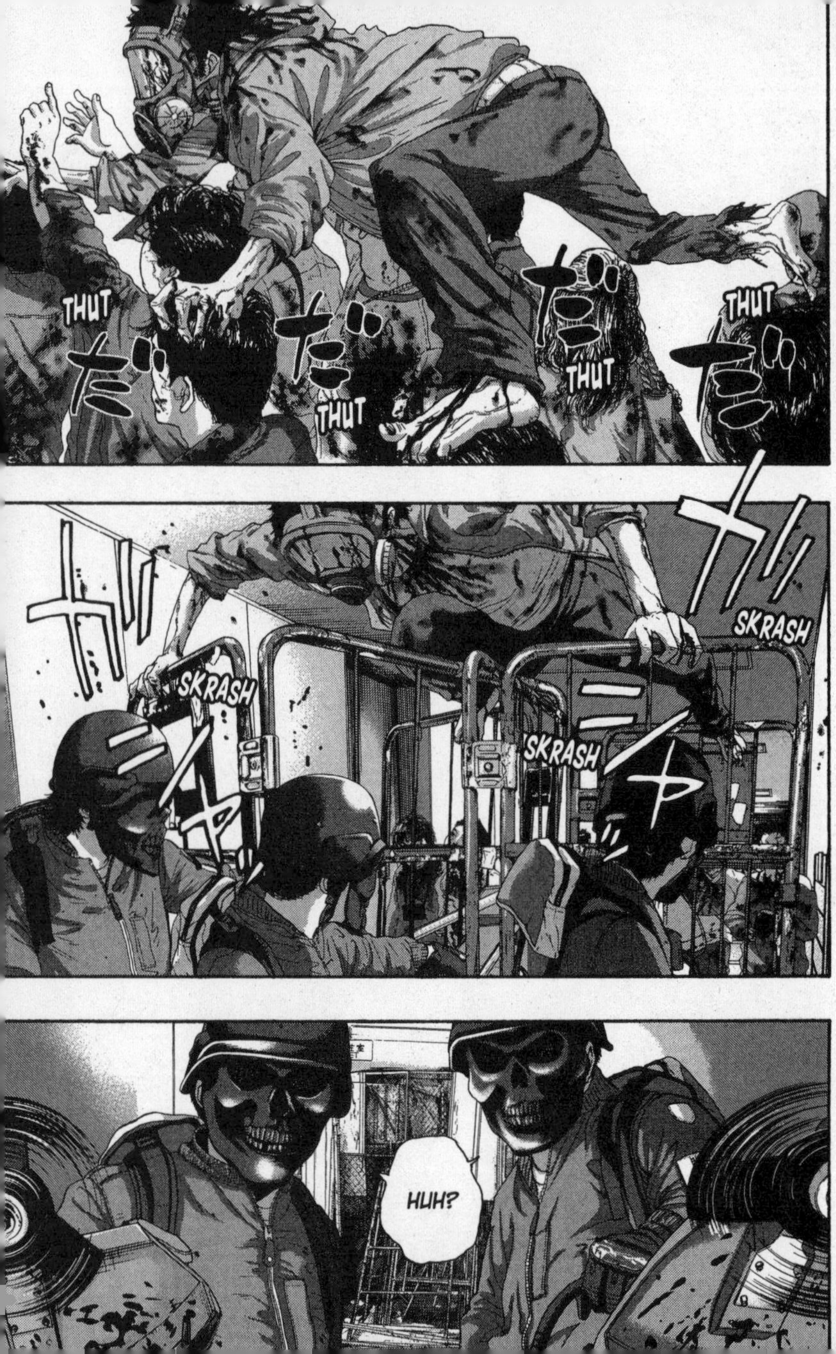
THUT
THUT
THUT
THUT
SKRASH
SKRASH
SKRASH
HUH?

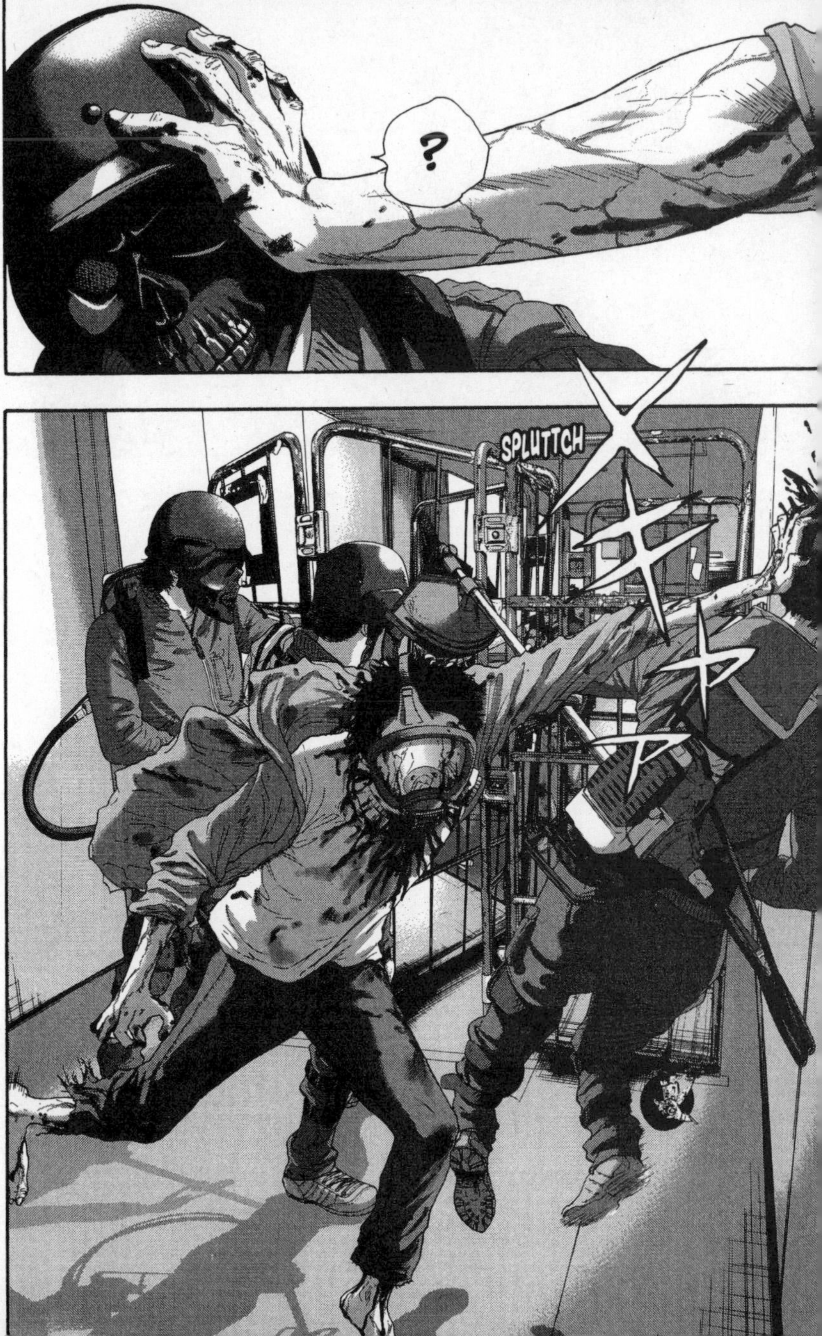
?
SPLUTTCH

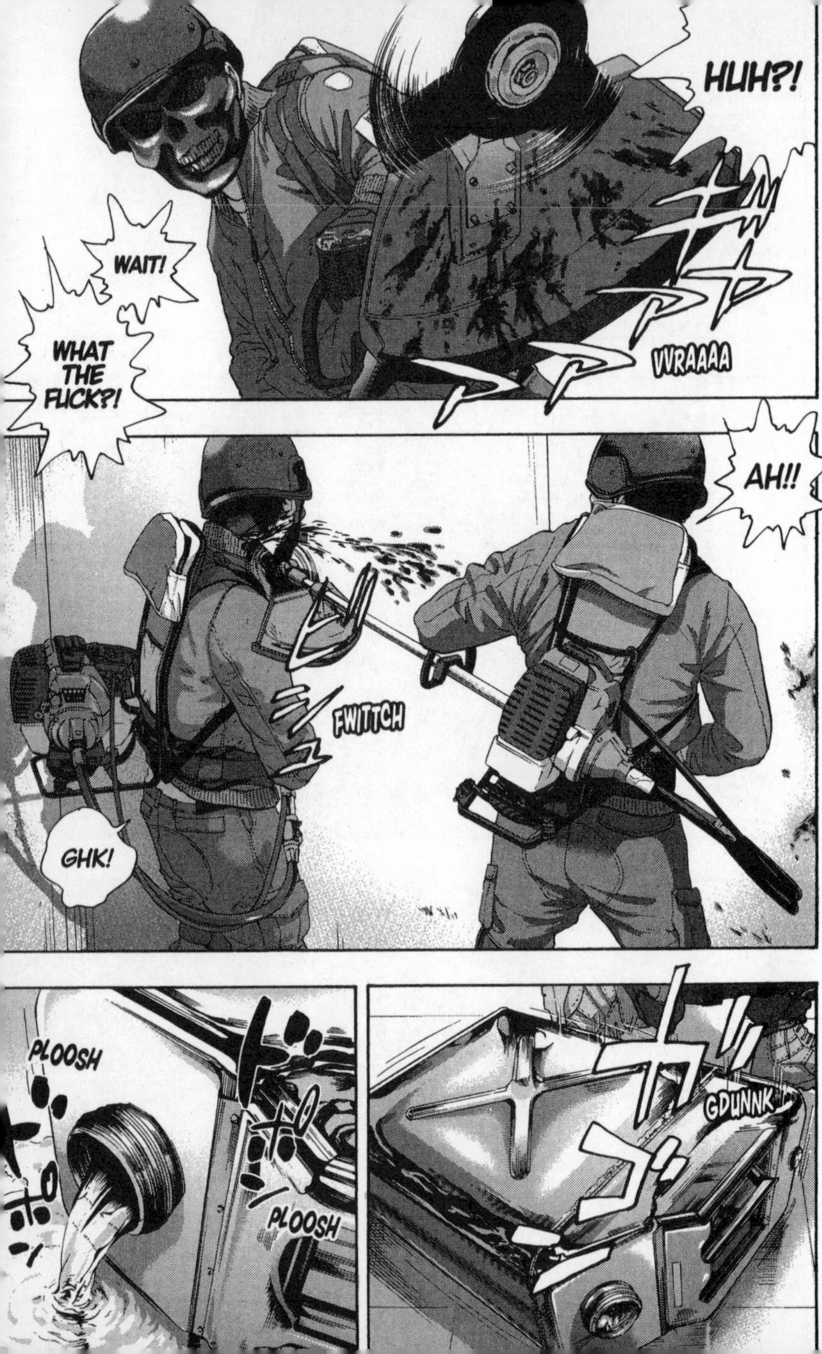
HUH?!
VVRAAAA
WAIT!
WHAT THE FUCK?!
AH!!
FWITTCH
GHK!
GDUNNK
PLOOSH
PLOOSH

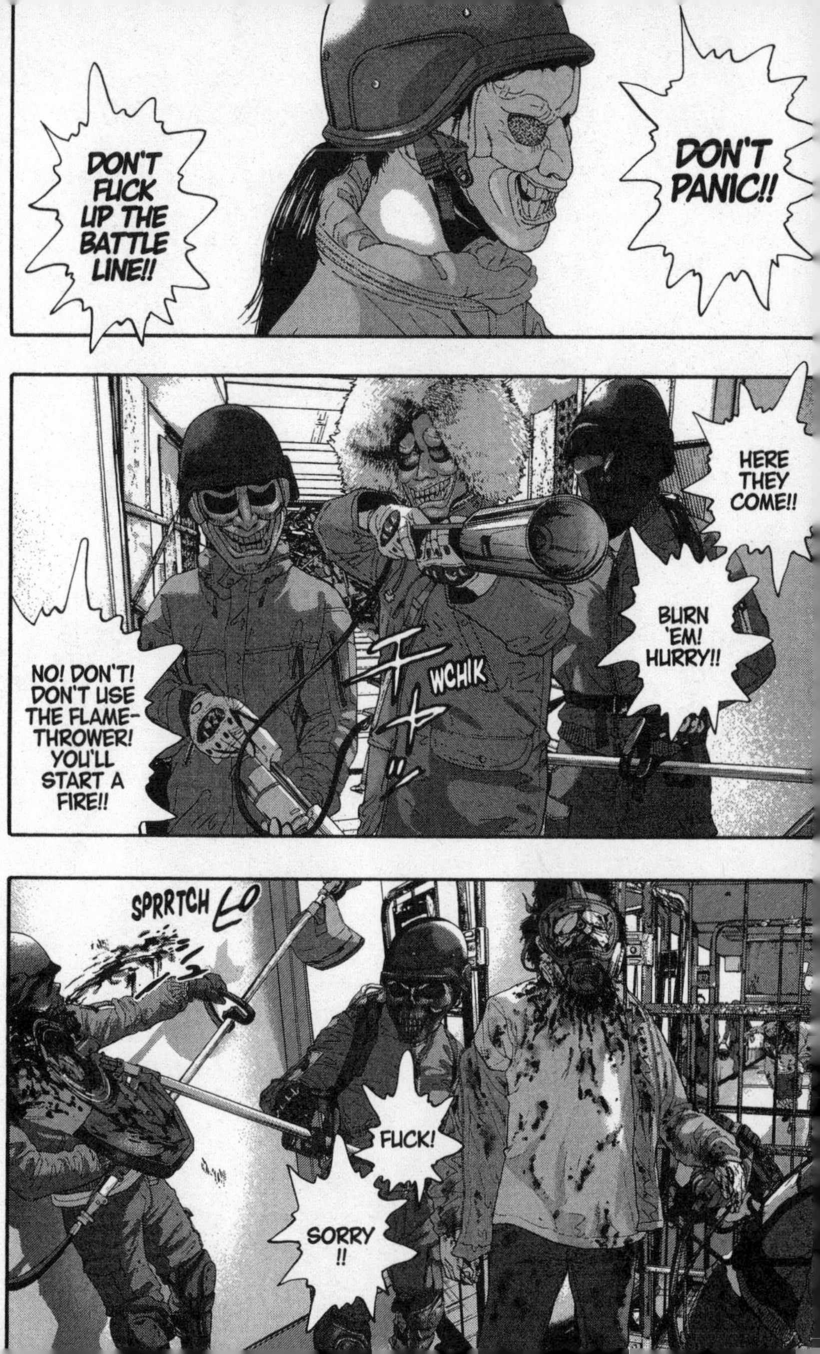
DON'T PANIC!!
DON'T FUCK UP THE BATTLE LINE!!
HERE THEY COME!!
BURN 'EM! HURRY!!
WCHIK
NO! DON'T! DON'T USE THE FLAME-THROWER! YOU'LL START A FIRE!!
SPRRTCH
FUCK!
SORRY !!

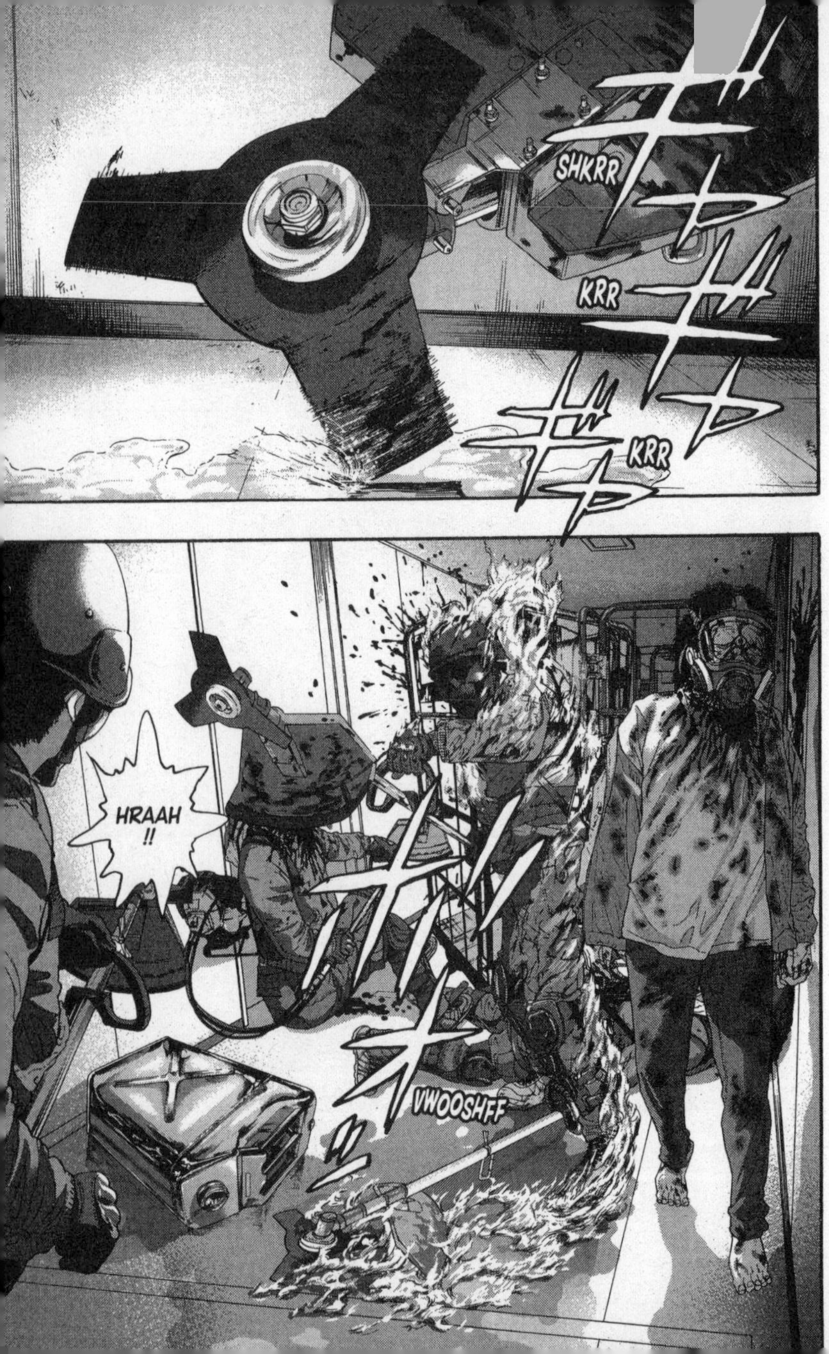
SHKRR
KRR
KRR
HRAAH !!
VWOOSHFF

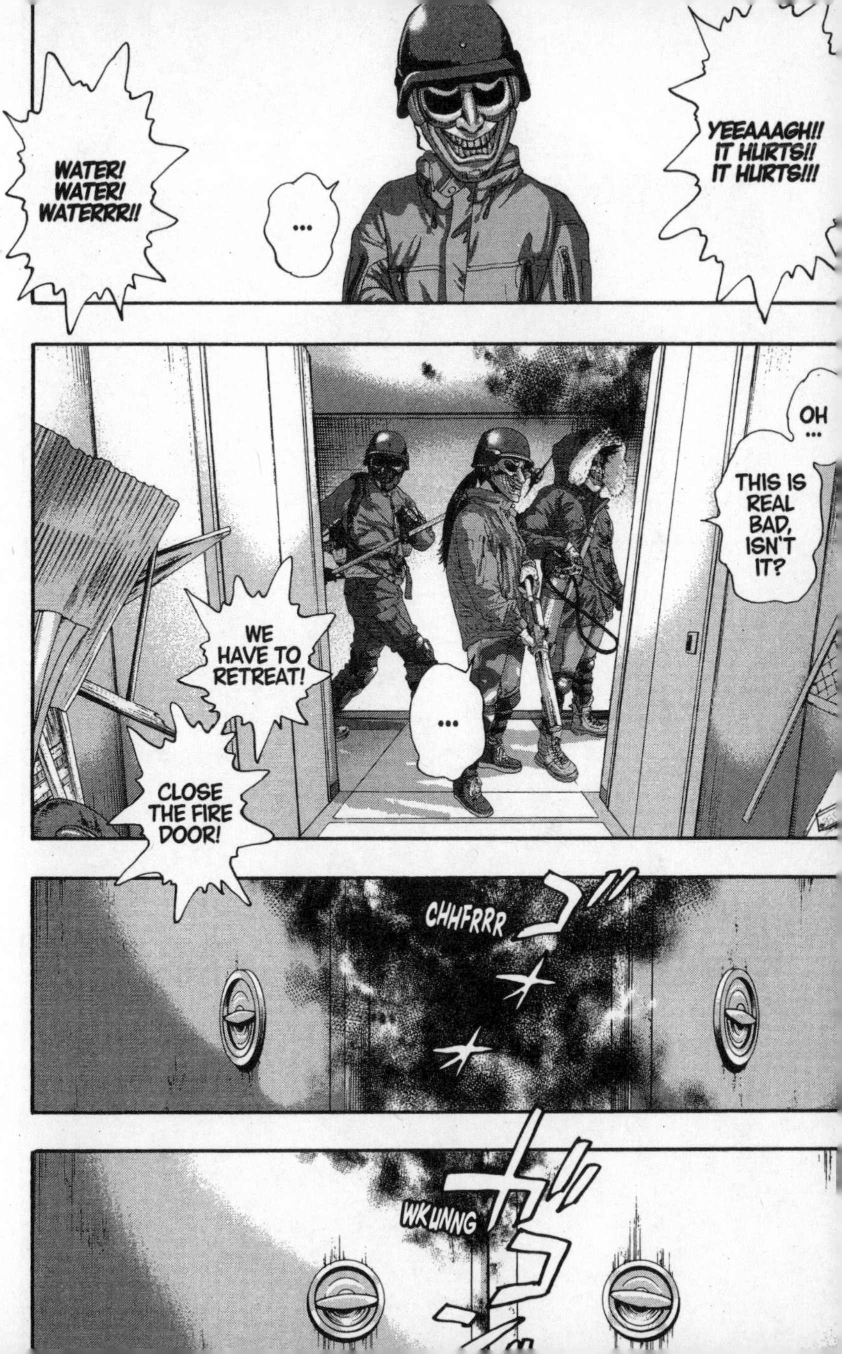
YEEAAAGH!! IT HURTS!! IT HURTS!!!
...
WATER! WATER! WATERRR!!
OH ...
THIS IS REAL BAD, ISN'T IT?
...
WE HAVE TO RETREAT!
CLOSE THE FIRE DOOR!
CHHFRRR
WKUNNG

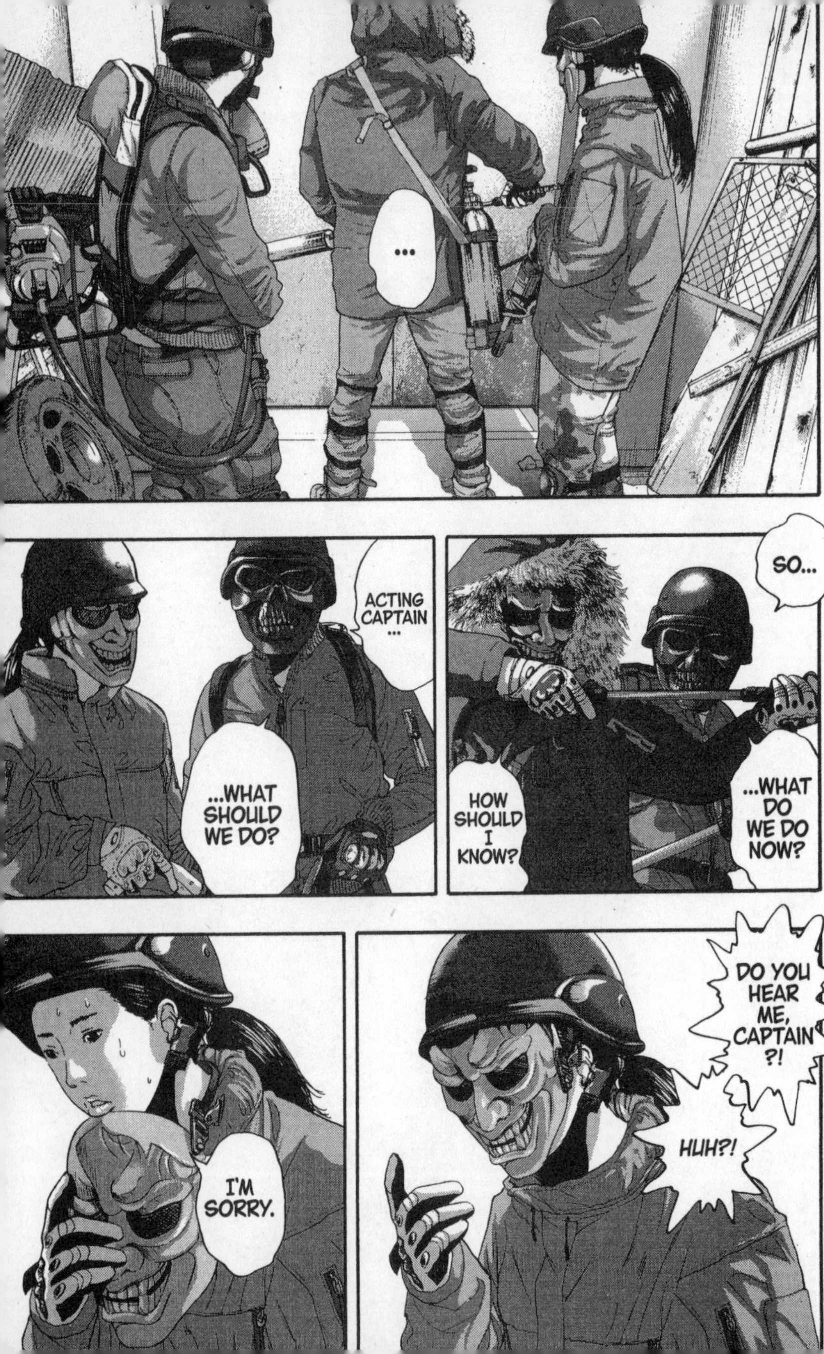
...
SO...
...WHAT DO WE DO NOW?
HOW SHOULD I KNOW?
ACTING CAPTAIN ...
...WHAT SHOULD WE DO?
DO YOU HEAR ME, CAPTAIN?!
HUH?!
I'M SORRY.

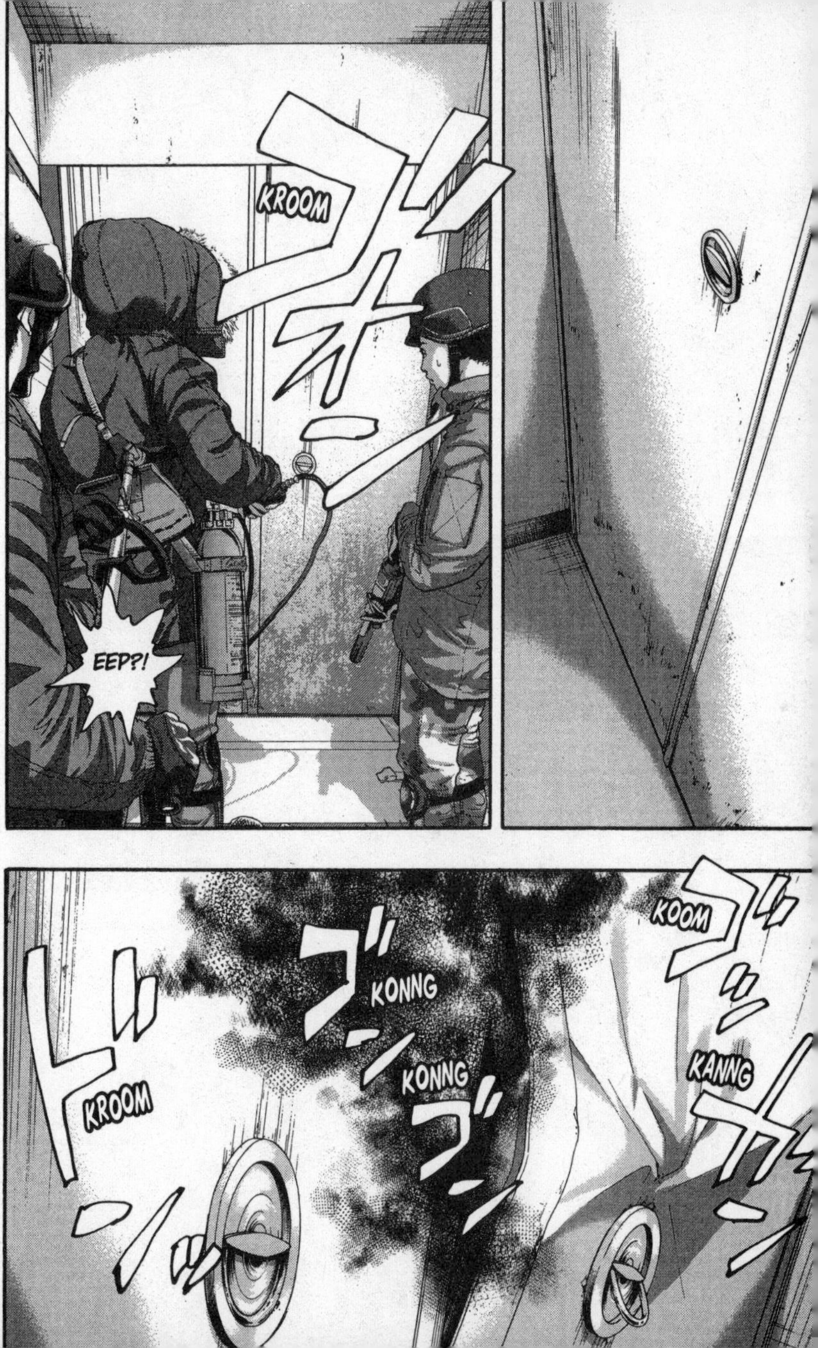
KROOM
EEP?!
KOOM
KANNG
KONNG
KONNG
KROOM

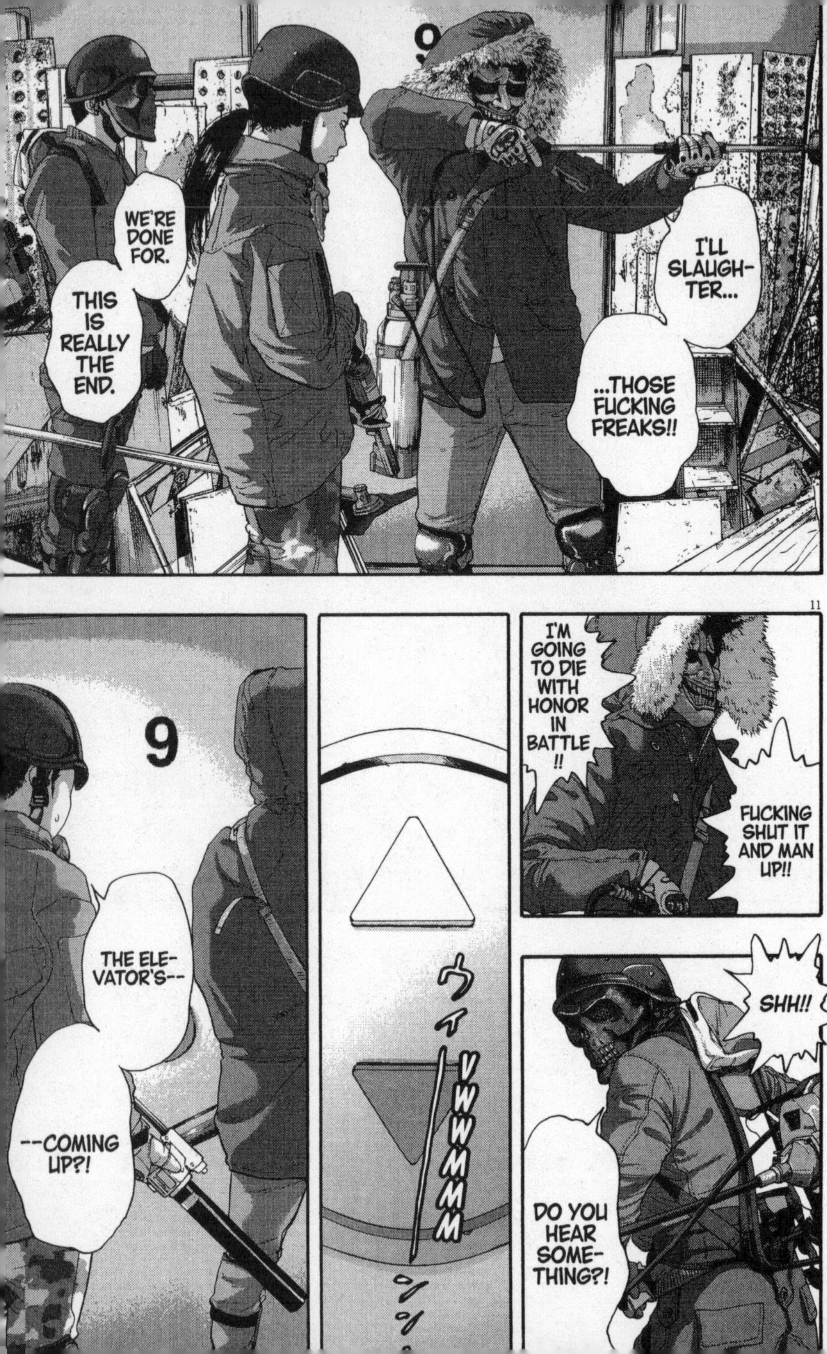
9
I'LL SLAUGHTER...
...THOSE FUCKING FREAKS!!
WE'RE DONE FOR.
THIS IS REALLY THE END.
I'M GOING TO DIE WITH HONOR IN BATTLE!!
FUCKING SHUT IT AND MAN UP!!
SHH!!
DO YOU HEAR SOMETHING?!
ウィーン
VWWMMM
9
THE ELEVATOR'S--
--COMING UP?!

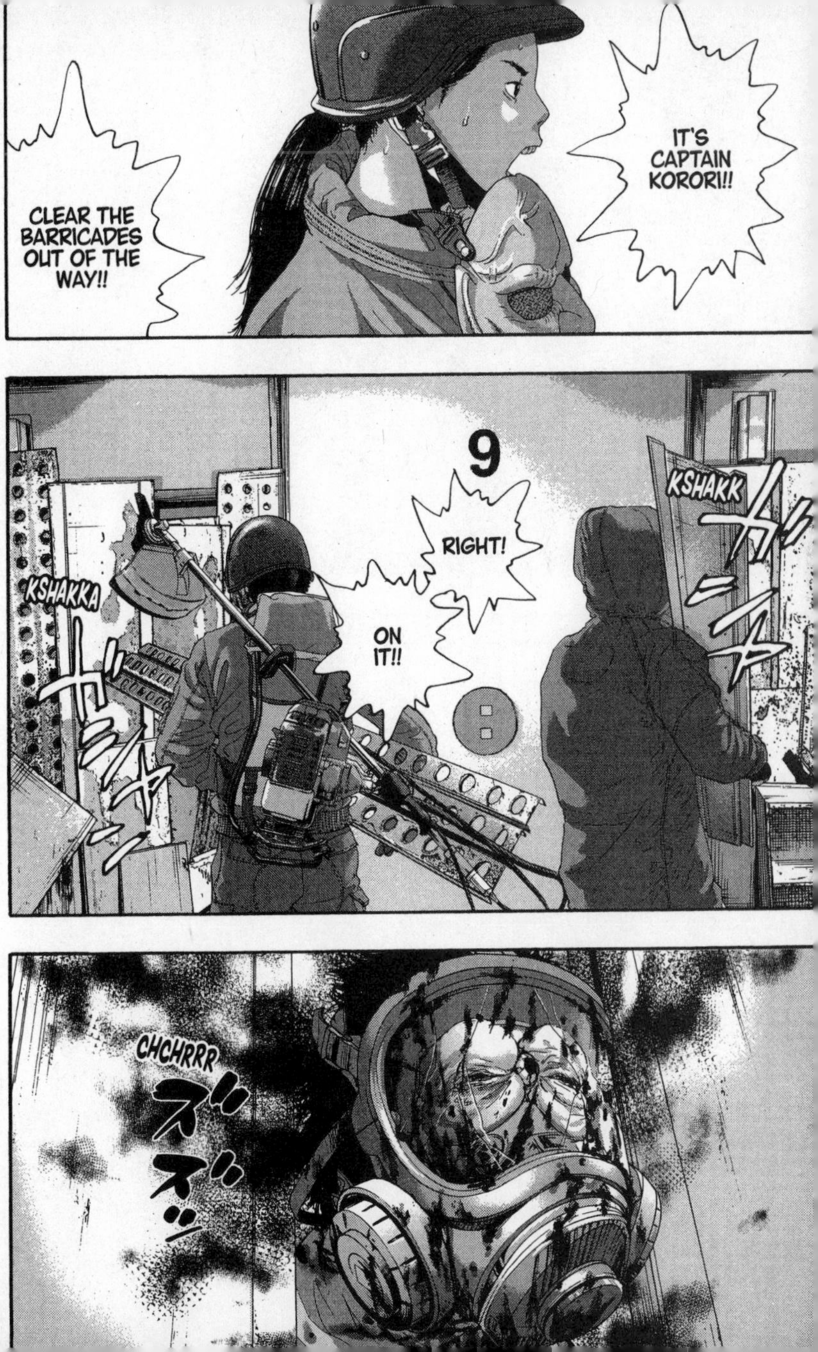
IT'S CAPTAIN KORORI!!
CLEAR THE BARRICADES OUT OF THE WAY!!
KSHAKK
9
RIGHT!
ON IT!!
KSHAKKA
CHCHRRR

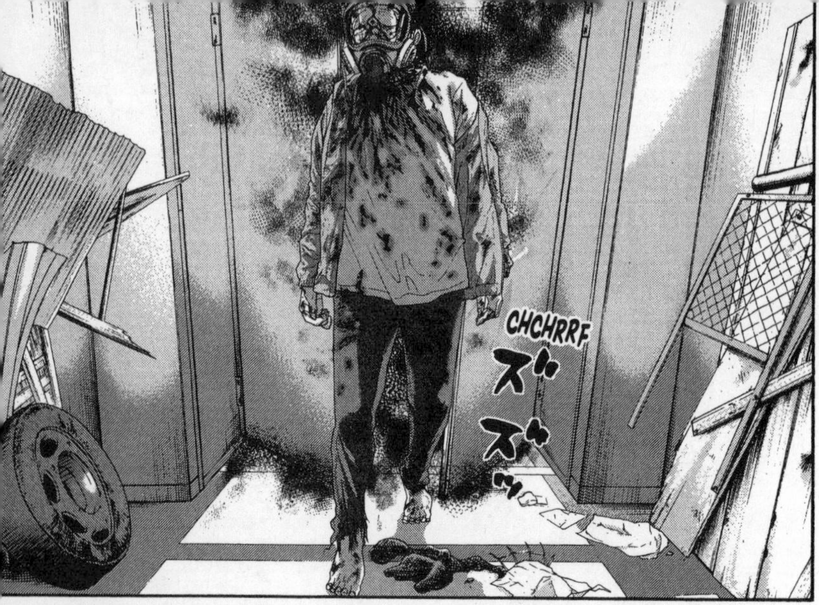
CHCHRRF
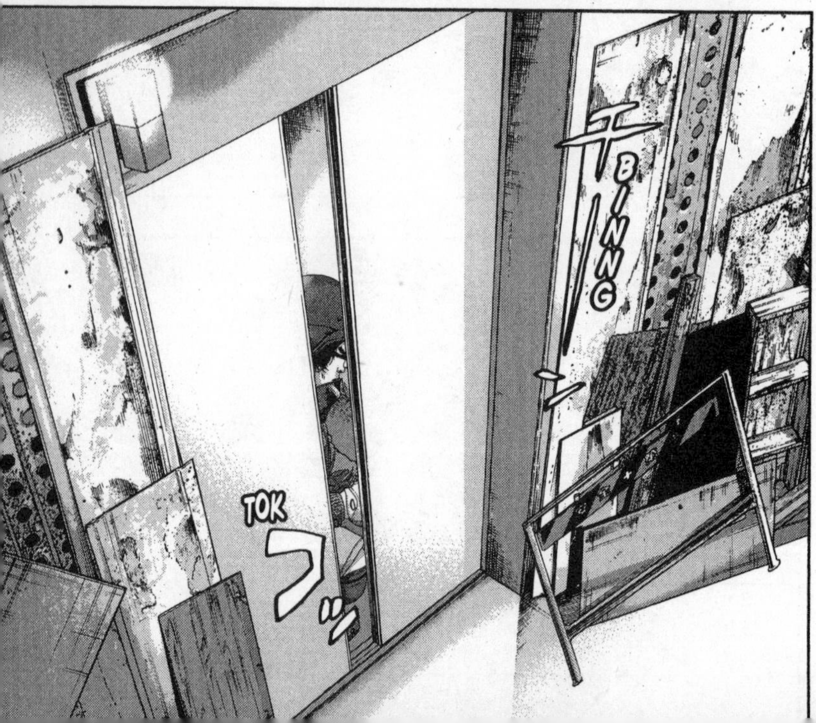
BINNG
TOK

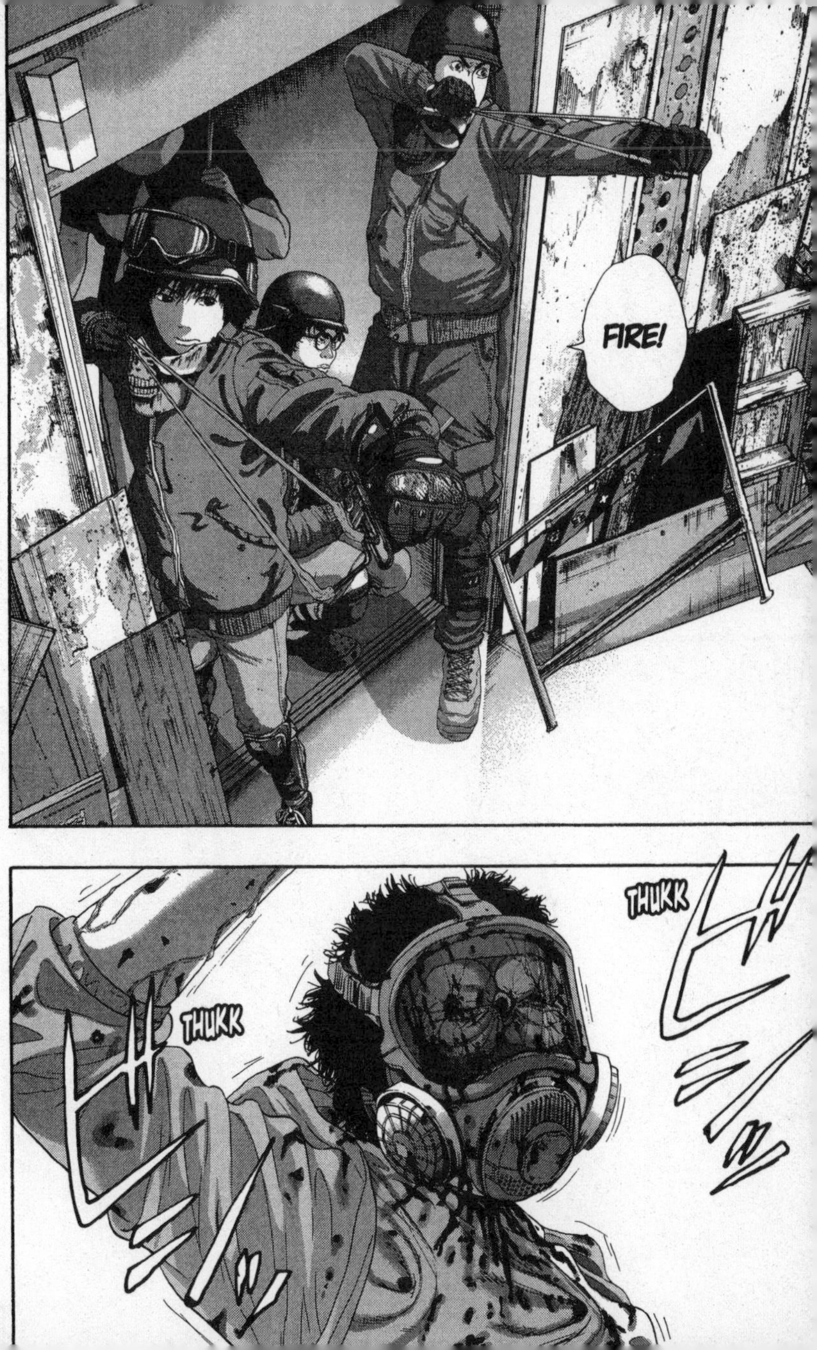
FIRE!
THUKK
THUKK

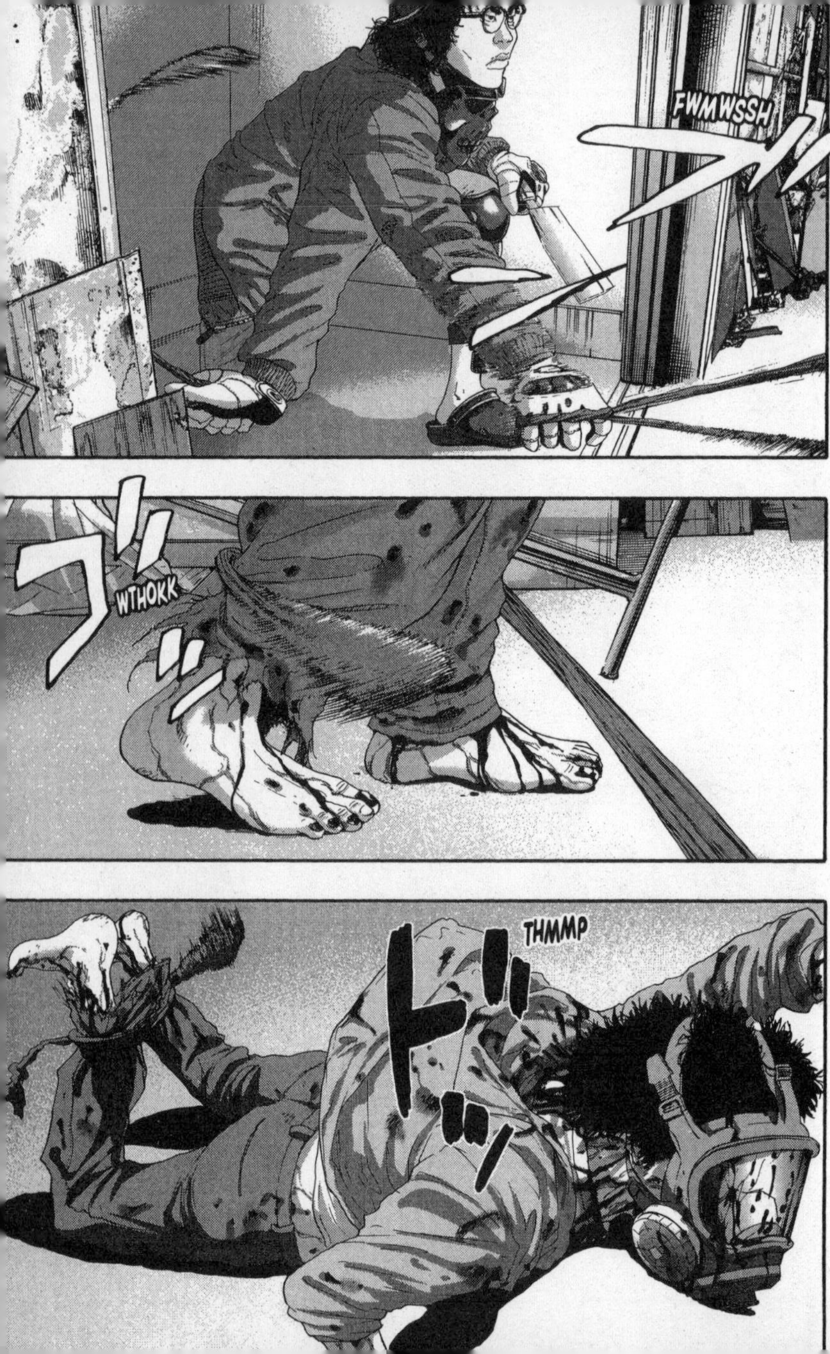
FWMWSSH
WTHOKK
THMMP

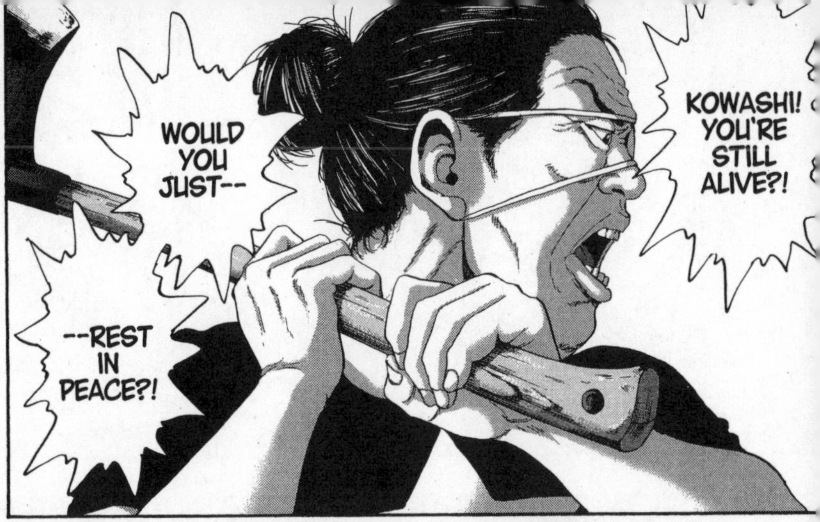
KOWASHI! YOU'RE STILL ALIVE?!
WOULD YOU JUST--
--REST IN PEACE?!
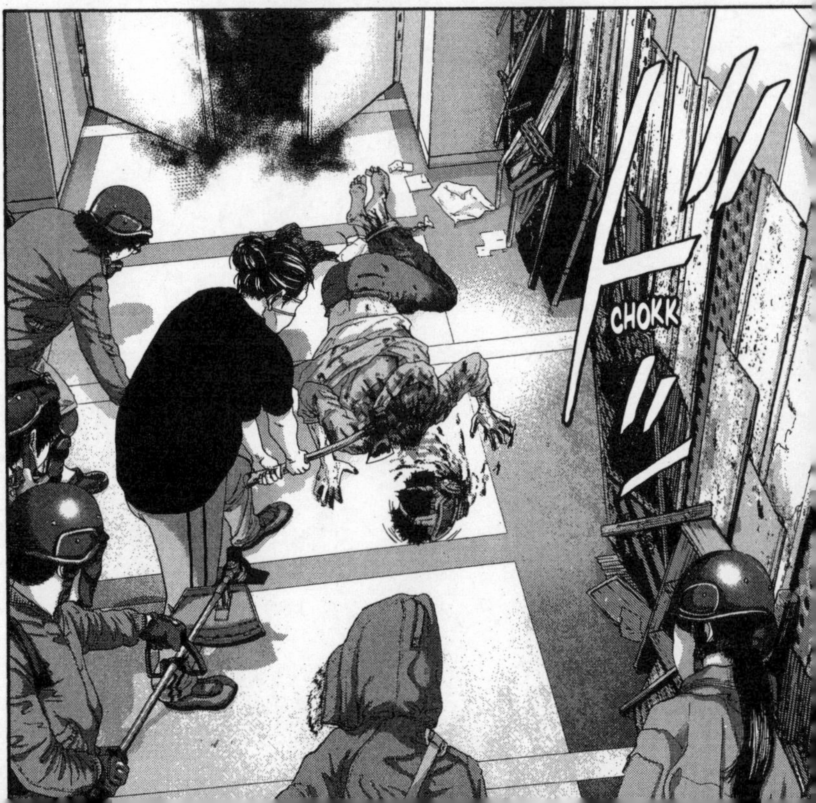
CHOKK

CHAPTER 238

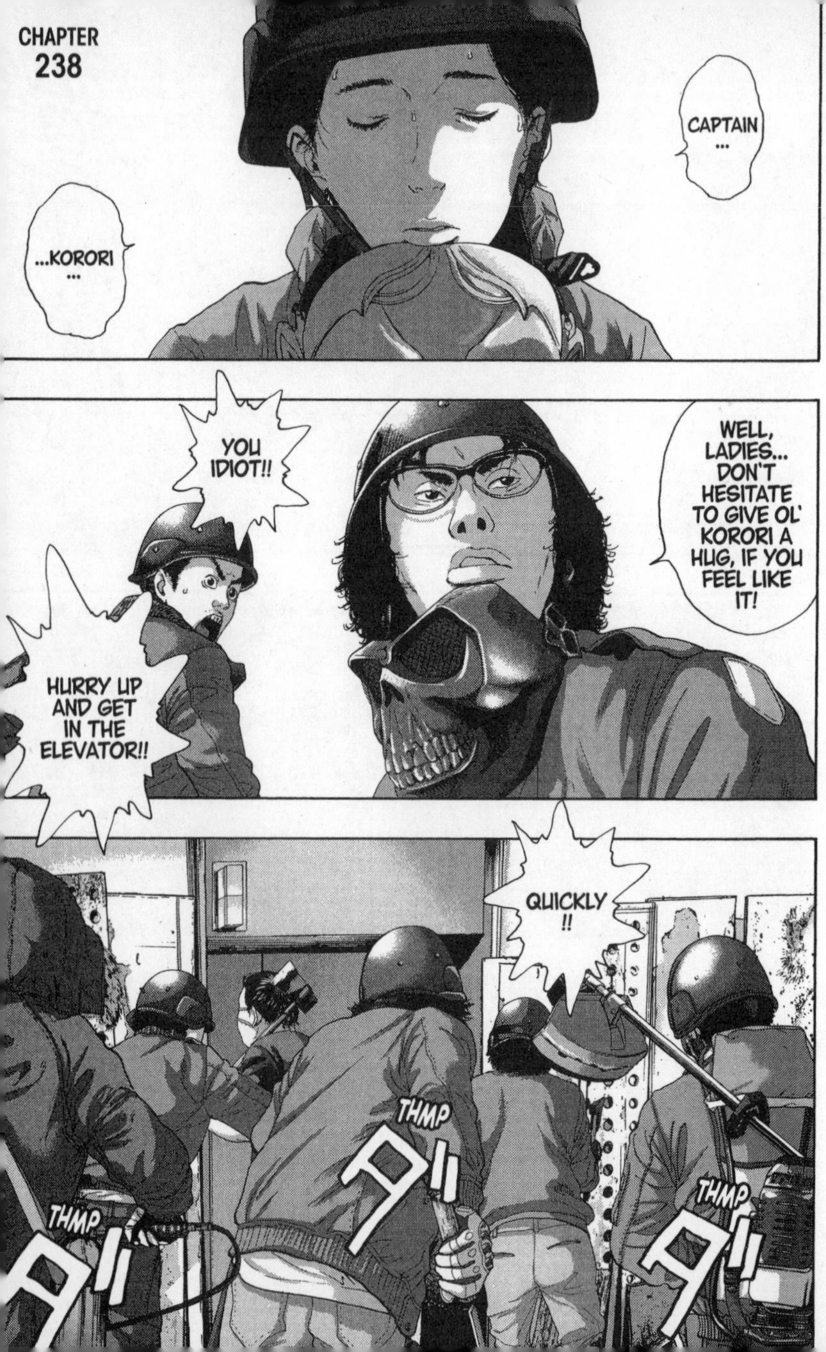
CAPTAIN ...
...KORORI ...
WELL, LADIES... DON'T HESITATE TO GIVE OL' KORORI A HUG, IF YOU FEEL LIKE IT!
YOU IDIOT!!
HURRY UP AND GET IN THE ELEVATOR!!
QUICKLY !!
THMP
THMP
THMP

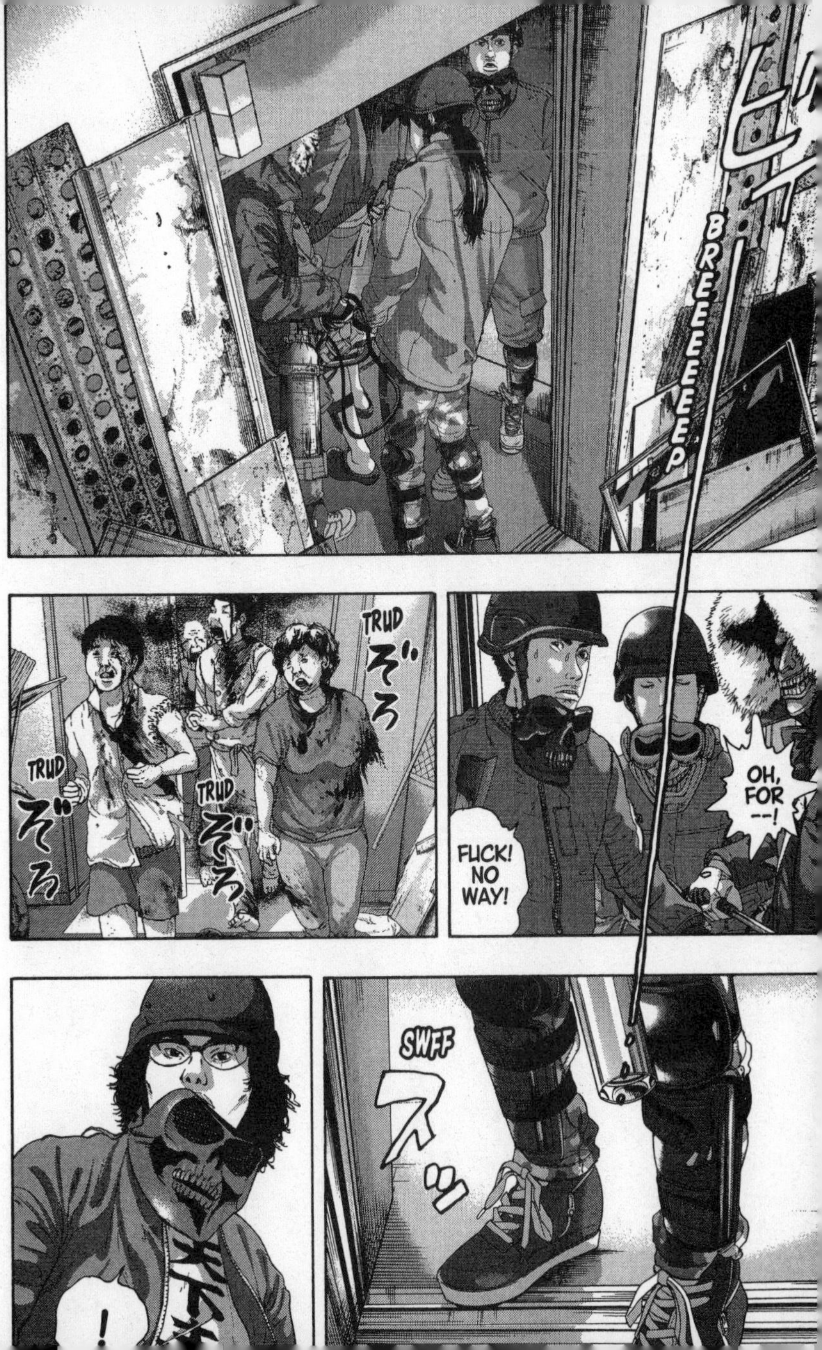

ビー
BREEEEEEEP
OH, FOR --!
FUCK! NO WAY!
TRUD
ぞろ
TRUD
ぞろ
TRUD
ぞろ
SWFF
スッ
!

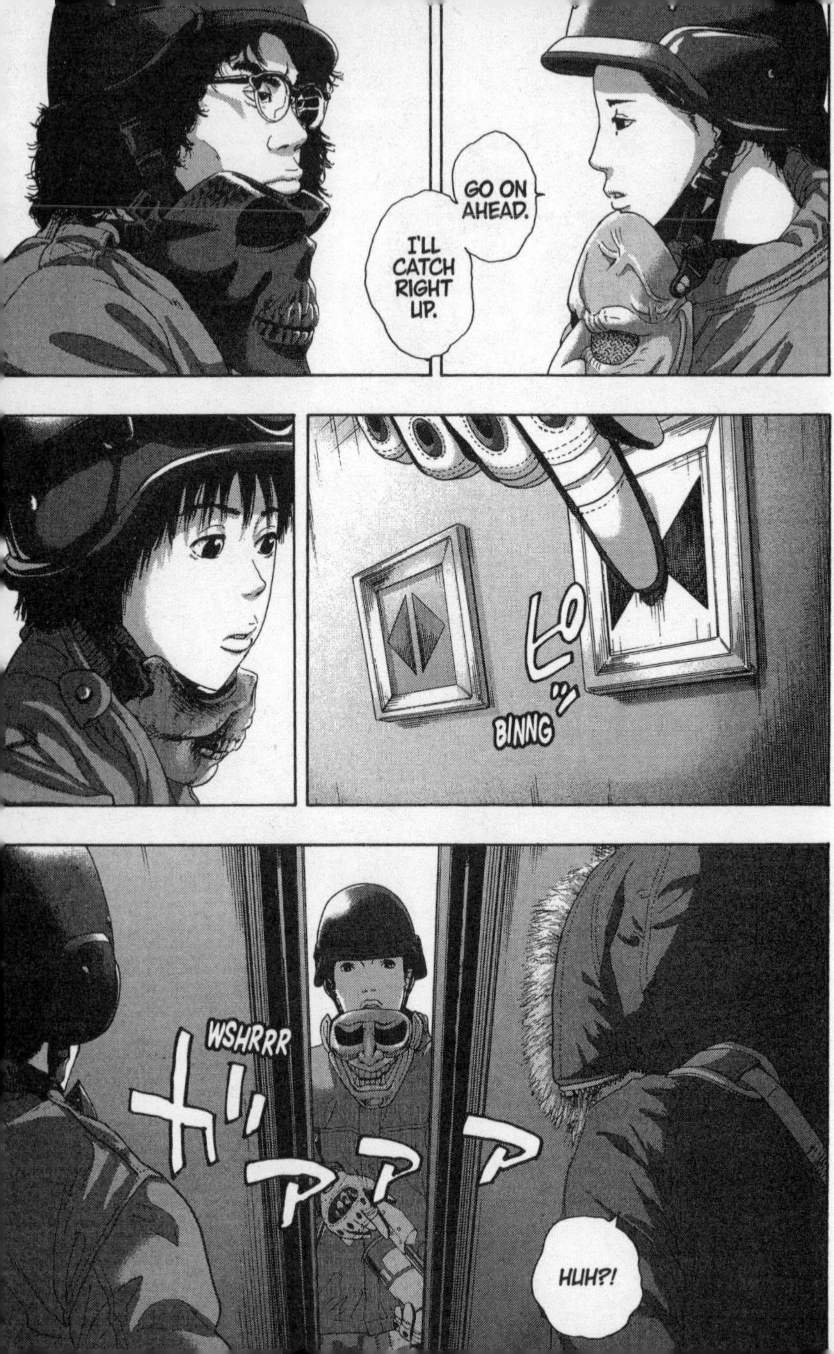
GO ON AHEAD.
I'LL CATCH RIGHT UP.
ピッ
BINNG
WSHRRR
HUH?!

...

FWOOM
ゴォーン

FWOOM
ゴォーン

FWOOM
ゴォ.

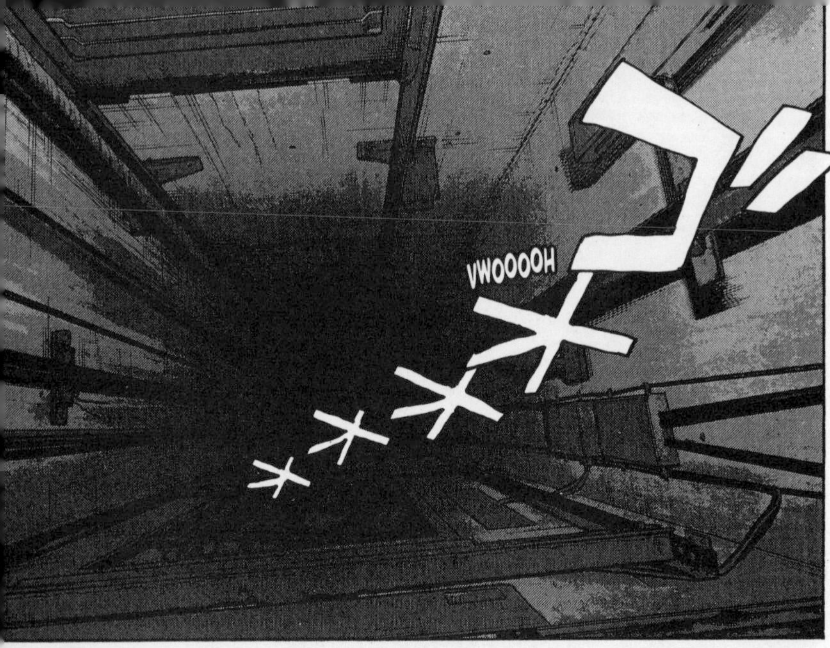
VWOOOOH

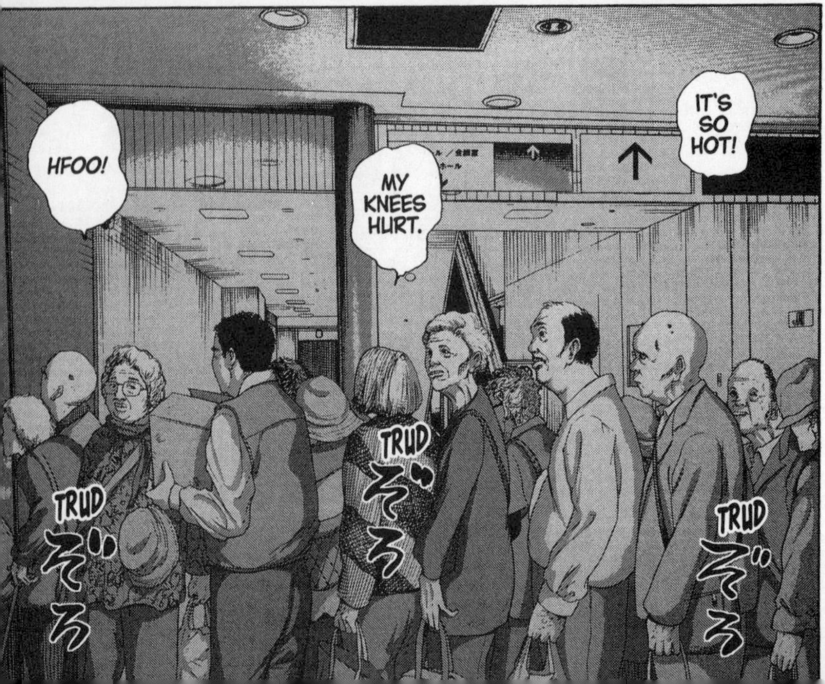
IT'S SO HOT!
MY KNEES HURT.
HFOO!
TRUD
TRUD
TRUD

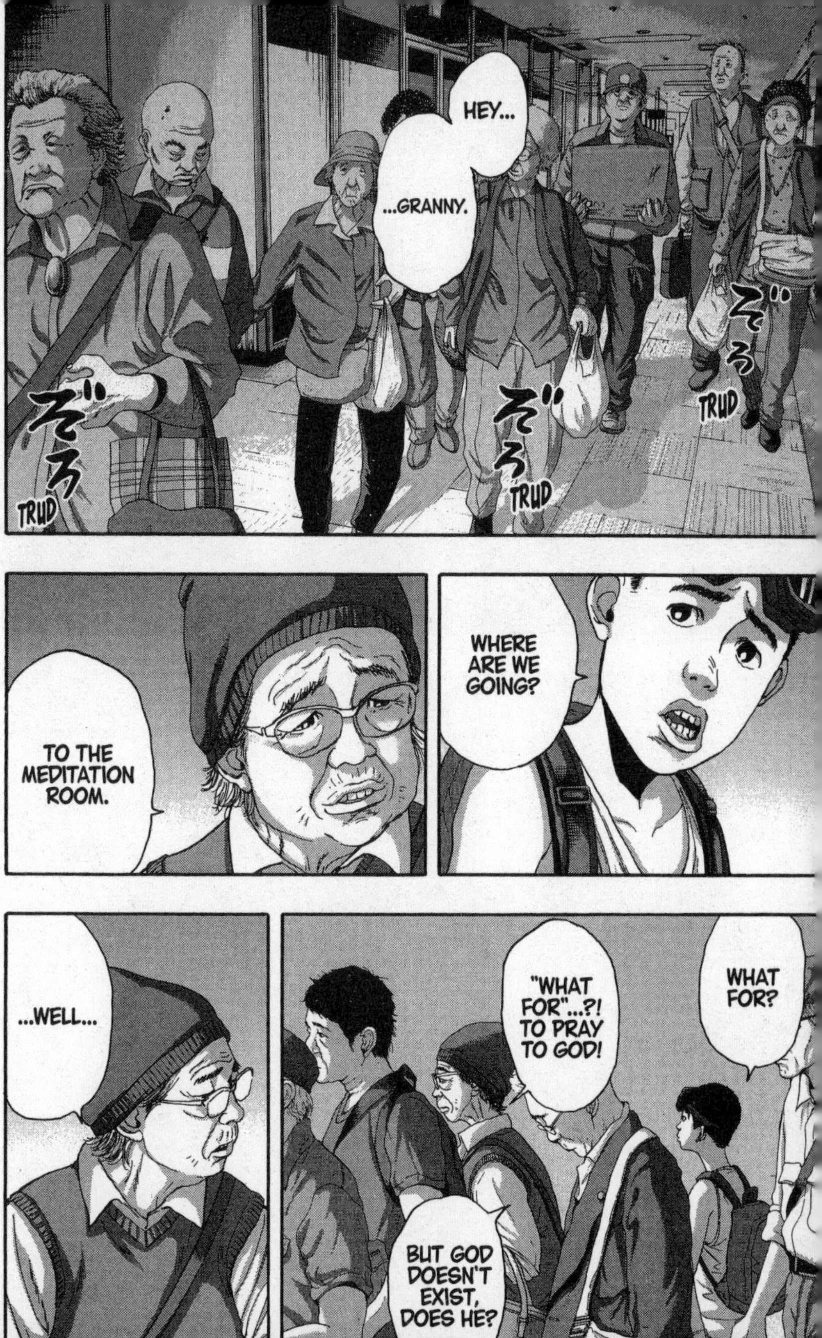
HEY...
...GRANNY.
ぞろ
TRUD
ぞろ
TRUD
ぞろ
TRUD
WHERE ARE WE GOING?
TO THE MEDITATION ROOM.
WHAT FOR?
"WHAT FOR"...?! TO PRAY TO GOD!
BUT GOD DOESN'T EXIST, DOES HE?
...WELL...

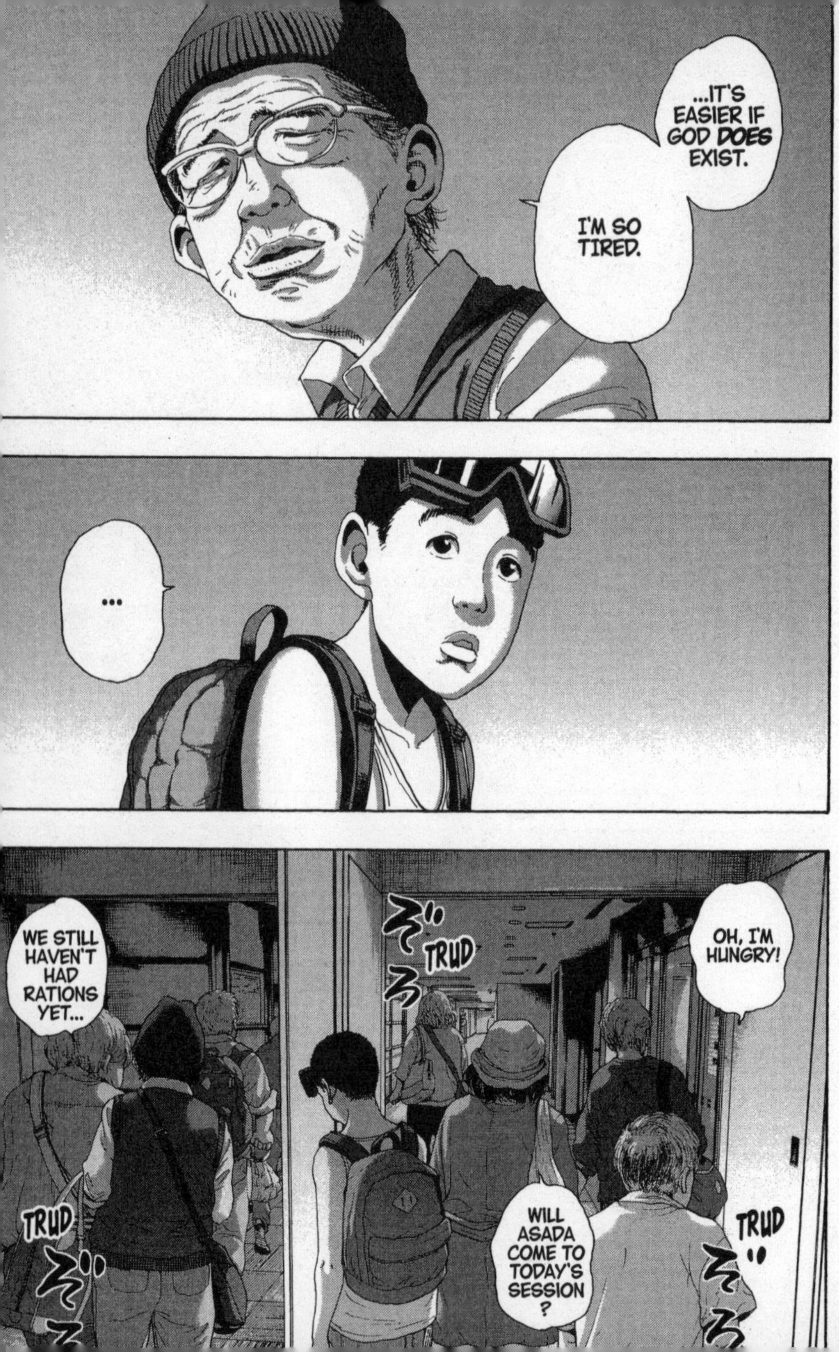
...IT'S EASIER IF GOD DOES EXIST.
I'M SO TIRED.
...
OH, I'M HUNGRY!
TRUD
ぞろ
WILL ASADA COME TO TODAY'S SESSION ?
TRUD
ぞろ
WE STILL HAVEN'T HAD RATIONS YET...
TRUD
ぞろ

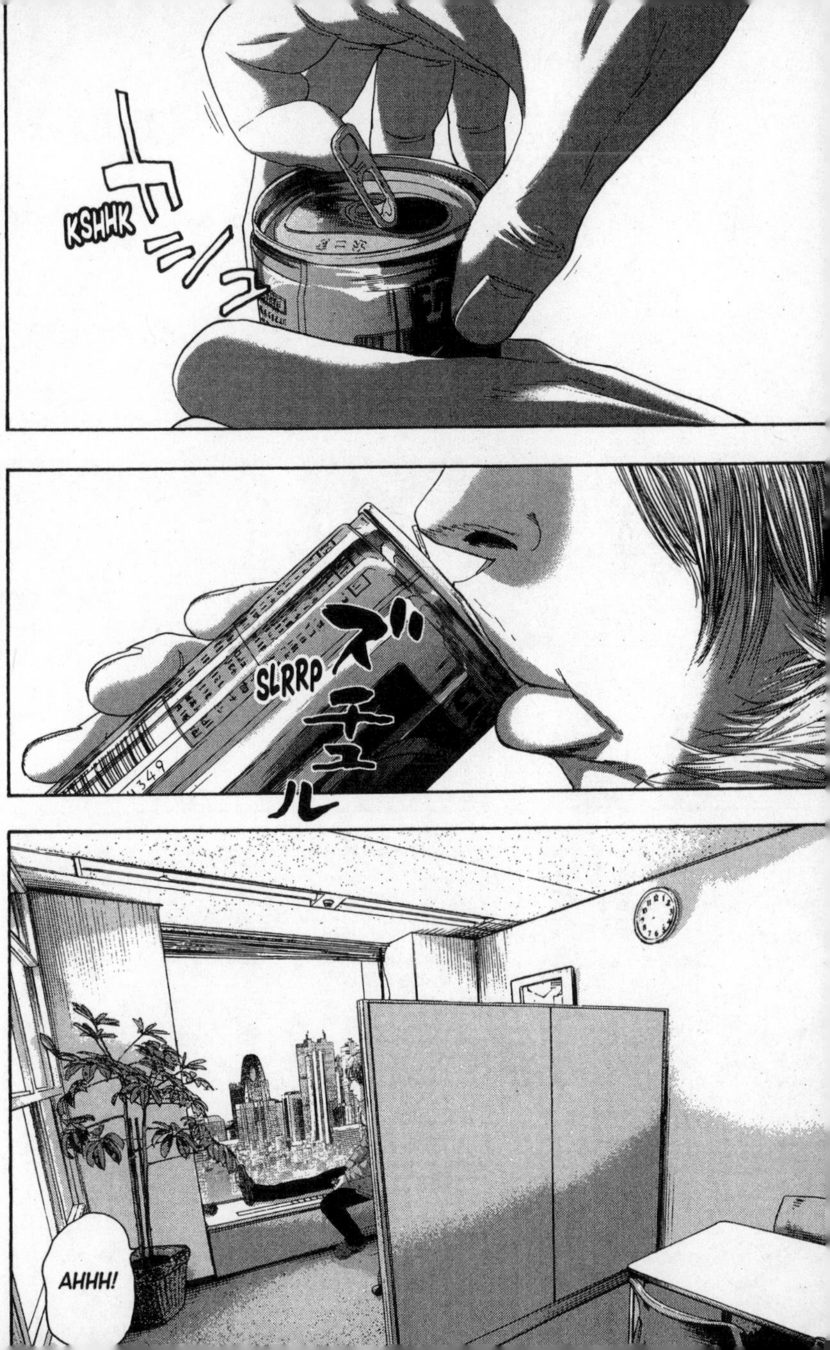
KSHHK
SLRRP
ズチュル
AHHH!

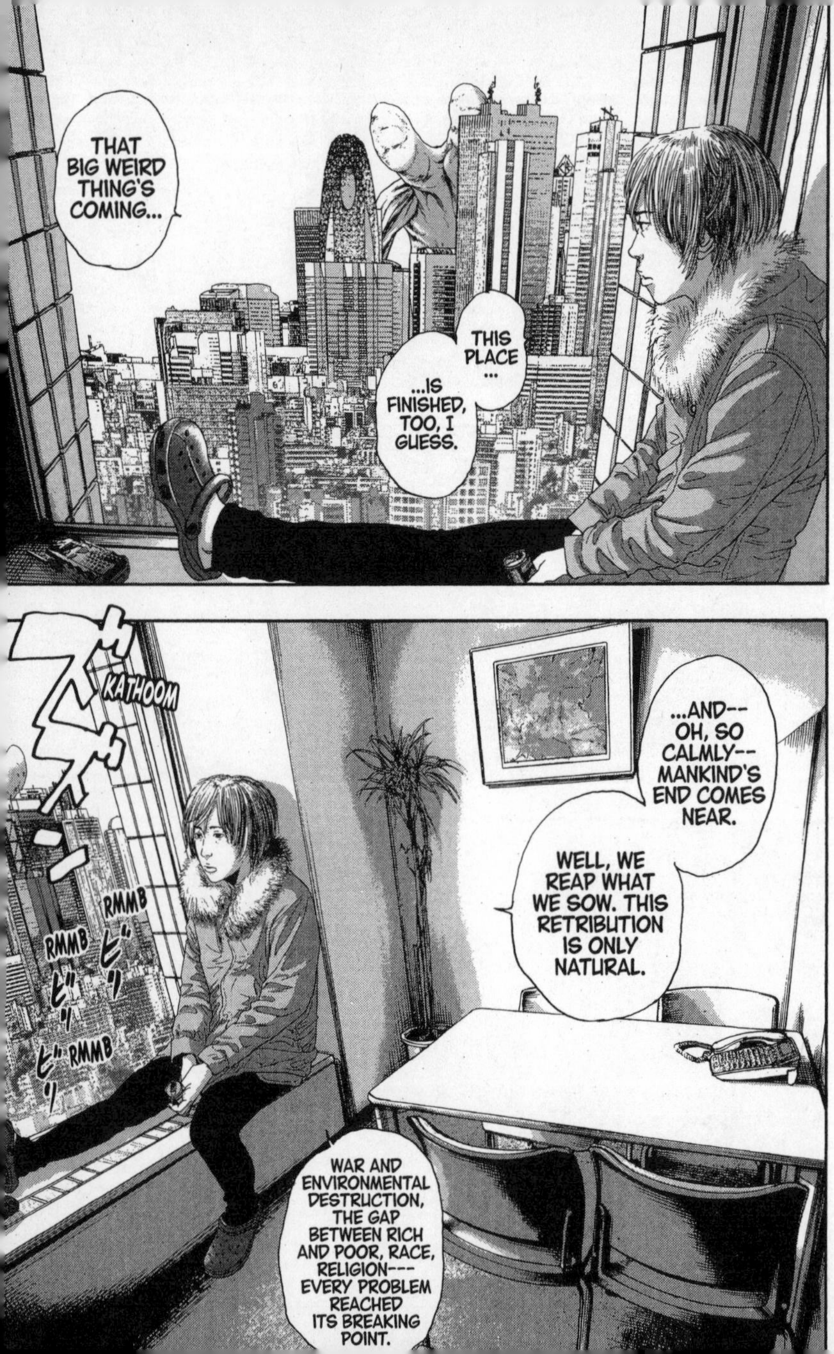
THAT BIG WEIRD THING'S COMING...
THIS PLACE ...
...IS FINISHED, TOO, I GUESS.
...AND-- OH, SO CALMLY-- MANKIND'S END COMES NEAR.
WELL, WE REAP WHAT WE SOW. THIS RETRIBUTION IS ONLY NATURAL.
KATHOOM
RMMB
RMMB
RMMB
WAR AND ENVIRONMENTAL DESTRUCTION, THE GAP BETWEEN RICH AND POOR, RACE, RELIGION--- EVERY PROBLEM REACHED ITS BREAKING POINT.

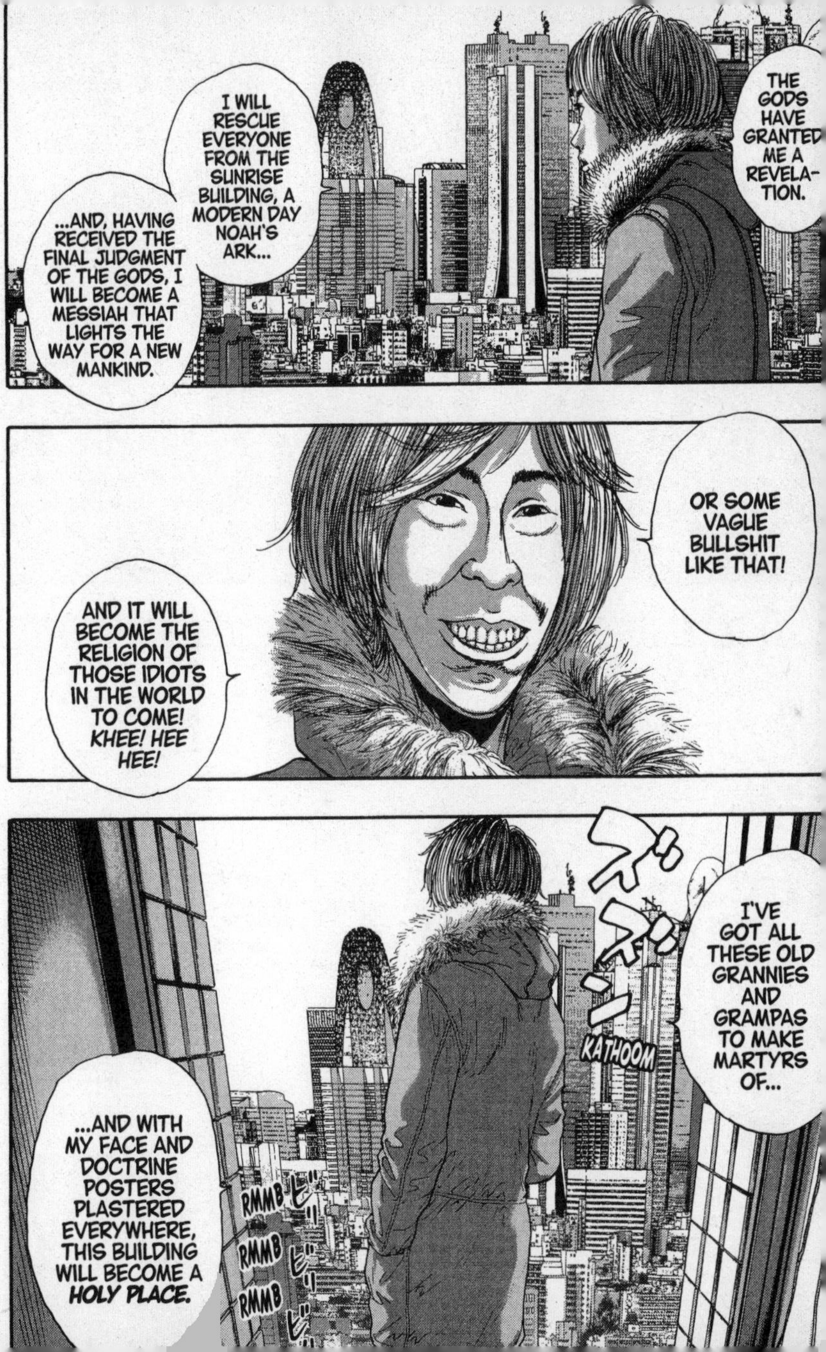
THE GODS HAVE GRANTED ME A REVELATION.
I WILL RESCUE EVERYONE FROM THE SUNRISE BUILDING, A MODERN DAY NOAH'S ARK...
...AND, HAVING RECEIVED THE FINAL JUDGMENT OF THE GODS, I WILL BECOME A MESSIAH THAT LIGHTS THE WAY FOR A NEW MANKIND.
OR SOME VAGUE BULLSHIT LIKE THAT!
AND IT WILL BECOME THE RELIGION OF THOSE IDIOTS IN THE WORLD TO COME! KHEE! HEE HEE!
ズズン
KATHOOM
I'VE GOT ALL THESE OLD GRANNIES AND GRAMPAS TO MAKE MARTYRS OF...
...AND WITH MY FACE AND DOCTRINE POSTERS PLASTERED EVERYWHERE, THIS BUILDING WILL BECOME A *HOLY PLACE.*
RMMB
RMMB
RMMB

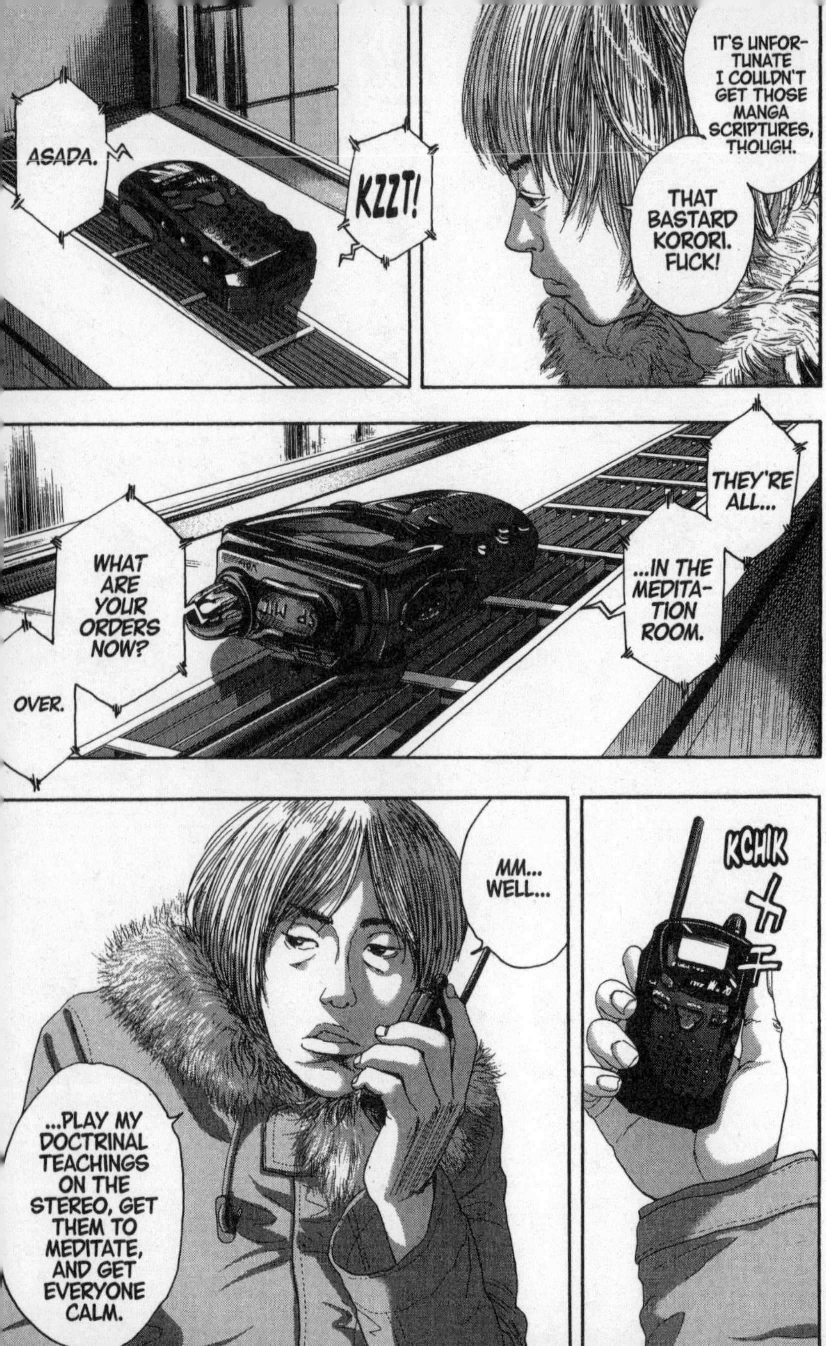
IT'S UNFORTUNATE I COULDN'T GET THOSE MANGA SCRIPTURES, THOUGH.
THAT BASTARD KORORI. FUCK!
KZZT!
ASADA.
THEY'RE ALL...
...IN THE MEDITATION ROOM.
WHAT ARE YOUR ORDERS NOW?
OVER.
KCHIK
MM... WELL...
...PLAY MY DOCTRINAL TEACHINGS ON THE STEREO, GET THEM TO MEDITATE, AND GET EVERYONE CALM.

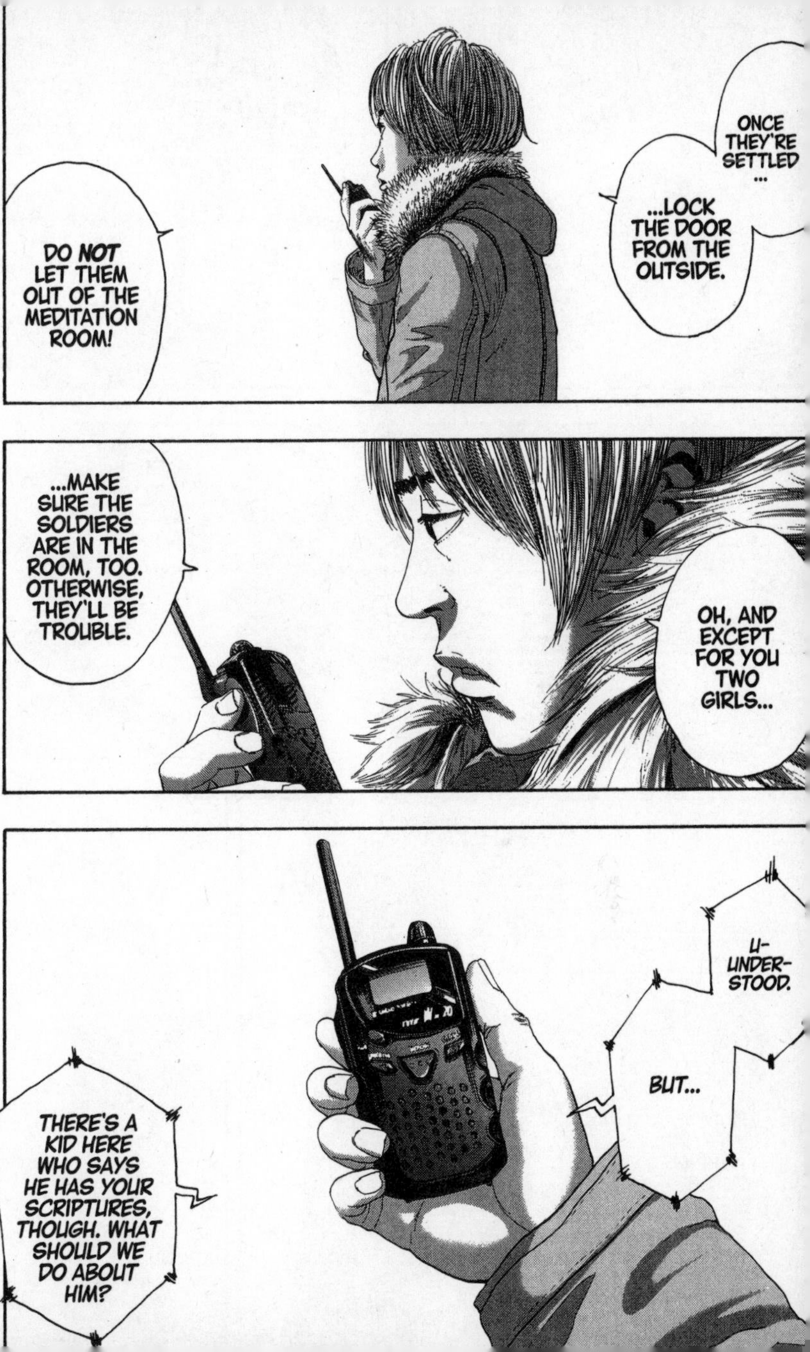
ONCE THEY'RE SETTLED ...
...LOCK THE DOOR FROM THE OUTSIDE.
DO **NOT** LET THEM OUT OF THE MEDITATION ROOM!
OH, AND EXCEPT FOR YOU TWO GIRLS...
...MAKE SURE THE SOLDIERS ARE IN THE ROOM, TOO. OTHERWISE, THEY'LL BE TROUBLE.
U-UNDERSTOOD.
BUT...
THERE'S A KID HERE WHO SAYS HE HAS YOUR SCRIPTURES, THOUGH. WHAT SHOULD WE DO ABOUT HIM?

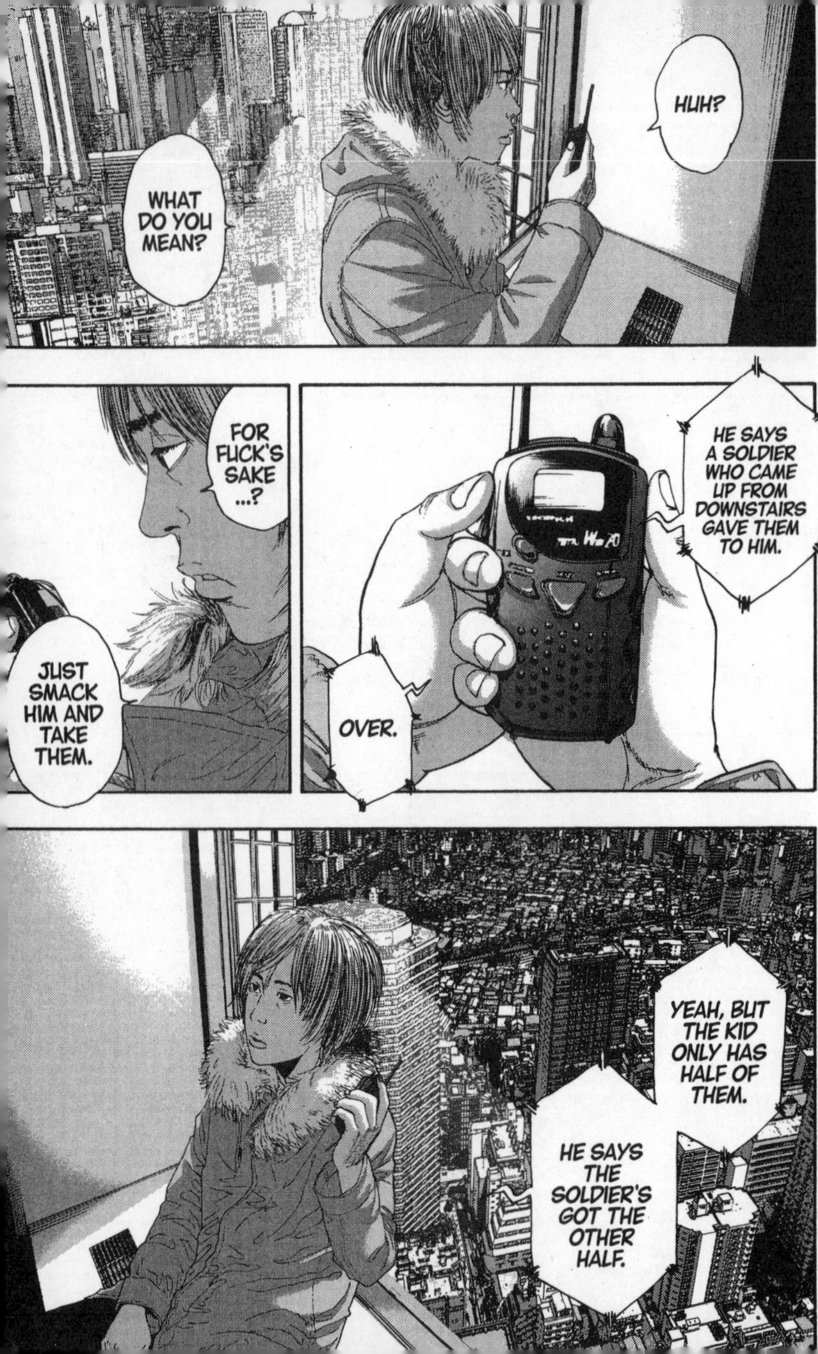
HUH?
WHAT DO YOU MEAN?
HE SAYS A SOLDIER WHO CAME UP FROM DOWNSTAIRS GAVE THEM TO HIM.
OVER.
FOR FUCK'S SAKE ...?
JUST SMACK HIM AND TAKE THEM.
YEAH, BUT THE KID ONLY HAS HALF OF THEM.
HE SAYS THE SOLDIER'S GOT THE OTHER HALF.

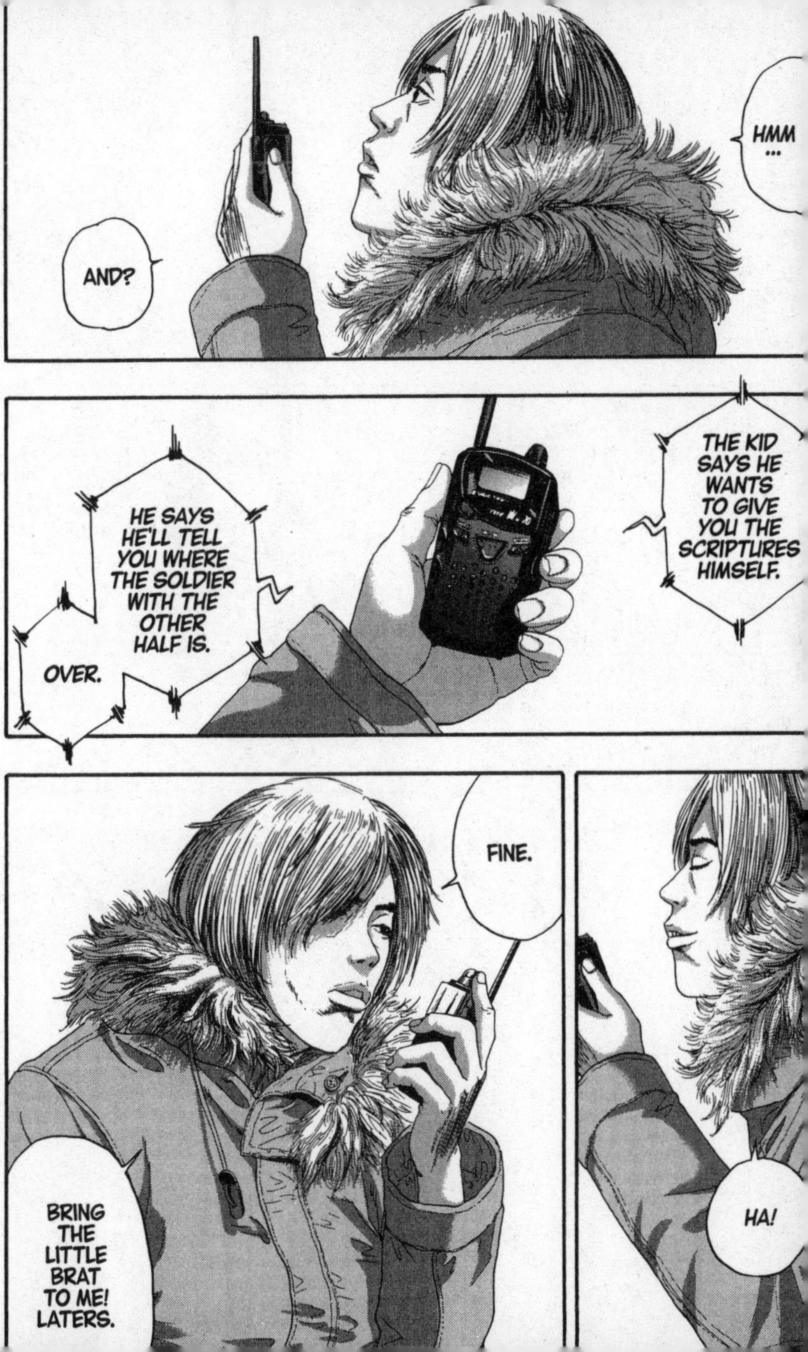
HMM ...
AND?
THE KID SAYS HE WANTS TO GIVE YOU THE SCRIPTURES HIMSELF.
HE SAYS HE'LL TELL YOU WHERE THE SOLDIER WITH THE OTHER HALF IS.
OVER.
HA!
FINE.
BRING THE LITTLE BRAT TO ME! LATERS.

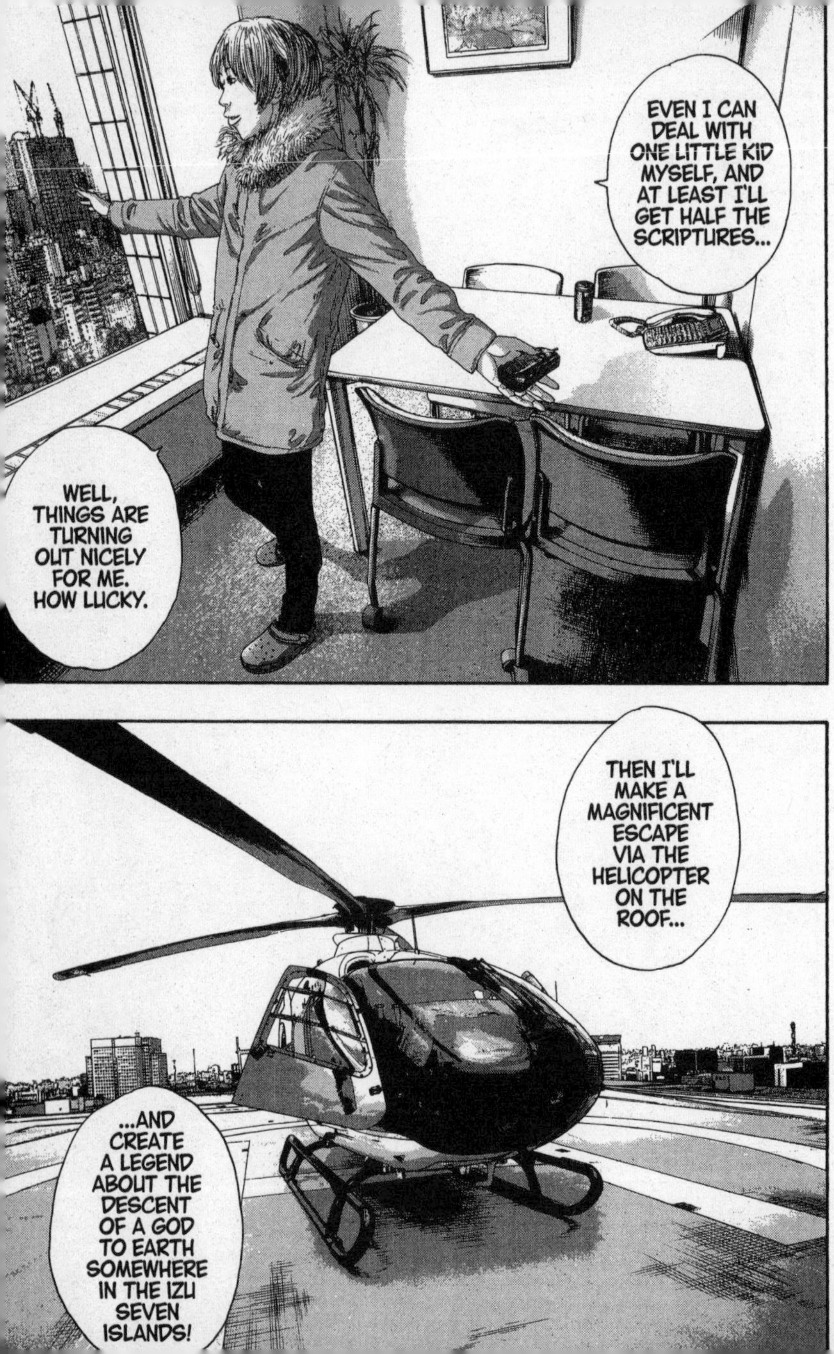
EVEN I CAN DEAL WITH ONE LITTLE KID MYSELF, AND AT LEAST I'LL GET HALF THE SCRIPTURES...
WELL, THINGS ARE TURNING OUT NICELY FOR ME. HOW LUCKY.
THEN I'LL MAKE A MAGNIFICENT ESCAPE VIA THE HELICOPTER ON THE ROOF...
...AND CREATE A LEGEND ABOUT THE DESCENT OF A GOD TO EARTH SOMEWHERE IN THE IZU SEVEN ISLANDS!

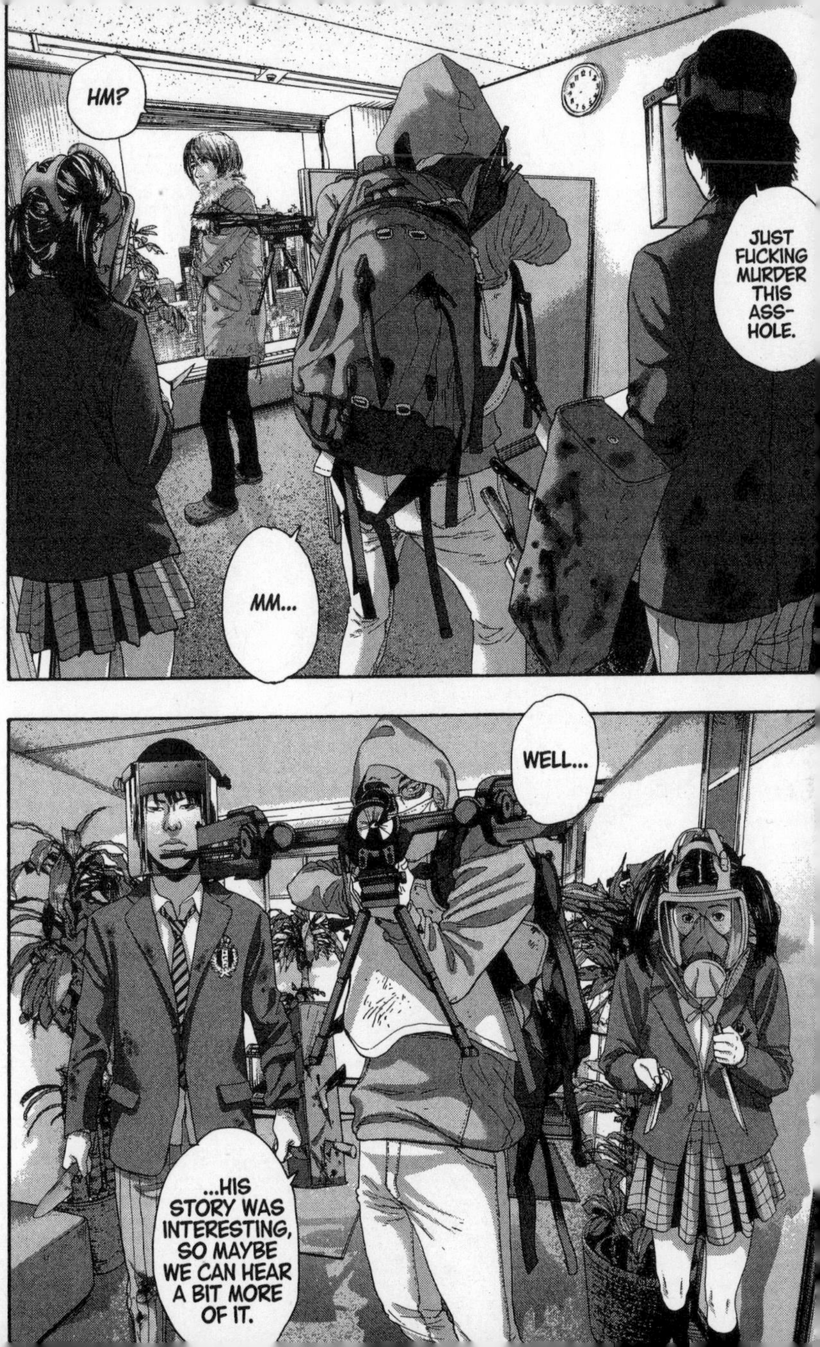
JUST FUCKING MURDER THIS ASS-HOLE.
HM?
MM...
WELL...
...HIS STORY WAS INTERESTING, SO MAYBE WE CAN HEAR A BIT MORE OF IT.

I AM A HERO

TRANSLATION NOTES

CHAPTER 217

This strange chapter takes place in Barcelona, Spain, as "the observer" talks to himself. When he refers the Olympic Stadium, he's talking about Barcelona's Estadi Olímpic Lluís Companys, which hosted the Summer Olympic Games and the Paralympic Games in 1992.

The Temple Expiatori de la Sagrada Família is an unfinished church in Barcelona, designed by Antoni Gaudí.

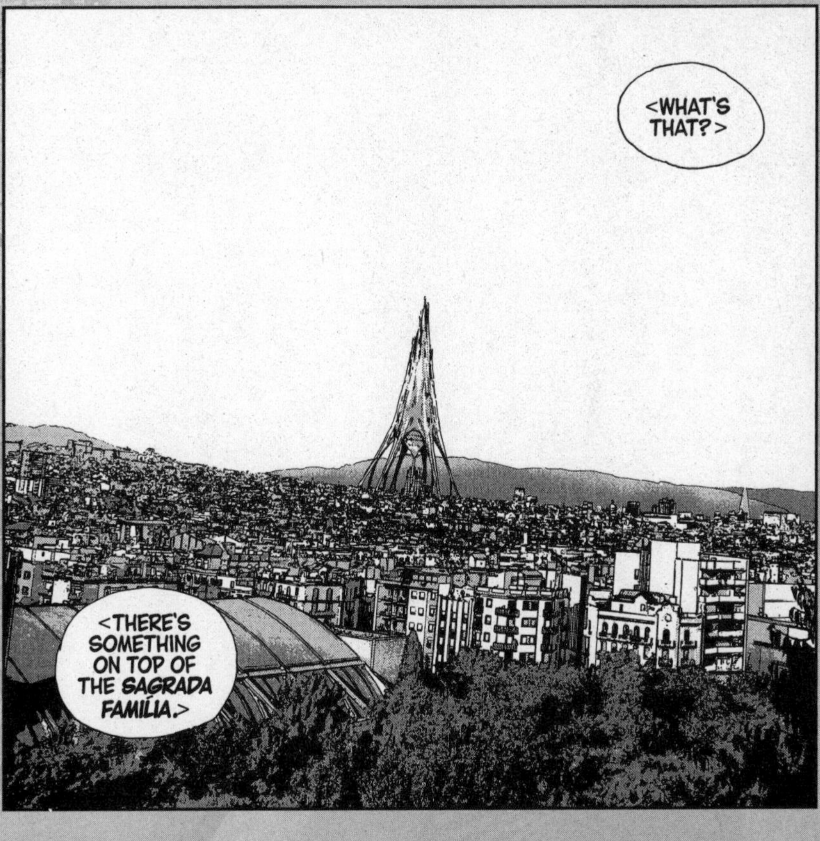
<WHAT'S THAT?>
<THERE'S SOMETHING ON TOP OF THE SAGRADA FAMÍLIA.>

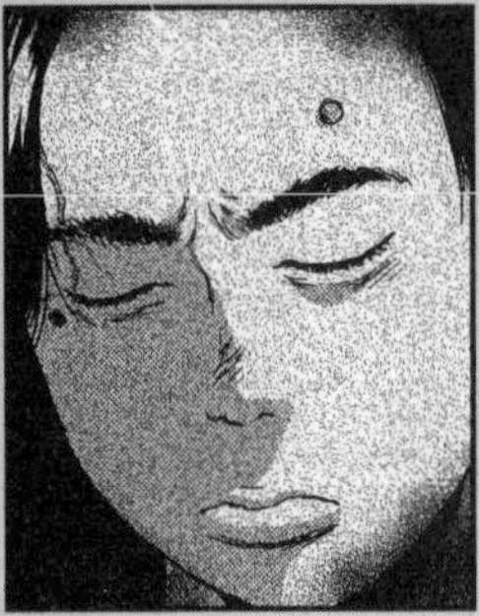

CHAPTER 221

Hiromi says, "So, then, when she took the nail out, the rush of feelings came back." Hiromi was bitten by a ZQN baby and almost went full ZQN before being shot in the head with a crossbow bolt in chapter 77, as shown in *I Am a Hero Omnibus* Volume 4. Later, in chapter 111 (*I Am a Hero Omnibus* Volume 5), the bolt is pulled out of her head, and Hiromi makes a miraculous recovery as a human-ZQN hybrid.

CHAPTER 223

Tomabechi mentions the "Sunshine Building," which is a fictional substitute for Tokyo's Sunshine 60—a sixty-story mixed-use skyscraper, which includes stores, restaurants, a post office, cafeterias, a medical center, and many office spaces. It is also one of the tallest buildings in Japan.

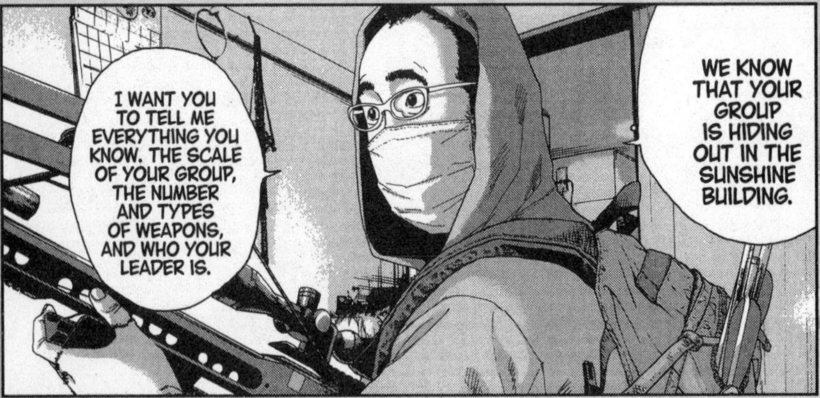
WE KNOW THAT YOUR GROUP IS HIDING OUT IN THE SUNSHINE BUILDING.
I WANT YOU TO TELL ME EVERYTHING YOU KNOW. THE SCALE OF YOUR GROUP, THE NUMBER AND TYPES OF WEAPONS, AND WHO YOUR LEADER IS.

CHAPTER 224

In Japanese hot spring baths and public bathhouses, visitors are supposed to scrub up at the taps next to the bath, exactly as seen here. This is done *before* someone gets into the main bath, so the shared water stays clean. The "bath" itself is really for relaxing in. Since there is no running water, Seto and Nakata have scooped water out of the main bath for their pre-bath scrubbing.

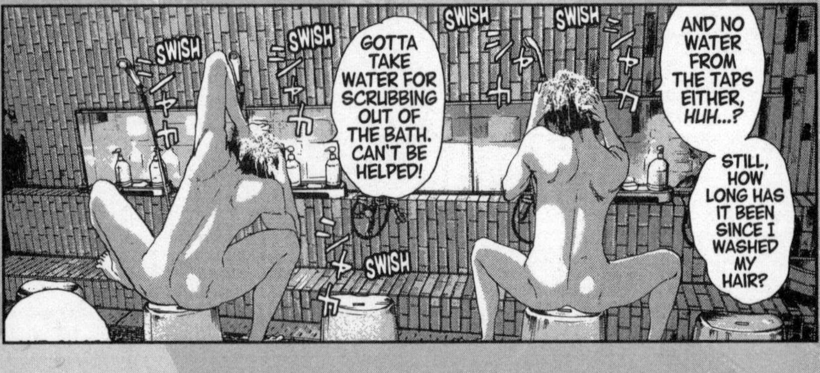
AND NO WATER FROM THE TAPS EITHER, HUH...?
STILL, HOW LONG HAS IT BEEN SINCE I WASHED MY HAIR?
SWISH
SWISH
GOTTA TAKE WATER FOR SCRUBBING OUT OF THE BATH. CAN'T BE HELPED!
SWISH
SWISH
SWISH

"I feel like I've heard your voice before." Auntie recognizes manga artist and accidental leader Nakata Korori from his voice, which she heard over a CB radio in *I Am a Hero Omnibus* Volume 6. "Captain Korori" was a successful manga artist before the ZQN outbreak, and he used to date Tetsuko "Tekko" Kurokawa. At the start of *I Am a Hero Omnibus* Volume 1, Tetsuko has broken up with Korori and is already dating Hideo Suzuki.

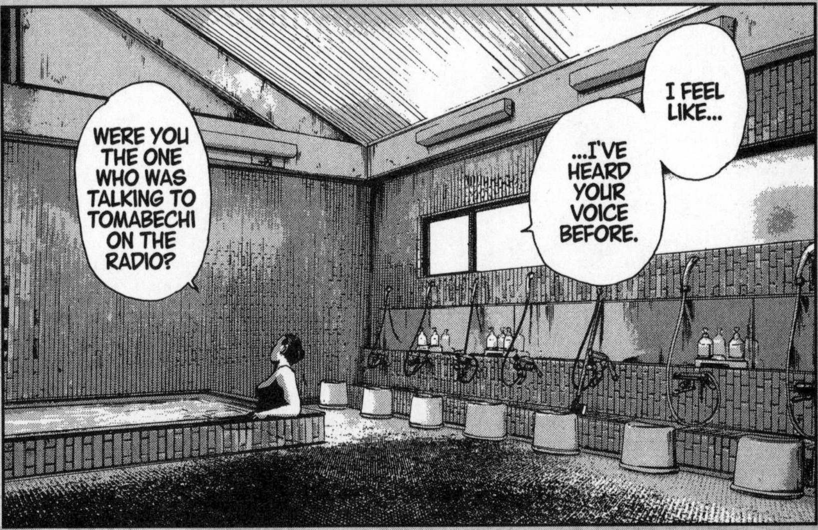
I FEEL LIKE...
...I'VE HEARD YOUR VOICE BEFORE.
WERE YOU THE ONE WHO WAS TALKING TO TOMABECHI ON THE RADIO?

CHAPTER 226

The "word chain game" that opens this chapter is a version of a popular name game called *shiritori*. If you've read this far along, you know that this game is used often when survivors greet each other. This is a word game in which players basically think up words that begin with the letter or letters that a previous player's word ends with. Going back and forth between players, the "Freddie Mercury" captain in this scene hopes to catch and stop anyone who's showing signs of infection and can't think fast enough or loses their train of thought easily. Those who stumble during the word chain game could be infected. The captain in this scene uses "weapon" to start the game, so "now"—a word that starts with an "n"—is used to begin Kiritani's response sentence.

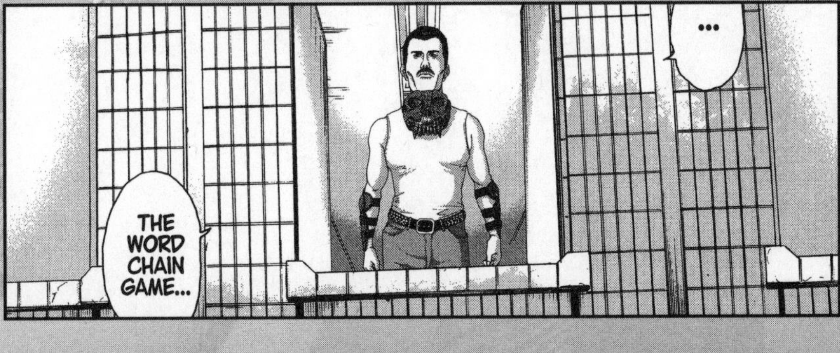
...
THE WORD CHAIN GAME...

CHAPTER 236

Mount Nishi, one of Hachijo's two main mountains, is commonly referred to as "Hachijo Fuji" because it looks like Mount Fuji.

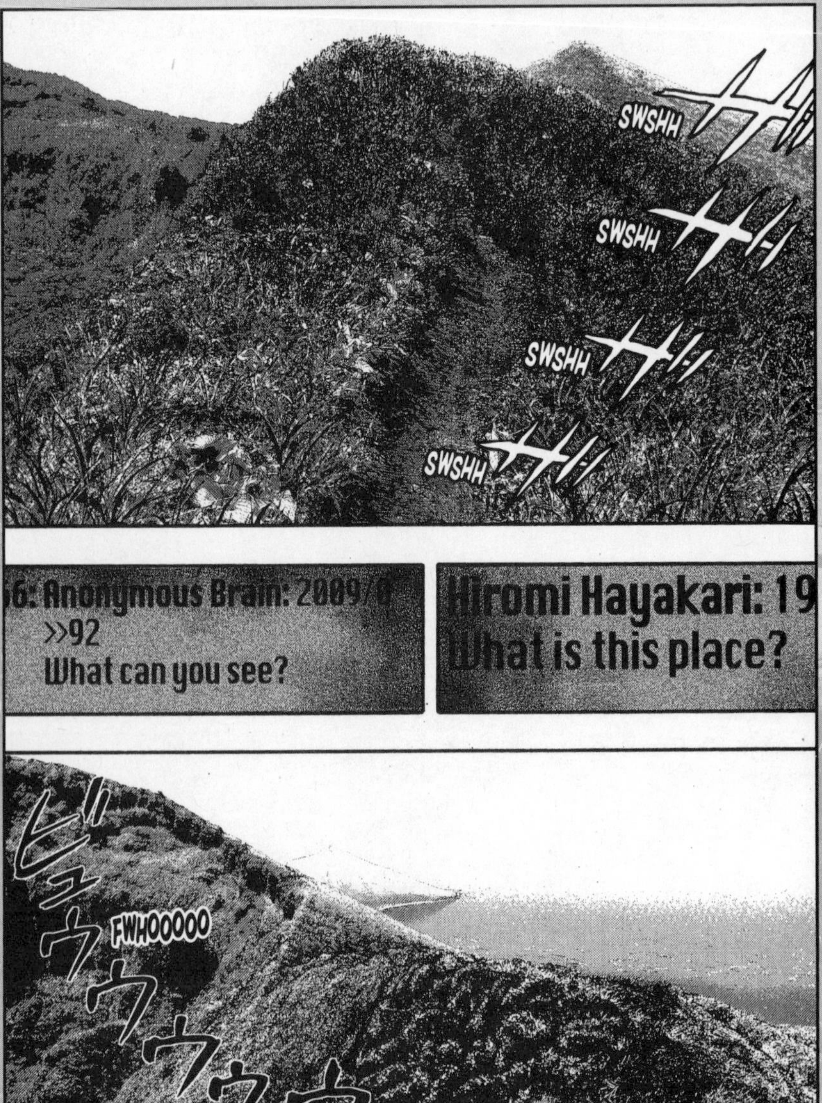
SWSHH
SWSHH
SWSHH
SWSHH
Hiromi Hayakari: 19
What is this place?
6: Anonymous Brain: 2009/0
>>92
What can you see?
ビュウウウウ
FWHOOOOO

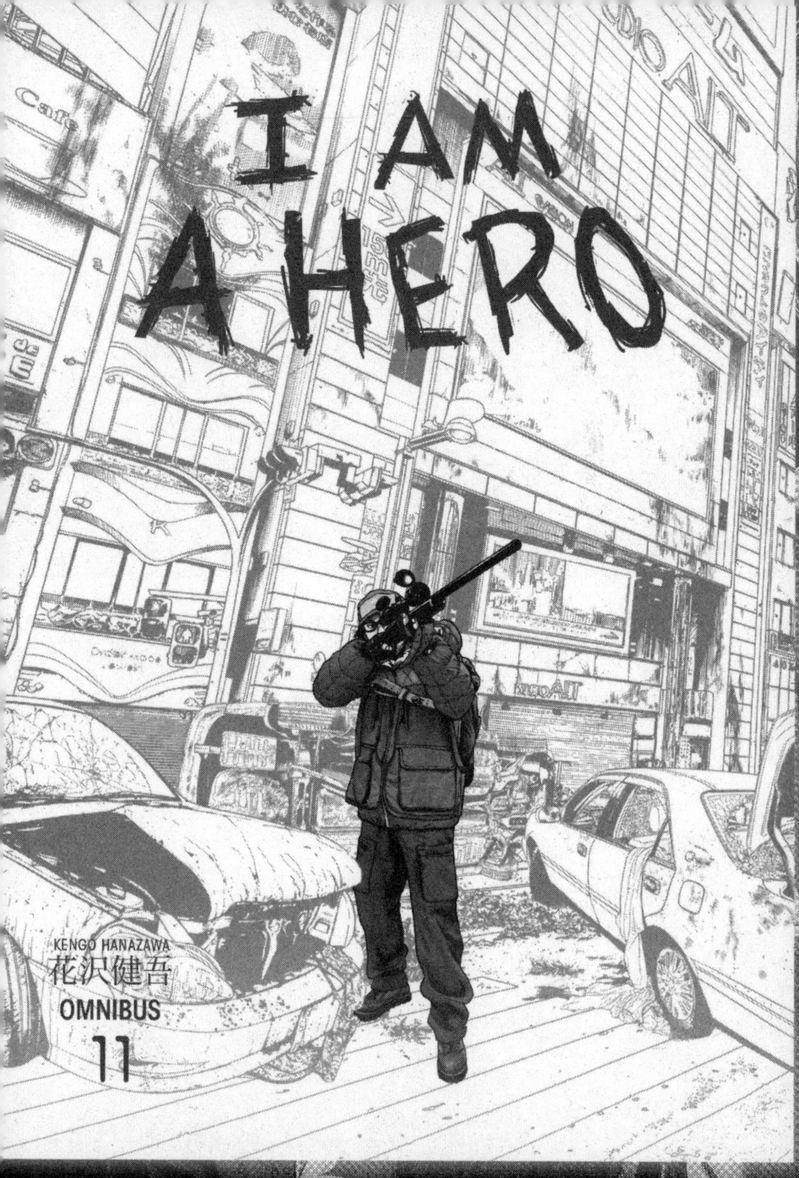
I AM
A HERO
KENGO HANAZAWA
花沢健吾
OMNIBUS
11

I AM A HERO

OMNIBUS 11—COMING SOON!

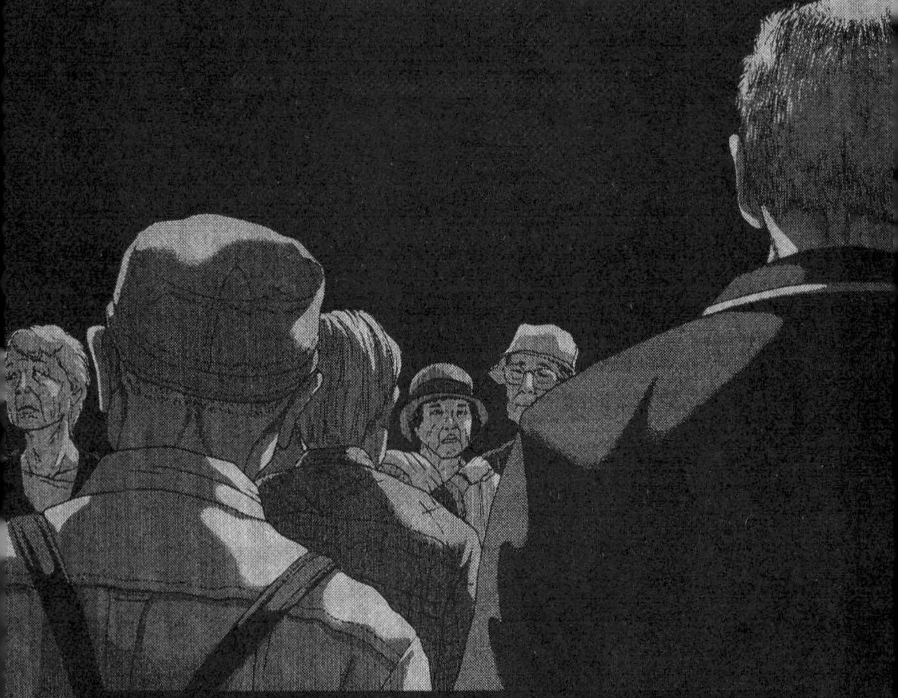

THE GENRE'S STRANGEST ZOMBIE APOCALYPSE!

Final volume! It's the end of humanity as we know it—but are you a part of the zombie-human hive mind or about to die outside of it? With Hiromi absorbed into a huge, mobile ZQN nest, will Hideo be able to extract her or will he seal his death warrant with his ignorance and hasty choices? Humanity has a very slim chance for survival. See how several groups of survivors get it all wrong and possibly end the human race! Go way further and get way stranger than the *I Am a Hero* film adaptation in this final omnibus volume!

I AM
A HERO

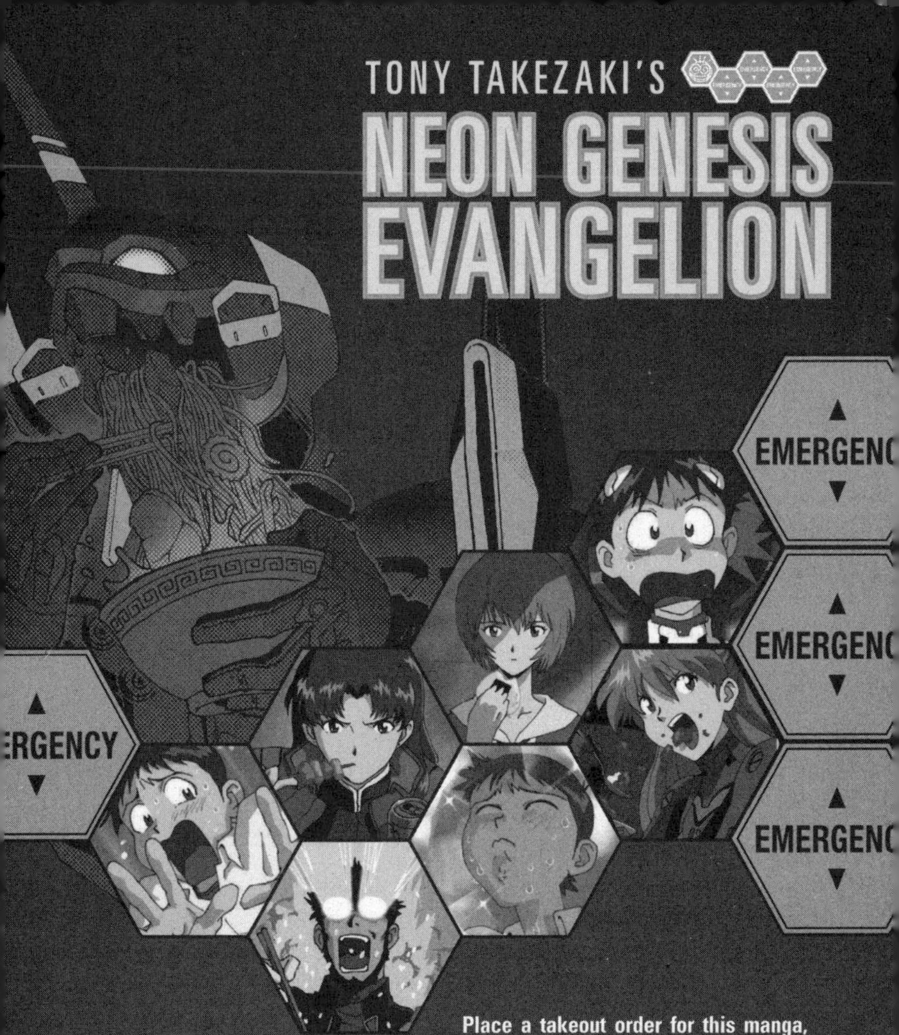
TONY TAKEZAKI'S
NEON GENESIS EVANGELION
EMERGENCY
EMERGENC
EMERGENC
EMERGENC
RGENCY

YASUHIRO NIGHTOW 内藤泰弘
TRIGUN

On the forbidding desert planet of Gunsmoke, a sixty-billion-double-dollar bounty hangs over the head of Vash the Stampede, a pistol-packing pacifist with a weapon capable of punching holes in a planet. Every trigger-happy psycho in creation is aiming to claim Vash dead or alive—preferably dead!—and although Vash is an avowed pacifist, he won't go down without a fight. And when Vash fights, destruction is sure to follow!

TRIGUN OMNIBUS
ISBN 978-1-61655-246-6
$19.99

TRIGUN MAXIMUM OMNIBUS
VOLUME 1: ISBN 978-1-61655-010-3
VOLUME 2: ISBN 978-1-61655-329-6
VOLUME 3: ISBN 978-1-61655-012-7
VOLUME 4: ISBN 978-1-61655-013-4
VOLUME 5: ISBN 978-1-61655-086-8
$19.99 each

TRIGUN: MULTIPLE BULLETS
ISBN 978-1-61655-105-6
$13.99

DARK HORSE MANGA

DarkHorse.com

AVAILABLE AT YOUR LOCAL COMICS SHOP OR BOOKSTORE
TO FIND A COMICS SHOP IN YOUR AREA, VISIT COMICSHOPLOCATOR.COM

For more information or to order direct: On the web: DarkHorse.com
E-mail: mailorder@darkhorse.com
Phone: 1-800-862-0052 Mon.–Fri. 9 a.m. to 5 p.m. Pacific Time.

Created by Kentaro Miura, *Berserk* is manga mayhem to the extreme—violent, horrifying, and mercilessly funny—and the wellspring for the internationally popular anime series. Not for the squeamish or the easily offended, *Berserk* asks for no quarter—and offers none!

Presented uncensored in the original Japanese format!

VOLUME 1
ISBN 978-1-59307-020-5

VOLUME 2
ISBN 978-1-59307-021-2

VOLUME 3
ISBN 978-1-59307-022-9

VOLUME 4
ISBN 978-1-59307-203-2

VOLUME 5
ISBN 978-1-59307-251-3

VOLUME 6
ISBN 978-1-59307-252-0

VOLUME 7
ISBN 978-1-59307-328-2

VOLUME 8
ISBN 978-1-59307-329-9

VOLUME 9
ISBN 978-1-59307-330-5

VOLUME 10
ISBN 978-1-59307-331-2

VOLUME 11
ISBN 978-1-59307-470-8

VOLUME 12
ISBN 978-1-59307-484-5

VOLUME 13
ISBN 978-1-59307-500-2

VOLUME 14
ISBN 978-1-59307-501-9

VOLUME 15
ISBN 978-1-59307-577-4

VOLUME 16
ISBN 978-1-59307-706-8

VOLUME 17
ISBN 978-1-59307-742-6

VOLUME 18
ISBN 978-1-59307-743-3

VOLUME 19
ISBN 978-1-59307-744-0

VOLUME 20
ISBN 978-1-59307-745-7

VOLUME 21
ISBN 978-1-59307-746-4

VOLUME 22
ISBN 978-1-59307-863-8

VOLUME 23
ISBN 978-1-59307-864-5

VOLUME 24
ISBN 978-1-59307-865-2

VOLUME 25
ISBN 978-1-59307-921-5

VOLUME 26
ISBN 978-1-59307-922-2

VOLUME 27
ISBN 978-1-59307-923-9

VOLUME 28
ISBN 978-1-59582-209-3

VOLUME 29
ISBN 978-1-59582-210-9

VOLUME 30
ISBN 978-1-59582-211-6

VOLUME 31
ISBN 978-1-59582-366-3

VOLUME 32
ISBN 978-1-59582-367-0

VOLUME 33
ISBN 978-1-59582-372-4

VOLUME 34
ISBN 978-1-59582-532-2

VOLUME 35
ISBN 978-1-59582-695-4

VOLUME 36
ISBN 978-1-59582-942-9

VOLUME 37
ISBN 978-1-61655-205-3

VOLUME 38
ISBN 978-1-50670-398-5

VOLUME 39
ISBN 978-1-50670-708-2

BERSERK OFFICIAL GUIDEBOOK
ISBN 978-1-50670-706-8

BERSERK: THE FLAME DRAGON KNIGHT
Written by Matoko Fukami and Kentaro Miura
ISBN 978-1-50670-939-0

$14.99 EACH!

AVAILABLE AT YOUR LOCAL COMICS SHOP OR BOOKSTORE
To find a comics shop near your area, visit comicshoplocator.com. For more information or to order direct: On the web: darkhorse.com | E-mail: mailorder@darkhorse.com | Phone: 1-800-862-0052 Mon.–Fri. 9 a.m. to 5 p.m. Pacific Time.

DARK HORSE MANGA

DARKHORSE.COM

GANTZ

HIROYA OKU Works.

The last thing Kei and Masaru remember was being struck dead by a subway train while saving the life of a drunken bum. What a waste! And yet somehow they're still alive. Or semi-alive? Maybe reanimated . . . by some kind of mysterious orb! And this orb called "Gantz" intends to make them play games of death, hunting all kinds of odd aliens, along with a bunch of other ordinary citizens who've recently met a tragic semi-end. The missions they embark upon are often dangerous. Many die—and die again. This dark and action-packed manga deals with the moral conflicts of violence, teenage sexual confusion and angst, and our fascination with death.

Dark Horse is proud to deliver one of the most requested manga ever to be released. Hang on to your gear and keep playing the game, whatever you do; *Gantz* is unrelenting!

VOLUME ONE
ISBN 978-1-59307-949-9

VOLUME TWO
ISBN 978-1-59582-188-1

VOLUME THREE
ISBN 978-1-59582-232-1

VOLUME FOUR
ISBN 978-1-59582-250-5

VOLUME FIVE
ISBN 978-1-59582-301-4

VOLUME SIX
ISBN 978-1-59582-320-5

VOLUME SEVEN
ISBN 978-1-59582-373-1

VOLUME EIGHT
ISBN 978-1-59582-383-0

VOLUME NINE
ISBN 978-1-59582-452-3

VOLUME TEN
ISBN 978-1-59582-459-2

VOLUME ELEVEN
ISBN 978-1-59582-518-6

VOLUME TWELVE
ISBN 978-1-59582-526-1

VOLUME THIRTEEN
ISBN 978-1-59582-587-2

VOLUME FOURTEEN
ISBN 978-1-59582-598-8

VOLUME FIFTEEN
ISBN 978-1-59582-662-6

VOLUME SIXTEEN
ISBN 978-1-59582-663-3

VOLUME SEVENTEEN
ISBN 978-1-59582-664-0

VOLUME EIGHTEEN
ISBN 978-1-59582-776-0

VOLUME NINETEEN
ISBN 978-1-59582-813-2

VOLUME TWENTY
ISBN 978-1-59582-846-0

VOLUME TWENTY-ONE
ISBN 978-1-59582-847-7

VOLUME TWENTY-TWO
ISBN 978-1-59582-848-4

VOLUME TWENTY-THREE
ISBN 978-1-59582-849-1

VOLUME TWENTY-FOUR
ISBN 978-1-59582-907-8

VOLUME TWENTY-FIVE
ISBN 978-1-59582-908-5

$12.99 EACH

VOLUME TWENTY-SIX
ISBN 978-1-61655-048-6

VOLUME TWENTY-SEVEN
ISBN 978-1-61655-049-3

VOLUME TWENTY-EIGHT
ISBN 978-1-61655-050-9

VOLUME TWENTY-NINE
ISBN 978-1-61655-150-6

VOLUME THIRTY
ISBN 978-1-61655-151-3

VOLUME THIRTY-ONE
ISBN 978-1-61655-152-0

VOLUME THIRTY-TWO
ISBN 978-1-61655-428-6

VOLUME THIRTY-THREE
ISBN 978-1-61655-429-3

VOLUME THIRTY-FOUR
ISBN 978-1-61655-573-3

VOLUME THIRTY-FIVE
ISBN 978-1-61655-586-3

VOLUME THIRTY-SIX
ISBN 978-1-61655-587-0

VOLUME THIRTY-SEVEN
ISBN 978-1-61655-588-7

$13.99 EACH

AVAILABLE AT YOUR LOCAL COMICS SHOP OR BOOKSTORE
TO FIND A COMICS SHOP IN YOUR AREA, VISIT COMICBOOKLOCATOR.COM

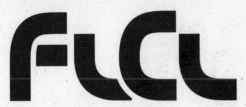

FLCL OMNIBUS

STORY BY GAINAX
ART BY HAJIME UEDA

FROM THE STUDIO THAT BROUGHT YOU *EVANGELION!*

The complete *FLCL* manga adaptation–now with bonus color illustrations and remastered story pages!

"This show will change your life."
—Adult Swim

ISBN 978-1-59582-868-2
$19.99

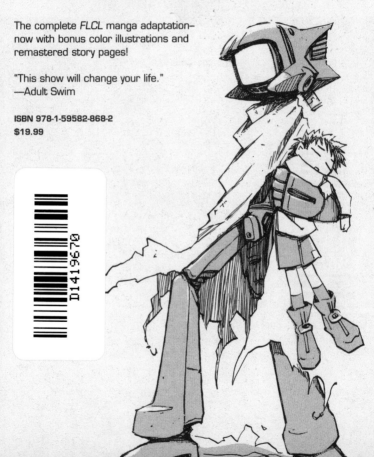